T0091609

Algorithms

A Top-Down Approach

Algorithms
A Top-Down Approach

RODNEY R HOWELL
Kansas State University, USA

 **World Scientific**

NEW JERSEY · LONDON · SINGAPORE · BEIJING · SHANGHAI · HONG KONG · TAIPEI · CHENNAI · TOKYO

Published by

World Scientific Publishing Co. Pte. Ltd.

5 Toh Tuck Link, Singapore 596224

USA office: 27 Warren Street, Suite 401-402, Hackensack, NJ 07601

UK office: 57 Shelton Street, Covent Garden, London WC2H 9HE

Library of Congress Control Number: 2022043934

British Library Cataloguing-in-Publication Data
A catalogue record for this book is available from the British Library.

ALGORITHMS
A Top-Down Approach

ISBN 978-981-126-383-5 (hardcover)
ISBN 978-981-126-384-2 (ebook for institutions)
ISBN 978-981-126-385-9 (ebook for individuals)

For any available supplementary material, please visit
https://www.worldscientific.com/worldscibooks/10.1142/13069#t=suppl

Desk Editors: Aanand Jayaraman/Steven Patt

Typeset by Stallion Press
Email: enquiries@stallionpress.com

Preface

This book gives an introduction to the design and analysis of algorithms. It is intended to introduce the reader to the theories of algorithm correctness and performance analysis, as well as to give a broad overview of algorithm design techniques. As the proper organization of data is essential to the efficiency of many algorithms, a significant portion of the text is devoted to design and analysis of data structures.

This book is motivated in part by the author's belief that people do not fully understand an algorithm until they are able to prove its correctness. For this reason, all of Chapter 2 and much of Chapter 4 are devoted to techniques for proving correctness. Outside of these two chapters, however, very few correctness proofs are given, as they would needlessly clutter the presentation with tedious details. Instead, all algorithms are presented in such a way as to facilitate a correctness proof. The particular approach used is *top-down*. This approach fits well with mathematical techniques of induction, proving loop invariants, and applying previously-shown theorems. By having an understanding of the mechanics of proving correctness, readers are equipped to gain a thorough understanding of an algorithm presented in a top-down way.

Correct use of notation, particularly asymptotic notation, is emphasized throughout. Although asymptotic notation is routinely abused in the literature, the author's experience is that students find such abuse confusing and misleading. As others have argued, nothing is gained by this abuse, so it is avoided in this book.

Algorithms are presented in a pseudo language defined with enough rigor to facilitate both performance analyses and correctness proofs. The essence of an algorithm is not tied to a particular programming language; hence, we have chosen a computational model and corresponding notation that we feel are appropriate for communicating algorithms to humans.

This text contains sufficient material for both an advanced undergraduate course and an introductory graduate-level course on the design and analysis of algorithms.

Prerequisite Material

This book is intended to be reasonably self-contained. However, a certain degree of maturity is assumed regarding the audience. Readers are expected to have enough experience in writing programs so as to be able to understand algorithms presented in a pseudo language. Experience with basic data structures, including stacks, queues, lists, and trees, will be helpful, as will experience in manipulating finite and infinite sums, solving recurrences, and performing combinatorial analyses. Though calculus and number theory are used occasionally, background in these fields of study is not assumed.

Organization

The outline of this book is as follows:

I. **Fundamentals** — the foundational material upon which the remainder of the text is based.

1. **Introduction** — introduction to the ideas of specification, correctness, and analysis of algorithms, as well as to the top-down approach.
2. **Proving Algorithm Correctness** — introduction to techniques for proving algorithm correctness.
3. **Analyzing Algorithms** — introduction to asymptotic notation and its use in analyzing worst-case performance of algorithms.

II. **Data Structures** — data structures commonly used with algorithms, including algorithms presented later in this text.

4. **Basic Techniques for Data Structures** — techniques for reasoning about and analyzing data structures. A more detailed discussion of the computational model and notation is presented. Amortized analysis is introduced.
5. **Priority Queues** — binary heaps, leftist heaps, skew heaps, and randomized heaps. Randomized algorithms and expected-case analysis are introduced.

6. **Storage/Retrieval I: Ordered Keys** — ordered arrays, binary search trees, AVL trees, splay trees, and skip lists.

7. **Storage/Retrieval II: Unordered Keys** — virtually initialized arrays and hashing, including universal hashing.

8. **Disjoint Sets** — structures for supporting MERGE and FIND operations on disjoint sets.

9. **Graphs** — introduction to graph theory and implementations of graphs.

III. **Algorithm Design Techniques** — an in-depth look at standard algorithmic design techniques.

10. **Divide and Conquer** — algorithms for sorting, selecting the kth smallest, multiplying polynomials, and multiplying/dividing integers.

11. **Optimization I: Greedy Algorithms** — algorithms for finding a minimum-cost spanning tree, finding shortest paths, scheduling, and generating Huffman codes.

12. **Optimization II: Dynamic Programming** — algorithms for finding shortest paths, optimal ordering of chained matrix multiplication, and knapsack problems.

IV. **Common Reduction Targets** — algorithms for problems to which many other problems can be reduced.

13. **Depth-First Search** — algorithms for topological sort, articulation points, and strongly connected components.

14. **Network Flow and Matching** — a study of network flow algorithms and their applications.

15. * **The Fast Fourier Transform** — a study of the Fast Fourier Transform algorithm and its application to problems such as integer multiplication.

V. **Intractable Problems** — dealing with problems for which we cannot find efficient solutions.

16. $\mathcal{NP}$-**Completeness** — an introduction to the theory of $\mathcal{NP}$-completeness, including proofs of $\mathcal{NP}$-completeness.

17. **Approximation Algorithms** — an introduction to design and analysis of approximation algorithms for $\mathcal{NP}$-complete problems.

Sections which may be omitted due to more mathematical content have titles prefixed with a "*".

An undergraduate course would consist of all of Part I (except Section 3.11) and most of Parts II and III. Parts IV and V are targeted more for graduate students, though selected topics could be used in an undergraduate course. A graduate-level course should also include all of Part I (though it could probably be covered rather quickly) and perhaps selected topics from Part II. The core of this course would come from Part III, supplemented by some or all of Parts IV and V.

Exercises

Each chapter includes a section of exercises intended to reinforce the chapter material. Some of the exercises are more challenging, and are therefore marked with "*" or "**" to indicate their level of difficulty. Exercises marked "*" will be challenging for most undergraduates, and exercises marked "**" will be challenging for most graduate students.

Web Site and Feedback

Various supplemental materials may be accessed online at

https://www.worldscientific.com/worldscibooks/10.1142/13069

Please send any feedback to rhowell@ksu.edu.

About the Author

Rodney R Howell is an Associate Professor in the Department of Computer Science at Kansas State University. He received a Ph.D. in Computer Science from the University of Texas at Austin in 1988. He has been a faculty member at Kansas State since that time. He has done research in Petri nets, self-stabilizing systems, and real-time scheduling theory. His research has been published in various international journals and peer-reviewed conference proceedings. He has taught courses in analysis of algorithm, data structures, and formal language theory, among other topics. He currently serves as his department's Undergraduate Programs Director.

Contents

Preface   v

About the Author   ix

List of Symbols   xvii

I Fundamentals   1

1. Introduction   3

    1.1   Specifications 3
    1.2   Algorithms 6
    1.3   Proving Algorithm Correctness 8
    1.4   Algorithm Analysis 9
    1.5   Data Structures 12
    1.6   A Case Study: Maximum Subsequence Sum 13
    1.7   Summary 19
    1.8   Exercises 20
    1.9   Notes 24

2. Proving Algorithm Correctness   25

    2.1   The Basics 25
    2.2   Handling Recursion 27
    2.3   Handling Iteration 29
    2.4   Combining Recursion and Iteration 37
    2.5   Mutual Recursion 45

2.6   Finding Errors   46
2.7   Summary   47
2.8   Exercises   48
2.9   Notes   53

3.   **Analyzing Algorithms**   **55**

3.1   Motivation   55
3.2   Big-O Notation   57
3.3   Big-Ω and Big-Θ   61
3.4   Operations on Sets   66
3.5   Smooth Functions and Summations   68
3.6   Analyzing While Loops   72
3.7   Analyzing Recursion   73
3.8   Analyzing Space Usage   81
3.9   Multiple Variables   82
3.10 Little-o and Little-ω   89
3.11 * Use of Limits in Asymptotic Analysis   92
3.12 Summary   95
3.13 Exercises   98
3.14 Notes 104

II   **Data Structures**   **107**

4.   **Basic Techniques for Data Structures**   **109**

4.1   Stacks 109
4.2   A Simple Stack Implementation 112
4.3   Expandable Arrays 121
4.4   The CONSLIST ADT 125
4.5   Amortized Analysis Using Potential Functions 131
4.6   Summary 141
4.7   Exercises 142
4.8   Notes 147

5.   **Priority Queues**   **149**

5.1   Sorted Arrays 150
5.2   Heaps 153
5.3   Leftist Heaps 159
5.4   Skew Heaps 165

5.5   Randomized Heaps 169

5.6   Sorting and Binary Heaps 179

5.7   Summary 187

5.8   Exercises 190

5.9   Notes 195

6.   Storage/Retrieval I: Ordered Keys   197

6.1   Binary Search Trees 200

6.2   AVL Trees 207

6.3   Splay Trees 216

6.4   Skip Lists 226

6.5   Summary 239

6.6   Exercises 240

6.7   Notes 244

7.   Storage/Retrieval II: Unordered Keys   245

7.1   Arrays with Virtual Initialization 245

7.2   Hashing 248

7.3   Deterministic Hash Functions 255

7.4   Universal Hashing 261

7.5   Number Theoretic Universal Hash Families 265

7.6   Perfect Hashing 275

7.7   Summary 283

7.8   Exercises 285

7.9   Notes 288

8.   Disjoint Sets   289

8.1   Using DISJOINTSETS in Scheduling 291

8.2   A Tree-Based Implementation 291

8.3   A Short Tree Implementation 294

8.4   * Path Compression 295

8.5   Summary 304

8.6   Exercises 305

8.7   Notes 307

9.   Graphs   309

9.1   Universal Sink Detection 312

9.2   Topological Sort 313

9.3   Adjacency Matrix Implementation 315

9.4   Adjacency List Implementation 318
9.5   Multigraphs 321
9.6   Summary 325
9.7   Exercises 325
9.8   Notes 327

III   Algorithm Design Techniques   329

10. Divide and Conquer   331

10.1   Polynomial Multiplication 332
10.2   Merge Sort 335
10.3   Quick Sort 337
10.4   Selection 342
10.5   Integer Division 348
10.6   * Newton's Method 355
10.7   Summary 363
10.8   Exercises 363
10.9   Notes 370

11. Optimization I: Greedy Algorithms   371

11.1   Job Scheduling 372
11.2   Minimum-Cost Spanning Trees 374
11.3   Single-Source Shortest Paths 379
11.4   Huffman Codes 380
11.5   Summary 384
11.6   Exercises 385
11.7   Notes 387

12. Optimization II: Dynamic Programming   389

12.1   Making Change 389
12.2   Chained Matrix Multiplication 393
12.3   All-Pairs Shortest Paths 395
12.4   The Knapsack Problem 397
12.5   Summary 400
12.6   Exercises 400
12.7   Notes 408

IV   Common Reduction Targets   409

13. Depth-First Search   411

   13.1   Ancestry in Rooted Trees 412
   13.2   Reachability in a Graph 417
   13.3   A Generic Depth-First Search 421
   13.4   Articulation Points 425
   13.5   Topological Sort Revisited 430
   13.6   Strongly Connected Components 432
   13.7   Summary 436
   13.8   Exercises 437
   13.9   Notes 439

14. Network Flow and Matching   441

   14.1   The Ford–Fulkerson Algorithm 443
   14.2   The Edmonds–Karp Algorithm 449
   14.3   Bipartite Matching 451
   14.4   Summary 460
   14.5   Exercises 460
   14.6   Notes 463

15. * The Fast Fourier Transform   465

   15.1   Convolutions 465
   15.2   Commutative Rings 477
   15.3   Integer Multiplication 481
   15.4   The Schönhage–Strassen Algorithm 492
   15.5   Summary 498
   15.6   Exercises 499
   15.7   Notes 500

V   Intractable Problems   501

16. $\mathcal{NP}$-Completeness   503

   16.1   Boolean Satisfiability 503
   16.2   The Set $\mathcal{P}$ 505
   16.3   The Set $\mathcal{NP}$ 508
   16.4   Restricted Satisfiability Problems 512
   16.5   Vertex Cover and Independent Set 518

16.6 Three-Dimensional Matching 522
16.7 Partitioning and Strong $\mathcal{NP}$-Completeness 526
16.8 Proof of Cook's Theorem 534
16.9 Summary 547
16.10 Exercises 548
16.11 Notes 553

17. Approximation Algorithms   **555**

17.1 Polynomial Turing Reducibility 555
17.2 Knapsack 557
17.3 Bin Packing 563
17.4 The Traveling Salesperson Problem 567
17.5 The Maximum Cut and Minimum Cluster Problems 572
17.6 Summary 577
17.7 Exercises 578
17.8 Notes 579

Bibliography   581

Index   587

List of Symbols

$\cdot$	operator for computing the component-wise product of two vectors of the same size	467
$\setminus$	set difference	91
$\leq_m^p$	polynomial many-one reducibility	509
$\leq_m^{pp}$	pseudopolynomial many-one reducibility	530
$\leq_T^{pp}$	pseudopolynomial Turing reducibility	556
$\leq_T^p$	polynomial Turing reducibility	568
$\otimes$	bitwise exclusive-or operator	264
$\alpha(n)$	a very slow-growing function — in some sense, an inverse of Ackermann's function	300
$\mathbb{C}$	the set of complex numbers	467
$E[f]$	expected value of f	171
$\widehat{f}(m,n)$	$\max\{f(i,j) \mid 0 \leq i \leq m, 0 \leq j \leq n\}$	85
$F^{(k)}(n)$	the function F applied k times to n	300
H_n	an element of the harmonic series	341
$I(e)$	indicator random variable for event e	236
λ	load factor of a hash table	254
$\binom{n}{j}$	binomial coefficients	242
$\mathbb{N}$	the set of natural numbers	
$n!$	n factorial	47
$\mathcal{NP}$	the set of all decision problems with polynomial-length proofs verifiable in a polynomial amount of time	508
O	asymptotic notation used to express upper bounds	57
o	asymptotic notation used to indicate a growth rate significantly slower than a given function	90

Ω	asymptotic notation used to express lower bounds	61
ω	asymptotic notation used to express a growth rate significantly faster than a given function	90
$\mathcal{P}$	the set of all decision problems decidable in a polynomial amount of time	507
$P(e)$	probability of e	170
$P(e_1 \mid e_2)$	conditional probability of e_1 given e_2	177
$\prod\limits_{a \in S} f(a)$	product of all values $f(a)$ where $a \in S$	232
$\mathbb{R}$	the set of real numbers	56
$\mathbb{R}^{\geq 0}$	the set of nonnegative real numbers	56
$\mathbb{R}^{>0}$	the set of positive real numbers	56
Θ	asymptotic notation used to express identical upper- and lower-bounds	62
$\lceil x \rceil$	the smallest integer no smaller than x	37
$\lfloor x \rfloor$	the largest integer no larger than x	37
$\times$	the operator forming the set of all ordered pairs of two given sets	84
$x \leftarrow y$	assign the value of y to x	10
$x \leftrightarrow y$	swap the values of x and y	8
$\mathbb{Z}$	the set of integers	441
$\mathbb{Z}^{>0}$	the set of positive integers	441
$\mathbb{Z}_m$	the set of natural numbers strictly less than m	478

Part I
Fundamentals

Chapter 1

Introduction

A large software system consists of many components, each designed to perform a specific task. The overall quality of a given system is determined largely by how well these components function individually and interact with each other and the external environment. The focus of this book is on individual components — algorithms and data structures — that can be used in a wide variety of software systems. In this chapter, we will present an overview of what these components are and how we will study them throughout the remainder of the book. In the course of this overview, we will illustrate a *top-down approach* for thinking about both algorithms and data structures. This approach will provide an essential framework for both designing and understanding algorithms and data structures.

1.1 Specifications

Before we can design or analyze any software component — including an algorithm or a data structure — we must first know what it is supposed to accomplish. A formal statement of what a software component is meant to accomplish is called a *specification*. Here, we will discuss specifically the specification of an algorithm. The specification of a data structure is similar, but a bit more involved. For this reason, we will wait until Chapter 4 to discuss the specification of data structures in detail.

Suppose, for example, that we wish to find the kth smallest element of an array of n numbers. Thus, if $k = 1$, we are looking for the smallest element in the array, or if $k = n$, we are looking for the largest. We will refer to this problem as the *selection problem*. Even for such a seemingly simple problem, there is a potential for ambiguity if we are not careful to state the problem precisely. For example, what do we expect from the algorithm if k

is larger than n? Do we allow the algorithm to change the array? Do all of the elements in the array need to be different? If not, what exactly do we mean by the kth smallest?

Specifically, we need to state the following:

- a *precondition*, which is a statement of the assumptions we make about the input to the algorithm and the environment in which it will be executed; and
- a *postcondition*, which is a statement of the required result of executing the algorithm, assuming the precondition is satisfied.

The precondition and postcondition, together with a *function header* giving a name and parameter list, constitute the *specification* of the algorithm. We say that the algorithm *meets its specification* if the postcondition is satisfied whenever the precondition is satisfied. Note that we guarantee nothing about the algorithm if its precondition is not satisfied.

The selection problem will have two parameters, an array A and a positive integer k. The precondition should specify what we are assuming about these parameters. For this problem, we will assume that

> We adopt the convention that if the last index is smaller than the first (e.g., $A[1..0]$), then the array has no elements.

the first element of A is indexed by 1 and the last element is indexed by some natural number (i.e., nonnegative integer) n; hence, we describe the array more precisely using the notation $A[1..n]$. We will assume that each element of $A[1..n]$ is a number; hence, our precondition must include this requirement. Furthermore, we will not require the algorithm to verify that k is within a proper range; hence, the precondition must require that $1 \leq k \leq n$, where $k \in \mathbb{N}$ ($\mathbb{N}$ is the mathematical notation for the set of natural numbers).

Now let us consider how we might specify a postcondition. We need to come up with a precise definition of the kth smallest element of $A[1..n]$. Consider first the simpler case in which all elements of $A[1..n]$ are distinct. In this case, we would need to return the element $A[i]$ such that exactly k elements of $A[1..n]$ are less than or equal to $A[i]$. However, this definition of the kth smallest element might be meaningless when $A[1..n]$ contains duplicate entries. Suppose, for example, that $A[1..2]$ contains two 0s and that $k = 1$. There is then no element $A[i]$ such that exactly 1 element of $A[1..2]$ is less than or equal to $A[i]$.

To better understand the case in which elements of A might be duplicated, let us consider a specific example. Let $A[1..8] = \langle 1, 5, 6, 9, 9, 9, 9, 10 \rangle$, and let $k = 5$. An argument could be made that 10 is the kth smallest because there are exactly k *distinct* values less than or equal to 10. However, if we were to adopt this definition, there would be no kth smallest element for $k = 6$. Because A is sorted, it would be better to conclude that the kth smallest is $A[k] = 9$. Note that all elements strictly less than 9 are in $A[1..4]$; i.e., there are strictly fewer than k elements less than the kth smallest. Furthermore, rearranging A would not change this fact. Likewise, observe that all the elements in $A[1..5]$ are less than or equal to 9; i.e., there are at least k elements less than or equal to the kth smallest. Again, rearranging A would not change this fact.

The above example suggests that the proper definition of the kth smallest element of an array $A[1..n]$ is the value x such that

- there are fewer than k elements $A[i] < x$ and
- there are at least k elements $A[i] \leq x$.

It is possible to show, though we will not do so here, that for any array $A[1..n]$ and any positive integer $k \leq n$, there is exactly one value x satisfying both of the above conditions. We will therefore adopt this definition of the kth smallest element.

The complete specification for the selection problem is shown in Figure 1.1. To express the data types of n and the elements of A, we use NAT to denote the natural number type and NUMBER to denote the number type. Note that NAT is a *subtype* of NUMBER — every NAT is also a NUMBER. In order to place fewer constraints on the algorithm, we have included in the postcondition a statement that the elements of $A[1..n]$ may be permuted (i.e., rearranged). In order for a specification to be precise, the postcondition must state when side-effects such as this may occur. In order to keep specifications from becoming overly wordy, we will adopt the convention that no values may be changed unless the postcondition explicitly allows the change.

Figure 1.1   Specification for the selection problem

Precondition: $A[1..n]$ is an array of NUMBERs, $1 \leq k \leq n$, k and n are NATs.

Postcondition: Returns the value x in $A[1..n]$ such that fewer than k elements of $A[1..n]$ are strictly less than x, and at least k elements of $A[1..n]$ are less than or equal to x. The elements of $A[1..n]$ may be permuted.

SELECT$(A[1..n], k)$

1.2   Algorithms

Once we have a specification, we need to produce an algorithm to implement that specification. This algorithm is a precise statement of the computational steps taken to produce the results required by the specification. An algorithm differs from a program in that it is usually not specified in a programming language. In this book, we describe algorithms using a notation that is precise enough to be implemented as a programming language, but which is designed to be read by humans.

A straightforward approach to solving the selection problem is as follows:

1. Sort the array in non-decreasing order.
2. Return the kth element.

If we already know how to sort, then we have solved our problem; otherwise, we must come up with a sorting algorithm. By using sorting to solve the selection problem, we say that we have *reduced* the selection problem to the sorting problem.

Solving a problem by reducing it to one or more simpler problems is the essence of the top-down approach to designing algorithms. One advantage to this approach is that it allows us to abstract away certain details so that we can focus on the main steps of the algorithm. In this case, we have a selection algorithm, but our algorithm requires a sorting algorithm before it can be fully implemented. This abstraction facilitates understanding of the algorithm at a high level. Specifically, if we know what is accomplished by sorting — but not necessarily how it is accomplished — then because the selection algorithm consists of very little else, we can readily understand what it does.

When we reduce the selection problem to the sorting problem, we need a specification for sorting as well. For this problem, the precondition will be that $A[1..n]$ is an array of NUMBERs, where $n \in \mathbb{N}$. Our postcondition will be that $A[1..n]$ is a permutation of its initial values such that for $1 \leq i < j \leq n$, $A[i] \leq A[j]$ — i.e., that $A[1..n]$ contains its initial values in nondecreasing order. Our selection algorithm is given in Figure 1.2. Note that SORT is only specified — its algorithm is not provided.

Let us now refine the SIMPLESELECT algorithm of Figure 1.2 by designing a sorting algorithm. We will reduce the sorting problem to the problem of inserting an element into a sorted array. In order to complete the reduction, we need to have a sorted array in which to insert. We have thus returned to our original problem. We can break this circularity, however, by using the top-down approach in a different way. Specifically, we reduce larger instances

---

Figure 1.2 An algorithm implementing the specification of Figure 1.1

SIMPLESELECT($A[1..n], k$)
    SORT($A[1..n]$)
    return $A[k]$

Precondition: $A[1..n]$ is an array of NUMBERs, n is a NAT.
Postcondition: $A[1..n]$ is a permutation of its initial values such that for $1 \leq i < j \leq n$, $A[i] \leq A[j]$.

SORT($A[1..n]$)

Figure 1.3 An algorithm implementing the specification of SORT, given in Figure 1.2

INSERTSORT($A[1..n]$)
    if $n > 1$
       INSERTSORT($A[1..n-1]$)
       INSERT($A[1..n]$)

Precondition: $A[1..n]$ is an array of NUMBERs such that n is a NAT, and for $1 \leq i < j \leq n-1$, $A[i] \leq A[j]$.
Postcondition: $A[1..n]$ is a permutation of its initial values such that for $1 \leq i < j \leq n$, $A[i] \leq A[j]$.

INSERT($A[1..n]$)

---

of sorting to smaller instances. In this application of the top-down approach, the simpler problem is actually a smaller instance of the same problem.

The algorithm is given in Figure 1.3. Though this application of the top-down approach may at first seem harder to understand, we can think about it in the same way as we did for SIMPLESELECT. If $n \leq 1$, the postcondition for SORT($A[1..n]$) (given in Figure 1.2) is clearly met. For $n > 1$, we use the specification of SORT to understand that INSERTSORT($A[1..n-1]$) sorts $A[1..n-1]$. Thus, the precondition for INSERT($A[1..n]$) is satisfied. We then use the specification of INSERT($A[1..n]$) to understand that when the algorithm completes, $A[1..n]$ is sorted.

The thought process outlined above might seem mysterious because it doesn't follow the sequence of steps in an execution of the algorithm. However, it is a much more powerful way to think about algorithms.

Figure 1.4   An algorithm implementing the specification of INSERT, given in Figure 1.3

RECURSIVEINSERT($A[1..n]$)
   if $n > 1$ **and** $A[n] < A[n-1]$
      $A[n] \leftrightarrow A[n-1]$
      RECURSIVEINSERT($A[1..n-1]$)

To complete the implementations of SIMPLESELECT and INSERTSORT, we need an algorithm for INSERT. We can again use the the top-down approach to reduce an instance of INSERT to a smaller instance of the same problem. According to the precondition (see Figure 1.3), $A[1..n-1]$ must be sorted in nondecreasing order; hence, if either $n = 1$ or $A[n] \geq A[n-1]$, the postcondition is already satisfied. Otherwise, $A[n-1]$ must be the largest element in $A[1..n]$. Therefore, if we swap $A[n]$ with $A[n-1]$, $A[1..n-2]$ is sorted in nondecreasing order and $A[n]$ is the largest element in $A[1..n]$. If we then solve the smaller instance $A[1..n-1]$, we will satisfy the postcondition.

The algorithm is shown in Figure 1.4. In this book, we will assume that a logical **and** or **or** is evaluated by first evaluating its first operand, then if necessary, evaluating its second operand. Thus, in evaluating the **if** statement in RECURSIVEINSERT, if $n \leq 1$, the second operand will not be evaluated, as the value of the expression must be **false**. We use the notation $x \leftrightarrow y$ to swap the values of variables x and y.

1.3   Proving Algorithm Correctness

Once we have an algorithm, we would like some assurance that it meets its specification. We have argued somewhat informally that the three algorithms, SIMPLESELECT, INSERTSORT, and RECURSIVEINSERT, meet their respective specifications; however, these arguments may not convince everyone. For example, it might not be clear that it is valid to assume that the recursive call to INSERTSORT in Figure 1.3 meets its specification. After all, the whole point of that discussion was to argue that INSERTSORT meets its specification. That argument might therefore seem circular.

In the next chapter, we will show how to prove formally that an algorithm meets its specification. These proofs will rest on solid mathematical foundations, so that a careful application of the techniques should give us confidence that a given algorithm is, indeed, correct. In particular, we will formally justify the reasoning used above — namely, that we can assume that a recursive call meets its specification, provided its input is of a smaller size than that of the original call, where the size is some natural number.

The ability to prove algorithm correctness is quite possibly the most underrated skill in the entire discipline of computing. First, knowing how to prove algorithm correctness also helps us in the design of algorithms. Specifically, once we understand the mechanics of correctness proofs, we can design the algorithm with a proof of correctness in mind. This approach makes designing correct algorithms much easier. Second, the exercise of working through a correctness proof — or even sketching such a proof — often uncovers subtle errors that would be difficult to find with testing alone. Third, this ability brings with it a capacity to understand specific algorithms on a much deeper level. Thus, the ability to prove algorithm correctness is a powerful tool for designing and understanding algorithms. Because these activities are closely related to programming, this ability greatly enhances programming abilities as well.

The proof techniques we will introduce fit nicely with the top-down approach to algorithm design. As a result, the top-down approach itself becomes an even more powerful tool for designing and understanding algorithms.

1.4 Algorithm Analysis

Once we have a correct algorithm, we need to be able to evaluate how well it does its job. This evaluation essentially boils down to an analysis of the resource usage of the algorithm, where the resources might be time or memory, for example. In Chapter 3, we will present tools for mathematically analyzing such resource usage. For now, let us discuss this resource usage less formally.

Consider the INSERTSORT algorithm given in Figures 1.3 and 1.4, for example. If we were to implement this algorithm in a programming language and run it on a variety of examples, we would discover that for sufficiently large inputs — typically a few thousand elements — the program will terminate abnormally due to a stack overflow. This problem is not, strictly speaking, an error in the algorithm, but instead is a reflection of the fact that it uses the machine's runtime stack inefficiently. Using the analysis tools of Chapter 3, it is possible to show that this algorithm's stack usage is linear in the size of the array. Because the runtime stack is usually much smaller than the total memory available, we usually would like the stack usage to be bounded by a slow-growing function of the size of the input — a logarithmic function, for example. Thus, if we were to do the analysis prior to implementing the algorithm, we could uncover the inefficiency earlier in the process.

Having uncovered an inefficiency, we would like to eliminate it. The runtime stack is used when performing function calls. Specifically, each time a function call is made, information is placed onto the stack. When the function returns, this information is removed. As a result, when an algorithm uses the runtime stack inefficiently, the culprit is almost always recursion. This in not to say that recursion always uses the stack inefficiently — indeed, we will see many efficient recursive algorithms in this book. The analysis tools of Chapter 3 will help us to determine when recursion is or is not used efficiently. For now, however, we will focus on removing the recursion.

It turns out that while recursion is the most obvious way to implement an algorithm designed using the top-down approach, it is by no means the only way. One alternative is to implement the top-down solution in a bottom-up way. The top-down solution for INSERTSORT is to reduce a large instance to a smaller instance and an instance of INSERT by first sorting the smaller instance, then applying INSERT. We can apply this same idea in a bottom-up fashion by observing that the first element of any nonempty array is necessarily sorted, then extending the sorted portion of the array by applying INSERT. In other words, we repeatedly apply INSERT to $A[1..2], A[1..3], \ldots, A[1..n]$. This can be done using a loop.

The bottom-up implementation works well for INSERTSORT because the recursive call is essentially the first step of the computation. However, the recursive call in RECURSIVEINSERT is necessarily the last step. Fortunately, there is a fairly straightforward way of removing the recursion from this type of algorithm, as well. When a reduction has the form that the solution to the simpler problem solves the original problem, we call this reduction a *transformation*. When we transform a large instance to a smaller instance of the same problem, the natural recursive algorithm is *tail recursive*, meaning that the last step is a recursive call.

Figure 1.5 illustrates how a typical tail recursive algorithm can be converted to an iterative algorithm. The loop iterates as long as the condition indicating the base case (i.e., the end of the recursion) is false. Each iteration performs all the computation in the recursive case except the recursive call. To simulate the recursive call, the formal parameters $p_1, \ldots, p_k$ are given the values of their corresponding actual parameters, $q_1, \ldots, q_k$, and the loop continues (a statement of the form "$x \leftarrow y$" assigns the value of y to the

---

Figure 1.5   Translation of a typical tail recursive algorithm to an iterative algorithm

---

TAILRECURSIVEALGORITHM($p_1, \ldots, p_k$)
  if ⟨BooleanCondition⟩
    ⟨BaseCase⟩
  else
    ⟨RecursiveCaseComputation⟩
    TAILRECURSIVEALGORITHM($q_1, \ldots, q_k$)

ITERATIVEALGORITHM($p_1, \ldots, p_k$)
  while not ⟨BooleanCondition⟩
    ⟨RecursiveCaseComputation⟩
    $p_1 \leftarrow q_1; \ldots; p_k \leftarrow q_k$
  ⟨BaseCase⟩

Figure 1.6   Iterative algorithm implementing the specification of INSERT, given in Figure 1.3

ITERATIVEINSERT($A[1..n]$)
  $j \leftarrow n$
  // **Invariant:** $A[1..n]$ is a permutation of its original values such that
  // for $1 \leq k < k' \leq n$, if $k' \neq j$, then $A[k] \leq A[k']$.
  while $j > 1$ **and** $A[j] < A[j-1]$
    $A[j] \leftrightarrow A[j-1]; j \leftarrow j-1$

---

variable x). Once the condition indicating the base case is true, the loop terminates, the base case is executed, and the algorithm terminates.

Figure 1.6 shows the result of eliminating the tail recursion from RECURSIVEINSERT. Because RECURSIVEINSERT is structured in a slightly different way from what is shown in Figure 1.5, we could not apply this translation verbatim. The tail recursion occurs, not in the **else** part, but in the **if** part, of the **if** statement in RECURSIVEINSERT. For this reason, we did not negate the condition when forming the **while** loop. The base case is then the empty **else** part of the **if** statement. Because there is no code in the base case, there is nothing to place after the loop. In order to avoid changing the value of n, we have copied its value to j, and used j in place of n throughout the algorithm. Furthermore, because the meaning of the statement "$A[1..j] \leftarrow A[1..j-1]$" is not clear, we instead simulated the recursion by the statement "$j \leftarrow j-1$".

Figure 1.7 Insertion sort implementation of SORT, specified in Figure 1.1

INSERTIONSORT($A[1..n]$)
    // **Invariant:** $A[1..n]$ is a permutation of its original values
    // such that $A[1..i-1]$ is in nondecreasing order.
    for $i \leftarrow 1$ **to** n
        $j \leftarrow i$
        // **Invariant:** $A[1..n]$ is a permutation of its original values
        // such that for $1 \leq k < k' \leq i$, if $k' \neq j$, then $A[k] \leq A[k']$.
        while $j > 1$ **and** $A[j] < A[j-1]$
            $A[j] \leftrightarrow A[j-1]$; $j \leftarrow j-1$

Prior to the loop in ITERATIVEINSERT, we have given a *loop invariant*, which is a statement that must be true at the beginning and end of each iteration of the loop. Loop invariants will be an essential part of

> *We consider each test of a loop exit condition to mark the beginning/end of an iteration.*

the correctness proof techniques that we will introduce in the next chapter. For now, however, we will use them to help us to keep track of what the loop is doing.

The resulting sorting algorithm, commonly known as insertion sort, is shown in Figure 1.7. Besides removing the two recursive calls, we have also combined the two functions into one. Also, we have started the **for** loop at 1, rather than at 2, as our earlier discussion suggested. As far as correctness goes, there is no difference which starting point we use, as the inner loop will not iterate when $i = 1$; however, it turns out that the correctness proof, which we will present in the next chapter, is simpler if we begin the loop at 1. Furthermore, the impact on performance is minimal.

While analysis techniques can be applied to analyze stack usage, a far more common application of these techniques is to analyze running time. For example, we can use these techniques to show that while INSERTIONSORT is not, in general, a very efficient sorting algorithm, there are important cases in which it is a very good choice. In Section 1.6, we will present a case study that demonstrates the practical utility of running time analysis.

1.5 Data Structures

One of the major factors influencing the performance of an algorithm is the way the data items it manipulates are organized. For this reason, it is essential that we include data structures in our study of algorithms. The themes that we have discussed up to this point all apply to data structures, but in a somewhat different way.

For example, a specification of a data structure must certainly include preconditions and postconditions for the operations on the structure. In addition, the specification must in some way describe the information represented by the structure, and how operations on the structure affect that information. As a result, proofs of correctness must take into account this additional detail.

While the analysis techniques of Chapter 3 apply directly to operations on data structures, it will be necessary to introduce a new technique that analyzes sequences of operations on a data structure. Furthermore, even the language we are using to express algorithms will need to be enriched in order to allow design and analysis of data structures. We will present all of these extensions in Chapter 4.

1.6 A Case Study: Maximum Subsequence Sum

We conclude this chapter by presenting a case study that illustrates the practical impact of algorithm efficiency. The inefficiencies that we will address all can be discovered using the analysis techniques of Chapter 3. This case study will also demonstrate the usefulness of the top-down approach in designing significantly more efficient algorithms.

Let us consider the problem of computing the maximum sum of any contiguous sequence in an array of numbers (see Figure 1.8). The numbers in the array may be positive, negative, or zero, and we consider the empty sequence to have a sum of 0. More formally, given an array $A[0..n-1]$ of numbers, where $n \in \mathbb{N}$, the *maximum subsequence sum* of A is defined to be

$$\max\left\{\sum_{k=i}^{j-1} A[k] \mid 0 \le i \le j \le n\right\}.$$

Note that when $i = j$, the sum has a beginning index of i and an ending index of $i-1$. By convention, we always write summations so that the index (k in this case) *increases* from its initial value (i) to its

> Similar conventions hold for products, except that an empty product is assumed to have a value of 1.

final value ($j - 1$). As a result of this convention, whenever the final value is less than the initial value, the summation contains no elements. Again by convention, such an empty summation is defined to have a value of 0. Thus, in the above definition, we are including the empty sequence and assuming

Figure 1.8 The subsequence with maximum sum may begin and end anywhere in the array, but must be contiguous

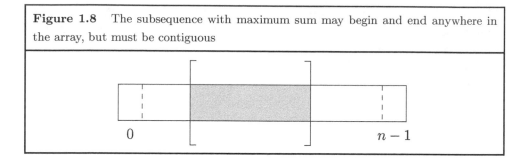

Figure 1.9 Specification for the maximum subsequence sum problem

Precondition: $A[0..n-1]$ is an array of NUMBERs, n is a NAT.
Postcondition: Returns the maximum subsequence sum of A.

MAXSUM($A[0..n-1]$)

its sum is 0. The specification for this problem is given in Figure 1.9. Note that according to this specification, the values in $A[0..n-1]$ may not be modified.

Example 1.1. Suppose $A[0..5] = \langle -1, 3, -2, 7, -9, 7 \rangle$. Then the subsequence $A[1..3] = \langle 3, -2, 7 \rangle$ has a sum of 8. By exhaustively checking all other contiguous subsequences, we can verify that this is, in fact, the maximum. For example, the subsequence $A[1..5]$ has a sum of 6.

Example 1.2. Suppose $A[0..3] = \langle -3, -4, -1, -5 \rangle$. Then all nonempty subsequences have negative sums. However, any empty subsequence (e.g., $A[0..-1]$) by definition has a sum of 0. The maximum subsequence sum of this array is therefore 0.

We can easily obtain an algorithm for this problem by translating the definition of a maximum subsequence sum directly into an iterative solution. The result is shown in Figure 1.10. By applying the analysis techniques of Chapter 3, it can be shown that the running time of this algorithm is proportional to n^3, where n is the size of the array.

In order to illustrate the practical ramifications of this analysis, we implemented this algorithm in the Java^{TM} programming language and ran it on a personal computer using randomly generated data sets of size 2^k for

---

Figure 1.10 A **simple algorithm** implementing the specification given in Figure 1.9

MAXSUMITER($A[0..n-1]$)
  $m \leftarrow 0$
  for $i \leftarrow 0$ **to** n
    for $j \leftarrow i$ **to** n
      $sum \leftarrow 0$
      for $k \leftarrow i$ **to** $j-1$
        $sum \leftarrow sum + A[k]$
      $m \leftarrow$ MAX(m, sum)
  return m

---

various values of k. On a data set of size $2^{10} = 1024$, MAXSUMITER required about 0.038 seconds, which seems reasonably fast. However, as the size of the array increased, the running time degraded quickly:

- $2^{11} = 2048$ elements: 0.36 seconds,
- $2^{12} = 4096$ elements: 3.0 seconds,
- $2^{13} = 8192$ elements: 24 seconds.

Note that as the size of the array doubles, the running time increases by roughly a factor of 8. This is not surprising if we realize that the running time should be cn^3 for some c, and $c(2n)^3 = 8cn^3$. We can therefore estimate that for a data set of size $2^{18} = 262{,}144$, the running time should be $8^5 = 32{,}768$ times as long as for 2^{13}. This running time is over a week!

If we want to solve this problem on large data sets, we clearly would like to improve the running time. A careful examination of Figure 1.10 reveals some redundant computation. Specifically, the inner loop computes sums of successively longer subsequences. Much work can be saved if we compute sums of successive sequences by simply adding the next element to the preceding sum. Furthermore, a small optimization can be made by running the outer loop to $n-1$, as the inner loop would not execute on this iteration. The result of this optimization is shown in Figure 1.11.

It turns out that this algorithm has a running time proportional to n^2, which is an improvement over n^3. To show how significant this improvement is, we again coded this algorithm and timed it for arrays of various sizes. The difference was dramatic — for an input of size 2^{18}, which we estimated would require over a week for MAXSUMITER to process, the running time

---

Figure 1.11   An algorithm for maximum subsequence sum (specified in Figure 1.9), optimized by removing an unnecessary loop from MAXSUMITER (Figure 1.10)

MAXSUMOPT($A[0..n-1]$)
  $m \leftarrow 0$
  for $i \leftarrow 0$ **to** $n-1$
    $sum \leftarrow 0$
    for $k \leftarrow i$ **to** $n-1$
      $sum \leftarrow sum + A[k]$
      $m \leftarrow$ MAX(m, sum)
  return m

---

of MAXSUMOPT was only 18 seconds. However, because $c(2n)^2 = 4cn^2$, we would expect the running time to increase by a factor of 4 each time the array size is doubled. This prediction proved to be true, as a data set of size $2^{19} = 524{,}288$ required about 70 seconds. Extrapolating this behavior, we would expect a data set of size $2^{24} = 16{,}777{,}216$ to require nearly 20 hours. (MAXSUMITER would require over 6,000 years to process a data set of this size.)

While MAXSUMOPT gives a dramatic speedup over MAXSUMITER, we would like further improvement if we wish to solve very large problem instances. Note that neither MAXSUMITER nor MAXSUMOPT was designed using the top-down approach. Let us therefore consider how we might solve the problem in a top-down way. For ease of presentation let us refer to the maximum subsequence sum of $A[0..n-1]$ as s_n. Suppose we can obtain s_{n-1} (i.e., the maximum subsequence sum of $A[0..n-2]$) for $n > 0$. Then in order to compute the overall maximum subsequence sum we need the maximum of s_{n-1} and all of the sums of subsequences $A[i..n-1]$ for $0 \leq i \leq n$. Thus, we need to solve another problem, that of finding the *maximum suffix sum* (see Figure 1.12), which we define to be

$$\max\left\{ \sum_{k=i}^{n-1} A[k] \mid 0 \leq i \leq n \right\}.$$

In other words, the maximum suffix sum is the maximum sum that we can obtain by starting at any index i, where $0 \leq i \leq n$, and adding together all elements from index i up to index $n-1$. (Note that by taking $i = n$, we include the empty sequence in this maximum.) We then have a top-down solution for computing the maximum subsequence sum:

Figure 1.12 The suffix with maximum sum may begin anywhere in the array, but must end at the end of the array

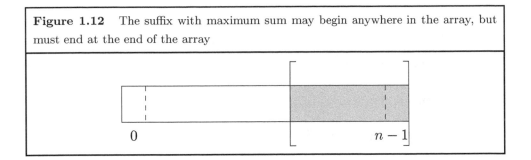

$$s_n = \begin{cases} 0 & \text{if } n = 0 \\ \max(s_{n-1}, t_n) & \text{if } n > 0, \end{cases} \qquad (1.1)$$

where t_n is the maximum suffix sum of $A[0..n-1]$.

Let us consider how to compute the maximum suffix sum t_n using the top-down approach. Observe that every suffix of $A[0..n-1]$ — except the empty suffix — ends with $A[n-1]$. If we remove $A[n-1]$ from all of these suffixes, we obtain all of the suffixes of $A[0..n-2]$. Thus, $t_{n-1} + A[n-1] = t_n$ unless $t_n = 0$. We therefore have

$$t_n = \max(0, A[n-1] + t_{n-1}). \qquad (1.2)$$

Using (1.1) and (1.2), we obtain the recursive solution given in Figure 1.13. Note that we have combined the algorithm for MAXSUFFIXTD with its specification.

Unfortunately, an analysis of this algorithm shows that it also has a running time proportional to n^2. What is worse, however, is that an analysis of its stack usage reveals that it is linear in n. Indeed, the program implementing this algorithm threw a STACKOVERFLOWERROR on an input of size 2^{15}.

While these results are disappointing, we at least have some techniques for improving the stack usage. Note that in both MAXSUMTD and MAXSUFFIXTD, the recursive calls don't depend on any of the rest of the computation; hence, we should be able to implement both algorithms in a bottom-up fashion in order to remove the recursion. Furthermore, we can simplify the resulting code with the realization that once t_i is computed (using (1.2)), we can immediately compute s_i using (1.1). Thus, we can compute both values within a single loop. The result is shown in Figure 1.14.

Because this algorithm uses no recursion, its stack usage is fixed (i.e., it does not grow as n increases). Furthermore, an analysis of its running time

Figure 1.13   A top-down solution for maximum subsequence sum, specified in Figure 1.9

MaxSumTD($A[0..n-1]$)
   if $n = 0$
      return 0
   else
      return Max(MaxSumTD($A[0..n-2]$), MaxSuffixTD($A[0..n-1]$))

Precondition: $A[0..n-1]$ is an array of Numbers, n is a Nat.
Postcondition: Returns the maximum suffix sum of A.

MaxSuffixTD($A[0..n-1]$)
   if $n = 0$
      return 0
   else
      return Max($0, A[n-1] + $ MaxSuffixTD($A[0..n-2]$))

Figure 1.14   A bottom-up calculation of the maximum subsequence sum, specified in Figure 1.9

MaxSumBU($A[0..n-1]$)
   $m \leftarrow 0; msuf \leftarrow 0$
   // **Invariant:** m is the maximum subsequence sum of $A[0..i-1]$,
   // $msuf$ is the maximum suffix sum for $A[0..i-1]$
   for $i \leftarrow 0$ **to** $n-1$
      $msuf \leftarrow$ Max($0, msuf + A[i]$)
      $m \leftarrow$ Max($m, msuf$)
   return m

reveals that it runs in a time linear in n. The program implementing this algorithm bears out that this is a significant improvement — this program used about a second on an array of size $2^{30} = 1,073,741,824$. By comparison, we estimate that on an array of this size, MaxSumOpt would require nearly 10 years, and that MaxSumIter would require over a billion years!

The running times of the Java™ implementations of all four algorithms are plotted on the graph in Figure 1.15. The code used to generate these results can be found on the textbook's web page.

Note that the performance improvement of MaxSumBU over either MaxSumIter or MaxSumOpt is better than what we can expect to obtain

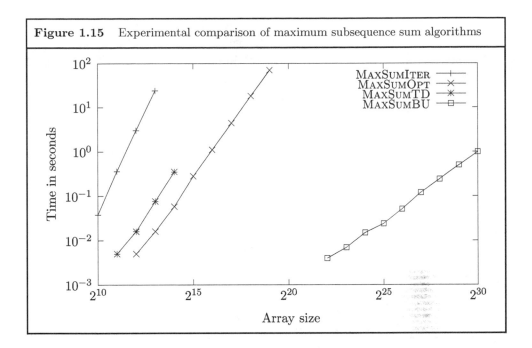

Figure 1.15 Experimental comparison of maximum subsequence sum algorithms

simply by using faster hardware. For example, to achieve with MAXSUMOPT the running time we measured for MAXSUMBU on an array of size 2^{24} would require hardware over 4,000,000 times faster. Even then, we would be able to process much larger inputs with MAXSUMBU. MAXSUMBU also has the advantage of being simpler than the other algorithms. Furthermore, because it makes only one pass through the input, it does not require that the data be stored in an array. Rather, it can simply process the data as it reads each element. As a result, it can be used for very large data sets that might not fit into main memory.

Thus, we can see the importance of efficiency in the design of algorithms. Furthermore, we don't have to code the algorithm and test it to see how efficient it is. Instead, we can get a fairly good idea of its efficiency by analyzing it using the techniques presented in Chapter 3. Finally, understanding these analysis techniques will help us to know where to look to improve algorithm efficiency.

1.7 Summary

The study of algorithms encompasses several facets. First, before an algorithm or data structure can be considered, a specification of the requirements must be made. Having a specification, we can then design the algorithm or data structure with a proof of correctness in mind. Once we have convinced ourselves that our solution is correct, we can then apply mathematical techniques to analyze its resource usage. Such an analysis gives us insight into how useful our solution might be, including cases in which it may or may not be useful. This analysis may also point to shortcomings upon which we might try to improve.

The top-down approach is a useful framework for designing correct, efficient algorithms. Furthermore, algorithms presented in a top-down fashion can be more easily understood. Together with the top-down approach, techniques such as bottom-up implementation and elimination of tail recursion — along with others that we will present later — give us a rich collection of tools for algorithm design. We can think of these techniques as algorithmic *design patterns*, as we use each of them in the design of a wide variety of algorithms.

In Chapters 2 and 3, we will provide the foundations for proving algorithm correctness and analyzing algorithms, respectively. In Part II, we will examine several of the most commonly-used data structures, including those that are frequently used by efficient algorithms. In Part III, we examine the most common approaches to algorithm design. In Part IV, we will study several specific algorithms to which many other problems can be reduced. Finally, in Part V, we will consider a class of problems believed to be computationally intractable and introduce some techniques for coping with them.

1.8   Exercises

Exercise 1.1. We wish to design an algorithm that takes an array $A[0..n-1]$ of numbers in nondecreasing order and a number x, and returns the location of the first occurrence of x in $A[0..n-1]$, or the location at which x could be inserted without violating the ordering if x does not occur in the array. Give a formal specification for this problem. The algorithm shown in Figure 1.16 should meet your specification.

Exercise 1.2. Give an iterative algorithm that results from removing the tail recursion from the algorithm shown in Figure 1.16. Your algorithm should meet the specification described in Exercise 1.1.

Exercise 1.3. Figure 1.17 gives a recursive algorithm for computing the dot product of two vectors, represented as arrays. Give a bottom-up implementation of this algorithm.

Figure 1.16 An algorithm satisfying the specification described in Exercise 1.1

FIND($A[0..n-1]$, x)
   if $n = 0$ **or** $A[n-1] < x$
      return n
   else
      return FIND($A[0..n-2], x$)

Figure 1.17 Algorithm for Exercise 1.3

Precondition: $A[1..n]$ and $B[1..n]$ are ARRAYS of NUMBERS, and n is a NAT.
Postcondition: Returns

$$\sum_{i=1}^{n} A[i]B[i].$$

DOTPRODUCT($A[1..n]$, $B[1..n]$)
   if $n = 0$
      return 0
   else
      return DOTPRODUCT($A[1..n-1], B[1..n-1]$) $+ A[n]B[n]$

Exercise 1.4. Figure 1.18 gives a specification for COPY.

(a) Show how to reduce COPY to a smaller instance of itself by giving a recursive algorithm. You may assume that A and B are distinct, non-overlapping arrays. Your algorithm should contain exactly one recursive call and no loops.

(b) Convert your algorithm from part (a) to an iterative algorithm by either removing tail recursion or implementing it bottom-up, whichever is more appropriate. Explain how you did your conversion.

(c) The specification of COPY does not prohibit the two arrays from sharing elements, for example, COPY($A[1..n-1], A[2..n]$). Modify your algorithm from part (a) to handle any two arrays of the same size. Specifically, you cannot assume that the recursive call does not change $A[1..n]$. Your algorithm should contain exactly one recursive call and no loops.

Figure 1.18   Specification of COPY

Precondition: n is a NAT.
Postcondition: For $1 \leq i \leq n$, $B[i]$ is modified to equal $A[i]$.

COPY$(A[1..n], B[1..n])$

Figure 1.19   Specification for FINDMAX

Precondition: $A[0..n-1]$ is an array of numbers, and n is a positive NAT.
Postcondition: Returns i such that $0 \leq i < n$ and for any j, $0 \leq j < n$,
$A[i] \geq A[j]$.

FINDMAX$(A[0..n-1])$

Exercise 1.5. A *palindrome* is a sequence of characters that is the same when read from left to right as when read from right to left. We wish to design an algorithm that recognizes whether an array of characters is a palindrome.

  (a) Give a formal specification for this problem. Use CHAR to denote the data type for a character.
  (b) Using the top-down approach, give an algorithm to solve this problem. Your algorithm should contain a single recursive call.
  (c) Give an iterative version of your algorithm from part (b) by either implementing it bottom-up or eliminating tail recursion, whichever is appropriate.

Exercise 1.6. FINDMAX is specified in Figure 1.19.

  (a) Using the top-down approach, give an algorithm for FINDMAX. Note that according to the specification, your algorithm may not change the values in A. Your algorithm should contain exactly one recursive call.
  (b) Give an iterative version of your algorithm from part (a) by either implementing it bottom-up or eliminating tail recursion, whichever is appropriate.
 * (c) Show how to reduce the sorting problem to FINDMAX (as specified in part (a)) and a smaller instance of sorting. Use the technique of

transformation, and remove the resulting tail recursion, so that your algorithm is iterative.

* **Exercise 1.7.** APPENDTOALL and SIZEOF are specified in Figure 1.20.

   (a) Show how to reduce APPENDTOALL to COPY (specified in Figure 1.18), SIZEOF, and a smaller instance of itself, by giving a recursive algorithm. Your algorithm should contain no loops and a single recursive call.

   (b) Convert your algorithm from part (a) to an iterative algorithm by either removing tail recursion or implementing it bottom-up, whichever is more appropriate. You do not need to provide algorithms for either COPY or SIZEOF.

* **Exercise 1.8.** ALLSUBSETS is specified in Figure 1.21.

   (a) Show how to reduce to ALLSUBSETS to COPY (specified in Figure 1.18), APPENDTOALL (specified in Figure 1.20), SIZEOF (specified in Figure 1.20), and a smaller instance of itself. Note that according to the specification, your algorithm may not change $A[1..n]$. Your algorithm should contain exactly one recursive call and no loops. (When calling COPY, your first array index does not need to be 1.)

   (b) Give an iterative version of your algorithm from part (a) by either implementing it bottom-up or eliminating tail recursion, whichever

---

Figure 1.20   Specifications of APPENDTOALL and SIZEOF

Precondition: $A[1..n]$ is an array of arrays and n is a NAT.
Postcondition: For $1 \leq i \leq n$, modifies $A[i]$ to contain an array whose size is 1 larger than its original size, and whose elements are the same as its original elements, with x added as its last element (i.e., x is appended to the end of each $A[i]$).

APPENDTOALL($A[1..n]$, x)

Precondition: A is an array.
Postcondition: Returns the number of elements in A.

SIZEOF(A)

Figure 1.21   Specification for ALLSUBSETS

Precondition: $A[1..n]$ is an ARRAY of distinct elements, and n is a NAT.
Postcondition: Returns an ARRAY $P[1..2^n]$ such that for $1 \leq i \leq 2^n$,
$P[i]$ is an ARRAY containing exactly one occurrence of each element of some
subset of the elements in $A[1..n]$, where each subset of $A[1..n]$ is represented
exactly once in $P[1..2^n]$.

ALLSUBSETS($A[1..n]$)

---

is appropriate. You do not need to provide algorithms for COPY,
APPENDTOALL, or SIZEOF.

1.9   Notes

The elements of top-down software design were introduced by Dijkstra [28]
and Wirth [122] in the late 1960s and early 1970s. As software systems
grew, however, these notions were found to be insufficient to cope with the
sheer size of large projects. As a result, they were eventually superseded by
object-oriented design and programming. The study of algorithms, however,
does not focus on large software systems, but on small components. Consequently, a top-down approach provides an ideal framework for designing and
understanding algorithms.

The maximum subsequence sum problem, as well as the algorithms
MAXSUMITER, MAXSUMOPT, and MAXSUMBU, was introduced by Bentley
[12]. The sorting algorithm suggested by Exercise 1.6 is *selection sort.*

Java is a registered trademark of Oracle and/or its affiliates.

Chapter 2

Proving Algorithm Correctness

In Chapter 1, we specified several problems and presented various algorithms for solving these problems. For each algorithm, we argued somewhat informally that it met its specification. In this chapter, we introduce a mathematical foundation for more rigorous proofs of algorithm correctness. Such proofs not only give us more confidence in the correctness of our algorithms, but also help us to find subtle errors. Furthermore, some of the tools we introduce here are also used in the context of analyzing algorithm performance.

2.1 The Basics

First consider the algorithm SIMPLESELECT, shown in Figure 1.2 on page 7. This algorithm is simple enough that ordinarily we would not bother to give a formal proof of its correctness; however, such a proof serves to illustrate the basic approach. Recall that in order for an algorithm to meet its specification, it must be the case that whenever the precondition is satisfied initially, the postcondition is also satisfied when the algorithm finishes.

Theorem 2.1. SIMPLESELECT *meets the specification given in Figure* 1.1.

Proof. First, we assume that the precondition for SIMPLESELECT($A[1..n]$) is satisfied initially; i.e., we assume that initially $A[1..n]$ is an array of numbers, $1 \leq k \leq n$, and both k and n are natural numbers. This assumption immediately implies the precondition for SORT($A[1..n]$), namely, that $A[1..n]$ is an array of numbers, and that n is a natural number. In order to talk about both the initial and final values of A without confusion, let us represent the final value of A by A' and use A only to denote its initial value. Because

SORT permutes A (we know this from its postcondition), A' contains the same collection of values as does A.

Suppose $A'[i] < A'[k]$ for some i, $1 \leq i \leq n$. Then $i < k$, for if $k < i$, $A'[k] > A'[i]$ violates the postcondition of SORT. Hence, there are fewer than k elements of A', and hence of A, with value less than $A'[k]$.

Now suppose $1 \leq i \leq k$. From the postcondition of SORT, $A'[i] \leq A'[k]$. Hence, there are at least k elements of A with value less than or equal to $A'[k]$. The returned value $A'[k]$ therefore satisfies the postcondition of SELECT. $\square$

Because of what it means for an algorithm to meet its specification, any proof of correctness will begin by assuming the precondition. The goal of the proof is then to prove that the postcondition is

> If the precondition is defined to be true, we don't need to assume it, because we know that true is true.

satisfied when the algorithm finishes. In order to reach this goal, we reason about the effect of each statement in turn. If a statement is a call to another algorithm, we use that algorithm's specification. Specifically, we must first make sure its precondition is satisfied (for otherwise, we cannot know what the algorithm does), then we conclude that its postcondition is satisfied when it finishes. We can then use this postcondition to continue our reasoning.

The proof of Theorem 2.1 illustrates a common difficulty with correctness proofs. In algorithms, variables typically change their values as the algorithm progresses. However, in proofs, a variable must maintain a single value in order to maintain consistent reasoning. In order to avoid confusion, we introduce different names for the value of the same variable at different points in the algorithm. It is customary to use the variable name from the algorithm to denote the initial value, and to add a "prime" ($'$) to denote its final value. If intermediate value must be considered, "double-primes" ($''$), superscripts, or subscripts can be used.

Although a variable should not change its value over the course of a proof, we do sometimes use the same variable with different values when proving different facts. For example, the variable i in the proof of Theorem 2.1 can have different values in the second and third paragraphs, respectively. It might be helpful to think of such usage as multiple local variables, each having the same name. Within each scope, the value of the variable does not change.

The proof of Theorem 2.1 is straightforward because the algorithm is straight-line — the flow of control proceeds sequentially from the first statement in the algorithm to the last. The addition of **if** statements complicates matters only slightly — we must simply apply case analysis. However, the addition of recursion and/or loops requires some additional machinery, which we will develop over the remainder of this chapter.

2.2   Handling Recursion

Let us now consider INSERTSORT from Figure 1.3 on page 7. To handle the **if** statement, we can consider two cases, depending on whether $n > 1$. In case $n > 1$, however, there is a recursive call to INSERTSORT. As is suggested in Section 1.2, we might simply use the specification of SORT just like we would for a call to any other algorithm. However, this type of reasoning is logically suspect — we are assuming the correctness of INSERTSORT in order to prove the correctness of INSERTSORT.

In order to break this circularity, we use the *principle of mathematical induction*. We will be using this principle throughout this text, so we will now take the time to present and prove it. The version we present is a technique for proving properties of the natural numbers. The property that we wish to prove in this case is that INSERTSORT($A[1..n]$) satisfies its specification for every natural number n. Let us now formally define what we mean by a property of the natural numbers, so that our statement of the induction principle will be clear.

Definition 2.2. A *property of the natural numbers* is a mapping

$$P : \mathbb{N} \to \{\mathsf{true}, \mathsf{false}\};$$

i.e., for a natural number n, $P(n)$ is either true or false.

Theorem 2.3 (Mathematical Induction Principle). *Let $P(n)$ be a property of the natural numbers. Suppose that every natural number n satisfies the following Induction Property:*

- *whenever $P(i)$ is* true *for every natural number $i < n$, $P(n)$ is also* true*.*

Then $P(n)$ is true *for every natural number n.*

Before we prove this theorem, let us consider how we can use it. Suppose we wish to prove a property $P(n)$ for every natural number n. Theorem 2.3 tells us that it is sufficient to prove the Induction Property. We can break this proof into two parts:

1. The *induction hypothesis*. We assume that for some arbitrary $n \in \mathbb{N}$, $P(i)$ is true for every natural number $i < n$.
2. The *induction step*. Using the induction hypothesis, we prove that $P(n)$ is true.

Some readers may be familiar with another version of induction consisting of three steps:

1. The *base case*. $P(0)$ is shown to be true.
2. The *induction hypothesis*. $P(n)$ is assumed to be true for some arbitrary natural number n.
3. The *induction step*. Using the induction hypothesis, $P(n+1)$ is proved.

Though this technique is also valid, the version given by Theorem 2.3 is more appropriate for the study of algorithms. To see why, consider how we are using the top-down approach. We associate with each input a natural number that in some way describes the size of the input. We then recursively apply the algorithm to one or more inputs of strictly smaller size. Theorem 2.3 tells us that in order to prove that this algorithm is correct for inputs of all sizes, we may assume that for arbitrary n, the algorithm is correct for all inputs of size less than n. Thus, we may reason about a recursive algorithm in the same way we reason about an algorithm that calls other algorithms, provided the size of the parameters is smaller for the recursive calls.

Now let us turn to the proof of Theorem 2.3.

Proof of Theorem 2.3. Suppose every natural number n satisfies the Induction Property given in the statement of the theorem. In order to derive a contradiction, assume that for some $n \in \mathbb{N}$, $P(n)$ = false. Specifically, let n be the smallest such value. Then for every $i < n$, $P(i)$ = true. By the Induction Property, $P(n)$ = true — a contradiction. We conclude that our assumption was invalid, so that $P(n)$ = true for every natural number n.□

Before we illustrate the use of this principle by proving the correctness of INSERTSORT, let us briefly discuss an element of style regarding induction proofs. One of the distinguishing features of this particular induction principle is the absence of a base case. However, in most proofs, there are special cases in which the induction hypothesis is not used. These are typically the smallest cases, where the induction hypothesis gives us little or no information. It would be a bit of a misnomer to use the term, "induction step", for such cases. It is stylistically better to separate these cases into one or more base cases. Hence, even though a base case is not required, we usually include one (or more).

Now we will illustrate the principle of induction by proving the correctness of INSERTSORT.

Theorem 2.4. INSERTSORT, *given in Figure* 1.3, *satisfies the specification of* SORT, *given in Figure* 1.2.

Proof. By induction on n.

Base: $n \leq 1$. In this case the algorithm does nothing, but its postcondition is vacuously satisfied (i.e., there are no i, j such that $1 \leq i < j \leq n$).

Induction Hypothesis: Assume that for some $n > 1$, for every $k < n$, INSERTSORT($A[1..k]$) satisfies its specification.

Induction Step: We first assume that initially, the precondition for INSERTSORT($A[1..n]$) is satisfied. Then the precondition for INSERTSORT($A[1..n-1]$) is also initially satisfied. By the Induction Hypothesis, we conclude that INSERTSORT($A[1..n-1]$) satisfies its specification; hence, its postcondition holds when it finishes. Let A'' denote the value of A after INSERTSORT($A[1..n-1]$) finishes. Then $A''[1..n-1]$ is a permutation of $A[1..n-1]$ in nondecreasing order, and $A''[n] = A[n]$. Thus, A'' satisfies the precondition of INSERT. Let A' denote the value of A after INSERT($A[1..n]$) is called. By the postcondition of INSERT, $A'[1..n]$ is a permutation of $A[1..n]$ in nondecreasing order. INSERTSORT therefore satisfies its specification. □

Because the algorithm contains an **if** statement, the proof requires a case analysis. The two cases are handled in the Base and the Induction Step, respectively. Note that the way we prove the Induction Step is very similar to how we proved Theorem 2.1. The only difference is that we have the Induction Hypothesis available to allow us to reason about the recursive call.

2.3 Handling Iteration

Let us now consider MAXSUMBU, shown in Figure 1.14 on page 18. This algorithm contains a **for** loop. As we did with recursion, we would like to be able to apply straight-line reasoning techniques. In Chapter 1, we used invariants in order to focus on a single loop iteration. Because we already know how to handle code without loops, focusing on a single iteration allows us to apply techniques we have already developed. Loop invariants therefore give us the power to reason formally about loops.

Suppose we wish to show that property P holds upon completion of a given loop. Suppose further that we can show each of the following:

1. **Initialization:** The invariant holds prior to the first loop iteration.
2. **Maintenance:** If the invariant holds at the beginning of an arbitrary loop iteration, then it must also hold at the end of that iteration.
3. **Termination:** The loop always terminates.
4. **Correctness:** Whenever the loop invariant and the loop exit condition both hold, then P must hold.

It is not hard to show by induction on the number of loop iterations that if both the initialization and maintenance steps hold, then the invariant holds at the end of each iteration. If the loop always terminates, then the invariant and the loop exit condition will both hold when this happens. The correctness step then guarantees that property P will hold after the loop completes. The above four steps are therefore sufficient to prove that P holds upon completion of the loop.

We now illustrate this proof technique by showing correctness of MAX-SUMBU. In our informal justification of this algorithm, we used equations (1.1) and (1.2); however, because we did not prove these equations, our proof of correctness should not use them.

Theorem 2.5. MAXSUMBU *satisfies its specification.*

Proof.   Suppose the precondition holds initially. We will show that when the loop finishes, m contains the maximum subsequence sum of $A[0..n-1]$, so that the postcondition is satisfied. Note that the loop invariant states that m is the maximum subsequence sum of $A[0..i-1]$.

Initialization: Before the loop iterates the first time, i has a value of 0. The maximum subsequence sum of $A[0..-1]$ is defined to be 0. m is initially assigned this value. Likewise, the maximum suffix sum of $A[0..-1]$ is defined to be 0, and *msuf* is initially assigned this value. Therefore, the invariant initially holds.

Maintenance: Suppose the invariant holds at the beginning of some iteration. We first observe that because the iteration occurs, $0 \leq i \leq n-1$; hence, $A[i]$ is a valid array location. Let *msuf'*, m' and i' denote the values of *msuf*, m and i, respectively, at the end of this iteration. Then

- $msuf' = \max(0, msuf + A[i])$;
- $m' = \max(m, msuf')$; and
- $i' = i + 1$.

For $0 \le j \le n$, let s_j denote the maximum subsequence sum of $A[0..j-1]$, and let t_j denote the maximum suffix sum of $A[0..j-1]$. From the invariant, $msuf = t_i$, and $m = s_i$. We need to show that $msuf' = t_{i'}$ and $m' = s_{i'}$.

Using the definition of a maximum suffix sum, we have

$$
\begin{aligned}
msuf' &= \max(0, msuf + A[i]) \\
&= \max(0, t_i + A[i]) \\
&= \max\left(0, \max\left\{\sum_{k=l}^{i-1} A[k] \mid 0 \le l \le i\right\} + A[i]\right) \\
&= \max\left\{0, A[i] + \sum_{k=l}^{i-1} A[k] \mid 0 \le l \le i\right\} \\
&= \max\left\{0, \sum_{k=l}^{i} A[k] \mid 0 \le l \le i\right\} \\
&= \max\left\{\sum_{k=l}^{i'-1} A[k] \mid 0 \le l \le i'\right\} \\
&= t_{i'}.
\end{aligned}
$$

Likewise, using the definitions of a maximum subsequence sum and a maximum suffix sum, we have

$$
\begin{aligned}
m' &= \max(m, msuf') \\
&= \max(s_i, t_{i'}) \\
&= \max\left(\max\left\{\sum_{k=l}^{h-1} A[k] \mid 0 \le l \le h \le i\right\}, \max\left\{\sum_{k=l}^{i'-1} A[k] \mid 0 \le l \le i'\right\}\right) \\
&= \max\left\{\sum_{k=l}^{h-1} A[k] \mid 0 \le l \le h \le i'\right\} \\
&= s_{i'}.
\end{aligned}
$$

Therefore, the invariant holds at the end of the iteration.

Termination: Because the loop is a **for** loop, it clearly terminates.

Correctness: The loop exits when $i = n$. Thus, from the invariant, m is the maximum subsequence sum of $A[0..n-1]$ when the loop terminates.

> In this textbook, a **for** loop always contains a single index variable, which either is incremented by a fixed positive amount each iteration until it exceeds a fixed value or is decremented by a fixed positive amount each iteration until it is less than a fixed value. The index cannot be changed otherwise. Such loops will always terminate.

□

As can be seen from the above proof, initialization and maintenance can be shown using techniques we have already developed. Furthermore, the correctness step is simply logical inference. In the case of Theorem 2.5, termination is trivial, because **for** loops always terminate. Note, however, that in order for such a proof to be completed, it is essential that a proper loop invariant be chosen. Specifically, the invariant must be chosen so that:

- it is true every time the loop condition is tested;
- it is possible to prove that if it is true at the beginning of an arbitrary iteration, it must also be true at the end of that iteration; and
- when coupled with the loop exit condition, it is strong enough to prove the desired correctness property.

Thus, if we choose an invariant that is too strong, it may not be true each time the loop condition is tested. On the other hand, if we choose an invariant that is too weak, we may not be able to prove the correctness property. Furthermore, even if the invariant is true on each iteration and is strong enough to prove the correctness property, it may still be impossible to prove the maintenance step. We will discuss this issue in more detail shortly.

For **while** loops, the proof of termination is usually nontrivial and in some cases quite difficult. An example that is not too difficult is ITERATIVEINSERT in Figure 1.6 (page 11). To prove termination of this loop, we need to show that each iteration makes progress toward satisfying the loop exit condition. The exit condition for this loop is that $j \leq 1$ or $A[j] \geq A[j-1]$. Usually, the way in which a loop will make progress toward meeting such a condition is that each iteration will decrease the difference between the two sides of an inequality. In this case, j is decreased by each iteration, and therefore becomes closer to 1. (The other inequality in the exit condition is not needed to prove termination — if it becomes true, the loop just terminates that much sooner.) We can therefore prove the following theorem.

Theorem 2.6. *The* **while** *loop in* ITERATIVEINSERT *always terminates.*

Proof. We first observe that each iteration of the **while** loop decreases j by 1. Thus, if the loop continues to iterate, eventually $j \leq 1$, and the loop then terminates. □

Proving termination of a **while** loop can be much more difficult than the proof of the above theorem. For example, consider the **while** loop shown in Figure 2.1. The mod operation, when applied to positive integers, gives the remainder obtained when an integer division is performed; thus, the **if** statement tests whether n is even. Though many people have studied this computation over a number of years, as of this writing, it is unknown whether this loop terminates for all initial integer values of n. This question is known as the *Collatz problem*.

On the other hand, when algorithms are designed using the top-down approach, proving termination of any resulting **while** loops becomes much easier. Even if an examination of the **while** loop condition does not help us to find a proof, we should be able to derive a proof from the reduction we used to solve the problem. Specifically, a loop results from the reduction of larger instances of a problem to smaller instances of the same problem, where the size of the instance is a natural number. We should therefore be able to prove that the expression denoting the size of the instance is a natural number that is decreased by every iteration. Termination will then follow.

For example, consider again the algorithm ITERATIVEINSERT. In the design of this algorithm (see Section 1.4), we reduced larger instances to smaller instances, where the size of an instance was n, the number of array elements. In removing the tail recursion from the algorithm, we replaced n by j. j should therefore decrease as the size decreases. We therefore base our correctness proof on this fact.

Figure 2.1 A loop whose termination for all n is unknown

while $n > 1$
    if $n \bmod 2 = 0$
        $n \leftarrow n/2$
    else
        $n \leftarrow 3n + 1$

Let us now consider an algorithm with nested loops, such as INSERTION-SORT, shown in Figure 1.7 on page 12. When loops are nested, we apply the same technique to each loop as we encounter it. Specifically, in order to prove maintenance for the outer loop, we need to prove that the inner loop satisfies some correctness property, which should in turn be sufficient to complete the proof of maintenance for the outer loop. Thus, nested within the maintenance step of the outer loop is a complete proof (i.e., initialization, maintenance, termination and correctness) for the inner loop.

When we prove initialization for the inner loop, we are not simply reasoning about the code leading to the first execution of that loop. Rather, we are reasoning about the code that initializes the loop on any iteration of the outer loop. For this reason, we cannot consider the initialization code for the outer loop when proving the initialization step for the inner loop. Instead, because the proof for the inner loop is actually a part of the maintenance proof for the outer loop, we can use any facts available for use in the proof of maintenance for the outer loop. Specifically, we can use the assumption that the invariant holds at the beginning of the outer loop iteration, and we can reason about any code executed prior to the inner loop during this iteration. We must then show that the invariant of the inner loop is satisfied upon executing this code.

We will now illustrate this technique by giving a complete proof that INSERTIONSORT meets its specification.

Theorem 2.7. INSERTIONSORT *meets its specification.*

Proof. We must show that when the **for** loop finishes, $A[1..n]$ is a permutation of its original values in nondecreasing order.

Initialization: (Outer loop) When the loop begins, $i = 1$ and the contents of $A[1..n]$ have not been changed. Because $A[1..i-1]$ is an empty array, it is in nondecreasing order.

Maintenance: (Outer loop) Suppose the invariant holds at the beginning of some iteration. Let $A'[1..n]$ denote the contents of A at the end of the iteration, and let i' denote the value of i at the end of the iteration. Then $i' = i+1$. We must show that the **while** loop satisfies the correctness property that $A'[1..n]$ is a permutation of the original values of $A[1..n]$, and that $A'[1..i'-1] = A'[1..i]$ is in nondecreasing order.

Initialization: (Inner loop) Because $A[1..n]$ has not been changed since the beginning of the current iteration of the outer loop, from the outer loop invariant, $A[1..n]$ is a permutation of its original values. From the outer loop invariant, $A[1..i-1]$ is in nondecreasing order; hence, because $j = i$, we have for $1 \leq k < k' \leq i$, where $k' \neq j$, $A[k] \leq A[k']$.

Maintenance: (Inner loop) Suppose the invariant holds at the beginning of some iteration. Let $A'[1..n]$ denote the contents of $A[1..n]$ following the iteration, and let j' denote the value of j following the iteration. Hence,

   (i) $A'[j] = A[j-1]$;
  (ii) $A'[j-1] = A[j]$;
 (iii) $A'[k] = A[k]$ for $1 \leq k \leq n$, $k \neq j$, and $k \neq j-1$; and
 (iv) $j' = j - 1$.

Thus, $A'[1..n]$ is a permutation of $A[1..n]$. From the invariant, $A'[1..n]$ is therefore a permutation of the original values of $A[1..n]$. Suppose $1 \leq k < k' \leq i$, where $k' \neq j' = j-1$. We must show that $A'[k] \leq A'[k']$. We consider three cases.

Case 1: $k' < j-1$. Then $A'[k] = A[k]$ and $A'[k'] = A[k']$. From the invariant, $A[k] \leq A[k']$; hence, $A'[k] \leq A'[k']$.

Case 2: $k' = j$. Then $A'[k'] = A[j-1]$. If $k = j-1$, then $A'[k] = A[j]$, and from the **while** loop condition, $A[j] < A[j-1]$. Otherwise, $k < j-1$ and $A'[k] = A[k]$; hence, from the invariant, $A[k] \leq A[j-1]$. In either case, we conclude that $A'[k] \leq A'[k']$.

Case 3: $k' > j$. Then $A'[k'] = A[k']$, and $A'[k] = A[l]$, where l is either k, j, or $j-1$. In each of these cases, $l < k'$; hence, from the invariant, $A[l] \leq A[k']$. Thus, $A'[k] \leq A'[k']$.

Termination (Inner loop): Each iteration decreases the value of j by 1; hence, if the loop keeps iterating, j must eventually be no greater than 1. At this point, the loop will terminate.

Correctness (Inner loop): Let $A'[1..n]$ denote the contents of $A[1..n]$ when the **while** loop terminates, and let i and j denote their values at this point. From the invariant, $A'[1..n]$ is a permutation of its original values. We must show that $A'[1..i]$ is in nondecreasing order. Let $1 \le k < k' \le i$. We consider two cases.

Case 1: $k' = j$. Then $j > 1$. From the loop exit condition, it follows that $A'[j-1] \le A'[j] = A'[k']$. From the invariant, if $k \ne j-1$, then $A'[k] \le A'[j-1]$; hence, regardless of whether $k = j-1$, $A'[k] \le A'[k']$.

Case 2: $k' \ne j$. Then from the invariant, $A'[k] \le A'[k']$.

This completes the proof for the inner loop, and hence the proof of maintenance for the outer loop.

Termination (Outer loop): Because the loop is a **for** loop, it must terminate.

Correctness (Outer loop): Let $A'[1..n]$ denote its final contents. From the invariant, $A'[1..n]$ is a permutation of its original values. From the loop exit condition $(i = n + 1)$ and the invariant, $A'[1..n]$ is in non-decreasing order. Therefore, the postcondition is satisfied.   □

Now that we have shown that INSERTIONSORT is correct, let us consider how we might have found the invariant for the inner loop. The inner loop implements a transformation of larger instances of the insertion problem, specified in Figure 1.3 on page 7, to smaller instances of the same problem. The loop invariant should therefore be related to the precondition for INSERT.

The current instance of the insertion problem is represented by $A[1..j]$. Therefore, a first choice for an invariant might be that $A[1..j]$ is a permutation of its original values, and that $A[1..j-1]$ is sorted. However, this invariant is not strong enough to prove the correctness property. To see why, observe that the loop exit condition allows the loop to terminate when $j = 1$. In this case, $A[1..j]$ has only one element, $A[1..j-1]$ is empty, and the invariant tells us almost nothing.

Clearly, we need to include in our invariant that $A[1..n]$ is a permutation of its initial values. Furthermore, we need more information about what has already been sorted. Looking at the invariant for the outer loop, we might try saying that both $A[1..j-1]$ and $A[j..i]$ are in nondecreasing order. By coupling this invariant with the loop exit condition (i.e, either $j = 1$ or $A[j-1] \le A[j]$), we can then show that $A[1..i]$ is sorted. Furthermore, it is possible to show that this invariant is true every time the loop condition is tested. However, it still is not sufficient to prove the maintenance step for this loop. To see why, observe that it tells us nothing about how $A[j-1]$

compares with $A[j+1]$. Thus, when $A[j-1]$ is swapped with $A[j]$, we cannot show that $A[j] \leq A[j+1]$.

We need to express in our invariant that when we choose two indices $k < k'$, where $k' \neq j$, we must have $A[k] \leq A[k']$. The invariant in Figure 1.7 states precisely this fact. Arriving at this invariant, however, required some degree of effort.

We mentioned in Section 1.4 that starting the **for** loop with $i = 1$, rather than $i = 2$, simplifies the correctness proof without affecting the correctness. We can now explain what we meant. Note that if we were to begin the **for** loop with $i = 2$, its invariant would no longer be established initially if $n = 0$. Specifically, $A[1..i-1] = A[1..1]$, and if $n = 0$, $A[1]$ is not a valid array location. A more complicated invariant — and consequently a more complicated proof — would therefore be required to handle this special case. By instead beginning the loop at 1, we have sacrificed a very small amount of run-time overhead for the purpose of simplifying the invariant.

2.4   Combining Recursion and Iteration

In this section, we will present an alternative approach to solving the selection problem, specified in Figure 1.1 on page 5. This approach will ultimately result in a recursive algorithm that also contains a loop. We will then show how to combine the techniques presented in the last two sections in order to prove such an algorithm to be correct.

We will reduce the selection problem to the following three problems:

- the *Dutch national flag problem*, defined below;
- the problem of finding the median of a nonempty array of numbers (see Figure 2.2 for a specification of this problem); and
- a smaller instance of the selection problem.

> Figure 2.2 uses the notation $\lceil x \rceil$, *pronounced the ceiling of* x, *to denote the smallest integer no smaller than* x. *Thus,* $\lceil 3/2 \rceil = 2$, *and* $\lceil -3/2 \rceil = -1$. *Likewise,* $\lfloor x \rfloor$, *pronounced the floor of* x, *denotes the largest integer no larger than* x. *Thus,* $\lfloor 3/2 \rfloor = 1$, *and* $\lfloor -3/2 \rfloor = -2$.

Somewhat informally, the input to the Dutch national flag problem is an array of items, each of which is colored either **red**, **white**, or **blue**. The goal is to arrange the items so that all of the **red** items precede all of the **white** items, which in turn precede all of the **blue** items. This order is the order of the colors appearing on the Dutch national flag, from top to bottom. We will modify the problem slightly by assuming that all items are numbers,

---

Figure 2.2   Specification of the median problem

Precondition: $A[1..n]$ is an array of numbers, and n is a positive integer.
Postcondition: Returns the median of $A[1..n]$; i.e., returns x such that fewer than $\lceil n/2 \rceil$ elements are less than x and at least $\lceil n/2 \rceil$ elements are less than or equal to x.

MEDIAN($A[1..n]$)

Figure 2.3   Specification of DUTCHFLAG

Precondition: $A[lo..hi]$ is an array of NUMBERs, lo and hi are INTs such that $hi \geq lo - 1$, and p is a NUMBER.
Postcondition: $A[lo..hi]$ is a permutation of its original values such that, all items less than p precede all items equal to p, which in turn precede all items greater than p. Returns an array $N[1..3]$ in which $N[1]$ is the number of items less than p, $N[2]$ is the number of items equal to p, and $N[3]$ is the number of items greater than p in $A[lo..hi]$.

DUTCHFLAG($A[lo..hi], p$)

---

and that a number is red if it is strictly less than some given value p, white if it is equal to p, or blue if it is strictly greater than p.

The formal specification of this problem is given in Figure 2.3. Note that we use the type INT to represent an integer. Notice also that because it may be important to know the number of items of each color, these values are returned in a 3-element array.

We can then find the kth smallest element in a nonempty array as follows:

1. Let p be the median element of the array.
2. Solve the resulting Dutch national flag problem.
3. If there are at least k red elements, return the kth smallest red element.
4. Otherwise, if there are at least k red and white elements combined, return p.
5. Otherwise, return the $(k - j)$th smallest blue element, where j is the number of red and white elements combined.

Note that after we have solved the Dutch national flag problem, all elements less than p appear first in the array, followed by all elements equal to p, followed by all elements greater than p. Furthermore, because steps 3 and 5 apply to portions of the array that do not contain p, these steps solve strictly smaller problem instances.

In what follows, we will develop a solution to the Dutch national flag problem. We will then combine that solution with the above reduction to obtain a solution to the selection problem (we will simply use the specification for MEDIAN). We will then prove that the resulting algorithm is correct.

In order to conserve resources, we will constrain our solution to the Dutch national flag problem to rearrange items by swapping them. We will reduce a large instance of the problem to a smaller instance. We begin by examining the last item. If it is blue, then we can simply ignore it and solve what is left. If it is red, we can swap it with the first item and again ignore it and solve what is left. If it is white, we need to find out where it belongs; hence, we temporarily ignore it and solve the remaining problem. We then swap it with the first blue item, or if there are no blue items, we can leave it where it is. This algorithm is shown in Figure 2.4.

If we were to implement this solution, or to analyze it using the techniques of Chapter 3, we would soon discover that its stack usage is too high. Furthermore, none of the recursive calls occur at either the beginning or the end of the computation; hence, the recursion is not tail recursion, and we cannot implement it bottom-up.

We can, however, use a technique called *generalization* that will allow us to solve the problem using a transformation. We first observe that the only reason we must wait until after the recursive calls to increment

---

Figure 2.4   A top-down implementation DUTCHFLAG, specified in Figure 2.3

DUTCHFLAGTD($A[lo..hi], p$)
  if $hi < lo$
    $N \leftarrow$ **new** ARRAY$[1..3]$; $N[1] \leftarrow 0$; $N[2] \leftarrow 0$; $N[3] \leftarrow 0$
  else if $A[hi] < p$
    $A[lo] \leftrightarrow A[hi]$; $N \leftarrow$ DUTCHFLAGTD($A[lo + 1..hi], p$)
    $N[1] \leftarrow N[1] + 1$
  else if $A[hi] = p$
    $N \leftarrow$ DUTCHFLAGTD($A[lo..hi - 1], p$)
    $A[hi] \leftrightarrow A[lo + N[1] + N[2]]$; $N[2] \leftarrow N[2] + 1$
  else
    $N \leftarrow$ DUTCHFLAGTD($A[lo..hi - 1], p$); $N[3] \leftarrow N[3] + 1$
  return N

the appropriate element of N is that the recursive call is responsible for constructing and initializing N. If instead, we could provide initial values for $N[1..3]$ to the recursive calls, we could then incorporate the color of the last element into these initial values. We therefore generalize the problem by requiring as input initial values for the number of items of each color. The returned array will then contain values representing the number of items of the corresponding color, plus the corresponding initial value from the input. By using 0 for all three initial values, we obtain the number of each color in the entire array; hence, we have defined a more general problem.

We can use this generalization to make two of the calls tail recursion. In order to be able to handle a white item, though, we need to modify our generalization slightly. Specifically, we need to know in advance where to put a white item. In order to be able to do this, let us specify that if w is given as the initial value for the number of white items, then the last w items in the array are white. Note that this variation is still a generalization of the original problem, because if $w = 0$, no additional constraints are placed on the input array.

Suppose we have an instance of this more general problem. If the initial value for the number of white items is equal to the number of elements in the array, then we can copy the initial values into $N[1..3]$ and return. Otherwise, we examine the item preceding the first known white item (see Figure 2.5). If it is red, we swap it with the first item and solve the smaller problem

Figure 2.5 The transformation for Dutch national flag.

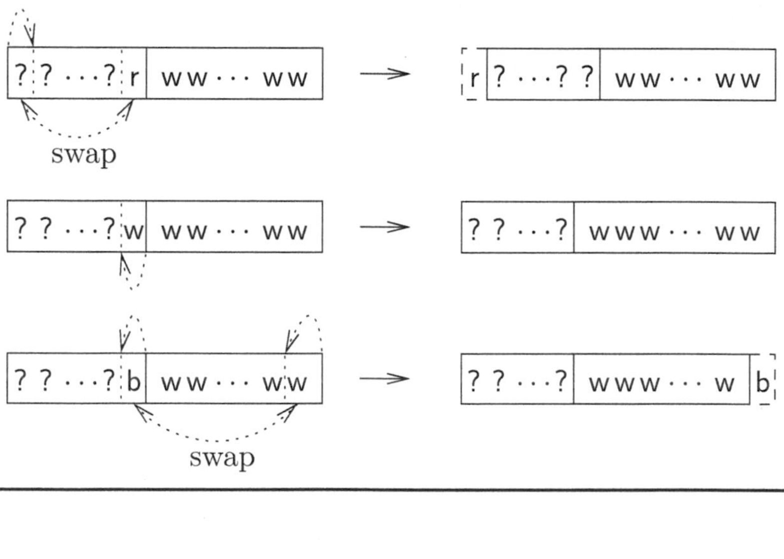

Figure 2.6   Tail recursive solution to a generalization of the Dutch national flag problem

---

Precondition: $A[lo..hi]$ is an array of NUMBERs whose last w items are equal to p, lo and hi are INTs such that $w \leq hi - lo + 1$, and r, w, and b are NATs.

Postcondition: $A[lo..hi]$ is a permutation of its original values such that all items less than p precede all items equal to p, which in turn precede all items greater than p. Returns an array $N[1..3]$ in which $N[1]$ is r plus the number of items less than p, $N[2]$ is the number of items equal to p, and $N[3]$ is b plus the number of items greater than p in $A[lo..hi]$.

DUTCHFLAGTAILREC($A[lo..hi], p, r, w, b$)
  if $w \geq hi - lo + 1$
    $N \leftarrow$ **new** ARRAY$[1..3]$; $N[1] \leftarrow r$; $N[2] \leftarrow w$; $N[3] \leftarrow b$
    return N
  else
    $j \leftarrow hi - w$
    if $A[j] < p$
      $A[j] \leftrightarrow A[lo]$
      return DUTCHFLAGTAILREC($A[lo + 1..hi], p, r + 1, w, b$)
    else if $A[j] = p$
      return DUTCHFLAGTAILREC($A[lo..hi], p, r, w + 1, b$)
    else
      $A[j] \leftrightarrow A[hi]$
      return DUTCHFLAGTAILREC($A[lo..hi - 1], p, r, w, b + 1$)

---

obtained by ignoring the first item. If it is white, we solve the problem that results from incrementing the initial number of white items. If it is blue, we swap it with the last element, and solve the smaller problem obtained by ignoring the last item. A recursive implementation of this strategy is shown in Figure 2.6.

The way we handle the case in which an item is white is suspicious in that the reduced instance is an array with the same number of elements. However, note that in each case, the number of elements of unknown color is decreased by the reduction. Thus, if we choose our definition of "size" to be the number of elements of unknown color, then our reduction does decrease the size of the problem in each case. Recall that our notion of size is any natural number which decreases in all "smaller" instances. Our reduction is therefore valid.

Figure 2.7 An algorithm for solving the selection problem, specified in Figure 1.1, using the median

---

$\text{SELECTBYMEDIAN}(A[1..n], k)$
   $p \leftarrow \text{MEDIAN}(A[1..n]); \; r \leftarrow 0; \; w \leftarrow 0; \; b \leftarrow 0$
   // **Invariant:** $r, w, b \in \mathbb{N}$, $r + w + b \leq n$, and $A[i] < p$ for $1 \leq i \leq r$,
   // $A[i] = p$ for $n - b - w < i \leq n - b$, and $A[i] > p$ for $n - b < i \leq n$.
   while $r + w + b < n$
      $j \leftarrow n - b - w$
      if $A[j] < p$
         $r \leftarrow r + 1; \; A[j] \leftrightarrow A[r]$
      else if $A[j] = p$
         $w \leftarrow w + 1$
      else
         $A[j] \leftrightarrow A[n - b]; \; b = b + 1$
   if $r \geq k$
      return $\text{SELECTBYMEDIAN}(A[1..r], k)$
   else if $r + w \geq k$
      return p
   else
      return $\text{SELECTBYMEDIAN}(A[1 + r + w..n], k - (r + w))$

Figure 2.7 shows the result of eliminating the tail recursion from DUTCH-FLAGTAILREC, incorporating it into the selection algorithm described earlier in this section, and making some minor modifications. First, *lo* and *hi* have been replaced by 1 and n, respectively. Second, the array N has been removed, and r, w, b are used directly instead. Finally, referring to Figure 2.6, note that when a recursive call is made, *lo* is incremented exactly when r is incremented, and *hi* is decremented exactly when b is incremented. Because we are replacing *lo* with 1, which cannot be changed, and *hi* with n, which we would rather not change, we instead use the expressions $r + 1$ and $n - b$, respectively. Thus, for example, instead of having a **while** loop condition of $w < hi - lo + 1$, we replace *lo* with $r + 1$ and *hi* with $n - b$, rearrange terms, and obtain $r + w + b < n$.

As we have already observed, the invariant for a loop implementing a transformation is closely related to the precondition for the problem. Thus, in order to obtain the loop invariant, we take the precondition for DUTCHFLAGTAILREC, remove "$A[lo..hi]$ is an array of NUMBERS", as this is understood, and replace *lo* with $r + 1$ and *hi* with $n - b$. This gives us most of the invariant. However, we must also take into account that the iterations do not actually change the size of the problem instance; hence, the invariant must also include a characterization of what has been done outside of $A[r + 1..n - b]$. The portion to the left is where **red** items have been placed, and the portion to the right is where **blue** items have been placed. We need to include these constraints in our invariant.

Note that in Figure 2.7, the last line of SELECTBYMEDIAN contains a recursive call in which the first parameter is $A[1 + r + w..n]$. However, the specification given in Figure 1.1 (page 5) states that the first parameter must be of the form $A[1..n]$. To accommodate such a mismatch, we adopt a convention that allows for automatic re-indexing of arrays when the specification requires a parameter to be an array whose beginning index is a fixed value. Specifically, we think of the sub-array $A[1 + r + w..n]$ as an array $B[1..n - (r + w)]$. B is then renamed to A when it is used as the actual parameter in the recursive call.

Let us now prove the correctness of SELECTBYMEDIAN. Because SELECTBYMEDIAN contains a loop, we must prove this loop's correctness using the techniques of Section 2.3. Specifically, we need the following lemma, whose proof we leave as an exercise.

Lemma 2.8. *If the precondition for* SELECTBYMEDIAN *is satisfied, then its* **while** *loop always terminates with* $A[1..n]$ *being a permutation of its original elements such that*

- $A[i] < p$ *for* $1 \leq i \leq r$;
- $A[i] = p$ *for* $r < i \leq r + w$; *and*
- $A[i] > p$ *for* $r + w < i \leq n$.

Furthermore, when the loop terminates, r, w, *and* b *are natural numbers such that* $r + w + b = n$.

We can then prove the correctness of SELECTBYMEDIAN using induction.

Theorem 2.9. SELECTBYMEDIAN *meets the specification of* SELECT *given in Figure 1.1.*

Proof. By induction on n.

Induction Hypothesis: Assume that for some $n \geq 1$, whenever $1 \leq m < n$, SELECTBYMEDIAN$(A[1..m], k)$ meets its specification, where $A[1..m]$ denotes (by re-indexing if necessary) any array with m elements.

Induction Step: Suppose the precondition is satisfied. By Lemma 2.8, the **while** loop will terminate with $A[1..n]$ being a permutation of its original elements such that $A[1..r]$ are less than p, $A[r+1..r+w]$ are equal to p, and $A[r+w+1..n]$ are greater than p. We consider three cases.

Case 1: $k \leq r$. In this case, there are at least k elements less than p, so the kth smallest is less than p. Because $A[1..r]$ are all the elements smaller than p, the kth smallest of $A[1..n]$ is the kth smallest of $A[1..r]$. Because p is an element of $A[1..n]$ that is not in $A[1..r]$, $r < n$. Furthermore, because $k \leq r$, the precondition of SELECT is satisfied by the recursive call SELECTBYMEDIAN$(A[1..r], k)$. By the Induction Hypothesis, this recursive call returns the kth smallest element of $A[1..r]$, which is the kth smallest of $A[1..n]$.

Case 2: $r < k \leq r + w$. In this case, there are fewer than k elements less than p and at least k elements less than or equal to p. p is therefore the kth smallest element.

Case 3: $r + w < k$. In this case, there are fewer than k elements less than or equal to p. The kth smallest must therefore be greater than p. It must therefore be in $A[r+w+1..n]$. Because every element in $A[1..r+w]$ is less than the kth smallest, the kth smallest must be the $(k-(r+w))$th smallest element in $A[r+w+1..n]$. Because p is an element of $A[1..n]$ that is not in $A[r+w+1..n]$, $r+w+1 > 1$, so that the number of elements in $A[r+w+1..n]$ is less than n. Let us refer to $A[r+w+1..n]$ as $B[1..n-(r+w)]$. Then because $r+w < k$, $1 \leq k-(r+w)$, and because $k \leq n$, $k-(r+w) \leq n-(r+w)$. Therefore, the precondition for SELECT is satisfied by the recursive call SELECTBYMEDIAN$(B[1..n-(r+w)], k-(r+w))$. By the Induction Hypothesis, this recursive call returns the $(k-(r+w))$th smallest element of $B[1..n-(r+w)] = A[r+w+1..n]$. This element is the kth smallest of $A[1..n]$. □

In some cases, a recursive call might occur inside a loop. For such cases, we would need to use the induction hypothesis when reasoning about the loop. As a result, it would be impossible to separate the proof into a lemma dealing with the loop and a theorem whose proof uses induction and the lemma. We would instead need to prove initialization, maintenance, termination, and correctness of the loop within the induction step of the induction proof.

2.5 Mutual Recursion

The techniques we have presented up to this point are sufficient for proving the correctness of most algorithms. However, one situation can occur which reveals a flaw in these techniques. Specifically, it is possible to prove correctness using these techniques, when in fact the algorithm is incorrect. The situation leading to this inconsistency is known as *mutual recursion*. In a simple case, we have one algorithm, A, which calls another algorithm, B, which in turn calls A. More generally, we may have a sequence of algorithms, $A_1, \ldots, A_n$, where A_i calls A_{i+1} for $1 \leq i < n$, and A_n calls A_1.

For example, suppose we were to implement MEDIAN, as specified in Figure 2.7, by reducing it to the selection problem. This reduction is straightforward, as it is easily seen that the median is just the $\lceil n/2 \rceil$nd smallest element. We therefore have the algorithm shown in Figure 2.8. Its proof of correctness is trivial.

We therefore have the algorithm SELECTBYMEDIAN, which correctly implements SELECT if we use a correct implementation of MEDIAN. We also have the algorithm MEDIANBYSELECT, which correctly implements MEDIAN if we use a correct implementation of SELECT. The problem arises when we use both of these implementations together. The proof of correctness for the resulting implementation contains circular reasoning. In fact, the implementation is not correct, as can be seen if we replace the call to MEDIAN in Figure 2.7 with the call, SELECTBYMEDIAN($A[1..n], \lceil n/2 \rceil$). We now have a recursive call whose argument is no smaller than that of the original call. As a result, we have infinite recursion.

Though we will not prove it here, it turns out that nontermination is the only way in which combining correct algorithms in a mutually recursive fashion can result in an incorrect implementation. Thus, if we can prove that the implementation terminates, we can conclude that it is correct. In Chapter 3, we will present techniques for showing not just termination, but the time it takes for an algorithm to terminate. These techniques will be general enough to apply to mutually recursive algorithms.

Figure 2.8 An implementation of MEDIAN, specified in Figure 2.7, using SELECT, as specified in Figure 1.1

MEDIANBYSELECT($A[1..n]$)
   return SELECT($A[1..n], \lceil n/2 \rceil$)

In Chapter 15, we will present algorithms that use mutual recursion. As we will see there, mutual recursion is sometimes useful for breaking a complicated algorithm into manageable pieces. Apart from that chapter, we will not dwell on mutual recursion. We should always be careful, however, when we combine algorithms, that we do not inadvertently introduce mutual recursion without proving termination of the implementation.

2.6 Finding Errors

The process of proving correctness of an algorithm is more than just an academic exercise. A proper correctness proof should give us confidence that a given algorithm is, in fact, correct. It therefore stands to reason that if a given algorithm is incorrect, the proof of correctness should fail at some point. The process of proving correctness can therefore help us to find errors in algorithms.

Suppose, for example, that in MaxSumBU (see Figure 1.14 on page 18), we had miscalculated *msuf* using the statement

$$msuf \leftarrow msuf + A[i].$$

We could have made such an error by forgetting that there is a suffix of $A[0..i]$ — the empty suffix — that does not end with $A[i]$. We would expect that a proof of correctness for such an erroneous algorithm should break down at some point.

This error certainly wouldn't affect the Initialization part of the proof, as the initialization code is unchanged. Likewise, the Correctness part doesn't depend directly on code within the loop, but only on the invariant and the loop exit condition. Because the Termination part is trivial, we are left with the Maintenance part. Because we have changed the calculation of *msuf*, we would expect that we would be unable to prove that the second part of the invariant is maintained (i.e., that *msuf* is the maximum suffix sum for $A[0..i-1]$).

Let us consider how this statement changes the Maintenance part of the proof of Theorem 2.5. The first change is that now $msuf' = msuf + A[i]$. This affects the derivation from $msuf'$ in the following way:

$$msuf' = msuf + A[i]$$
$$= t_i + A[i]$$

$$= \max \left\{ \sum_{k=l}^{i-1} A[k] \mid 0 \le l \le i \right\} + A[i]$$

$$= \max \left\{ A[i] + \sum_{k=l}^{i-1} A[k] \mid 0 \le l \le i \right\}$$

$$= \max \left\{ \sum_{k=l}^{i} A[k] \mid 0 \le l \le i \right\}$$

$$= \max \left\{ \sum_{k=l}^{i'-1} A[k] \mid 0 \le l \le i' - 1 \right\}.$$

However,

$$t_{i'} = \max \left\{ \sum_{k=l}^{i'-1} A[k] \mid 0 \le l \le i' \right\}.$$

Note that the set on the right-hand side of this last equality has one more element than does the set on the right-hand side of the preceding equality. This element is generated by $l = i'$, which results in an empty sum having a value of 0. All of the remaining elements are derived from values $l \le i' - 1$, which result in nonempty sums of elements from $A[0..i]$. Thus, if $A[0..i]$ contains only negative values, $msuf' < t_{i'}$. It is therefore impossible to prove that these values are equal.

A failure to come up with a proof of correctness does not necessarily mean the algorithm is incorrect. It may be that we have not been clever enough to find the proof. Alternatively, it may be that an invariant has not been stated properly, as discussed in Section 2.3. Such a failure always reveals, however, that we do not yet understand the algorithm well enough to prove that it is correct.

2.7 Summary

We have introduced two main techniques for proving algorithm correctness, depending on whether the algorithm uses recursion or iteration:

- The correctness of a recursive algorithm should be shown using induction.
- The correctness of an iterative algorithm should be shown by proving initialization, maintenance, termination, and correctness for each of the loops.

Some algorithms might contain both recursion and iteration. In such cases, both techniques should be used. Because the algorithm is recursive, its correctness should be shown using induction. In order to complete the induction, the loops will need to be handled by proving initialization, maintenance, termination, and correctness. In Chapter 4, we will see how these techniques can be extended to proving the correctness of data structures.

Though correctness proofs are useful for finding errors in algorithms and for giving us confidence that algorithms are correct, they are also quite tedious. On the other hand, if an algorithm is fully specified and designed in a top-down fashion, and if proper loop invariants are provided, working out the details of a proof is usually not very hard. For this reason, we will not provide many correctness proofs in the remainder of this text, but will leave them as exercises. We will instead give top-down designs of algorithms and provide invariants for most of the loops contained in them.

2.8   Exercises

Exercise 2.1. Induction can be used to prove solutions for summations. Use induction to prove each of the following:

(a) The *arithmetic series*:

$$\sum_{i=1}^{n} i = \frac{n(n+1)}{2}. \tag{2.1}$$

(b) The *geometric series*:

$$\sum_{i=0}^{n} x^i = \frac{x^{n+1} - 1}{x - 1}, \tag{2.2}$$

for any real $x \neq 1$.

Exercise 2.2. Let

$$f(n) = \begin{cases} 1 & \text{if } n = 0 \\ \displaystyle\sum_{i=0}^{n-1} f(i) & \text{if } n > 0. \end{cases}$$

Use induction to prove that for all $n > 0$, $f(n) = 2^{n-1}$.

* Exercise 2.3. The *Fibonacci sequence* is defined as follows:

$$F_n = \begin{cases} n & \text{if } 0 \leq n \leq 1 \\ F_{n-1} + F_{n-2} & \text{if } n > 1. \end{cases} \tag{2.3}$$

Use induction to prove each of the following properties of the Fibonacci sequence:

(a) For every $n > 0$,

$$F_{n-1}F_n + F_n F_{n+1} = F_{2n} \tag{2.4}$$

and

$$F_n^2 + F_{n+1}^2 = F_{2n+1}. \tag{2.5}$$

[**Hint:** Prove both equalities together in a single induction argument.]
(b) For every $n \in \mathbb{N}$,

$$F_n = \frac{\phi^n - (-\phi)^{-n}}{\sqrt{5}}, \tag{2.6}$$

where ϕ is the *golden ratio*:

$$\phi = \frac{1 + \sqrt{5}}{2}.$$

Exercise 2.4. Prove that RECURSIVEINSERT, shown in Figure 1.4 on page 8, meets is specification, given in Figure 1.3 on page 7.

Exercise 2.5. Prove that MAXSUFFIXTD and MAXSUMTD, given in Figure 1.13 (page 18), meet their specifications. For MAXSUMTD, use the specification of MAXSUM given in Figure 1.9 (page 14).

Exercise 2.6. Prove that DOTPRODUCT, shown in Figure 1.17 on page 21, meets its specification.

Exercise 2.7. Prove that FACTORIAL, shown in Figure 2.9, meets its specification. $n!$ (pronounced, "n factorial") denotes the product $1 \cdot 2 \cdots n$ (0! is defined to be 1).

Exercise 2.8. A minor modification of MAXSUMOPT is shown in Figure 2.10 with its loop invariants. Prove that it meets the specification of MAXSUM, given in Figure 1.9 (page 14).

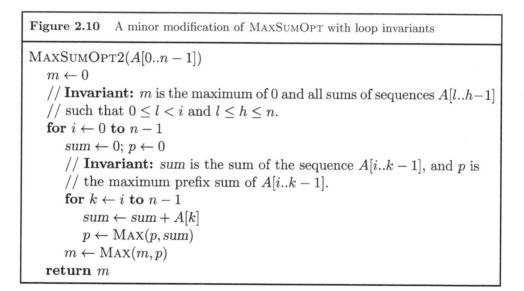

Figure 2.9   Algorithm for FACTORIAL

Precondition: n is a NAT.
Postcondition: Returns $n!$.

FACTORIAL(n)
  $p \leftarrow 1$
  // **Invariant:** $p = (i-1)!$
  for $i \leftarrow 1$ **to** n
    $p \leftarrow ip$
  return p

Figure 2.10   A minor modification of MAXSUMOPT with loop invariants

MAXSUMOPT2($A[0..n-1]$)
  $m \leftarrow 0$
  // **Invariant:** m is the maximum of 0 and all sums of sequences $A[l..h-1]$
  // such that $0 \le l < i$ and $l \le h \le n$.
  for $i \leftarrow 0$ **to** $n-1$
    $sum \leftarrow 0; p \leftarrow 0$
    // **Invariant:** sum is the sum of the sequence $A[i..k-1]$, and p is
    // the maximum prefix sum of $A[i..k-1]$.
    for $k \leftarrow i$ **to** $n-1$
      $sum \leftarrow sum + A[k]$
      $p \leftarrow$ MAX(p, sum)
    $m \leftarrow$ MAX(m, p)
  return m

Exercise 2.9. A minor modification of MAXSUMITER is shown in Figure 2.11 with its loop invariants. Prove that it meets the specification of MAXSUM, given in Figure 1.9 (page 14).

Exercise 2.10. Prove that DUTCHFLAGTD, given in Figure 2.4 (page 39), meets its specification, given in Figure 2.3 (page 38).

* Exercise 2.11. Figure 2.12 shows a slightly optimized version of INSERTIONSORT. Prove that INSERTIONSORT2 meets the specification given in Figure 1.2 on page 7. You will need to find appropriate invariants for each of the loops.

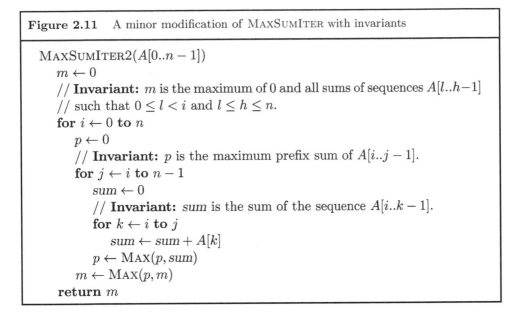

Figure 2.11 A minor modification of MaxSumIter with invariants

MaxSumIter2($A[0..n-1]$)
   $m \leftarrow 0$
   // **Invariant:** m is the maximum of 0 and all sums of sequences $A[l..h-1]$
   // such that $0 \leq l < i$ and $l \leq h \leq n$.
   for $i \leftarrow 0$ **to** n
      $p \leftarrow 0$
      // **Invariant:** p is the maximum prefix sum of $A[i..j-1]$.
      for $j \leftarrow i$ **to** $n-1$
         $sum \leftarrow 0$
         // **Invariant:** sum is the sum of the sequence $A[i..k-1]$.
         for $k \leftarrow i$ **to** j
            $sum \leftarrow sum + A[k]$
         $p \leftarrow$ Max(p, sum)
      $m \leftarrow$ Max(p, m)
   return m

Figure 2.12 A slightly optimized version of InsertionSort

InsertionSort2($A[1..n]$)
   for $i \leftarrow 2$ **to** n
      $j \leftarrow i;\ t \leftarrow A[j]$
      while $j > 1$ **and** $A[j-1] > t$
         $A[j] \leftarrow A[j-1];\ j \leftarrow j-1$
      $A[j] \leftarrow t$

Exercise 2.12. Prove that DutchFlagTailRec, shown in Figure 2.6 on page 41, meets its specification.

Exercise 2.13. Prove Lemma 2.8 (page 43).

* Exercise 2.14. Prove that Permutations, shown in Figure 2.13, meets it specification. Use the specifications of Copy, AppendToAll, and Factorial from Figures 1.18, 1.20, and 2.9, respectively.

Exercise 2.15. Prove that SwapColors, shown in Figure 2.14, meets its specification. Note that the second conjunct in the **while** condition is comparing two boolean values; thus, it is true whenever exactly one of $A[i]$ and $A[j]$ equals p.

Figure 2.13   Algorithm for PERMUTATIONS

Precondition: $A[1..n]$ is an array of distinct elements, and n is a NAT.
Postcondition: Returns an array $P[1..n!]$ of all of the permutations of $A[1..n]$, where each permutation is itself an array $A_i[1..n]$.

PERMUTATIONS($A[1..n]$)
   $P \leftarrow$ **new** ARRAY$[1..\text{FACTORIAL}(n)]$
   if $n = 0$
      $P[1] \leftarrow$ **new** ARRAY$[1..0]$
   else
      $k \leftarrow 1$; $nmin1fac \leftarrow$ FACTORIAL$(n - 1)$
      // **Invariant:** $P[1..k - 1]$ contains all of the permutations of $A[1..n]$
      // such that for $1 \leq j < k$, $P[j][n]$ is in $A[1..i - 1]$.
      for $i \leftarrow 1$ **to** n
         $B \leftarrow$ **new** ARRAY$[1..n - 1]$
         COPY$(A[1..i - 1], B[1..i - 1])$; COPY$(A[i + 1..n], B[i..n - 1])$
         $C \leftarrow$ PERMUTATIONS$(B[1..n - 1])$
         APPENDTOALL$(C[1..nmin1fac], A[i])$
         COPY$(C[1..nmin1fac], P[k..k + nmin1fac - 1])$
         $k \leftarrow k + nmin1fac$
   return P

Figure 2.14   The algorithm for Exercise 2.15

Precondition: $A[lo..hi]$ is an array of NUMBERs, lo and hi are INTs, and p is a NUMBER such that either all occurrences of p in $A[lo..hi]$ precede all occurrences of other values, or all occurrences of p follow all occurrences of other values. We will refer to the first group of elements (i.e., either those equal to p or those not equal to p, whichever comes first) as yellow, and the other elements as green.
Postcondition: $A[lo..hi]$ is a permutation of its initial values such that all green elements precede all yellow elements.

SWAPCOLORS($A[lo..hi], p$)
   if $lo \leq hi + 1$
      $i \leftarrow lo$; $j \leftarrow hi$
      // **Invariant:** $lo \leq i \leq j + 1 \leq hi + 1$ and $A[lo..hi]$ is a
      // permutation of its original values such that $A[k]$ is green for
      // $lo \leq k < i$, $A[k]$ is yellow for $j < k \leq hi$, and in $A[i..j]$,
      // all yellow elements precede all green elements.
      while $i < j$ **and** $(A[i] = p) \neq (A[j] = p)$
         $A[i] \leftrightarrow A[j]$; $i \leftarrow i + 1$; $j \leftarrow j - 1$

Figure 2.15 Buggy algorithm for Exercise 2.16

DUTCHFLAGFIVEBANDS($A[lo..hi], p$)
  $i \leftarrow lo; \; j \leftarrow lo; \; k \leftarrow hi; \; l \leftarrow hi$
  // **Invariant:** $lo \leq i \leq j \leq hi, \; lo \leq k \leq l \leq hi, \; A[lo..i-1]$ all equal p,
  // $A[i..j-1]$ are all less than p, $A[k..l]$ are all greater than p, and
  // $A[l+1..hi]$ all equal p.
  while $j < k$
    if $A[j] < p$
      $j \leftarrow j + 1$
    else if $A[j] = p$
      $A[j] \leftrightarrow A[i]; \; i \leftarrow i + 1; \; j \leftarrow j + 1$
    else if $A[k] = p$
      $A[k] \leftrightarrow A[l]; \; k \leftarrow k - 1; \; l \leftarrow l - 1$
    else if $A[k] > p$
      $k \leftarrow k - 1$
    else
      $A[j] \leftrightarrow A[k]; \; j \leftarrow j + 1; \; k \leftarrow k - 1$
  $N \leftarrow$ **new** ARRAY$[1..3]$
  $N[1] \leftarrow j - i; \; N[2] \leftarrow i - lo + hi - l; \; N[3] \leftarrow l - k$
  SWAPCOLORS($A[lo..j], p$)
  SWAPCOLORS($A[k..hi], p$)
  return $N[1..3]$

Exercise 2.16. Figure 2.15 contains an algorithm for reducing the Dutch national flag problem to the problem solved in Figure 2.14. However, the algorithm contains several errors. Work through a proof that this algorithm meets its specification (given in Figure 2.3 on page 38), pointing out each place at which the proof fails. At each of these places, suggest a small change that could be made to correct the error. In some cases, the error might be in the invariant, not the algorithm itself.

* Exercise 2.17. Reduce the sorting problem to the Dutch national flag problem and one or more smaller instances of itself.

2.9 Notes

The techniques presented here for proving correctness of algorithms are based on Hoare logic [63]. More complete treatments of techniques for proving program correctness can be found in Apt and Olderog [6] or Francez [44]. Our presentation of proofs using invariants is patterned after Cormen, *et al.* [25].

A discussion of the Dutch national flag problem and the iterative solution used in SELECTBYMEDIAN are given by Dijkstra [29]. The Collatz problem was first posted by Lothar Collatz in 1937. An up-to-date summary of its history is maintained by Eric Weisstein [119].

Chapter 3

Analyzing Algorithms

In Chapter 1, we saw that different algorithms for the same problem can have dramatically different performance. In this chapter, we will introduce techniques for mathematically analyzing the performance of algorithms. These analyses will enable us to predict, to a certain extent, the performance of programs using these algorithms.

3.1 Motivation

Perhaps the most common performance measure of a program is its running time. The running time of a program depends not only on the algorithms it uses, but also on such factors as the speed of the processor(s), the amount of main memory available, the speeds of devices accessed, and the impact of other software utilizing the same resources. Furthermore, the same algorithm can perform differently when coded in different languages, even when all other factors remain unchanged. When analyzing the performance of an algorithm, we would like to learn something about the running time of any of its implementations, regardless of the impact of these other factors.

Suppose we divide an execution of an algorithm into a sequence of *steps*, each of which does some fixed amount of work. For example, a step could be comparing two values or performing a single arithmetic operation. Assuming the values used are small enough to fit into a single machine word, we could reasonably expect that any processor could execute each step in a bounded amount of time. Some of these steps might be faster than others, but for any given processor, we should be able to identify both a lower bound $l > 0$ and an upper bound $u \geq l$ on the amount of time required for any single execution step, assuming no other programs are being executed by that processor. Thus, if we simply count execution steps, we obtain an estimate on the running time, accurate to within a factor of u/l.

Obviously, these bounds will be different for different processors. Thus, if an analysis of an algorithm is to be independent of the platform on which the algorithm runs, the analysis must *ignore constant factors*. In other words, our analyses will be unable to conclude, for example, that algorithm A is twice as fast (or a million times as fast) as algorithm B. By ignoring constant factors, we therefore lose a great deal of precision in measuring performance. However, we will see that this loss of precision leads us to focus on the more dramatic differences in algorithm performance. These differences are important enough that they tend to transcend the differences in platforms on which an algorithm is executed.

Because we are ignoring constant factors, it only makes sense to consider the behavior of an algorithm on an infinite set of inputs. To see why, consider that the execution times of two algorithms on the same single input are always related by a constant factor — we simply divide the number of steps in one execution by the number of steps in the other. This argument can be extended to any finite set of inputs by dividing the number of steps in the longest execution of one algorithm by the number of steps in the shortest execution of the other.

Mathematically, we will describe the running time of an algorithm by a function $f : \mathbb{N} \to \mathbb{N}$. The input to f is a natural number representing the size of an input. $f(n)$ then represents the number of steps taken by the algorithm on some particular input of size n. The context will determine which input of size n we are considering, but usually we will be interested in the *worst-case* input — an input of size n resulting in the maximum number of execution steps.

Our analysis will then focus on this function f, not its value at specific points. More precisely, we will focus our attention on the behavior of $f(n)$ as n increases. This behavior is known as the *asymptotic* behavior of f. Most algorithms behave well enough if their inputs are small enough. By focusing on asymptotic behavior, we can see how quickly the algorithm's performance will degrade as it processes larger inputs.

Throughout the remainder of this chapter, we will define various notations that allow us to relate the asymptotic behaviors of various functions to each other. In this context, all functions will be of the form $f : \mathbb{N} \to \mathbb{R}^{\geq 0}$, where $\mathbb{R}^{\geq 0}$ denotes the set of nonnegative real numbers (likewise, we will use $\mathbb{R}$ to denote the set of all real numbers and $\mathbb{R}^{>0}$ to denote the set of positive real numbers). Each of the notations we introduce will relate a set of functions to one given function f based on their respective asymptotic growth rates. Typically, f will be fairly simple, e.g., $f(n) = n^2$. In this way, we will be able describe the growth rates of complicated — or even unknown — functions using well-understood functions like n^2.

3.2 Big-*O* Notation

Definition 3.1. Let $f : \mathbb{N} \to \mathbb{R}^{\geq 0}$. $O(f(n))$ is defined to be the set of all functions $g : \mathbb{N} \to \mathbb{R}^{\geq 0}$ such that for some natural number n_0 and some strictly positive real number c, $g(n) \leq cf(n)$ whenever $n \geq n_0$.

> $O(f(n))$ is pronounced "big-Oh of f of n".

The above definition formally defines big-*O* notation. Let us now dissect this definition to see what it means. We start with some specific function f which maps natural numbers to nonnegative real numbers. $O(f(n))$ is then defined to be a set whose elements are all functions. Each of the functions in $O(f(n))$ maps natural numbers to nonnegative real numbers. Furthermore, if we consider any function $g(n)$ in $O(f(n))$, then for every sufficiently large n (i.e., $n \geq n_0$), $g(n)$ cannot exceed $f(n)$ by more than some fixed constant factor (i.e., $g(n) \leq cf(n)$). Thus, all of the functions in $O(f(n))$ grow no faster than some constant multiple of f as n becomes sufficiently large. Note that the constants n_0 and c may differ for different f and g, but are the same for all n.

Note that big-*O* notation is defined solely in terms of mathematical functions — not in terms of algorithms. Presently, we will show how it can be used to analyze algorithms. First, however, we will give a series of examples illustrating some of its mathematical properties.

Example 3.2. Let $f(n) = n^2$, and let $g(n) = 2n^2$. Then $g(n) \in O(f(n))$ because $g(n) \leq 2f(n)$ for every $n \geq 0$. Here, the constant n_0 is 0, and the constant c is 2.

Example 3.3. Let $f(n) = n^2$, and let $g(n) = 3n + 10$. We wish to show that $g(n) \in O(f(n))$. Hence, we need to find a positive real number c and a natural number n_0 such that $3n + 10 \leq cn^2$ whenever $n \geq n_0$. If $n > 0$, we can divide both sides of this inequality by n, obtaining an equivalent inequality, $3 + 10/n \leq cn$. The left-hand side of this inequality is maximized when n is minimized. Because we have assumed $n > 0$, 1 is the minimum value of n. Thus, if we can satisfy $cn \geq 13$, the original inequality will be satisfied. This inequality can be satisfied by choosing $c = 13$ and $n \geq 1$. Therefore, $g(n) \in O(f(n))$.

Example 3.4. $n^3 \notin O(n^2)$ because $n^3 = n(n^2)$, so that whatever values we pick for n_0 and c, we can find an $n \geq n_0$ such that $n(n^2) > cn^2$. Note that in this example, we are using n^3 and n^2 to denote functions.

Example 3.5. $1000 \in O(1)$. Here, 1000 and 1 denote constant functions — functions whose values are the same for all n. Thus, for every $n \geq 0$, $1000 \leq 1000(1)$.

Example 3.6. $O(n) \subseteq O(n^2)$; i.e., every function in $O(n)$ is also in $O(n^2)$. To see this, note that for any function $f(n) \in O(n)$, there exist a positive real number c and a natural number n_0 such that $f(n) \leq cn$ whenever $n \geq n_0$. Furthermore, $n \leq n^2$ for all $n \in \mathbb{N}$. Therefore, $f(n) \leq cn^2$ whenever $n \geq n_0$.

Example 3.7. $O(n^2) = O(4n^2 + 7n)$; i.e., the sets $O(n^2)$ and $O(4n^2 + 7n)$ contain exactly the same functions. It is easily seen that $O(n^2) \subseteq O(4n^2+7n)$ using an argument similar to that of Example 3.6. Consider any function $f(n) \in O(4n^2 + 7n)$. There exist a positive real number c and a natural number n_0 such that $f(n) \leq c(4n^2 + 7n)$ whenever $n \geq n_0$. Furthermore, $4n^2+7n \leq 11n^2$ for all $n \in \mathbb{N}$. Letting $c' = 11c$, we therefore have $f(n) \leq c'n^2$ whenever $n \geq n_0$. Therefore, $f(n) \in O(n^2)$. Note that although $O(n^2)$ and $O(4n^2+7n)$ denote the same set of functions, the preferred notation is $O(n^2)$ because it is simpler.

We have chosen to use functions that map natural numbers to non-negative real numbers because these functions make our definitions clean. Furthermore, they fit what we would expect a function describing the running time of an algorithm to look like — the size of the problem is a natural number, and the running time is a non-negative real number. However, we sometimes want to express a running time as being in a set such as $O(2^n/n)$. Strictly speaking, this doesn't make sense because $2^0/0$ is undefined. However, because asymptotic notation focuses on the behavior of the function for sufficiently large n, this single undefined function value doesn't affect anything. To accommodate such exceptions to our definition, we will assume that such functions are "patched" so that undefined or negative values are replaced by 0 (e.g., we assume that $2^0/0 = 0$). We must be careful, however, that the functions have only a finite number of negative or undefined values.

Let us now illustrate the use of big-O notation by analyzing the running time of MAXSUMBU from Figure 1.14 on page 18. The initialization statements prior to the loop, including the initialization of the loop index i, require a fixed number of steps. Their running time is therefore bounded by some constant a. Likewise, the number of steps required by any single iteration of the loop (including the loop test and the increment of i) is bounded by some constant b. Because the loop iterates n times, the total number of steps required by the loop is at most bn. Finally, the last loop condition test and the **return** statement require a number of steps bounded by some constant c. The running time of the entire algorithm is therefore bounded by $a + bn + c$, where a, b, and c are fixed positive constants. The running time of MAXSUMBU is in $O(n)$, because $a + bn + c \leq (a + b + c)n$ for all $n \geq 1$.

We can simplify the above analysis somewhat using the following theorem.

Theorem 3.8. *Suppose $f_1(n) \in O(g_1(n))$ and $f_2(n) \in O(g_2(n))$. Then*

1. $f_1(n)f_2(n) \in O(g_1(n)g_2(n))$; *and*
2. $f_1(n) + f_2(n) \in O(\max(g_1(n), g_2(n)))$.

(By $f_1(n)f_2(n)$, we mean the function that maps n to the product of $f_1(n)$ and $f_2(n)$. Likewise, $\max(g_1(n), g_2(n))$ denotes the function that maps n to the maximum of $g_1(n)$ and $g_2(n)$.)

Proof. Because $f_1(n) \in O(g_1(n))$ and $f_2(n) \in O(g_2(n))$, there exist positive real numbers c_1 and c_2 and natural numbers n_1 and n_2 such that

$$f_1(n) \leq c_1 g_1(n) \text{ whenever } n \geq n_1 \tag{3.1}$$

and

$$f_2(n) \leq c_2 g_2(n) \text{ whenever } n \geq n_2. \tag{3.2}$$

Because both of the above inequalities involve only nonnegative numbers, we may multiply the inequalities, obtaining

$$f_1(n)f_2(n) \leq c_1 c_2 g_1(n)g_2(n),$$

whenever $n \geq \max(n_1, n_2)$. Let $c = c_1 c_2$ and $n_0 = \max(n_1, n_2)$. Then

$$f_1(n)f_2(n) \leq c g_1(n)g_2(n),$$

whenever $n \geq n_0$. Therefore, $f_1(n)f_2(n) \in O(g_1(n)g_2(n))$.

If we add inequalities (3.1) and (3.2), we obtain

$$f_1(n) + f_2(n) \leq c_1 g_1(n) + c_2 g_2(n)$$
$$\leq c_1 \max(g_1(n), g_2(n)) + c_2 \max(g_1(n), g_2(n))$$
$$= (c_1 + c_2) \max(g_1(n), g_2(n)),$$

whenever $n \geq \max(n_1, n_2)$. Therefore, $f_1(n) + f_2(n) \in O(\max(g_1(n), g_2(n)))$.
□

Let us now apply these two theorems to obtain a simpler analysis of the running time of MAXSUMBU. Recall that in our original analysis, we concluded that the running time of a single iteration of the loop is bounded by a fixed constant. We can therefore conclude that the running time of a single iteration is in $O(1)$. Because there are n iterations, the running time for the entire loop is bounded by the product of n and the running time of a single iteration. By Theorem 3.8 part 1, the running time of the loop is in $O(n)$. Clearly, the running times of the code segments before and after the loop are each in $O(1)$. The total running time is then the sum of the running times of these segments and that of the loop. By applying Theorem 3.8 part 2 twice, we see that the running time of the algorithm is in $O(n)$ (because $\max(1, n) \leq n$ whenever $n \geq 1$).

Recall that the actual running time of the program implementing MAXSUMOPT (Figure 1.11 on page 16) was much slower than that of MAXSUMBU. Let us now analyze MAXSUMOPT to see why this is the case.

We will begin with the inner loop. It is easily seen that each iteration runs in $O(1)$ time. The number of iterations of this loop varies from 1 to n. Because the number of iterations is in $O(n)$, we can conclude that this loop runs in $O(n)$ time. It is then easily seen that a single iteration of the outer loop runs in $O(n)$ time. Because the outer loop iterates n times, this loop, and hence the entire algorithm, runs in $O(n^2)$ time.

It is tempting to conclude that this analysis explains the difference in running times of the implementations of the algorithms; i.e., because n^2 grows much more rapidly than does n, MAXSUMOPT is therefore much slower than MAXSUMBU. However, this conclusion is not yet warranted, because we have only shown upper bounds on the running times of the two algorithms. In particular, it is perfectly valid to conclude that the running time of MAXSUMBU is in $O(n^2)$, because $O(n) \subseteq O(n^2)$. Conversely, we have not shown that the running time of MAXSUMOPT is not in $O(n)$.

In general, big-O notation is useful for expressing upper bounds on the growth rates of functions. In order to get a complete analysis, however, we need additional notation for expressing lower bounds.

3.3   Big-Ω and Big-Θ

Definition 3.9. Let $f : \mathbb{N} \to \mathbb{R}^{\geq 0}$. $\Omega(f(n))$ is defined to be the set of all functions $g : \mathbb{N} \to \mathbb{R}^{\geq 0}$ such that for some natural number n_0 and some strictly positive real number c, $g(n) \geq cf(n)$ whenever $n \geq n_0$.

> $\Omega(f(n))$ *is pronounced "big-Omega of f of n".*

Note that the definition of Ω is identical to the definition of O, except that the inequality, $g(n) \leq cf(n)$, is replaced by the inequality, $g(n) \geq cf(n)$. Thus, Ω notation is used to express a lower bound in the same way that O notation is used to express an upper bound. Specifically, if $g(n) \in \Omega(f(n))$, then for sufficiently large n, $g(n)$ is at least some constant multiple of $f(n)$. This constant multiple is only required to be a positive real number, so it may be very close to 0.

Example 3.10. Let $f(n) = 3n + 10$ and $g(n) = n^2$. We wish to show that $g(n) \in \Omega(f(n))$. We therefore need to find a positive real number c and a natural number n_0 such that $n^2 \geq c(3n + 10)$ for every $n \geq n_0$. We have already found such values in Example 3.3: $c = 1/13$ and $n_0 = 1$.

The above example illustrates a duality between O and Ω, namely, that for any positive real number c, $g(n) \leq cf(n)$ iff $f(n) \geq g(n)/c$. The following theorem summarizes this duality.

Theorem 3.11. *Let* $f : \mathbb{N} \to \mathbb{R}^{\geq 0}$ *and* $g : \mathbb{N} \to \mathbb{R}^{\geq 0}$. *Then* $g(n) \in O(f(n))$ *iff* $f(n) \in \Omega(g(n))$.

By applying Theorem 3.11 to Examples 3.2, 3.4, 3.6, and 3.7, we can see that $n^2 \in \Omega(2n^2)$, $n^2 \notin \Omega(n^3)$, $\Omega(n^2) \subseteq \Omega(n)$, and $\Omega(n^2) = \Omega(4n^2 + 7n)$.

When we analyze the growth rate of a function g, we would ideally like to find a simple function f such that $g(n) \in O(f(n))$ and $g(n) \in \Omega(f(n))$. Doing so would tell us that the growth rate of $g(n)$ is the same as that of $f(n)$, within a constant factor in either direction. We therefore have another notation for expressing such results.

Definition 3.12. Let $f : \mathbb{N} \to \mathbb{R}^{\geq 0}$. $\Theta(f(n))$ is defined to be

> $\Theta(f(n))$ *is pronounced "big-Theta of f of n".*

$$O(f(n)) \cap \Omega(f(n)).$$

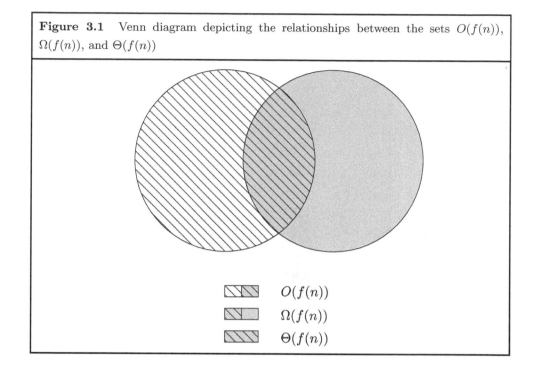

Figure 3.1 Venn diagram depicting the relationships between the sets $O(f(n))$, $\Omega(f(n))$, and $\Theta(f(n))$

$O(f(n))$

$\Omega(f(n))$

$\Theta(f(n))$

In other words, $\Theta(f(n))$ is the set of all functions belonging to both $O(f(n))$ and $\Omega(f(n))$ (see Figure 3.1). We can restate this definition by the following theorem, which characterizes $\Theta(f(n))$ in terms similar to the definitions of O and Ω.

Theorem 3.13. $g(n) \in \Theta(f(n))$ *iff there exist positive constants c_1 and c_2 and a natural number n_0 such that*

$$c_1 f(n) \leq g(n) \leq c_2 f(n) \tag{3.3}$$

whenever $n \geq n_0$.

Proof. We must prove the implication in two directions.

$\Rightarrow$: Suppose $g(n) \in \Theta(f(n))$. Then $g(n) \in O(f(n))$ and $g(n) \in \Omega(f(n))$. By the definition of Ω, there exist a positive real number c_1 and a natural number n_1 such that $c_1 f(n) \leq g(n)$ whenever $n \geq n_1$. By the definition of O, there exist a positive real number c_2 and a natural number n_2 such that $g(n) \leq c_2 f(n)$ whenever $n \geq n_2$. Let $n_0 = \max(n_1, n_2)$. Then (3.3) holds whenever $n \geq n_0$.

$\Leftarrow$: Suppose (3.3) holds whenever $n \geq n_0$. From the first inequality, $g(n) \in \Omega(f(n))$. From the second inequality, $g(n) \in O(f(n))$. Therefore, $g(n) \in \Theta(f(n))$. $\square$

The definition of Θ also gives us the following corollary to Theorem 3.11.

Corollary 3.14. *Let $f : \mathbb{N} \to \mathbb{R}^{\geq 0}$ and $g : \mathbb{N} \to \mathbb{R}^{\geq 0}$. Then $g(n) \in \Theta(f(n))$ iff $f(n) \in \Theta(g(n))$.*

In order to apply these definitions to the analysis of algorithms, a few more results regarding manipulation of the notation are helpful. The following theorem is analogous to Theorem 3.8. Its proof is left as an exercise.

Theorem 3.15. *Suppose $f_1(n) \in \Omega(g_1(n))$ and $f_2(n) \in \Omega(g_2(n))$. Then*

1. $f_1(n)f_2(n) \in \Omega(g_1(n)g_2(n))$; *and*
2. $f_1(n) + f_2(n) \in \Omega(\max(g_1(n), g_2(n)))$.

By combining Theorems 3.8 and 3.15, we obtain the following corollary.

Corollary 3.16. *Suppose $f_1(n) \in \Theta(g_1(n))$ and $f_2(n) \in \Theta(g_2(n))$. Then*

1. $f_1(n)f_2(n) \in \Theta(g_1(n)g_2(n))$; *and*
2. $f_1(n) + f_2(n) \in \Theta(\max(g_1(n), g_2(n)))$.

The following two theorems are also useful for simplifying expressions using asymptotic notation. The proofs of both are left as exercises.

Theorem 3.17. *Let $f(n) : \mathbb{N} \to \mathbb{R}^{\geq 0}$ and $g(n) : \mathbb{N} \to \mathbb{R}^{\geq 0}$ such that $f(n) \in O(g(n))$ (or equivalently, $g(n) \in \Omega(f(n))$). Then:*

1. $O(f(n)) \subseteq O(g(n))$.
2. $\Omega(g(n)) \subseteq \Omega(f(n))$.

Theorem 3.18. *Let $f(n) : \mathbb{N} \to \mathbb{R}^{\geq 0}$ and $g(n) : \mathbb{N} \to \mathbb{R}^{\geq 0}$ such that $f(n) \in \Theta(g(n))$. Then $\Theta(f(n)) = \Theta(g(n))$.*

Let us now use the above definitions and results to continue our analysis of MAXSUMBU. Clearly, the body of the loop must take some positive number of steps, so its running time is in $\Omega(1)$. Furthermore, the loop iterates n times. We may therefore use Theorem 3.15 to conclude that the running time of the algorithm is in $\Omega(n)$. Because we have already shown the running time to be in $O(n)$, it therefore is in $\Theta(n)$.

Let us now analyze the lower bound for MAXSUMOPT. Again, the inner loop has a running time in $\Omega(1)$. Its number of iterations ranges from 1 to n, so the best lower bound we can give on the number of iterations is in $\Omega(1)$.

Using this lower bound, we conclude that the running time of the inner loop is in $\Omega(1)$. Because the outer loop iterates n times, the running time of the algorithm is in $\Omega(n)$.

Unfortunately, this lower bound does not match our upper bound of $O(n^2)$. In some cases, we may not be able to make the upper and lower bounds match. In most cases, however, if we work hard enough, we can bring them together.

Clearly, the running time of a single iteration of the inner loop will require a constant number of steps in the worst case. Let $a > 0$ denote that constant. The loop iterates $n - i$ times, so that the total number of steps required by the inner loop is $(n - i)a$. An iteration of the outer loop requires a constant number of steps apart from the inner loop. Let $b > 0$ denote that constant. The loop iterates n times. However, because the number of steps required for the inner loop depends on the value of i, which is different for each iteration of the outer loop, we must be more careful in computing the total number of steps required by the outer loop. That number is given by

$$b + \sum_{i=0}^{n-1}(n - i)a = b + a\sum_{i=0}^{n-1}(n - i).$$

The above summation can be simplified if we observe that the quantity $(n - i)$ takes on the values $n, n - 1, \ldots, 1$. We can therefore rewrite the sum by taking the terms in the opposite order:

$$1 + 2 + \cdots + n = \sum_{i=1}^{n} i.$$

Thus, the number of steps required by the inner loop is

$$b + a\sum_{i=1}^{n} i.$$

We can now use (2.1) from page 48 to conclude that the number of steps taken by the outer loop is

$$b + \frac{an(n + 1)}{2}.$$

The above expression is a polynomial in n with degree 2. The following theorem gives us a way to characterize polynomials using asymptotic notation.

Theorem 3.19. *Let $p(n)$ be a polynomial of degree k whose coefficient for n^k is positive, and let $f(n)$: $\mathbb{N} \to \mathbb{R}^{\geq 0}$ such that for some $n_0 \in \mathbb{N}$, $f(n) = p(n)$ whenever $n \geq n_0$. Then $f(n) \in \Theta(n^k)$.*

> We state the theorem in this way to make it clear that $p(n)$ is allowed to be negative for $n < n_0$. $f(n)$ can be the "patched" version of $p(n)$, though this is not required.

Proof. Let

$$p(n) = \sum_{i=0}^{k} a_i n^i.$$

Then let $A = \max\{a_i \mid 0 \leq i \leq k\}$ and $n_1 = \max\{1, n_0\}$. Note that because $a_k > 0$, $A > 0$. Then whenever $n \geq n_1$,

$$f(n) = p(n)$$

$$= \sum_{i=0}^{k} a_i n^i$$

$$\leq \sum_{i=0}^{k} A n^i$$

$$\leq A \sum_{i=0}^{k} n^k$$

because $n \geq 1$. Thus,

$$f(n) \leq A \sum_{i=0}^{k} n^k$$

$$= A(k+1)n^k.$$

Letting $c_1 = A(k+1)$, we have $f(n) \leq c_1 n^k$ whenever $n \geq n_1$.

Now let $A' = \min\{0, a_i \mid 0 \leq i < k\}$. Then whenever $n \geq n_1$,

$$f(n) = p(n)$$

$$= a_k n^k + \sum_{i=0}^{k-1} a_i n^i$$

$$\geq a_k n^k + \sum_{i=0}^{k-1} A' n^i$$

$$= a_k n^k + A' \sum_{i=0}^{k-1} n^i$$

$$\geq a_k n^k + A' \sum_{i=0}^{k-1} n^{k-1}$$

because $A' \leq 0$ and $n \geq 1$. Because the summation in the above expression evaluates to kn^{k-1}, we have

$$f(n) \geq (a_k n + A'k)n^{k-1}.$$

Now let $n_2 = \max\{n_1, \lceil -2A'k/a_k \rceil\}$. When $n \geq n_2$, we have

$$n \geq \left\lceil \frac{-2A'k}{a_k} \right\rceil$$

$$\geq \frac{-2A'k}{a_k}$$

$$\frac{-a_k n}{2} \leq A'k.$$

Thus,

$$f(n) \geq (a_k n + A'k)n^{k-1}$$

$$\geq (a_k n - \frac{a_k n}{2})n^{k-1}$$

$$= \frac{a_k n^k}{2}.$$

Letting $c_2 = a_k/2$, $f(n) \geq c_2 n^k$ whenever $n \geq n_2$. From Theorem 3.13, $f(n) \in \Theta(n^k)$. $\square$

By the above theorem, the running time of MaxSumOpt is in $\Theta(n^2)$.

This is a rather tedious analysis for such a simple algorithm. Fortunately, there are techniques for simplifying analyses. In the next two sections, we will present some of these techniques.

3.4 Operations on Sets

Asymptotic analysis can be simplified if we extend operations on functions to operations on sets of functions. Such an extension will allow us to streamline our notation without the need to introduce new constants or functions representing the running times of various code segments.

Definition 3.20. Let $\circ$ be a binary operation on functions of the form $f : \mathbb{N} \to \mathbb{R}^{\geq 0}$ (for example, $\circ$ might represent addition or multiplication). Let f be such a function, and let A and B be sets of such functions. We then define:

- $f \circ A = \{f \circ g \mid g \in A\}$;
- $A \circ f = \{g \circ f \mid g \in A\}$; and
- $A \circ B = \{g \circ h \mid g \in A, h \in B\}$.

Example 3.21. $n^2 + \Theta(n^3)$ is the set of all functions that can be written $n^2 + g(n)$ for some $g(n) \in \Theta(n^3)$. This set includes such functions as

- $n^2 + 3n^3$;
- $(n^3 + 1)/2$, which can be written $n^2 + (\frac{n^3+1}{2} - n^2)$ (note that $\frac{n^3+1}{2} - n^2 \geq 0$ for all natural numbers n); and
- $n^3 + 2n$, which can be written $n^2 + (n^3 + 2n - n^2)$.

Because all functions in this set belong to $\Theta(n^3)$, $n^2 + \Theta(n^3) \subseteq \Theta(n^3)$.

Example 3.22. $O(n^2) + O(n^3)$ is the set of functions that can be written $f(n) + g(n)$, where $f(n) \in O(n^2)$ and $g(n) \in O(n^3)$. Functions in this set include:

- $2n^2 + 3n^3$;
- $2n$, which can be written as $n + n$; and
- $2n^3$, which can be written as $0 + 2n^3$.

Because all functions in this set belong to $O(n^3)$, $O(n^2) + O(n^3) \subseteq O(n^3)$.

Definition 3.23. Let A be a set of functions of the form $f : \mathbb{N} \to \mathbb{R}^{\geq 0}$. We define

$$\sum_{i=k}^{n} A(i)$$

to be the set of all functions $g : \mathbb{N} \to \mathbb{R}^{\geq 0}$ such that

$$g(n) = \sum_{i=k}^{n} f(i)$$

for some $f \in A$. We define products analogously.

Example 3.24.

$$\sum_{i=1}^{n} \Theta(i^2)$$

is the set of all functions of the form

$$\sum_{i=1}^{n} f(i)$$

such that $f(i) \in \Theta(i^2)$.

Example 3.25. $f(n) \in f(n-1) + \Theta(n)$ for $n \geq 1$. This is an example of an *asymptotic recurrence*. The meaning is that f is a function satisfying a recurrence of the form

$$f(n) = \begin{cases} f(n-1) + h(n) & \text{for } n \geq 1 \\ h(n) & \text{otherwise,} \end{cases}$$

for some $h(n) \in \Theta(n)$. Note that because $h(0)$ may have any nonnegative value, so may $f(0)$.

We can use the above definitions to simplify our analysis of the lower bound for MaxSumOpt. Instead of introducing the constant a to represent the running time of a single iteration of the inner loop, we can simply use $\Omega(1)$ to represent the lower bound for this running time. We can therefore conclude that the total running time of the inner loop is in

$$\sum_{k=i}^{n-1} \Omega(1).$$

While this notation allows us to simplify the expression of bounds on running times, we still need a way of manipulating such expressions as the one above. In the next section, we present powerful tools for performing such manipulation.

3.5   Smooth Functions and Summations

Asymptotic analysis involving summations can be simplified by applying a rather general property of summations. This property relies on the fact that our summations typically involve well-behaved functions — functions that obey three important properties. The following definitions characterize these properties.

Definition 3.26. Let $f : \mathbb{N} \to \mathbb{R}^{\geq 0}$. f is said to be *eventually non-decreasing* if there is a natural number n_0 such that $f(n) \leq f(n+1)$ whenever $n \geq n_0$.

Definition 3.27. Let $f : \mathbb{N} \to \mathbb{R}^{\geq 0}$. f is said to be *eventually positive* if there is a natural number n_0 such that $f(n) > 0$ whenever $n \geq n_0$.

Definition 3.28. Let $f : \mathbb{N} \to \mathbb{R}^{\geq 0}$ be an eventually non-decreasing and eventually positive function. f is said to be *smooth* if there exist a real number c and a natural number n_0 such that $f(2n) \leq cf(n)$ whenever $n \geq n_0$.

Example 3.29. $f(n) = n$ is a smooth function. Clearly, f is eventually non-decreasing and eventually positive, and $f(2n) = 2f(n)$ for all $n \in \mathbb{N}$.

Example 3.30. $f(n) = 2^n$ is not smooth. f is eventually non-decreasing, and eventually positive, but $f(2n) = 2^{2n} = f^2(n)$ for all $n \in \mathbb{N}$. Because f is unbounded, for any real c, $f(2n) > cf(n)$ for all sufficiently large n.

We will soon discuss in more detail which functions are smooth. First, however, let's see why this notion is important. Suppose we want to give asymptotic bounds for a summation of the form

$$\sum_{i=1}^{g(n)} \Omega(f(i))$$

for some smooth function f. The following theorem, whose proof is outlined in Exercise 3.13, can then be applied.

Theorem 3.31. *Let $f : \mathbb{N} \to \mathbb{R}^{\geq 0}$ be a smooth function, $g : \mathbb{N} \to \mathbb{N}$ be an eventually non-decreasing and unbounded function, and let X denote either O, Ω, or Θ. Then*

$$\sum_{i=1}^{g(n)} X(f(i)) \subseteq X(g(n)f(g(n))).$$

Thus, if we know that f is smooth, we have an asymptotic solution to the summation. We therefore need to examine the property of smoothness more closely. The following theorem can be used to show a wide variety of functions to be smooth.

> We leave as an exercise the proof that this containment is proper.

Theorem 3.32. *Let $f : \mathbb{N} \to \mathbb{R}^{\geq 0}$ and $g : \mathbb{N} \to \mathbb{R}^{\geq 0}$ be smooth functions, and let $c \in \mathbb{R}^{\geq 0}$. Then the following functions are smooth:*

- $f(n) + g(n)$;
- $f(n)g(n)$;

- $f^c(n)$; *and*
- $f(g(n))$, *provided g is unbounded.*

The proof is left as an exercise. Knowing that $f(n) = n$ is smooth, we can apply Theorem 3.32 to conclude that any polynomial is smooth. In fact, such functions as $\sqrt{n}$ and $n^{\sqrt{2}}$ are also smooth. We can extend this idea to logarithms as well. In particular, let $\lg x$ denote the base-2 logarithm; i.e.,

$$2^{\lg x} = x \tag{3.4}$$

for all positive x.

Example 3.33. $\lg n$ is smooth. Clearly $\lg n$ is eventually non-decreasing and eventually positive. Furthermore, $\lg(2n) = 1 + \lg n \le 2 \lg n$ whenever $n \ge 2$.

Thus far, the only example we have seen of a non-smooth function is 2^n. Indeed, almost any polynomial-bounded, eventually non-decreasing, eventually positive function we encounter will turn out to be smooth. However, we can contrive exceptions. For example, we leave it as an exercise to show that $2^{2^{\lfloor \lg \lg n \rfloor}} \in O(n)$, but is not smooth.

We can now continue the analysis of the lower bound for MAXSUMOPT. As we showed in the previous section, the lower bound on the running time of the inner loop is in

$$\sum_{k=i}^{n-1} \Omega(1).$$

In order to apply Theorem 3.31, we need to rewrite the sum so that the summation index begins at 1:

$$\sum_{k=i}^{n-1} \Omega(1) = \sum_{k=1}^{n-i} \Omega(1).$$

Theorem 3.31 still does not quite apply because the upper limit, $n - i$, is not a function of one variable. In order to overcome this difficulty, we can introduce an *auxiliary variable* N, which we define to be $n - i$. Because $i < n$ in the algorithm, this definition makes sense — N is a natural number. The lower bound can now be expressed as

$$\sum_{k=1}^{N} \Omega(1).$$

We can now apply Theorem 3.31 by letting $g(N) = N$ and $f(k) = 1$. Because N is eventually non-decreasing and unbounded, and because 1 is smooth, we can conclude that the running time of the inner loop is in $\Omega(g(N)f(g(N))) = \Omega(N)$. The lower bound for the algorithm is therefore in

$$\sum_{i=0}^{n-1} \Omega(N).$$

Again, Theorem 3.31 does not immediately apply to this summation. First, the lower limit of the index i is 0, not 1 as required by Theorem 3.31. Furthermore, the theorem requires the expression inside the asymptotic notation to be a function of the summation index i, not of N.

In order to take care of the latter problem, we observe that as i ranges from 0 to $n-1$, N (or $n-i$) takes on each of the integer values from n to 1. We can therefore write the above sum as:

$$\sum_{N=1}^{n} \Omega(N).$$

In order to apply Theorem 3.31, we let $g(n) = n$ and $f(N) = N$. $g(n)f(g(n))$ is therefore n^2. From Theorem 3.31 the running time of MAXSUMOPT is in $\Omega(n^2)$. Note that this is the same bound that we obtained in Section 3.3, but instead of using Equation (2.1), we used the more general (and hence, more widely applicable) Theorem 3.31.

To further illustrate the power of Theorem 3.31, let's now analyze the running time of MAXSUMITER, given in Figure 1.10 on page 15. A single iteration of the inner loop has a running time in $\Theta(1)$. The total running time of this loop is therefore in

$$\sum_{k=i}^{j-1} \Theta(1) = \sum_{k=1}^{j-i} \Theta(1).$$

Letting $J = j - i$, which is a natural number because $j \geq i$, from Theorem 3.31, this running time is in $\Theta(J)$. The total running time of the middle loop is then in

$$\sum_{j=i}^{n} \Theta(J) = \sum_{J=0}^{n-i} \Theta(J).$$

This summation does not immediately fit the form of Theorem 3.31, as the starting value of the summation index J is 0, not 1. We can rewrite this sum as

$$\sum_{J=0}^{n-i} \Theta(J) = \sum_{J=1}^{n-i+1} \Theta(J-1).$$

What we have done here is simply to shift the range of J upward by 1 (i.e., from $0, \ldots, n-i$ to $1, \ldots, n-i+1$), and to compensate for this shift by subtracting 1 from each occurrence of J in the expression being summed. Now from Theorem 3.19, $J-1 \in \Theta(J)$, and from Theorem 3.18, $\Theta(J-1) = \Theta(J)$; hence, the running time of the middle loop is in

$$\sum_{J=1}^{n-i-1} \Theta(J).$$

Finally, we let $N = n - i + 1$, which is a natural number because $i \leq n$. This gives us a running time of

$$\sum_{J=1}^{N} \Theta(J).$$

Applying Theorem 3.31 to the above sum, we find that the running time of the middle loop is in $\Theta(N^2)$. The running time of the outer loop is then in

$$\sum_{i=0}^{n} \Theta(N^2) = \sum_{N=1}^{n+1} \Theta(N^2).$$

Applying Theorem 3.31 to this sum, we find that the running time of this loop is in

$$\Theta((n+1)^3) = \Theta(n^3)$$

by Theorems 3.19 and 3.18.

3.6   Analyzing While Loops

To analyze algorithms with **while** loops, we can use the same techniques as we have used to analyze **for** loops. For example, consider INSERTIONSORT, shown in Figure 1.7 on page 12. Let us consider the **while** loop. The value of j begins at i and decreases by 1 on each loop iteration. Furthermore, if its value reaches 1, the loop terminates. The loop therefore iterates at most

$i - 1$ times. Because each iteration runs in $\Theta(1)$ time, the **while** loop runs in $O(i)$ time in the worst case.

In order to be able to conclude that the loop runs in $\Theta(i)$ time in the worst case, we must determine that for arbitrarily large i, the loop may iterate until $j = 1$. This is certainly the case if, prior to the beginning of the loop, $A[i]$ is strictly less than every element in $A[1..i - 1]$. Thus, the **while** loop runs in $\Theta(i)$ time in the worst case.

It is now tempting to use Theorem 3.31 to conclude that the entire algorithm's running time is in

$$\Theta(1) + \sum_{i=1}^{n} \Theta(i) \subseteq \Theta(1) + \Theta(n^2)$$

$$= \Theta(n^2).$$

However, we must be careful, because we have not shown that the **while** loop runs in $\Omega(i)$ time for *every* iteration of the **for** loop; hence the running time of the **for** loop might not be in

$$\sum_{i=1}^{n} \Theta(i).$$

We must show that there are inputs of size n, for every sufficiently large n, such that the **while** loop iterates $i - 1$ times for each iteration of the **for** loop. It is not hard to show that an array of distinct elements in decreasing order will produce the desired behavior. Therefore, the algorithm indeed operates in $\Theta(n^2)$ time.

3.7 Analyzing Recursion

Before we consider how to analyze recursion, let us first consider how to analyze non-recursive function calls. For example, consider SIMPLESELECT from Figure 1.2 on page 7. This algorithm is easy to analyze if we know the running time of SORT. Suppose we use INSERTIONSORT (Figure 1.7, page 12). We saw in the last section that INSERTIONSORT runs in $\Theta(n^2)$ time. The running time of SIMPLESELECT is therefore in

$$\Theta(1) + \Theta(n^2) \subseteq \Theta(n^2).$$

Suppose now that we wish to analyze an algorithm that makes one or more recursive calls. For example, consider MAXSUFFIXTD from Figure 1.13 on page 18. We analyze such an algorithm in exactly the same way. Specifically, this algorithm has a running time in $\Theta(1)$ plus whatever is required by the recursive call. The difficulty here is in how to determine the running time of the recursive call without knowing the running time of the algorithm.

The solution to this difficulty is to express the running time as a recurrence. Specifically, let $f(n)$ denote the worst-case running time of MAXSUFFIXTD on an array of size n. Then for $n > 0$, we have the equation,

$$f(n) = g(n) + f(n-1) \tag{3.5}$$

where $g(n) \in \Theta(1)$ is the worst-case running time of the body of the function, excluding the recursive call. Note that $f(n-1)$ has already been defined to be the worst-case running time of MAXSUFFIXTD on an array of size $n-1$; hence, $f(n-1)$ gives the worst-case running time of the recursive call.

The solution of arbitrary recurrences is beyond the scope of this book. However, asymptotic solutions are often much simpler to obtain than are exact solutions. First, we observe that (3.5) can be simplified using set operations:

$$f(n) \in f(n-1) + \Theta(1) \tag{3.6}$$

for $n > 0$.

It turns out that most of the recurrences that we derive when analyzing algorithms fit into a few general forms. With asymptotic solutions to these general forms, we can analyze recursive algorithms without using a great deal of detailed mathematics. (3.6) fits one of the most basic of these forms. The following theorem, whose proof is outlined in Exercise 3.23, gives the asymptotic solution to this form.

Theorem 3.34. *Let*

$$f(n) \in af(n-1) + X(b^n g(n))$$

for $n > n_0$, where $n_0 \in \mathbb{N}$, $a \geq 1$ and $b \geq 1$ are real numbers, $g(n)$ is a smooth function, and X is either O, Ω, or Θ. Then

$$f(n) \in \begin{cases} X(b^n g(n)) & \text{if } a < b \\ X(na^n g(n)) & \text{if } a = b \\ X(a^n) & \text{if } a > b. \end{cases}$$

When we apply this theorem to the analysis of algorithms, a in the recurrence denotes the number of recursive calls. The set $X(b^n g(n))$ contains the function giving the running time of the algorithm, excluding recursive calls. Note that the expression $b^n g(n)$ is general enough to describe a wide variety of functions. However, the main restriction on the applicability of this theorem is that $f(n)$ is in terms of $f(n-1)$, so that it applies only to those algorithms whose recursive calls reduce the size of the problem by 1.

Let us now see how Theorem 3.34 can be applied to the analysis of MaxSuffixTD. (3.6) fits the form given in Theorem 3.34, where $a = 1$, $b = 1$, $g(n) = 1$, and $X = \Theta$. Therefore, the second case of Theorem 3.34 applies. Substituting the values for X, a, and $g(n)$ in that solution, we obtain $f(n) \in \Theta(n)$.

Knowing that MaxSuffixTD operates in $\Theta(n)$ time, we can now analyze MaxSumTD in the same way. In this case, the time required excluding the recursive call is in $\Theta(n)$, because a call to MaxSuffixTD is made. Letting $f(n)$ denote the running time for MaxSumTD on an array of size n, we see that

$$f(n) \in f(n-1) + \Theta(n)$$

for $n > 0$. Again, this recurrence fits the form of Theorem 3.34 with $a = 1$, $b = 1$, $g(n) = n$, and $X = \Theta$. The second case again holds, so that the running time is in $\Theta(n^2)$.

It is no coincidence that both of these analyses fit the second case of Theorem 3.34. Note that unless a and b are both 1, Theorem 3.34 yields an exponential result. Thus, efficient algorithms will always fit the second case if this theorem applies. As a result, we can observe that an algorithm that makes more than one recursive call of size $n-1$ will yield an exponential-time algorithm.

We have included the first and third cases in Theorem 3.34 because they are useful in deriving a solution for certain other types of recurrences. To illustrate how these recurrences arise, we consider another solution to the maximum subsequence sum problem (see Section 1.6).

The technique we will use is called *divide-and-conquer*. This technique, which we will examine in detail in Chapter 10, involves reducing the size of recursive calls to a fixed fraction of the size of the original call. For example, we may attempt to make recursive calls on arrays of half the original size.

We therefore begin this solution by dividing a large array in half, as nearly as possible. The subsequence giving us the maximum sum can then lie in one of three places: entirely in the first half, entirely in the second half, or partially in both halves, as shown in Figure 3.2. We can find the maximum subsequence sum of each half by solving the two smaller problem instances recursively. If we can then find the maximum sum of any sequence

Figure 3.2   When applying divide-and-conquer, the maximum subsequence sum may not lie entirely in either half

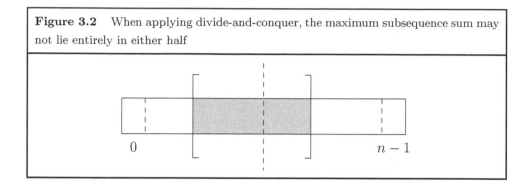

that begins in the first half and ends in the second half, then the maximum of these three values is the overall maximum subsequence sum.

For example, consider again the array $A[0..5] = \langle -1, 3, -2, 7, -9, 7 \rangle$ from Example 1.1 (page 14). The maximum subsequence sum of the first half, namely, of $A[0..2] = \langle -1, 3, -2 \rangle$, has a value of 3. Likewise, the maximum subsequence sum of the second half, $\langle 7, -9, 7 \rangle$, is 7. In examining the two halves, we have missed the actual maximum, $A[1..3] = \langle 3, -2, 7 \rangle$, which resides in neither half. However, notice that such a sequence that resides in neither half can be expressed as a suffix of the first half followed by a prefix of the last half; e.g., $\langle 3, -2, 7 \rangle$ can be expressed as $\langle 3, -2 \rangle$ followed by $\langle 7 \rangle$.

Let us define the *maximum prefix sum* analogously to the maximum suffix sum as follows:

$$\max \left\{ \sum_{k=0}^{i-1} A[k] \mid 0 \leq i \leq n \right\}.$$

It is not hard to see that the maximum sum of any sequence crossing the boundary is simply the maximum suffix sum of the first half plus the maximum prefix sum of the second half. For example, returning to Example 1.1, the maximum suffix sum of the first half is 1, obtained from the suffix $\langle 3, -2 \rangle$. Likewise, the maximum prefix sum of the second half is 7, obtained from the prefix $\langle 7 \rangle$. The sum of these two values gives us 8, the maximum subsequence sum.

Note that when we create smaller instances by splitting the array in half, one of the two smaller instances — the upper half — does not begin with index 0. For this reason, let us describe the input array more generally, as $A[lo..hi]$. We can then modify the definitions of maximum subsequence sum, maximum suffix sum, and maximum prefix sum by replacing 0 with lo and $n-1$ with hi. We will discuss the ranges of lo and hi shortly.

We must be careful that each recursive call is of a strictly smaller size. We wish to divide the array in half, as nearly as possible. We begin by finding the midpoint between *lo* and *hi*; i.e.,

$$mid = \left\lfloor \frac{lo + hi}{2} \right\rfloor.$$

Note that if $hi > lo$, then $lo \le mid < hi$. In this case, we can split $A[lo..hi]$ into $A[lo..mid]$ and $A[mid + 1..hi]$, and both sub-arrays are smaller than the original. However, a problem occurs when $lo = hi$ — i.e., when the array contains only one element — because in this case $mid = hi$. In fact, it is impossible to divide an array of size 1 into two subarrays, each smaller than the original. Fortunately, it is easy to solve a one-element instance directly. Furthermore, it now makes sense to consider an empty array as a special case, because it can only occur when we begin with an empty array, and not as a result of dividing a nonempty array in half. We will therefore require in our precondition that $lo \le hi$, and that both are natural numbers.

We can compute the maximum suffix sum as in MAXSUMBU (see Figure 1.14 on page 18), and the maximum prefix sum in a similar way. The entire algorithm is shown in Figure 3.3. Note that the specification has been changed from the one given in Figure 1.9. However, it is a trivial matter to give an algorithm that takes as input $A[0..n-1]$ and calls MAXSUMDC if $n > 0$, or returns 0 if $n = 0$. Such an algorithm would satisfy the specification given in Figure 1.9.

This algorithm contains two recursive calls on arrays of size $\lfloor n/2 \rfloor$ and $\lceil n/2 \rceil$, respectively. In addition, it calls MAXSUFFIXBU on an array of size $\lfloor n/2 \rfloor$ and MAXPREFIXBU on an array of size $\lceil n/2 \rceil$. These two algorithms are easily seen to have running times in $\Theta(n)$; hence, if $f(n)$ denotes the worst-case running time of MAXSUMDC on an array of size n, we have

$$f(n) \in f(\lfloor n/2 \rfloor) + f(\lceil n/2 \rceil) + \Theta(n) \tag{3.7}$$

for $n > 1$.

This equation does not fit the form of Theorem 3.34. However, suppose we focus only on those values of n that are powers of 2; i.e., let $n = 2^k$ for some $k > 0$, and let $g(k) = f(2^k) = f(n)$. Then

$$g(k) = f(2^k)$$
$$\in 2f(2^{k-1}) + \Theta(2^k)$$
$$= 2g(k-1) + \Theta(2^k) \tag{3.8}$$

Figure 3.3   Divide-and-conquer algorithm for maximum subsequence sum, specified in Figure 1.9

Precondition: $A[lo..hi]$ is an array of NUMBERs, $lo \leq hi$, and both lo and hi are NATs.
Postcondition: Returns the maximum subsequence sum of $A[lo..hi]$.

MAXSUMDC($A[lo..hi]$)
  if $lo = hi$
    return MAX($0, A[lo]$)
  else
    $mid \leftarrow \lfloor (lo + hi)/2 \rfloor; mid1 \leftarrow mid + 1;$
    $sum1 \leftarrow$ MAXSUMDC($A[lo..mid]$)
    $sum2 \leftarrow$ MAXSUMDC($A[mid1..hi]$)
    $sum3 \leftarrow$ MAXSUFFIXBU($A[lo..mid]$) + MAXPREFIXBU($A[mid1..hi]$)
    return MAX($sum1, sum2, sum3$)

Precondition: $A[lo..hi]$ is an array of NUMBERs, $lo \leq hi$, and both lo and hi are NATs.
Postcondition: Returns the maximum suffix sum of $A[lo..hi]$.

MAXSUFFIXBU($A[lo..hi]$)
  $m \leftarrow 0$
  // **Invariant:** m is the maximum suffix sum of $A[lo..i-1]$
  for $i \leftarrow lo$ **to** hi
    $m \leftarrow$ MAX($0, m + A[i]$)
  return m

Precondition: $A[lo..hi]$ is an array of NUMBERs, $lo \leq hi$, and both lo and hi are NATs.
Postcondition: Returns the maximum prefix sum of $A[lo..hi]$.

MAXPREFIXBU($A[lo..hi]$)
  $m \leftarrow 0$
  // **Invariant:** m is the maximum prefix sum of $A[i+1..hi]$
  for $i \leftarrow hi$ **to** lo **by** -1
    $m \leftarrow$ MAX($0, m + A[i]$)
  return m

---

for $k > 0$. Theorem 3.34 applies to (3.8), yielding $g(k) \in \Theta(k2^k)$. Because $n = 2^k$, we have $k = \lg n$, so that

$$f(n) = g(k) = g(\lg n). \tag{3.9}$$

It is now tempting to conclude that because $g(\lg n) \in \Theta(n \lg n)$, $f(n) \in \Theta(n \lg n)$; however, (3.9) is valid only when n is a power of 2. In order to conclude that $f(n) \in \Theta(n \lg n)$, we must know something about $f(n)$ for *every* sufficiently large n. However, we can show by induction on n that $f(n)$ is eventually non-decreasing (the proof is left as an exercise). This tells us that for sufficiently large n, when $2^k \le n \le 2^{k+1}$, $f(2^k) \le f(n) \le f(2^{k+1})$. From the fact that $f(2^k) = g(k) \in \Theta(k2^k)$, there exist positive real numbers c_1 and c_2 such that $c_1 k 2^k \le f(n) \le c_2(k+1)2^{k+1}$. Furthermore, because $n \lg n$ is smooth, there is a positive real number d such that for sufficiently large m, $2m \lg(2m) \le dm \lg m$. Hence, substituting 2^k for m, we have $2^{k+1}(k+1) \le d2^k k$. Putting it all together, we have

$$f(n) \le c_2(k+1)2^{k+1}$$

$$\le c_2 d k 2^k$$

$$\le c_2 d n \lg n$$

$$\in O(n \lg n).$$

Likewise,

$$f(n) \ge c_1 k 2^k$$

$$\ge \frac{c_1(k+1)2^{k+1}}{d}$$

$$\ge \frac{c_1 n \lg n}{d}$$

$$\in \Omega(n \lg n).$$

Thus, $f(n) \in \Theta(n \lg n)$. The running time of MAXSUMDC is therefore slightly worse than that of MAXSUMBU.

The above technique is often useful when we have a recurrence which is not of a form for which we have a solution. More importantly, however, we can generalize this technique to prove the following theorem; the details are left as an exercise.

Theorem 3.35. *Let $a \ge 1$ and $q \ge 0$ be real numbers, and let $n_0 \ge 1$ and $b \ge 2$ be integers. Let $g : \mathbb{N} \to \mathbb{R}^{\ge 0}$ be such that $g'(n) = g(n_0 b^n)$ is smooth. Finally, let $f : \mathbb{N} \to \mathbb{R}^{\ge 0}$ be an eventually non-decreasing function satisfying*

$$f(n) \in af(n/b) + X(n^q g(n)),$$

whenever $n = n_0 b^k$ for a positive integer k, where X is either O, Ω, or Θ. Then

$$f(n) \in \begin{cases} X(n^q g(n)) & \text{if } a < b^q \\ X(n^q g(n) \lg n) & \text{if } a = b^q \\ X(n^{\log_b a}) & \text{if } a > b^q. \end{cases}$$

Let us first see that (3.7) fits the form of Theorem 3.35. As we have already observed, f is eventually non-decreasing (this requirement is typically met by recurrences obtained in the analysis of algorithms). When $n = 2^k$, (3.7) simplifies to

$$f(n) \in 2f(n/2) + \Theta(n).$$

Therefore, we can let $n_0 = 1$, $a = b = 2$, $q = 1$, and $g(n) = 1$. This yields $g'(n) = g(2^n) = 1$, which is smooth. Therefore, the second case applies, yielding $f(n) \in \Theta(n \lg n)$.

An important prerequisite for applying Theorem 3.35 is that $g(n_0 b^n)$ is smooth. Due to the exponential term, any function that satisfies this property must be in $O(\lg^k n)$ for some fixed k. This is not really a restriction, however, because the term expressing the non-recursive part of the analysis may be in $X(n^q g(n))$ for arbitrary real $q \geq 0$; hence, we can express most polynomially-bounded functions. What is important is that we separate this function into a polynomial part and a "polylogarithmic" part, because the degree of the polynomial affects the result.

Example 3.36. Let $f : \mathbb{N} \to \mathbb{R}^{\geq 0}$ be an eventually non-decreasing function such that

$$f(n) \in 3f(n/2) + \Theta(n^2 \lg n),$$

whenever $n = 2^k$ for a positive integer k. We then let $n_0 = 1$, $a = 3$, $b = 2$, $q = 2$, and $g(n) = \lg n$. Then

$$\begin{aligned} g'(n) &= g(2^n) \\ &= \lg 2^n \\ &= n \end{aligned}$$

is smooth. We can therefore apply Theorem 3.35. Because $b^q = 2^2 = 4$ and $a = 3$, the first case applies. Therefore, $f(n) \in \Theta(n^2 \lg n)$.

Example 3.37. Let $f : \mathbb{N} \to \mathbb{R}^{\geq 0}$ be an eventually non-decreasing function such that

$$f(n) \in 4f(n/3) + O(n \lg^2 n),$$

whenever $n = 5 \cdot 3^k$ for a positive integer k. We then let $n_0 = 5$, $a = 4$, $b = 3$, $q = 1$, and $g(n) = \lg^2 n$. Then

$$\begin{aligned} g'(n) &= g(5 \cdot 3^n) \\ &= \lg^2(5 \cdot 3^n) \\ &= \lg^2 5 + n^2 \lg^2 3 \end{aligned}$$

is smooth. We can therefore apply Theorem 3.35. Because $b^q = 3$ and $a = 4$, the third case applies. Therefore, $f(n) \in O(n^{\log_3 4})$ ($\log_3 4$ is approximately 1.26).

3.8 Analyzing Space Usage

As we mentioned earlier, running time is not the only performance measure we may be interested in obtaining. For example, recall that the implementation of MAXSUMTD from Figure 1.13 on page 18 terminated with a STACKOVERFLOWERROR on an input of 32,768 elements. As we explained in Section 1.6, this error was caused by high stack usage due to the recursion. In contrast, the implementation of MAXSUMDC can handle an input of several million elements, even though it, too, is recursive. In order to see why, we can analyze the space usage of these algorithms using the techniques we have already developed.

Let us first consider MAXSUFFIXTD from Figure 1.13. Because there is no need to copy the array in order to perform the recursive call, this algorithm requires only a constant amount of space, ignoring that needed by the recursive call. (We typically do not count the space occupied by the input or the output in measuring the space usage of an algorithm.) Thus, the total space usage is given by

$$f(n) \in f(n-1) + \Theta(1) \tag{3.10}$$

for $n > 0$. From Theorem 3.34, $f(n) \in \Theta(n)$.

Already this is enough to tell us why MAXSUMTD has poor space performance. If MAXSUFFIXTD requires $\Theta(n)$ space, then MAXSUMTD surely must require $\Omega(n)$ space. Furthermore, it is easily seen from the above analysis that the space used is almost entirely from the runtime stack;

hence, the stack usage is in $\Theta(n)$. We typically would not have a runtime stack capable of occupying space proportional to an input of, say, a million elements.

Let us now complete the analysis of MaxSumTD. Ignoring the space usage of the recursive call, we see that MaxSumTD uses $\Theta(n)$ space, due to the space usage of MaxSuffixTD. However, this does not mean that the following recurrence describes the total space usage:

$$f(n) \in f(n-1) + \Theta(n),$$

for $n > 0$. The reason is that the call made to MaxSuffixTD can reuse the space used by the recursive call. Furthermore, any calls made to MaxSuffixTD as a result of the recursive call will be on arrays of fewer than n elements, so they may reuse the space used by MaxSuffixTD($A[0..n-1]$). Therefore, the total space used by all calls to MaxSuffixTD is in $\Theta(n)$. Ignoring this space, the space used by MaxSumTD is given by

$$f(n) \in f(n-1) + \Theta(1),$$

for $n > 0$, so that $f(n) \in \Theta(n)$. The total space used is therefore in $\Theta(n) + \Theta(n) = \Theta(n)$.

Now let's consider MaxSumDC. MaxSuffixBU and MaxPrefixBU each use $\Theta(1)$ space. Because the two recursive calls can reuse the same space, the total space usage is given by

$$f(n) \in f(\lceil n/2 \rceil) + \Theta(1)$$

for $n > 1$. Applying Theorem 3.35, we see that $f(n) \in \Theta(\lg n)$. Because $\lg n$ is such a slow-growing function (e.g., $\lg 10^6 < 20$), we can see that MaxSumDC is a much more space-efficient algorithm than MaxSumTD. Because the space used by both algorithms is almost entirely from the runtime stack, MaxSumDC will not have the stack problems that MaxSumTD has.

3.9   Multiple Variables

Consider the algorithm AddMatrices shown in Figure 3.4. Applying the techniques we have developed so far, we can easily see that the inner loop runs in $\Theta(n)$ time. Furthermore, the outer loop iterates exactly m times. It is tempting at this point to say that the algorithm runs in $\Theta(mn)$ time; however, we must be careful here because we have defined asymptotic notation for single-variable functions only. In this section, we discuss how to apply asymptotic analysis to functions on more than one variable.

Figure 3.4   An algorithm to add two matrices

Precondition: $A[1..m, 1..n]$ and $B[1..m, 1..n]$ are arrays of NUMBERS, and m and n are positive NATS.

Postcondition: Returns the sum of $A[1..m, 1..n]$ and $B[1..m, 1..n]$; i.e., returns the array $C[1..m, 1..n]$ such that for $1 \leq i \leq m$ and $1 \leq j \leq n$, $C[i, j] = A[i, j] + B[i, j]$.

ADDMATRICES($A[1..m, 1..n], B[1..m, 1..n]$)
   $C \leftarrow$ **new** ARRAY$[1..m, 1..n]$
   for $i \leftarrow 1$ **to** m
      for $j \leftarrow 1$ **to** n
         $C[i, j] \leftarrow A[i, j] + B[i, j]$
   return $C[1..m, 1..n]$

We would like to extend the definitions to multiple variables in as straightforward a manner as possible. For example, we would like for $O(f(m, n))$ to include all functions $g : \mathbb{N} \times \mathbb{N} \to \mathbb{R}^{\geq 0}$ such that for

> For sets A and B, $A \times B$ denotes the set of all ordered pairs (a, b) such that $a \in A$ and $b \in B$.

some $c \in \mathbb{R}^{>0}$ and $n_0 \in \mathbb{N}$, $g(m, n) \leq cf(m, n)$ whenever certain conditions hold. The question is what exactly these "certain conditions" should be. Should the inequality be required to hold whenever at least one of m or n is at least n_0? Or should it be required to hold only when both m and n are at least n_0?

Suppose first that we were to require that the inequality hold whenever at least one of m or n is at least n_0. Unfortunately, a consequence of such a definition would be that $mn + 1 \notin O(mn)$. To see why, observe that whatever values we choose for c and n_0, when $m = 0$ and $n \geq n_0$, $mn + 1 > cmn$. As a result, working with asymptotic notation would become much messier with multiple variables than with a single variable.

On the other hand, only requiring the inequality to hold when both m and n are at least n_0 also presents problems. Consider, for example, how we would analyze the rather silly algorithm shown in Figure 3.5. We can observe that the first of the inner loops iterates 2^n times, and that the second iterates in times. However, the first loop is only executed when $i = 0$; hence, when both i and n are sufficiently large, only the second loop is executed. We could therefore legitimately conclude that the body of the outer loop runs in $O(in)$ time. Unfortunately, this would lead to an incorrect analysis of the algorithm because the first inner loop will always execute once, assuming m is a NAT.

Figure 3.5 An algorithm illustrating difficulties with asymptotic notation with multiple variables

---

Precondition: m and n are NATs.
Postcondition: true.

$\mathrm{F}(m, n)$
    for $i \leftarrow 0$ **to** $m - 1$
        if $i = 0$
            for $j \leftarrow 1$ **to** 2^n
                // Do nothing
        else
            for $j \leftarrow 1$ **to** in
                // Do nothing

Thus, we can see that if we want to retain the properties of asymptotic notation on a single variable, we must extend it to multiple variables in a way that is not straightforward. Unfortunately, the situation is worse than this — it can be shown that it is impossible to extend the notation to multiple variables in a way that retains the properties of asymptotic notation on a single variable. What we can do, however, is to extend it so that these properties are retained whenever the function inside the asymptotic notation is strictly non-decreasing. Note that restricting the functions in this way does not avoid the problems discussed above, as the functions inside the asymptotic notation in this discussion are all strictly non-decreasing. We therefore must use some less straightforward extension.

The definition we propose for $O(f(m, n))$ considers all values of a function $g(m, n)$, rather than ignoring values when m and/or n are small. However, it allows even infinitely many values of $g(m, n)$ to be large in comparison to $f(m, n)$, provided that they are not too large in comparison to the overall growth rate of f. In order to accomplish these goals, we first give the following definition.

> *We say that a function $f : \mathbb{N} \times \mathbb{N} \to \mathbb{R}^{\geq 0}$ is strictly non-decreasing if, for every $m \in \mathbb{N}$ and $n \in \mathbb{N}$, $f(m, n) \leq f(m + 1, n)$ and $f(m, n) \leq f(m, n + 1)$.*

Definition 3.38. For a function $f : \mathbb{N} \times \mathbb{N} \to \mathbb{R}^{\geq 0}$, we define $\widehat{f} : \mathbb{N} \times \mathbb{N} \to \mathbb{R}^{\geq 0}$ so that

$$\widehat{f}(m, n) = \max\{f(i, j) \mid 0 \leq i \leq m, 0 \leq j \leq n\}.$$

Using the above definition, we can now define big-O for 2-variable functions.

Definition 3.39. For a function $f : \mathbb{N} \times \mathbb{N} \to \mathbb{R}^{\geq 0}$, we define $O(f(m, n))$ to be the set of all functions $g : \mathbb{N} \times \mathbb{N} \to \mathbb{R}^{\geq 0}$ such that there exist $c \in \mathbb{R}^{>0}$ and $n_0 \in \mathbb{N}$ so that

$$g(m, n) \leq cf(m, n)$$

and

$$\widehat{g}(m, n) \leq c\widehat{f}(m, n),$$

whenever $m \geq n_0$ and $n \geq n_0$.

Likewise, we can define big-Ω and big-Θ for 2-variable functions.

Definition 3.40. For a function $f : \mathbb{N} \times \mathbb{N} \to \mathbb{R}^{\geq 0}$, we define $\Omega(f(m, n))$ to be the set of all functions $g : \mathbb{N} \times \mathbb{N} \to \mathbb{R}^{\geq 0}$ such that there exist $c \in \mathbb{R}^{>0}$ and $n_0 \in \mathbb{N}$ so that

$$g(m, n) \geq cf(m, n)$$

and

$$\widehat{g}(m, n) \geq c\widehat{f}(m, n),$$

whenever $m \geq n_0$ and $n \geq n_0$.

Definition 3.41. For a function $f : \mathbb{N} \times \mathbb{N} \to \mathbb{R}^{\geq 0}$,

$$\Theta(f(m, n)) = O(f(m, n)) \cap \Omega(f(m, n)).$$

We extend these definitions to more than two variables in the obvious way. Using the above definitions, it is an easy matter to show that Theorem 3.11 extends to more than one variable. The proof is left as an exercise.

Theorem 3.42. *Let* $f : \mathbb{N} \times \mathbb{N} \to \mathbb{R}^{\geq 0}$ *and* $g : \mathbb{N} \times \mathbb{N} \to \mathbb{R}^{\geq 0}$. *Then* $g(m, n) \in O(f(m, n))$ *iff* $f(m, n) \in \Omega(g(m, n))$.

We would now like to show that the theorems we have presented for single variables extend to multiple variables, provided the functions within the asymptotic notation are strictly non-decreasing. Before we do this, however, we will first prove a theorem that will allow us to simplify the proofs of the individual properties.

Theorem 3.43. *Let* $f : \mathbb{N} \times \mathbb{N} \to \mathbb{R}^{\geq 0}$ *be a strictly non-decreasing function. Then*

1. $O(f(m, n))$ *is the set of all functions* $g : \mathbb{N} \times \mathbb{N} \to \mathbb{R}^{\geq 0}$ *such that there exist* $c \in \mathbb{R}^{>0}$ *and* $n_0 \in \mathbb{N}$ *such that*

$$\widehat{g}(m, n) \leq c\widehat{f}(m, n),$$

whenever $m \geq n_0$ *and* $n \geq n_0$.

2. $\Omega(f(m, n))$ *is the set of all functions* $g : \mathbb{N} \times \mathbb{N} \to \mathbb{R}^{\geq 0}$ *such that there exist* $c \in \mathbb{R}^{>0}$ *and* $n_0 \in \mathbb{N}$ *such that*

$$g(m, n) \geq cf(m, n),$$

whenever $m \geq n_0$ *and* $n \geq n_0$.

Proof. From the definitions, for any function $g(m, n)$ in $O(f(m, n))$ or in $\Omega(f(m, n))$, respectively, there are a $c \in \mathbb{R}^{>0}$ and an $n_0 \in \mathbb{N}$ such that whenever $m \geq n_0$ and $n \geq n_0$, the corresponding inequality above is satisfied. We therefore only need to show that if there are $c \in \mathbb{R}^{>0}$ and $n_0 \in \mathbb{N}$ such that whenever $m \geq n_0$ and $n \geq n_0$, the given inequality is satisfied, then $g(m, n)$ belongs to $O(f(m, n))$ or $\Omega(f(m, n))$, respectively.

We first observe that if f is strictly non-decreasing, then

$$\widehat{f}(m, n) = f(m, n),$$

for all natural numbers m and n. Furthermore, for any function $g : \mathbb{N} \times \mathbb{N} \to \mathbb{R}^{\geq 0}$,

$$\widehat{g}(m, n) \geq g(m, n).$$

Now suppose $c \in \mathbb{R}^{>0}$ and $n_0 \in \mathbb{N}$ such that whenever $m \geq n_0$ and $n \geq n_0$, $\widehat{g}(m, n) \leq c\widehat{f}(m, n)$. Then for $m \geq n_0$ and $n \geq n_0$,

$$g(m, n) \leq \widehat{g}(m, n)$$
$$\leq c\widehat{f}(m, n)$$
$$= cf(m, n).$$

Hence, $g(m, n) \in O(f(m, n))$.

Likewise, suppose now that $c \in \mathbb{R}^{>0}$ and $n_0 \in \mathbb{N}$ such that whenever $m \geq n_0$ and $n \geq n_0$, $g(m, n) \geq cf(m, n)$. Then for $m \geq n_0$ and $n \geq n_0$,

$$\widehat{g}(m, n) \geq g(m, n)$$
$$\geq cf(m, n)$$
$$= c\widehat{f}(m, n).$$

Therefore, $g(m, n) \in \Omega(f(m, n))$. $\qquad\qquad\square$

As a result of the above theorem, in order to prove properties about either $O(f(m,n))$ or $\Omega(f(m,n))$, where f is strictly non-decreasing, we only need to prove one of the two inequalities in the definition. Consider, for example, the following extension to Theorem 3.8.

Theorem 3.44. *Suppose* $f_1(m,n) \in O(g_1(m,n))$ *and* $f_2(m,n) \in O(g_2(m,n))$, *where* g_1 *and* g_2 *are strictly non-decreasing. Then*

1. $f_1(m,n)f_2(m,n) \in O(g_1(m,n)g_2(m,n))$; *and*
2. $f_1(m,n) + f_2(m,n) \in O(\max(g_1(m,n), g_2(m,n)))$.

Proof. We will only show part 3.44; part 3.44 will be left as an exercise. Because $f_1(m,n) \in O(g_1(m,n))$ and $f_2(m,n) \in O(g_2(m,n))$, there exist positive real numbers c_1 and c_2 and natural numbers n_1 and n_2 such that whenever $m \geq n_1$ and $n \geq n_1$,

$$\widehat{f_1}(m,n) \leq c_1\widehat{g_1}(m,n),$$

and whenever $m \geq n_2$ and $n \geq n_2$,

$$\widehat{f_2}(m,n) \leq c_2\widehat{g_2}(m,n).$$

In what follows we will let

$$\widehat{f_1f_2}(m,n) = \max\{f_1(i,j)f_2(i,j) \mid 0 \leq i \leq m, 0 \leq j \leq n\}.$$

We first observe that for any natural numbers m and n,

$$\widehat{f_1f_2}(m,n) \leq \widehat{f_1}(m,n)\widehat{f_2}(m,n).$$

Furthermore, because both g_1 and g_2 are strictly non-decreasing, so is g_1g_2.
Let $n_0 = \max(n_1, n_2)$. Then whenever $m \geq n_0$ and $n \geq n_0$,

$$\begin{aligned}
\widehat{f_1f_2}(m,n) &\leq \widehat{f_1}(m,n)\widehat{f_2}(m,n) \\
&\leq c_1\widehat{g_1}(m,n)c_2\widehat{g_2}(m,n) \\
&= c_1c_2\widehat{g_1}(m,n)\widehat{g_2}(m,n) \\
&= c\widehat{g_1g_2}(m,n),
\end{aligned}$$

where $c = c_1c_2$. From Theorem 3.43,

$$f_1(m,n)f_2(m,n) \in O(g_1(m,n)g_2(m,n)).$$

$\square$

In a similar way, the following extension to Theorem 3.15 can be shown. The proof is left as an exercise.

Theorem 3.45. *Suppose* $f_1(m,n) \in \Omega(g_1(m,n))$ *and* $f_2(m,n) \in \Omega(g_2(m,n))$, *where* g_1 *and* g_2 *are strictly non-decreasing. Then*

1. $f_1(m,n)f_2(m,n) \in \Omega(g_1(m,n)g_2(m,n))$; *and*
2. $f_1(m,n) + f_2(m,n) \in \Omega(\max(g_1(m,n), g_2(m,n)))$.

We therefore have the following corollary.

Corollary 3.46. *Suppose* $f_1(m,n) \in \Theta(g_1(m,n))$ *and* $f_2(m,n) \in \Theta(g_2(m,n))$, *where* g_1 *and* g_2 *are strictly non-decreasing. Then*

1. $f_1(m,n)f_2(m,n) \in \Theta(g_1(m,n)g_2(m,n))$; *and*
2. $f_1(m,n) + f_2(m,n) \in \Theta(\max(g_1(m,n), g_2(m,n)))$.

Before we can extend Theorem 3.31 to more than one variable, we must first extend the definition of smoothness. In order to do this, we must first extend the definitions of eventually non-decreasing and eventually positive.

Definition 3.47. Let $f : \mathbb{N} \times \mathbb{N} \to \mathbb{R}^{\geq 0}$. f is said to be *eventually non-decreasing* if there is a natural number n_0 such that $f(m,n) \leq f(m+1,n)$ and $f(m,n) \leq f(m,n+1)$ whenever both $m \geq n_0$ and $n \geq n_0$.

Definition 3.48. Let $f : \mathbb{N} \times \mathbb{N} \to \mathbb{R}^{\geq 0}$. f is said to be *eventually positive* if there is a natural number n_0 such that $f(m,n) > 0$ whenever both $m \geq n_0$ and $n \geq n_0$.

Definition 3.49. Let $f : \mathbb{N} \times \mathbb{N} \to \mathbb{R}^{\geq 0}$ be an eventually non-decreasing and eventually positive function. f is said to be *smooth* if there exist a real number c and a natural number n_0 such that $f(2m,n) \leq cf(m,n)$ and $f(m,2n) \leq cf(m,n)$ whenever both $m \geq n_0$ and $n \geq n_0$.

The following extension to Theorem 3.31 can now be shown — the proof is left as an exercise.

Theorem 3.50. *Let* $f : \mathbb{N} \times \mathbb{N} \to \mathbb{R}^{\geq 0}$ *be a strictly non-decreasing smooth function. Let* $g : \mathbb{N} \to \mathbb{N}$ *be an eventually non-decreasing and unbounded function, and let* X *denote either* O, Ω, *or* Θ. *Then*

$$\sum_{i=1}^{g(m)} X(f(i,n)) \subseteq X(g(m)f(g(m),n)).$$

Having the above theorems, we can now complete the analysis of ADD-MATRICES. Because we are analyzing the algorithm with respect to two parameters, we view n as the 2-variable function $f(m, n) = n$, and we view m as the 2-variable function $g(m, n) = m$. We can then apply Corollary 3.46 to $\Theta(m)\Theta(n)$ to obtain a running time in $\Theta(mn)$. Alternatively, because n is smooth, we could apply Theorem 3.50 to obtain

$$\sum_{i=1}^{m} \Theta(n) \subseteq \Theta(mn).$$

The results from this section give us the tools we need to analyze iterative algorithms with two natural parameters. Furthermore, all of these results can be easily extended to more than two parameters. Recursive algorithms, however, present a greater challenge. In order to analyze recursive algorithms using more than one natural parameter, we need to be able to handle asymptotic recurrences in more than one variable. This topic is beyond the scope of this book.

3.10 Little-o and Little-ω

Occasionally, we would like to use asymptotic notation without ignoring constant factors. Consider, for example, $f(n) = 3n^2 + 7n + 2$. As n increases, the $7n + 2$ term becomes less relevant. In fact, as n increases, the ratio $3n^2/f(n)$ approaches 1. We might therefore wish to say that $f(n)$ is $3n^2$, plus some low-order terms. We would like to be able to express the fact that these low-order terms are insignificant as n increases. To this end, we give the following definitions.

Definition 3.51. Let $f : \mathbb{N} \to \mathbb{R}^{\geq 0}$. $o(f(n))$ is the set of all functions $g : \mathbb{N} \to \mathbb{R}^{\geq 0}$ such that for every positive real number c, there is a natural number n_0 such that $g(n) < cf(n)$ whenever $n \geq n_0$.

> $o(f(n))$ is pronounced *"little-oh of f of n"*.

Definition 3.52. Let $f : \mathbb{N} \to \mathbb{R}^{\geq 0}$. $\omega(f(n))$ is the set of all functions $g : \mathbb{N} \to \mathbb{R}^{\geq 0}$ such that for every positive real number c, there is a natural number n_0 such that $g(n) > cf(n)$ whenever $n \geq n_0$.

> $\omega(f(n))$ is pronounced *"little-omega of f of n"*.

Example 3.53. $7n + 2 \in o(n^2)$. In proof, suppose $c > 0$. We need to find a natural number n_0 such that $7n + 2 < cn^2$ whenever $n \geq n_0$. We first observe that this inequality holds if $n > 0$ and $(7 + 2/n)/c < n$. The left-hand side of this inequality is maximized when $n = 1$; therefore, if $n \geq \lfloor 9/c \rfloor + 1$, $7n + 2 < cn^2$.

Figure 3.6 Venn diagram depicting the relationships between the sets $O(f(n))$, $\Omega(f(n))$, $\Theta(f(n))$, $o(f(n))$, and $\omega(f(n))$

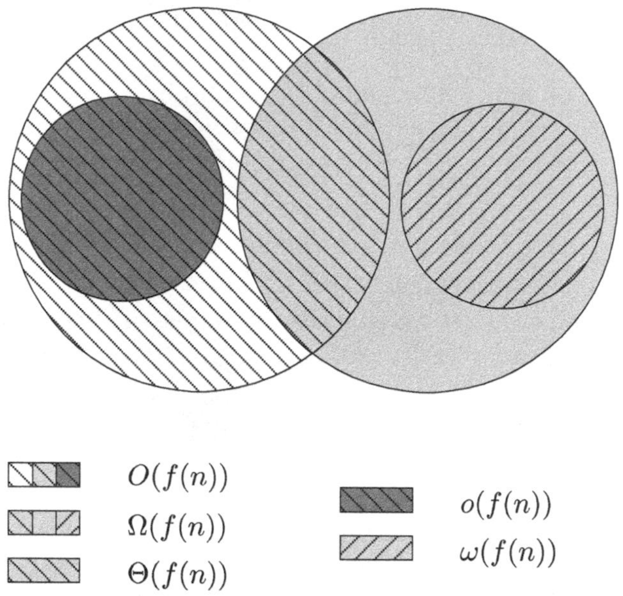

Thus, if $f(n) = 3n^2 + 7n + 2$, then $f(n) \in 3n^2 + o(n^2)$.

These definitions are similar to the definitions of O and Ω, respectively, except that the inequalities hold for *every* positive real number c, rather than for *some* positive real number c. Thus, $g(n) \in o(f(n))$ is a strictly stronger statement than $g(n) \in O(f(n))$, and $g(n) \in \omega(f(n))$ is a strictly stronger statement than $g(n) \in \Omega(f(n))$ (see Figure 3.6). This idea is formalized by the following theorem.

Theorem 3.54. *Let* $f : \mathbb{N} \to \mathbb{R}^{\geq 0}$ *be an eventually positive function. Then*

1. $o(f(n)) \subseteq O(f(n)) \setminus \Theta(f(n))$; *and*
2. $\omega(f(n)) \subseteq \Omega(f(n)) \setminus \Theta(f(n))$,

where $A \setminus B$ *denotes the set of elements in* A *but not in* B.

Proof. We will only prove part 1; the proof of part 2 is symmetric. Let $g(n) \in o(f(n))$, and let c be any positive real number. Then there is a natural number n_0 such that $g(n) < cf(n)$ whenever $n \geq n_0$. Hence, $g(n) \in O(f(n))$. Furthermore, because the choice of c is arbitrary, we can conclude that $g(n) \notin \Omega(f(n))$; hence, $g(n) \notin \Theta(f(n))$. $\qquad\square$

It may seem at this point that the above theorem could be strengthened to say that $o(f(n)) = O(f(n)) \setminus \Theta(f(n))$ and $\omega(f(n)) = \Omega(f(n)) \setminus \Theta(f(n))$. Indeed, for functions f and g that we typically encounter in the analysis of algorithms, it will be the case that if $g(n) \in O(f(n)) \setminus \Theta(f(n))$ then $g(n) \in o(f(n))$. However, there are exceptions. For example, let $f(n) = n$, and let $g(n) = 2^{2^{\lfloor \lg \lg n \rfloor}}$. Then $g(n) \in O(f(n))$ because $g(n) \leq f(n)$ for all $n \in \mathbb{N}$. Furthermore, when $n = 2^{2^k} - 1$ for $k > 0$, $g(n) = 2^{2^{k-1}} = \sqrt{n+1}$; hence, $g(n) \notin \Theta(f(n))$. Finally, when $n = 2^{2^k}$, $g(n) = n$, so $g(n) \notin o(f(n))$.

Note that we have the same duality between o and ω as between O and Ω. We therefore have the following theorem.

Theorem 3.55. *Let $f : \mathbb{N} \to \mathbb{R}^{\geq 0}$ and $g : \mathbb{N} \to \mathbb{R}^{\geq 0}$. Then $g(n) \in o(f(n))$ iff $f(n) \in \omega(g(n))$.*

Given the above results, we might expect o and ω to have some properties similar to those of other forms of asymptotic notation. One example of such a property is expressed in the following theorem, which is analogous to Theorems 3.8 and 3.15. Its proof is left as an exercise.

Theorem 3.56. *Suppose $f_1(n) \in o(g_1(n))$, $f_2(n) \in o(g_2(n))$, $f_3(n) \in \omega(g_3(n))$, and $f_4(n) \in \omega(g_4(n))$. Then*

1. $f_1(n)f_2(n) \in o(g_1(n)g_2(n))$.
2. $f_1(n) + f_2(n) \in o(\max(g_1(n), g_2(n)))$.
3. $f_3(n)f_4(n) \in \omega(g_3(n)g_4(n))$.
4. $f_3(n) + f_4(n) \in \omega(\max(g_3(n), g_4(n)))$.

The following theorems express relationships between common functions using o-notation.

Theorem 3.57. *Let $p, q \in \mathbb{R}^{\geq 0}$ such that $p < q$, and suppose $f(n) \in O(n^p)$ and $g(n) \in \Omega(n^q)$. Then $f(n) \in o(g(n))$.*

Proof. Because $f(n) \in O(n^p)$, there exist a positive real number c_1 and a natural number n_1 such that

$$f(n) \leq c_1 n^p \tag{3.11}$$

whenever $n \geq n_1$. Because $g(n) \in \Omega(n^q)$, there exist a positive real number c_2 and a natural number n_2 such that

$$g(n) \geq c_2 n^q \tag{3.12}$$

whenever $n \geq n_2$. Combining (3.11) and (3.12), we have

$$f(n) \leq \frac{c_1 g(n)}{c_2 n^{q-p}}$$

whenever $n \geq \max(n_1, n_2)$. Let c be an arbitrary positive real number. Let $n_0 = \max(n_1, n_2, \lceil (c_1/(c_2 c))^{1/(q-p)} \rceil) + 1$. Then when $n \geq n_0$, $n^{q-p} > c_1/(c_2 c)$ because $q > p$. We therefore have,

$$f(n) \leq \frac{c_1 g(n)}{c_2 n^{q-p}}$$

$$< cg(n).$$

Therefore, $f(n) \in o(g(n))$. □

Theorem 3.58. *Let p and q be any positive real numbers. Then*

1. *$O(\lg^p n) \subseteq o(n^q)$; and*
2. *$O(n^p) \subseteq o(2^{qn})$.*

The proof of Theorem 3.58 requires some additional techniques, which we present in the next section.

3.11   * Use of Limits in Asymptotic Analysis

The astute reader may have noticed a relationship between asymptotic analysis and the concept of a limit. Both of these concepts involve the behavior of a function $f(n)$ as n increases. In order to examine this relationship precisely, we now give the formal definition of a limit.

Definition 3.59. Let $f : \mathbb{N} \to \mathbb{R}$, and let $u \in \mathbb{R}$. We say that

$$\lim_{n \to \infty} f(n) = u,$$

if for every positive real number c, there is a natural number n_0 such that $|f(n) - u| < c$ whenever $n \geq n_0$. Likewise, for a function $g : \mathbb{R}^{\geq 0} \to \mathbb{R}$, we say that

$$\lim_{x \to \infty} g(x) = u,$$

if for every positive real number c, there is a real number x_0 such that $|g(x) - u| < c$ whenever $x \geq x_0$.

Note that for $f : \mathbb{N} \to \mathbb{R}$ and $g : \mathbb{R}^{\geq 0} \to \mathbb{R}$, if $f(n) = g(n)$ for every $n \in \mathbb{N}$, it follows immediately from the above definition that

$$\lim_{n \to \infty} f(n) = \lim_{x \to \infty} g(x),$$

whenever the latter limit exists. It is also possible to define infinite limits, but for our purposes we only need finite limits as defined above. Given this definition, we can now formally relate limits to asymptotic notation.

Theorem 3.60. *Let $f : \mathbb{N} \to \mathbb{R}^{\geq 0}$ and $g : \mathbb{N} \to \mathbb{R}^{\geq 0}$. Then*

1. $g(n) \in o(f(n))$ *iff* $\lim_{n \to \infty} g(n)/f(n) = 0$ *and*
2. $g(n) \in \Theta(f(n))$ *if* $\lim_{n \to \infty} g(n)/f(n) = x > 0$.

Note that part 3.60 is an "if and only if", whereas part 3.60 is an "if". The reason for this is that there are four possibilities, given arbitrary f and g:

1. $\lim_{n \to \infty} g(n)/f(n) = 0$. In this case $g(n) \in o(f(n))$ and $f(n) \in \omega(g(n))$.
2. $\lim_{n \to \infty} f(n)/g(n) = 0$. In this case $f(n) \in o(g(n))$ and $g(n) \in \omega(f(n))$.
3. $\lim_{n \to \infty} g(n)/f(n) = x > 0$. In this case, $g(n) \in \Theta(f(n))$ and $f(n) \in \Theta(g(n))$. (Note that $\lim_{n \to \infty} f(n)/g(n) = 1/x > 0$.)
4. Neither $\lim_{n \to \infty} g(n)/f(n)$ nor $\lim_{n \to \infty} f(n)/g(n)$ exists. In this case, we can only conclude that $g(n) \notin o(f(n))$ and $f(n) \notin o(g(n))$ — we do not have enough information to determine whether $g(n) \in \Theta(f(n))$.

Proof of Theorem 3.60

1. This follows immediately from the definitions of limit and o.
2. Suppose $\lim_{n \to \infty} g(n)/f(n) = x > 0$. Then for every positive real number c, there is a natural number n_0 such that

$$x - c < g(n)/f(n) < x + c$$

whenever $n \geq n_0$. Multiplying the above inequalities by $f(n)$, we have

$$(x - c)f(n) < g(n) < (x + c)f(n).$$

Because these inequalities hold for every positive real number c, and because $x > 0$, we may choose $c = x/2$, so that both $x - c$ and $x + c$ are positive. Therefore, $g(n) \in \Theta(f(n))$. $\qquad \square$

A powerful tool for evaluating limits of the form given in Theorem 3.60 is L'Hôpital's rule, which we present without proof in the following theorem.

Theorem 3.61 (L'Hôpital's rule). *Let* $f : \mathbb{R}^{\geq 0} \to \mathbb{R}$ *and* $g : \mathbb{R}^{\geq 0} \to \mathbb{R}$ *be functions such that* $\lim_{x \to \infty} 1/f(x) = 0$ *and* $\lim_{x \to \infty} 1/g(x) = 0$. *Let* f' *and* g' *denote the derivatives of* f *and* g, *respectively. If* $\lim_{x \to \infty} g'(x)/f'(x) = u \in \mathbb{R}$, *then* $\lim_{x \to \infty} g(x)/f(x) = u$.

> We are implicitly assuming that for sufficiently large x, the derivatives are defined and $f'(x) \neq 0$.

With this theorem, we can now prove Theorem 3.58.

Proof of Theorem 3.58

1. We will use L'Hôpital's rule to show that $\lim_{x \to \infty} \lg x / x^{q/p} = 0$. It will therefore follow that $\lim_{x \to \infty} \lg^p x / x^q = 0$. From Theorem 3.60, it will then follow that $\lg^p n \in o(n^q)$. We leave it as an exercise to show that if $g(n) \in o(f(n))$, then $O(g(n)) \subseteq o(f(n))$.

   We first note that because both $\lg x$ and $x^{q/p}$ are non-decreasing and unbounded (because q and p are both positive), $\lim_{x \to \infty} 1/\lg x = 0$ and $\lim_{x \to \infty} 1/x^{q/p} = 0$. In order to compute the derivative of $\lg x$, we first observe that $\lg x \ln 2 = \ln x$, where $\ln$ denotes the natural logarithm or base-e logarithm, where $e \approx 2.718$. Thus, the derivative of $\lg x$ is $1/(x \ln 2)$. The derivative of $x^{q/p}$ is

   $$qx^{\frac{q}{p}-1}/p.$$

   Using L'Hôpital's rule,

   $$\lim_{x \to \infty} \frac{\lg x}{x^{q/p}} = \lim_{x \to \infty} \frac{1}{qx^{\frac{q}{p}-1} x \ln 2/p}$$

   $$= \lim_{x \to \infty} \frac{p}{qx^{\frac{q}{p}} \ln 2}$$

   $$= 0.$$

   Hence, $\lim_{x \to \infty} \lg^p x / x^q = 0$. Therefore, $\lg^p n \in o(n^q)$ and $O(\lg^p n) \subseteq o(n^q)$.

2. Because $\lim_{x \to \infty} \lg^p x / x^q = 0$ and 2^x is non-decreasing and unbounded, it follows that

   $$\lim_{x \to \infty} x^p / 2^{qx} = \lim_{x \to \infty} \lg^p(2^x)/(2^x)^q$$

   $$= 0.$$

   Therefore, $n^p \in o(2^{qn})$ and $O(n^p) \subseteq o(2^{qn})$. $\square$

3.12   Summary

Asymptotic notation can be used to express the growth rates of functions in a way that ignores constant factors and focuses on the behavior as the function argument increases. We can therefore use asymptotic notation to analyze performance of algorithms in terms of such measures as worst-case running time or space usage. O and Ω are used to express upper and lower bounds, respectively, while Θ is used to express the fact that the upper and lower bounds are tight. o gives us the ability to abstract away low-order terms when we don't want to ignore constant factors. ω provides a dual for o.

Analysis of iterative algorithms typically involves summations. Theorem 3.31 gives us a powerful tool for obtaining asymptotic solutions for summations. Analysis of recursive algorithms, on the other hand, typically involves recurrence relations. Theorems 3.34 and 3.35 provide asymptotic solutions for the most common forms of recurrences.

The analyses of the various algorithms for the maximum subsequence sum problem illustrate the utility of asymptotic analysis. We saw that the five algorithms have worst-case running times shown in Figure 3.7. These results correlate well with the actual running times shown in Figure 1.15.

The results of asymptotic analyses can also be used to predict performance degradation. If an algorithm's running time is in $\Theta(f(n))$, then as n increases, the running time of an implementation must lie between $cf(n)$ and $df(n)$ for some positive real numbers c and d. In fact, for most algorithms, this running time will approach $cf(n)$ for a single positive real number c. Assuming that this convergence occurs, if we run the algorithm on sufficiently large input, we can approximate c by dividing the actual running time by $f(n)$, where n is the size of the input.

Figure 3.7   Asymptotic worst-case running times of maximum subsequence sum algorithms

Algorithm	Running Time
MAXSUMITER	$\Theta(n^3)$
MAXSUMOPT	$\Theta(n^2)$
MAXSUMTD	$\Theta(n^2)$
MAXSUMDC	$\Theta(n \lg n)$
MAXSUMBU	$\Theta(n)$

For example, our implementation of MaxSum-Iter took 24 seconds to process an input of size $2^{13} = 8{,}192$. Dividing 24 by $(8{,}192)^3$, we obtain a value of $c = 4.4 \times 10^{-11}$. Evaluating cn^3 for $n = 2^{12}$,

> The results of floating-point computations in this discussion are all rounded to two significant digits.

we obtain a value of 3.0 seconds. This matches the actual running time measured on an input of size 2^{13}. Thus, the running time does appear to be converging to cn^3 for sufficiently large n.

Figure 3.8 shows a plot of the functions estimating the running times of the various maximum subsequence sum implementations, along with the measured running times from Figure 1.15. The functions were derived via the technique outlined above using the timing information from Figure 1.15, taking the largest data set tested for each algorithm. We have extended both axes to show how these functions compare as n grows as large as $2^{30} = 1{,}073{,}741{,}824$.

For example, consider MaxSumIter and MaxSumBU. As we have already shown, the function estimating the running time of MaxSumIter is $f(n) = (4.4 \times 10^{-11})n^3$. We were able to run MaxSumBU on an array of size 2^{30} — it ran in 0.99 seconds. On the other hand, we estimate the running time for MaxSumIter on an array of this size to be $f(2^{30}) = 5.4 \times 10^{16}$ seconds,

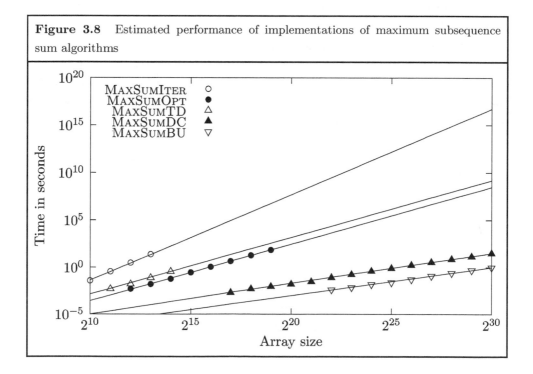

Figure 3.8   Estimated performance of implementations of maximum subsequence sum algorithms

or over 1.7 billion years! Even if we could speed up the processor by a factor of one million, this implementation would still require over 1700 years.

Though this example clearly illustrates the utility of asymptotic analysis, a word of caution is in order. Asymptotic notation allows us to focus on growth rates while ignoring constant factors. However, constant factors can be relevant. For example, two linear-time algorithms will not yield comparable performance if the hidden constants are very different.

For a more subtle example, consider the functions $\lg^{16} n$ and $\sqrt{n}$, shown in Figure 3.9. From Theorem 3.58, $O(\lg^{16} n) \subseteq o(\sqrt{n})$, so that as n increases, $\lg^{16} n$ grows much more slowly than does $\sqrt{n}$. However, consider $n = 2^{32} = 4{,}294{,}967{,}296$. For this value, $\sqrt{n} = 2^{16} = 65{,}536$, whereas

$$\lg^{16} n = 32^{16} = 1{,}208{,}925{,}819{,}614{,}629{,}174{,}706{,}176.$$

$\lg^{16} n$ remains larger than $\sqrt{n}$ until $n = 2^{256}$ — a 78-digit number. After that, $\sqrt{n}$ does grow much more rapidly than does $\lg^{16} n$, but it is hard to see any practical value in studying the behaviors of these functions at such large values.

Finally, the running time analyses we have seen in this chapter have all been worst-case analyses. For some algorithms, the worst case is much worse than typical cases, so that in practice, the algorithm performs much better than a worst-case analysis would suggest. Later, we will see other kinds of

Figure 3.9 Functions illustrating the practical limitations of asymptotic notation

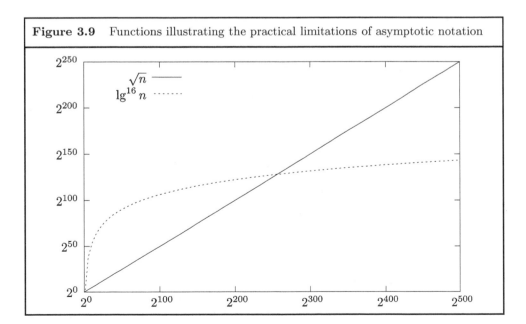

analyses that may be more appropriate in such cases. However, we must realize that there is a limit to what can be determined analytically.

3.13 Exercises

Exercise 3.1. Prove that if $g(n) \in O(f(n))$, then $O(g(n)) \subseteq O(f(n))$.

Exercise 3.2. Prove that for any $f : \mathbb{N} \to \mathbb{R}^{\geq 0}$, $f(n) \in \Theta(f(n))$.

Exercise 3.3. Prove that if $f(n) \in O(g(n))$ and $g(n) \in O(h(n))$, then $f(n) \in O(h(n))$.

Exercise 3.4. Suppose $f(n) \in \Theta(g(n))$. Prove that for each $X \in \{O, \Omega, \Theta\}$, $X(f(n)) = X(g(n))$.

Exercise 3.5. Prove Theorem 3.15.

Exercise 3.6. Prove Theorem 3.17.

Exercise 3.7. Prove Theorem 3.18. [*Hint*: You might find Theorem 3.17 useful for showing containment in one direction.]

Exercise 3.8. For each of the following, give functions $f(n) \in \Theta(n)$ and $g(n) \in \Theta(n)$ that satisfy the given property.

    a. $f(n) - g(n) \in \Theta(n)$.
    b. $f(n) - g(n) \notin \Theta(n)$.

Exercise 3.9. Suppose that $g_1(n) \in \Theta(f_1(n))$ and $g_2(n) \in \Theta(f_2(n))$, where g_2 and f_2 are eventually positive. Prove that $g_1(n)/g_2(n) \in \Theta(f_1(n)/f_2(n))$.

Exercise 3.10. Show that the result in Exercise 3.9 does not necessarily hold if we replace Θ by O.

Exercise 3.11. Let $f : \mathbb{N} \to \mathbb{R}^{\geq 0}$ and $g : \mathbb{N} \to \mathbb{R}^{\geq 0}$, where g is eventually positive. Prove that $f(n) \in O(g(n))$ iff there is a positive real number c such that $f(n) \leq cg(n)$ whenever $g(n) > 0$.

* Exercise 3.12. Let $f(n) = 2^{2^{\lfloor \lg \lg n \rfloor}}$, where we assume that $f(n) = 0$ for $n \leq 1$.

    a. Show that $f(n) \in O(n)$.
    b. Show that $f(n)$ is not smooth; i.e., show that for every $c \in \mathbb{R}^{>0}$ and every $n_0 \in \mathbb{N}$, there is some $n \geq n_0$ such that $f(2n) > cf(n)$. [*Hint*: Consider a sufficiently large value of n having the form $2^{2^k - 1}$.]

* **Exercise 3.13.** The goal of this exercise is to prove Theorem 3.31. Let $f : \mathbb{N} \to \mathbb{R}^{\geq 0}$ be a smooth function, $g : \mathbb{N} \to \mathbb{N}$ be an eventually non-decreasing and unbounded function, and $h : \mathbb{N} \to \mathbb{R}^{\geq 0}$.

a. Show that if $h(n) \in O(f(n))$, then there exist natural numbers n_0 and n_1, a positive real number c, and a non-negative real number d such that for every $n \geq n_1$,

$$\sum_{i=1}^{g(n)} h(i) \leq d + \sum_{i=n_0}^{g(n)} cf(g(n)).$$

b. Use part (a) to prove that

$$\sum_{i=1}^{g(n)} O(f(i)) \subseteq O(g(n)f(g(n))).$$

c. Show that if $h(n) \in \Omega(f(n))$, then there exist natural numbers n_0 and n_1 and positive real numbers c and d such that for every $n \geq n_0$,

$$f(n) \geq f(2n)/d,$$

and for every $n \geq n_1$, both

$$\sum_{i=1}^{g(n)} h(i) \geq \sum_{i=\lceil g(n)/2 \rceil}^{g(n)} cf(\lceil g(n)/2 \rceil),$$

and

$$g(n) \geq 2n_0$$

hold.

d. Use part (c) to prove that

$$\sum_{i=1}^{g(n)} \Omega(f(i)) \subseteq \Omega(g(n)f(g(n))).$$

e. Use parts (b) and (d) to prove that

$$\sum_{i=1}^{g(n)} \Theta(f(i)) \subseteq \Theta(g(n)f(g(n))).$$

* Exercise 3.14. Prove that for every smooth function $f : \mathbb{N} \to \mathbb{R}^{\geq 0}$ and every eventually non-decreasing and unbounded function $g : \mathbb{N} \to \mathbb{N}$, and every $X \in \{O, \Omega, \Theta\}$,

$$\sum_{i=1}^{g(n)} X(f(i)) \neq X(g(n)f(g(n))).$$

[*Hint*: First identify a property that every function in the set on the left-hand side must satisfy, but which functions in the set on the right-hand side need not satisfy.]

Exercise 3.15. Prove Theorem 3.32.

Exercise 3.16. Analyze the worst-case running time of the following code fragments, assuming that n represents the problem size. Express your result as simply as possible using Θ-notation.

a. **for** $i \leftarrow 0$ **to** $2n$
    for $j \leftarrow 0$ **to** $3n$
        $k \leftarrow k + i + j$

b. **for** $i \leftarrow 1$ **to** n^2
    for $j \leftarrow i$ **to** i^3
        $k \leftarrow k + 1$

* c. $i \leftarrow n$
   while $i > 0$
       for $j \leftarrow 1$ **to** i^2
           $x \leftarrow (x + j)/2$
       $i \leftarrow \lfloor i/2 \rfloor$

Exercise 3.17. Give asymptotic solutions to the following asymptotic recurrences. In each case, you may assume that $f : \mathbb{N} \to \mathbb{R}^{\geq 0}$ is an eventually non-decreasing function.

a.

$$f(n) \in 2f(n-1) + \Theta(1),$$

for $n > 0$.

b.

$$f(n) \in f(n-1) + \Omega(n \lg n),$$

for $n > 0$.

c.

$$f(n) \in 4f(n/2) + O(\lg^2 n),$$

whenever $n = 3 \cdot 2^k$ for a positive integer k.

d.

$$f(n) \in 5f(n/3) + \Theta(n^2),$$

whenever $n = 3^k$ for a positive integer k.

e.

$$f(n) \in 3f(n/2) + O(n),$$

whenever $n = 8 \cdot 2^k$ for a positive integer k.

Exercise 3.18. Analyze the worst-case running time of SELECTBYMEDIAN, shown in Figure 2.7, assuming that MEDIAN is implemented to run in $\Theta(n)$ time. Express your result as simply as possible using Θ-notation.

Exercise 3.19. Analyze the worst-case running time of the following functions. Express your result as simply as possible using Θ-notation.

a. SLOWSORT($A[1..n]$)
   if $n = 2$ **and** $A[1] > A[2]$
     $A[1] \leftrightarrow A[2]$
   else if $n > 2$
     SLOWSORT($A[1..n-1]$)
     SLOWSORT($A[2..n]$)
     SLOWSORT($A[1..n-1]$)

b. FINDMAX($A[1..n]$)
   if $n = 0$
     error
   else if $n = 1$
     return $A[1]$
   else
     return MAX(FINDMAX($A[1..\lfloor n/2 \rfloor]$), FINDMAX($A[\lfloor n/2 \rfloor + 1..n]$))

c. FINDMIN($A[1..n]$)
    if $n = 0$
        error
    else if $n = 1$
        return $A[1]$
    else
        $B \leftarrow$ **new** ARRAY$[1..\lceil n/2 \rceil]$
        for $i \leftarrow 1$ **to** $\lfloor n/2 \rfloor$
            $B[i] \leftarrow$ MIN$(A[2i - 1], A[2i])$
        if $n \bmod 2 = 1$
            $B[\lceil n/2 \rceil] \leftarrow A[n]$
        return FINDMIN($B[1..\lceil n/2 \rceil]$)

Exercise 3.20. Analyze the worst-case space usage of each of the functions given in Exercise 3.19. Express your result as simply as possible using Θ-notation.

* Exercise 3.21. Prove that if $f : \mathbb{N} \rightarrow \mathbb{R}^{\geq 0}$ is smooth and $g(n) \in \Theta(n)$, then $f(g(n)) \in \Theta(f(n))$.

* Exercise 3.22. Prove that for any smooth function $g : \mathbb{N} \rightarrow \mathbb{R}^{\geq 0}$, there is a natural number k such that $g(n) \in O(n^k)$.

* Exercise 3.23. The goal of this exercise is to prove Theorem 3.34. Let

$$f(n) \in af(n - 1) + X(b^n g(n))$$

for $n > n_0$, where $n_0 \in \mathbb{N}$, $a \geq 1$ and $b \geq 1$ are real numbers, $g(n)$ is a smooth function, and X is either O, Ω, or Θ. In what follows, let n_1 be any natural number such that $n_1 \geq n_0$ and whenever $n \geq n_1$, $0 < g(n) \leq g(n + 1)$.

a. Prove by induction on n that if X is O, then there is a positive real number c such that for $n \geq n_1$,

$$f(n) \leq a^{n-n_1} f(n_1) + ca^n \sum_{i=n_1+1}^{n} (b/a)^i g(i).$$

b. Prove by induction on n that if X is Ω, then there is a positive real number d such that

$$f(n) \geq a^{n-n_1} f(n_1) + da^n \sum_{i=n_1+1}^{n} (b/a)^i g(i).$$

c. Use parts (a) and (b), together with Equation (2.2), to show that if $a < b$, then $f(n) \in X(b^n g(n))$.

d. Use parts (a) and (b), together with Theorem 3.31, to show that if $a = b$, then $f(n) \in X(na^n g(n))$.

e. Suppose $a > b$, and let $r = \sqrt{a/b}$. Show that there is a natural number $n_2 \geq n_0$ such that for every $n \geq n_2$, $0 < g(n) \leq g(n+1)$ and

$$\sum_{i=n_2+1}^{n} (b/a)^i g(i) \leq \frac{r}{r-1}.$$

[*Hint*: Use the result of Exercise 3.22 and Theorem 3.58 to show that for sufficiently large i, $g(i) \leq r^i$; then apply Equation (2.2).]

f. Use parts (a), (b), and (e) to show that if $a > b$, then $f(n) \in X(a^n)$.

Exercise 3.24. Let $f : \mathbb{N} \to \mathbb{R}^{\geq 0}$ be a function satisfying (3.7). Prove by induction on n that $f(n) \leq f(n+1)$ for $n \geq 1$.

Exercise 3.25. Prove Theorem 3.35.

Exercise 3.26. Show that COPY, specified in Figure 1.18 on page 22, can be implemented to run in $\Theta(n)$ time, $\Theta(n)$ space, and $\Theta(1)$ stack space, where n is the size of both of the arrays. Note that function calls use space from the stack, but constructed arrays do not. Also recall that the parameters $A[1..n]$ and $B[1..n]$ should not be included in the analysis of space usage. Your algorithm should work correctly even for calls like COPY($A[1..n-1], A[2..n]$) (see Exercise 1.4).

Exercise 3.27. Prove Theorem 3.42.

Exercise 3.28. Complete the proof of Theorem 3.44.

Exercise 3.29. Prove Theorem 3.45.

* Exercise 3.30. Prove Theorem 3.50. [*Hint*: First work Exercise 3.13, but note that not all parts of that exercise extend directly to multiple variables.]

Exercise 3.31. Let $A[1..n]$ be an array of numbers. An *inversion* is a pair of indices $1 \leq i < j \leq n$ such that $A[i] > A[j]$. The number of inversions in A is a way to quantify how nearly sorted A is — the fewer inversions A has, the more nearly sorted it is. Let I denote the number of inversions in A. Show that INSERTIONSORT (Figure 1.7, page 12) runs in $\Theta(n + I)$ time in the worst case. (Thus, INSERTIONSORT is very efficient when the array is nearly sorted.) Note that because the analysis is in terms of two variables, "worst case" refers to the worst-case input for *each* pair of values n and I.

Exercise 3.32. Prove Theorem 3.56.

Exercise 3.33. Prove that if $g(n) \in o(f(n))$, then $O(g(n)) \subseteq o(f(n))$.

** Exercise 3.34. Find two smooth functions $f : \mathbb{N} \to \mathbb{R}^{\geq 0}$ and $g : \mathbb{N} \to \mathbb{R}^{\geq 0}$ such that $g(n) \in O(f(n))$, but $g(n)$ is in neither $\Theta(f(n))$ nor $o(f(n))$.

Exercise 3.35. Prove that for any real numbers $a > 1$ and $b > 1$,

$$O(\log_a n) = O(\log_b n).$$

* Exercise 3.36. Prove that

$$\lg(n!) \in \Theta(n \lg n).$$

3.14   Notes

Asymptotic notation predates electronic computing by several decades. Big-O notation was introduced by Bachman [7] in 1894, but with a meaning slightly different from our definition. In the original definition, $O(f(n))$ was used to denote a specific, but unknown, function belonging to the set we have defined to be $O(f(n))$. According to the original definition, it was proper to write,

$$2n^2 + 7n - 4 = O(n^2).$$

However, one would never have written,

$$O(n^2) = 2n^2 + 7n - 4.$$

Thus, the "=" symbol was used to denote not equality, but a relation that is not even symmetric.

Over the years, many have observed that a set-based definition, as we have given here, is more sound mathematically. In fact, Brassard [16] claims that as long ago as 1962, a set-based treatment was taught consistently in Amsterdam. It was Brassard's paper [16], however, that in 1985 first made a strong case for using set-based notation consistently. Though we are in full agreement with his position, use of the original definition is still widespread. Alternatively, some authors give set-based definitions, then abuse the notation by using "=" instead of "∈" or "⊆". For a justification of this practice, see Knuth [82] or Cormen, *et al.* [25]. For more information on the development of asymptotic notation, including variations not discussed here, see Brassard [16].

The definitions of asymptotic notation on multiple variables are from [67]. We have been careful to use multiple variables in asymptotic notation only when the problem being analyzed has multiple natural parameters. Otherwise, it makes sense to avoid the additional overhead of multiple variables and to introduce auxiliary variables instead. This avoids problems such as the expression potentially becoming negative when it includes a difference of two values.

The first edition of Knuth [82] introduced the study of the analysis of running times of algorithms. The notion of a smooth function is due to Brassard [16]. Many techniques exist for solving summations and recurrences; a good resource is Graham *et al.* [59].

Part II
Data Structures

Chapter 4

Basic Techniques for Data Structures

Algorithms must manipulate data, often in large quantities. Therefore, the way in which an algorithm stores and accesses data can have a significant impact on performance. The principles developed in the first three chapters apply to data structures, but in a somewhat different way than to algorithms. In this chapter, we will examine the ways in which top-down design, correctness proofs, and performance analysis can be applied to data structures. We will use rather simple data structures as examples. In succeeding chapters, we will apply these techniques to more involved structures.

4.1 Stacks

One of the strengths of both top-down design and object-oriented design is their use of abstraction to express high-level solutions to problems. In fact, we can apply abstraction to the problems themselves to obtain high-level solutions to many similar problems. Such high-level solutions are known as *design patterns*. For example, consider the "undo" operation in a word processor. We have some object that is undergoing a series of modifications. An application of the "undo" operation restores the object to its state prior to the last modification. Subsequent applications of "undo" restore the object to successively earlier states in its history.

We have captured the essence of the "undo" operation without specifying any of the details of the object being modified or the functionality of the document formatter in which it will appear. In fact, our description is general enough that it can apply to other applications, such as a spreadsheet or the search tree viewer on this book's web site. We have therefore specified a design pattern for one aspect of functionality of an application.

We may apply the top-down approach to designing an implementation of the undo operation specified above. We first observe that we need to store a history of the edits applied to the edited object. These edits must be represented in such a way that we can undo or invert them. Furthermore, we only need *last-in-first-out* (LIFO) access to the history of edits. This suggests that the history of edits should be stored in a stack. We can then implement undo by popping the top edit from the stack, and applying its inverse to the edited object. If the stack is empty, then no undo is possible. Likewise, when edits are performed, each edit must be pushed onto the stack.

Let us now make these ideas a bit more formal. In order to be able to reason about this solution, we must have a formal definition of a stack and its operations. We therefore define a stack as a finite sequence of elements $\langle a_1, \ldots, a_n \rangle$, together with the operations specified in Figure 4.1. A mathematical structure, together with a specification of operations on that structure, is known as an *abstract data type* (ADT). The operations specified are the *interface* of the ADT. If we have a stack S, we refer to its POP operation by S.POP(). We refer to the POP operation of the STACK ADT by STACK.POP(). The STACK() operation is a specification of a *constructor*, meaning that it is possible to construct an instance of any implementation without supplying any arguments.

Figure 4.1   The STACK ADT

Precondition: true.
Postcondition: Constructs an empty STACK.

STACK()

Precondition: true.
Postcondition: a is added to the end of the represented sequence.

STACK.PUSH(a)

Precondition: The stack is nonempty.
Postcondition: The last element of the represented sequence is removed and returned.

STACK.POP()

Precondition: true.
Postcondition: Returns true iff the represented sequence is empty.

STACK.IsEMPTY()

In practice, we might want additional operations such as an operation that returns the top element without changing the sequence; however, the above operations are sufficient for now. Later, we will add to this set.

Note that the definition of an ADT is purely mathematical; i.e., it defines a stack as a sequence, which is a mathematical object. It says nothing about how a stack is to be implemented. Such a mathematical definition is sufficient for proving the correctness of UNDO, shown in Figure 4.3, together with the specification of the EDITABLE ADT in Figure 4.2. Such a proof is, in fact, trivial. Note that by specifying in the precondition that the stack is nonempty, we place on the caller the responsibility of checking this condition prior to calling UNDO.

Continuing with the top-down approach, we need to design an implementation for the STACK ADT. In what follows, we will first consider a simple approach that does not quite meet the specification. We will then consider two full implementations of the STACK ADT.

Figure 4.2   Specification of the EDITABLE ADT

Precondition: *op* is an EDITOP.
Postcondition: Applies *op* to this EDITABLE.

EDITABLE.APPLY(*op*)

Precondition: *op* is an EDITOP.
Postcondition: Applies the inverse operation of *op* to this EDITABLE.

EDITABLE.APPLYINVERSE(*op*)

Figure 4.3   An algorithm to undo an editing operation

Precondition: *history* is a nonempty STACK containing the sequence of EDITOps performed on the EDITABLE *x*.
Postcondition: The last element *e* has been removed from *history*, and the inverse of *e* has been applied to *x*.

UNDO(*history*, *x*)
    e ← *history*.POP()
    x.APPLYINVERSE(*e*)

4.2   A Simple Stack Implementation

The first step in designing an implementation for a data structure is to decide upon a *representation* of the data. Perhaps the simplest representation of a stack is an array storing the sequence of elements. Because we will want to push additional elements onto the stack, we should use an array larger than the number of elements. We therefore need a way to find the last element of the sequence, or the top element of the stack. We can accomplish this by keeping track of the number of elements in the stack.

Such a representation is a bit too simple, because the size of the array limits the size of the stack — i.e., once we have constructed the array, we have limited the size of the sequence we can represent. In order to accommodate this shortcoming, we will associate with each of these stacks a *capacity*, which gives the maximum number of elements it can hold. Later, we will consider how this restriction might be removed. As a result of this restriction, we must modify our specification of the PUSH operation so that if n is strictly less than the stack's capacity, then PUSH(a) adds a to the end of the sequence. In order to be able to check this condition, we will replace the ISEMPTY operation with a more general SIZE operation that returns the number of elements in the stack.

Our representation, therefore, consists of:

- an ARRAY *elements*[1..*M*] for some $M \geq 0$; and
- a NAT *size*.

The value M above is not an explicit part of the representation, but we assume that we can obtain its value by using the function SIZEOF, specified in Figure 1.20 on page 23. In order to make sense of a given representation, we need an *interpretation*, which relates a given set of values for the variables in the representation to a specific instance of the formal definition. The variables used by the interpretation may include not only the representation variables, but also variables that may be accessed using the representation variables. In our present example, *elements*[1..*size*] describes the stack $\langle elements[1], \ldots, elements[size] \rangle$, and SIZEOF(*elements*) gives the capacity of the stack.

The above interpretation is problematic when *size* is outside the bounds of the array. We therefore need a mechanism to ensure that the values of a given representation are valid. To this end we use a *structural invariant*. This invariant is a statement about the values of the representation variables, and perhaps other variables that can be accessed using the representation variables. It should be true at virtually all times. The only exception is that we allow it to be temporarily violated while an operation is modifying the structure, provided that it is true by the time the operation completes. The structural invariant for our present example will be:

$$0 \leq \textit{size} \leq \textsc{SizeOf}(\textit{elements}). \tag{4.1}$$

The values of the representation variables, together with all values used by the interpretation and the structural invariant, comprise the *state* of the data structure. Thus, the state of our stack implementation consists of the value of *size*, the array *elements*, and the values stored in *elements*[1..*size*]. (We will clarify shortly the distinction between the array and the values stored in the array.)

We can now complete our implementation by giving algorithms for the SimpleStack constructor and operations. These algorithms are shown in Figure 4.4.

Note that the preconditions and postconditions for the constructor and operations are stated in terms of the definition of a stack, not in terms of our chosen representation. For example, the precondition for the Push operation could have been stated as,

$$\textit{size} < \textsc{SizeOf}(\textit{elements}).$$

However, preconditions and postconditions for operations on data structures should specify the externally observable behavior of the operation, and hence should not refer to the representation of the structure. Thus, the preconditions and postconditions still make sense even if we change the representation.

The performance of these operations can be analyzed using the techniques given in Chapter 3. It is easily seen that each of the operations Push, Pop, and Size operate in $\Theta(1)$ time. Analysis of the constructor is more problematic because we must include the time for constructing an array. This time depends on such factors as how the operating system allocates memory and whether the elements are initialized to some default value. For the sake of simplicity, we will assume that the memory can be allocated in constant time, and that the array will not be initialized. Thus, the time to construct a new array is in $\Theta(1)$, and the constructor operates in $\Theta(1)$ time.

Proving correctness of operations on a data structure is similar to proving correctness of ordinary algorithms. There are five parts:

Figure 4.4   The data type SimpleStack, which does not quite implement the Stack ADT

Structural Invariant: $0 \leq size \leq \text{SizeOf}(elements)$.

Precondition: cap is a Nat.
Postcondition: The constructed stack is empty, and its capacity is cap.

SimpleStack(cap)
    $size \leftarrow 0$; $elements \leftarrow$ **new** Array$[1..cap]$

Precondition: The number of elements in the represented sequence is strictly less than the capacity.
Postcondition: a is added to the end of the represented sequence.

SimpleStack.Push(a)
    if $size < \text{SizeOf}(elements)$
        $size \leftarrow size + 1$; $elements[size] \leftarrow a$
    else
        error

Precondition: The represented sequence is nonempty.
Postcondition: The last element of the represented sequence is removed and returned.

SimpleStack.Pop()
    if $size > 0$
        $size \leftarrow size - 1$; **return** $elements[size + 1]$
    else
        error

Precondition: true.
Postcondition: Returns the length of the represented sequence.

SimpleStack.Size()
    return $size$

---

1. **Initialization:** If the precondition holds at the beginning of a constructor invocation, then the postcondition holds upon completion of the constructor. If the constructor terminates normally, then the structural invariant holds after the data structure has been constructed, regardless of the truth of the precondition. (If the constructor terminates abnormally,

i.e., with an error condition, then we assume the structure has not been constructed.)

2. **Maintenance:** If the structural invariant holds prior to the beginning of an operation, then it holds following completion of that operation.

3. **Security:** If the structural invariant holds, then the state can only be modified by invoking one of this structure's operations.

4. **Termination:** Each operation and constructor terminates.

5. **Correctness:** If the structural invariant and the precondition hold prior to the beginning of an operation, then the postcondition holds following the completion of that operation.

We have already seen four of these five parts in proofs of algorithm correctness. Security is needed not only to make sure that malicious or untrusted code cannot violate the intended purpose of the data structure, but also to guarantee that the structural invariant is maintained between operations. In order to guarantee security, we need a mechanism for restricting access to the representation variables. Before we can discuss this mechanism, however, we first need to provide some details about the computational model we are assuming. We will tackle all of this shortly; however, let us first give an example of the other four parts via a correctness proof for SIMPLESTACK. We will first state security as a lemma to be proved later, then we will show that SIMPLESTACK meets its specification.

Lemma 4.1. *Security holds for* SIMPLESTACK.

Theorem 4.2. SIMPLESTACK *meets its specification.*

Proof. We must show initialization, maintenance, security, termination, and correctness.

Initialization: First, suppose the precondition to the constructor is met; i.e., that *cap* is a NAT. Then the constructor will terminate normally with *size* = 0, which we interpret as meaning the represented sequence is empty. Because we interpret SIZEOF(*elements*), which is *cap*, to be the capacity of the stack, the postcondition is therefore met. Furthermore, regardless of the truth of the precondition, if the constructor terminates without error, *size* will be 0 and *elements* will refer to an array. Because an array cannot have a negative number of elements, its size is at least 0. Therefore, the structural invariant holds ($0 \leq size \leq$ SIZEOF(*elements*)).

Maintenance: Suppose the structural invariant holds prior to the execution of an operation. We will only consider the operation PUSH(a); proofs for the other two operations are left as an exercise.

The size of *elements* is not changed by this operation. The value of *size* is only changed if it is strictly less than the size of *elements*. In this case, because it is incremented by 1, the value of *size* will remain nonnegative, but will not exceed the size of *elements*. The structural invariant therefore holds after this operation completes.

Security: Follows from Lemma 4.1.

Termination: Because there are no loops or recursive calls, all constructors and operations terminate.

Correctness: Suppose the structural invariant holds prior to the execution of an operation. We will only consider the operation PUSH(a); proofs for the other two operations are left as an exercise.

Suppose the precondition holds, i.e., that the number of elements in the stack is strictly less than the stack's capacity. Because we interpret the size of *elements* to be the stack's capacity and the value of *size* to be the number of elements in the stack, it follows that $size < $ SIZEOF(*elements*). The **if** condition is therefore **true**. *size* is therefore incremented by 1, which we interpret as increasing the number of elements on the stack by 1. a is then assigned to *elements*[*size*], which we interpret as the last element of the represented sequence. The postcondition is therefore met.   □

As the above proof illustrates, initialization, maintenance, termination, and correctness can be shown using the techniques introduced in Chapter 2, although the specific statements to be shown are somewhat different. Proving security, on the other hand, not only uses different techniques, it also requires a more detailed specification of the underlying computational model that we are assuming. We have chosen a model that is reasonably simple and consistent, and which may be implemented easily in a variety of programming languages. In what follows, we will give its details.

One characteristic of our model involves the way in which data items are associated with variables. With each data item, there is a *reference* that uniquely identifies it (i.e., two distinct references may not identify the same data item). Furthermore, a reference may not itself be a data item; i.e., a reference may not refer to another reference. It is the reference, not the data item itself, that will be stored in a variable. We do not specify anything else regarding the reference, but often a reference will be implemented as the address in memory at which the data item resides. However, we will assume that a constant like the integer 3 also has a reference. In this case the reference may simply be the binary encoding of 3.

Such a distinction between a data constant and its reference may seem artificial, but it allows for a uniform treatment of variables and data. Thus, when variable assignments are made, the reference to the assigned data item is stored in the modified variable. Likewise, when formal parameters take their values from actual parameters, the references are copied from the actual parameters to the formal parameters.

Given the distinction between a data item and its reference, we can now define more precisely the state of a SIMPLESTACK. It must first include the values of the reference variables, namely *size* (a reference to an integer) and *elements* (a reference to an array). Because the interpretation uses the values of *elements*[1..*size*], these values, which are references to arbitrary data items, are also part of the state. However, the values of the data items to which the references in *elements*[1..*size*] refer are *not* included in the state. Thus, if *elements*[*size*] contains a reference to an array A, that reference is a part of the state of the stack, but the contents of A are not. In particular, if the value stored in *elements*[*size*] changes, then the stack contents change, but if the contents of A change, the stack contents do not change — A is still the item at the top of the stack.

Our model uses a simple hierarchical type system. Each implementation has a unique type. This type may be a subtype of one or more interfaces (i.e., ADTs) that it implements. Thus, if an implementation A implements ADTs B and C, then any instance of type A also belongs to types B and C. We do not allow implementations to be subtypes of other implementations, so our model includes no inheritance. Our algorithms will not always specify the type of a data item if its type is irrelevant to the essence of the algorithm. For example, we have not specified the type of the parameter a for the STACK.PUSH operation in Figure 4.4 because we do not care what kind of data is stored in the stack.

When the data type of a parameter is important, we can specify it in the precondition, as we have done for the constructor in Figure 4.4. Unless we explicitly state otherwise, when we state in a precondition that a variable refers to an item of some particular type, we mean that this variable must be non-nil. Note, however, that a precondition does not affect the execution of the code. When it is important that the type actually be checked (e.g., for maintaining a structural invariant), we will attach a type declaration in the parameter list, as in the two-argument constructor in Figure 4.10 (page 129). A type declaration applies to a single parameter only, so that in this example, L is of type CONSLIST, but a is untyped. We interpret a type declaration as generating an error if the value passed to that parameter is not nil and does not refer to an instance of the declared type.

As we have already suggested, the elements of a particular data type may have operations associated with them. Thus, each instance of the STACK type has a PUSH operation and a POP operation. For the sake of consistency, we will consider that when a constructor is invoked, it belongs to the data item that it is constructing. In addition, the elements of a data type may have *internal functions* associated with them. Internal functions are just like operations, but with restricted access, as described below.

In order to control the way in which a data structure can be changed, we place the following restrictions on how representation variables and internal functions can be accessed:

- Write access to a representation variable of an instance of data type A is given only to the operations, constructors, and internal functions of that instance.
- Read access to a representation variable of an instance of data type A is given only to operations, constructors, and internal functions of instances of type A.
- Access to an internal function of an instance of a data type A is given only to operations, constructors, and internal functions of that instance.

These restrictions are severe enough that we will often need to relax them. In order to relax either of the first two restrictions, we can provide *accessor operations*. Because we frequently need to do this, we will adopt some conventions that allow us to avoid cluttering our algorithms with trivial code.

- If we want to provide read access to a variable *var* in the representation of type A, we define the operation $A.\text{VAR}()$, which simply returns *var*. Using this convention, we could have omitted operation SIMPLESTACK.SIZE() from Figure 4.4.
- If we want to provide write access to *var*, we define the operation $A.\text{SETVAR}(x)$, which assigns the value of x to *var*.

Explicitly allowing write access does not technically violate security, because any changes are made by invoking operations of the data structure. What can be problematic is allowing read access. For example, suppose we were to allow read access to the variable *elements* in the representation of a stack. Using this reference, a user's code could change the contents of that array. Because this array's contents belong to the state of the data structure, security would then be violated. We must therefore check for the following conditions, each of which might compromise security:

- An operation returns a reference to a portion of the state of the structure. This condition can include an operation that gives explicit read access to a representation variable. This condition will violate security if the reference refers to a data item whose value can change.
- An operation causes the data item to which one of its parameters refers to be a part of the state of the structure. Under this condition, the code that invokes the operation has a copy of the parameter, and hence has access to the state of the structure. If the data item in question can be changed, security is violated.
- A reference to a portion of the state is copied to the state of another instance of the same type. For example, if S and T are of type SIMPLESTACK, and their *elements* variables have the same value, then the operation $S.\text{PUSH}(x)$ could change the contents of T. Thus, if a shared data item can be changed, security is violated.

We can now illustrate the technique of proving security by proving Lemma 4.1.

Proof of Lemma 4.1 Read access is explicitly given to *size*. However, *size* refers to a NAT, which cannot be changed. The only other values returned are references to elements stored in the stack, and the values of these elements are not part of the state of the stack. Likewise, the only parameters are the capacity and the parameter to PUSH, neither of which refers to a data item that becomes a part of the state of the stack. Finally, no operations copy any part of the state of a SIMPLESTACK to the state of another SIMPLESTACK. We therefore can conclude that SIMPLESTACK is secure. □

> Specifically, the variable *size* can receive a different value, and hence refer to a different NAT; however, the NATs themselves cannot change.

Designing secure data structures is sometimes rather challenging. In fact, there are occasions when security becomes too much of a burden — for example, when we are designing a data structure to be used only locally within some algorithm. In such a case, it may be easier to prove that our algorithm doesn't violate the security of the data structure, rather than to prove that such a violation is impossible. If we define a data structure for which we can prove initialization, maintenance, termination, and correctness, we say that this structure is *insecure*, but otherwise satisfies its specification.

Together, initialization, maintenance, and security are almost sufficient to prove that the structural invariant holds between execution of any operations on the structure. The only caveat is similar to the difficulty associated with mutual recursion, as was discussed in Section 2.5. Suppose that during execution of some operation x.OP1, a function call is made while the structural invariant is false. Suppose that through some sequence of nested

Figure 4.5   Illustration of a callback — when x.OP2() is called, the structural invariant of x is false

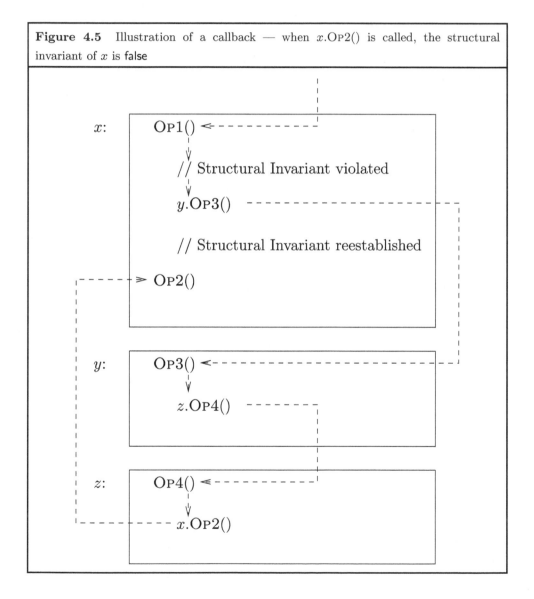

calls, some operation $x.\text{OP2}$ is then called (see Figure 4.5). At this point, the structural invariant is false, and the operation's correctness cannot be guaranteed. This scenario is known as a *callback*. Note that it does not matter how long the sequence of nested calls is. In particular, the function call made by $x.\text{OP1}$ may be a direct call to $x.\text{OP2}$, or it may be a recursive call.

Though callbacks are common in software systems, they are more problematic than beneficial in the design of data structures. Furthermore, as is the case for mutual recursion, callbacks may be impossible to detect when we are designing a single data structure, as we may need to call a function whose implementation we don't have. For these reasons, we will assume that if a callback is attempted, a runtime error results. Our correctness proofs will then rest on the assumption that data structures and algorithms are not combined in such a way as to result in a callback.

Given this assumption, once initialization, maintenance, and security are shown, it can be shown by induction that the structural invariant holds between execution of any operations that construct or alter an instance of the data structure. Note that the structural invariant will hold

> A locking mechanism can be used to cause any callback to generate a runtime error.

after the structure is constructed, regardless of whether preconditions to operations are met. Thus, we can be convinced that a structural invariant holds even if operations are not invoked properly. Because we can know that the structural invariant holds, we can then use it in addition to the precondition in proving the correctness of an individual operation.

4.3   Expandable Arrays

SIMPLESTACK does not quite implement the STACK ADT because each SIMPLESTACK must be constructed with a fixed capacity. We will now present a true implementation of STACK.

We can use the basic idea from SIMPLESTACK if we have a way to perform a PUSH when the array is full. Our solution will be to construct a new, larger array, and to copy the elements in the stack to this new array. This new array then replaces the original array. We now have room to add the new element.

Though this idea is simple, there are some performance issues to consider. In particular, $\Theta(n)$ time is required to copy n elements from one array to another. We might be willing to pay this performance price occasionally, but if we are not careful, the overall performance of manipulating a stack may be significantly degraded. Suppose, for example, that the new array contains only one more location than the original array. Consider what happens if we push n elements onto such a stack, where n is much larger than the size of the original array. After the original array is filled, each PUSH requires $\Theta(i)$ time, where i is number of elements currently in the stack. It is not hard to see that the total time for pushing all n elements is in $\Theta(n^2)$, assuming the size of the original array is a fixed constant.

In order to avoid this bad performance, when we need to allocate a new array, we should make sure that it is significantly larger than the array we are replacing. As we will see shortly, we can achieve this goal by doubling the size of the array. The EXPANDABLEARRAYSTACK implementation shown in Figure 4.6 implements this idea. In order for this to work, however, the size of the array must always be non-zero; hence, we will need to include this restriction in the structural invariant. Note that we have added a constructor that was not specified in the interface (Figure 4.1). The no-argument constructor simply invokes this new constructor with a default value for its argument.

At this point it is tempting to apply the top-down design principle by defining an ADT for an expandable array. However, when an idea is simple enough, designing an ADT often becomes more cumbersome than it is worth. To attain the full functionality of an expandable array, we would need operations to perform each of the following tasks:

- reading from and writing to arbitrary locations;
- obtaining the current size of the array; and
- explicitly expanding the array (we might want to do this before the array is full) to a size we choose.

Furthermore, we might wish to redistribute the data in the larger array when we expand it. It therefore seems best to characterize the expandable array design pattern as the practice of moving data from one array to a new one of at least twice the size whenever the current array becomes too full.

Clearly, the worst-case running time of the PUSH operation shown in Figure 4.6 is in $O(n)$, where n is the number of elements in the stack. Furthermore, for any $n > 0$, if we construct a stack with the constructor call EXPANDABLEARRAYSTACK(n), then when the $(n + 1)$-st element is pushed onto the stack, $\Omega(n)$ time is required. Therefore, the worst-case running time of the PUSH operation is in $\Theta(n)$. All other operations clearly require $\Theta(1)$ time.

The above analysis seems inadequate because in any actual use of a stack, the $\Theta(n)$ behavior will occur for only a few operations. If an EXPANDABLEARRAYSTACK is used by some algorithm, the slow operations

---

Figure 4.6 EXPANDABLEARRAYSTACK implementation of STACK

Structural Invariant: $0 \leq \mathit{size} \leq \text{SIZEOF}(\mathit{elements})$, and $\text{SIZEOF}(\mathit{elements}) > 0$.

EXPANDABLEARRAYSTACK()
  EXPANDABLEARRAYSTACK(10)

Precondition: *cap* is a strictly positive NAT.
Postcondition: An empty stack is constructed.

EXPANDABLEARRAYSTACK(*cap*)
  if $cap > 0$
    $\mathit{size} \leftarrow 0$; $\mathit{elements} \leftarrow$ **new** ARRAY$[1..cap]$
  else
    error

EXPANDABLEARRAYSTACK.PUSH(*a*)
  if $\mathit{size} = \text{SIZEOF}(\mathit{elements})$
    $el \leftarrow$ **new** ARRAY$[1..2 \cdot \mathit{size}]$
    for $i \leftarrow 1$ **to** size
      $el[i] \leftarrow \mathit{elements}[i]$
    $\mathit{elements} \leftarrow el$
  $\mathit{size} \leftarrow \mathit{size} + 1$; $\mathit{elements}[\mathit{size}] \leftarrow a$

EXPANDABLEARRAYSTACK.POP()
  if $\mathit{size} > 0$
    $\mathit{size} \leftarrow \mathit{size} - 1$
    return $\mathit{elements}[\mathit{size} + 1]$
  else
    error

EXPANDABLEARRAYSTACK.ISEMPTY()
  return $\mathit{size} = 0$

may be few enough that they do not significantly impact the algorithm's overall performance. In such a case, it makes sense to consider the worst-case performance of an entire sequence of operations, rather than a single operation. This idea is the basis for *amortized analysis*.

With amortized analysis, we consider an arbitrary sequence of operations performed on an initially empty data structure. We then do a form of worst-case analysis of this sequence of operations. Clearly, longer sequences will have longer running times. In order to remove the dependence upon the length of the sequence, we *amortize* the total running time of the sequence over the individual operations in the sequence. For the time being, this amortization will simply be to compute the average running time for an individual operation in the sequence; later in this chapter we will generalize this definition. The analysis is still worst-case because the sequence is arbitrary — we are finding the worst-case amortized time for the operations on the data structure.

For example, consider any sequence of n operations on an initially empty stack constructed with EXPANDABLEARRAYSTACK(k). We first analyze the worst-case running time of such a sequence. We can use the techniques presented in Chapter 3, but the analysis is easier if we apply a new technique. We first analyze the running time ignoring all iterations of the **for** loop in the PUSH operation and any loop overhead that results in the execution of an iteration. Having ignored this code, it is easily seen that each operation requires $\Theta(1)$ time, so that the entire sequence requires $\Theta(n)$ time.

We now analyze the running time of all iterations of the **for** loop throughout the entire sequence of operations. In order to accomplish this, we must compute the total number of iterations. The array will be expanded to size $2k$ the first time the stack reaches size $k + 1$. For this first expansion, the **for** loop iterates k times. The array will be expanded to size $4k$ the first time the stack reaches size $2k + 1$. For this expansion, the loop iterates $2k$ times. In general, the array will be expanded to size $2^{i+1}k$ the first time the stack reaches size $2^i k + 1$, and the loop will iterate $2^i k$ times during this expansion. Because the sequence contains n operations, the stack can never exceed size n. Therefore, in order to compute an upper bound on the total number of iterations, we must sum $2^i k$ for all $i \geq 0$ such that

$$2^i k + 1 \leq n$$
$$2^i \leq (n - 1)/k$$
$$i \leq \lg(n - 1) - \lg k.$$

The total number of iterations is therefore at most

$$\sum_{i=0}^{\lfloor \lg(n-1)-\lg k \rfloor} 2^i k = k \sum_{i=0}^{\lfloor \lg(n-1)-\lg k \rfloor} 2^i$$

$$= k(2^{\lfloor \lg(n-1)-\lg k \rfloor+1} - 1) \qquad \text{by (2.2)}$$

$$\leq k 2^{\lg(n-1)-\lg k+1}$$

$$= \frac{k 2^{\lg(n-1)+1}}{2^{\lg k}}$$

$$= 2(n - 1).$$

Because each loop iteration requires $\Theta(1)$ time, the time required for all loop iterations is in $O(n)$. Combining this result with the earlier analysis that ignored the loop iterations, we see that the entire sequence runs in $\Theta(n)$ time.

Now to complete the amortized analysis, we must average the total running time over the n operations in the sequence. By Exercise 3.9 on page 98, if $f(n) \in \Theta(n)$, then $f(n)/n \in \Theta(1)$. Therefore, the worst-case amortized time for the stack operations is in $\Theta(1)$. We conclude that, although an individual PUSH operation may be expensive, the expandable array yields a stack that performs well on any sequence of operations starting from an initially empty stack.

4.4 The CONSLIST ADT

On this textbook's web site is a search tree viewer that allows users to insert and remove strings from various kinds of search trees (see Chapter 6) and to view the results. Included are "Back" and "Forward" buttons that allow the user to step through the history of the trees created. Two stacks are used, one to store the history, and one to store the "future" after the user has stepped back into the history. Also included is a "Clone" button, which causes an identical window to be created, with identical history and future. This new window can be manipulated independently from the first. In order to accomplish this independence, the two stacks must be cloned.

Let us consider how we might clone an EXPANDABLEARRAYSTACK. In order to simplify the discussion, we will restrict our attention to *shallow cloning*. Shallow cloning consists of cloning only the state of the structure, and not the items contained in the structure. Thus, if a data item is stored in a stack which is then cloned, any subsequent changes to that data item will be reflected in both stacks. However, changes to one of the stacks will not affect the other. In order to perform a shallow clone of an EXPANDABLEARRAYSTACK, the array must clearly be copied, so that the two stacks can be manipulated independently. Copying one array to another requires $\Theta(n)$ time, where n is the number of elements copied.

We might be able to improve on this running time if we can use a data structure that facilitates *non-destructive updates*. An update is said to be *non-destructive* if it does not change any of the existing structure, but instead builds a new structure, perhaps using some or all of the existing structure. If all updates are non-destructive (i.e., the structure is *immutable*), it is possible for different structures to share substructures that are common to both. This sharing can sometimes lead to improved efficiency; for example, to clone an immutable structure all that we need to copy is the reference to it.

In order to apply this idea to stacks, it is helpful to think of a finite sequence as nested ordered pairs. In particular, a sequence of length $n > 0$ is an ordered pair consisting of a sequence of length $n - 1$ followed by an element. As a special case, the sequence of length 0 is denoted (). Thus, the sequence $\langle a_1, a_2, a_3 \rangle$ can be thought of as the pair $((((), a_1), a_2), a_3)$. If we think of this sequence as a STACK S, then we can think of $S.\textsc{Push}(a_4)$ as a function returning a new sequence $(((((), a_1), a_2), a_3), a_4)$. Note that this new sequence can be constructed simply by pairing S with a_4, leaving S unchanged.

Nested pairs form the basic data structure in the programming language Lisp and its derivatives. The Lisp function to build an ordered pair is called CONS. Based on this background is the ADT known as a CONSLIST. It is useful to think of a nonempty CONSLIST as a pair $(head, tail)$, where *head* is an element and *tail* is a CONSLIST. (Note that the two components of the pair are in the reverse order of that described in the above paragraph.)

More formally, we define a CONSLIST to be a finite sequence $\langle a_1, \ldots, a_n \rangle$, together with the operations specified in Figure 4.7. Note that none of these

> We use BOOL to denote the type whose only values are true and false.

operations changes the CONSLIST. We therefore say that a CONSLIST is an immutable structure, meaning that though the elements in the sequence may change their state, the sequence itself will not change.

In what follows, we will show how to implement STACK using a CONSLIST. We will have thus applied top-down design to the task of implementing STACK, as we will have reduced this problem to the problem of implementing CONSLIST. The resulting STACK implementation will support constant-time PUSH, POP, and shallow cloning, which we will support via an additional

---

Figure 4.7 The CONSLIST ADT

Precondition: true
Postcondition: Constructs a CONSLIST representing an empty sequence.

CONSLIST()

Precondition: L is a CONSLIST $\langle a_1, \ldots a_n \rangle$.
Postcondition: Constructs a CONSLIST representing the sequence $\langle a, a_1, \ldots, a_n \rangle$.

CONSLIST(a, L)

Precondition: true.
Postcondition: Returns a BOOL that is **true** iff the represented sequence is empty.

CONSLIST.ISEMPTY()

Precondition: The represented sequence is nonempty.
Postcondition: Returns the first element of the sequence.

CONSLIST.HEAD()

Precondition: The represented sequence $\langle a_1, \ldots a_n \rangle$ is nonempty.
Postcondition: Returns a CONSLIST representing the sequence $\langle a_2, \ldots, a_n \rangle$.

CONSLIST.TAIL()

---

constructor. We will then complete the design by showing how to implement CONSLIST.

Our STACK representation will be a CONSLIST *elements*. We interpret *elements* as storing the stack in reverse order; i.e., the head of *elements* is the top element on the stack. The structural invariant will be that *elements* refers to a CONSLIST. The implementation is shown in Figure 4.8. The one-argument constructor is used to construct a shallow clone.

Again, all constructors and operations can easily be seen to run in $\Theta(1)$ time, and proving initialization, maintenance, termination, and correctness is straightforward. Regarding security, we note that *elements* is shared when the one-argument constructor is used; however, because a CONSLIST is immutable, this sharing cannot violate security. The full correctness proof is left as an exercise.

Figure 4.8 ConsListStack implementation of Stack

Structural Invariant: *elements* refers to a ConsList.

ConsListStack()
   elements ← **new** ConsList()

Precondition: *S* refers to a ConsListStack.
Postcondition: The constructed stack is a shallow clone of the stack *S*.

ConsListStack(*S*)
   elements ← *S.elements*

ConsListStack.Push(*a*)
   elements ← **new** ConsList(*a, elements*)

ConsListStack.Pop()
   if *elements*.IsEmpty()
     error
   else
     top ← *elements*.Head(); *elements* ← *elements*.Tail()
     return *top*

ConsListStack.IsEmpty()
   return *elements*.IsEmpty()

We will now complete the implementation of ConsListStack by implementing ConsList. Our representation consists of the following:

- a readable Bool *isEmpty*;
- a readable element *head*; and
- a readable ConsList *tail*.

If *isEmpty* is **true**, then we interpret the ConsList to represent an empty sequence. Otherwise, we interpret *head* as the first element of the sequence, and *tail* as the remainder of the sequence. As our structural invariant, we require a ConsList to represent a finite sequence according to the above interpretation. The representation of the ConsList $\langle a_1, a_2, a_3, a_4 \rangle$ is illustrated in Figure 4.9.

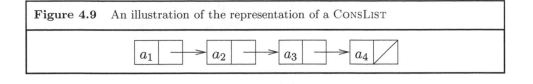

Figure 4.9   An illustration of the representation of a CONSLIST

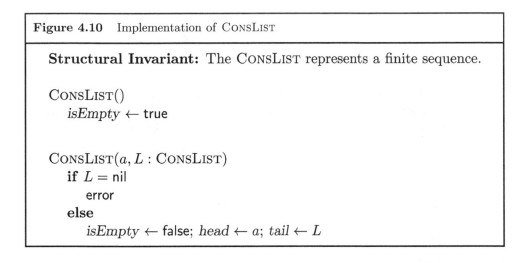

Figure 4.10   Implementation of CONSLIST

Structural Invariant: The CONSLIST represents a finite sequence.

CONSLIST()
    isEmpty ← true

CONSLIST(a, L : CONSLIST)
    if $L =$ nil
        error
    else
        isEmpty ← false; *head* ← a; *tail* ← L

Because our representation fits so closely with the definition of a CONSLIST, the implementation is trivial — the operations are simply the accessors for the three representation variables. Note that our specification says nothing about the contents of *head* and *tail* when *isEmpty* is true; hence, if these accessors are called for an empty list, arbitrary values may be returned. The implementation is shown in Figure 4.10. Because we will only present a single implementation of CONSLIST, we use the same name for the implementation as for the interface.

It is easily seen that each constructor and operation runs in $\Theta(1)$ time. We will now prove that the implementation meets its specification.

Theorem 4.3. *The* CONSLIST *implementation meets its specification.*

Proof.

Initialization: We consider the two constructors as separate cases.

Case 1: CONSLIST(). Because *isEmpty* is set to true, we interpret the constructed CONSLIST as representing an empty sequence. The structural invariant and postcondition therefore hold.

Case 2: CONSLIST(a, L : CONSLIST). If this constructor terminates normally, then L refers to a CONSLIST. Let us therefore assume that this is the case. Let L represent the sequence $\langle a_1, \ldots, a_n \rangle$. *isEmpty* is set to false, so the constructed instance is interpreted to be the nonempty sequence $\langle a, a_1, \ldots, a_n \rangle$. Because this is a finite sequence, the structural invariant and postcondition both hold.

Maintenance: Because no operations change any representation variables, maintenance holds trivially.

Security: Read access is explicitly given to the three representation variables. However, *isEmpty* and *tail* are immutable, so this read access cannot result in changes to either of them. Because *head* refers to a data item that is not a part of the state, changes that may result from reading this reference do not affect the security of the CONSLIST. Finally, although the parameter L to the two-argument constructor is copied to a representation variable, because it refers to an immutable data item, security is not violated.

Termination: Because there are no loops or recursion, all constructors and operations terminate.

Correctness: The only operations simply provide read access, and so are trivially correct.   □

Example 4.4. Suppose we construct an empty CONSLISTSTACK S, then push data items a_1, a_2, and a_3 in sequence onto S. Figure 4.11(a) illustrates the result of these operations. Suppose we then construct T using CONSLISTSTACK(S). At this point $T.elements$ is equal to $S.elements$. If we then execute $T.$POP() twice, $T.elements$ is assigned $T.elements.$TAIL().TAIL(), as shown in Figure 4.11(b). Note that this does not affect the contents of S. If we then push a_4 onto T, we obtain the result shown in Figure 4.11(c). Again, the contents of S are unchanged.

We conclude our discussion of CONSLISTs by noting that there are some disadvantages to this implementation of STACK. The running time of the PUSH operations is likely to be slower than either of the other implementations because new memory is always allocated. Furthermore, this memory is never explicitly released, so this implementation should only be coded in a language that provides automatic garbage collection.

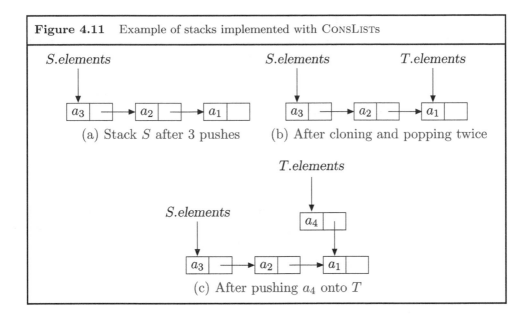

Figure 4.11 Example of stacks implemented with ConsLists

(a) Stack S after 3 pushes   (b) After cloning and popping twice

(c) After pushing a_4 onto T

The idea behind a ConsList can be modified to form a mutable structure if we allow the value of *tail* to be modified. It is difficult to define a general-purpose ADT based on this idea other than to allow write access to *tail*. If we do this, then there is little security; i.e., the user can construct complicated linked structures that share data or perhaps form loops. Nevertheless, if we are careful, we can use this idea as a building block for several more advanced data structures. We will therefore refer to this idea as the *linked list* design pattern.

4.5 Amortized Analysis Using Potential Functions

In Section 4.3, we introduced the technique of amortized analysis. The actual analysis was rather straightforward, mainly because the worst case is easily identifiable. For many data structures, amortized analysis is not so straightforward. Furthermore, we would like to be able to amortize in a more general way than simply averaging over all operations in a sequence. Specifically, we would like to be able to amortize in such a way that operations on small structures receive smaller amortized cost than operations on large structures. For example, if n represents the size of a structure, we would like to be able to speak about an amortized running time in $O(\lg n)$. In this section, we introduce a more general notion of amortized cost and present a corresponding technique for performing amortized analysis.

In order to motivate this technique, it is helpful to think of amortized analysis using an analogy. Suppose we have a daily budget for gasoline for a car. We want to track our gasoline purchases to ensure that we don't exceed this budget. Further suppose that we begin tracking these expenses when the tank is full. We may then have several days in which we spend no money on gasoline. At some point, we will refill the tank, thus incurring a large expense which may be greater than our daily budget. However, if we amortize this cost over all of the days since we last filled the tank, we will hopefully find that we have remained within our daily budget for each of these days.

One way to monitor our budget more closely is to consider the potential cost of filling the tank at the end of each day. Specifically, suppose that we have a very precise gas gauge on our car. In order to keep the analogy simple, we will also suppose that the cost of gasoline remains constant. At the end of each day, we could then measure the amount of gasoline in the tank and compute the cost of potentially filling the tank at that point.

For example, suppose gasoline costs $3 per gallon. Further suppose that on consecutive days, we find that our 10-gallon tank contains 8 gallons and 6.5 gallons, respectively. On the first day, the potential cost of filling the tank was $6, as the tank would hold 2 additional gallons (see Figure 4.12). On the second day, the potential cost was $10.50, as the tank would hold 3.5 additional gallons. Assuming that no gasoline was added to the tank that day, the cost of the gasoline used that day was then $4.50 — the difference in the two potential costs.

On days in which we fill the tank, the computation is only slightly more complicated. Note that on these days, the potential cost is likely to decrease. For example, suppose that the previous day's level (day 4 in Figure 4.12) was 3 gallons, today's level is 9 gallons, and that we spent $24 to purchase 8 gallons of gasoline. The potential cost of filling the tank has decreased from $21 to $3; hence, the change in potential cost is negative $18. However, we should include the cost of the gasoline we actually purchased, resulting in an amortized cost of $6 for that day. In general, we compute the amortized cost by adding the actual cost to the change in potential cost.

Note that this amortization process is somewhat pessimistic, as we are assessing costs before we actually incur them; however, it is a safe way of verifying our budget. Specifically, suppose we sum up the amortized costs for any sequence of days, beginning with a day in which the tank is full. The sum of changes in potential costs will be the net change in potential cost. Because the tank is initially full, the initial potential cost is 0; hence the net change in potential cost is the final potential cost. The remainder of

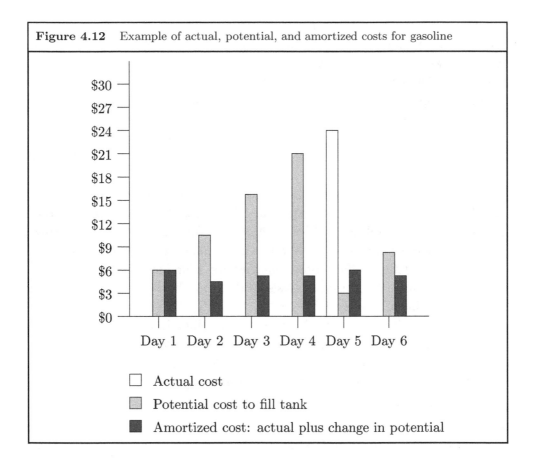

Figure 4.12 Example of actual, potential, and amortized costs for gasoline

the sum of amortized costs is the sum of actual costs of gasoline purchases. Thus, the sum of amortized costs is the sum of actual costs plus the final potential cost. Because the potential cost can never be negative (the tank can't be "overfull"), the sum of the amortized costs will be at least the sum of the actual costs.

Let us now consider how we might apply this technique to the amortized analysis of a data structure such as an EXPANDABLEARRAYSTACK. The potential gasoline cost is essentially a measure of how "bad" the state of the gas tank is. In a similar way, we could measure how "bad" the state of an EXPANDABLEARRAYSTACK is by considering how full the array is — the closer the array is to being filled, the closer we are to an expensive operation. We can formalize this measure by defining a *potential function* Φ, which maps states of a data structure into the nonnegative real numbers, much like the potential gasoline cost maps "states" of the gas tank into nonnegative real numbers.

As we assumed our potential gasoline cost to be initially 0, so also we require that Φ maps the initial state (usually an empty data structure) to 0. Each operation, by changing the state of the data structure, also changes the value of Φ. An increase in Φ corresponds to using gasoline, whereas a decrease in Φ corresponds to adding gasoline to the tank (though not necessarily filling it, as Φ might not reach 0). Thus, for EXPANDABLEARRAYSTACK, we would want the potential function to increase when a PUSH that does not expand the array is performed, but to decrease when either a POP or a PUSH that expands the array is performed.

Let σ denote the state of a data structure prior to some operation, and let σ' denote the state of that structure following the operation. We then define the change in Φ to be $\Phi(\sigma') - \Phi(\sigma)$. We further define the *amortized cost* of the operation relative to Φ to be the actual cost plus the change in Φ.

The above defines what a potential function is and suggests how it might be used to perform amortized analysis. It does not, however, tell us precisely how we can obtain a potential function. We will address this issue in detail shortly; for now however, we will show that an amortized analysis using *any* valid potential function will give a true upper bound on amortized cost. The proof is essentially the same argument that we gave justifying our use of the potential gasoline cost for amortized analysis.

Theorem 4.5. *Let Φ be a valid potential function for some data structure; i.e., if σ_0 is the initial state of the structure, then $\Phi(\sigma_0) = 0$, and if σ is any state of the structure, then $\Phi(\sigma) \geq 0$. Then for any sequence of operations from the initial state σ_0, the sum of the amortized costs of the operations relative to Φ is at least the sum of the actual costs of the operations.*

Proof.   Let $o_1, \ldots, o_m$ be a sequence of operations from σ_0, and let σ_i be the state of the data structure after operation o_i has been performed. Also, let c_i be the actual cost of o_i applied to state σ_{i-1}. Then

$$\sum_{i=1}^{m} (c_i + \Phi(\sigma_i) - \Phi(\sigma_{i-1})) = \sum_{i=1}^{m} c_i + \sum_{i=1}^{m} \Phi(\sigma_i) - \sum_{i=0}^{m-1} \Phi(\sigma_i)$$

$$= \sum_{i=1}^{m} c_i + \Phi(\sigma_m) - \Phi(\sigma_0)$$

$$\geq \sum_{i=1}^{m} c_i,$$

because $\Phi(\sigma_m) \geq 0$ and $\Phi(\sigma_0) = 0$. $\square$

This notion of amortized cost is therefore meaningful and more general than the one introduced in Section 4.3. Specifically, because an amortized cost is defined for each operation, we can analyze this cost much like we would analyze the actual running time of an operation. Note, however, that this notion of amortization only provides an upper bound. For this reason, we only use O-notation (not Ω or Θ) when we perform this type of analysis.

This technique can now be used to analyze the amortized performance of EXPANDABLEARRAYSTACK. However, finding an appropriate potential function for this analysis turns out to be a bit tricky. As Theorem 4.5 implies, we can perform an amortized analysis using any valid potential function; however, a poor choice of potential function may result in a poor upper bound on the amortized cost. For example, we could choose as our potential function the constant function 0 — i.e., for each state, the potential is 0. This function meets the requirements of a potential function; however, because the change in potential will always be 0, the amortized cost relative to this potential function is the same as the actual cost. Finding a potential function that yields constant amortized cost for the EXPANDABLEARRAYSTACK operations requires a bit of insight.

For this reason, before we give a potential-function analysis for EXPAND-ABLEARRAYSTACK, we will begin with a simpler example. In particular, consider the ADT BINARYCOUNTER, specified in Figure 4.13. A BINARYCOUNTER maintains a value that is initially 1. The INCREMENT operation can be used to increment the value by 1, and the VALUE operation can be used to retrieve the value as a CONSLIST of 1s and 0s, least significant bit first. It is unlikely that this ADT has any useful purpose; however, the implementation shown in Figure 4.14 yields an amortized analysis that is simple enough to illustrate clearly the potential-function technique.

This implementation uses a single readable representation variable, *value*. The structural invariant states that *value* refers to the CONSLIST specified by the VALUE operation. We leave it as an exercise to show that this implementation satisfies its specification.

Let us now analyze the worst-case running time of INCREMENT. In the worst case, the first loop can iterate n times, where n is the length of *value*. This case occurs when *value* consists entirely of 1s; however, when *value* begins with a 0, this loop will not iterate at all. It is easily seen that the second loop always iterates the same number of times as the first loop; hence, in the worst case, the INCREMENT operation runs in $\Theta(n)$ time, or in $\Theta(\lg v)$ time, where v is the value represented.

Figure 4.13   Specification of the BINARYCOUNTER ADT

Precondition: true.
Postcondition: Constructs a counter with value 1.

BINARYCOUNTER()

Precondition: true.
Postcondition: Increases the counter value by 1.

BINARYCOUNTER.INCREMENT()

Precondition: true.
Postcondition: Returns a CONSLIST of 0s and 1s ending with a 1 and giving the binary representation of the counter value, with the least significant bit first; i.e. if the sequence is $\langle a_0, \ldots, a_n \rangle$, the value represented is

$$\sum_{i=0}^{n} a_i 2^i.$$

BINARYCOUNTER.VALUE()

We wish to show that the amortized costs of the ITERBINCOUNTER operations are in $O(1)$. We first need to identify the actual costs. Observe that the VALUE operation runs in $\Theta(1)$ time and does not change the structure; hence, we can ignore this operation (we will be ignoring only some constant time for each operation). Because the two loops in INCREMENT iterate the same number of times, the running time of INCREMENT is proportional to the number of iterations of the **while** loop, plus some constant. We can therefore use the number of iterations of the **while** loop as the actual cost of this operation. Note that the actual cost varies from 0 to n, depending on the current value represented.

The next step is to define an appropriate potential function. This step is usually the most challenging part of this technique. While finding a suitable potential function requires some creativity, there are several guidelines we can apply.

First, we can categorize operations of a data structure according to two criteria relevant to amortized analysis:

- the actual cost of the operation; and
- how much it degrades or improves future performance of the data structure.

Figure 4.14   ITERBINCOUNTER implementation of BINARYCOUNTER, specified in
Figure 4.13

Structural Invariant: *value* is a CONSLIST of 0s and 1s ending with a 1.
The sequence represented by this CONSLIST gives the current value of the
BINARYCOUNTER in binary, with the least significant bit first.

ITERBINCOUNTER()
   value ← **new** CONSLIST(1, **new** CONSLIST())

ITERBINCOUNTER.INCREMENT()
   $k ← 0$; $c ←$ *value*
   // **Invariant:** *value* contains k 1s, followed by c.
   while not c.ISEMPTY() **and** c.HEAD() $= 1$
      $k ← k + 1$; $c ← c$.TAIL()
   if c.ISEMPTY()
      $c ←$ **new** CONSLIST($1, c$)
   else
      $c ←$ **new** CONSLIST($1, c$.TAIL())
   // **Invariant:** c contains $i - 1$ 0s and a 1, followed by the CONSLIST
   // obtained by removing all initial 1s and the first 0 (if any) from *value*.
   for $i ← 1$ **to** k
      $c ←$ **new** CONSLIST($0, c$)
   value ← c

Using the above criteria, we can divide operations into four categories:

1. Operations that cost little and improve future performance. ITERBIN-
   COUNTER contains no such operation; however, we needn't be too
   concerned with operations of this type because they cause no problems
   for our analysis.
2. Operations that cost little but degrade future performance. The INCRE-
   MENT operation when the head of *value* is 0 is an example of this type.
   It performs no loop iterations, but causes *value* to have at least one
   leading 1, so that the next INCREMENT will perform at least one iteration.
3. Operations that cost much but improve future performance. The INCRE-
   MENT operation when *value* has many leading 1s is an example of this
   type. It performs a loop iteration for each leading 1, but replaces these
   leading 1s with 0s. Thus, the next INCREMENT will not perform any

iterations. In fact, a number of INCREMENT operations will be required before we encounter another expensive one.

4. Operations that cost much and degrade future performance. Our ITERBINCOUNTER includes no operations of this type. In fact, operations of this type usually make amortized analysis futile.

The key to finding an appropriate potential function is in striking a good balance between operations of types 2 and 3 above. Consider an operation of type 3. The potential function needs to decrease enough to cancel out the high cost of the operation. On the other hand, it cannot increase too much on an operation of type 2, or this operation's amortized cost will be too high. We are trying to show that the INCREMENT operation has a constant amortized cost. Therefore, an operation of type 2 must increase the potential function by at most a constant value. Furthermore, an operation of type 3 requires k iterations, so our potential function must have a decrease of roughly k for such an operation. In addition, any potential function must be 0 initially and always nonnegative.

Based upon the above discussion, it would appear that the number of leading 1s in *value* would be a good measure of the structure's degradation. Let us therefore consider using as our potential function the number of leading 1s. Unfortunately, we immediately encounter a problem with this function — it is not initially 0, because an ITERBINCOUNTER initially has one leading 1. This function is therefore not a valid potential function. We could make a small adjustment by subtracting 1 from the number of leading 1s; however, the resulting function will then go negative whenever there are no leading 1s.

Before we look for an alternative potential function, we should make one more observation regarding the number of leading 1s. Suppose *value* begins with a 0, which is followed by a large number of 1s. When an INCREMENT is performed on this state, the leading 0 is replaced by a 1, thus causing the number of leading 1s to increase by a large amount. Hence, even if the number of leading 1s qualified as a valid potential function, it wouldn't be an appropriate one — the amortized cost of this operation would be high due to the large increase in potential caused by a single operation.

This observation suggests that it is not just the leading 1s that degrade the structure, but that all of the 1s in *value* contribute to the degradation. We might therefore consider using the total number of 1s in *value* as our potential function. Again, this number is initially 1, not 0; however, from the structural invariant, *value* will always contain at least one 1. Therefore, if we subtract 1 from the number of 1s in *value*, we obtain a valid potential function.

Let us now analyze the amortized cost of INCREMENT relative to this potential function. Suppose the actual cost is k (i.e., the loops both iterate k times). The change in potential is simply the number of 1s in *value* after the operation, minus the number of 1s in *value* before the operation (the two -1s cancel each other when we subtract). The **while** loop removes k 1s from c. The **if** statement adds a 1. The **for** loop does not change the number of 1s. The total change is therefore $1 - k$. The amortized cost is then the actual cost plus the change in potential, or

$$k + (1 - k) = 1.$$

We can therefore conclude that the amortized running time of the ITERBIN-COUNTER operations is in $O(1)$.

Let us now use this technique to analyze the amortized performance of EXPANDABLEARRAYSTACK. We first observe that operations which result in an error run in $\Theta(1)$ time and do not change the state of the structure; hence, we can ignore these operations. As we did in Section 4.3, we will again amortize the number of loop iterations; i.e., the actual cost of an operation will be the number of loop iterations performed by that operation. An operation that does not require expanding the array performs no loop iterations, and an operation that requires expanding the array performs n loop iterations, where n is the size of the stack prior to the operation.

We now need an appropriate potential function. We first note that the POP operation not only is cheap, but it also improves the state of the stack by making more array locations available. We therefore don't need to focus on this operation when looking for a potential function. Instead, we need to focus on the PUSH operation. A PUSH that does not expand the array is inexpensive, but degrades the future performance by reducing the number of available array locations. We therefore want the potential function to increase by at most a constant in this case. A PUSH that requires an array expansion is expensive — requiring n iterations — but improves the performance of the structure by creating additional array locations. We want the potential function to decrease by roughly n in this case.

We mentioned earlier that we wanted the potential function to be a measure of how full the array is. Perhaps the most natural measure is n/k, where n is the number of elements in the stack and k is the size of the array. This function is 0 when n is 0 and is always nonnegative. Furthermore, because $n \leq k$, n/k never exceeds 1; hence, no operation can increase this function by more than 1. However, this also means that no operation causes it to decrease by more than 1. Therefore, it does not fit the characteristics we need for a tight amortized analysis.

In order to overcome this problem, let us try multiplying n/k by some value in order to give it more of a range. Because we need for the function to decrease by about n when we expand the array, it will need to have grown by about n after we have done n PUSHes; hence, it needs to exhibit at least linear growth. n/k is bounded by a constant; hence, to cause it to be linear in n, we would want to multiply it by a function that is linear in n. This suggests that we might want to try some function of the form an^2/k, where a is some positive real number to be determined later.

Using this potential function, consider the amortized cost of a PUSH operation that expands the array. Prior to the operation, $n = k$. Therefore, the change in potential is

$$\frac{a(n+1)^2}{2n} - \frac{an^2}{n} = \frac{an^2 + 2an + a - 2an^2}{2n}$$

$$= -\frac{an}{2} + a + \frac{a}{2n}$$

$$\leq -\frac{an}{2} + a + \frac{a}{2}$$

$$= -\frac{an}{2} + \frac{3a}{2}.$$

When we add the actual cost of n, we need the result to be bounded by a fixed constant. We can accomplish this by setting $a = 2$. The potential function $2n^2/k$ therefore results in an amortized cost of no more than 3 in this case.

Now let us consider the amortized cost of a PUSH operation that does not expand the array. Because n increases by 1 and k does not change, the change in the potential function $2n^2/k$ is

$$\frac{2(n+1)^2}{k} - \frac{2n^2}{k} = \frac{2n^2 + 4n + 2 - 2n^2}{k}$$

$$= \frac{4n + 2}{k}$$

$$= 4\left(\frac{n + \frac{1}{2}}{k}\right)$$

$$< 4$$

because k must be strictly larger than n, and both are integers. Because no loop iterations are performed in this case, the actual cost is 0; hence, the amortized cost is less than 4.

In order to complete the analysis, we must consider the POP operation. Because n is initially positive and decreases by 1, and because k remains the same, the change in potential is

$$\frac{2(n-1)^2}{k} - \frac{2n^2}{k} = \frac{2n^2 - 4n + 2 - 2n^2}{k}$$

$$= \frac{2 - 4n}{k}$$

$$< 0.$$

The actual cost is 0. The amortized cost is therefore less than 0.

In each case, the amortized cost is in $O(1)$. Because the time for each loop iteration and the time required by each operation apart from the loop iterations are both in $O(1)$, we conclude that the amortized running time of the stack operations is in $O(1)$.

4.6   Summary

We have shown how the top-down design paradigm can be applied to the design of data structures. In many cases, we can reduce the implementation of an ADT to the implementation of simpler or lower-level ADTs. In other cases, we can reduce the implementation to a common design pattern. The algorithms we have used for implementing the operations of ADTs have been quite simple. As we examine more advanced data structures in the following chapters, we will see that the algorithms in the implementations also use the top-down approach as presented in Chapter 1.

Applying the top-down approach yields clean techniques for proving that implementations of ADTs meet their specifications. The techniques are similar to those presented in Chapter 2, but additionally require proving security of the implementations. Borrowing some ideas from modular and object-oriented languages, we have supplied a computational model that facilitates security in a straightforward way. This model also facilitates the implementation of immutable structures, which in some cases yield performance benefits by eliminating the need to copy data. However, use of immutable structures tends to increase the amount of dynamic memory allocation and requires the presence of an automatic garbage collector.

The analysis techniques of Chapter 3 can be applied to data structures as well. In addition, amortized analysis is sometimes useful for analyzing structures for which operations are occasionally expensive. By amortizing the cost, we can see that sequences of operations may be less expensive than a simple worst-case analysis would suggest. Potential functions provide a general approach to amortized analysis.

4.7   Exercises

Exercise 4.1. Complete the proof of Theorem 4.2 by giving proofs of maintenance and correctness for the two missing cases.

Exercise 4.2. Prove that CONSLISTSTACK, shown in Figure 4.8 on page 128, meets its specification, given in Figure 4.1 on page 110.

* Exercise 4.3. Give an algorithm for APPEND, specified in Figure 4.15. Your algorithm should run in $O(n)$ time, where n is the number of elements in x.

Exercise 4.4. Prove that ITERBINCOUNTER, shown in Figure 4.14 (page 137), meets the specification shown in Figure 4.13 (page 136).

Exercise 4.5. Let $f(n)$ denote the number of 1s in *value* after n calls to INCREMENT on a new ITERBINCOUNTER. Prove by induction on n that the total number of iterations of the **while** loop in these n calls is

$$n - f(n) + 1.$$

Exercise 4.6. Figure 4.16 gives an alternative implementation of the INCREMENT operation for the BINARYCOUNTER ADT.

a. Prove that the implementation that uses this algorithm meets its specification.

Figure 4.15   Specification for APPEND

Precondition: x and y are CONSLISTs representing the sequences $\langle x_1, x_2, \ldots, x_n \rangle$ and $\langle y_1, y_2, \ldots, y_m \rangle$, respectively.
Postcondition: Returns a CONSLIST representing the sequence $\langle x_1, x_2, \ldots, x_n, y_1, y_2, \ldots, y_m \rangle$.

APPEND(x, y)

> **Figure 4.16** Implementation of the INCREMENT operation for BINARYCOUNTER, specified in Figure 4.13
>
> ---
>
> RECBINCOUNTER.INCREMENT()
>   *value* ← INC(*value*)
>
> — **Internal Functions Follow** —
>
> **Precondition:** c is a CONSLIST of 0s and 1s not ending in 0.
> **Postcondition:** Returns a CONSLIST representing $c + 1$, where the CONSLISTs are interpreted as the binary representation of natural numbers, least significant bit first.
>
> RECBINCOUNTER.INC(c)
>   **if** c.ISEMPTY()
>   **return new** CONSLIST(1, c)
>   **else if** c.HEAD() = 0
>   **return new** CONSLIST(1, c.TAIL())
>   **else**
>   **return new** CONSLIST(0, INC(c.TAIL()))

b. It is easily seen that the running time of INCREMENT is proportional to the number of calls made (including recursive calls) to the internal function INC. Using a potential function, show that the amortized number of calls to INC is in $O(1)$.

Exercise 4.7. Analyze the amortized cost of the EXPANDABLEARRAYSTACK operations using the number of iterations performed as the actual cost and

$$\frac{4n^3}{3k^2}$$

as the potential function, where n is the number of elements in the stack and k is the size of the array.

Exercise 4.8. Let $c > 1$ be a fixed real number. Suppose we modify Figure 4.6 so that the new array is of size $\lceil c \cdot size \rceil$. Using the potential function approach, show that the amortized running time of the stack operations is in $O(1)$.

Exercise 4.9. With EXPANDABLEARRAYSTACK, it is possible that the stack reaches a state in which it is using much more space than it requires.

This can happen if a large number of elements are pushed onto the stack, then most are removed. One solution is to modify the POP operation so that if the number of elements drops below half the size of the array, then we copy the elements to a new array of half the size. Give a convincing argument that this solution would not result in $O(1)$ amortized running time.

Exercise 4.10. An alternative to the solution sketched in the above exercise is to reduce the size of the array by half whenever it becomes less than $1/4$ full, but is still non-empty.

  a. Give a modified POP operation to implement this idea.

 * b. Using the technique of Section 4.3, show that the stack operations have an amortized running time in $O(1)$ when this scheme is used. You may assume that the array is initially of size 4.

** c. Repeat the above analysis using a potential function. [**Hint:** Your potential function will need to increase as the size of the array diverges from $2n$, where n is the number of elements in the stack.]

Exercise 4.11. A *queue* is similar to a stack, but it provides *first in first out* (FIFO) access to the data items. Instead of the operations PUSH and POP, it has operations ENQUEUE and DEQUEUE — ENQUEUE adds an item to the end of the sequence, and DEQUEUE removes the item from the beginning of the sequence.

a. Give an ADT for a queue.
b. Using the linked list design pattern, give an implementation of your ADT for which all operations run in $\Theta(1)$ time.
c. Prove that your implementation meets its specification.

Exercise 4.12. A certain data structure contains operations that each consists of a sequence of zero or more POPs from a stack, followed by a single PUSH. The stack is initially empty, and no POP is attempted when the stack is empty.

a. Prove that in any sequence of n operations on an initialized structure, there are at most $2n$ stack operations (i.e., PUSHes and POPs).
b. Use a simple potential function to show that the amortized number of stack operations is bounded by a constant.

Exercise 4.13. A STRING, as specified in Figure 4.17, represents a finite sequence of CHARs, or characters.

a. Give an implementation of STRING for which

Figure 4.17 The STRING ADT

Precondition: $A[0..n-1]$ is an array of CHARs, and n is a NAT.
Postcondition: Constructs a STRING representing the sequence of CHARs in A.

STRING($A[0..n-1]$)

Precondition: x is a STRING.
Postcondition: Adds the sequence of CHARs represented by x to the end of this STRING.

APPEND(x)

Precondition: i and *len* are NATs such that $i +$ *len* does not exceed the length of this STRING.
Postcondition: Returns   the   STRING   representing   the   sequence $\langle a_i, a_{i+1}, \ldots, a_{i+len-1} \rangle$, where $\langle a_0, \ldots, a_{n-1} \rangle$ is the sequence represented by this STRING.

SUBSTRING(i, *len*)

Precondition: i is a NAT strictly less than the length of this STRING.
Postcondition: Returns the CHAR a_i, where $\langle a_0, \ldots, a_{n-1} \rangle$ is the sequence represented by this STRING.

GETCHARACTER(i)

Precondition: true.
Postcondition: Returns the length of the represented sequence.

LENGTH()

- the constructor runs in $O(n)$ amortized time;
- APPEND runs in $O(m)$ amortized time, where m is the length of x;
- SUBSTRING runs in $O(len)$ amortized time; and
- GETCHARACTER and LENGTH run in $\Theta(1)$ time in the worst case.

For the purpose of defining amortized running times, think of the constructor and the SUBSTRING operation as appending CHARs to an empty string. Prove the above running times for your implementation.

b. Prove that your implementation meets its specification.

Exercise 4.14. Figure 4.18 gives an ADT for an immutable arbitrary-precision natural number. Such an ADT is useful for defining algorithms for

---

Figure 4.18　BIGNUM ADT

Precondition: $A[0..n-1]$ is an array whose values are all either 0 or 1.
Postcondition: Constructs a BIGNUM representing

$$\sum_{i=0}^{n-1} A[i]2^i.$$

BIGNUM($A[0..n-1]$)

Precondition: v refers to a BIGNUM.
Postcondition: Returns 1 if the value of this BIGNUM is greater than v, 0 if it is equal to v, or -1 if it is less than v.

BIGNUM.COMPARETO(v)

Precondition: v refers to a BIGNUM.
Postcondition: Returns a BIGNUM representing the sum of the value of this BIGNUM and v.

BIGNUM.ADD(v)

Precondition: v refers to a BIGNUM no greater than the value of this BIGNUM.
Postcondition: Returns a BIGNUM representing the value of this BIGNUM minus v.

BIGNUM.SUBTRACT(v)

Precondition: i is an integer.
Postcondition: Returns the floor of the BIGNUM obtained by multiplying this BIGNUM by 2^i.

BIGNUM.SHIFT(i)

Precondition: true.
Postcondition: Returns the number of bits in the binary representation of this BIGNUM with no leading zeros.

BIGNUM.NUMBITS()

Precondition: *start* and *len* are natural numbers.
Postcondition: Returns an array $A[0..len-1]$ containing the values of bit positions *start* through *start* + *len* − 1; zeros are assigned to the high-order positions if necessary.

GETBITS(*start*, *len*)

operating on natural numbers which may not fit in a single machine word. We can implement this ADT using a single representation variable, $bits[0..n-1]$, which is an array of 0s and 1s. The structural invariant is that all elements of $bits$ are either 0 or 1, and that if $\textsc{SizeOf}(bits) \neq 0$,

$$bits[\textsc{SizeOf}(bits) - 1] = 1.$$

If $n = \textsc{SizeOf}(bits)$, the represented number is then

$$\sum_{i=0}^{n-1} bits[i]2^i.$$

Note that the least significant bit has the lowest index; hence, it might be helpful to think of the array with index 0 at the far right, and indices increasing from right to left.

a. Complete this implementation of BIGNUM such that

- NUMBITS runs in $\Theta(1)$ time;
- SHIFT and GETBITS run in $\Theta(n)$ time, where n is the number of bits in the result;
- the constructor and the remaining operations run in $\Theta(n)$ time, where n is the number of bits in the largest number involved in the operation.

b. Prove that your implementation meets its specification.

4.8 Notes

The phenomenon that occurs when multiple copies are made of the same reference is known in the literature as *aliasing*. The problem is thoroughly discussed by, e.g., Aho *et al.* [3] and Muchnick [94].

Use of immutable structures has its roots in functional programming, though it has carried over to some degree to languages from other paradigms. Paulson [97] gives a nice introduction to functional programming using ML, where immutable data types are the norm.

The search tree viewer posted on this textbook's web site contains complete Java implementations of CONSLIST and CONSLISTSTACK. Deep cloning is simulated in this code because only immutable items are placed on the stacks.

Exercise 4.12 is due to Tarjan [113], who gives an excellent survey of amortized analysis. He credits D. Sleator for the potential function method of amortized analysis.

Chapter 5

Priority Queues

In many applications, we need data structures which support the efficient storage of data items and their retrieval in order of a pre-determined *priority*. Consider priority-based scheduling, for example. Jobs become available for execution at various times, and as jobs complete, we wish to schedule the available job having highest priority. These priorities may be assigned, for example, according to the relative importance of each job's being executed in a timely manner. In order to support this form of storage and retrieval, we define a PRIORITYQUEUE as a set of items, each having an associated number giving its priority, together with the operations specified in Figure 5.1.

We sometimes wish to have operations MINPRI-ORITY() and REMOVEMIN() instead of MAXPRI-ORITY() and REMOVEMAX(). The specifications of these operations are the same as those of MAXPRIORITY and REMOVEMAX, respectively, except that minimum priorities are used instead of maximum

> *Strictly speaking, we should use a multiset, because we do not prohibit multiple occurrences of the same item. However, because we ordinarily would not insert multiple occurrences, we will call it a set.*

priorities. We call the resulting ADT an INVERTEDPRIORITYQUEUE. It is a straightforward matter to convert any implementation of PRIORITYQUEUE into an implementation of INVERTEDPRIORITYQUEUE.

In order to facilitate implementations of PRIORITYQUEUE, we will use a data structure KEYED for pairing data items with their respective priorities. This structure will consist of two readable representation variables, *key* and *data*. We will use a rather general interpretation, namely, that *key* and *data* are associated with each other. This generality will allow us to reuse the structure in later chapters with somewhat different contexts. Its structural invariant will simply be true. It will contain a constructor that takes two inputs, x and k, and produces an association with k as the key and x as the data. It will contain no additional operations.

Figure 5.1   The PRIORITYQUEUE ADT

Precondition: true.
Postcondition: Constructs an empty PRIORITYQUEUE.

PRIORITYQUEUE()

Precondition: p is a NUMBER.
Postcondition: Adds x to the set with priority p.

PRIORITYQUEUE.PUT(x, p)

Precondition: The represented set is not empty.
Postcondition: Returns the maximum priority of any item in the set.

PRIORITYQUEUE.MAXPRIORITY()

Precondition: The represented set is not empty.
Postcondition: An item with maximum priority is removed from the set and returned.

PRIORITYQUEUE.REMOVEMAX()

Precondition: true.
Postcondition: Returns the number of items in the set.

PRIORITYQUEUE.SIZE()

5.1   Sorted Arrays

Our first implementation of PRIORITYQUEUE maintains the data in an expandable array, sorted in nondecreasing order of priorities. The representation consists of two variables:

- *elements*$[0..M-1]$: an array of KEYED items, each containing a data item with its associated priority as its key, in order of priorities; and
- *size*: an integer giving the number of data items.

Implementation of the REMOVEMAX operation is then trivial — after verifying that *size* is nonzero, we simply decrement *size* by 1 and then return *elements*[*size*].DATA(). Clearly, this can be done in $\Theta(1)$ time. Similarly, the MAXPRIORITY operation can be trivially implemented to run in $\Theta(1)$ time.

In order to implement PUT(x, p), we must find the correct place to insert x so that the order of the priorities is maintained. Let us therefore reduce the PUT operation to the problem of finding the correct location to insert a given priority p. This location is the index i, $0 \leq i \leq size$, such that

- if $0 \leq j < i$, then $elements[j].\text{KEY}() < p$; and
- if $i \leq j < size$, then $p \leq elements[j].\text{KEY}()$.

Because the priorities are sorted, $elements[i].\text{KEY}() = p$ iff there is an item in the array whose priority is p. Furthermore, if no such item exists, i gives the location at which such an item should be inserted.

We can apply the top-down approach to derive a search technique called *binary search*. Assume we are looking for the insertion point in an array $A[lo..hi - 1]$; i.e., the insertion point i will be in the range $lo \leq i \leq hi$. Further assume that $lo < hi$, for otherwise, we must have $lo = i = hi$. Recall that the divide-and-conquer technique, introduced in Section 3.7, reduces large instances to smaller instances that are a fixed fraction of the size of the original instance. In order to apply this technique, we first look at the priority of the middle data item — the item with index $mid = \lfloor (lo+hi)/2 \rfloor$. If the key of this item is greater than or equal to p, then i can be no greater than mid, which in turn is strictly less than hi. Otherwise, i must be strictly greater than mid, which in turn is greater than or equal to lo. We will therefore have reduced our search to a strictly smaller search containing about half the elements from the original search.

Note that this reduction is actually a transformation — a reduction in which the solution to the smaller problem is exactly the solution to the original problem. Recall from Section 2.4 that a transformation can be implemented as a loop in a fairly straightforward way. Specifically, each iteration of the loop will reduce a large instance to a smaller instance. When the loop terminates, the instance will be the base case, where $lo = hi$.

Prior to the loop, lo and hi must have values 0 and $size$, respectively. Our invariant will be that $0 \leq lo \leq hi \leq size$, that items with indices less than lo have a key less than p, and that elements with indices greater than or equal to hi have a key greater than or equal to p. Thus, the index i to be returned will always be in the range $lo \leq i \leq hi$. When the loop terminates, we will have $lo = hi$; hence, we can return either lo or hi. This algorithm is given as the FIND function in Figure 5.2, where a partial implementation of SORTEDARRAYPRIORITYQUEUE is given. The EXPAND function copies the contents of its argument into an array of twice the original size, as in Section 4.3. The remainder of the implementation and its correctness proof are left as an exercise.

Figure 5.2 SORTEDARRAYPRIORITYQUEUE implementation (partial) of the PRIOR-
ITYQUEUE ADT

Structural Invariant: $0 \leq size \leq$ SIZEOF($elements$), where $elements$ is
an array of KEYED items whose keys are numbers in nondecreasing order.

SORTEDARRAYPRIORITYQUEUE.PUT($x, p :$ NUMBER)
   $i \leftarrow$ FIND(p)
   if $size =$ SIZEOF($elements$)
      $elements \leftarrow$ EXPAND($elements$)
   for $j \leftarrow size - 1$ **to** i **by** -1
      $elements[j + 1] \leftarrow elements[j]$
   $elements[i] \leftarrow$ **new** KEYED(x, p); $size \leftarrow size + 1$

— **Internal Functions Follow** —

Precondition: The structural invariant holds, and p is a NUMBER.
Postcondition: Returns the index i, $0 \leq i \leq size$, such that if $0 \leq j < i$,
then $elements[j]$.KEY() $< p$ and if $i \leq j < size$, then
$p \leq elements[j]$.KEY().

SORTEDARRAYPRIORITYQUEUE.FIND(p)
   $lo \leftarrow 0$; $hi \leftarrow size$
   // **Invariant:** $0 \leq lo \leq hi \leq size$,
   // if $0 \leq j < lo$, then $elements[j]$.KEY() $< p$,
   // and if $hi \leq j < size$, then $elements[j]$.KEY() $\geq p$.
   while $lo < hi$
      $mid \leftarrow \lfloor (lo + hi)/2 \rfloor$
      if $elements[mid]$.KEY() $\geq p$
         $hi \leftarrow mid$
      else
         $lo \leftarrow mid + 1$
   return lo

Let us now analyze the running time of FIND. Clearly, each iteration of
the **while** loop runs in $\Theta(1)$ time, as does the code outside the loop. We
therefore only need to count the number of iterations of the loop.

Let $f(n)$ denote the number of iterations, where $n = hi - lo$ gives the
number of elements in the search range. One iteration reduces the number of
elements in the range to either $\lfloor n/2 \rfloor$ or $\lceil n/2 \rceil - 1$. The former value occurs

whenever the key examined is greater than or equal to p. The worst case therefore occurs whenever we are looking for a key smaller than any key in the set. In the worst case, the number of iterations is therefore given by the following recurrence:

$$f(n) = f(\lfloor n/2 \rfloor) + 1$$

for $n > 1$. From Theorem 3.35, $f(n) \in \Theta(\lg n)$. Therefore, FIND runs in $\Theta(\lg n)$ time.

Let us now analyze the running time of PUT. Let n be the value of *size*. The first statement requires $\Theta(\lg n)$ time, and based on our analysis in Section 4.3, the EXPAND function should take $O(n)$ time in the worst case. Because we can amortize the time for EXPAND, let us ignore it for now. Clearly, everything else outside the **for** loop and a single iteration of the loop run in $\Theta(1)$ time. Furthermore, in the worst case (which occurs when the new key has a value less than all other keys in the set), the loop iterates n times. Thus, the entire algorithm runs in $\Theta(n)$ time in the worst case, regardless of whether we count the time for EXPAND.

5.2 Heaps

The SORTEDARRAYPRIORITYQUEUE has very efficient MAXPRIORITY and REMOVEMAX operations, but a rather slow PUT operation. We could speed up the PUT operation considerably by dropping our requirement that the array be sorted. In this case, we could simply add an element at the end of the array, expanding it if necessary. This operation is essentially the same as the EXPANDABLEARRAYSTACK.PUSH operation, which has an amortized running time in $\Theta(1)$. However, we would no longer be able to take advantage of the ordering of the array in finding the maximum priority. As a result, we would need to search the entire array. The running times for the MAXPRIORITY and REMOVEMAX operations would therefore be in $\Theta(n)$ time, where n is the number of elements in the priority queue.

In order to facilitate efficient implementations of all three operations, let us try applying the top-down approach to designing an appropriate data structure. Suppose we have a non-empty set of elements. Because we need to be able to find and remove the maximum priority quickly, we should keep track of it. When we remove it, we need to be able to locate the new maximum quickly. We can therefore organize the remaining elements into two (possibly empty) priority queues. (As we will see, using two priority queues for these remaining elements can yield significant performance advantages

Figure 5.3   A heap — each priority is no smaller than any of its children

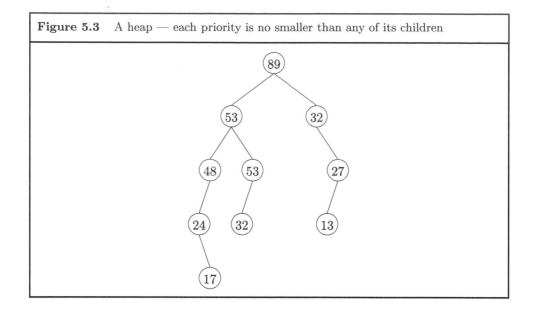

over a single priority queue.) Assuming for the moment that both of these priority queues are nonempty, the new overall maximum must be the larger of the maximum priorities from each of these priority queues. We can therefore find the new maximum by comparing these two priorities. The cases in which one or both of the two priority queues are empty are likewise straightforward.

We can implement the above idea by arranging the priorities into a *heap*, as shown in Figure 5.3. This structure will be the basis of all of the remaining PRIORITYQUEUE implementations presented in this chapter. In this figure, integer priorities of several data items are shown inside circles, which we will call *nodes*. The structure is referenced by its *root node*, containing the priority 89. This value is the maximum of the priorities in the structure. The remaining priorities are accessed via one of two references, one leading to the left, and the other leading to the right. Each of these two groups of priorities forms a priority queue structured in a similar way. Thus, as we follow any path downward in the heap, the values of the priorities are non-increasing.

A heap is a special case of a more general structure known as a *tree*. Let N be a finite set of nodes, each containing a data item. We define a *rooted tree* comprised of N recursively as:

- a special object which we will call the *empty tree* if $N = \varnothing$; or
- a *root node* $x \in N$, together with a finite sequence $\langle T_1, \ldots, T_k \rangle$ of *children*, where

– each T_i is a rooted tree comprised of some (possibly empty) set $N_i \subseteq N \setminus \{x\}$ (i.e., each element of each N_i is an element of N, but not the root node);

– $\bigcup_{i=1}^{k} N_i = N \setminus \{x\}$ (i.e., the elements in all of the sets N_i together form the set N, without the root node); and

– for $i \neq j$, $N_i \cap N_j = \varnothing$ (i.e., no two of these sets have any elements in common).

Thus, the structure shown in Figure 5.3 is a rooted tree comprised of 10 nodes. Note that the data items contained in the nodes are not all distinct; however, the nodes themselves are distinct. The root node contains 89. Its first child is a rooted tree comprised of six nodes and having a root node containing 53.

When a node c is a child of a node p, we say that p is the *parent* of c. Also, two children of a given node are called *siblings*. Thus, in Figure 5.3, the node containing 48 has one node containing 53 as its parent and another as its sibling. We refer to a non-empty tree whose children are all empty as a *leaf*. Thus, in Figure 5.3, the subtree whose root contains 13 is a leaf.

We define the *size* of a rooted tree to be the number of nodes which comprise it. Another important measure of a non-empty rooted tree is its *height*, which we define recursively to be one plus the maximum height of its non-empty children; if it has no non-empty children, we say its height is 0. Thus, the height is the maximum of the distances from the root to the leaves, where we define the distance as the number of steps we must take to get from one node to the other. For example, the tree in Figure 5.3 has size 10 and height 4.

When we draw rooted trees, we usually do not draw empty trees. For example, in Figure 5.3, the subtree whose root contains 24 has two children, but the first is empty. This practice can lead to ambiguity; for example, it is not clear whether the subtree rooted at 13 contains any children, or if they might all be empty. For this and other reasons, we often consider restricted classes of rooted trees. Here, we wish to define a *binary tree* as a rooted tree in which each non-empty subtree has exactly two children, either (or both) of which may be empty. In a binary tree, the first child is called the *left* child, and the other is called the *right* child. If we then state that the rooted tree in Figure 5.3 is a binary tree, it is clear that the subtree rooted at 13, because it is nonempty, has two empty children.

It is rather difficult to define an ADT for either trees or binary trees in such a way that it can be implemented efficiently. The difficulty is in

---

Figure 5.4   Constructor for BINARYTREENODE

Precondition: true.
Postcondition: Constructs a BINARYTREENODE with all three variables nil.

BINARYTREENODE()
    root ← nil; *leftChild* ← nil; *rightChild* ← nil

---

enforcing as a structural invariant the fact that no two children have nodes in common. In order for an operation to maintain this invariant when adding a new node, it would apparently need to examine the entire structure to see if the new node is already in the tree. As we will see, maintaining this invariant becomes much easier for specific applications of trees. It therefore seems best to think of a rooted tree as a mathematical object, and to mimic its structure in defining a heap implementation of PRIORITYQUEUE.

In order to build a heap, we need to be able to implement a single node. For this purpose, we will define a data type BINARYTREENODE. Its representation will contain three variables:

- *root*: the KEYED data item stored in the node;
- *leftChild*: the BINARYTREENODE representing the root of the left child; and
- *rightChild*: the BINARYTREENODE representing the root of the right child.

We will provide read/write access to all three of these variables, and our structural invariant is simply true. The only constructor is shown in Figure 5.4, and no additional operations are included. Clearly, BINARYTREENODE meets its specification (there is very little specified), and each operation and constructor runs in $\Theta(1)$ time.

We can now formally define a heap as a binary tree containing KEYED elements such that if the tree is non-empty, then

- the item stored at the root has the maximum key in the tree and
- both children are heaps.

Based on the above definition, we can define a representation for PRIORITYQUEUE using two variables:

- *elements*: a BINARYTREENODE; and
- *size*: a natural number.

Our structural invariant will be that *elements* is a heap whose size is given by *size*. We interpret the contents of the nodes comprising this heap as the set of items stored in the priority queue, together with their associated priorities.

Implementation of MAXPRIORITY is now trivial — we just return the key of the root. To implement REMOVEMAX, we must remove the root (provided the heap is non-empty) and return the data from its contents. When we remove the root, we are left with the two children, which must then be combined into one heap. We therefore will define an internal function MERGE, which takes as input two heaps h_1 and h_2 with no nodes in common (i.e., the two heaps share no common structure, though they may have keys in common), and returns a single heap containing all of the nodes from h_1 and h_2. Note that we can also use the MERGE function to implement PUT if we first construct a single-node heap from the element we wish to insert.

Let us consider how to implement MERGE. If either of the two heaps h_1 and h_2 is nil (i.e., empty), we can simply return the other heap. Otherwise, the root of the result must be the root of either h_1 or h_2, whichever root contains a KEYED item with larger key (a tie can be broken arbitrarily). Let L denote the heap whose root contains the maximum key, and let S denote the other heap. Then we must form a heap whose root is the root of L and whose two children are heaps containing the nodes in the following three heaps:

- the left child of L;
- the right child of L; and
- S.

We can form these two children by recursively merging two of these three heaps.

A simple implementation, which we call SIMPLEHEAP, is shown in Figure 5.5. Note that we can maintain the structural invariant because we can ensure that the precondition to MERGE is always met (the details are left as an exercise). Note also that the above discussion leaves some flexibility in the implementation of MERGE. In fact, we will see shortly that this particular implementation performs rather poorly. As a result, we will need to find a better way of choosing the two heaps to merge in the recursive call, and/or a better way to decide which child the resulting heap will be.

Let us now analyze the running time of MERGE. Suppose h_1 and h_2 together have n nodes. Clearly, the running time excluding the recursive call is in $\Theta(1)$. In the recursive call, $L.\text{RIGHTCHILD}()$ has at least one fewer node than does L; hence the total number of nodes in the two heaps in the

---

Figure 5.5 SIMPLEHEAP implementation of PRIORITYQUEUE

Structural Invariant: *elements* is a heap whose size is given by *size*.

SIMPLEHEAP()
 elements ← nil; *size* ← 0

SIMPLEHEAP.PUT(x, p : NUMBER)
 h ← **new** BINARYTREENODE(); h.SETROOT(**new** KEYED(x, p))
 elements ← MERGE(*elements, h*); *size* ← *size* + 1

SIMPLEHEAP.MAXPRIORITY()
 return *elements*.ROOT().KEY()

SIMPLEHEAP.REMOVEMAX()
 x ← *elements*.ROOT().DATA(); *size* ← *size* − 1
 elements ← MERGE(*elements*.LEFTCHILD(), *elements*.RIGHTCHILD())
 return x

— **Internal Functions Follow** —

Precondition: h_1 and h_2 are (possibly nil) BINARYTREENODEs
representing heaps with no nodes in common.
Postcondition: Returns a heap containing all of the nodes in h_1 and h_2.

SIMPLEHEAP.MERGE(h_1, h_2)
  if h_1 = nil
    return h_2
  else if h_2 = nil
    return h_1
  else
    if h_1.ROOT().KEY() > h_2.ROOT().KEY()
      L ← h_1; S ← h_2
    else
      L ← h_2; S ← h_1
    L.SETRIGHTCHILD(MERGE(L.RIGHTCHILD(), S))
    return L

recursive call is no more than $n - 1$. The total running time is therefore bounded above by

$$f(n) \in f(n - 1) + O(1)$$
$$\subseteq O(n)$$

by Theorem 3.34.

At first it might seem that the bound of $n - 1$ on the number of nodes in the two heaps in the recursive call is overly pessimistic. However, upon close examination of the algorithm, we see that not only does this describe the worst case, it actually describes every case. To see this, notice that nowhere in the algorithm is the left child of a node changed after that node is created. Because each left child is initially empty, no node ever has a nonempty left child. Thus, each heap is single path of nodes going to the right.

The SIMPLEHEAP implementation therefore amounts to a linked list in which the keys are kept in non-increasing order. The PUT operation will therefore require $\Theta(n)$ time in the worst case, which occurs when we add a node whose key is smaller than any in the heap. In the remainder of this chapter, we will examine various ways of taking advantage of the branching potential of a heap in order to improve the performance.

5.3 Leftist Heaps

In order to improve the performance of merging two heaps, it would make sense to try to reach one of the base cases as quickly as possible. In SIMPLEHEAP.MERGE, the base cases occur when one of the two heaps is empty. In order to simplify the discussion, let us somewhat arbitrarily decide that one of the two heaps to be merged in the recursive call will always be S. We therefore need to decide which child of L to merge with S. In order to reach a base case as quickly as possible, it would make sense to use the child having an empty subtree nearest to its root.

Let us define, for a given binary tree T, the *null path length* to be the length of the shortest path from the root to an empty subtree. Specifically, if T is empty, then its null path length is 0; otherwise, it is 1 plus the minimum of the null path lengths of its children. Now if, in the recursive call, we were to merge S with the child of L having smaller null path length, then the sum of the null path lengths of the two heaps would always be smaller for the recursive call than for the original call. The running time is therefore proportional to the sum of the null path lengths. This is advantageous due to the following theorem.

Theorem 5.1. *For any binary tree T with n nodes, the null path length of T is at most $\lg(n+1)$.*

The proof of this theorem is typical of many proofs of properties of trees. It proceeds by induction on n using the following general strategy:

- For the base case, prove that the property holds when $n = 0$ — i.e., for an empty tree.
- For the induction step, apply the induction hypothesis to one or more of the children of a nonempty tree.

Proof of Theorem 5.1. By induction on n.

Base: $n = 0$. Then by definition, the null path length is $0 = \lg 1$.

Induction Hypothesis: Assume for some $n > 0$ that for $0 \leq i < n$, the null path length of any tree with i nodes is at most $\lg(i+1)$.

Induction Step: Let T be a binary tree with n nodes. Then because the two children together contain $n - 1$ nodes, they cannot both contain more than $(n-1)/2$ nodes; hence, one of the two children has no more than $\lfloor(n-1)/2\rfloor$ nodes. By the induction hypothesis, this child has a null path of at most $\lg(\lfloor(n-1)/2\rfloor + 1)$. The null path length of T is therefore at most

$$1 + \lg(\lfloor(n-1)/2\rfloor + 1) \leq 1 + \lg((n+1)/2)$$
$$= \lg(n+1).$$

$\square$

By the above theorem, if we can always choose the child with smaller null path length for the recursive call, then the merge will operate in $O(\lg n)$ time, where n is the number of nodes in the larger of the two heaps. We can develop slightly simpler algorithms if we build our heaps so that the right-hand child always has the smaller null path length, as in Figure 5.6(a). We therefore define a *leftist tree* to be a binary tree which, if nonempty, has two leftist trees as children, with the right-hand child having a null path length no larger than that of the left-hand child. A *leftist heap* is then a leftist tree that is also a heap.

> The term "leftist" refers to the tendency of these structures to be heavier on the left.

In order to implement a leftist heap, we will use an implementation of a leftist tree. The leftist tree implementation will take care of maintaining the proper shape of the tree. Because we will want to combine leftist trees

Figure 5.6 Example of performing a LEFTISTHEAP.REMOVEMAX operation

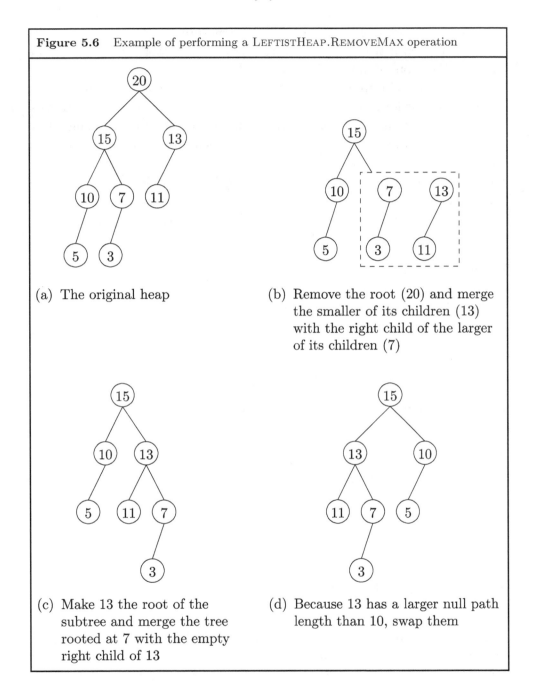

(a) The original heap

(b) Remove the root (20) and merge the smaller of its children (13) with the right child of the larger of its children (7)

(c) Make 13 the root of the subtree and merge the tree rooted at 7 with the empty right child of 13

(d) Because 13 has a larger null path length than 10, swap them

to form larger leftist trees, we must be able to handle the case in which two given leftist trees have nodes in common. The simplest way to handle this situation is to define the implementation to be an immutable structure.

Because no changes can be made to the structure, we can treat all nodes as distinct, even if they are represented by the same storage (in which case they are the roots of identical trees).

In order to facilitate fast computation of null path lengths, we will record the null path length of a leftist tree in one of its representation variables. Thus, when forming a new leftist tree from a root and two existing leftist trees, we can simply compare the null path lengths to decide which tree should be used as the right child. Furthermore, we can compute the null path length of the new leftist tree by adding 1 to the null path length of its right child.

For our representation of LEFTISTTREE, we will therefore use four variables:

- *root*: a KEYED item;
- *leftChild*: a LEFTISTTREE;
- *rightChild*: a LEFTISTTREE; and
- *nullPathLength*: a NAT.

We will allow read access to all variables. Our structural invariant will be that this structure is a leftist tree such that

- *nullPathLength* gives its null path length; and
- *root* = nil iff *nullPathLength* = 0.

Specifically, we will allow the same node to occur more than once in the structure — each occurrence will be viewed as a copy. Because the structure is immutable, such sharing is safe. The implementation of LEFTISTTREE is shown in Figure 5.7. Clearly, each of these constructors runs in $\Theta(1)$ time.

We now represent our LEFTISTHEAP implementation of PRIORITYQUEUE using two variables:

- *elements*: a LEFTISTTREE; and
- *size*: a natural number.

Our structural invariant is that *elements* is a leftist heap whose size is given by *size*, and whose nodes are KEYED items. We interpret these KEYED items as the represented set of elements with their associated priorities. The implementation of LEFTISTHEAP is shown in Figure 5.8.

Based on the discussion above, MERGE runs in $O(\lg n)$ time, where n is the number of nodes in the larger of the two leftist heaps. It follows that PUT and REMOVEMAX operate in $O(\lg n)$ time, where n is the number of

---

Figure 5.7 The LEFTISTTREE data structure.

Structural Invariant: This structure forms a leftist tree with *nullPathLength* giving its null path length, and *root* = nil iff *nullPathLength* = 0.

Precondition: true.
Postcondition: Constructs an empty LEFTISTTREE.

LEFTISTTREE()
    root ← nil; *leftChild* ← nil; *rightChild* ← nil; *nullPathLength* ← 0

Precondition: x is a non-nil KEYED item.
Postcondition: Constructs a LEFTISTTREE containing x at its root and having two empty children.

LEFTISTTREE(x : KEYED)
    if x = nil
        error
    else
        root ← x; *nullPathLength* ← 1
        leftChild ← **new** LEFTISTTREE()
        rightChild ← **new** LEFTISTTREE()

Precondition: x, t_1, and t_2 are non-nil, x is KEYED, and t_1 and t_2 are LEFTISTTREES.
Postcondition: Constructs a LEFTISTTREE containing x at its root and having children t_1 and t_2.

LEFTISTTREE(x : KEYED, t_1 : LEFTISTTREE, t_2 : LEFTISTTREE)
    if x = nil **or** t_1 = nil **or** t_2 = nil
        error
    else if t_1.*nullPathLength* ≥ t_2.*nullPathLength*
        leftChild ← t_1; *rightChild* ← t_2
    else
        leftChild ← t_2; *rightChild* ← t_1
    root ← x; *nullPathLength* ← 1 + *rightChild*.*nullPathLength*

---

items in the priority queue. Though it requires some work, it can be shown that the lower bound for each of these running times is in $\Omega(\lg n)$.

It is easy to see that the stack space usage of MERGE is proportional to the depth of recursion, which in turn is proportional to the running time.

Figure 5.8 LEFTISTHEAP implementation of PRIORITYQUEUE

Structural Invariant: *elements* is a leftist heap whose size is given by *size* and whose nodes are KEYED items.

LEFTISTHEAP()
    elements ← **new** LEFTISTTREE(); *size* ← 0

LEFTISTHEAP.PUT(x, p : NUMBER)
    elements ← MERGE(*elements*, **new** LEFTISTTREE(**new** KEYED(x, p)))
    size ← *size* + 1

LEFTISTHEAP.MAXPRIORITY()
    return *elements*.ROOT().KEY()

LEFTISTHEAP.REMOVEMAX()
    x ← *elements*.ROOT().DATA()
    elements ← MERGE(*elements*.LEFTCHILD(), *elements*.RIGHTCHILD())
    size ← *size* − 1
    return x

— **Internal Functions Follow** —

Precondition: h_1 and h_2 are LEFTISTTREEs storing heaps.
Postcondition: Returns a LEFTISTTREE containing the elements of h_1 and h_2 in a heap.

LEFTISTHEAP.MERGE(h_1, h_2)
    if h_1.ROOT() = nil
        return h_2
    else if h_2.ROOT() = nil
        return h_1
    else if h_1.ROOT().KEY() > h_2.ROOT().KEY()
        L ← h_1; S ← h_2
    else
        L ← h_2; S ← h_1
    t ← MERGE(L.RIGHTCHILD(), S)
    return new LEFTISTTREE(L.ROOT(), L.LEFTCHILD(), t)

Therefore, MERGE, and hence PUT and REMOVEMAX, uses $\Theta(\lg n)$ stack space in the worst case. The remaining space usage is in $\Theta(1)$.

Example 5.2. Consider the leftist heap shown in Figure 5.6(a). Suppose we were to perform a REMOVEMAX on this heap. To obtain the resulting heap, we must merge the two children of the root. The larger of the two keys is 15; hence, it becomes the new root. We must then merge its right child with the original right child of 20 (see Figure 5.6(b)). The larger of the two roots is 13, so it becomes the root of this subtree. The subtree rooted at 7 is then merged with the empty right child of 13. Figure 5.6(c) shows the result without considering the null path lengths. We must therefore make sure that in each subtree that we've formed, the null path length of the right child is no greater than the null path length of the left child. This is the case for the subtree rooted at 13, but not for the subtree rooted at 15. We therefore must swap the children of 15, yielding the final result shown in Figure 5.6(d).

A PUT operation is performed by creating a single-node heap from the element to be inserted, then merging the two heaps as in the above example. The web site that accompanies this textbook contains a program for viewing and manipulating various kinds of heaps, including leftist heaps and the heaps discussed in the remainder of this chapter. This heap viewer can be useful for generating other examples in order to understand the behavior of heaps.

It turns out that in order to obtain $O(\lg n)$ worst-case performance, it is not always necessary to follow the shortest path to a nonempty subtree. For example, if we maintain a tree such that for each of its n nodes, the left child has at least as many nodes as the right child, then the distance from the root to the rightmost subtree is still no more than $\lg(n+1)$. As a result, we can use this strategy for obtaining $O(\lg n)$ worst-case performance for the PRIORITYQUEUE operations (see Exercise 5.7 for details). However, we really don't gain anything from this strategy, as it is now necessary to maintain the size of each subtree instead of each null path length. In the next two sections, we will see that it is possible to achieve good performance without maintaining any such auxiliary information.

5.4   Skew Heaps

In this section, we consider a simple modification to SIMPLEHEAP that yields good performance without the need to maintain auxiliary information such as null path lengths. The idea is to avoid the bad performance of SIMPLEHEAP

Figure 5.9   The SKEWHEAP.MERGE internal function

Precondition: h_1 and h_2 are (possibly nil) BINARYTREENODES representing heaps with no nodes in common.
Postcondition: Returns a heap containing all of the nodes in h_1 and h_2.

SKEWHEAP.MERGE(h_1, h_2)
    if h_1 = nil
       return h_2
    else if h_2 = nil
       return h_1
    else
       if h_1.ROOT().KEY() > h_2.ROOT().KEY()
          $L \leftarrow h_1$; $S \leftarrow h_2$
       else
          $L \leftarrow h_2$; $S \leftarrow h_1$
       $t \leftarrow$ MERGE(L.RIGHTCHILD(), S)
       L.SETRIGHTCHILD(L.LEFTCHILD()); L.SETLEFTCHILD(t)
       return L

---

by modifying MERGE to swap the children after the recursive call. We call this modified structure a *skew heap*. The MERGE function for SKEWHEAP is shown in Figure 5.9; the remainder of the implementation of SKEWHEAP is the same as for SIMPLEHEAP.

Example 5.3. Consider again the heap shown in Figure 5.6(a), and suppose it is a skew heap. Performing a REMOVEMAX on this heap proceeds as shown in Figure 5.6 through part (c). At this point, however, for each node at which a recursive MERGE was performed, the children of this node are swapped. These nodes are 13 and 15. The resulting heap is shown in Figure 5.10.

In order to understand why such a simple modification might be advantageous, observe that in MERGE, when S is merged with L.RIGHTCHILD(), we might expect the resulting heap to have a tendency to be larger than L.LEFTCHILD(). As we noted at the end of the previous section, good worst-case behavior can be obtained by ensuring that the left child of each node has at least as many nodes as the right child. Intuitively, we might be able to approximate this behavior by swapping the children after every recursive call. However, this swapping does not always avoid expensive operations.

Suppose, for example, that we start with an empty skew heap, then insert the sequence of keys $2, 1, 4, 3, \ldots, 2i, 2i - 1, 0$, for some $i \geq 1$. Figure 5.11

Figure 5.10 The result of performing a REMOVEMAX on the skew heap shown in Figure 5.6(a)

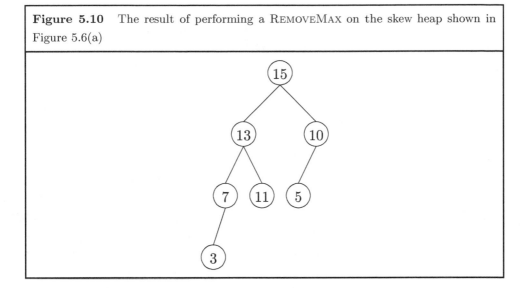

Figure 5.11 Construction of a bad skew heap

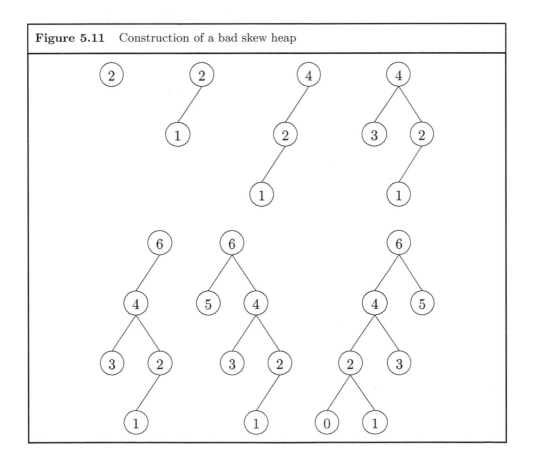

shows this sequence of insertions for $i = 3$. Note that each time an even key is inserted, because it is the largest in the heap, it becomes the new root and the original heap becomes its left child. Then when the next key is inserted, because it is smaller than the root, it is merged with the empty right child, then swapped with the other child. Thus, after each odd key is inserted, the heap will contain all the even keys in the rightmost path (i.e., the path beginning at the root and going to the right until it reaches an empty subtree), and for $i \geq 1$, key $2i$ will have key $2i - 1$ as its left child. Finally, when key 0 is inserted, because it is the smallest key in the heap, it will successively be merged with each right child until it is merged with the empty subtree at the far right. Each of the subtrees on this path to the right is then swapped with its sibling. Clearly, this last insertion requires $\Theta(i)$ running time, and i is proportional to the number of nodes in the heap.

The bad behavior described above results because a long rightmost path is constructed. Note, however, that $2i$ PUT operations were needed to construct this path. Each of these operations required only $\Theta(1)$ time. Furthermore, after the $\Theta(i)$ operation, no long rightmost paths exist from any node in the heap (see Figure 5.11). This suggests that a skew heap might have good amortized running time.

A good measure of the actual cost of the SKEWHEAP operations is the number of calls to MERGE, including recursive calls. In order to derive a bound on the amortized cost, let us try to find a good potential function. Based upon the above discussion, let us say that a node is *good* if its left child has at least as many nodes as its right child; otherwise, it is *bad*. We now make two key observations, whose proofs are left as exercises:

- In any binary tree with n nodes, the number of good nodes in the rightmost path is no more than $\lg(n + 1)$.
- In the MERGE function, if L is a bad node initially, it will be a good node in the resulting heap.

Due to these observations, we use as our potential function the number of bad nodes in the heap. Because the number of good nodes in each of the two rightmost paths is logarithmic, the potential function can increase by only a logarithmic amount on any MERGE. Furthermore, because any bad node encountered becomes good, the resulting change in potential will cancel the actual cost associated with this call, leaving only a logarithmic number of calls whose actual costs are not canceled. As a result, we should expect the amortized costs of the SKEWHEAP operations to be in $O(\lg n)$, where n is the number of elements in the priority queue (the details of the analysis are left as an exercise). Thus, a SKEWHEAP provides a simple, yet efficient, implementation of PRIORITYQUEUE.

We should caution, however, that it does not make sense to amortize space usage, as this usage does not accumulate over time. Specifically, the worst-case stack space usage of MERGE, as for leftist heaps, is proportional to its worst-case running time. Hence, the worst-case stack space usage is in $\Theta(n)$. On the other hand, it is possible to reorganize this algorithm so that it uses iteration, rather than recursion. Although the algorithm given in Figure 5.9 is not tail recursive, it is possible to order the operations so that the recursion can be removed in a similar way. We leave the details as an exercise. Removing the recursion in this way reduces the total space usage to $\Theta(1)$.

5.5   Randomized Heaps

For all of the heap implementations we have seen so far, the merge uses the right child in the recursive call. This choice is not necessary for the correctness of any of the algorithms, but does impact their performance.

Figure 5.12   The RANDOMIZEDHEAP.MERGE internal function

Precondition: h_1 and h_2 are (possibly nil) BINARYTREENODEs representing heaps with no nodes in common.
Postcondition: Returns a heap containing all of the nodes in h_1 and h_2.

RANDOMIZEDHEAP.MERGE(h_1, h_2)
   if $h_1 = $ nil
      return h_2
   else if $h_2 = $ nil
      return h_1
   else
      if h_1.ROOT().KEY() $>$ h_2.ROOT().KEY()
         $L \leftarrow h_1; S \leftarrow h_2$
      else
         $L \leftarrow h_2; S \leftarrow h_1$
      if FLIPCOIN() $= $ heads
         L.SETLEFTCHILD(MERGE(L.LEFTCHILD(), S))
      else
         L.SETRIGHTCHILD(MERGE(L.RIGHTCHILD(), S))
      return L

SIMPLEHEAP.MERGE performs badly because all recursive calls use right children, and their results all form right children. Leftist heaps and skew heaps avoid this bad performance by using the results of the recursive calls as left children, at least part of the time. Another approach is to use different children in different calls. Specifically, when we make a recursive call, we can flip a coin to determine which child to use.

The resulting MERGE function is shown in Figure 5.12; the remainder of the implementation of RANDOMIZEDHEAP is identical to the implementations of SIMPLEHEAP and SKEWHEAP. We assume that the FLIPCOIN function returns **heads** or **tails** randomly with uniform probability. Thus, each call to FLIPCOIN returns **heads** with probability 1/2, regardless of the results of any prior calls. This function can typically be implemented using a built-in random number generator. Most platforms provide a function returning random values uniformly distributed over the range of signed integers on that platform. In a standard signed integer representation, the negative values comprise exactly half the range. The FLIPCOIN function can therefore generate a random integer and return **heads** iff that integer is negative.

It usually makes no sense to analyze the worst-case running time for a randomized algorithm, because the running time usually depends on random events. For example, if a given heap consists of a single path with n nodes, the algorithm could follow exactly that path. However, this could only happen for one particular sequence of n coin flips. If any of the flips differ from this sequence, the algorithm reaches a base case and terminates at that point. Because the probability of flipping this exact sequence is very small for large n, a worst-case analysis seems inappropriate. Perhaps more to the point, a worst-case analysis would ignore the effect of randomization, and so does not seem appropriate for a randomized algorithm.

Instead, we can analyze the *expected* running time of a randomized algorithm. The goal of expected-case analysis is to bound the average performance over all possible executions on a worst-case input. For an ordinary deterministic algorithm, there is only one possible execution on any given input, but for randomized algorithms, there can be many possible executions depending on the random choices made.

Expected-case analysis is based on the expected values of random variables over discrete probability spaces. A *discrete probability space* is a countable set of *elementary events*, each having a *probability*.

> A set is said to countable *if each element can be labeled with a unique natural number.*

For an elementary event e in a discrete probability space S, we denote the probability of e by $P(e)$. For any discrete probability space S, we require that $0 \leq P(e) \leq 1$ and that

$$\sum_{e \in S} P(e) = 1.$$

As a simple example, consider the flipping of a fair coin. The probability space is $\{\mathsf{heads}, \mathsf{tails}\}$, and each of these two elementary events has probability $1/2$. For a more involved example, let T be a binary tree, and consider the probability space $Path_T$ consisting of paths from the root of T to empty subtrees. We leave as an exercise to show that if T has n nodes, then it has $n + 1$ empty subtrees; hence $Path_T$ has $n + 1$ elements. In order that it be a probability space, we need to assign a probability to each path. The probability of a given path of length k should be the same as the probability of the sequence of k coin flips that yields this path in the MERGE algorithm; thus, if the path corresponds to k flips, its probability should be 2^{-k}. We leave as an exercise to prove that the sum of these probabilities is 1 for any binary tree.

An important element of expected-case analysis is the notion of a *discrete random variable*, which is a function $f : S \to \mathbb{R}$, where S is a discrete probability space. In this text, we will restrict our random variables to nonnegative values. For an example of a random variable, let $len_T(e)$ give the length of a path e in the probability space $Path_T$ defined above. The *expected value* of a random variable f over a probability space S is defined to be

> More precisely, $len_T(e)$ is the number of coin flips that are needed to generate e.

$$E[f] = \sum_{e \in S} f(e)P(e).$$

Thus, by multiplying the value of the random variable for each elementary event by the probability of that elementary event, we obtain an average value for that variable. Note that it is possible for an expected value to be infinite. If the summation converges, however, it converges to a unique value, because all terms are nonnegative.

Example 5.4. Let T be a binary tree with n nodes, such that all paths from the root to empty subtrees have the same length. Because the probability of each path is determined solely by its length, all paths must have the same probability. Because there are $n + 1$ paths and the sum of their probabilities is 1, each path must have probability $1/(n+1)$. In this case, $E[len_T]$ is simply the arithmetic mean, or simple average, of all of the lengths:

$$E[len_T] = \sum_{e \in Path_T} len_T(e)P(e)$$

$$= \frac{1}{n+1} \sum_{e \in Path_T} len_T(e).$$

Furthermore, because the lengths of all of the paths are the same, $E[len_T]$ must be this length, which we will denote by k.

We have defined the probability of a path of length k to be 2^{-k}. Furthermore, we have seen that all probabilities are $1/(n+1)$. We therefore have

$$2^{-k} = 1/(n+1).$$

Solving for k, we have

$$k = \lg(n+1).$$

Thus, $E[len_T] = \lg(n+1)$.

The discrete random variable len_T is always a natural number. When this is the case, its expected value is often easier to analyze. To show why, we first need to define an *event*, which is any subset of the elementary events in a discrete probability space. The probability of an event A is the sum of the probabilities of its elementary events; i.e.,

$$P(A) = \sum_{e \in A} P(e).$$

Note that because the sum of the probabilities of all elementary events in a discrete probability space is 1, the probability of an event is never more than 1.

The following theorem gives a technique for computing expected values of discrete random variables that range over the natural numbers. It uses predicates like "$f = i$" to describe events; e.g., the predicate "$f = i$" defines the event in which f has the value i, and $P(f = i)$ is the probability of this event.

Theorem 5.5. *Let $f : S \to \mathbb{N}$ be a discrete random variable. Then*

$$E[f] = \sum_{i=1}^{\infty} P(f \geq i).$$

The idea behind the proof is that $P(f = i) = P(f \geq i) - P(f \geq i+1)$. The definition of $E[f]$ then yields

$$E[f] = \sum_{e \in S} f(e)P(e)$$

$$= \sum_{i=0}^{\infty} iP(f = i)$$

$$= \sum_{i=0}^{\infty} i(P(f \geq i) - P(f \geq i+1))$$

$$= \sum_{i=0}^{\infty} (iP(f \geq i) - iP(f \geq i+1)).$$

In the above sum, the negative portion $iP(f \geq i+1)$ of the ith term cancels most of the positive portion $(i+1)P(f \geq i+1)$ of the $(i+1)$st term. The result of this cancellation is the desired sum. However, in order for this reasoning to be valid, it must be the case that the "leftover" term, $-iP(f \geq i+1)$, converges to 0 as i approaches infinity if $E[f]$ is finite. We leave the details as an exercise.

Example 5.6. Let T be a binary tree in which each of the n nodes has an empty left child; i.e., the nodes form a single path going to the right. Again, the size of $Path_T$ is $n + 1$, but now the probabilities are not all the same. The length of the path to the rightmost empty subtree is n; hence, its probability is 2^{-n}. For $1 \leq i \leq n$, there is exactly one path that goes right $i - 1$ times and left once. The probabilities for these paths are given by 2^{-i}. We therefore have

$$E[len_T] = \sum_{e \in Path_T} len_T(e)P(e)$$

$$= n2^{-n} + \sum_{i=1}^{n} i2^{-i}.$$

Because we have no formula to evaluate the above summation, let us instead apply Theorem 5.5. The probability that a given path has length at least i, for $1 \leq i \leq n$, is the probability that $i-1$ coin flips all yield **tails**. This probability is 2^{1-i}. The probability that a given path has length at least i

for $i > n$ is 0. By Theorem 5.5, we therefore have

$$E[len_T] = \sum_{i=1}^{\infty} P(len_T \geq i)$$

$$= \sum_{i=1}^{n} 2^{1-i}$$

$$= \sum_{i=0}^{n-1} (1/2)^i$$

$$= \frac{(1/2)^n - 1}{(1/2) - 1} \qquad \text{(by (2.2))}$$

$$= 2 - 2^{1-n}.$$

Thus, $E[len_T] < 2$.

In order to be able to analyze the expected running time of RANDOM-IZEDHEAP.MERGE, we need to know $E[len_T]$ for a worst-case binary tree T with n nodes. Examples 5.4 and 5.6 give two extreme cases — a completely balanced tree and a completely unbalanced tree. We might guess that the worst case would be one of these extremes. Because $\lg(n + 1) \geq 2 - 2^{1-n}$ for all $n \in \mathbb{N}$, a good guess would be that $\lg(n + 1)$ is an upper bound for the worst case. We can show that this is indeed the case, but we need to use the following theorem relating the sum of logarithms to the logarithm of a sum.

Theorem 5.7. *If x and y are positive real numbers, then*

$$\lg x + \lg y \leq 2 \lg(x + y) - 2.$$

Proof.   We first note that $\lg x + \lg y = \lg xy$. We will therefore show that the right-hand side of the inequality is at least $\lg xy$. Using the fact that $\lg 4 = 2$, we have

$$2 \lg(x + y) - 2 = \lg((x + y)^2) - \lg 4$$

$$= \lg\left(\frac{x^2 + 2xy + y^2}{4}\right).$$

In order to isolate $\lg xy$, let us now subtract xy from the fraction in the above equation. This yields

$$2\lg(x+y) - 2 = \lg\left(\frac{x^2 + 2xy + y^2}{4}\right)$$

$$= \lg\left(xy + \frac{x^2 - 2xy + y^2}{4}\right)$$

$$= \lg\left(xy + \frac{(x-y)^2}{4}\right)$$

$$\geq \lg xy,$$

because $(x-y)^2/4$ is always nonnegative and the $\lg$ function is non-decreasing. □

We can now show that $\lg(n+1)$ is an upper bound for $E[len_T]$ when T is a binary tree with n nodes.

Theorem 5.8. *Let T be any binary tree with size n, where $n \in \mathbb{N}$. Then $E[len_T] \leq \lg(n+1)$.*

Proof. By induction on n.

Base: $n = 0$. Then only one path to an empty tree exists, and its length is 0. Hence, $E[len_T] = 0 = \lg 1$.

Induction Hypothesis: Assume that for some $n > 0$, if S is any binary tree with size $i < n$, then $E[len_S] \leq \lg(i+1)$.

Induction Step: Suppose T has size n. Because $n > 0$, T is nonempty. Let L and R be the left and right children, respectively, of T. We then have

$$E[len_T] = \sum_{e \in Path_T} len_T(e)P(e)$$

$$= \sum_{e \in Path_L} (len_L(e) + 1)\frac{P(e)}{2} + \sum_{e \in Path_R} (len_R(e) + 1)\frac{P(e)}{2}, \quad (5.1)$$

because the probability of any path from the root of a child of T to any empty subtree is twice the probability of the path from the root of T to the same empty subtree, and its length is one less.

Because the two sums in (5.1) are similar, we will simplify just the first one. Thus,

$$\sum_{e \in Path_L} (len_L(e) + 1) \frac{P(e)}{2} = \frac{1}{2} \left(\sum_{e \in Path_L} len_L(e)P(e) + \sum_{e \in Path_L} P(e) \right)$$

$$= \frac{1}{2} \left(\sum_{e \in Path_L} len_L(e)P(e) + 1 \right),$$

because in $Path_L$, the sum of the probabilities is 1. We now observe that

$$\sum_{e \in Path_L} len_L(e)P(e) = E[len_L].$$

Applying a similar simplification to the second sum in 5.1, we have

$$E[len_T] = 1 + (E[len_L] + E[len_R])/2.$$

Suppose L has size i. Then R has size $n - i - 1$. Because $0 \le i < n$, the Induction Hypothesis applies to both L and R. Thus,

$$E[len_T] \le 1 + (\lg(i + 1) + \lg(n - i))/2$$

$$\le 1 + (2\lg(n + 1) - 2)/2 \qquad \text{(by Theorem 5.7)}$$

$$= \lg(n + 1).$$

$\square$

The fact that the expected length of a randomly chosen path in a binary tree of size n is never more than $\lg(n+1)$ gives us reason to believe that the expected running time of RANDOMIZEDHEAP.MERGE is in $O(\lg n)$. However, MERGE operates on two binary trees. We therefore need a bound on the expected sum of the lengths of two randomly chosen paths, one from each of two binary trees. Hence, we will combine two probability spaces $Path_S$ and $Path_T$ to form a new discrete probability space $Paths_{S,T}$. The elementary events of this space will be pairs consisting of an elementary event from $Path_S$ and an elementary event from $Path_T$.

We need to assign probabilities to the elementary events in $Paths_{S,T}$. In so doing, we need to reflect the fact that the lengths of any two paths from S and T are independent of each other; i.e., knowing the length of one path tells us nothing about the length of the other path. Let e_1 and e_2 be events over a discrete probability space S. We say that e_1 and e_2 are *independent* if $P(e_1 \cap e_2) = P(e_1)P(e_2)$.

Suppose we were to define a new discrete probability space S_{e_2} including only those elementary events in the event e_2. The sum of the probabilities of these elementary events is $P(e_2)$. If we were to scale all of these probabilities by dividing by $P(e_2)$, we would achieve a total probability of 1 while preserving the ratio of any two probabilities. The probability of event e_1 within S_{e_2} would be given by

$$P(e_1 \mid e_2) = \frac{P(e_1 \cap e_2)}{P(e_2)}, \tag{5.2}$$

where the probabilities on the right-hand side are with respect to S. We call $P(e_1 \mid e_2)$ the *conditional probability of e_1 given e_2*. Note that if $P(e_2) \neq 0$, independence of e_1 and e_2 is equivalent to $P(e_1) = P(e_1 \mid e_2)$. Thus, two events are independent if knowledge of one event does not affect the probability of the other.

The definition of independence tells us how to assign the probabilities in $Paths_{S,T}$. Let e_1 be the event such that the path in S is s, and let e_2 be the event such that the path in T is t. Then $e_1 \cap e_2$ is the elementary event consisting of paths s and t. We need $P(e_1 \cap e_2) = P(e_1)P(e_2)$ in order to achieve independence. However, $P(e_1)$ should be the probability of s in $Paths_S$, and $P(e_2)$ should be the probability of t in $Path_T$. Thus the probability of an elementary event in $Paths_{S,T}$ must be the product of the probabilities of the constituent elementary events from $Paths_S$ and $Path_T$. It is then not hard to verify that $P(e_1)$ and $P(e_2)$ are the probabilities of s in $Paths_S$ and of t in $Path_T$, respectively.

We now extend the discrete random variables len_S and len_T to the space $Paths_{S,T}$ so that len_S gives the length of the path in S and len_T gives the length of the path in T. Because neither the lengths of the paths nor their probabilities change when we make this extension, it is clear that their expected values do not change either.

The running time of RANDOMIZEDHEAP.MERGE is clearly proportional to the lengths of the paths followed in the two heaps S and T. These paths may or may not go all the way to an empty subtree, but if not, we can extend them to obtain elementary events s and t in $Paths_S$ and $Path_T$, respectively. The running time is then bounded above by $c(len_S(s) + len_T(t))$, where c is some fixed positive constant. The expected running time of MERGE is therefore bounded above by $E[c(len_S + len_T)]$. In order to bound this expression, we need the following theorem.

Theorem 5.9 (Linearity of Expectation). *Let f, g, and h_i be discrete random variables for all $i \in \mathbb{N}$, and let $a \in \mathbb{R}^{\geq 0}$. Then*

$$E[af + g] = aE[f] + E[g],$$

and

$$E\left[\sum_{i=0}^{\infty} h_i\right] = \sum_{i=0}^{\infty} E[h_i].$$

The proof of this theorem is straightforward and left as an exercise. It is important to realize not only what this theorem says, but also what it doesn't say. For example, it is not necessarily the case that $E[fg] = E[f]E[g]$, or that $E[2^f] = 2^{E[f]}$ — see Exercise 5.18 for specific counterexamples. We must therefore be very careful in working with expected values, as they do not always behave as our intuition might suggest.

Applying Theorems 5.9 and 5.7 to our analysis, we now see that

$$E[c(len_S + len_T)] = c(E[len_S] + E[len_T])$$
$$\leq c(\lg(|S| + 1) + \lg(|T| + 1))$$
$$\leq 2c\lg(|S| + |T| + 2),$$

where $|S|$ and $|T|$ denote the sizes of S and T, respectively. Thus, the expected running time of MERGE is in $O(\lg n)$, where n is the total number of nodes in the two heaps. It follows that the expected running times of PUT and REMOVEMAX are also in $O(\lg n)$.

A close examination of Example 5.4 reveals that the bound of $\lg(n + 1)$ on $E[len_T]$ is reached when $n + 1$ is a power of 2. Using the fact that $\lg$ is smooth, we can then show that the expected running time of MERGE is in $\Omega(\lg n)$; the details are left as an exercise. Thus, the expected running times of PUT and REMOVEMAX are in $\Theta(\lg n)$.

It is also clear that the stack space usage of MERGE is proportional to the depth of recursion, which is proportional to the running time. As a result, the expected stack space usage of MERGE, and hence of PUT and REMOVEMAX, is in $\Theta(\lg n)$. While this result is positive, it might be worthwhile to consider the worst-case stack space usage, as high stack space usage will cause a program to terminate abnormally. In the worst case, all nodes in a single tree can be in the same path, and MERGE can follow this path to the end. Hence, in the worst case, MERGE, PUT, and REMOVEMAX can use $\Theta(n)$ stack space. On the other hand, the recursion can be removed in a similar way as we suggested for SKEWHEAP.MERGE. Doing so would reduce the total space usage to $\Theta(1)$.

5.6 Sorting and Binary Heaps

In Section 3.6, we saw how to sort an array in $\Theta(n^2)$ time. A priority queue can be used to improve this performance. Using either a LEFTISTHEAP or a SKEWHEAP, we can insert n elements in $\Theta(n \lg n)$ time, by Theorem 3.31. We can then sort the items in the heap by removing the maximum in $\Theta(\lg n)$ time and sorting the remainder. It is easily seen that this entire algorithm runs in $\Theta(n \lg n)$ time.

In order to improve further the performance of sorting, we would like to avoid the need to use an auxiliary data structure. Specifically, we would like to keep the data items in a single array, which is partitioned into an unsorted part followed by a sorted part, as illustrated in Figure 5.13(a). The unsorted part will, in essence, be a representation of a priority queue — we will explain the details of this representation in what follows. This priority queue will contain keys that are no larger than any of the keys in the sorted part. When we remove the maximum element from the priority queue, this frees up an array location, as shown in Figure 5.13(b). We can put the element that we removed from the priority queue into this location. Because

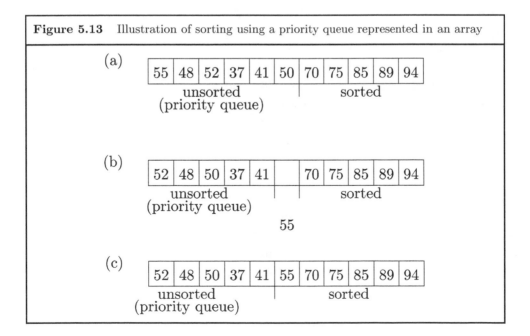

Figure 5.13   Illustration of sorting using a priority queue represented in an array

Figure 5.14   A binary heap

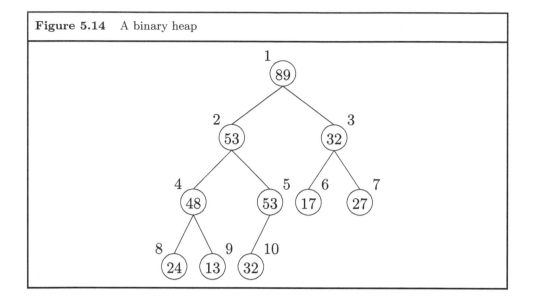

this key is at least as large as any key in the priority queue, but no larger than any key in the sorted part, we can extend the sorted part to include this location (see Figure 5.13(c)).

We therefore need to be able to represent a heap using an array. One way to accomplish this is to number the nodes left-to-right by levels, as shown in Figure 5.14. The numbers we have assigned to the nodes can be used as array indices. In order to avoid ambiguity, there should be no "missing" nodes; i.e., each level except possibly the last should be completely full, and all of the nodes in the last level should be as far to the left as possible. This scheme for storing a heap is known as a *binary heap*.

Note that a binary heap is very nearly balanced. We saw in Example 5.4 that in a completely balanced binary tree with n nodes, the length of any path to an empty subtree is $\lg(n+1)$. This result holds only for tree sizes that can be completely balanced. However, it is not hard to show that for any n, if a binary tree with n nodes is balanced as nearly as possible, the length of the longest path to an empty subtree is $\lceil \lg(n + 1) \rceil$ (or equivalently, the height is $\lceil \lg(n+1) \rceil - 1$). We will show that this fact allows us to implement both PUT and REMOVEMAX for a binary heap in $\Theta(\lg n)$ time.

Note that each level of a binary heap, except the first and possibly the last, contains exactly twice as many nodes as the level above it. Thus, if we were to number the levels starting with 0 for the top level, then each level i (except possibly the last) contains exactly 2^i nodes. It follows from (2.2) that levels 0 through $i - 1$, where i is strictly less than the total number of levels, have a total of $2^i - 1$ nodes. Let x be the jth node on level i. x would then have index $2^i - 1 + j$. Suppose x has a left child, y. In order to compute its index, we observe that level i has $j - 1$ nodes to the left of x. Each of these nodes has two children on level $i + 1$ to the left of node y. Therefore, the index of y is

$$2^{i+1} - 1 + 2(j - 1) + 1 = 2^{i+1} + 2j - 2,$$

or exactly twice the index of its parent. Likewise, if x has a right child, its index is 1 greater than that of y.

As a result of these relationships, we can use simple calculations to find either child or the parent of a node at a given location. Specifically, the left and right children of the element at location i are the elements at locations $2i$ and $2i + 1$, respectively, provided they exist. Furthermore, the parent of the element at location $i > 1$ is at location $\lfloor i/2 \rfloor$.

Let us consider how we can implement a binary heap as a data structure. We will use two representation variables:

- *elements*[0..m]: an array of KEYED items; and
- *size*: a NAT.

We allow read access to *size*. For reasons that will become clear shortly, *elements*[0] will act as a sentinel element, and will have as its key the maximum allowable value. For convenience, we will use a constant **sentinel** to represent such a data item.

> A sentinel element *is an extra element added to a data structure in order to indicate when a traversal of that structure has reached the end.*

Note because $\lfloor 1/2 \rfloor = 0$, we can treat *elements*[0] as if it were the parent of *elements*[1].

The structural invariant will be:

- *size* $\leq$ SIZEOF(*elements*);
- *elements*[0] = **sentinel**; and
- for $1 \leq i \leq$ *size*, *elements*[i].KEY() $\leq$ *elements*[$\lfloor i/2 \rfloor$].KEY().

We interpret *elements*[1..*size*] as the elements of the set being represented, together with their associated priorities.

Unfortunately, the algorithms for merging heaps don't work for binary heaps because they don't maintain the balanced shape. Therefore, let us consider how to insert an element x into a binary heap. If *size* is 0, then we can simply make x the root. Otherwise, we need to compare x.KEY() with the key of the root. The larger of the two will be the new root, and we can then insert the other into one of the children. We select which child based on where we need the new leaf.

In this insertion algorithm, unless the tree is empty, there will always be a recursive call. This recursive call will always be on the child in the path that leads to the location at which we want to add the new node. Note that the keys along this path from the root to the leaf are in nonincreasing order. As long as the key to be inserted is smaller than the key to which it is compared, it will be the inserted element in the recursive call. When it is compared with a smaller key, that smaller key is used in the recursive call. When this happens, the key passed to the recursive call will always be at least as large as the root of the subtree in which it is being inserted; thus, it will become the new root, and the old root will be used in the recursive call. Thus, the entire process results in inserting the new key at the proper point in the path from the root to the desired insertion location.

For example, suppose we wish to insert the priority 35 into the binary heap shown in Figure 5.15(a). We first find the path to the next insertion point. This path is $\langle 89, 32, 17 \rangle$. The proper position of 35 in this path is between 89 and 32. We insert 35 at this point, pushing the following priorities downward. The result is shown in Figure 5.15(b).

Because we can easily find the parent of a node in a BINARYHEAP, we can implement this algorithm bottom-up by starting at the location of the

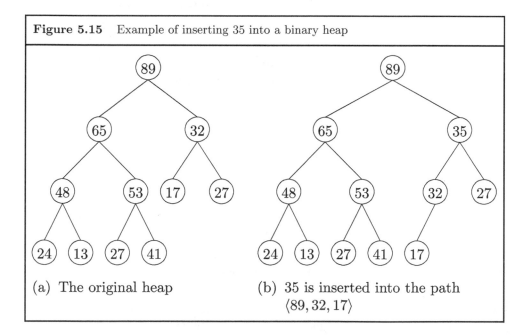

Figure 5.15 Example of inserting 35 into a binary heap

(a) The original heap

(b) 35 is inserted into the path $\langle 89, 32, 17 \rangle$

new leaf and shifting elements downward one level until we reach a location where the new element will fit. This is where having a sentinel element is convenient — we know we will eventually find some element whose key is at least as large as that of x. The resulting algorithm is shown in Figure 5.16. We assume that EXPAND(A) returns an array of twice the size of A, with the elements of A copied to the first half of the returned array.

The REMOVEMAX operation is a bit more difficult. We need to remove the root because it contains the element with maximum priority, but in order to preserve the proper shape of the heap, we need to remove a specific leaf. We therefore first save the value of the root, then remove the proper leaf. We need to form a new heap by replacing the root with the removed leaf. In order to accomplish this, we use the MAKEHEAP algorithm shown in Figure 5.17. For ease of presentation, we assume t is formed with BINARYTREENODEs, rather than with an array. If the key of x is at least as large as the keys of the roots of all children of t, we can simply replace the root of t with x, and we are finished. Otherwise, we need to move the root of the child with larger key to the root of t and make a heap from this child and x. This is just a smaller instance of the original problem.

We can simplify MAKEHEAP somewhat when we use it with a binary heap. First, we observe that once we have determined that at least one child is nonempty, we can conclude that the left child must be nonempty. We also observe that the reduction is a transformation to a smaller instance; i.e.,

---

Figure 5.16   The BINARYHEAP.PUT operation

BINARYHEAP.PUT(x, p : NUMBER)
    size ← *size* + 1
    if *size* > SIZEOF(*elements*)
        elements ← EXPAND(*elements*)
    i ← *size*; *elements*[i] ← *elements*[$\lfloor i/2 \rfloor$]
    // **Invariant:** $1 \leq i \leq$ *size*, *elements*[1..*size*] forms a heap,
    // *elements*[0..*size*] contains the elements originally in
    // *elements*[0..*size* − 1], with *elements*[i] and *elements*[$\lfloor i/2 \rfloor$]
    // being duplicates, and $p >$ *elements*[j].KEY() for
    // $2i \leq j \leq \max(2i + 1, size)$.
    while $p >$ *elements*[i].KEY()
        i ← $\lfloor i/2 \rfloor$; *elements*[i] ← *elements*[$\lfloor i/2 \rfloor$]
    elements[i] ← **new** KEYED(x, p)

Figure 5.17   The MAKEHEAP algorithm

Precondition: x is a KEYED element and t is a BINARYTREENODE whose children are both heaps.
Postcondition: Forms a heap from t containing x and the elements of t's children without changing the shape of t.

MAKEHEAP(x, t)
   $L \leftarrow t.\text{LEFTCHILD}()$; $R \leftarrow t.\text{RIGHTCHILD}()$
   if $L = $ nil **and** $R = $ nil
     $t.\text{SETROOT}(x)$
   else
     if $L \neq $ nil
       if $R \neq $ nil **and** $L.\text{ROOT}().\text{KEY}() < R.\text{ROOT}().\text{KEY}()$
         largerChild $\leftarrow R$
       else
         largerChild $\leftarrow L$
     else
       largerChild $\leftarrow R$
     if $x.\text{KEY}() \geq$ *largerChild*$.\text{ROOT}().\text{KEY}()$
       $t.\text{SETROOT}(x)$
     else
       $t.\text{SETROOT}($*largerChild*$.\text{ROOT}())$
       MAKEHEAP$(x, $*largerChild*$)$

MAKEHEAP is tail recursive. We can therefore implement it using a loop. In order to simplify the statement of the loop invariant, we make use of the fact that the entire tree is initially a heap, so that the precondition of MAKEHEAP could be strengthened to specify that t is a heap. (Later we will use MAKEHEAP in a context in which we need the weaker precondition.) Figure 5.18 gives the entire REMOVEMAX operation without a separate MAKEHEAP function. Note that *elements*[*size*+1] in Figure 5.18 corresponds to x in Figure 5.17, *elements*[i] corresponds to t, and j corresponds to *largerChild*.

Notice that in REMOVEMAX, i is initialized to 1, the root of the heap, and on each iteration that does not cause the **while** condition to be false, i is set to j, the index of its larger child. Furthermore, on each iteration, *elements*[i] is set to either *elements*[$size + 1$] or *elements*[j]. In the latter case, the larger child of *elements*[i] is copied to *elements*[i], and in the former case, the removed leaf is placed in its proper location. Thus, as in the PUT

Figure 5.18 The BINARYHEAP.REMOVEMAX operation.

BINARYHEAP.REMOVEMAX()
  if *size* = 0
    error
  else
    $m \leftarrow elements[1].\text{DATA}(); size \leftarrow size - 1; i \leftarrow 1$
    // **Invariant:** *elements*[1..*size*] forms a heap; $1 \leq i \leq size + 1$;
    // *elements*[1..*i* − 1], *elements*[*i* + 1..*size* + 1], and *m* are
    // the elements in the original set;
    // $elements[size + 1].\text{KEY}() \leq elements[\lfloor i/2 \rfloor].\text{KEY}()$;
    // and *m* has maximum key.
    while $elements[i] \neq elements[size + 1]$
      $j \leftarrow 2i$
      if *j* > *size*
        $elements[i] \leftarrow elements[size + 1]$
      else
        if $j < size$ **and** $elements[j].\text{KEY}() < elements[j + 1].\text{KEY}()$
          $j \leftarrow j + 1$
        if $elements[j].\text{KEY}() \leq elements[size + 1].\text{KEY}()$
          $elements[i] \leftarrow elements[size + 1]$
        else
          $elements[i] \leftarrow elements[j]; i \leftarrow j$
    return *m*

---

operation, an element is inserted into a path in the heap; however, in this case, the path follows the larger of the children of a node, and the elements preceding the insertion location are moved upward.

For example, suppose we were to perform a REMOVEMAX on the binary heap shown in Figure 5.19(a). We would remove 89 and find the path that follows the larger child of each node. This path is $\langle 65, 48, 33 \rangle$. We would then insert 41, the last leaf, into this path between 48 and 33, moving the preceding priorities upward. The result is shown in Figure 5.19(b).

It is easily seen that both PUT and REMOVEMAX operate in $\Theta(\lg n)$ time, excluding any time needed to expand the array. Furthermore, as we saw in Section 4.3, we can amortize the cost of array expansion to constant time per insertion. The amortized running time for PUT is therefore in $\Theta(\lg n)$, and the worst-case time for REMOVEMAX is in $\Theta(\lg n)$.

We now return to the sorting problem. In order to sort an array A, we first need to arrange it into a binary heap. One approach is first to make

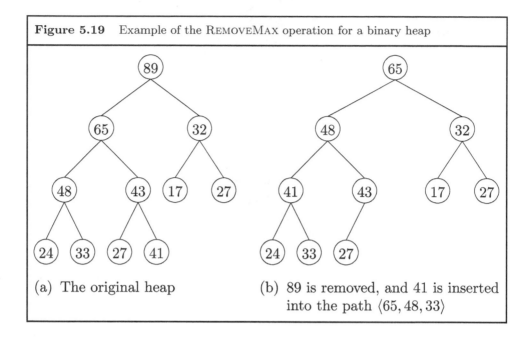

Figure 5.19   Example of the REMOVEMAX operation for a binary heap

(a) The original heap

(b) 89 is removed, and 41 is inserted into the path $\langle 65, 48, 33 \rangle$

$A[1..n-1]$ into a heap, then to insert $A[n]$. We can easily implement this bottom-up. The resulting algorithm does $n-1$ insertions into heaps of sizes ranging from 1 to $n-1$. The total running time is therefore in

$$\sum_{i=1}^{n-1} \Theta(\lg i) \subseteq \Theta((n-1)\lg(n-1)) \quad \text{(from Theorem 3.31)}$$

$$= \Theta(n \lg n).$$

We can do better, however, by viewing the array $A[1..n]$ as a binary tree in which the parent of $A[i]$ is $A[\lfloor i/2 \rfloor]$ for $i > 1$. With this view in mind, the natural approach seems to be to make the children into heaps first, then use MAKEHEAP to make the entire tree into a heap. The resulting algorithm is easiest to analyze when the tree is completely balanced — i.e., when $n+1$ is a power of 2. Let $N = n+1$, and let $f(N)$ give the worst-case running time for this algorithm. When N is a power of 2, we have

$$f(N) \in 2f(N/2) + \Theta(\lg N).$$

From Theorem 3.35, $f(N) \in \Theta(N) = \Theta(n)$.

This implementation of MAKEHEAP must be more general than the implementation used for BINARYHEAP. Specifically, we must be able to apply MAKEHEAP to arbitrary subtrees in order to be able to use it to form the heap initially. In order to allow us to express the specification of Figure 5.17 in terms of a binary heap, we introduce the notation TREE(A, k, n) to denote the binary tree formed by using $A[k]$ as the root, TREE($A, 2k, n$) as the left child, and TREE($A, 2k + 1, n$) as the right child, provided $k \leq n$. If $k > n$, TREE(A, k, n) denotes an empty tree. Thus, TREE($A, 1, n$) denotes the binary tree T implied by the array $A[1..n]$, and for $k \leq n$, TREE(A, k, n) denotes the subtree of T rooted at $A[k]$. The full implementation of HEAPSORT is shown in Figure 5.20.

It is not hard to show that MAKEHEAP operates in $\Theta(\lg(n/k))$ time in the worst case. It is easily seen that the first **for** loop in HEAPSORT operates in $O(n \lg n)$ time, though in fact a careful analysis shows that it runs in $\Theta(n)$ time, as suggested by the above discussion. It is not hard to show, using Theorem 3.31, that the second **for** loop operates in $\Theta(n \lg n)$ time in the worst case. Therefore, HEAPSORT runs in $\Theta(n \lg n)$ time in the worst case.

The only BINARYHEAP method that uses more than $O(1)$ space is the recursive method MAKEHEAP. This algorithm uses stack space proportional to its depth of recursion, which is in turn proportional to its running time. Thus, it uses $\Theta(\lg(n/k))$ stack space, which in the worst case is in $\Theta(\lg n)$. The stack space usage for HEAPSORT is therefore in $\Theta(\lg n)$.

5.7 Summary

A heap provides a clean framework for implementing a priority queue. Although LEFTISTHEAPs yield $\Theta(\lg n)$ worst-case performance for the operations PUT and REMOVEMAX, the simpler SKEWHEAPs and RANDOMIZEDHEAPs yield $O(\lg n)$ amortized and $\Theta(\lg n)$ expected costs, respectively, for these operations. On the other hand, stack space usage for these two implementations may be problematic unless the algorithms are restructured to use iteration rather than recursion. BINARYHEAPs, while providing no asymptotic improvements over LEFTISTHEAPs, nevertheless tend to be more efficient in practice because they require less dynamic memory allocation. They also provide the basis for HEAPSORT, a $\Theta(n \lg n)$ in-place sorting algorithm that uses $\Theta(\lg n)$ stack space in the worst case. A summary of the running times of the PRIORITYQUEUE operations for the various implementations is shown in Figure 5.21.

For the implementations that use a MERGE function, it is possible to provide MERGE as an operation. However, this operation is not very appropriate for the PRIORITYQUEUE ADT because we may need to require

---

Figure 5.20 HEAPSORT implementation of SORT, specified in Figure 1.1

HEAPSORT($A[1..n]$)
  // **Invariant:** $A[1..n]$ is a permutation of its original elements such
  // that for $2(i+1) \leq j \leq n$, $A[\lfloor j/2 \rfloor] \geq A[j]$.
  for $i \leftarrow \lfloor n/2 \rfloor$ **to** 1 **by** -1
    MAKEHEAP($A[1..n], i, A[i]$)
  // **Invariant:** $A[1..n]$ is a permutation of its original elements such
  // that for $2 \leq j \leq i$, $A[\lfloor j/2 \rfloor] \geq A[j]$, and
  // $A[1] \leq A[i+1] \leq A[i+2] \leq \cdots \leq A[n]$.
  for $i \leftarrow n$ **to** 2 **by** -1
    $t \leftarrow A[i]$; $A[i] \leftarrow A[1]$; MAKEHEAP($A[1..i-1], 1, t$)

Precondition: $A[1..n]$ is an array of NUMBERs such that TREE($A, 2k, n$) and TREE($A, 2k+1, n$) form heaps, $1 \leq k \leq n$, and x is a NUMBER.
Postcondition: TREE(A, k, n) is a heap containing a permutation of the original values of TREE($A, 2k, n$), TREE($A, 2k+1, n$), and x, and no other elements of A have changed.

MAKEHEAP($A[1..n], k, x$)
  $A[k] \leftarrow$ sentinel; $i \leftarrow k$
  // **Invariant:** TREE(A, k, n) forms a heap; $k \leq i \leq n$;
  // $A[i]$ belongs to TREE(A, k, n);
  // the elements of TREE(A, k, n), excluding $A[i]$, are the elements initially
  // in TREE($A, 2k, n$) and TREE($A, 2k+1, n$);
  // all other elements of A have their initial values;
  // and if $i \geq 2k$, then $x < A[\lfloor i/2 \rfloor]$.
  while $A[i] \neq x$
    $j \leftarrow 2i$
    if $j > n$
      $A[i] \leftarrow x$
    else
      if $j < n$ **and** $A[j] < A[j+1]$
        $j \leftarrow j+1$
      if $A[j] \leq x$
        $A[i] \leftarrow x$
      else
        $A[i] \leftarrow A[j]$; $i \leftarrow j$

Figure 5.21 Running times for the PRIORITYQUEUE operations for various implementations.

	PUT	REMOVEMAX
SORTEDARRAYPRIORITYQUEUE	$\Theta(n)$	$\Theta(1)$
SIMPLEHEAP	$\Theta(n)$	$\Theta(1)$
LEFTISTHEAP	$\Theta(\lg n)$	$\Theta(\lg n)$
SKEWHEAP	$O(\lg n)$ amortized	$O(\lg n)$ amortized
RANDOMIZEDHEAP	$\Theta(\lg n)$ expected	$\Theta(\lg n)$ expected
BINARYHEAP	$\Theta(\lg n)$ amortized	$\Theta(\lg n)$

Notes:

- n is the number of elements in the priority queue.
- Unless otherwise noted, all running times are worst-case.
- The constructor and the MAXPRIORITY and SIZE operations all run is $\Theta(1)$ worst-case time for all implementations.

the two priority queues to be of the same type. For example, if we added a MERGE operation to LEFTISTHEAP, we would need to require that the parameter is also a LEFTISTHEAP — MERGE(PRIORITYQUEUE) would be insufficient. Furthermore, we would need to be concerned with security because the resulting heap would share storage with the original heaps.

Using an immutable structure, as we did for LEFTISTHEAP, would take care of the security issue. With such implementations, the MERGE operation could be done in $\Theta(\lg n)$ worst-case time for a LEFTISTHEAP, or in $\Theta(\lg n)$ expected time for a RANDOMIZEDHEAP, where n is the sum of the sizes of the two priority queues. The amortized time for SKEWHEAP.MERGE, however, is not in $O(\lg n)$ unless we restrict the sequences of operations so that after two priority queues are merged, the original priority queues are not used in any subsequent operations; otherwise, we can repeatedly perform the same expensive MERGE.

In Section 5.5, we introduced the basics of expected-case analysis for randomized algorithms. Specifically, we showed how discrete random variables can be defined and manipulated in order to analyze expected running time. In Section 6.4, we will develop this theory more fully.

5.8   Exercises

Exercise 5.1. Complete the implementation of SORTEDARRAYPRIORITY-QUEUE shown in Figure 5.2 by adding a constructor and implementations of the MAXPRIORITY and REMOVEMAX operations. Prove that your implementation meets its specification.

Exercise 5.2. Prove that SIMPLEHEAP, shown in Figure 5.5, meets its specification.

Exercise 5.3. Show the result of first inserting the sequence of priorities below into a leftist heap, then executing one REMOVEMAX.

$$34, 12, 72, 15, 37, 49, 17, 55, 45$$

Exercise 5.4. Prove that LEFTISTTREE, shown in Figure 5.7, meets its specification.

Exercise 5.5. Prove that LEFTISTHEAP, shown in Figure 5.8, meets its specification.

* Exercise 5.6. Prove that for any $n \in \mathbb{N}$, if we insert a sequence of n strictly decreasing priorities into an initially empty leftist heap, we obtain a leftist heap with null path length $\lfloor \lg(n + 1) \rfloor$.

Exercise 5.7. Instead of keeping track of the null path lengths of each node, a variation on LEFTISTTREE keeps track of the number of nodes in each subtree, and ensures that the left child has as many nodes as the right child. We call this variation a LEFTHEAVYTREE.

a. Give an implementation of LEFTHEAVYTREE. The structure must be immutable, and each constructor must require only $\Theta(1)$ time.
b. Prove by induction on the number of nodes n in the tree that in any LEFTHEAVYTREE, the distance from the root to the rightmost empty subtree is no more than $\lg(n + 1)$.
c. Using the result of part 5.7, show that if we use LEFTHEAVYTREES instead of LEFTISTTREES in the implementation of LEFTISTHEAP, the running times of the operations are still in $O(\lg n)$, where n is the number of elements in the priority queue.

Figure 5.22   The HASPRIORITY interface

Precondition: true.

Postcondition: Returns a number representing a priority.

HASPRIORITY.PRIORITY()

Exercise 5.8. Repeat Exercise 5.3 using a skew heap instead of a leftist heap.

Exercise 5.9. Prove that SKEWHEAP, obtained by replacing the MERGE function in SIMPLEHEAP (Figure 5.5) with the function shown in Figure 5.9, meets its specification.

* Exercise 5.10. Another way of specifying a priority queue is to define an interface HASPRIORITY, as shown in Figure 5.22. Rather than supplying two arguments to the PUT operation, we could instead specify that it takes a single argument of type HASPRIORITY, where the priority of the item is given by its PRIORITY operation. Discuss the potential security problems for this approach. How could these problems be avoided if such a specification were adopted?

Exercise 5.11. The goal of this exercise is to complete the analysis of the amortized running times of the SKEWHEAP operations.

  a. Prove by induction on n that in any binary tree T with n nodes, the number of good nodes on its rightmost path is no more than $\lg(n+1)$, where the definition of a good node is as in Section 5.4.
  b. Prove that in the SKEWHEAP.MERGE operation (shown in Figure 5.9 on page 166) if L is initially a bad node, then it is a good node in the resulting heap.
  c. Given two skew heaps to be merged, let us define the potential of each node to be 0 if the node is good, or 1 if the node is bad. Using the results from parts (a) and (b) above, prove that the actual cost of the MERGE operation, plus the sum of the potentials of the nodes in the resulting heap, minus the sum of potentials of the nodes in the two original heaps, is in $O(\lg n)$ where n is the number of keys in the two heaps together.
  d. Using the result of part (c), prove that the amortized running times of the SKEWHEAP operations are in $O(\lg n)$, where n is the number of nodes in the heap.

* Exercise 5.12. Restructure SKEWHEAP.MERGE to replace the recursion with a loop. Your algorithm should use only $\Theta(1)$ space (apart from the space already used by the heaps). Prove that the data structure obtained by replacing the MERGE function in SIMPLEHEAP with this revised function meets the specification given in Figure 5.1.

Exercise 5.13. Prove that RANDOMIZEDHEAP, obtained by replacing the MERGE function in SIMPLEHEAP (Figure 5.5) with the function shown in Figure 5.12, meets specification given in Figure 5.1.

Exercise 5.14. Prove by induction on n that any binary tree with n nodes has exactly $n + 1$ empty subtrees.

Exercise 5.15. Prove by induction on the number of nodes in a binary tree T, that the sum of the probabilities in $Path_T$ is 1.

Exercise 5.16. The goal of this exercise is to prove Theorem 5.5. Let $f : S \to \mathbb{N}$ be a discrete random variable.

a. Prove by induction on n that

$$\sum_{i=0}^{n} iP(f = i) = \sum_{i=1}^{n} P(f \geq i) - nP(f \geq n+1).$$

b. Prove that for every $n \in N$,

$$\sum_{i=0}^{\infty} iP(f = i) \geq \sum_{i=0}^{n} iP(f = i) + nP(f \geq n+1).$$

c. Using the fact that if $g(i) \geq 0$ for all i, then

$$\sum_{i=0}^{\infty} g(i) = \lim_{n \to \infty} \sum_{i=0}^{n} g(i),$$

prove that if $E[f]$ is finite, then

$$\lim_{n \to \infty} nP(f \geq n+1) = 0.$$

d. Prove Theorem 5.5.

Exercise 5.17. Prove Theorem 5.9.

Exercise 5.18. Let S be the set of all sequences of four flips of a fair coin, where each sequence has probability $1/16$. Let h be the discrete random variable giving the number of **heads** in the sequence.

a. Compute $E[h]$.
b. Compute $E[h^2]$, and show that $E[h^2] \neq (E[h])^2$.
c. Compute $E[2^h]$, and show that $E[2^h] \neq 2^{E[h]}$.

Exercise 5.19. Use Example 5.4 to show that the expected running time of RANDOMIZEDHEAP.MERGE, shown in Figure 5.12, is in $\Omega(\lg n)$ in the worst case, where n is the number of elements in the two heaps combined.

Exercise 5.20. Complete the implementation of BINARYHEAP by adding a constructor and a MAXPRIORITY operation to the operations shown in Figures 5.16 and 5.18. Prove that the resulting implementation meets its specification.

Exercise 5.21. Repeat Exercise 5.3 using a binary heap instead of a leftist heap. Show the result as both a tree and an array.

Exercise 5.22. Prove that HEAPSORT, shown in Figure 5.20, meets its specification.

Exercise 5.23. Prove that the first loop in HEAPSORT runs in $\Theta(n)$ time in the worst case.

Exercise 5.24. Prove that HEAPSORT runs in $\Theta(n \lg n)$ time in the worst case.

Exercise 5.25. We can easily modify the SORT specification (Figure 1.2 on page 7) so that instead of sorting numbers, we are sorting KEYED items in nondecreasing order of their keys. HEAPSORT can be trivially modified to meet this specification. Any sorting algorithm meeting this specification is said to be *stable* if the resulting sorted array always has elements with equal keys in the same order as they were initially. Show that HEAPSORT, when modified to sort KEYED items, is not stable.

Exercise 5.26. Consider the following scheduling problem. We have a collection of jobs, each having a natural number *ready time* r_i, a positive integer *execution time* e_i, and a positive integer *deadline* d_i, such that $d_i \geq r_i + e_i$. At each natural number time instant t, we wish to schedule the job with minimum deadline satisfying the following conditions

- $t \geq r_i$ (i.e., the job is ready);
- if the job has already been executed for $a < e_i$ time units, then $t + e_i - a \leq d_i$ (i.e., the job can meet its deadline).

Note that this scheduling strategy may preempt jobs, and that it will discard jobs that have been delayed so long that they can no longer meet their deadlines. Give an algorithm to produce such a schedule, when given a sequence of jobs ordered by ready time. Your algorithm should store the ready jobs in an INVERTEDPRIORITYQUEUE. (You do not need to give an implementation of INVERTEDPRIORITYQUEUE.) Show that your algorithm operates in $O(k \lg n)$ time, where k is length of the schedule and n is the number of jobs. You may assume that $k \geq n$ and that PUT and REMOVEMIN both operate in $\Theta(\lg n)$ time in the worst case.

Exercise 5.27. The game of craps consists of a sequence of rolls of two six-sided dice with faces numbered 1 through 6. The first roll is known as the *come-out* roll. If the come-out roll is a 7 or 11 (the sum of the top faces of the two dice), the shooter wins. If the come-out roll is a 2, 3, or 12, the shooter loses. Otherwise, the result is known as the *point*. The shooter continues to roll until the result is either the point (in which case the shooter wins) or a 7 (in which case the shooter loses).

 a. For each of the values 2 through 12, compute the probability that any single roll is that value.
 b. A *field bet* can be made on any roll. For each dollar bet, the payout is determined by the roll as follows:

   • 2 or 12: \$3 (i.e., the bettor pays \$1 and receives \$3, netting \$2);
   • 3, 4, 9, 10 or 11: \$2;
   • 5, 6, 7, or 8: 0.

   Calculate the expected payout for a field bet.
 c. A *pass-line bet* is a bet, placed prior to the come-out roll, that the shooter will win. For each dollar bet, the payout for a win is \$2, whereas the payout for a loss is 0. Compute the expected payout for a pass-line bet. [**Hint:** The problem is much easier if you define a finite probability space, ignoring those rolls that don't affect the outcome. In order to do this you will need to use conditional probabilities (e.g., given that the roll is either a 5 or a 7, the probability that it is a 5).]

Exercise 5.28. Let S be a discrete probability space, and let f be a discrete random variable over S. Let a be any positive real number. Prove *Markov's Inequality*:

$$P(f \geq a) \leq E[f]/a. \tag{5.3}$$

5.9 Notes

Both heaps and heap sort were introduced by Williams [121]. The linear-time construction of a binary heap is due to Floyd [41]. Leftist heaps were introduced by Crane [26]; see also Knuth [84]. Skew heaps were introduced by Sleator and Tarjan [108]. Randomized heaps were introduced by Gambin and Malinowski [48].

Other implementations of priority queues have been defined based on the idea of a heap. For example, binomial queues were introduced by Vuillemin [116]. Lazy binomial queues and Fibonacci heaps, each of which provide PUT and REMOVEMAX operations with amortized running times in $O(1)$ and $O(\lg n)$, respectively, were introduced by Fredman and Tarjan [46].

The information on craps in Exercise 5.27 is taken from Silberstang [106].

Chapter 6

Storage/Retrieval I: Ordered Keys

In this chapter, we begin an examination of data structures for general storage and retrieval. We will assume that with each data item is associated a key that uniquely identifies the data item. An example of this kind of key might be a bank account number. Thus, if we provide a bank's database with a customer's account number, we should be able to retrieve that customer's account information.

We will let KEY denote the type to which the keys belong. We will assume that, even though the KEY may not be a numeric type, it is still possible to sort elements of this type using a comparison operator $\leq$. Moreover, we assume that we need an efficient way to obtain data items in order of their keys. In the next chapter, we will examine data structures that do not require these two assumptions.

In order to facilitate arbitrary processing of all of the items in the data structure, we provide the VISITOR interface, shown in Figure 6.1. We can then define an implementation of VISITOR so that its VISIT() operation does whatever processing we wish on a data item. (The use of this interface is known as the *visitor pattern*.)

We then define a DICTIONARY as a finite set of data items, each having a unique key of type KEY, together with the operations shown in Figure 6.2. In the next chapter, we will examine implementations of this ADT. In this chapter, we will explore several implementations of the ORDEREDDICTIONARY ADT, which is the extension of the DICTIONARY ADT obtained by adding the interface shown in Figure 6.3.

Example 6.1. Suppose we would like to print all of the data items in an instance of ORDEREDDICTIONARY in order of keys. We can accomplish this by implementing VISITOR so that its VISIT operation prints its argument.

Figure 6.1   The VISITOR interface

Precondition: true.
Postcondition: Completes without an error. May modify the state of x.

VISITOR.VISIT(x)

Figure 6.2   The DICTIONARY ADT

Precondition: true.
Postcondition: Constructs an empty DICTIONARY.

DICTIONARY()

Precondition: k is a KEY.
Postcondition: Returns the element with key k, or nil if no item with key k is contained in the set.

DICTIONARY.GET(k)

Precondition: $x \neq$ nil, and k is a KEY that is not associated with any item in the set.
Postcondition: Adds x to the set with key k.

DICTIONARY.PUT(x, k)

Precondition: k is a KEY.
Postcondition: If there is an item with key k in the set, this item is removed.

DICTIONARY.REMOVE(k)

Precondition: true.
Postcondition: Returns the number of items in the set.

DICTIONARY.SIZE()

Such an implementation, PRINTER, is shown in Figure 6.4. Note that we have strengthened the postcondition over what is specified in Figure 6.1. This is allowable because an implementation with a stronger postcondition and/or a weaker precondition is still consistent with the specification. Having defined PRINTER, we can print the contents of the ORDEREDDICTIONARY d with

---

Figure 6.3   Interface extending DICTIONARY to ORDEREDDICTIONARY

Precondition: v is a VISITOR.

Postcondition: Applies v.VISIT(x) to every item x in the set in order of their keys.

ORDEREDDICTIONARY.VISITINORDER(v)

Figure 6.4   PRINTER implementation of VISITOR

Structural Invariant: true.

Precondition: true.
Postcondition: Prints x.

PRINTER.VISIT(x)
   print x

---

the statement,

$$d.\text{VISITINORDER}(\textbf{new } \text{PRINTER}()).$$

In order to implement ORDEREDDICTIONARY, it is possible to store the data items in a sorted array, as we did with SORTEDARRAYPRIORITYQUEUE in Section 5.1. Such an implementation has similar advantages and disadvantages to those of SORTEDARRAYPRIORITYQUEUE. Using binary search, we can find an arbitrary data item in $\Theta(\lg n)$ time, where n is the number of items in the dictionary. Thus, the GET operation can be implemented to run in $\Theta(\lg n)$ time. However, to add or remove an item requires $\Theta(n)$ time in the worst case. Thus, PUT and REMOVE are inefficient using such an implementation. The fact that the elements of an array are located contiguously allows random access, which, together with the fact that the elements are sorted, facilitates the fast binary search algorithm. However, it is exactly this contiguity that causes updates to be slow, because in order to maintain sorted order, elements must be moved to make room for new elements or to take the place of those removed.

If we were to use a linked list instead of an array, we would be able to change the structure without moving elements around, but we would no longer be able to use binary search. The "shape" of a linked list demands a sequential search; hence, look-ups will be slow. In order to provide fast updates and retrievals, we need a linked structure on which we can approximate a binary search.

6.1 Binary Search Trees

Consider the binary tree structure shown in Figure 6.5. Integer keys of several data items are shown in the nodes. Note that the value of the root is roughly the median of the keys in the structure; i.e., about half of the remaining keys are smaller. The smaller keys are all in the left child, whereas the larger keys are all in the right child. The two children are then structured in a similar way. Thus, if our search target is smaller than the key at the current node, we look in the left child, and if it is larger, we look in the right child. Because this type of search approximates a binary search, this structure is called a *binary search tree*.

More formally we define a *binary search tree (BST)* to be a binary tree satisfying the following properties:

- Each node contains a data item together with its key.
- If the BST is nonempty, then both of its children are BSTs, and the key in its root node is

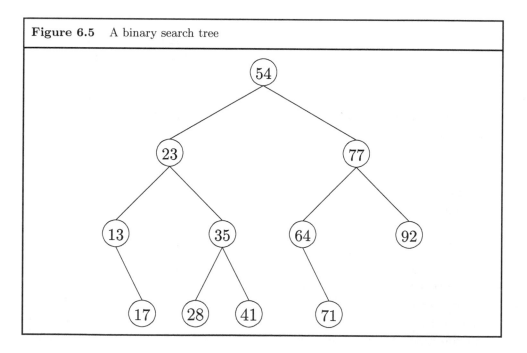

Figure 6.5   A binary search tree

– strictly larger than all keys in its left child;
– strictly smaller than all keys in its right child.

We can represent a binary search tree with the following variables:

- *elements*, which refers to a BINARYTREENODE (see Section 5.2);
- *size*, which is an integer giving the number of data items in the set.

We interpret *elements* as representing a binary search tree as follows. If its *root* variable is nil, then the represented BST is empty. Otherwise, its *root* variable is a KEYED item (see page 149) containing the data item stored in the root with its associated key, and its *leftChild* and *rightChild* variables represent the left and right children, respectively. Our structural invariant is that *elements* refers to a binary search tree according to the above interpretation, and that *size* gives the number of nodes in the represented binary search tree. Note that this invariant implies that all non-nil *root* variables in the BINARYTREENODEs refer to KEYED items.

Because both GET and REMOVE require that we find a node with a given key, we will design an internal function FIND(k, t) to find the node in the BST rooted at t with key k. If no such key exists in the tree, FIND(k, t) will return a reference to the empty subtree in which it could be inserted; thus, we can also use FIND in implementing PUT.

Consider how we might implement FIND(k, t). If t is empty, then obviously it does not contain the key. Otherwise, we should first check the root. If we don't find our key, we should see how it compares with the key at the root. Proceeding top-down, we can then find the key in either the left or right child, depending on the outcome of the comparison. This algorithm is a transformation, and so can be implemented as a loop, as is shown in Figure 6.6.

Complete implementations of GET and PUT are shown in Figure 6.6. The implementation of REMOVE requires a bit more work, however. Once we find the node containing the key k, we need to be able to remove that node t while maintaining a binary search tree. If t has no nonempty children, all we need to do is remove it (i.e., make the subtree empty). If t has only one nonempty child, we can safely replace the node to which t refers by that child. The difficulty comes when t has two nonempty children. In order to take care of this case, we replace t with the node in its right child having smallest key. That node must have an empty left child, so we can easily remove it. Furthermore, because it is in the right child of t, its key is greater

---

Figure 6.6   BSTDICTIONARY implementation of ORDEREDDICTIONARY, part 1

Structural Invariant: *elements* refers to a BST, and *size* gives the number of nodes in the represented BST.

BSTDICTIONARY()
   elements ← **new** BINARYTREENODE(); *size* ← 0

BSTDICTIONARY.GET(k)
   return FIND(k, *elements*).ROOT().DATA()

BSTDICTIONARY.PUT(x, k)
   if $x = $ nil
     error
   else
     $t \leftarrow$ FIND(k, *elements*)
     if t.ROOT() = nil
       size ← *size* + 1
       t.SETROOT(**new** KEYED(x, k))
       t.SETLEFTCHILD(**new** BINARYTREENODE())
       t.SETRIGHTCHILD(**new** BINARYTREENODE())

— **Internal Functions Follow** —

Precondition: k is a key and t is a BINARYTREENODE representing a BST.

Postcondition: Returns the BINARYTREENODE in t with key k, or in which k could be inserted if k is not in t.

BSTDICTIONARY.FIND(k, t)
   // **Invariant:** k belongs in the subtree represented by t
   while t.ROOT() $\neq$ nil **and** $k \neq t$.ROOT().KEY()
     if $k < t$.ROOT().KEY()
       $t \leftarrow t$.LEFTCHILD()
     else
       $t \leftarrow t$.RIGHTCHILD()
   return t

than any key in the left child of t; hence, moving it to the root of t maintains the BST structure.

We can find the smallest key in a nonempty BST by first looking at the left child of the root. If it is empty, then the root contains the smallest key. Otherwise, the smallest key is in the left child. This is a transformation, and so can be implemented using a loop. The complete implementation of REMOVE is shown in Figure 6.7. Figure 6.8 shows the result of deleting 54 from the BST shown in Figure 6.5. Specifically, because 54 has two children, it is replaced by the smallest key (64) in its right child, and 64 is replaced by its right child (71).

The VISITINORDER operation requires us to apply v.VISIT to each data item in the BST, in order of keys. If the BST is empty, then there is nothing to do. Otherwise, we must visit all of the data items in the left child prior to visiting the root, then we must visit all of the data items in the right child. Because the left and right children are themselves BSTs, they comprise smaller instances of this problem. Applying the top-down approach in a straightforward way, we obtain the recursive internal function TRAVERSEINORDER shown in Figure 6.7.

The above algorithm implemented by TRAVERSEINORDER is known as an *inorder traversal*. Inorder traversal applies strictly to binary trees, but two other traversals apply to rooted trees in general. A *preorder* traversal visits the root prior to recursively visiting all of its children, whereas a *postorder* traversal visits the root after recursively visiting all of its children.

Let us now analyze the running time of FIND. Let n be the number of data items in the BST. Clearly, the time required outside the loop and the time for a single iteration of the loop are each in $\Theta(1)$. We therefore need to analyze the worst-case number of iterations of the loop. Initially, t refers to a BST with n nodes. A single iteration has the effect of resetting t to refer to one of its children. In the worst case, this child may contain all nodes except the root. Thus, in the worst case, the loop may iterate n times. This can happen, for example, if all left children are empty, so that *elements* refers to a BST that consists of a single chain of nodes going to the right (see Figure 6.9). The worst-case running time is therefore in $\Theta(n)$.

Example 6.2. Suppose we build a BSTDICTIONARY by inserting n items with integer keys $1, 2, \ldots, n$, in that order. As each key is inserted, it is larger than any key already in the BST. It is therefore inserted to the right of every key already in the BST. The result is shown in Figure 6.9. It is easily seen that to insert key i requires $\Theta(i)$ time. The total time to build the BSTDICTIONARY is therefore in $\Theta(n^2)$, by Theorem 3.31.

Figure 6.7   BSTDICTIONARY implementation of ORDEREDDICTIONARY, part 2

BSTDICTIONARY.REMOVE(k)
  $t \leftarrow$ FIND(k, *elements*)
  if t.ROOT() $\neq$ nil
    if t.LEFTCHILD().ROOT() = nil
      COPY(t.RIGHTCHILD(), t)
    else if t.RIGHTCHILD().ROOT() = nil
      COPY(t.LEFTCHILD(), t)
    else
      $m \leftarrow t$.RIGHTCHILD()
      // **Invariant:** The smallest key in the right child of t is in the
      // subtree rooted at m.
      while m.LEFTCHILD().ROOT() $\neq$ nil
        $m \leftarrow m$.LEFTCHILD()
      t.SETROOT(m.ROOT()); COPY(m.RIGHTCHILD(), m)

BSTDICTIONARY.VISITINORDER(v)
  TRAVERSEINORDER(*elements*, v)

— Internal Functions Follow —

Precondition: *source* and *dest* are BINARYTREENODEs.
Postcondition: Copies the contents of *source* to *dest*.

BSTDICTIONARY.COPY(*source*, *dest*)
  dest.SETROOT(*source*.ROOT())
  dest.SETLEFTCHILD(*source*.LEFTCHILD())
  dest.SETRIGHTCHILD(*source*.RIGHTCHILD())

Precondition: t is a BINARYTREENODE representing a BST, and v is a
VISITOR
Postcondition: Applies v.VISIT to every node in t in order of their keys.

BSTDICTIONARY.TRAVERSEINORDER(t, v)
  if t.ROOT() $\neq$ nil
    TRAVERSEINORDER(t.LEFTCHILD(), v)
    v.VISIT(t.ROOT().DATA())
    TRAVERSEINORDER(t.RIGHTCHILD(), v)

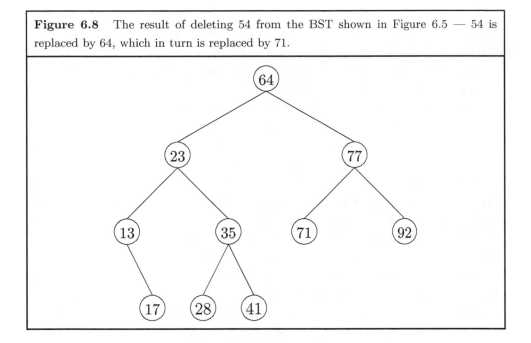

Figure 6.8 The result of deleting 54 from the BST shown in Figure 6.5 — 54 is replaced by 64, which in turn is replaced by 71.

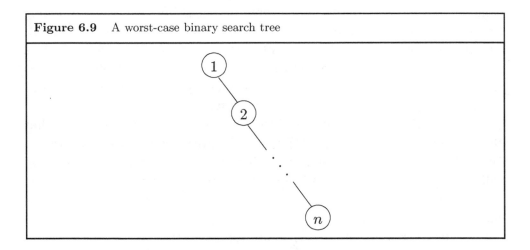

Figure 6.9 A worst-case binary search tree

The worst-case performance of a binary search tree is no better than either a sorted array or a sorted linked list for implementing ORDERED-DICTIONARY. In fact, in the worst case, a binary search tree degenerates into a sorted linked list, as Figure 6.9 shows. However, the performance of a binary search tree is not nearly as bad as the worst-case analysis suggests. In practice, binary search trees often yield very good performance.

In order to help us to understand better the performance of a binary search tree, let us analyze the worst-case running time of FIND in a somewhat different way. Instead of analyzing the running time in terms of the number of data items, let us instead analyze it in terms of the height of the tree. The analysis is similar, because again in the worst case the child selected in the loop has height one less than the entire subtree. Thus, the worst-case running time of FIND is in $\Theta(h)$, where h is the height of the tree.

What this analysis tells us is that in order to achieve good performance from a binary search tree, we need a tree whose height is not too large. In practice, provided the pattern of insertions and deletions is somewhat random, the height of a binary search tree tends to be in $\Theta(\lg n)$. It is not hard to see that the worst-case running time of GET, PUT, and REMOVE are all in $\Theta(h)$. Thus, if the height of the tree is logarithmic, we can achieve good performance. In the next section, we will show how we can modify our implementation to guarantee logarithmic height in the worst case, and thereby achieve logarithmic performance from these three operations.

Before we leave ordinary binary search trees, however, let us analyze the worst-case running time of TRAVERSEINORDER, which does not use the FIND function. We cannot analyze this operation completely because we cannot analyze v.VISIT without knowing how it is implemented. Assuming the correctness of TRAVERSEINORDER (whose proof we leave as an exercise), we can nevertheless conclude that v.VISIT is called exactly once for each data item, and so must take at least $\Omega(n)$ time. What we would like to analyze is the time required for everything else. This amounts to analyzing the overhead involved in applying v.VISIT to every data item.

Ignoring the call to v.VISIT and the recursive calls, it is easily seen that the remaining code runs in $\Theta(1)$ time. However, setting up a recurrence describing the worst-case running time, including the recursion but excluding calls to v.VISIT, is not easy. We must make two recursive calls, but all we know about the sizes of the trees in these calls is that their sum is one less than the size of the entire tree.

Let us therefore take a different approach to the analysis. As we have already argued, v.VISIT is called exactly once for each data item. Furthermore, it is easily seen that, excluding the calls made on empty trees, v.VISIT is called exactly once in each call to TRAVERSEINORDER. A total of exactly n calls are therefore made on nonempty trees. The calls made on empty trees make no further recursive calls. We can therefore obtain the total number of recursive calls (excluding the initial call made from VISITINORDER) by counting the recursive calls made by each of the calls on nonempty trees. Because each of these calls makes two recursive calls, the total number of recursive calls is exactly $2n$. Including the initial call the total number of calls made to TRAVERSEINORDER is $2n + 1$. Because each of these calls runs in $\Theta(1)$ time (excluding the time taken by $v.$VISIT), the total time is in $\Theta(n)$. Note that we cannot hope to do any better than this because the specification requires that $v.$VISIT be called n times.

Because TRAVERSEINORDER is recursive, we should also consider the stack space usage. Again, analyzing the stack space in terms of the number of nodes is rather difficult, but it turns out to be much easier to do the analysis in terms of the height of the tree. As with FIND, this analysis also gives us useful information about the performance of TRAVERSEINORDER.

Let $f(h)$ be the worst-case stack space used by TRAVERSEINORDER on a tree of height h. Then if $h > 0$, $f(h)$ is in $\Theta(1)$ plus the maximum of the amount of space used the two recursive calls in the worst case. Because at least one of the two children has height $h - 1$, $f(h) \geq f(h - 1)$; i.e., $f(h)$ is nondecreasing. Then in the worst case, the maximum space used by one of the recursive calls is $f(h - 1)$. We therefore have the following recurrence:

$$f(h) \in f(h - 1) + \Theta(1),$$

for $h > 0$. By Theorem 3.34, $f(h) \in \Theta(h)$. In the worst case, $h = n - 1$, where n is the number of data items; hence, the worst-case stack space usage is in $\Theta(n)$.

The above analysis tells us that if we want to keep the stack space usage for TRAVERSEINORDER reasonable, we need to ensure that the heights of the trees are small. Thus, ensuring that the height of a binary tree is in $\Theta(\lg n)$ would ensure not only good performance for FIND, but also good stack space usage for TRAVERSEINORDER.

6.2 AVL Trees

In this section, we present a variant of binary search trees that guarantees logarithmic height. As a result, we obtain an implementation of ORDERED-DICTIONARY for which the GET, PUT, and REMOVE operations all run in $\Theta(\lg n)$ time.

The key to keeping the height of a binary tree relatively small is in maintaining balance. The trick is to be able to achieve balance without too much overhead; otherwise the overhead in maintaining balance may result in poor overall performance. Consequently, we need to be careful how we define "balance", so that our balance criterion is not too difficult to maintain.

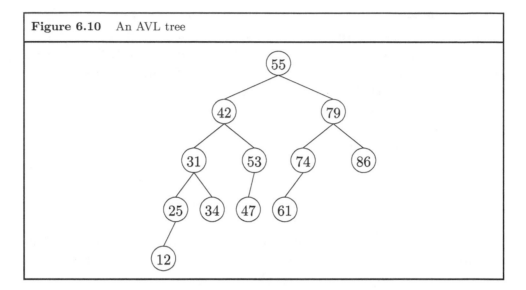

Figure 6.10 An AVL tree

The balance criterion that we choose is that in any subtree, the heights of the two children differ by at most 1. For the purpose of this definition, we consider an empty tree to have height -1, or one less than the height of a tree containing a single node. A binary search tree obeying this balance criterion is known as an *AVL tree*; "AVL" stands for the names of its inventors, Adel'son-Vel'skiĭ and Landis.

Figure 6.10 shows an AVL tree of height 4 containing integer keys. Note that its balance is not perfect – it is not hard to construct a binary tree of height 3 with even more nodes. Nevertheless, the children of each nonempty subtree have heights differing by at most 1, so it is an AVL tree.

Before we begin designing an AVL tree implementation of ORDERED-DICTIONARY, let us first derive an upper bound on the height of an AVL tree with n nodes. We will not derive this bound directly. Instead, we will first derive a lower bound on the number of nodes in an AVL tree of height h. We will then transform this lower bound into our desired upper bound.

Consider an AVL tree with height h having a minimum number of nodes. By definition, both children of a nonempty AVL tree must also be AVL trees. By definition of the height of a tree, at least one child must have height $h - 1$. By definition of an AVL tree, the other child must have height at least $h - 2$. In order to minimize the number of nodes in this child, its height must be exactly $h - 2$, provided $h \geq 1$. Thus, the two children are AVL trees of heights $h - 1$ and $h - 2$, each having a minimum number of nodes.

The above discussion suggests a recurrence giving the minimum number of nodes in an AVL tree of height h. Let $g(h)$ give this number. Then for

$h \geq 1$, the number of nodes in the two children are $g(h-1)$ and $g(h-2)$. Then for $h \geq 1$,

$$g(h) = g(h-1) + g(h-2) + 1, \tag{6.1}$$

where $g(-1) = 0$ (the number of nodes in an empty tree) and $g(0) = 1$ (the number of nodes in a tree of height 0).

Example 6.3. Consider the subtree rooted at 25 in Figure 6.10. It is of height 1, and its two children are minimum-sized subtrees of height 0 and -1, respectively. It is therefore a minimum-sized AVL tree of height 1, so $g(1) = 2$. Likewise, the subtrees rooted at 53 and 74 are also minimum-sized AVL trees of height 1. The subtrees rooted at 31 and 79 are then easily seen to be minimum-sized AVL trees of height 2, so $g(2) = 4$. In like manner it can be seen that $g(3) = 7$, $g(4) = 12$, and the entire tree is a minimum-sized AVL tree of height 4.

Recurrence (6.1) does not fit any of the forms we saw in Chapter 3. However, it is somewhat similar to the form of Theorem 3.34. Recall that we only need a lower bound for $g(n)$. In what follows, we will derive a recurrence that fits the form of Theorem 3.34 and gives a lower bound for $g(n)$.

We first observe that g must be a nondecreasing function. Thus, for $h \geq 1$, if

$$g_1(h) = 2g_1(h-2) + 1,$$

where $g_1(h) = g(h)$ for $h < 1$, then

$$g_1(h) \leq g(h), \tag{6.2}$$

for all $h \geq -1$.

Now if we let $g_2(h) = g_1(2h)$ for all h, we obtain

$$\begin{aligned}
g_2(h) &= g_1(2h) \\
&= 2g_1(2h-2) + 1 \\
&= 2g_1(2(h-1)) + 1 \\
&= 2g_2(h-1) + 1.
\end{aligned}$$

g_2 then fits the form of Theorem 3.34. Applying this theorem, we obtain

$$g_2(h) \in \Theta(2^h).$$

Thus, for sufficiently large h, there is a positive real number c_1 such that

$$g_1(2h) = g_2(h)$$

$$\geq c_1 2^h.$$

Then for sufficiently large even h,

$$g_1(h) \geq c_1 2^{h/2}.$$

For sufficiently large odd h, we have

$$g_1(h) \geq g_1(h-1)$$

$$\geq c_1 2^{(h-1)/2} \quad \text{(because } h-1 \text{ is even)}$$

$$= \frac{c_1}{\sqrt{2}} 2^{h/2},$$

so that for some positive real number c_2 and all sufficiently large h,

$$g_1(h) \geq c_2 2^{h/2}. \tag{6.3}$$

Combining (6.3) with (6.2), we obtain

$$c_2 2^{h/2} \leq g(h),$$

for sufficiently large h. Applying lg to both sides and rearranging terms, we obtain

$$h \leq 2(\lg g(h) - \lg c_2)$$

$$\in O(\lg g(h)).$$

Because $g(h)$ is the minimum number of nodes in an AVL tree of height h, it follows that the height of an AVL tree is in $O(\lg n)$, where n is the number of nodes. By a similar argument, it can be shown that the height is in $\Omega(\lg n)$ as well. We therefore have the following theorem.

Theorem 6.4. *The worst-case height of an AVL tree is in $\Theta(\lg n)$, where n is the number of nodes.*

By Theorem 6.4, if we can design operations that run in time linear in the height of an AVL tree, these operations will run in time logarithmic in the size of the data set. Certainly, adding or deleting a node will change the heights of some of the subtrees in an AVL tree; hence, these operations must re-establish balance. Computing the height of a binary tree involves finding the longest path, which apparently requires examining the entire tree. However, we can avoid recomputing heights from scratch if we record the height of each subtree. If the heights of both children are known, computing the height of the tree is straightforward.

We therefore define the data type AVLNODE, which is just like BINARY-TREENODE, except that it has an additional representation variable, *height*. This variable is used to record the height of the tree as an integer. As for the other three variables, we allow read/write access to *height*. The constructor for AVLNODE is just like the constructor for BINARYTREENODE, except that it also initializes *height* to -1.

To represent an ORDEREDDICTIONARY using an AVL tree, we again use two variables, *elements* and *size*, as we did for BSTDICTIONARY. In this representation, however, *elements* will refer to an AVLNODE. Our structural invariant is that *elements* represents an AVL tree. We interpret this statement as implying that each *height* variable gives the height of the subtree at which it is rooted, or -1 if that subtree is empty.

We can define a FIND function for this implementation as we did for BSTDICTIONARY; in fact, because an AVL tree is a binary search tree, the same function will work. As we have already shown the running time of BSTDICTIONARY.FIND to be in $\Theta(h)$, where h is the height of the tree, we can conclude that this function has a running time in $\Theta(\lg n)$. However, this function is not useful in implementing the PUT or REMOVE operations because we might need to change the shape of the tree at some other location in order to maintain the balance criterion.

Let us therefore consider how PUT might be implemented. More generally, let us consider how a data item x might be inserted into an arbitrary AVL tree t, which may be a subtree of a larger AVL tree. If t is empty, we can replace it with a single-node AVL tree containing x. Otherwise, we'll need to compare keys and insert into the appropriate child. However, we are not yet finished, because the insertion into the child will have changed its shape; hence, we need to compare the heights of the two children and restore balance if necessary. Note that this reduction is not a transformation, due to the additional work required following the insertion into the child.

In order to complete the insertion function, we need to be able to restore the balance criterion after an insertion into one of the children. Clearly, if we insert into one particular child, the other child will be unchanged. Furthermore, if we specify the insertion function to cause the result to be an AVL tree, we know that both children will be AVL trees; hence, we only need to worry about restoring balance at the root. Before we can talk about how to restore balance at the root, we should consider how much difference there might be in the heights of the children. It stands to reason that an

Figure 6.11   A single rotate right

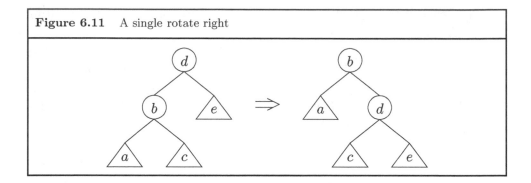

insertion should either leave the height unchanged or increase it by 1. We will therefore include this condition in the postcondition of our insertion function.

Based on the above discussion, it suffices to show how to balance a binary search tree whose children are AVL trees having a height difference of exactly 2. This restoration of balance is accomplished via *rotations*. Consider, for example, the rotation shown in Figure 6.11. In this figure, circles denote single nodes, and triangles denote arbitrary subtrees, which in some cases may be empty. All nodes and subtrees are labeled in a way that corresponds to the order of nodes in a BST (e.g., subtree c is to the right of node b and to the left of node d). The rotation shown is known as a *single rotate right*. It is accomplished by promoting node b to the root, then filling in the remaining pieces in the only way that maintains the ordering of keys in the BST. Suppose that in the "before" picture, the right child (e) has height h and the left child has height $h+2$. Because the left child is an AVL tree, one of its two children has a height of $h+1$ and the other has a height of either h or $h+1$. Suppose subtree a has a height of $h+1$. Then it is easily seen that this rotation results in an AVL tree.

The rotation shown in Figure 6.11 does not restore balance, however, if subtree a has height h. Because the left child in the "before" picture has height $h+2$, subtree c must have height $h+1$ in this case. After the rotation, the left child has height h, but the right child has height $h+2$. To take care of this case, we need another kind of rotation called a *double rotate right*, shown in Figure 6.12. It is accomplished by promoting node d to the root and again filling in the remaining pieces in the only way that maintains the ordering of keys. Suppose that subtrees a and g have height h and that the subtree rooted at d in the "before" picture has height $h+1$. This is then the case for which a single rotate fails to restore balance. Subtrees c and e

Figure 6.12   A double rotate right

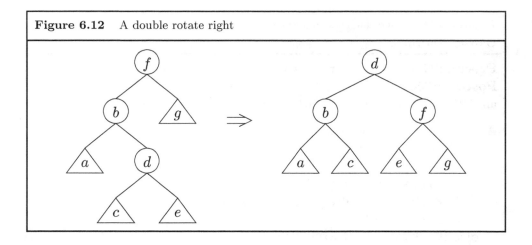

may have heights of either h or $h - 1$ (though at least one must have height h). It is therefore easily seen that following the rotation, balance is restored.

These two rotations handle the cases in which the left child has height 2 greater than the right child. When the right child has height 2 greater than the left child a single rotate left or a double rotate left may be applied. These rotations are simply mirror images of the rotations shown in Figures 6.11 and 6.12.

To complete our discussion of the insertion function, we must convince ourselves that if it changes the height of the tree, then it increases it by exactly 1. This is clearly the case if no rotation is done. Let us then consider the rotations shown in Figures 6.11 and 6.12. If either of these rotations is applied, then the data item must have been inserted into the left child, causing its height to increase from $h+1$ to $h+2$. The overall height of the tree had to have been $h + 2$ prior to the insertion. Following a single rotate right, it is easily seen that the height is either $h + 2$ or $h + 3$. Likewise, following a double rotate right, it is easily seen that the height is $h + 2$. Thus, the result of the insertion is to either leave the height unchanged or increase it by 1.

The insertion algorithm is shown as AVLDICTIONARY.INSERT in Figure 6.13. The BALANCE function can also be used by the deletion algorithm. The remainder of the AVLDICTIONARY implementation, including the rotations, is left as an exercise. Note that the rotations must ensure that all *height* values except that of the root are correct. Specifically, the heights of node d in Figure 6.11 and nodes b and f in Figure 6.12 must be recomputed.

Figure 6.13 Some internal functions for AVLDICTIONARY implementation of ORDEREDDICTIONARY

Precondition: t represents an AVL tree, and x is a KEYED item.
Postcondition: Inserts x into t if its key is not already there, resulting in an AVL tree whose height is either unchanged or increased by 1.

AVLDICTIONARY.INSERT(x, t)
  if t.HEIGHT() $= -1$
    t.SETROOT(x)
    t.SETLEFTCHILD(**new** AVLNODE())
    t.SETRIGHTCHILD(**new** AVLNODE())
    t.SETHEIGHT(0)
  else if x.KEY() $<$ t.ROOT().KEY()
    INSERT(x, t.LEFTCHILD())
    BALANCE(t)
  else if x.KEY() $>$ t.ROOT().KEY()
    INSERT(x, t.RIGHTCHILD())
    BALANCE(t)

— **Internal Functions Follow** —

Precondition: t refers to a nonempty AVLNODE representing a BST. The children of t are AVL trees whose heights differ by at most 2.
Postcondition: Arranges t into an AVL tree.

AVLDICTIONARY.BALANCE(t)
  $l \leftarrow t$.LEFTCHILD()
  $r \leftarrow t$.RIGHTCHILD()
  if l.HEIGHT() $= r$.HEIGHT() $+ 2$
    if l.LEFTCHILD().HEIGHT() $> r$.HEIGHT()
      SINGLEROTATERIGHT(t)
    else
      DOUBLEROTATERIGHT(t)
  else if r.HEIGHT() $= l$.HEIGHT() $+ 2$
    if r.RIGHTCHILD().HEIGHT() $> l$.HEIGHT()
      SINGLEROTATELEFT(t)
    else
      DOUBLEROTATELEFT(t)
  t.SETHEIGHT(MAX(l.HEIGHT(), r.HEIGHT()) $+ 1$)

Example 6.5. Suppose we were to insert the key 39 into the AVL tree shown in Figure 6.14(a). Using the ordinary BST insertion algorithm, 39 should be made the right child of 35, as shown in Figure 6.14(b). To complete the insertion, we must check the balance along the path to 39, starting at the bottom. Both 35 and 23 satisfy the the balance criterion; however, the left child of 42 has height 2, whereas the right child has height 0. We therefore need to perform a rotation at 42. To determine which rotation is appropriate, we compare the height of the left child of the left child of 42 (i.e., the subtree rooted at 11) with the right child of 42. Because both of these subtrees have height 0, a double rotate right is required at 42. To accomplish this rotation, we promote 35 to the root of the subtree (i.e., where 42 currently is), and place the nodes 23 and 42, along with the subtrees rooted at 11, 39, and 50, at the only locations that preserve the order of the BST. The result of this rotation is shown in Figure 6.14(c). Because the balance criterion is satisfied at 54, this tree is the final result.

It is not hard to see that each of the rotations can be implemented to run in $\Theta(1)$ time, and that BALANCE therefore runs in $\Theta(1)$ time. Let us

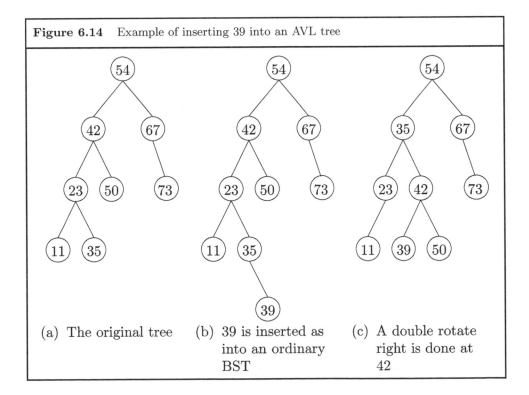

Figure 6.14 Example of inserting 39 into an AVL tree

(a) The original tree

(b) 39 is inserted as into an ordinary BST

(c) A double rotate right is done at 42

now analyze INSERT. Excluding the recursion, this function clearly runs in $\Theta(1)$ time. At most one recursive call is made, and its second parameter has height strictly less than the height of t; in the worst case, it is 1 less. If h is the height of t, then the worst-case running time of INSERT is given by

$$f(h) \in f(h-1) + \Theta(1),$$

for $h > 0$. By Theorem 3.34, $f(h) \in \Theta(h)$. By Theorem 6.4, INSERT therefore runs in $\Theta(\lg n)$ time, where n is the size of the data set. Clearly, PUT can be written to operate in $\Theta(\lg n)$ time.

The same analysis shows that the stack space usage of PUT is in $\Theta(\lg n)$. We leave as an exercise the design and analysis of an algorithm for REMOVE.

6.3   Splay Trees

While a worst-case bound of $\Theta(\lg n)$ for ORDEREDDICTIONARY accesses is good, bounding the worst case does not always result in the best performance. For example, in many applications, the so-called "80-20" rule holds; i.e., 80% of the accesses involve roughly 20% of the data items. This rule then applies recursively, so that 64% of the accesses involve roughly 4% of the data items. In order to get good performance in such an environment, we would like to structure the data so that the most commonly-accessed data items can be accessed more quickly.

One variation of a binary search tree that attempts to achieve this kind of performance is a *splay tree*. Structurally, a splay tree is simply a binary search tree. Operationally, however, it is *self-adjusting* — when it accesses an item, it brings that item to the root of the tree via a series of rotations. (The VISITINORDER operation is an exception to this rule, as it accesses all of the data items.) As a result, the more frequently accessed items tend to remain closer to the root.

No attempt is made to ensure any sort of balance in a splay tree. As a result, the operations run in $\Theta(n)$ time in the worst case. However, when a long path is traversed, the rotations have the effect of shortening it by roughly half. Thus, an expensive operation improves future performance. As a result, the amortized running times of GET, PUT, and REMOVE are all in $O(\lg n)$.

To get a rough idea of how rotations improve the data structure, suppose we have a long zig-zag path from the root to some node b; i.e., by starting from the root, then taking first the left child, then the right child, and continuing to alternate, we eventually reach b. We could then bring b to the root of the tree by a series of double rotations, each promoting b by two levels. Now referring to Figure 6.12, note that the distance between the root and any descendant of d decreases by 1 for each rotation. The number of rotations is half the distance from the root to d, so each descendant of d ends up closer to the root by half the original distance between the root and d.

Unfortunately, single rotations are not as effective in improving the structure. Notice that in Figure 6.11, nodes in subtree c do not get any closer to the root as a result of the rotation. As a result, we need a new kind of double rotation that can be applied when the node to be promoted is not a "zig-zag" from its grandparent. So that we might distinguish between the various double rotations, we will refer to the rotation of Figure 6.12 as a *zig-zag right*, and to its mirror image as a *zig-zag left*. A *zig-zig right* is shown in Figure 6.15. Note that by this rotation, the distance between the root and any descendant of a is decreased by at least 1.

Our representation, interpretation, and structural invariant will be the same as for BSTDICTIONARY. The only differences will occur in the actual implementations of the operations. In fact, the implementation of VISITIN-ORDER will also be the same as for BSTDICTIONARY.

Let us consider how we can implement a FIND function. First, we observe that no value needs to be returned, because if the key we are looking for exists, we will bring it to the root of the tree. Hence, after invoking the FIND function, the GET operation only needs to look in the root to see if the desired key is there. Second, we don't want to bring a node representing an empty subtree to the root. For this reason, we will need to verify that a node is nonempty at some point before rotating it to the root. It therefore seems reasonable to include as part of the precondition that the tree is nonempty.

Figure 6.15 A zig-zig right rotation

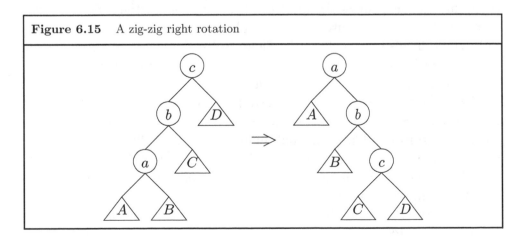

We therefore begin by comparing the given key k to the key at the root of the given tree t. If the keys don't match, we will need to look in the appropriate child, after verifying that it is nonempty. However, we want to do a double rotation whenever possible, so rather than using a recursive call at this point, we should go ahead and make another comparison. If we find the key k, or if the appropriate grandchild is empty, we do a single rotation. Otherwise, we recursively look for k in the appropriate grandchild and do a double rotation. The algorithm is shown in Figure 6.16.

Example 6.6. Suppose we were to do a FIND on 60 in the splay tree shown in Figure 6.17(a). Because the length of the path to 60 is odd, we must begin with a single rotation. Figure 6.17(b) shows the result of doing a single rotate left at 53. We then proceed with double rotations to bring 60 to the root. In this case, only one rotation — a zig-zag left — is required. The result is shown in Figure 6.17(c).

The insertion algorithm cannot use FIND because it must insert a new data item when an empty subtree is found. However, it can be patterned after the FIND algorithm. The main difference is that because a data item is inserted into an empty tree, we will always rotate that node to the root. We therefore do not need to restrict its use to nonempty trees. The details are left as an exercise.

The deletion algorithm can, however, use FIND. Suppose we want to delete key k. We can use FIND(k, *elements*) to move k to the root if it is present. If the right child is empty, we can simply make the left child the new root. Otherwise, we can use another internal function, FINDMIN(*elements*.RIGHTCHILD()), to move the minimum key m in the right child to the root of the right child. At this point, the right child has an empty left child, because there are no keys with values between k and its right child. The result is shown in Figure 6.18. We can therefore complete the deletion by making A the left child of m and making m the root (see Figure 6.18). The algorithm is given in Figure 6.19.

Let us now analyze the amortized running times of GET, PUT, and REMOVE for SPLAYDICTIONARY. It is not hard to see that all of the recursive algorithms have constant running time, excluding recursive calls. Furthermore, each time a recursive call is made, a rotation is done. It is therefore sufficient to analyze the total number of rotations. Each rotation, therefore, will have an actual cost of 1.

In order to amortize the number of rotations, we need to find an appropriate potential function. Intuitively, an operation involving many

---

Figure 6.16 The FIND internal function for the SPLAYDICTIONARY implementation of ORDEREDDICTIONARY.

Precondition: k is a KEY and t is a reference to a BINARYTREENODE representing a nonempty BST.

Postcondition: If a data item with key k is in t, then t is rearranged into a BST with k at the root.

SPLAYDICTIONARY.FIND(k, t)
   if $k < t$.ROOT().KEY()
     if t.LEFTCHILD().ROOT() $\neq$ nil
       if $k < t$.LEFTCHILD().ROOT().KEY()
         if t.LEFTCHILD().LEFTCHILD().ROOT() $\neq$ nil
           FIND(k, t.LEFTCHILD().LEFTCHILD()); ZIGZIGRIGHT(t)
         else
           SINGLEROTATERIGHT(t)
       else if $k > t$.LEFTCHILD().ROOT().KEY()
         if t.LEFTCHILD().RIGHTCHILD().ROOT() $\neq$ nil
           FIND(k, t.LEFTCHILD().RIGHTCHILD()); ZIGZAGRIGHT(t)
         else
           SINGLEROTATERIGHT(t)
       else
         SINGLEROTATERIGHT(t)
   else if $k > t$.ROOT().KEY()
     if t.RIGHTCHILD().ROOT() $\neq$ nil
       if $k < t$.RIGHTCHILD().ROOT().KEY()
         if t.RIGHTCHILD().LEFTCHILD().ROOT() $\neq$ nil
           FIND(k, t.RIGHTCHILD().LEFTCHILD()); ZIGZAGLEFT(t)
         else
           SINGLEROTATELEFT(t)
       else if $k > t$.RIGHTCHILD().ROOT().KEY()
         if t.RIGHTCHILD().RIGHTCHILD().ROOT() $\neq$ nil
           FIND(k, t.RIGHTCHILD().RIGHTCHILD()); ZIGZIGLEFT(t)
         else
           SINGLEROTATELEFT(t)
       else
         SINGLEROTATELEFT(t)

---

rotations should improve the overall balance of the tree. The potential function should in some way measure this balance, decreasing as the balance increases. If the tree is very unbalanced, as in Figure 6.9, many of the subtrees

Figure 6.17   Example of doing a Find on 60 in a splay tree

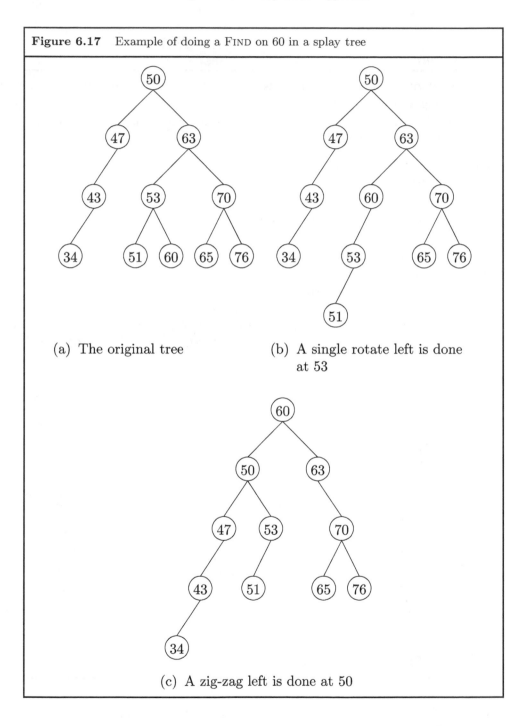

(a) The original tree

(b) A single rotate left is done
     at 53

(c) A zig-zag left is done at 50

Figure 6.18 The splay tree after the calls to FIND and FINDMIN in REMOVE

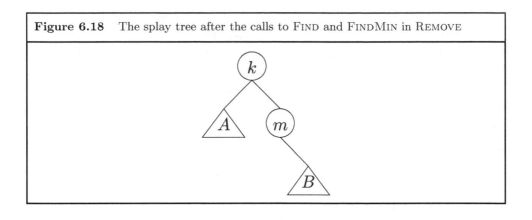

Figure 6.19 The REMOVE operation for the SPLAYDICTIONARY implementation of ORDEREDDICTIONARY

SPLAYDICTIONARY.REMOVE(k)
  if *elements*.ROOT() $\neq$ nil
    FIND(k, *elements*)
    if *elements*.ROOT().KEY() $= k$
      $l \leftarrow$ *elements*.LEFTCHILD()
      $r \leftarrow$ *elements*.RIGHTCHILD()
      if r.ROOT() $=$ nil
        elements $= l$
      else
        FINDMIN(r); r.SETLEFTCHILD(l); *elements* $\leftarrow r$

— **Internal Functions Follow** —

Precondition: t is a BINARYTREENODE representing a nonempty BST.
Postcondition: Arranges t into a BST whose smallest key is at the root.

SPLAYDICTIONARY.FINDMIN(t)
  if t.LEFTCHILD().ROOT() $\neq$ nil
    if t.LEFTCHILD().LEFTCHILD().ROOT() $=$ nil
      SINGLEROTATERIGHT(t)
    else
      FINDMIN(t.LEFTCHILD().LEFTCHILD())
      ZIGZIGRIGHT(t)

have a comparatively large number of nodes, whereas in a balanced tree, most of the subtrees have only a few nodes. It would therefore make sense to define the potential function to depend on the number of nodes in each subtree.

An example of such a potential function is the sum of the sizes of all of the subtrees. However, this potential function will not work. Consider what happens when 0 is inserted into the tree in Figure 6.9. It is inserted to the left of 1, then rotated to the root via a single rotate right. The original tree therefore ends up as the right child of the result. The potential function therefore increases by the number of nodes in the result. With an increase this large, we cannot achieve a logarithmic amortized cost.

In order to scale back the growth of the potential function, let us try applying the lg function to the size of each nonempty subtree. Specifically, let $|t|$ denote the number of nodes in a subtree t. We then define our potential function $\Phi(T)$ to be the sum of all $\lg |t|$ such that t is a nonempty subtree of the entire tree T. In what follows, we will show that for each of the three operations, the amortized cost with respect to Φ is in $O(\lg n)$.

Because most of the rotations will be double rotations, let us begin by analyzing a zig-zag rotation. We will be focusing on the three subtrees that are changed by the zig-zag rotation, as shown in Figure 6.20; thus T_a, T_b, and T_c denote the subtrees rooted at a, b, and c, respectively, prior to the rotation, and T_a', T_b', and T_c' denote the subtrees rooted at these nodes following the rotation. The amortized cost of the rotation will be the actual cost (i.e., 1)

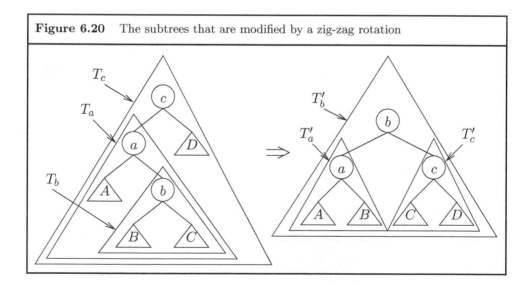

Figure 6.20   The subtrees that are modified by a zig-zag rotation

plus the change in the potential function Φ. Noting that $|T'_b| = |T_c|$, we conclude that the change in Φ is

$$\lg|T'_a| + \lg|T'_c| - \lg|T_a| - \lg|T_b|. \tag{6.4}$$

We need to simplify the above expression. It will be much easier to use if we can bound it in terms of subtrees of the original tree. In particular, we would like to get an expression involving only $|T_b|$ and $|T_c|$ so that, when the amortized costs of all rotations in one operation are added together, perhaps most terms will cancel out.

Let us therefore apply Theorem 5.7 (page 174) to $\lg|T'_a| + \lg|T'_c|$ in (6.4). We know that $|T'_a| + |T'_c| \le |T_c|$. By Theorem 5.7, we have $\lg|T'_a| + \lg|T'_c| \le 2\lg|T_c| - 2$. Using the fact that $|T_a| > |T_b|$ and adding in the actual cost, we obtain the following upper bound on the amortized cost of a zig-zag rotation:

$$2\lg|T_c| - 2 - 2\lg|T_b| + 1 = 2(\lg|T_c| - \lg|T_b|) - 1. \tag{6.5}$$

Let us now analyze the amortized cost of a zig-zig rotation. Referring to Figure 6.21 and adopting the same notational conventions as above, we see that the change in Φ is

$$\lg|T'_b| + \lg|T'_c| - \lg|T_a| - \lg|T_b|. \tag{6.6}$$

In order to get a tight bound for this expression in terms of $\lg|T_c| - \lg|T_a|$, we need to be a bit more clever. We would again like to use Theorem 5.7. Note that $|T_a| + |T'_c| \le |T_c|$; however, $\lg|T_a| + \lg|T'_c|$ does not occur in (6.6).

Figure 6.21   The subtrees that are modified by a zig-zig rotation

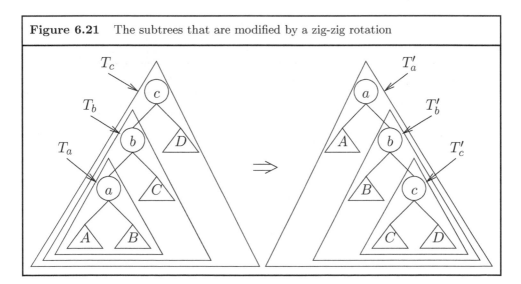

Let us therefore both add and subtract $\lg |T_a|$ to (6.6). Adding in the actual cost, applying Theorem 5.7, and simplifying, we obtain the following bound on the amortized cost of a zig-zig rotation:

$$\lg |T_b'| + \lg |T_c'| + \lg |T_a| - 2\lg |T_a| - \lg |T_b| + 1$$
$$\leq \lg |T_b'| + 2\lg |T_c| - 2 - 2\lg |T_a| - \lg |T_b| + 1$$
$$\leq 3\lg |T_c| - 3\lg |T_a| - 1$$
$$= 3(\lg |T_c| - \lg |T_a|) - 1. \tag{6.7}$$

Finally, let us analyze the amortized cost of a single rotate. We refer to Figure 6.22 for this analysis. Clearly, the amortized cost is bounded by

$$\lg |T_b'| - \lg |T_a| + 1 \leq \lg |T_b| - \lg |T_a| + 1. \tag{6.8}$$

Because each operation will do at most two single rotations (recall that a deletion can do a single rotation in both the FIND and the FINDMIN), the "+ 1" in this bound will not cause problems.

We can now analyze the amortized cost of a FIND. We first combine bounds (6.5), (6.7), and (6.8) into a single recurrence defining a function $f(k,t)$ bounding the amortized cost of FIND(k,t). Suppose FIND(k,t) makes a recursive call on a subtree s and performs a double rotation. We can then combine (6.5) and (6.7) to define:

$$f(k,t) = 3(\lg |t| - \lg |s|) + f(k,s).$$

Figure 6.22 The subtrees that are modified by a single rotation

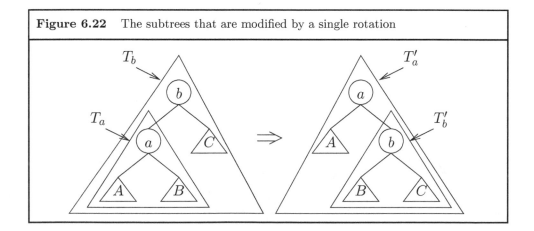

For the base of the recurrence, suppose that either no rotation or a single rotate is done. Using (6.8), we can define

$$f(k, t) = 3(\lg |t| - \lg |s|) + 1,$$

where s is the child rotated upward or t if no rotation is done.

It is easily seen that the above recurrence telescopes; i.e., when the value for $f(k, s)$ is substituted into the value for $f(k, t)$, the $\lg |s|$ terms cancel. The entire recurrence therefore simplifies to

$$f(k, t) = 3(\lg |t| - \lg |s|) + 1$$

where s is the subtree whose root is rotated to the root of t. Clearly, $f(k, t) \in O(\lg n)$, where n is the number of nodes in t. The amortized cost of FIND, and hence of GET, is therefore in $O(\lg n)$.

The analysis of PUT is identical to the analysis of FIND, except that we must also account for the change in Φ when the new node is added to the tree. When the new node is added, prior to any subsequent rotations, it is a leaf. Let s denote the empty subtree into which the new leaf is inserted. The insertion causes each of the ancestors of s, including s itself, to increase in size by 1. Let t be one of these ancestors other than the root, and let t' be the same subtree after the new node is inserted. Note that t' has no more nodes than does the parent of t. If we think of the insertion as replacing the parent of t by t', then this replacement causes no increase in Φ. The only node for which this argument does not apply is the root. Therefore, the increase in Φ is no more than $\lg(n + 1)$, where n is the number of nodes in the tree prior to the insertion. The entire amortized cost of PUT is therefore in $O(\lg n)$.

Finally, let us consider the REMOVE operation. The FIND has an amortized cost in $O(\lg n)$. Furthermore, the amortized analysis of FIND also applies to FINDMIN, so that it is also in $O(\lg n)$. Finally, it is easily seen that the actual removal of the node does not increase Φ. The amortized cost of REMOVE is therefore in $O(\lg n)$ as well.

As we observed for skew heaps (see Section 5.4), amortized analysis is inappropriate for analyzing stack space usage. We leave it as an exercise to show that the worst-case stack space usage for PUT is in $\Theta(n)$. To avoid this large stack space usage, the algorithms can be reformulated to use iteration with an explicit stack, rather than using the runtime stack for recursive calls. As a result, the total space usage is still in $\Theta(n)$, but the stack space usage is in $\Theta(1)$. We leave the details as an exercise.

6.4 Skip Lists

We conclude this chapter by returning to the idea of using an ordered linked list to implement ORDEREDDICTIONARY. Recall that the difficulty with this idea is that items must be accessed sequentially, so that a binary search cannot be used to find an item. A *skip list* overcomes this difficulty by using additional references to skip over portions of the list (see Figure 6.23). Using these additional references, a binary search can be approximated.

The main building block for a skip list is the data type SKIPLISTNODE, which represents a data item, its key, a *level* $n \geq 1$, and a sequence of n values, each of which is either a SKIPLISTNODE or *empty*. The representation consists of three variables:

- *data*: a data item; and
- *key*: a KEY;
- *links*[1..*n*]: an array of (possibly nil) SKIPLISTNODEs.

We interpret *data* as the represented data item, *key* as its associated key, SIZEOF(*links*) as the *level* of the SKIPLISTNODE, and *links*[*i*] as the *i*th element of the sequence, where *empty* is represented by nil. We allow read access to *key* and *data*. The complete implementation is shown in Figure 6.24.

We represent the ORDEREDDICTIONARY with four variables:

- *start*: a non-nil SKIPLISTNODE;
- *end*: a non-nil SKIPLISTNODE;
- *maxLevel*: a NAT; and
- *size*: a NAT.

Figure 6.23   A skip list

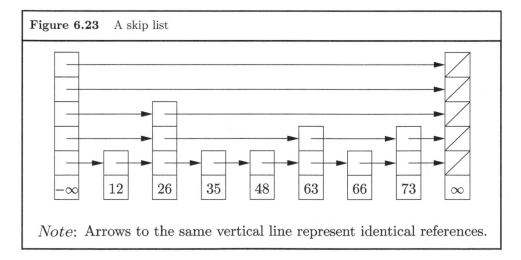

Note: Arrows to the same vertical line represent identical references.

Figure 6.24   The data type SKIPLISTNODE

Structural Invariant: true.

Precondition: x is a data item, k is a KEY, and n is a non-zero NAT.
Postcondition: Constructs a SKIPLISTNODE containing data x with key k and level n. All n elements of the sequence are *empty*.

SKIPLISTNODE(x, k, n)
   $data \leftarrow x$; $key \leftarrow k$; $links \leftarrow$ **new** ARRAY$[1..n]$
   for $i \leftarrow 1$ **to** n
     $links[i] \leftarrow$ nil

Precondition: true.
Postcondition: Returns the level.

SKIPLISTNODE.LEVEL()
   return SIZEOF($links$)

Precondition: i is a non-zero NAT no greater than the level.
Postcondition: Returns the ith element of the sequence, or nil if that element is *empty*.

SKIPLISTNODE.LINK(i)
   return $links[i]$

Precondition: i is a non-zero NAT no greater than the level, and s is a (possibly nil) reference to a SKIPLISTNODE.
Postcondition: Sets the ith element of the sequence to s, or to *empty* if s is nil.

SKIPLISTNODE.SETLINK(i, s : SKIPLISTNODE)
   $links[i] \leftarrow s$

We interpret the represented set to be the data items in the linked list beginning with *start* and ending with *end*, using the variables *links*[1] to obtain the next element in the list; the data items in *start* and *end* are excluded from the set.

    Our structural invariant is:

- Both *start* and *end* have a level of $M \geq maxLevel$.
- *start.key* = *minKey*, which is the smallest possible key.
- *end.key* = *maxKey*, which is the largest possible key.

- There is a sequence of SKIPLISTNODEs with length $size + 2$ obtained by starting with *start* and following the *links*[1] reference in each SKIPLISTNODE until *end* is reached. We will refer to this sequence as the level-1 sequence.
- For $1 < i \leq M$, there is a sequence obtained in the same way as above, but using the *links*[i] variables instead of the *links*[1] variables. We will refer to this sequence as the level-i sequence. The level-i sequence is the subsequence of the level-$(i-1)$ sequence containing those SKIPLISTNODEs having level i or greater.
- The keys in each sequence are strictly increasing in value.
- *maxLevel* is the maximum level of any SKIPLISTNODE in the above sequences, excluding *start* and *end*. If *start* and *end* are the only SKIPLISTNODEs in the sequences, $maxLevel = 1$.

In order to be able to approximate a binary search with this data structure, the level-i sequence should include roughly every second node from the level-$(i-1)$ sequence, for $1 < i \leq maxLevel$. However, as is suggested by Figure 6.23, we will not explicitly maintain this property. Instead, we will use randomization to produce a structure that we expect, on average, to approximate this property.

When we insert a new data item, we first determine the level of its SKIPLISTNODE via a series of flips of a fair coin. As long as the outcome of a coin flip is heads, we continue flipping. We stop flipping when the outcome is tails. The level of the SKIPLISTNODE is the total number of flips. Because we flip the coin at least once, every level will be at least 1. Because the coin is fair, the probability of tails is $1/2$; hence, we would expect about half of the SKIPLISTNODEs to have level 1. The probability of flipping heads then tails is $(1/2)^2 = 1/4$, so we would expect about $1/4$ of the SKIPLISTNODEs to have level 2. In general, the probability of flipping $i-1$ heads followed by 1 tails is 2^{-i}. We would therefore expect the fraction of nodes having level i to be about 2^{-i}. Because the coin is fair, these levels should be randomly distributed over the level-1 sequence.

Suppose a given SKIPLISTNODE has level l. In order to insert it into the skip list, we need to insert it into its proper location in the level-i sequence for each i, $1 \leq i \leq l$. For the purpose of finding these insertion points, we will design a function FIND(k, l), which will return an array of references such that at index i, $1 \leq i \leq l$, is the reference to the SKIPLISTNODE of level at least i having the largest key strictly less than k. We will then be able to use this function not only in the PUT operation, but also in the GET and REMOVE operations. The PUT operation is shown in Figure 6.25.

Figure 6.25 SKIPLISTDICTIONARY implementation (partial) of ORDEREDDIC-
TIONARY

SKIPLISTDICTIONARY()
  $start \leftarrow$ **new** SKIPLISTNODE(nil, minKey, 100)
  $end \leftarrow$ **new** SKIPLISTNODE(nil, maxKey, 100)
  for $i \leftarrow 1$ **to** 100
    $start.$SETLINK(i, end)
  $size \leftarrow 0$; $maxLevel \leftarrow 1$

SKIPLISTDICTIONARY.PUT(x, k)
  if $x =$ nil
    error
  else
    $l \leftarrow 1$
    while FLIPCOIN() = heads
      $l \leftarrow l + 1$
    $p \leftarrow$ FIND(k, l)
    if $p[1].$LINK(1).KEY() $\neq k$
      $maxLevel \leftarrow$ MAX($maxLevel, l$); $q \leftarrow$ **new** SKIPLISTNODE(x, k, l)
      for $i \leftarrow 1$ **to** l
        $q.$SETLINK($i, p[i].$LINK(i)); $p[i].$SETLINK(i, q)

— **Internal Functions Follow** —

Precondition: k is a KEY and l is a non-zero NAT, no larger than the
levels of *start* or *end*.

Postcondition: Returns an array $A[1..l]$ such that $A[i]$ refers to the
SKIPLISTNODE of level i or larger having the largest key strictly less than
k.

SKIPLISTDICTIONARY.FIND(k, l)
  $A \leftarrow$ **new** ARRAY[1..l]; $p \leftarrow start$
  for $i \leftarrow$ MAX($maxLevel, l$) **to** 1 **by** -1
    while $p.$LINK(i).KEY() $< k$
      $p \leftarrow p.$LINK(i)
    if $i \leq l$
      $A[i] \leftarrow p$
  return A

The partial implementation shown in Figure 6.25 does not explicitly handle the case in which the level of a new node exceeds the level of *start* and *end*. In what follows, we will assume that these arrays are expanded as needed using the expandable array design pattern. Later, we will argue that for all practical purposes, a fixed-sized array can be used. In the meantime, we note that the time needed to expand the array is proportional to the number of iterations of the **while** loop in PUT, so we need not amortize this cost.

We will devote the remainder of this section to analyzing the expected running time of PUT. This analysis is rather involved, but it uses some important new tools for analyzing expected running times. Furthermore, much of this analysis can be applied directly to the analyses of GET and REMOVE; we therefore leave these analyses as exercises. In view of the sometimes counter-intuitive nature of expected values, we will proceed with care.

We will partition the algorithm into five parts:

- the **while** loop;
- the call to FIND;
- the construction of a new SKIPLISTNODE;
- the **for** loop; and
- the remainder of the algorithm for the case in which $x \neq$ nil.

At this point, let us observe that a worst-case input must have $x \neq$ nil and k as a new key, not already in the set. On any such input, the overall running time is the sum of the running times of the above five parts. By the linearity of expectation, the expected running time of the algorithm on a worst-case input is therefore the sum of the expected running times of these five parts on a worst-case input.

We begin by analyzing the **while** loop. We define the discrete probability space *Seq* to be the set of all finite sequences of flips containing zero or more heads, followed by exactly one tails. Note that for each positive integer i, there is exactly one sequence in *Seq* with length i; hence, *Seq* is countable. As we have already argued, the probability of achieving a sequence of length i is 2^{-i}. In order to conclude that *Seq* is a discrete probability space, we must show that

$$\sum_{i=1}^{\infty} 2^{-i} = 1.$$

This fact follows from the following theorem, using $c = 2$ and $a = -1$.

Theorem 6.7. *For any real numbers a and c such that $c > 1$,*

$$\sum_{i=0}^{\infty} c^{a-i} = \frac{c^{a+1}}{c-1}.$$

Proof.

$$\sum_{i=0}^{\infty} c^{a-i} = \lim_{n \to \infty} \sum_{i=0}^{n} c^{a-i}$$

$$= c^a \lim_{n \to \infty} \sum_{i=0}^{n} (1/c)^i$$

$$= c^a \lim_{n \to \infty} \frac{(1/c)^{n+1} - 1}{\frac{1}{c} - 1} \quad \text{from } (2.2)$$

$$= c^a \lim_{n \to \infty} \frac{c - (1/c)^n}{c - 1}$$

$$= \frac{c^{a+1}}{c-1}$$

because $1/c < 1$. □

We now define the discrete random variable *len* over *Seq* such that *len*(e) is the length of the sequence of flips. Note that $E[\textit{len}]$ gives us the expected number of times the **while** loop condition is tested, as well as the expected final value of l. As a result, it also gives us the expected number of iterations of the **for** loop, provided k is not already in the set.

Because *len*(e) is always a natural number, we can apply Theorem 5.5 (page 172) to obtain $E[\textit{len}]$. The probability that a sequence has length at least i is the probability that $i - 1$ flips all result in heads, or 2^{1-i}. Thus,

$$E[\textit{len}] = \sum_{i=1}^{\infty} 2^{1-i}$$

$$= 2$$

from Theorem 6.7. We can therefore expect the **while** loop in PUT to iterate once, yielding an expected value of 2 for l, on average. Hence, the **for** loop, if it executes, iterates twice on average. The expected running times of both loops are therefore in $\Theta(1)$ for a worst-case input.

In order to determine the expected running time of the SKIPLISTNODE constructor, we need to analyze it again, but this time doing an expected-case analysis using *len* as its third parameter. Using the same analysis as we did for the **for** loop in PUT, we see that its expected running time is in $\Theta(1)$.

In order to complete the expected-case analysis of PUT, we need to analyze FIND. We will begin by defining an appropriate discrete probability space. Let Seq^n be the set of all n-tuples of elementary events from Seq; i.e., each elementary event in Seq^n is an n-tuple $\langle e_1, \ldots, e_n \rangle$ such that each e_i is a sequence of coin flips containing zero or more **heads**, followed by exactly one **tails**. Such an n-tuple describes the "shape" of a skip list by recording, for each of the n data elements, the sequence of coin flips which generated the level of the SKIPLISTNODE containing it.

In order to show that Seq^n is countable, we can label each n-tuple $\langle e_1, \ldots, e_n \rangle \in Seq^n$ with the natural number

$$p_1^{len(e_1)} p_2^{len(e_2)} \cdots p_n^{len(e_n)},$$

where p_i is the ith prime. Because each elementary event in Seq is uniquely identified by its length, and because each positive integer has a unique prime factorization, each tuple has a unique label; hence, Seq^n is countable.

We need to define the probabilities of elements in Seq^n. In order to do this properly, we need to extend the definition of independence given in Section 5.5 to more than two events. We say that a set S of events is *pairwise independent* if for every pair of events $e_1, e_2 \in S$, e_1 and e_2 are independent. If for every subset $T \subseteq S$ containing at least two events,

> This $\prod$-notation denotes the product of the probabilities $P(e)$ for all events e in T.

$$P\left(\bigcap_{e \in T} e \right) = \prod_{e \in T} P(e),$$

then we say the events in S are *mutually independent*. We leave as an exercise to show that pairwise independence does not necessarily imply mutual independence, even for 3-element sets of events.

Returning to Seq^n, let len_{ij} denote the event that component i has length j, for $1 \le i \le n$, $j > 1$. In any set $\{ len_{i_1 j_1}, \ldots, len_{i_m j_m} \}$ with $2 \le m \le n$ and all the i_ks different, the events should be mutually

> In other words, the probability that all of the events in T occur is the product of the probabilities for each of these events.

independent. Furthermore, in order to be consistent with Seq, we want $P(len_{ij}) = 2^{-j}$ for $1 \le i \le n$ and $j > 1$. We can satisfy these constraints by setting the probability of elementary event $\langle e_1, \ldots, e_n \rangle$ to the product of the probabilities in *Seq* of $e_1, \ldots, e_n$; i.e.,

$$P(\langle e_1, \ldots, e_n \rangle) = \prod_{i=1}^{n} 2^{-len(e_i)}.$$

It can be shown by a straightforward induction on n that the sum of the probabilities of the elementary events in Seq^n is 1. Seq^n is therefore a discrete probability space.

We now need to determine what comprises a worst-case input to FIND. As we suggested earlier, the components of an elementary event in Seq^n correspond to the n data elements in a skip list. The length of a component gives the level of the skip list element. Apart from the number of elements in the structure, the shape of a skip list is determined completely at random, independent of the data elements inserted or the order in which they are inserted. Specifically, the keys in the data elements determine their order, but their levels are determined solely by coin flips. Thus, in order to determine a worst-case input, we needn't worry about how the structure was constructed — we need only concern ourselves with the parameters to FIND. Both of these values can affect the running time.

In order to determine the worst-case input, we need to consider the behavior of the **while** loop. For a given value of i, the **while** loop iterates once for each key at level i that is

- less than k; and
- greater than the largest key less than k at any level $j > i$ (or $-\infty$ if there is no such key).

It is easily seen that at any level i, the expected number of iterations is maximized when the number of keys less than k is maximized, because the levels of these keys are determined randomly. The worst-case input therefore has k greater than any key in the data set.

We therefore define $tail_i(e)$, where $e = \langle e_1, \ldots, e_n \rangle \in Seq^n$, to be the largest natural number j such that some suffix of e contains j components with length exactly i and no components longer than i. Thus, if e contains at least one component strictly longer than i, then $tail_i(e)$ is the number of components with length i that follow the last component strictly longer than i. Otherwise, $tail_i(e)$ is simply the number of components with length i.

Example 6.8. Let e represent the skip list shown in Figure 6.23 on page 226. Then

- $tail_1(e) = 0$ because there are no level-1 nodes following the last node with level greater than 1;

- $tail_2(e) = 2$ because there are 2 level-2 nodes following the last node with level greater than 2; and
- $tail_3(e) = 1$ because there is 1 level-3 node, and there are no nodes with level greater than 3.

Suppose e describes some skip list with n elements, and suppose this skip list's FIND function is called with a key larger than any in the list. The running time of FIND is then proportional to the number of times the **while** loop condition is tested. On iteration i of the **for** loop, the **while** loop will iterate exactly $tail_i(e)$ times, but will be tested $tail_i(e) + 1$ times, including the test that causes the loop to terminate. The expected running time of FIND on a worst-case input is therefore proportional to:

$$E\left[\sum_{i=1}^{\max(maxLevel,l)} (tail_i + 1)\right]$$

$$= E\left[\left(\sum_{i=1}^{\max(maxLevel,l)} tail_i\right) + \max(maxLevel, l)\right]$$

$$= E\left[\sum_{i=1}^{\max(maxLevel,l)} tail_i\right] + E[\max(maxLevel, l)]. \qquad (6.9)$$

Let us first consider the first term in (6.9). It is tempting to apply linearity of expectation to this term; however, note that $maxLevel$ is a random variable, as its value depends on the levels of the nodes in the skip list. Theorem 5.9 therefore does not apply to this term. In particular, note that for any positive n and i, there is a non-zero probability that there is at least one node at level i; hence, there is a non-zero probability that $tail_i$ is positive.

The proper way to handle this kind of a summation, therefore, is to convert it to an infinite sum. The term inside the summation should be equal to $tail_i$ when $i \le \max(maxLevel, l)$, but should be 0 for all larger i. In this case, it is easy to derive such a term, as $tail_i = 0$ when $i > maxLevel$. We therefore have:

$$E\left[\sum_{i=1}^{\max(maxLevel,l)} tail_i\right] = E\left[\sum_{i=1}^{\infty} tail_i\right]$$

$$= \sum_{i=1}^{\infty} E[tail_i]. \qquad (6.10)$$

By Theorem 5.5,

$$E[tail_i] = \sum_{j=1}^{\infty} P(tail_i \geq j).$$

Suppose that there are at least j components with length at least i. In order for $tail_i \geq j$, the ith coin flip in each of the last j of these components must be tails. The probability that j independent coin flips are all tails is 2^{-j}. However, this is not the probability that $tail_i \geq j$, but rather the conditional probability given that there are at least j components with length at least i. Let num_i denote the number of components whose length is at least i. We then have

$$P(tail_i \geq j \mid num_i \geq j) = 2^{-j}.$$

Fortunately, this conditional probability is closely related to $P(tail_i \geq j)$. Specifically, in order for $tail_i \geq j$, it must be the case that $num_i \geq j$. Thus, the event $tail_i \geq j$ is a subset of the event $num_i \geq j$. Therefore, from (5.2) we have

$$P(tail_i \geq j) = P((tail_i \geq j) \cap (num_i \geq j))$$

$$= P(num_i \geq j)P(tail_i \geq j \mid num_i \geq j)$$

$$= P(num_i \geq j)2^{-j}.$$

Unfortunately, computing the exact value of $P(num_i \geq j)$ is rather difficult. We will therefore content ourselves with observing that because it is a probability, it can be no more than 1. We therefore have,

$$E[tail_i] = \sum_{j=1}^{\infty} P(tail_i \geq j)$$

$$= \sum_{j=1}^{\infty} P(num_i \geq j)2^{-j}$$

$$\leq \sum_{j=1}^{\infty} 2^{-j}$$

$$= 1$$

from Theorem 6.7.

This bound seems quite good, perhaps even surprisingly so. It tells us that on any iteration of the **for** loop, we can expect the **while** loop to iterate no more than once, on average. Still, this bound does not give a finite bound for (6.10). However, we have already observed that for any $e \in Seq^n$, $tail_i(e)$ will be 0 for all but finitely many i. This follows because there are only finitely many nonempty levels. Consequently, we might want to use the fact that $tail_i(e) \le num_i(e)$; hence, $E[tail_i] \le E[num_i]$.

While this bound would yield a finite bound for (6.10), it unfortunately is still too loose, as $num_1(e) = n$ for every $e \in Seq^n$. We would like to derive a logarithmic upper bound, if possible. However, we can use a combination of the two bounds. In particular, the bound of 1 seems to be a good upper bound as long as it is less than $E[num_i]$. Once i is large enough that $E[num_i] \le 1$, $E[num_i]$ would be a better bound. If we can determine the smallest value of i such that $E[num_i] \le 1$, we should be able to break the infinite sum into two sums and derive tight bounds for each of them.

In order to analyze $E[num_i]$, we observe that for $e \in Seq^n$, $num_i(e)$ is a count of the number of components whose lengths are at least i. Furthermore, we can express the fact that a component has a length of at least i as an event in Seq. The standard technique for counting events is to use an *indicator random variable*. Specifically, consider the event in Seq that $len \ge i$; i.e., this event is the set of sequences of coin flips consisting of at least $i - 1$ **heads**, followed by exactly one **tails**. The *indicator* for this event is then defined to be

$$I(len \ge i)(e_j) = \begin{cases} 1 & \text{if } len(e_j) \ge i \\ 0 & \text{otherwise.} \end{cases}$$

We can then express num_i as follows:

$$num_i(\langle e_1, \dots, e_n \rangle) = \sum_{j=1}^{n} I(len \ge i)(e_j).$$

The utility of indicator random variables is shown by the following theorem, whose proof follows immediately from Theorem 5.5.

Theorem 6.9. *Let e be any event in a discrete probability space. Then $E[I(e)] = P(e)$.*

Applying the above theorem, we obtain

$$E[num_i] = E\left[\sum_{j=1}^{n} I(len \ge i)\right]$$

$$= E[nI(len \ge i)]$$

$$= nE[I(\text{len} \geq i)]$$

$$= nP(\text{len} \geq i)$$

$$= n2^{1-i}.$$

Clearly, $E[num_i] > 1$ iff $i < 1 + \lg n$. This suggests that *maxLevel* should typically be about $\lg n$ (however, this is not a proof of the expected value of *maxLevel*). Because we already know that the **while** loop is expected to iterate no more than once for each level, this suggests that the overall running time is logarithmic in n (assuming l is sufficiently small). While we don't have quite enough yet to show this, we can now show a logarithmic bound on the first term in (6.9):

$$\sum_{i=1}^{\infty} E[tail_i] \leq \sum_{i=1}^{\infty} (\min(1, E[num_i]))$$

$$= \sum_{i=1}^{\lceil \lg n \rceil} 1 + \sum_{i=\lceil \lg n \rceil + 1}^{\infty} n2^{1-i}$$

$$= \lceil \lg n \rceil + n \sum_{i=0}^{\infty} 2^{-\lceil \lg n \rceil - i}$$

$$= \lceil \lg n \rceil + n2^{1-\lceil \lg n \rceil}$$

$$\leq \lceil \lg n \rceil + n2^{1-\lg n}$$

$$= \lceil \lg n \rceil + 2. \tag{6.11}$$

In order to complete the analysis of FIND, we must consider the second term in (6.9), namely, $E[\max(maxLevel, l)]$. It would be nice if we could use a property like the linearity of expectation to conclude that this value is equal to $\max(E[maxLevel], E[l])$; however, such a property does not necessarily hold (see Exercise 6.16). On the other hand, because *maxLevel* and l are nonnegative, we can use the fact that $\max(maxLevel, l) \leq maxLevel + l$. Therefore,

$$E[\max(maxLevel, l)] \leq E[maxLevel + l]$$

$$= E[maxLevel] + E[l]. \tag{6.12}$$

For the case in which FIND is called from PUT, we know that $E[l] = 2$. We therefore need to evaluate $E[maxLevel]$. Note that *maxLevel* is the number of nonempty levels. We can therefore use another indicator random variable to express *maxLevel* — specifically,

$$maxLevel = \sum_{i=1}^{\infty} I(num_i > 0).$$

We therefore have

$$E[maxLevel] = E\left[\sum_{i=1}^{\infty} I(num_i > 0)\right]$$

$$= \sum_{i=1}^{\infty} E[I(num_i > 0)]. \qquad (6.13)$$

Clearly, $I(num_i > 0)(e) \le 1$ for all $e \in Seq^n$, so that $E[I(num_i > 0)] \le 1$. Furthermore, $I(num_i > 0)(e) \le num_i(e)$, so that $E[I(num_i > 0)] \le E[num_i]$. We therefore have $E[I(num_i > 0)] \le \min(1, E[num_i])$, which is the same upper bound we showed for $E[tail_i]$. Therefore, following the derivation of (6.11), we have

$$E[maxLevel] \le \lceil \lg n \rceil + 2. \qquad (6.14)$$

Now combining (6.9), (6.10), (6.11), (6.12), and (6.14), it follows that the expected number of tests of the **while** loop condition is no more than

$$2(\lceil \lg n \rceil + 2) + 2 \in O(\lg n),$$

for a worst-case input when FIND is called by PUT. The expected running time of FIND in this context is therefore in $O(\lg n)$.

A matching lower bound for the expected running time of FIND can also be shown — the details are outlined in Exercise 6.18. We can therefore conclude that the expected running time of FIND when called from PUT on a worst-case input is in $\Theta(\lg n)$.

We can now complete the analysis of PUT. We have shown that the expected running times for both loops and the constructor for SKIPLIST-NODE are all in $\Theta(1)$. The expected running time of $\text{FIND}(k, l)$ is in $\Theta(\lg n)$. The remainder of the algorithm clearly runs in $\Theta(1)$ time. The total time is therefore expected to be in $\Theta(\lg n)$ for a worst-case input. We leave as exercises to design GET and REMOVE to run in $\Theta(\lg n)$ expected time, as well.

Earlier, we suggested that for all practical purposes, fixed-sized arrays could be used for both *start.elements* and *end.elements*. We can now justify that claim by observing that

$$P(num_i > 0) = E[I(num_i > 0)]$$
$$\leq E[num_i]$$
$$= n2^{1-i}.$$

Thus, the probability that some element has a level strictly greater than 100 is at most $n2^{-100}$. Because $2^{-20} < 10^{-6}$, this means that for $n \leq 2^{80} \approx 10^{24}$, the probability that a level higher than 100 is reached is less than one in a million. Such a small probability of error can safely be considered negligible.

6.5   Summary

A summary of the running times of the operations for the various implementations of ORDEREDDICTIONARY is given in Figure 6.26. $\Theta(\lg n)$-time implementations of the GET, PUT, and REMOVE operations for the ORDEREDDICTIONARY interface can be achieved in three ways:

- A balanced binary search tree, such as an AVL tree, guarantees $\Theta(\lg n)$ performance in the worst case.
- A splay tree is a binary search tree that guarantees $O(\lg n)$ amortized performance by rotating the items accessed to the root. This has an additional benefit of leaving frequently accessed items near the root, so that they are accessed more quickly.
- A skip list uses randomization to achieve $\Theta(\lg n)$ expected performance for worst-case inputs.

The worst-case stack space usage for each of the AVL tree operations is in $\Theta(\lg n)$. Because the skip list implementation uses no recursion, its worst-case stack space usage is in $\Theta(1)$. However, unless the splay tree implementation is revised to remove the recursion (see Exercise 6.14), its worst-case stack space usage is in $\Theta(n)$.

Section 6.4 introduced the use of indicator random variables for analyzing randomized algorithms. The application of this technique involves converting the expected value of a random variable to the expected values of indicator random variables and ultimately to probabilities. Theorems 5.5, 5.9, and 6.9 are useful in performing this conversion. The probabilities are then computed using the probabilities of the elementary events and the laws of probability

---

Figure 6.26 Running times of the SMALLCAPS{OrderedDictionary} operations for various implementations

	GET	PUT	REMOVE
BSTDICTIONARY	$\Theta(n)$	$\Theta(n)$	$\Theta(n)$
AVLDICTIONARY	$\Theta(\lg n)$	$\Theta(\lg n)$	$\Theta(\lg n)$
SPLAYDICTIONARY	$O(\lg n)$ amortized	$O(\lg n)$ amortized	$O(\lg n)$ amortized
SKIPLISTDICTIONARY	$\Theta(\lg n)$ expected	$\Theta(\lg n)$ expected	$\Theta(\lg n)$ expected

Notes:

- n is the number of elements in the dictionary.
- The constructor and the SIZE operation each run in $\Theta(1)$ worst-case time for each implementation.
- The VISITINORDER operation runs in $\Theta(n)$ worst-case time for each implementation, assuming that the VISIT operation for the given VISITOR runs in $\Theta(1)$ time.
- Unless otherwise noted, all running times are worst-case.

---

theory. Because we are only interested in asymptotic bounds, probabilities which are difficult to compute exactly can often be bounded by probabilities that are easier to compute.

6.6 Exercises

Exercise 6.1. Prove the correctness of BSTDICTIONARY.TRAVERSEINORDER, shown in Figure 6.7.

Exercise 6.2. Draw the result of inserting the following keys in the order given into an initially empty binary search tree:

$$34, 65, 75, 54, 19, 45, 11, 23, 90, 15$$

Exercise 6.3. Draw the result of deleting each of the following keys from the tree shown in Figure 6.10, assuming that it is an ordinary binary search tree. The deletions are not cumulative; i.e., each deletion operates on the original tree.

a. 55

b. 74

c. 34

Exercise 6.4. Repeat Exercise 6.2 for an AVL tree.

Exercise 6.5. Repeat Exercise 6.3 assuming the tree is an AVL tree.

Exercise 6.6. Repeat Exercise 6.2 for a splay tree.

Exercise 6.7. Repeat Exercise 6.3 assuming the tree is a splay tree.

Exercise 6.8. Complete the implementation of AVLDICTIONARY, shown in Figure 6.13, so that GET, PUT, and REMOVE run in $\Theta(\lg n)$ time in the worst case, and so that PUT and REMOVE use $\Theta(\lg n)$ stack space in the worst case. Prove the correctness, running time, and stack space usage of the resulting implementation.

Exercise 6.9. The *depth* of a node in a tree is its distance from the root; specifically the root has depth 0 and the depth of any other node is 1 plus the depth of its parent. Prove by induction on the height h of any AVL tree that every leaf has depth at least $h/2$.

* Exercise 6.10. Prove that when a node is inserted into an AVL tree, at most one rotation is performed.

** Exercise 6.11. Prove that if $2^m - 1$ keys are inserted into an AVL tree in increasing order, the result is a perfectly balanced tree. [*Hint:* You will need to describe the shape of the tree after n insertions for arbitrary n, and prove this by induction on n.]

Exercise 6.12. A *red-black tree* is a binary search tree whose nodes are colored either red or black such that

- if a node is red, then the roots of its non-empty children are black; and
- from any given node, every path to any empty subtree has the same number of black nodes.

We call the number of black nodes on a path from a node to an empty subtree to be the *black-height* of that node. In calculating the black-height of a node, we consider that the node itself is on the path to the empty subtree.

a. Prove by induction on the height of a red-black tree that if the black-height of the root is b, then the tree has at least $2^b - 1$ black nodes.
b. Prove that if a red-black tree has height h, then it has at least $2^{h/2} - 1$ nodes.
c. Prove that if a red-black tree has n nodes, then its height is at most $2\lg(n+1)$.

Exercise 6.13. Give a splay-tree implementation of PUT based on SPLAY-DICTIONARY.FIND, shown in Figure 6.16. You do not need to include algorithms for the rotations. Prove its correctness, assuming the rotations are correct.

* Exercise 6.14. Give a splay-tree implementation that does not use recursion. Instead, use loops with an explicit stack. You do not need to include algorithms for the rotations. Prove its correctness, assuming the rotations are correct.

Exercise 6.15. Prove by induction on n that the sum of the probabilities of the elementary events in Seq^n is 1.

Exercise 6.16. Let $S = \{\text{heads}, \text{tails}\}$ be the discrete probability space in which $P(\text{heads}) = P(\text{tails}) = 1/2$.

a. Using the definition of expected value, compute

$$E[\max(I(\text{heads}), I(\text{tails}))].$$

b. Using Theorem 6.9, compute

$$\max(E[I(\text{heads})], E[I(\text{tails})]).$$

Your answer should be different from your answer in part (a).

Exercise 6.17. Prove that if f and g are discrete random variables in a discrete probability space, then

$$E[\max(f, g)] \geq \max(E[f], E[g]).$$

* Exercise 6.18. The goal of this exercise is to show a lower bound on the expected running time of SKIPLISTDICTIONARY.FIND.

a. Prove that $P(num_i > 0) = 1 - (1 - 2^{1-i})^n$. [*Hint:* First compute $P(num_i = 0)$.]

b. Prove the *binomial theorem*, namely, for any real a, b, and natural number n,

$$(a + b)^n = \sum_{j=0}^{n} \binom{n}{j} a^{n-j} b^j, \tag{6.15}$$

where

$$\binom{n}{j} = \frac{n!}{j!(n-j)!}$$

are the *binomial coefficients* for $0 \leq j \leq n$. [*Hint:* Use induction on n.]

c. Using the results of parts (a) and (b), prove that for $i \leq \lg n + 1$,

$$P(num_i > 0) > 1/2.$$

d. Using the result of part (c), Exercise 6.17, and (6.13), prove that

$$E[\max(maxLevel, l)] \in \Omega(\lg n),$$

and hence, the expected running time of FIND is in $\Omega(\lg n)$.

Exercise 6.19. Give algorithms for SKIPLISTDICTIONARY.GET and SKIP-LISTDICTIONARY.REMOVE. Prove that they meet their specifications and run in expected $\Theta(\lg n)$ time for worst-case input. Note that in both cases, you will need to modify the analysis of SKIPLISTDICTIONARY.FIND to use the appropriate value for $E[l]$. You may use the result of Exercise 6.18 for the lower bounds.

Exercise 6.20. Suppose we define a discrete probability space consisting of all ordered pairs of flips of a fair coin. This probability space contains four elementary events, each having probability $1/4$. We define the following three events:

- e_1: the first flip is heads;
- e_2: the second flip is heads; and
- e_3: the two flips are different.

Show that the three events are pairwise independent, but not mutually independent.

* Exercise 6.21. Let *len* be as defined in Section 6.4. For each of the following, either find the expected value or show that it diverges (i.e., that it is infinite).

a. $E[2^{len}]$.
b. $E[\sqrt{2^{len}}]$.

Exercise 6.22. Let $A[1..n]$ be a random permutation of the positive integers less than or equal to n, such that each permutation is equally likely. Recall from Exercise 3.31 (page 103) that an inversion is a pair of indices $1 \leq i < j \leq n$ such that $A[i] > A[j]$. Determine the expected number of inversions in A. [*Hint:* Use an indicator random variable for the event that (i, j) is an inversion.]

Exercise 6.23. As in the above exercise, let $A[1..n]$ be a random permutation of the positive integers less than or equal to n, such that each permutation is equally likely. What is the expected number of indices i such that $A[i] = i$?

6.7 Notes

AVL trees, which comprise the first balanced binary search tree scheme, were introduced by Adel'son-Vel'skiĭ and Landis [1]. Splay trees were introduced by Sleator and Tarjan [107]. Red-black trees, mentioned in Exercise 6.12, were introduced by Bayer [8] (see also Gubias and Sedgewick [60]). Balance in red-black trees is maintained using the same rotations as for splay trees. As a result, keys can be accessed in $\Theta(\lg n)$ time in the worst case. Because heights don't need to be calculated, they tend to perform better than AVL trees and are widely used in practice. A somewhat simpler version of red-black trees, known as AA-trees, was introduced by Andersson [5].

All of the above trees can be manipulated by the tree viewer on this textbook's web site. The implementations of these trees within this package are all immutable.

Another important balanced search tree scheme is the B-tree, introduced by Bayer and McCreight [9]. A B-tree is a data structure designed for accessing keyed data from an external storage device. B-trees therefore have high branching factor in order to minimize the number of device accesses needed. Red-black trees and AA-trees are actually simulations of B-trees with a maximum branching factor of 4 (called 2-3-4 trees) and 3 (called 2-3 trees), respectively.

Skip lists were introduced by Pugh [100].

Chapter 7

Storage/Retrieval II: Unordered Keys

In the last chapter, we considered the problem of storage and retrieval, assuming that we also need to be able to access keys in a predefined order. In this chapter, we drop this assumption; i.e., we will be considering implementations of DICTIONARY (see Figure 6.2, p. 204) rather than ORDEREDDICTIONARY. The structures we defined in the last chapter all utilized the ordering on the keys to guide the searches. Hence, it might seem that there is nothing to be gained by neglecting to keep the keys in order. However, we will see that *disorder* can actually be more beneficial when it comes to locating keys quickly.

7.1 Arrays with Virtual Initialization

A simple implementation of DICTIONARY is to store all of the elements in an array indexed by keys. Though this approach is simple, it has several difficulties. The first difficulty is in using a key as an array index. For example, if our keys are strings, we must somehow be able to interpret them as natural numbers. Another difficulty is that we may have no fixed bound on the size of our keys. In this case, we would not know how large an array to construct. An expandable array would not yield a satisfactory solution because however we determine the size of the array, the next key can be so large that a new array must be constructed. Thus, we would have to expand the array each time a new key is inserted. Such an approach is clearly too expensive.

In spite of these difficulties, there is still a theoretically interesting approach using keys as array indices, provided we are willing to make some assumptions. First, we assume that each key is a natural number (or equivalently, each key can be treated as a natural number). Second, we assume that there is a known upper bound on the values of all of the keys. Even with these assumptions, it can still be the case that the range of the keys is much larger than the number of keys. For example, suppose our data set consists of 5,000 items keyed by 9-digit natural numbers (e.g., Social Security Numbers). An array of 1 billion elements is required to store these 5,000 items. Initializing such an array would be very expensive.

Note, however, that once an array is initialized, storage and retrieval can both be done in $\Theta(1)$ time in the worst case. What we need is a technique for initializing an array in $\Theta(1)$ time while maintaining constant-time accesses to elements. We will now present such a technique, known as *virtual initialization*. This technique involves keeping track of which array elements have been initialized in a way that facilitates making this determination quickly. We assume that the environment provides a facility for allocating an array in $\Theta(1)$ time without initializing its locations. We will call the resulting data structure a VARRAY.

In addition to an array *elements*$[0..n-1]$ to store the data, we also need an array *used*$[0..n-1]$ of NATs to keep track of which locations of *elements* are used to store data. We use a NAT *num* to keep track of how many locations of *elements* store data items. Thus, *used*$[0..num-1]$ will be indices at which data items are stored in *elements*. Finally, in order to facilitate a quick determination of whether *elements*$[i]$ contains a data element, we use a third array *loc*$[0..n-1]$ such that *loc*$[i]$ stores the index in *used* at which i is stored, if indeed i is in *used*$[0..num-1]$. The structural invariant is that $0 \leq num \leq n$, and for $0 \leq i < num$, *loc*$[used[i]] = i$. We interpret *elements*$[i]$ as giving the data item at location i if $0 \leq loc[i] < num$ and *used*$[loc[i]] = i$; otherwise, we interpret the value stored at location i as nil.

For example, Figure 7.1 shows a VARRAY with 10 locations, storing 35 at location 4, 17 at location 7, and nil at all other locations. Note that for $i = 4$ or $i = 7$, $0 \leq loc[i] < num$ and *used*$[loc[i]] = i$. For other values of i, it is possible that *loc*$[i]$ stores a natural number less than *num*; however, if this is the case, then *used*$[loc[i]]$ is either 4 or 7, so that *used*$[loc[i]] \neq i$.

To initialize all locations of the VARRAY to nil, we simply set *num* to 0. In this way, there is no possible value of *loc*$[i]$ such that $0 \leq loc[i] < num$, so we interpret all locations as being nil. To retrieve the value at location i, we first determine whether $0 \leq loc[i] < num$ and *used*$[loc[i]] = i$. Note, however, that *loc*$[i]$ may not yet have been initialized, so that it may not even refer to a NUMBER. Therefore, we must first verify that it is a NAT. If all these tests are passed, we return *elements*$[i]$; otherwise, we return nil.

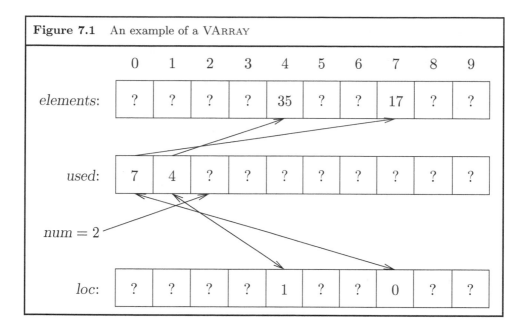

Figure 7.1 An example of a VARRAY

To store x at location i of the VARRAY, we must first determine as above whether *elements*[i] is currently being used to store a data item — i.e., whether $0 \leq loc[i] < num$ and *used*[*loc*[i]] = i. If so, we can simply store x in *elements*[i]. Otherwise, we must also update the other representation variables to reflect the fact that we are using location i to store a data item. In particular, we must store i in *used*[*num*], store *num* in *loc*[i], and increment *num*. As a result, we interpret *elements*[i] as storing x, and the structural invariant is maintained. The entire implementation of VARRAY is shown in Figure 7.2.

It is easily seen that the constructor and all operations of VARRAY operate in $\Theta(1)$ time. However, it uses $\Theta(n)$ space, where n is the size of the range of indices, not the number of elements stored. Thus, if a VARRAY is used to implement a DICTIONARY, its space usage will be proportional to the number of possible keys. This number may be much larger than the number of keys actually stored in the DICTIONARY.

In the remainder of this chapter, we will examine techniques for improving the space usage while maintaining fast storage and retrieval. Though we cannot guarantee $\Theta(1)$ worst-case access time when we reduce the space usage, we can achieve amortized expected access time proportional to the length of the key, even if the keys are not natural numbers and have an unbounded range. Consequently, if the keys do have a fixed range, the amortized expected access time is in $\Theta(1)$.

Figure 7.2   Implementation of VARRAY

Structural Invariant: $0 \leq num \leq n$, and for $0 \leq i < num$, $loc[used[i]] = i$.

Precondition: n is a NAT.
Postcondition: Constructs a VARRAY with locations $0, \ldots, n-1$, all initialized to nil.

VARRAY(n)
    elements ← **new** ARRAY$[0..n-1]$; *used* ← **new** ARRAY$[0..n-1]$
    loc ← **new** ARRAY$[0..n-1]$; *num* ← 0

Precondition: true.
Postcondition: Sets all locations to nil.

VARRAY.CLEAR()
    num ← 0

Precondition: i is a NAT less than the number of locations.
Postcondition: Returns the value stored at location i.

VARRAY.GET(i)
    if *loc*$[i]$ **isType** NAT **and** *loc*$[i] < num$ **and** *used*$[loc[i]] = i$
        return *elements*$[i]$
    else
        return nil

Precondition: i is a NAT less than the number of locations.
Postcondition: Sets the value stored at location i to x.

VARRAY.PUT(x, i)
    if not ISNAT(*loc*$[i]$) **or** *loc*$[i] \geq num$ **or** *used*$[loc[i]] \neq i$
        loc$[i]$ ← *num*; *used*$[num]$ ← i; *num* ← *num* + 1
    elements$[i]$ ← x

7.2   Hashing

The technique we will develop over the remainder of this chapter is known as *hashing*. The basic idea behind hashing is to convert each key k to an index $h(k)$ using a *hash function* h, so that for all k, $0 \leq h(k) < m$ for some positive integer m. $h(k)$ is then used as an index into a *hash table*, which is an array $T[0..m-1]$. We then store the data item at that index.

Typically, the universe of keys is much larger than m, the size of the hash table. By choosing our array size m to be close to the number of elements we need to store, we eliminate the space usage problem discussed in Section 7.1. However, because the number of possible keys will now be greater than m, we must deal with the problem that h must map more than one potential key to the same index. When two actual keys map to the same index, it is known as a *collision*.

The potential for collisions is not just a theoretical issue unlikely to occur in practice. Suppose, for example, that we were to randomly and independently assign indices to n keys, so that for any given key k and index i, $0 \leq i < m$, the probability that k is assigned i is $1/m$. We can model this scenario with a discrete probability space consisting of the m^n n-tuples of natural numbers less than m. Each tuple is equally likely, and so has probability m^{-n}. We can then define the random variable *coll* as the number of collisions; i.e., $coll(\langle i_1, \ldots, i_n \rangle)$ is the number of ordered pairs (i_j, i_k) such that $i_j = i_k$ and $j < k$.

coll can be expressed as the sum of indicator random variables as follows:

$$coll(\langle i_1, \ldots, i_n \rangle) = \sum_{j=1}^{n-1} \sum_{k=j+1}^{n} I(i_j = i_k).$$

Therefore,

$$E[coll] = E\left[\sum_{j=1}^{n-1} \sum_{k=j+1}^{n} I(i_j = i_k)\right]$$

$$= \sum_{j=1}^{n-1} \sum_{k=j+1}^{n} E[I(i_j = i_k)]$$

$$= \sum_{j=1}^{n-1} \sum_{k=j+1}^{n} P(i_j = i_k).$$

For each choice of i, j, and i_j, i_k can take on m possible values, one of which is i_j. Because the probabilities of all elementary events are equal, it is easily seen that $P(i_j = i_k) = 1/m$ for $j < k$. Hence,

$$E[coll] = \sum_{j=1}^{n-1} \sum_{k=j+1}^{n} 1/m$$

$$= \frac{1}{m} \sum_{j=1}^{n-1} (n-j)$$

$$= \frac{1}{m} \sum_{j=1}^{n-1} j \qquad \text{(reversing the sum)}$$

$$= \frac{n(n-1)}{2m}$$

by (2.1).

For example, if our hash table has 500,000 locations and we have more than a thousand data elements, we should expect at least one collision, on average. In general, it requires too much space to make the table large enough so that we can reasonably expect to have no collisions.

Several solutions to the collision problem exist, but the most common is to use a linked list to store all data elements that are mapped to the same location. The approach we take here is similar, but we will use a CONSLIST instead of a linked list. Using a CONSLIST results in somewhat simpler code, and likely would not result in any significant performance degradation. This approach is illustrated in Figure 7.3.

In the remainder of this section, we will ignore the details of specific hash functions and instead focus on the other implementation details of a

Figure 7.3   Illustration of a hash table.

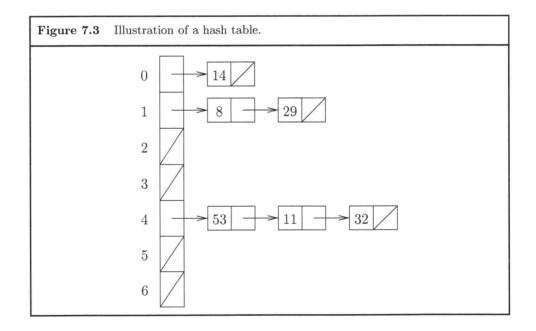

Figure 7.4 The HashFunction ADT

Precondition: $n \geq 1$ is an INT.
Postcondition: Constructs a HashFunction for some table size that is at least n and strictly less than $3n$.

HashFunction(n)

Precondition: k refers to a KEY.
Postcondition: Returns the index i associated with k by this HashFunction. i is a NAT strictly less than the table size.

HashFunction.Index(k)

Precondition: true.
Postcondition: Returns the table size for this HashFunction.

HashFunction.Size()

---

hash table. In order to approach the use of hash functions in a general way, we use the HashFunction ADT, shown in Figure 7.4. Note that because there are no operations to change the hash function, the HashFunction ADT specifies an immutable data type. In remaining sections of this chapter, we will consider various ways of implementing a HashFunction. As we will see in the next section, not all hash table sizes are appropriate for every HashFunction implementation. For this reason, we allow the user to select an approximate table size, but leave it up to the HashFunction to determine the exact table size.

Our HashTable representation of Dictionary then consists of three variables:

- *hash*: a HashFunction whose associated table size is some positive integer m;
- *table*[$0..m - 1$]: an array of ConsLists; and
- *size*: a readable NAT.

Our structural invariant is that:

- for $0 \leq i < hash.\text{Size}()$, *table*[$i$] is a ConsList containing only KEYED items;
- for each KEYED item x in *table*[i], $0 \leq i < m$, $hash.\text{Index}(x.\text{Key}()) = i$; and
- the total number of KEYED items in the ConsLists is given by *size*.

Figure 7.5   The HASHTABLE implementation of DICTIONARY (partial)

Structural Invariant: For $0 \leq i < hash.\text{SIZE}()$, $table[i]$ is a CONSLIST containing only KEYED items; for each KEYED item x in $table[i]$, $0 \leq i < m$, $hash.\text{INDEX}(x.\text{KEY}()) = i$; and the total number of KEYED items in the CONSLISTs is given by $size$.

HASHTABLE()
    $size \leftarrow 0$; $hash \leftarrow$ **new** HASHFUNCTION(100)
    $table \leftarrow$ **new** ARRAY$[0..hash.\text{SIZE}() - 1]$
    for $i \leftarrow 0$ **to** SIZEOF($table$) $- 1$
        $table[i] \leftarrow$ **new** CONSLIST()

HASHTABLE.GET(k)
    $i \leftarrow hash.\text{INDEX}(k)$; $L \leftarrow table[i]$
    while not $L.\text{IsEMPTY}()$
        if $L.\text{HEAD}().\text{KEY}() = k$
            return $L.\text{HEAD}().\text{DATA}()$
        $L \leftarrow L.\text{TAIL}()$
    return nil

We interpret the KEYED items in the CONSLISTs to contain the elements of the data set together with their associated keys.

Accessing a data item given a key k is now straightforward — we simply compute $hash.\text{INDEX}(k)$ and search the CONSLIST at this location in $table$; see Figure 7.5. The worst-case time for any such operation is easily seen to be proportional to the time to compute the index plus the length of the CONSLIST.

Let us now consider the worst-case length of a CONSLIST in $table$. Unfortunately, it can be quite bad. The following theorem shows that under reasonable assumptions, all keys can map to the same index; hence, in the worst case, the running time of a hash table access is in $\Omega(n)$.

Theorem 7.1. *Let T be a hash table with m locations, and suppose the universe U of possible keys contains more than $m(n-1)$ elements. Then for any function h mapping U to natural numbers less than m, there is some natural number $i < m$ such that h maps at least n keys in U to i.*

The proof of the above theorem is simply the observation that if it were not true — i.e., if h maps at most $n-1$ elements to each i — then the size of U could be at most $m(n-1)$. Though this result looks bad, what it tells us is that we really want h to produce a random distribution of the keys so that the list lengths are more evenly distributed throughout the table.

For the remainder of this section, therefore, we will assume that the key distribution is modeled by a discrete probability space *hashDist*. The elementary events in *hashDist* are the same as those in the probability distribution defined above: all n-tuples of natural numbers less than m. Again, the n positions in the tuple correspond to n keys, and their values give their indices in the hash table. Regarding probabilities, however, we will make a weaker assumption, namely, the probability that any two given distinct positions are equal is at most ϵ, where $0 < \epsilon < 1$. Our earlier probability space satisfies this property for $\epsilon = 1/m$, but we will see in Sections 7.4 and 7.5 that other spaces do as well.

In what follows, we will analyze the expected length of the CONSLIST searched for an arbitrary key, assuming a distribution modeled by *hashDist*. In the next section we will show how to define deterministic hash functions that approximate this distribution well enough to work very well in practice. Then in Sections 7.4 and 7.5, we will show how to guarantee this behavior using randomization.

For a given search in the hash table, suppose there are a total of n keys in the table together with the key for which we are searching. Thus, if the given key is in the hash table, there are n keys in the hash table; otherwise, there are $n-1$. We will use *hashDist* to model the distribution of these n keys, where the nth key is the one for which we are searching. Let *len* be the discrete random variable giving the number of positions equal to position n in a given element of *hashDist*. Then if the given key is in the hash table, $E[len]$ gives the expected length of the CONSLIST searched; otherwise, $E[len] - 1$ gives this expected length.

We can express *len* as the sum of indicator random variables as follows:

$$len = \sum_{j=1}^{n} I(i_j = i_n),$$

where i_j denotes position j of an elementary event. Applying linearity of expectation, we have

$$E[len] = \sum_{j=1}^{n} E[I(i_j = i_n)]$$

$$= \sum_{j=1}^{n} P(i_j = i_n).$$

Now using the fact that $P(i_j = i_n) \leq \epsilon$ when $j \neq n$, we have

$$E[len] = \sum_{j=1}^{n} P(i_j = i_n)$$

$$\leq P(i_n = i_n) + \sum_{j=1}^{n-1} \epsilon$$

$$= 1 + \epsilon(n - 1).$$

The above value is the expected length of the CONSLIST searched when the key is found in a table containing n keys. If the key is not in the table, $n - 1$ gives the number of keys in the table, and $E[len]$ is one greater than the expected length of the CONSLIST. Thus, if we let n denote the number of keys in the table, the length of the CONSLIST searched is expected to be $n\epsilon$.

In either case, the length of the CONSLIST is linear in n if ϵ is a fixed constant. However, ϵ may depend upon m. Thus, if $\epsilon \leq c/m$ for some positive constant c and we use an expandable array for the table, we can keep the expected length bounded by a constant. Let $\lambda = n/m$ be known as the *load factor* of the hash table. Using the expandable array design pattern, we can ensure that $\lambda \leq d$, where d is a fixed positive real number of our choosing. Thus, the expected list length is bounded by

$$1 + \epsilon n \leq 1 + cn/m$$

$$= 1 + c\lambda$$

$$\leq 1 + cd$$

$$\in O(1).$$

In order to implement the expandable array pattern for a hash table, we will need to change the hash function to take advantage of the larger range of indices. In copying elements to the new table, we therefore need to apply the new hash function to each element in order to find its proper location. This technique is called *rehashing*. We leave it as an exercise to show that as long as the size of the table increases by at least a factor of 2 and at most a factor of 6, the amortized cost of rehashing is proportional to the cost of hashing a single key. The HASHTABLE.PUT operation, which employs rehashing, is shown in Figure 7.6.

Figure 7.6 The PUT operation for HASHTABLE

HASHTABLE.PUT(x, k)
   $i \leftarrow hash.$INDEX(k); $L \leftarrow table[i]$
   while not $L.$ISEMPTY$()$
     if $L.$HEAD$().$KEY$() = k$
       error
     $L \leftarrow L.$TAIL$()$
   $table[i] \leftarrow$ **new** CONSLIST(**new** KEYED$(x, k), table[i])$
   $size \leftarrow size + 1$
   if $size/$SIZEOF$(table) > \lambda$
     $hash \leftarrow$ **new** HASHFUNCTION$(2 \cdot$ SIZEOF$(table))$
     $t \leftarrow$ **new** ARRAY$[0..hash.$SIZE$() - 1]$
     for $j \leftarrow 0$ **to** SIZEOF$(t) - 1$
       $t[j] \leftarrow$ **new** CONSLIST$()$
     for $j \leftarrow 0$ **to** SIZEOF$(table) - 1$
       $L \leftarrow table[j]$
       while not $L.$ISEMPTY$()$
         $y \leftarrow L.$HEAD$()$; $i \leftarrow hash.$INDEX$(y.$KEY$())$
         $t[i] \leftarrow$ **new** CONSLIST$(y, t[i])$; $L \leftarrow L.$TAIL$()$
     $table \leftarrow t$

We conclude that as long as the hash function is designed so that the probability of two arbitrary keys colliding is no more than c/m, where m is the number of locations in the hash table and c is a positive real number, the amortized expected running time of a hash table access is in $\Theta(1)$ plus the time needed to compute the hash function. We can keep the constant bounding the look-up time quite small by bounding λ by a small constant, provided c is not much larger than 1. A bound of 3/4 on λ, for example, gives a nice trade-off between space and time.

7.3 Deterministic Hash Functions

In this section, we will consider the design of a deterministic hash function. Theorem 7.1 guarantees that any realistic deterministic hash function will result in linear-time accesses in the worst case. However, it is possible to construct a deterministic hash function for which such cases are very unlikely to occur in practice.

We will assume that our keys are represented as natural numbers. This assumption does not result in any loss of generality, because all data types can be viewed as sequences of bytes, or more generally, as w-bit components. We can view each component as a natural number less than 2^w. The sequence $\langle k_1, \ldots, k_l \rangle$ then represents the natural number

$$\sum_{i=1}^{l} k_i 2^{w(l-i)};$$

thus, we view the key as encoding a natural number in radix 2^w. We must realize, however, that the keys may be very large, so that they do not fit in a single machine word.

The basic idea of the *division method* is simple. For a natural number k, we define

$$h(k) = k \bmod m,$$

where m is the number of array locations in the hash table. Thus, $0 \leq k \bmod m < m$. The table shown in Figure 7.3 uses the division method.

It is not hard to show that

$$(xy + z) \bmod m = (x(y \bmod m) + z) \bmod m$$

(see Exercise 7.5). This relationship gives us a top-down solution to the problem of computing $h(k)$ for large k. If z is the last w-bit component of k, we can write $k = 2^w y + z$, where y is the value obtained by removing the component z from k. We then have

$$\begin{aligned} h(k) &= (2^w y + z) \bmod m \\ &= (2^w (y \bmod m) + z) \bmod m \\ &= (2^w h(y) + z) \bmod m. \end{aligned}$$

We can therefore compute $h(k)$ bottom-up by starting with the first component of k and repeatedly multiplying by 2^w, adding the next component, and taking the result mod m.

The division method is illustrated in Figure 7.7, where an implementation of HASHFUNCTION is presented. The representation of HASHFUNCTION is a NAT *size*, and the structural invariant is *size* > 0. We assume the existence of a function TOARRAY(x, w), which returns an array of NATs, each strictly less than 2^w, and which together give a representation of x. It is easily seen that INDEX runs in time linear in the length of the key.

Figure 7.7 The INDEX operation for the DIVISIONMETHOD implementation of HASHFUNCTION

DIVISIONMETHOD.INDEX(k)
   components[1..*l*] ← TOARRAY(k, w); $h ← 0$
   for $i ← 1$ **to** l
      $h ← (h \cdot 2^w + components[i])$ mod *size*
   return h

One advantage of the division method is that it can be applied quickly. Because the multiplication is by a power of 2, it can be implemented by shifting to the left by w bits. The addition then adds a w-bit number to a number whose binary representation ends in w zeros; hence, the addition can be accomplished via a bitwise or. Otherwise, there is only an application of the mod operator for each word of the key.

The effectiveness of the division method as a hash function depends on the value chosen for the table size. Knowing that we cannot prevent bad cases from ever occurring, the best we can do is to try to avoid bad behavior on cases which may be likely to occur. If data were random, our job would be much simpler, because we could take advantage of this randomness to generate a random distribution in the table. Real data sets, however, tend to contain patterns. We need our hash function to perform well in the presence of these patterns.

Suppose, for example, that the table size $m = 255$, and that each byte of the key is a character encoded in ASCII. From the binomial theorem ((6.15) on page 242), we can write the key as

$$\sum_{i=1}^{l} 256^{l-i} k_i = \sum_{i=1}^{l} (255 + 1)^{l-i} k_i$$

$$= \sum_{i=1}^{l} \sum_{j=0}^{l-i} \binom{l-i}{j} 255^j k_i.$$

Each term of the inner sum such that $j > 0$ is divisible by 255; hence, computing the key mod 255 yields:

$$\left(\sum_{i=1}^{l} 256^{i-1} k_i \right) \bmod 255 = \sum_{i=1}^{l} k_i \bmod 255.$$

Thus, applying this hash function to the key is equivalent to applying it to the sum of the bytes in the key. Because addition is commutative, we can see that the hash function would yield the same value for any permutation of the bytes in the key; hence every permutation of the same bytes would hash to the same location. Such behavior is undesirable. Similar behavior can occur for other values very near powers of 2.

As another example, suppose that all of the keys are even numbers. If m is even, then $k \bmod m$ will always be even. As a result, only half the locations in the table are used, so we could expect the lists to be at least twice as long. More generally, if even keys are more likely than odd keys, even m will cause the division method to perform poorly. This tells us that m should not be even.

We can generalize the above arguments to conclude that m should ideally be a *prime number* — a number with no factors other than itself and 1 — and not too close to a power of two. It turns out that these restrictions are nearly always sufficient to yield good performance from the division method.

The constructor DIVISIONMETHOD(n) therefore needs to select a table size m that is a prime number in the range $n \leq m < 3n$, such that m is not too close to a power of 2. Searching for such a number can be somewhat expensive.

Fortunately, we can simplify the search in practice. Consider the following sequence of prime numbers:

2	5	11	23	47	97
197	397	797	1597	3203	6421
12853	25717	51437	102877	205759	411527
823117	1646237	3292489	6584983	13169977	26339969
52679969	105359939	210719881	421439783	842879579	1685759167

Suppose we were to initialize an array with these values, beginning with index 1. Then for $2 \leq n \leq 2^{30} = 1{,}073{,}741{,}824$, the value at location $\lceil \lg n \rceil$ is at least n and strictly less than $3n$. Thus, by adding an extra 2 at location 0, we can easily find a prime table size in the correct range for all $n \leq 2^{30}$, which is sufficiently large for most applications. Furthermore, except for the first three or four of these values, none are close to any power of 2. We can avoid using the first three or four sizes by setting the initial size to be sufficiently large, but even if we were to use them, rehashing guarantees that they will only be used for very small data sets.

One drawback to the PUT operation as shown in Figure 7.6, is that when rehashing is performed, all of the hash values must be recomputed from scratch. When the division method is used on long keys, this can lead to a significant amount of computation.

An improvement is to use a combination of two hash functions. The first hash function produces an index in a range that may be too large to be used as a table size, but which is small enough to fit into a single machine word. This first hash function is called a *compression map*. The second hash function is then applied to the result of the compression map to produce an index into the actual table. Because the compression map generates an index that will fit into a single machine word, the computation of the hash table index from the compression map index can be done quickly; for example the division method would consist of a single mod operation. Thus, if we save the result of the compression map with the element we are storing, we can perform rehashing by applying a new hash function to the stored compression map index. We leave the implementation details of such a scheme as an exercise.

The division method could be used for both of the hash functions in such a scheme. However, if the modulus is near the maximum value that can be stored in a single machine word, double-word arithmetic is required. An alternative that avoids double-word arithmetic for computing the compression map is *polynomial hashing*.

In order to motivate polynomial hashing, let's consider what happens when we pack four bytes, k_1, k_2, k_3, and k_4, into a 4-byte word. If we wish to retain all of the information, we might produce the value

$$k_1 256^3 + k_2 256^2 + k_3 256 + k_4.$$

Polynomial hashing generalizes this technique by producing, for a given key $\langle k_1, \ldots, k_l \rangle$,

$$\left(\sum_{i=1}^{l} k_i r^{l-i} \right) \bmod 2^w,$$

where w is the number of bits in a machine word, excluding any sign bit. The final "mod 2^w" describes the effect of overflow in a w-bit unsigned integer. Thus, if an unsigned integer is used, this operation need not be explicitly performed.

One reason this technique is popular is that it can be computed quickly. Note that

$$\sum_{i=1}^{l} k_i r^{l-i} = k_l + \sum_{i=1}^{l-1} k_i r^{l-i}$$

$$= k_l + r \sum_{i=1}^{l-1} k_i r^{l-1-i}.$$

This gives us a top-down solution that can be applied bottom-up in the same way as we applied the division method directly to large keys. Specifically, we start with k_1 and repeatedly multiply by r and add the next k_i. This procedure requires one multiplication and one addition for each component of the key. Furthermore, all computation can be done with single-word arithmetic.

In order for this method to work well, r must be chosen properly. We first note that 256 is a poor choice, because $256^i \bmod 2^w = 0$ for all $i \geq w/8$; thus only the first $w/8$ components of the key are used in computing the hash value. More generally, r should never be even, because $(c2^j)^i \bmod 2^w = 0$ for $j > 0$ and $i \geq w/j$. Furthermore, not all odd values work well. For example, $r = 1$ yields $r^i = 1$ for all i, so that the result is simply the sum of the components, mod 2^w. This has the disadvantage of causing all permutations of a key to collide.

More generally, if r is odd, $r^i \bmod 2^w$ will repeat its values in a cyclic fashion. In other words, for every odd r there is a natural number n such that $r^{n+i} \bmod 2^w = r^i$ for all $i \in \mathbb{N}$. Fortunately, there are only a few values of r (like 1) that have short cycles. In order to avoid these short cycles, we would like to choose r so that this cycle length is as large as possible. It is beyond the scope of this book to explain why, but it turns out that this cycle length is maximized whenever $r \bmod 8$ is either 3 or 5.

We can run into other problems if r is small and the component size is smaller than w. Suppose, for example that $r = 3$, $w = 32$, and each component is one byte. For any key containing fewer than 15 components, the polynomial-hash value will be less than 2^{31}. We have therefore reduced the range of possible results by more than half — much more for shorter keys. As a result, more collisions than necessary are introduced. A similar phenomenon occurs if r is very close to 2^w.

If we avoid these problems, polynomial hashing usually works well as a compression map. To summarize, we should choose r so that $r \bmod 8$ is either 3 or 5, and not too close to either 0 or 2^w. This last condition can typically be satisfied if we choose an r with 5-9 bits (i.e., between 16 and 512). The division method can then be used to obtain an index into the table. Because it will be applied to a single word, its computation consists of a single mod operation.

7.4 Universal Hashing

Though the techniques discussed so far are widely used and work well in practice, we cannot prove much of anything useful about their performance. In this section, we consider how to use randomization to yield a hashing strategy with provably good expected behavior.

We cannot simply store data items in random array locations because we would then be unable to find them quickly. We can, however, randomly select a hash function from a set of alternatives. If the set of potential hash functions is chosen well, we can prove that the resulting hash table will be expected to have few collisions.

Let U be our universe of keys, and let $\mathcal{H}$ be some countable set of hash functions of the form $h : U \to M$, where M is the set of natural numbers less than m. Let us also suppose that each element of $\mathcal{H}$ has some probability, so that $\mathcal{H}$ is a discrete probability space. Two distinct keys k_1 and k_2 collide for $h \in \mathcal{H}$ iff $h(k_1) = h(k_2)$. Taking $h(k_1)$ and $h(k_2)$ as random variables over $\mathcal{H}$, we see that the probability that these keys collide is $P(h(k_1) = h(k_2))$. If two values from M are chosen independently with uniform probability, then the probability that they are the same is $1/m$. We therefore say that a $\mathcal{H}$ is a *universal family* of hash functions if for any two keys in U, the probability that they collide is no more than $1/m$. As we showed in Section 7.2, this probability bound implies that for any hash table access, the expected length of the list searched is in $\Theta(1)$.

Several universal families of hash functions have been defined, but most of them require some number theory in order to prove that they are universal families. In what follows, we present a universal family that is easier to understand at the cost of requiring a bit more computational overhead. Then in the next section, we will show how number theory can be utilized to define universal families whose hash functions can be computed more efficiently.

Suppose each key $k \in U$ is encoded by l bits. Ideally, we would like to generate each function mapping U into M with equal probability. However, doing so is too expensive. There are 2^l keys in U, and m possible values to which each could be mapped. The total number of possible hash functions is therefore m^{2^l}. Uniquely identifying one of these functions therefore requires at least $\lg m^{2^l} = 2^l \lg m$ bits. If, for example, each key is 32 bits and our hash table size is 256, four gigabytes of storage would be needed just to identify the hash function.

Instead, we will randomly generate a table location for each of the l bit positions. Let these locations be $t_1, \ldots, t_l$. We will assume that m is a power of 2 so that each of these locations is encoded using $\lg m$ bits. A given key k will select the subsequence of $\langle t_1, \ldots, t_l \rangle$ such that t_i is included iff the ith bit of k is a 1. Thus, each key selects a unique subsequence of locations. The hash table location of k is then given by the bitwise exclusive-or of the locations in the subsequence; in other words, the binary encoding of the hash location has a 1 in position j iff the number of selected locations having a 1 in position j is odd.

Example 7.1. Suppose our keys contain 4 bits, and we want to use a hash table with 8 locations. We then randomly generate 4 table locations, one for each of the 4 bit positions in the keys:

- $t_1 = 3$, or 011 in binary;
- $t_2 = 6$, or 110 in binary;
- $t_3 = 0$, or 000 in binary;
- $t_4 = 3$, or 011 in binary.

Note that these locations don't need to be distinct.

Now let us compute the hash value for the keys 5 and 11, whose binary encodings are 0101 and 1011. The key 5 selects the locations t_2 and t_4, whose binary encodings are 110 and 011, respectively. The bitwise exclusive-or of these two values is 101 because the first and third bit positions each have an odd number of 1, but the second has an even number. The key 5 therefore is placed in location 5. Likewise, the key 11 selects the locations t_1, t_3, and t_4, whose binary encodings are 011, 000, and 011, respectively. The bitwise exclusive-or of these three values is 000 because each of the three bit positions contains an even number of 1s. The hash value for 11 is therefore 0.

To see why we use the exclusive-or operation, suppose we have a bit value x that is 1 with probability p, $0 \le p \le 1$. Suppose we then assign a value to bit y by flipping a fair coin; i.e., y has a value of 1 with probability $1/2$, independent of the value of x. The exclusive-or of x and y is 1 iff the values of x and y are different. The probability of this event is therefore

$$\frac{p}{2} + \frac{1-p}{2} = \frac{1}{2}.$$

Thus, the probability distribution of the exclusive-or of two independent random bits is uniform if at least one of the two has uniform probability distribution. We can easily conclude that the method outlined above for selecting a hash function results in each key mapping to any given table location with probability $1/m$.

However, knowing that each key maps to any given table location with probability $1/m$ is not sufficient to conclude that any two keys collide with probability at most $1/m$. Suppose, for example, that we were to select a hash function by randomly generating a natural number $i < m$ with uniform probability. The hash function then maps all keys to i. For any given key k, this strategy maps k to any given location with probability $1/m$. However, because all keys map to the same location, the probability that two given keys collide is 1 for each pair of keys.

Before we try to prove that this family of hash functions is universal, we will define it more formally. In order to accommodate a formal definition, we must first define a discrete probability space that will represent the set of hash functions. Let $S_{l,m}$ be the set of all l-tuples of bit strings of length $\lg m$, where l is a positive integer and m is a power of 2. Each of these l-tuples will represent a hash function. Note that $S_{l,m}$ has m^l elements. We therefore assign each element of $S_{l,m}$ a probability of m^{-l}; hence, $S_{l,m}$ is a discrete probability space in which each elementary event has the same probability.

We can now formally define a hash function corresponding to each element in $S_{l,m}$. Let *select* be the function that takes a sequence $s = \langle t_1, \ldots, t_n \rangle$ of bit strings all having the same length, together with a bit string $k_1 \cdots k_n$, and returns the subsequence of s such that t_i is included iff $k_i = 1$. Furthermore, let X be the function that takes a sequence of bit strings each having the same length and returns their bitwise exclusive-or. Given $s = \langle t_1, \ldots, t_l \rangle \in S_{l,m}$, let $h_s : U \to M$ such that

$$h_s(k) = X(select(s, k)).$$

We now define

$$\mathcal{H}_{l,m}^1 = \{ h_s \mid s \in S_{l,m} \}.$$

Each element $h \in \mathcal{H}_{l,m}^1$ corresponds to the event consisting of all sequences $s \in S_{l,m}$ such that $h = h_s$. We leave it as an exercise to show that for each $h \in \mathcal{H}_{l,m}^1$, there is exactly one such s; hence, there is a one-to-one correspondence between elementary events in $S_{l,m}$ and hash functions in $\mathcal{H}_{l,m}^1$. We will now show that for every distinct $k, k' \in U$, $P(h(k) = h(k')) = 1/m$, so that $\mathcal{H}_{l,m}^1$

is a universal family of hash functions. In the proof and the implementation that follows, we use $\otimes$ to denote bitwise exclusive-or.

Theorem 7.2. *Let l be a positive integer and m be a power of 2. Then $\mathcal{H}^1_{l,m}$ is a universal family of hash functions.*

Proof.   Suppose k and k' are two keys differing in bit position i. Without loss of generality, suppose the ith bit of k is 0 and the ith bit of k' is 1. Let k'' be the key obtained from k' by changing the ith bit to 0. Let t_j be the discrete random variable giving the value of the jth component of s for $s \in S_{l,m}$, and let $h(x)$ be the random variable giving the hash value of $x \in U$. Then $h(k') = h(k'') \otimes t_i$. Thus, $h(k) = h(k')$ iff $h(k) = h(k'') \otimes t_i$.

Because the ith bits of both k and k'' are 0, we can evaluate $h(k)$ and $h(k'')$ knowing only $t_1, \ldots, t_{i-1}, t_{i+1}, \ldots t_l$. For each choice of these values, there is exactly one value of t_i for which $h(k) = h(k'') \otimes t_i$, namely $t_i = h(k) \otimes h(k'')$. There are then m^{l-1} hash functions for which k and k' collide. Because each hash function occurs with probability m^{-l},

$$P(h(k) = h(k')) = m^{l-1}m^{-l}$$
$$= 1/m.$$

To represent an instance of this family, we use a readable NAT *size* and an array *indices*[1..l] of NATs; we assume for now that l, the number of bits in a key, is fixed. Our structural invariant is that *size* $= 2^i$ for some natural number i, and that for $1 \le j \le l$, *indices*[j] < *size*. The implementation is shown in Figure 7.8. It uses a function RANDOM, which takes a positive integer n as input and returns, with uniform probability, any natural number strictly less than n. It is easily seen that both the constructor and the INDEX operation run in $\Theta(l)$ time, assuming RANDOM runs in $\Theta(1)$ time.

If we use this implementation of HASHFUNCTION with the HASHTABLE implementation shown in Figures 7.5 and 7.6, the expected search time is in $\Theta(1)$. Furthermore, it is not hard to show that the expected amortized cost of rehashing is in $\Theta(l)$.

In many applications, the key lengths may vary, and we may not know the maximum length in advance. Such situations can be handled easily, provided we may pad keys with zeros without producing other valid keys. This padding may be done safely if the length of the key is encoded within the key, or if each key is terminated by some specific value. We can therefore consider each key as having infinite length, but containing only finitely many 1s. We can ensure that we have bit strings for *indices*[1..i] for some i. If we encounter a key with a 1 in bit position $j > i$, we can generate bit strings for positions

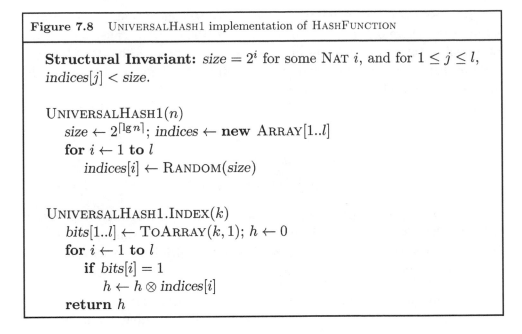

Figure 7.8   UNIVERSALHASH1 implementation of HASHFUNCTION

Structural Invariant: $size = 2^i$ for some NAT i, and for $1 \leq j \leq l$, $indices[j] < size$.

UNIVERSALHASH1(n)
  $size \leftarrow 2^{\lceil \lg n \rceil}$; $indices \leftarrow$ **new** ARRAY$[1..l]$
  for $i \leftarrow 1$ **to** l
    $indices[i] \leftarrow$ RANDOM($size$)

UNIVERSALHASH1.INDEX(k)
  $bits[1..l] \leftarrow$ TOARRAY($k, 1$); $h \leftarrow 0$
  for $i \leftarrow 1$ **to** l
    if $bits[i] = 1$
      $h \leftarrow h \otimes indices[i]$
  return h

$i + 1$ through j at that time. Note that neither of these strategies add any significant overhead — they simply delay the generation of the bit strings. We leave the implementation details as an exercise.

7.5   Number Theoretic Universal Hash Families

In this section, we will use some elementary number theory to obtain universal families whose hash functions resemble those of Section 7.3. The resulting functions may require less overhead than do the functions in $\mathcal{H}^1_{l,m}$. We first need the following fact from number theory:

Theorem 7.3. *Let a, b, and m be natural numbers such that $0 < a < m$ and $b < m$. Then the equation*

$$ai \bmod m = b$$

has a unique solution in the range $0 \leq i < m$ iff a and m are relatively prime (i.e., 1 is the greatest common divisor of a and m).

Proof.   Because we will only need to use this theorem in one direction, we will only prove one implication and leave the other as an exercise.

$\Leftarrow$: Suppose a and m are relatively prime. We will show that if $ai \bmod m = aj \bmod m$, where $0 \le i < m$ and $0 \le j < m$, then $i = j$. Thus, each of the m possible values of i will result in a distinct value of $ai \bmod m$. Because only m distinct values of $ai \bmod m$ are possible, it will follow that one of the values of i must yield $ai \bmod m = b$.

Suppose $ai \bmod m = aj \bmod m$. Then there exist natural numbers q_1 and q_2 such that

$$ai - q_1 m = aj - q_2 m$$
$$a(i - j) = (q_1 - q_2)m,$$

so that $a(i - j)$ is divisible by m. Because a and m are relatively prime, it must be the case that $(i - j)$ is divisible by m. Given the ranges for i and j, it must be the case that $|i - j| < m$. The only multiple of m with absolute value strictly less than m is 0; hence, $i = j$. $\square$

For our next universal family, we will interpret the keys as natural numbers and assume that there is some maximum value for a key. Let p be a prime number strictly larger than this maximum key value. Our hash functions will consist of two steps. The first step will map each key to a unique natural number less than p. We will design this part so that, depending on which hash function is used, a distinct pair of keys will be mapped with uniform probability to any of the pairs of distinct natural numbers less than p. The second step will apply the division method to scale the value to an appropriate range.

For the first step, let

$$h_{p,a,b}(k) = (ak + b) \bmod p, \qquad (7.1)$$

for a and b strictly less than p. Consider distinct keys k and k'. We then have

$$(h_{p,a,b}(k) - h_{p,a,b}(k')) \bmod p = ((ak + b) \bmod p - (ak' + b) \bmod p) \bmod p$$
$$= a(k - k') \bmod p,$$

from Exercise 7.5. Because $k - k' \ne 0$ and p is prime, Theorem 7.3 tells us that for each natural number $j < p$, there is a unique a, $0 \le a < p$, such that

$$j = a(k - k') \bmod p$$
$$= (h_{p,a,b}(k) - h_{p,a,b}(k')) \bmod p,$$

independent of the value of b. Because $h_{p,0,b}(k) - h_{p,0,b}(k') = 0$, each positive $a < p$ yields a distinct positive value of $(h_{p,a,b}(k) - h_{p,a,b}(k')) \bmod p$. Furthermore, for a given positive a, each choice of b clearly results in a distinct value for $h_{p,a,b}(k)$.

Each choice of a and b, where $0 < a < p$ and $0 \le b < p$, therefore results in a unique pair of distinct values $h_{p,a,b}(k)$ and $h_{p,a,b}(k')$. Because the number of choices of a and b is exactly the same as the number of pairs of distinct values $h_{p,a,b}(k)$ and $h_{p,a,b}(k')$, each of these pairs can be produced by exactly one choice of a and b. We therefore have the following lemma.

Lemma 7.4. *Let p be a prime number, and let k and k' be distinct natural numbers strictly less than p. If a and b are chosen independently and uniformly such that $1 \le a < p$ and $0 \le b < p$, then $h_{p,a,b}(k)$ and $h_{p,a,b}(k')$ are any pair of distinct natural numbers less than p with uniform probability.*

To apply the second step of the hash function, let

$$f_m(i) = i \bmod m,$$

where m is a positive integer and i is a natural number. We then define

$$\mathcal{H}^2_{p,m} = \{f_m \circ h_{p,a,b} \mid 0 < a < p,\ 0 \le b < p\},$$

where $\circ$ denotes function composition (i.e., $f_m \circ h_{p,a,b}(k) = f_m(h_{p,a,b}(k))$). We define the probability of each element of $\mathcal{H}^2_{p,m}$ by selecting a and b independently with uniform probability. We can then show the following theorem.

Theorem 7.5. *For any prime number p and positive integer m, $\mathcal{H}^2_{p,m}$ is a universal family of hash functions.*

Proof. Let k and k' be two distinct keys. As we argued above, $h_{p,a,b}(k)$ and $h_{p,a,b}(k')$ are distinct natural numbers less than p, and each possible pair of distinct values can be obtained by exactly one pair of values for a and b. $f_m(h_{p,a,b}(k)) = f_m(h_{p,a,b}(k'))$ iff $h_{p,a,b}(k) \bmod m = h_{p,a,b}(k') \bmod m$ iff $h_{p,a,b}(k) - h_{p,a,b}(k')$ is divisible by m. For any natural number $i < p$, there are strictly fewer than p/m natural numbers $j < p$ (other than i) such that $i - j$ is divisible by m. Because the number of these values of j is an integer, it is at most $(p-1)/m$. Because there are p possible values of $h_{p,a,b}(k)$ and $p(p-1)$ possible pairs of values for $h_{p,a,b}(k)$ and $h_{p,a,b}(k')$, each of which is equally likely, the probability that $f_m(h_{p,a,b}(k)) = f_m(h_{p,a,b}(k'))$ is at most

$$\frac{p\left(\frac{p-1}{m}\right)}{p(p-1)} = \frac{1}{m}.$$

$\square$

Note that by the above theorem, $\mathcal{H}_{p,m}^2$ is universal for any positive m. As a result, the size of the hash table does not need to be a particular kind of number, such as a prime number or a power of 2, in order for this strategy to yield good expected performance. However, the restriction that p is a prime number larger than the value of the largest possible key places some limitations on the effectiveness of this approach. Specifically, if there is no upper bound on the length of a key, we cannot choose a p that is guaranteed to work. Furthermore, even if an upper bound is known, unless it is rather small, the sizes of p, a, and b would make the cost of computing the hash function too expensive.

Let us therefore treat keys as sequences of natural numbers strictly smaller than some value p, which we presume to be not too large (e.g., small enough to fit in a single machine word). Furthermore, let us choose p to be a prime number. Let $\langle k_1, \ldots, k_l \rangle$ be a key, and let $s = \langle a_1, \ldots, a_l \rangle$ be a sequence of natural numbers, each of which is strictly less than p. We then define

$$h_{p,s}(\langle k_1, \ldots, k_l \rangle) = \left(\sum_{i=1}^{l} a_i k_i \right) \bmod p.$$

We first observe that we cannot guarantee that $h_{p,s}(k) \neq h_{p,s}(k')$ for each distinct pair of keys k and k'. The reason for this is that there are potentially more keys than there are values of $h_{p,s}$. However, suppose k and k' are distinct keys, and let $k_i \neq k_i'$, where $1 \leq i \leq l$. Let us arbitrarily fix the values of all a_j such that $j \neq i$, and let

$$c = \left(\sum_{j=1}^{i-1} a_j k_j' + \sum_{j=i+1}^{l} a_j k_j' - \sum_{j=1}^{i-1} a_j k_j - \sum_{j=i+1}^{l} a_j k_j \right) \bmod p.$$

Then

$$(h_{p,s}(k) - h_{p,s}(k')) \bmod p = \left(\sum_{j=1}^{l} a_j k_j - \sum_{j=1}^{l} a_j k_j' \right) \bmod p$$

$$= (a_i(k_i - k_i') - c) \bmod p.$$

Because $0 \leq c < p$, the above value is 0 iff

$$a_i(k_i - k_i') \bmod p = c.$$

Because $k_i \neq k_i'$ and p is prime, $k_i - k_i'$ and p are relatively prime. From Theorem 7.3, the above equation has a unique solution for a_i such that $0 \leq a_i < p$. Thus, for each choice of $a_1, \ldots, a_{i-1}, a_{i+1}, \ldots, a_l$, there is exactly one choice of a_i such that $(h_{p,s}(k) - h_{p,s}(k') \bmod p) = 0$. Note that from the range of $h_{p,s}$, the only way $(h_{p,s}(k) - h_{p,s}(k')) \bmod p = 0$ is if $h_{p,s}(k) = h_{p,s}(k')$. We therefore have the following lemma.

Lemma 7.6. *Let p be a prime number and l a positive integer. In addition, let $s = \langle a_1, \ldots, a_l \rangle$, where each a_j is chosen independently and uniformly such that $0 \leq a_j < p$. Then the probability that $h_{p,s}(k) = h_{p,s}(k')$ for distinct keys k and k' is $1/p$.*

We now define

$$\mathcal{H}_{p,l}^3 = \{h_{p,s} \mid s = \langle a_1, \ldots, a_l \rangle,\ 0 \leq a_i < p \text{ for } 1 \leq i \leq l\}. \qquad (7.2)$$

We define the probability of each element of $\mathcal{H}_{p,l}^3$ by selecting each a_i independently with uniform probability. Note that the range of each hash function in $\mathcal{H}_{p,l}^3$ is the set of natural numbers strictly less than p. Therefore, based on the above discussion, we have the following theorem.

Theorem 7.7. *For any prime number p and positive integer l, $\mathcal{H}_{p,l}^3$ is a universal family of hash functions.*

If we know in advance the approximate size of our data set and the maximum key length, we can select an appropriate prime value for p and randomly select the appropriate hash function from $\mathcal{H}_{p,l}^3$. Because we can apply the mod operation after each addition, we are always working with values having no more than roughly twice the number of bits as p; hence, we can compute this hash function reasonably quickly for each key. Furthermore, even if we don't know the maximum key length, we can generate the multipliers a_i as we need them.

However, if we don't know in advance the approximate size of the data set, we may need to use rehashing. For the sake of efficiency, we would like to avoid the need to apply a new hash function to the entire key. Furthermore, as we will see in the next section, it would be useful to have a universal family that is appropriate for large keys and for which the table size is unrestricted.

A straightforward attempt to achieve these goals is to combine $\mathcal{H}^3_{p,l}$ with $\mathcal{H}^2_{p,m}$. Specifically, we define

$$\mathcal{H}^4_{p,l,m} = \{h_1 \circ h_2 \mid h_1 \in \mathcal{H}^2_{p,m}, h_2 \in \mathcal{H}^3_{p,l}\}.$$

Hash functions in this family are of the form,

$$h(k) = h_{p,a,b}(h_{p,s}(k)) \bmod m$$

$$= \left(a \sum_{i=1}^{l} a_i k_i + b\right) \bmod p \bmod m, \qquad (7.3)$$

where a, b, and each a_i are natural numbers, and $a \neq 0$. We define the probability of each element of $\mathcal{H}^4_{p,l,m}$ by selecting a, b, and each a_i independently with uniform probability. (We leave it as an exercise to show that the same probability distribution for $\mathcal{H}^4_{p,l,m}$ can be achieved by setting $a = 1$ and selecting b and each a_i independently with uniform probability.)

Because $\mathcal{H}^2_{p,m}$ is a universal family, it causes any pair of distinct keys to collide with probability at most $1/m$. However, $\mathcal{H}^3_{p,l}$ also causes distinct keys to collide with probability $1/p$. When the function from $\mathcal{H}^2_{p,m}$ is applied to equal values, it yields equal values. We must therefore be careful in analyzing the probability of collisions for $\mathcal{H}^4_{p,l,m}$.

Let us first consider the case in which two distinct keys k and k' are mapped to distinct values by $h_{p,s} \in \mathcal{H}^3_{p,l}$. From Lemma 7.6, the probability that this occurs is

$$1 - \frac{1}{p} = \frac{p-1}{p}.$$

Furthermore, from Lemma 7.4, $h_{p,a,b}(h_{p,s}(k))$ and $h_{p,a,b}(h_{p,s}(k'))$ are with uniform probability any pair of distinct natural numbers less than p, provided a and b are chosen independently with uniform probability such that $1 \leq a < p$ and $0 \leq b < p$. Because there are $p(p-1)$ pairs of distinct natural numbers less than p, this probability is

$$\frac{1}{p(p-1)}.$$

Therefore, given any two distinct keys k and k', and any two distinct natural numbers i and j strictly less than p, the probability that $h_{p,a,b}(h_{p,s}(k)) = i$

and $h_{p,a,b}(h_{p,s}(k')) = j$ is

$$\left(\frac{p-1}{p}\right)\left(\frac{1}{p(p-1)}\right) = \frac{1}{p^2}.$$

Now consider the case in which $h_{p,s}(k) = h_{p,s}(k')$. From Lemma 7.6, this case occurs with probability $1/p$. For any value of a, $1 \leq a < p$, and any value of i, $0 \leq i < p$, there is exactly one value of b such that $0 \leq b < p$ and

$$(ah_{p,s}(k) + b) \bmod p = i.$$

Thus, each value of i is reached with probability $1/p$. Therefore, for each natural number $i < p$, the probability that $h_{p,a,b}(h_{p,s}(k)) = h_{p,a,b}(h_{p,s}(k')) = i$ is $1/p^2$.

Thus, for a hash function h chosen from $\mathcal{H}^4_{p,l,m}$, $h(k) = i \bmod m$ and $h(k') = j \bmod m$, where i and j are natural numbers less than p chosen independently with uniform probability. Furthermore, $i \bmod m = j \bmod m$ iff $i - j$ is divisible by m. Because $p - (p \bmod m)$ is divisible by m, for any i, exactly 1 of every m values j such that $0 \leq j < p - (p \bmod m)$ is such that $i - j$ is divisible by m. Likewise, for any j, exactly 1 of every m values i such that $0 \leq i < p - (p \bmod m)$ is such that $i - j$ is divisible by m (see Figure 7.9). Thus, of the $p^2 - (p \bmod m)^2$ pairs in which at least one value is less than $p - (p \bmod m)$, exactly

$$\frac{p^2 - (p \bmod m)^2}{m}$$

pairs result in collisions. Of the remaining $(p \bmod m)^2$ pairs, only those in which $i = j$ result in collisions. There are exactly $p \bmod m$ such pairs. Thus, the probability of a collision is exactly

$$\frac{p^2 - (p \bmod m)^2}{mp^2} + \frac{p \bmod m}{p^2} = \frac{p^2 + m(p \bmod m) - (p \bmod m)^2}{mp^2}$$

$$= \frac{1}{m} + \frac{(m - (p \bmod m))(p \bmod m)}{mp^2}. \quad (7.4)$$

Clearly, $m - (p \bmod m)$ is always positive and $p \bmod m$ is always nonnegative. Furthermore, because p is prime, the only way $p \bmod m$ can be 0 is if $m = 1$ or $m = p$. A hash table of size 1 is simply a CONSLIST, and selecting $m = p$ would defeat the purpose of combining $\mathcal{H}^3_{p,l}$ with $\mathcal{H}^2_{p,m}$. Thus, for all reasonable values of m, the second fraction on the right-hand side of (7.4) is strictly positive; therefore, $\mathcal{H}^4_{p,l,m}$ is not a universal family.

Figure 7.9   Pairs resulting in collisions when applying mod

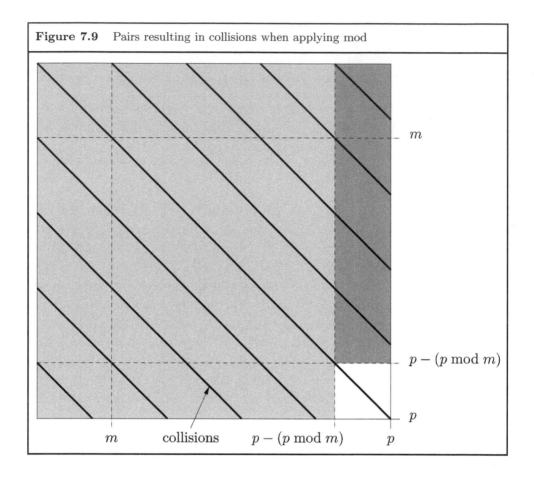

However, recall from Section 7.2 that $\Theta(1)$ amortized expected performance can be achieved using rehashing if the probability of collisions is bounded by c/m for some positive real number c. We therefore define a family of hash functions to be *c-universal* if for each pair of distinct keys, the probability of a collision is at most c/m. In what follows, we will derive a c such that $\mathcal{H}^4_{p,l,m}$ is c-universal whenever $1 < m < p$.

Specifically, we need to find a real number c such that whenever p is prime and $1 < m < p$,

$$\frac{c}{m} \geq \frac{1}{m} + \frac{(m - (p \bmod m))(p \bmod m)}{mp^2}$$

$$c \geq 1 + \frac{(m - (p \bmod m))(p \bmod m)}{p^2}. \tag{7.5}$$

Let us fix p at an arbitrary prime value and try to maximize the right-hand side of (7.5). Suppose $m < p/2$. Then $p - (p \bmod m) > m$, and

$$p \bmod (p - p \bmod m) = p \bmod m.$$

Thus, by replacing m with $p - p \bmod m$ in (7.5), we increase the value of the expression. In order to maximize its value, we therefore need $m \geq p/2$. Because p is prime, we cannot have $m = p/2$, so we can assume $m > p/2$.

If $m > p/2$, then $p \bmod m = p - m$. It therefore suffices to maximize

$$(m - (p - m))(p - m) = (2m - p)(p - m)$$
$$= -(2m^2 - 3mp + p^2),$$

or equivalently, to minimize

$$f(m) = 2m^2 - 3mp + p^2.$$

There are several ways to find the minimum value of a quadratic, but one way that does not involve calculus is by the technique of completing the square. A quadratic of the form $(ax - b)^2$ is clearly nonnegative for all values of $a, x,$ and b. Furthermore, it reaches a value of 0 (its minimum) at $x = b/a$. We can therefore minimize $f(m)$ by finding a value d such that $f(m) - d$ is of the form

$$(am - b)^2 = a^2m^2 - 2abm + b^2.$$

Because $f(m) - d$ reaches a minimum value of 0 at $m = b/a$, $f(m)$ reaches a minimum value of d at the same point.

In order to make the coefficient of m^2 have a value of 2, a must be $\sqrt{2}$. To find the coefficient b, we must solve

$$3mp = 2\sqrt{2}bm,$$
$$b = \frac{3p}{2\sqrt{2}}.$$

To find d, we must then solve

$$p^2 - d = \left(\frac{3p}{2\sqrt{2}}\right)^2$$
$$= \frac{9p^2}{8},$$
$$d = -\frac{p^2}{8}.$$

Thus, $-f(m)$ — and hence the numerator of the second term in the right-hand side of (7.5) — is never more than $p^2/8$. Furthermore, this value is achieved (assuming for the moment that m varies over the real numbers) when

$$m = \frac{\frac{3p}{2\sqrt{2}}}{\sqrt{2}}$$
$$= \frac{3p}{4}.$$

We conclude that the right-hand side of (7.5) is bounded above by

$$1 + \frac{p^2/8}{p^2} = 9/8.$$

We therefore have the following theorem.

Theorem 7.8. *For any prime number p and positive integers l and m such that $1 < m < p$, $\mathcal{H}^4_{p,l,m}$ is 9/8-universal.*

The upper bound of 9/8 can be reached when $m = 3p/4$; however, in order for this equality to be satisfied, p must be a multiple of 4, and hence cannot be prime. We can, however, come arbitrarily close to this bound by using a sufficiently large prime number p and setting m to either $\lfloor 3p/4 \rfloor$ or $\lceil 3p/4 \rceil$. Practically speaking, though, such values for m are much too large. In practice, m would be much smaller than p, and as a result, the actual probability of a collision would be much closer to $1/m$.

By choosing p to be of an appropriate size, we can choose a single h of the form

$$h(k) = \left(a \sum_{i=1}^{l} a_i k_i + b \right) \bmod p,$$

and change m as we need to rehash. For example, if the maximum array size on a given platform is $2^{31} - 1$, which by happy coincidence is prime, we can set p to this value. We can then break the keys into 2- or 3-byte components and randomly select a, b, and $a_1, \ldots, a_l$. We can select any value of $m < 2^{31} - 1$ as our table size, but a power of 2 works particularly well, because $h(k) \bmod m$ is just the low-order $\lg m$ bits of $h(k)$. As we compute the hash value $h(k) \bmod m$ for each key k, we save the value $h(k)$. Note that this value can be computed using 64-bit arithmetic and stored as a 32-bit (signed or unsigned) integer. If we need to rehash, we double the size of the table. We can then compute the new hash values for each k by looking up $h(k)$ and computing $h(k) \bmod 2m$.

If $p = 2^{31} - 1$ and m is a power of 2, then $p \bmod m = m - 1$. Substituting this value into (7.4), we see that the probability of a collision is

$$\frac{1}{m} + \frac{m-1}{mp^2} < \frac{1}{m} + \frac{1}{(2^{31}-1)^2}$$
$$< \frac{1}{m} + 2^{-61}.$$

7.6   Perfect Hashing

In this section, we consider a restricted form of DICTIONARY for which PUT and REMOVE are not allowed; i.e., updates will never be made to the structure after it is created. In order for such a structure to be useful, we need to modify the constructor to receive as input the elements to be stored. The formal specification of the IMMUTABLEDICTIONARY ADT is shown in Figure 7.10.

If we expect to make a large number of accesses to an IMMUTABLEDICTIONARY, it might make sense to invest more time in constructing it if we

---

Figure 7.10   The IMMUTABLEDICTIONARY ADT

Precondition: *elements*$[0..n-1]$ is an array of non-nil items, *keys*$[0..n-1]$ is an array of distinct KEYS, $n \in \mathbb{N}$.
Postcondition: Constructs a IMMUTABLEDICTIONARY containing all of the items in *elements*$[0..n-1]$ using *keys*$[i]$ as the key for *elements*$[i]$ for $0 \le i < n$.

IMMUTABLEDICTIONARY(*elements*$[0..n-1]$, *keys*$[0..n-1]$)

Precondition: k is a key.
Postcondition: Returns the item with key k, or nil if no item with key k is contained in the set.

IMMUTABLEDICTIONARY.GET(k)

Precondition: true.
Postcondition: Returns the number of items in the set.

IMMUTABLEDICTIONARY.SIZE()

can then guarantee that accesses will be fast. To achieve this goal, we use a technique called *perfect hashing*.

One of the drawbacks to hashing is that we can't guarantee that there will be no collisions. In fact, we can't even guarantee that all of keys don't hash to the same location. Universal hashing gives us an expectation that the resulting hash table will not have too many collisions. Thus, even though we might be unlucky and choose a hash function that yields poor performance on our data set, if we randomly select several different hash functions, we can expect to find one that yields a small number of collisions.

With perfect hashing, our goal is to produce a hash table with no collisions. Unfortunately, as we saw in Section 7.2, unless the size of the hash table is much larger than the number of keys, we can expect to have at least one collision. With a reasonable table size, we would probably need to try many different hash functions before we found one that yielded no collisions.

We can avoid this difficulty, however, by employing a two-level approach (see Figure 7.11). Instead of using a CONSLIST to store all of the elements that hash to a certain location, we use a secondary hash table with its own hash function. The secondary hash tables that store more than one element are much larger than the number of elements they store. As a result, we will be able to find a hash function for each secondary hash table such that no collisions occur. Furthermore, we will see that the sizes of the secondary hash tables can be chosen so that the total number of locations in all of the hash tables combined is linear in the number of elements stored.

Let us first determine an appropriate size m for a secondary hash table in which we need to store n distinct keys. We saw in Section 7.2 that in order for the expected number of collisions to be less than 1, if the probability that two keys collide is $1/m$, then m must be nearly n^2. We will therefore assume that $m \geq n^2$.

Let $\mathcal{H}_m$ be a c-universal family of hash functions. We wish to determine an upper bound on the number of hash functions we would need to select from $\mathcal{H}_m$ before we can expect to find one that produces no collisions among the given keys. Let *coll* be the discrete random variable giving the total number of collisions, as defined in Section 7.2, produced by a hash function $h \in \mathcal{H}_m$ on distinct keys $k_1, \ldots, k_n$. As we showed in Section 7.2,

$$E[coll] = \sum_{i=1}^{n-1} \sum_{j=i+1}^{n} P(h(k_i) = h(k_j)).$$

Figure 7.11 The structure of a perfect hash table

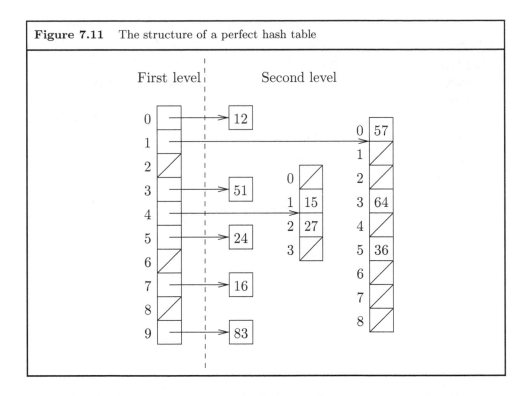

Because the probability that any two distinct keys collide is no more than $c/m \leq c/n^2$, we have

$$E[coll] \leq \sum_{i=1}^{n-1} \sum_{j=i+1}^{n} \frac{c}{n^2}$$

$$= \frac{c}{n^2} \sum_{i=1}^{n-1} (n - i)$$

$$= \frac{c}{n^2} \sum_{i=1}^{n-1} i \qquad \text{(reversing the sum)}$$

$$= \frac{cn(n-1)}{2n^2} \qquad \text{(by (2.1))}$$

$$< c/2.$$

From Markov's Inequality (5.3) on page 194, the probability that there is at least one collision is therefore less than $c/2$.

Suppose, for example, that $c = 1$, as for a universal hash family. Then the probability that a randomly chosen hash function results in no collisions is greater than $1/2$. If $c = 9/8$, as for $\mathcal{H}^4_{p,l,m}$, then the probability is greater than $7/16$. Suppose we repeatedly select hash functions and try storing the keys in the table. Because the probability that there are no collisions is positive whenever $c < 2$, we will eventually find a hash function that produces no collisions.

Let us now determine how many hash functions we would expect to try before finding one that results in no collisions. Let *reps* be the discrete random variable giving this number. For a given positive integer i, $P(reps \geq i)$ is the probability that $i - 1$ successive hash functions fail; i.e.,

$$P(reps \geq i) < (c/2)^{i-1}$$
$$= (2/c)^{1-i}.$$

From Theorem 5.5,

$$E[reps] = \sum_{i=1}^{\infty} P(reps \geq i)$$
$$< \sum_{i=1}^{\infty} (2/c)^{1-i}.$$

Suppose $c < 2$. Then we can re-index the sum to begin at 0 and apply Theorem 6.7, yielding

$$E[reps] < \sum_{i=0}^{\infty} (2/c)^{-i}$$
$$= \frac{2/c}{(2/c) - 1}$$
$$= \frac{2}{2 - c}.$$

Note that the above value is a fixed constant for fixed $c < 2$. Thus, the expected number of attempts at finding an appropriate secondary hash function is bounded by a fixed constant. For example, with $c = 1$, the value of this constant is less than 2, or with $c = 9/8$, the value is less than $16/7$. As a result, we would expect that the number of times a secondary hash function is applied to any key during the process placing keys in secondary hash tables is bounded by a constant.

We must now ensure that the total space used by the primary and secondary hash tables (and hence the time needed to initialize them) is linear in n, the total number of keys. Suppose the primary hash table has

m locations. Further suppose that n_i keys are mapped to index i in the primary hash table. We will then construct a HASHFUNCTION by passing n_i^2 to the constructor of an implementation providing a c-universal hash family. Due to the specification of the HASHFUNCTION constructor, the actual HASHFUNCTION constructed may contain up to $3n_i^2 - 1$ locations when $n_i > 0$. The size of the table constructed is therefore linear in n_i^2. The actual space used by all of the secondary hash tables is therefore linear in

$$\sum_{i=0}^{m-1} n_i^2.$$

Let *sumsq* be a discrete random variable denoting the above sum. The expected space usage of the secondary hash tables is then linear in $E[sumsq]$. In order to analyze $E[sumsq]$, we first observe that n_i^2 is closely related to the number of collisions at index i. The number of collisions at index i is $n_i(n_i - 1)/2$, so that

$$
\begin{aligned}
E[coll] &= E\left[\sum_{i=0}^{m-1} \frac{n_i(n_i - 1)}{2}\right] \\
&= \frac{1}{2}\left(E\left[\sum_{i=0}^{m-1} n_i^2\right] - E\left[\sum_{i=0}^{m-1} n_i\right]\right) \\
&= (E[sumsq] - E[n])/2 \\
&= (E[sumsq] - n)/2.
\end{aligned}
$$

Rearranging terms, we have

$$E[sumsq] = 2E[coll] + n.$$

By reasoning as in Section 7.2, it is easily seen that if the probability that two keys collide is at most c/m, then

$$E[coll] \leq \frac{cn(n - 1)}{2m}.$$

Hence,

$$
\begin{aligned}
E[sumsq] &= 2E[coll] + n \\
&\leq \frac{cn(n - 1)}{m} + n.
\end{aligned}
\tag{7.6}
$$

Thus, if $m \in \Theta(n)$, the expected number of locations in the primary hash table and all of the secondary hash tables is in $\Theta(n)$. In particular, if $m \geq n$, then $E[sumsq] \leq (c+1)n$. It turns out that the value of m that minimizes

$$\frac{cn(n-1)}{m} + n + m,$$

is roughly n (see Exercise 7.17); hence, we will construct our primary hash function by passing n to constructor for an appropriate implementation of HASHFUNCTION.

Of course, we could be unlucky in selecting a primary hash function, so that the number of secondary locations is much larger than what we expect. For example, if it happens that all keys hash to the same location, then a single secondary hash table with at least n^2 locations will be used. In order to guarantee linear space usage in the worst case, we therefore need to select primary hash functions repeatedly until we get one that yields a reasonable total space usage. Because the space usage is linear in *sumsq*, we don't need to construct the actual secondary hash tables in order to determine whether the space usage is reasonable — we can instead simply compute *sumsq*. We should therefore determine some maximum acceptable value for *sumsq*.

In order to ensure a reasonable probability of success, we don't want this maximum value to be too small. From Markov's Inequality (5.3), the probability that a discrete random variable is at least twice its expected value is at most $1/2$, provided its expected value is strictly positive. Based on (7.6) above, because we will be using a primary table size of at least n, it makes sense to use $2(c+1)n$ as the maximum allowable value for *sumsq*. Furthermore, our derivations have assumed that $c < 2$; hence, we can simplify the maximum allowable value to $6n$. By using this maximum, we would expect to select no more than 2 primary hash functions, on average, and still guarantee linear space usage.

We represent an IMMUTABLEDICTIONARY with the following variables:

- *table*$[0..m-1]$: an array of (possibly nil) arrays of (possibly nil) KEYED elements;
- *hash*: a HASHFUNCTION;
- *functions*$[0..m-1]$: an array of (possibly nil) HASHFUNCTIONs; and
- *size*: a readable NAT.

Our structural invariant is that:

- the size of *hash* is the number of locations m in *table*;
- for $0 \leq i < m$, *table*$[i]$ is nil iff *functions*$[i]$ is nil;

- if $table[i] \neq$ nil, then the array stored there is indexed $0..s - 1$, where s is the size of $functions[i]$;
- if an element with key k is stored at $table[i][j]$, then $hash.\text{INDEX}(k) = i$ and $functions[i].\text{INDEX}(k) = j$; and
- $size = n$, the total number of keys stored.

We interpret the KEYED items stored as the elements of the IMMUTABLE-DICTIONARY, together with their associated keys.

The implementation of the constructor is shown in Figure 7.12. Based on the above discussion, the first **repeat** loop is expected to iterate no more than twice. Furthermore, it is easily seen that each iteration of this loop runs in $\Theta(nf(l) + g(n))$ time in the worst case, where $g(n)$ is the time required by the HASHFUNCTION constructor, and $f(l)$ is the time required by the INDEX operation on keys of length l. In order to simplify the discussion that follows, we will assume that the HASHFUNCTION constructor runs in $O(n)$ time; consequently, the expected running time of this loop is in $\Theta(nf(l))$. The effect of this loop is to create a HASHFUNCTION $hash$ and an array $t[0..hash.\text{SIZE}() - 1]$ that is essentially an ordinary hash table for $hash$.

The analysis of the remainder of the algorithm is somewhat more involved, but again relies heavily on the above discussion. The outer loop constructs a secondary hash table for each $t[i]$ and places it in $table[i]$. Each iteration of the **repeat** loop generates a hash function and attempts to construct a secondary hash table for the elements at $t[i]$. It iterates until it has a secondary hash table with no collisions. By the above discussion, the expected number of iterations is in $\Theta(1)$. Let n_i be the number of elements at $t[i]$. Then the **for** loop iterates n_i^2 times, and the **while** loop iterates n_i times in the worst case. Therefore, the **repeat** loop requires $\Theta(n_i^2 + n_i f(l))$ expected time.

The expected running time of the entire **for** loop is then in

$$\sum_{i=0}^{m-1} \Theta(n_i^2 + n_i f(l)) = \sum_{i=0}^{m-1} \Theta(n_i^2) + \sum_{i=0}^{m-1} \Theta(n_i f(l))$$

$$= \Theta\left(\sum_{i=0}^{m-1} n_i^2\right) + \Theta\left(f(l) \sum_{i=0}^{m-1} n_i\right)$$

$$= \Theta((c + 1)n) + \Theta(nf(l))$$

$$= \Theta(nf(l)).$$

The total expected running time of the constructor is therefore in $\Theta(nf(l))$.

Figure 7.12   Constructor for PERFECTHASH implementation of IMMUTABLEDIC-
TIONARY

PERFECTHASH(*elements*[0..*n* − 1], *keys*[0..*n* − 1])
  size ← *n*
  repeat
    hash ← **new** HASHFUNCTION(*n*); *m* ← *hash*.SIZE()
    t ← **new** ARRAY[0..*m* − 1]; *count* ← **new** ARRAY[0..*m* − 1]
    for *i* ← 0 **to** *m* − 1
      t[*i*] ← **new** CONSLIST(); *count*[*i*] ← 0
    for *i* ← 0 **to** *n* − 1
      h ← *hash*.INDEX(*keys*[*i*])
      t[*h*] ← **new** CONSLIST(**new** KEYED(*elements*[*i*], *keys*[*i*]), *t*[*h*])
      count[*h*] ← *count*[*h*] + 1
    sum ← 0
    for *i* ← 0 **to** *m* − 1
      sum ← *sum* + *count*[*i*]^2
  until *sum* ≤ 6*n*
  table ← **new** ARRAY[0..*m* − 1]; *functions* ← **new** ARRAY[0..*m* − 1]
  for *i* ← 0 **to** *m* − 1
    if *t*[*i*].ISEMPTY()
      table[*i*] = nil; *functions*[*i*] = nil
    else
      repeat
        functions[*i*] = **new** HASHFUNCTION(*count*[*i*]^2)
        table[*i*] = **new** ARRAY[0..*functions*[*i*].SIZE() − 1]
        for *j* ← 0 **to** SIZEOF(*table*[*i*]) − 1
          table[*i*][*j*] ← nil
        L ← *t*[*i*]; *coll* = false
        while not *L*.ISEMPTY() **and not** *coll*
          h ← *functions*[*i*].INDEX(*L*.HEAD().KEY())
          if *table*[*i*][*h*] = nil
            table[*i*][*h*] ← *L*.HEAD(); *L* ← *L*.TAIL()
          else
            if *table*[*i*][*h*].KEY() = *L*.HEAD().KEY()
              error
            else
              coll ← true
      until *L*.ISEMPTY()

Thus, for $\mathcal{H}^2_{p,m}$, the constructor runs in $\Theta(n)$ expected time, and for $\mathcal{H}^4_{p,l,m}$, the constructor runs in $\Theta(nl)$ expected time. It is not hard to show that the constructor runs in $\Theta(nl)$ expected time for $\mathcal{H}^1_{l,m}$ as well; the details are left as an exercise.

It is easily seen that the space required by the IMMUTABLEDICTIONARY is in $\Theta(n)$ in the worst case. However, the hidden constants can be rather large. Specifically, the primary hash table can contain nearly $3n$ locations, and the secondary hash tables can contain a total of nearly $18n$ locations. As a result, nearly $21n$ array locations can be used to store n data items. However, observe that the constructor for the family $\mathcal{H}^1_{l,m}$ will return a hash function with size less than $2n$, and the constructors for the families $\mathcal{H}^2_{p,m}$ and $\mathcal{H}^4_{p,l,m}$ both return hash functions with size n. Furthermore, if we were to fix a specific c-universal family of hash functions, we could reduce the bound on the first **repeat** loop to $2(c+1)n$.

Combining the above results, we see that the worst-case total number of array locations can be reduced to:

- $10n$ for $\mathcal{H}^1_{l,m}$;
- $5n$ for $\mathcal{H}^2_{p,m}$; or
- $21n/4$ for $\mathcal{H}^4_{p,l,m}$.

Finally, we observe that because $E[sumsq] < (c+1)n$, the expected total number of array locations is no more than

- $6n$ for $\mathcal{H}^1_{l,m}$;
- $3n$ for $\mathcal{H}^2_{p,m}$; or
- $25n/8$ for $\mathcal{H}^4_{p,l,m}$.

These last bounds hold regardless of whether we change the bound on the first **repeat** loop.

The GET operation is shown in Figure 7.13. It clearly runs in $\Theta(f(l))$ time, where $f(l)$ is the time needed to compute the hash function on a key of length l.

7.7 Summary

If keys are natural numbers, we can implement DICTIONARY using a VARRAY and thus achieve constant-time accesses in the worst case. However, the space usage of a VARRAY makes it impractical. For this reason, hash tables are the preferred implementation in practice. Furthermore, hashing can be done for arbitrary types of keys.

Figure 7.13   The PERFECTHASH.GET operation

PERFECTHASH.GET(*k*)
  h ← *hash*.INDEX(*k*)
  if *table*[*h*] = nil
    return nil
  else
    return *table*[*h*][*functions*[*h*].INDEX(*k*)]

Deterministic hashing yields data accesses that, in practice, run in amortized time proportional to the length of the key, independent of the number of data items in the set. This compares very well to the structures presented in Chapter 6, which give $\Theta(\lg n)$ access times, where n is the number of data items in the set. In our analyses in Chapter 6, we did not consider the key length. Our analyses thus implicitly assumed that keys could be compared in constant time. Each of the structures in Chapter 6 require $\Theta(\lg n)$ comparisons in either the worst, amortized, or expected case, depending on the structure. In the worst case, each of these comparisons requires a time proportional to the length of the key. As a result, the performance of deterministic hashing is usually significantly better in practice than those structures given in Chapter 6. The trade-off is that hash tables do not permit fast access to all of the keys in a predetermined order.

The division method, which computes the value of the key mod the table size, is the most common type of hash function. In order for this method to work well, the table size should be a prime number that is not too close to a power of 2. The division method is often combined with polynomial hashing in order to produce a single-word index, which can then be converted to locations in tables of different sizes. Polynomial hashing involves multiplying each component of the key by a radix raised to successively higher powers, retaining only those bits that will fit in a single machine word. The radix r should use 5 to 9 bits, and should be such that r mod 8 is either 3 or 5.

Though it works very well in practice, in the worst case, deterministic hashing results in accesses having a running time in $\Theta(n)$. We can achieve better theoretical results using universal hashing, in which a hash function is selected at random from a universal family of hash functions. When universal hashing is used, data accesses have an expected amortized running time proportional to the key length.

Perfect hashing is an application of universal hashing which produces an IMMUTABLEDICTIONARY. Using the inherent randomization in universal hashing, we can construct an IMMUTABLEDICTIONARY in expected time linear in the sum of the key lengths. Retrievals can then be performed by computing two hash functions — no searching is required. However, if the keys are long, the cost of computing a second hash function may exceed the cost of searching for the key in an ordinary hash table.

7.8 Exercises

Exercise 7.1. Prove that VARRAY, shown in Figure 7.2, meets its specification.

Exercise 7.2. Give an algorithm that takes as input an array $A[1..n]$ of natural numbers and returns an array $B[1..n]$ such that for $1 \leq i \leq n$, $B[i]$ gives the last location in A that contains $A[i]$. Your algorithm must run in $O(n)$ time in the worst case, and you may make no assumptions about how large the elements in A are. Prove the correctness and time complexity of your algorithm. [**Hint:** Use a VARRAY.]

Exercise 7.3. Complete the implementation of HASHTABLE shown in Figures 7.5 (p. 252) and 7.6 (p. 255) by adding a REMOVE operation as specified in Figure 6.2 (p. 204).

Exercise 7.4. Prove that if the cost of rehashing, as implemented in Figure 7.6 (p. 255), is amortized over all PUT and REMOVE operations, the amortized cost of rehashing is proportional to the cost of computing the index for a single key.

Exercise 7.5. Prove the following for all integers x and y and all positive integers m:

a. $(x + (y \bmod m)) \bmod m = (x + y) \bmod m$.
b. $(x(y \bmod m)) \bmod m = (xy) \bmod m$.
c. $(-(x \bmod m)) \bmod m = (-x) \bmod m$.

Exercise 7.6. Show the hash table that results from inserting the following keys in the order listed, assuming the division method is used with a table of size 13:

$$27, 36, 14, 40, 42, 15, 25, 2.$$

You may assume that no rehashing is done. How does the number of collisions, as defined by the random variable *coll* in Section 7.2, compare with the expected number, assuming that distinct keys collide with probability $1/13$?

Exercise 7.7. Give a modified version of HASHTABLE.PUT(x, k) (see Figure 7.6) which uses a compression map, as described in Section 7.3. Use the HASHFUNCTION ADT to represent both hash functions (i.e., both the compression map and the function to compute the index in the hash table). You may need to define an additional data structure in order to save results of the compression map for use in rehashing (you need to be able to retrieve these values quickly).

Exercise 7.8. Give an implementation of HASHFUNCTION that uses polynomial hashing, as described in Section 7.3. You may assume that the variable r contains an appropriate value to use as the radix, and that the variable w contains the number of bits in a machine word. The size should be the smallest power of 2 that is no smaller than the parameter given to the constructor. For clarity, your implementation should include the mod operation rather than relying on overflow (we don't assume any explicit bounds on integer variables in our algorithms).

* Exercise 7.9. Prove that for each $h \in \mathcal{H}^1_{l,m}$ there is exactly one $s \in S_{l,m}$ such that $h_s = h$. [**Hint:** Prove that if $s \neq s'$, then $h_s \neq h_{s'}$. In order to do this, it is sufficient to find a k such that $h_s(k) \neq h_{s'}(k)$.]

* Exercise 7.10. Modify UNIVERSALHASH1 (Figure 7.8) to handle varying-length keys of unbounded length. Use the expandable-array design pattern to store the randomly-generated indices. Show that when this implementation is used with HASHTABLE (shown in Figures 7.5 and 7.6), the amortized expected running time of the DICTIONARY operations is in $O(l)$, where l is the number of bits in the longest key in the table. You may assume that the actual running time of REMOVE(k) is proportional to the running time of *hash*.INDEX(k) plus the length of the CONSLIST at the resulting index.

* Exercise 7.11. Complete the proof of Theorem 7.3.

Exercise 7.12. Implement HASHFUNCTION to provide $\mathcal{H}^2_{p,m}$. You may assume the variable p contains a prime number larger than any key. You may also assume that all values will fit into integer variables.

Exercise 7.13. Implement HASHFUNCTION to provide $\mathcal{H}^3_{p,l}$. You may assume the variable p contains a prime number larger than w bits, where w is another variable. You may also assume that if a, b, and c are all natural numbers less than p, then $ab + c$ will fit in an integer variable; however, you may not assume that arbitrarily many of these values added together will fit.

* Exercise 7.14. Suppose we were to modify the definition of $\mathcal{H}_{p,l}^3$ (7.2) so that for each a_i, $1 \leq a_i < p$. Show that for every $l \geq 2$ and prime number p, the resulting family of hash functions is not universal. Specifically, show that there are two distinct keys that collide with probability strictly greater than $1/p$. [**Hint:** First consider $l = 2$, then generalize.]

Exercise 7.15. Implement HASHFUNCTION to provide $\mathcal{H}_{p,l,m}^4$ using the same assumptions as for Exercise 7.13.

Exercise 7.16. Let p be a prime number and l and m be positive integers such that $m < p$.

*a. Prove that for every $h \in \mathcal{H}_{p,l,m}^4$ and every positive integer $a < p$, there is exactly one choice of natural numbers $b, a_1, \ldots, a_l$ less than p such that

$$h(\langle k_1, \ldots, k_l \rangle) = \left(a \sum_{i=1}^{l} a_i k_i + b \right) \bmod p \bmod m$$

for every l-tuple $\langle k_1, \ldots, k_l \rangle$ of natural numbers less than p.

b. Consider the following two methods of randomly selecting a hash function h of the form given by equation (7.3):

   i. Select a with uniform probability from the positive integers less than p, and select $b, a_1, \ldots, a_l$ independently with uniform probability from the natural numbers less than p.

   ii. Set a to 1, and select $b, a_1, \ldots, a_l$ independently with uniform probability from the natural numbers less than p.

Prove that for any $h \in \mathcal{H}_{p,l,m}^4$, h is chosen with the same probability by both methods.

* Exercise 7.17. In terms of c and n, find the value of $m \in \mathbb{R}^{\geq 0}$ that minimizes

$$\frac{cn(n-1)}{m} + n + m,$$

assuming $c \in \mathbb{R}^{>0}$, $n \in \mathbb{N}$, and $n > 1$.

Exercise 7.18. Prove that the constructor for PERFECTHASH runs in $\Theta(nl)$ expected time if $\mathcal{H}_{l,m}^1$ is used as the universal hash family, where m is a power of 2.

7.9 Notes

Virtual initialization was suggested by Aho *et al.* [2, Exercise 2.12].

The first description of hashing in the literature was by Dumey [33], who also introduced the division method. However, the concept appears to have been discovered a few years earlier at IBM by H. P. Luhn and independently by Gene M. Amdahl, Elaine M. Boehme, N. Rochester, and Arthur L. Samuel. Knuth [84] gives a detailed treatment of deterministic hashing.

Universal hashing was introduced by Carter and Wegman [19]. They presented the universal families $\mathcal{H}_{l,m}^1$ and $\mathcal{H}_{p,m}^2$. The notion of a c-universal family is closely related to the notion of an ϵ-universal family defined by Cormen *et al.* [25].

The perfect hashing strategy given in Section 7.6 is due to Fredman *et al.* [45].

Chapter 8

Disjoint Sets

In order to motivate the topic of this chapter, let us consider the following problem. We want to design an algorithm to schedule a set of jobs on a single server. Each job requires one unit of execution time and has its own deadline. We must assign a job with deadline d to some time slot t, where $1 \leq t \leq d$. Furthermore, no two jobs can be assigned to the same time slot. If we can't find a time slot for some jobs, we simply won't schedule them. One way to construct such a schedule is to assign each job in turn to the latest available time slot prior to its deadline, provided there is such a time slot. The challenge here is to find an efficient way of locating the latest available time slot prior to the deadline.

One way to think about this problem is to partition the time slots into *disjoint sets* — i.e., a collection of sets such that no two sets have any element in common. In this case, each set will contain a non-empty range of time slots such that the first has not been assigned to a job, but all the rest have been assigned to jobs. In order to be able to handle the case in which time slot 1 has been assigned a job, we will also include a time slot 0, which we will consider to be always available.

Suppose, for example, that we have scheduled jobs in time slots 1, 2, 5, 7, and 8. Each set must have a single available time slot, which must be the smallest time slot in that set; thus, the elements 0, 3, 4, 6, and all elements greater than 8 must be in different sets and must each be the smallest element of its set. If 10 is the latest deadline, our disjoint sets will therefore be $\{0, 1, 2\}$, $\{3\}$, $\{4, 5\}$, $\{6, 7, 8\}$, $\{9\}$, and $\{10\}$. If we then wish to schedule a job with deadline 8, we need to find the latest available time slot prior to 8. This is simply the first time slot in the set containing 8 — namely, 6. Thus, in order to find this time slot, we need to be able to determine which set contains the deadline 8, and what is the first time slot in that set.

When we then schedule the job at time slot 6, the set $\{6, 7, 8\}$ no longer contains an available time slot. We therefore need to merge the set $\{6, 7, 8\}$ with the set containing 5, namely, $\{4, 5\}$.

The operations of finding the set containing a given element and merging two sets are typical of many algorithms that manipulate disjoint sets. The operation of finding the smallest element of a given set is not as commonly needed, so we will ignore this operation for now; however, as we will see shortly, it is not hard to use an array to keep track of this information. Furthermore, we often need to manipulate objects other than NATs; however, we can always store these objects in an array and use their indices as the elements of the disjoint sets. For this reason, we will simplify matters by assuming that the elements of the disjoint sets are the NATs $0..n-1$. In general, the individual sets will be allowed to contain non-consecutive integers.

The DISJOINTSETS ADT, shown in Figure 8.1, specifies the data structure we need. Each of the sets contains an element that is distinguished as its *representative*. The FIND operation simply returns that representative. Thus, if two calls to FIND return the same result, we know that both elements belong to the same set. The MERGE operation takes two representatives, combines the sets identified by these elements, and returns the resulting set's representative. In this chapter, we will consider how the DISJOINTSETS ADT can be implemented efficiently. Before we do this, however, let us take a closer look at how the DISJOINTSETS ADT can be used to implement the scheduling algorithm outlined above.

Figure 8.1   The DISJOINTSETS ADT

Precondition: n is a positive NAT.
Postcondition: Constructs a DISJOINTSETS object in which each element in $0..n-1$ forms a singleton set and is the representative of that set.

DISJOINTSETS(n)

Precondition: k is a NAT less than the size of the universe of elements.
Postcondition: Returns the representative of the partition containing k.

DISJOINTSETS.FIND(k)

Precondition: i and j are representatives of two different partitions.
Postcondition: Merges the partitions containing i and j into a new partition and returns the representative of the new partition.

DISJOINTSETS.MERGE(i, j)

8.1 Using DISJOINTSETS in Scheduling

We will use an instance of the DISJOINTSETS ADT to maintain the disjoint sets in the scheduling algorithm outlined above. In order to find the time slot in which to schedule a job, we first need to find the time interval containing the last time slot prior to the job's deadline. We can use the FIND operation for this purpose. Assuming that we can obtain the available time slot in a given partition, and assuming this time slot is not 0, we have the time slot i in which to schedule the job. We then need to combine this partition with the one immediately preceding it. We can find the preceding partition with FIND($i - 1$). We can then combine the two partitions using MERGE.

We need one additional data structure in order to be able to find the available slot in an interval, given the representative of that interval. For this purpose, we can use an array $avail[0..n]$ such that if j is the representative of an interval, then $avail[j]$ is the available time slot in that interval. Initially, $avail[i] = i$ for all i. Suppose we schedule a job at time i. We then merge the interval containing i with the preceding interval. Let j be the representative of the preceding interval prior to the merger. Then $avail[j]$ is the available element in the resulting interval. If k is the value returned by the call to MERGE, then we can update $avail$ by assigning to $avail[k]$ the value $avail[j]$. Because no other representatives change, no other updates are needed. The entire algorithm is shown in Figure 8.2.

8.2 A Tree-Based Implementation

In this section, we will consider a tree-based implementation of the DISJOINTSETS ADT, as illustrated in Figure 8.3. Each partition will be represented by a tree. The nodes of the tree will be the elements of the partition. The element at the root of the tree will be the representative of that partition. Because we will need to find the root from an arbitrary node in the tree, the children will maintain references to their parents, rather than vice versa. Note that because parents do not need to reference children, a node can have arbitrarily many children.

Given a value k, we need to be able to find the parent of the node representing k. In order to accommodate this functionality, we will use an array $parent[0..n - 1]$ to represent the trees. Specifically, $parent[k]$ will give the parent of k in its tree, or if k is the root, $parent[k]$ will be k. Thus, $parent$ will be the only representation variable. Our structural invariant will be that for $0 \le i < n$:

Figure 8.2 Scheduling algorithm using DISJOINTSETS

Precondition: *deadlines*[1..*m*] contains positive NATs no larger than *n*.
Postcondition: Returns an array *sched*[1..*n*] of NATs no larger than *m*
such that if *sched*[*i*] > 0, then *i* ≤ *deadlines*[*sched*[*i*]].

SCHEDULE(*deadlines*[1..*m*], *n*)
    sched ← **new** ARRAY[1..*n*]; *avail* ← **new** ARRAY[0..*n*]
    intervals ← **new** DISJOINTSETS(*n* + 1); *avail*[0] ← 0
    // **Invariant:** For 1 ≤ *j* < *i*, *sched*[*j*] = 0 and *avail*[*j*] = *j*.
    for *i* ← 1 **to** *n*
        sched[*i*] ← 0; *avail*[*i*] ← *i*
    // **Invariant:** For 1 ≤ *s* ≤ *n*, *sched*[*s*] ≤ *m* and if *sched*[*s*] > 0, then
    // *s* ≤ *deadlines*[*sched*[*s*]]. Each partition in *intervals* contains a range
    // of natural numbers *u*, *u* + 1, ... *u* + *d* such that *sched*[*u*] = 0,
    // *sched*[*u* + *v*] > 0 for 1 ≤ *v* ≤ *d*, and for the representative *w* of this
    // partition, *avail*[*w*] = *u*.
    for *i* ← 1 **to** *m*
        k ← *intervals*.FIND(*deadlines*[*i*]); *t* ← *avail*[*k*]
        if *t* ≠ 0
            sched[*t*] ← *i*; *j* ← *intervals*.FIND(*t* − 1)
            k ← *intervals*.MERGE(*j*, *k*); *avail*[*k*] ← *avail*[*j*]
    return *sched*

Figure 8.3 A tree-based implementation of DISJOINTSETS.

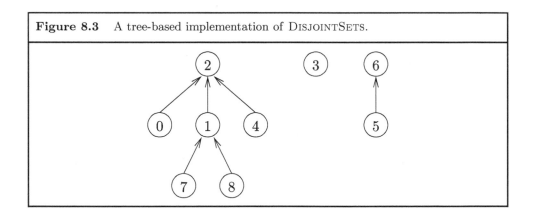

- 0 ≤ *parent*[*i*] < *n*; and
- there is a finite sequence *parent*[*i*], *parent*[*parent*[*i*]], ..., *k* such that *parent*[*k*] = *k*.

Note that this invariant implies that the values in the universe are grouped into trees, where the root *k* of a tree is denoted by *parent*[*k*] = *k*.

Figure 8.4 TREEDISJOINTSETS implementation of DISJOINTSETS

Structural Invariant: For $0 \leq i < n$, $0 \leq parent[i] < n$ and there is a finite sequence $parent[i], parent[parent[i]], ..., k$ such that $parent[k] = k$.

TREEDISJOINTSETS(n)
    $parent \leftarrow$ **new** ARRAY$[0..n-1]$
    // **Invariant:** For $0 \leq j < i$, $parent[j] = j$.
    for $i \leftarrow 0$ **to** $n-1$
        $parent[i] \leftarrow i$

TREEDISJOINTSETS.FIND(k)
    $i \leftarrow k$
    // **Invariant:** i is an ancestor of k.
    while $parent[i] \neq i$
        $i \leftarrow parent[i]$
    return i

TREEDISJOINTSETS.MERGE(i, j)
    if $i = j$ **or** $i \neq parent[i]$ **or** $j \neq parent[j]$
        error
    else
        $parent[i] \leftarrow j$
        return j

The MERGE and FIND operations are now straightforward. MERGE simply makes one tree a child of the root of the other, and FIND follows the *parent* references until the root is reached. The full implementation is shown in Figure 8.4.

Clearly, the constructor operates in $\Theta(n)$ time, and MERGE operates in $\Theta(1)$ time. The number of iterations of the **while** loop in FIND is the depth of k, which in the worst case is the height of the tree. Clearly, the height is at most $n - 1$. Unfortunately, this height can be achieved by the sequence

$$\text{MERGE}(0, 1), \text{MERGE}(1, 2), \ldots, \text{MERGE}(n - 2, n - 1).$$

Thus, the worst-case running time for FIND is in $\Theta(n)$.

Because the constructor will only be executed once for each structure, $\Theta(n)$ is not a bad running time. However, we will probably need to execute

FIND repeatedly. We would therefore like to improve its performance. In the next section we will examine a simple way to do this.

8.3   A Short Tree Implementation

Because the worst-case running time for FIND is proportional to the height of the tree, we can improve the worst-case performance by controlling heights of the trees. In order to accomplish this, when we merge two trees, we will always make the tree with smaller height the child of the root of the other tree. If both trees have the same height, we arbitrarily choose one as the child. Note that by using this technique, the only way we can increase the height of a tree is to merge it with another tree of the same height. We will show that as a result, the heights of the trees are always at most logarithmic in their number of nodes.

As we did in analyzing the heights of AVL trees (Section 6.2), let us compute the minimum number of nodes required to achieve a tree of height h, assuming we always make the tree with smaller height the child. Let $f(h)$ give this number. Then $f(0) = 1$. In order to build a tree with height $h > 0$ using the fewest nodes, we must merge two trees of height $h-1$, each having the fewest nodes possible. Thus, each of the two merged trees must have $f(h-1)$ nodes. The total number of nodes is given by the recurrence

$$f(h) = 2f(h-1).$$

It is easily seen that $f(h) = 2^h$, so that $h = \lg f(h)$. Thus, if k is the number of nodes in a tree of height h, we have

$$h = \lg f(h)$$
$$\leq \lg k.$$

We conclude that if the universe contains n elements, then no tree has a height greater than $\lg n$.

In order to be able to merge trees in this way, we need to keep track of the height of each tree. For this purpose, we include an additional representation variable $height[0..n-1]$. Our structural invariant will then be that for $0 \leq i < n$, $height[i]$ is the maximum of 0 and $height[j] + 1$ for all $j \neq i$ such that $parent[j] = i$, and that $0 \leq parent[i] < n$. Note that because $height[parent[i]] > height[i]$ whenever $parent[i] \neq i$, each value i must have an ancestor j such that $parent[j] = j$; thus, the elements of the universe must be grouped into trees rooted at nodes with $parent[i] = i$.

Figure 8.5   SHORTDISJOINTSETS implementation of DISJOINTSETS

Structural Invariant: For $0 \leq i < n$, $height[i]$ is the maximum of 0 and $height[j] + 1$ for all $j \neq i$ such that $parent[j] = i$, and $0 \leq parent[i] < n$.

SHORTDISJOINTSETS(n)
 $parent \leftarrow$ **new** ARRAY$[0..n-1]$; $height \leftarrow$ **new** ARRAY$[0..n-1]$
 for $i \leftarrow 0$ **to** $n-1$
  $parent[i] \leftarrow i$; $height[i] \leftarrow 0$

SHORTDISJOINTSETS.MERGE(i, j)
 if $i = j$ **or** $i \neq parent[i]$ **or** $j \neq parent[j]$
  error
 else if $height[i] \leq height[j]$
  $parent[i] \leftarrow j$
  if $height[i] = height[j]$
   $height[j] \leftarrow height[j] + 1$
  return j
 else
  $parent[j] \leftarrow i$
  return i

The constructor and MERGE operation for this implementation are shown in Figure 8.5. The FIND operation is implemented exactly as TREEDISJOINTSETS.FIND in Figure 8.4.

As in the previous implementation, the constructor runs in $\Theta(n)$ time, and MERGE runs in $\Theta(1)$ time. Based on the above discussion, FIND runs in $\Theta(\lg n)$ time.

8.4   * Path Compression

In order to improve the performance of a FIND, we would like to decrease the distance from a node to the root as much as possible. An effective way of

> *An internal function is used in order to avoid making a callback.*

accomplishing this is to modify the FIND so that it changes the parent of every node it encounters to be the root of its tree. This technique is called *path compression*. We implement this technique using a recursive internal function, COMPRESS. If the given node k is not the root, COMPRESS first performs a recursive COMPRESS on k's parent. If we treat the distance between a node and the root as the size of a call to FIND, we see that such a recursive call is valid. Furthermore, it compresses the path from k's parent to the root and returns the root. It can therefore complete its task by making k a child of the root and returning the root. The resulting FIND algorithm is shown in Figure 8.6.

The rest of the implementation is the same as for SHORTDISJOINTSETS; however, because path compression can decrease the height of a node i without updating *height*[i], this value is no longer guaranteed to give the height of node i. For this reason, we will change the name of this array to *rank* and weaken the structural invariant so that *rank*[i] is at least the height of i. The precise meaning of *rank*[i] is now rather elusive, other than the fact that it gives an upper bound on the height of i.

Clearly, the running time of COMPRESSEDDISJOINTSETS.FIND is in $O(h)$, where h is the height of the tree. Furthermore, the height of a tree in this implementation can certainly be no larger than it would have been if no path compression had been done; hence, the upper bound of $O(\lg n)$ shown for SHORTDISJOINTSETS.FIND also holds for

---

Figure 8.6   The FIND algorithm for the COMPRESSEDDISJOINTSETS implementation of DISJOINTSETS

Structural Invariant: For $0 \leq i < n$, $0 \leq parent[i] < n$ and there is a finite sequence $parent[i], parent[parent[i]], ..., k$ such that $parent[k] = k$.

COMPRESSEDDISJOINTSETS.FIND(k)
   return COMPRESS(k)

// Internal function

Precondition: k is a NAT less than the size of the universe of elements, and the structural invariant holds.

Postcondition: Returns the representative of the partition containing k, and makes each other element that was an ancestor of k a child of the representative. The structural invariant holds.

COMPRESSEDDISJOINTSETS.COMPRESS(k)
   if $parent[k] \neq k$
      $parent[k] \leftarrow$ COMPRESS($parent[k]$)
   return $parent[k]$

COMPRESSEDDISJOINTSETS.FIND. Because we can still construct a tree with height in $\Theta(\lg n)$ with a sequence of MERGEs, we conclude that COMPRESSEDDISJOINTSETS.FIND runs in $\Theta(\lg n)$ time in the worst case. Clearly, COMPRESSEDDISJOINTSETS.MERGE runs in $\Theta(1)$ time, so that in the worst case, the asymptotic performance of COMPRESSEDDISJOINTSETS is identical to that of SHORTDISJOINTSETS.

On the other hand, because each path compression has the tendency to improve the performance of subsequent FINDs, we might suspect that the amortized performance of this structure is improved. Indeed, we will show that the amortized performance of the MERGE and FIND operations for COMPRESSEDDISJOINTSETS is "almost" constant.

In order to perform an amortized analysis, we need to assign actual costs to the operations. The running time of FIND(i) is proportional to the number of nodes on the path from i to the root of its tree. Another way to say this is that the running time is proportional to the number of locations of the *parent* array that are accessed. Let us therefore define the actual cost of an operation to be the number of locations accessed in the *parent* array. The actual cost of MERGE is therefore 2.

The key to a good amortized analysis is finding a good potential function. Let S be the set of all possible states of some COMPRESSEDDISJOINTSETS with size n. We need a function $\Phi : S \to \mathbb{R}^{\geq 0}$ such that the initial state is mapped to 0. To arrive at this function, we will define, for a given state $s \in S$, a potential for each node; i.e., we will define a function $\phi_s : U \to \mathbb{N}$, where $U = \{i \in \mathbb{N} \mid i < n\}$. We will then define the potential function to be the sum of the potentials of all of the nodes:

$$\Phi(s) = \sum_{i=0}^{n-1} \phi_s(i).$$

Let $rank_s$ and $parent_s$ denote the values of the *rank* and *parent* arrays in state s. We will define our potential function based on these values. Let ϵ denote the initial state. Thus, for $0 \leq i < n$, $rank_\epsilon[i] = 0$. In order for Φ to be a valid potential function, we need $\Phi(\epsilon) = 0$. To accomplish this, we let $\phi_s(i) = 0$ if $rank_s[i] = 0$ for $0 \leq i < n$ and any state s. Note that a node can only obtain a non-zero rank when a MERGE makes it the parent of another node; thus, $rank_s[i] = 0$ iff i is a leaf.

We have two operations we need to consider as we define $\phi_s(i)$ for non-leaf i. MERGE is a cheap operation, having an actual cost of 2, whereas FIND is more expensive in the worst case. We therefore need to amortize the cost of an expensive FIND over preceding MERGEs. This means that we need the potential function to increase by some amount — say $\alpha(n)$, where α is some appropriate function — for at least some of the MERGES. The MERGE operation only operates on roots, so let us focus our attention there. When a MERGE is performed, the rank of one node — a root — may increase by 1, but otherwise, no ranks increase (see Figure 8.5, and recall that the *rank* array replaces the *height* array in this algorithm). Therefore, let us define $\phi_s(i)$ to be $\alpha(n)rank_s[i]$ if i is a root (i.e., if $parent_s[i] = i$).

Note that the above definitions are consistent with each other: if i is both a leaf and a root, its rank is 0, and hence its potential is 0 by either of the above definitions. Furthermore, if we can ensure that a MERGE causes the potential of no node other than the root of the resulting tree to increase, we will have a bound of $\alpha(n) + 2$ on the amortized cost of MERGE with respect to Φ. We still need to define the potentials for nodes that are neither leaves nor roots in such a way that an expensive FIND causes Φ to decrease enough to offset much of the actual cost.

Consider the effect of FIND(j) on a node i that is neither a leaf nor a root. i's rank doesn't change, but its parent may. In particular, it may receive a parent with different rank than its original parent. It is not hard to show as a structural invariant that if $parent[i] \neq i$, then $rank[parent[i]] > rank[i]$. We would therefore like the potential of i to decrease, generally speaking, as $rank[parent[i]]$ increases. Furthermore, in order that its potential does not increase when a MERGE changes it from a root to a non-root, we should have $\phi_s(i) \leq \alpha(n)rank_s[i]$ for all states s and nodes i.

As a first approximation to a definition of $\phi_s(i)$, where i is neither a leaf nor a root, suppose we let $\phi_s(i) = (\alpha(n) - f(s, i))rank_s[i]$, where f is some function that depends on the ranks of i and its parent in s and obeys the constraint

$$0 \leq f(s, i) < \alpha(n).$$

If f does not decrease when i receives a parent of higher rank, ϕ_s would satisfy the constraints outlined above. However, it would suffer the disadvantage that its value is always a multiple of $rank_s[i]$. In order to give us more control over how much the potential function changes, we would like for this function to have a larger range when $rank_s[i]$ is fixed, as it is when i is not a root. Therefore, we wish to find, for each state s, a function

$$\phi_s(i) = (\alpha(n) - f(s, i))rank_s[i] - g(s, i),$$

where f is as above and g is some function that depends on the ranks of i and its parent in s and obeys the constraint

$$0 < g(s, i) \leq rank_s[i].$$

Let us consider the nodes examined during the operation FIND(j) on some state s. These nodes are the ancestors of j. Let us restrict our attention to those ancestors that have nonzero rank and are not the root. (Note that as a result, we ignore at most two ancestors.) Let A_k be a function describing the relationship between the ranks of i and its parent for any non-root i, where $k = f(s, i)$; i.e., $rank_s[parent_s[i]] \geq A_{f(s,i)}(rank_s[i])$. When the path compression is done, the parent of i may have the same rank (if i had already been a child of the root), or it may be very little more than the rank of i's original parent. However, suppose that in the original state s, i has a proper ancestor i' other than the root such that $f(s, i') = f(s, i) = k$. Because i' is not a root, the rank of i's new parent is at least the rank of the original parent of i'. Therefore, if A_k is nondecreasing, we have

$$rank_{s'}[parent_{s'}[i]] \geq rank_s[parent_s[i']]$$
$$\geq A_k(rank_s[i'])$$
$$\geq A_k(rank_s[parent_s[i]]).$$

Thus, each time a path compression moves a non-leaf i having a proper ancestor i' (other than the root) with $f(s, i) = f(s, i') = k$, the rank of i's parent increases by at least the application of the function A_k. Furthermore, because $0 \leq f(s, i) < \alpha(n)$, there can be at most $\alpha(n)$ nodes i on the path from j to the root, other than leaves or the root, that do not have a proper ancestor i' with $f(s, i') = f(s, i)$. Thus, if we can decrease the potential of each i having a proper ancestor i' with $f(s, i') = f(s, i)$, without increasing any potentials, then we will have a bound of $\alpha(n) + 2$ on the amortized cost of a FIND with respect to Φ.

The behavior described above gives us some insight into how we might define f, g, and each A_k. First, we would like g to give the maximum number of times $A_{f(s,i)}$ can be applied to the rank of i without exceeding the rank of i's parent. Thus, if i has a proper ancestor i' with $f(s, i') = f(s, i)$, and if $f(s', i) = f(s, i)$, then $g(s', i) > g(s, i)$. As a result, the potential of i decreases. In order to keep $g(s, i)$ within the proper range, we should define $f(s, i)$ and A_k so that if we apply $A_{f(s,i)}$ more than $rank_s(i)$ times to $rank_s(i)$, we must attain a value of at least $A_{f(s,i)+1}(rank_s[i])$. Then if we define $f(s,i)$ to be the maximum k such that $rank_s[parent_s[i]] \geq A_k(rank_s[i])$, we can never have $rank_s[parent_s[i]] \geq A_{f(s,i)+1}(rank_s[i])$.

We still need to define the functions A_k. In order to facilitate this definition, we first define the *iteration operator* for functions. Let $F : \mathbb{N} \to \mathbb{N}$. We then define

$$F^{(0)}(n) = n$$

$$F^{(k)}(n) = F(F^{(k-1)}(n)) \quad \text{for } k > 0.$$

For example, if $F(n) = 2n$, then $F^{(2)}(n) = 4n$ and $F^{(3)}(n) = 8n$; more generally, $F^{(k)}(n) = 2^k n$.

We now define:

$$A_k(n) = \begin{cases} n+1 & \text{if } k = 0 \\ A_{k-1}^{(n+1)}(n) & \text{if } k \geq 1. \end{cases}$$

We can then define, for each node i that is neither a leaf nor a root,

$$f(s,i) = \max\{k \mid rank_s[parent_s[i]] \geq A_k(rank_s[i])\}$$

and

$$g(s,i) = \max\{k \mid rank_s[parent_s[i]] \geq A_{f(s,i)}^{(k)}(rank_s[i])\}.$$

Finally, we need $f(s,i) < \alpha(n)$ whenever i is neither a leaf nor a root. Thus, we need to ensure that whenever i is neither a leaf nor a root, we have

$$A_{\alpha(n)}(rank_s[i]) > rank_s[parent_s[i]].$$

We have shown that without path compression, the height of a tree never exceeds $\lg n$; hence, with path compression, the rank of a node never exceeds $\lg n$. It therefore suffices to define

$$\alpha(n) = \min\{k \mid A_k(1) > \lg n\}.$$

As the subscript k increases, $A_k(1)$ increases very rapidly. We leave it as an exercise to show that

$$A_4(1) \geq 2^{2^{\cdot^{\cdot^{\cdot^2}}}},$$

where there are 2051 2s on the right-hand side. It is hard to comprehend just how large this value is, for if the right-hand side contained only six 2s, the number of bits required to store it would be $2^{65536} + 1$. By contrast, the number of elementary particles in the universe is currently estimated to be no more than about 2^{300}. Hence, there is not nearly enough matter in the universe to store $A_4(1)$ in binary. Because $\alpha(n) \leq 4$ for all $n < 2^{A_4(1)}$, we can see that α grows very slowly.

To summarize, we define our potential function Φ so that

$$\Phi(s) = \sum_{i=0}^{n-1} \phi_s(i),$$

where

$$\phi_s(i) = \begin{cases} 0 & \text{if } rank_s[i] = 0 \\ \alpha(n)rank_s[i] & \text{if } parent_s[i] = i \\ (\alpha(n) - f(s,i))rank_s[i] - g(s,i) & \text{otherwise,} \end{cases}$$

for α, f, and g as defined above. Before we can complete the amortized analysis, we need to show that both f and g satisfy the properties outlined in the discussion above.

Lemma 8.1. *Let s be a state of a* COMPRESSEDDISJOINTSETS *of size n, and let $0 \leq i < n$ such that $parent_s[i] \neq i$ and $rank_s[i] > 0$. Then*

$$0 \leq f(s,i) < \alpha(n).$$

Proof. First, because the rank of the parent of i is strictly larger than that of i, we have

$$rank_s[parent_s[i]] \geq rank_s[i] + 1$$
$$= A_0(rank_s[i]),$$

from the definition of A_0. Thus, from the definition of f, $f(s,i) \geq 0$.

It is not hard to show that each A_k is nondecreasing — we leave the details as an exercise. Using this fact, along with the definition of α and the fact that no rank exceeds $\lg n$, we have

$$A_{\alpha(n)}(rank_s[i]) \geq A_{\alpha(n)}(1)$$
$$> \lg n$$
$$\geq rank_s[parent_s[i]].$$

Thus, from the definition of f, $f(s,i) < \alpha(n)$. □

Lemma 8.2. *Let s be a state of a* COMPRESSEDDISJOINTSETS *of size n, and let $0 \leq i < n$ such that $parent_s[i] \neq i$ and $rank_s[i] > 0$. Then*

$$0 < g(s,i) \leq rank_s[i].$$

Proof. First, from the definition of f, we have

$$rank_s[parent_s[i]] \geq A_{f(s,i)}(rank_s[i])$$
$$= A_{f(s,i)}^{(1)}(rank_s[i]).$$

Thus, from the definition of g, $g(s,i) > 0$.

Now from the definitions of A and f, we have

$$A_{f(s,i)}^{(rank_s[i]+1)}(rank_s[i]) = A_{f(s,i)+1}(rank_s[i])$$
$$> rank_s[parent_s[i]].$$

Thus, $g(s,i) \leq rank_s[i]$. $\qquad\square$

We are now ready to show that the amortized costs of MERGE and FIND are in $O(\alpha(n))$.

Theorem 8.3. *With respect to Φ, the amortized cost of* MERGE *on a* COMPRESSEDDISJOINTSETS *of size n is in $O(\alpha(n))$.*

Proof. Suppose we do MERGE(i,j) in state s, yielding state s'. Without loss of generality, assume j is made the parent of i. Then i is the only node whose parent changes, and j is the only node whose rank may change; hence, the potentials for all other nodes remain unchanged. The change in potential for node i is given by

$$\phi_{s'}(i) - \phi_s(i) = (\alpha(n) - f(s',i))rank_{s'}[i] - g(s',i) - \alpha(n)rank_s[i]$$
$$< \alpha(n)(rank_{s'}[i] - rank_s[i])$$
$$= 0.$$

The change in potential for node j is given by

$$\phi_{s'}(j) - \phi_s(j) = \alpha(n)rank_{s'}[j] - \alpha(n)rank_s[j]$$
$$\leq \alpha(n),$$

because the rank of j can increase by at most 1. The change in Φ is therefore less than $\alpha(n)$. Because the actual cost is 2, the amortized cost is less than $\alpha(n) + 2 \in O(\alpha(n))$. $\qquad\square$

Theorem 8.4. *With respect to Φ, the amortized cost of* FIND *on a* COMPRESSEDDISJOINTSETS *of size n is in $O(\alpha(n))$.*

Proof. Suppose we perform FIND(j) on state s. Let s' be the resulting state. Suppose there are d nodes on the path from j to the root in s. Then the actual cost of the operation is d. We will show that as a result of this operation, at least $d - \alpha(n) - 2$ nodes decrease in potential, and no nodes increase in potential. As a result, we will have shown the amortized cost to be at most $\alpha(n) + 2 \in O(\alpha(n))$.

First, we will show that no potentials increase as a result of FIND(j). Because the FIND operation does not change any ranks and does not change which nodes are roots, no leaves or roots can change potential. The potential for any other node i can change only due to changes in f and g. Because i cannot receive a parent with a smaller rank as a result of path compression, $f(s', i) \geq f(s, i)$. If $f(s', i) = f(s, i)$, then clearly $g(s', i) \geq g(s, i)$. In this case, the potential does not increase. If, on the other hand, $f(s', i) > f(s, i)$, from Lemma 8.2 and the fact that path compression leaves all ranks unchanged, $g(s, i) - g(s', i) < \text{rank}_s[i]$. Then

$$
\begin{aligned}
\phi_{s'}(i) - \phi_s(i) = \quad & (\alpha(n) - f(s', i))\text{rank}_{s'}[i] - g(s', i) \\
- \quad & (\alpha(n) - f(s, i))\text{rank}_s[i] + g(s, i) \\
< \quad & (f(s, i) - f(s', i))\text{rank}_s[i] + \text{rank}_s[i] \\
\leq \quad & 0.
\end{aligned}
$$

In this case, the potential of i decreases.

The only nodes whose parents change are ancestors of j, and no ranks change. Hence, the only nodes whose potentials change are ancestors of j. The ancestors of j include a root and at most one leaf. For the other ancestors i, from Lemma 8.1, there can be at most $\alpha(n)$ distinct values for $f(s, i)$. For a given value k, each node i with $f(s, i) = k$ except the one nearest the root has a proper ancestor i' with $f(s, i') = k$. We will show that all of these nodes — i.e., at least $d - \alpha(n) - 2$ of the d ancestors of j — decrease in potential as a result of the FIND.

Let i be an ancestor of j in s such that i is neither a leaf nor a root and such that for some proper ancestor i' of i other than the root, $f(s, i) = f(s, i') = k$. We have already shown that if $f(s', i) > f(s, i)$, the potential of i decreases. Therefore, suppose $f(s', i) = f(s, i) = k$. Then

$$
\begin{aligned}
\text{rank}_{s'}[\text{parent}_{s'}[i]] &\geq \text{rank}_s[\text{parent}_s[i']] \\
&\geq A_k(\text{rank}_s[i']) && \text{(definition of } f) \\
&\geq A_k(\text{rank}_s[\text{parent}_s[i]]) \\
&\geq A_k(A_k^{(g(s,i))}(\text{rank}_s[i])) && \text{(definition of } g) \\
&= A_k^{(g(s,i)+1)}(\text{rank}_s[i]) \\
&= A_k^{(g(s,i)+1)}(\text{rank}_{s'}[i]).
\end{aligned}
$$

Because $f(s', i) = k$, $g(s', i) > g(s, i)$, so that $\phi_{s'}(i) < \phi_s(i)$. □

The above theorems show that the amortized running times of MERGE and FIND are in $O(\alpha(n))$. However, α appears to be a somewhat contrived function. We have argued intuitively that α increases very slowly, but we have not formally compared it with any better-known slow-growing function like lg or lg lg. We address this issue more formally in the Exercises. For now, we will simply state that the collection of functions A_k form a variation of *Ackermann's function*, and that α is one way of defining its inverse. There have actually been several different 2- or 3-variable functions that have been called Ackermann's function, and all grow at roughly the same rapid rate.

8.5 Summary

Tree-based implementations of disjoint sets provide very efficient MERGE and FIND operations, particularly when path compression is used. The worst-case running times for these operations are in $\Theta(1)$ and $\Theta(\lg n)$, respectively, for both SHORTDISJOINTSETS and COMPRESSEDDISJOINTSETS. The latter implementation yields nearly constant amortized running time. A summary of the running times of the operations for the different implementations is shown in Figure 8.7. As we will see in later chapters, these structures are very useful in the design of efficient algorithms.

Figure 8.7   Comparison of running times of the DISJOINTSETS operations for various implementations

	FIND
TREEDISJOINTSETS	$\Theta(n)$
SHORTDISJOINTSETS	$\Theta(\lg n)$
COMPRESSEDDISJOINTSETS	$O(\alpha(n))$ amortized

Notes:

- n is the number of elements in the universe of the sets.
- The constructor runs in $\Theta(n)$ worst-case time for each implementation.
- The MERGE operation runs in $\Theta(1)$ worst-case time for each operation.
- Unless otherwise noted, all running times are worst-case.

8.6 Exercises

Exercise 8.1. Draw the trees that result from the following sequence of operations:

$t \leftarrow$ **new** TREEDISJOINTSETS(8)
$t.$MERGE$(0, 1)$
$t.$MERGE$(t.$FIND$(1), 2)$
$t.$MERGE$(3, 4)$
$t.$MERGE$(5, 6)$
$t.$MERGE$(t.$FIND$(3), t.$FIND$(6))$
$t.$MERGE$(t.$FIND$(3), t.$FIND$(0))$

Exercise 8.2. Repeat Exercise 8.1 using a SHORTDISJOINTSETS implementation.

Exercise 8.3. Repeat Exercise 8.1 using a COMPRESSEDDISJOINTSETS implementation.

Exercise 8.4. Prove that SCHEDULE, shown in Figure 8.2, meets its specification.

Exercise 8.5. Prove that an algorithm that returns an array $sched[1..n]$ containing all 0s meets the specification of SCHEDULE (Figure 8.2).

Exercise 8.6. Analyze the worst-case running time of SCHEDULE (Figure 8.2) assuming the TREEDISJOINTSETS implementation of DISJOINTSETS. Your analysis should be in terms of n, and you may assume that $m \leq n$. Express your result as simply as possible using Θ-notation.

Exercise 8.7. Repeat Exercise 8.6 assuming the SHORTDISJOINTSETS implementation of DISJOINTSETS.

Exercise 8.8. Repeat Exercise 8.7 assuming the COMPRESSEDDISJOINT-SETS implementation of DISJOINTSETS. Express the best result you can as simply as possible using big-O notation.

Exercise 8.9. Prove that TREEDISJOINTSETS, shown in Figure 8.4, meets the DISJOINTSETS specification, given in Figure 8.1.

Exercise 8.10. Prove that SHORTDISJOINTSETS, shown in Figure 8.5, meets the DISJOINTSETS specification, given in Figure 8.1.

Exercise 8.11. Prove that COMPRESSEDDISJOINTSETS, described in Section 8.4, meets the DISJOINTSETS specification, given in Figure 8.1. Use as the structural invariant that for $0 \leq i < n$,

- if $rank[i] = 0$ then there is no j, such that $0 \le j < n$, $j \ne i$, and $parent[j] = i$; and
- if $rank[i] > 0$, then
  - there is some j such that $0 \le j < n$, $j \ne i$, and $parent[j] = i$; and
  - $rank[i] > \max\{rank[j] \mid 0 \le j < n, j \ne i, parent[j] = i\}$.

Exercise 8.12. Suppose that we modify SHORTDISJOINTSETS so that in the MERGE operation we make the tree with fewer nodes a child of the root of the other tree (choosing arbitrarily if both trees have the same number of nodes). Prove by induction on k that any tree with $k > 0$ nodes formed in this way will have height at most $\lg k$.

* Exercise 8.13. Suppose that we modify TREEDISJOINTSETS so that in the MERGE operation we flip a fair coin to determine which node will be the new root. Analyze the worst-case expected running time of FIND for such an implementation. Express your answer as simply as possible using Θ-notation. In showing the lower bound, describe a sequence of operations for an arbitrarily large universe of elements such that the last FIND is expected to require the stated running time.

Exercise 8.14. Prove by induction on i that $A_0^{(i)}(n) = n+i$, so that $A_1(n) = 2n + 1$.

Exercise 8.15. Using the result of Exercise 8.14, prove by induction on i that $A_1^{(i)}(n) = 2^i(n+1) - 1$, so that $A_2(n) = 2^{n+1}(n+1) - 1$.

Exercise 8.16. Prove by induction on k that each A_k is non-decreasing.

Exercise 8.17. Using the results of Exercises 8.15 and 8.16, prove by induction on i that

$$A_2^{(i)}(n) \ge 2^{2^{\cdot^{\cdot^{\cdot^{2^n}}}}},$$

where the right-hand side has i 2s.

Exercise 8.18. Using the result of Exercise 8.15, evaluate $A_3(1)$.

Exercise 8.19. Using the result of Exercises 8.17 and 8.18, show that

$$A_4(1) \ge 2^{2^{\cdot^{\cdot^{\cdot^{2}}}}},$$

where the right-hand side has 2051 2s.

Exercise 8.20. For the following, you may use the results of Exercises 8.15 and 8.16.

a. Prove by induction on i that for each $i \in \mathbb{N}$,

$$\lg^{(i)}(n) \geq \min\{k \mid A_2^{(i)}(k) \geq n\}.$$

b. Prove by induction on k that for $k \geq 4$, $A_k(1) \geq A_2^{(k)}(k)$.
c. Using the results of parts (a) and (b), prove that for each $i \in \mathbb{N}$, there is an $n_i \in \mathbb{N}$ such that whenever $n \geq n_i$, $\alpha(n) \leq \lg^{(i)}(n)$.
d. Using the result of part (c), prove that for each $i \in \mathbb{N}$, $\alpha(i) \in o(\lg^{(i)} n)$.

* Exercise 8.21. Let

$$\lg^* n = \min\{k \mid \lg^{(k)} n \leq 1\}.$$

Prove that $\alpha(n) \in o(\lg^* n)$.

8.7 Notes

The TREEDISJOINTSETS implementation of DISJOINTSETS is due to Galler and Fischer [47]. The improvement of Section 8.3 is presented by Hopcroft and Ullman [66], who credit McIlroy and Morris with having implemented it.

The improvement using path compression is credited to Tritter by Knuth [82]. The amortized analysis of this structure yielding results similar to those presented here was done by Tarjan [111,112]. The analysis given here is based on the presentation by Cormen *et al.* [25], which is based on a proof due to Kozen [87].

Exercise 8.12 is from Brassard and Bratley [17].

Chapter 9

Graphs

Often we need to model relationships that can be expressed using a set of pairs. Examples include distances between points on a map, links in a communications network, precedence constraints between tasks, and compatibility of items or people. In some cases, the relationship is symmetric; e.g., if A is compatible with B, then B is compatible with A. In other cases, the relationship is asymmetric; e.g., the requirement that A precedes B is not the same as the requirement that B precedes A. All of these relationships can be modeled using graphs. Having modeled the relationship, we can then apply graph algorithms for extracting such information as a shortest path between two points or a valid ordering of tasks.

There are two kinds of graphs, depending on whether the relationship to be modeled is symmetric or asymmetric. For symmetric relationships, we define an *undirected graph* to be a pair (V, E), where V is a finite set of *vertices* (or *nodes*) and E is a set of 2-element subsets of V. We refer to the elements of E as *edges*. We can represent undirected graphs pictorially as in Figure 9.1, where vertices are denoted by circles and edges are denoted by line segments or curves connecting their constituent vertices. We often say that an edge $\{u, v\}$ is *incident on* vertices u and v, and that u and v are therefore *adjacent*.

For modeling asymmetric relationships, we define a *directed graph* to be a pair (V, E), where again V is a finite set of vertices or nodes, but E is a set of

> In some cases, we drop the requirement that the elements be distinct.

ordered pairs of distinct elements of V. Again, we refer to the elements of E as edges. In order to differentiate the edges of an undirected graph from the edges of a directed graph, we sometimes refer to the former as *undirected edges* and to the latter as *directed edges*. We can represent directed graphs in a manner similar to our depiction of undirected graphs, using arrows to

Figure 9.1 An undirected graph

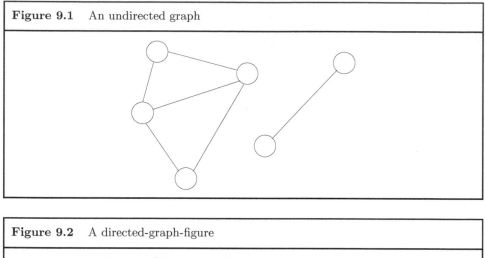

Figure 9.2 A directed-graph-figure

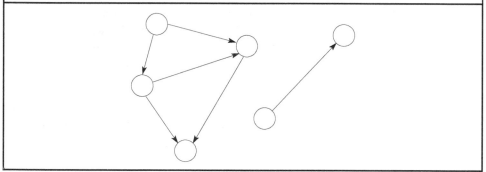

indicate the directions of the edges. Conventionally, we draw the edge (u, v) as an arrow from u to v (see Figure 9.2). For a directed edge (u, v) we say that v is adjacent to u, but not vice versa (unless (v, u) is also an edge in the graph).

We usually want to associate some additional information with the vertices and/or the edges. For example, if the graph is used to represent distances between points on a map, we would want to associate a distance with each edge. In addition, we might want to associate the name of a city with each vertex. In order to simplify our presentation, we will focus our attention on the edges of a graph and any information associated with them. Specifically, as we did for disjoint sets in the previous chapter, we will adopt the convention that the vertices of a graph will be designated by natural numbers $0, \ldots, n - 1$. If additional information needs to be associated with vertices, it can be stored in an array indexed by the numbers designating the vertices. While some applications might require more flexibility, this scheme is sufficient for our purposes.

Figure 9.3 The GRAPH ADT

Precondition: n is a NAT.
Postcondition: Constructs a GRAPH with vertices $0, \ldots, n - 1$ and no edges.

GRAPH(n)

Precondition: true.
Postcondition: Returns the number of vertices in the graph.

GRAPH.SIZE()

Precondition: i and j are NATs less than the number of vertices, $i \neq j$, and x refers to a non-nil item.
Postcondition: Associates x with the edge (i, j), adding this edge if necessary.

GRAPH.PUT(i, j, x)

Precondition: i and j are NATs less than the number of vertices.
Postcondition: Returns the data item associated with edge (i, j), or nil if (i, j) is not in the graph.

GRAPH.GET(i, j)

Precondition: i is a NAT less than the number of vertices.
Postcondition: Returns a CONSLIST of EDGEs representing the edges proceeding from vertex i, where an edge (i, j) with data x is represented by an EDGE with *source* $= i$, *dest* $= j$, and *data* $= x$.

GRAPH.ALLFROM(i)

Although in practice it may be beneficial to define separate ADTs for directed and undirected graphs, respectively, it will simplify our presentation if we specify a single GRAPH ADT, as shown in Figure 9.3. This actually specifies a directed graph, but we can use it to represent an undirected graph if we make sure that whenever (i, j) is an edge, then (j, i) is an edge with the same associated information. We can therefore use the same ADT for both types of graph, though the specification itself will never guarantee that the graph is undirected.

This specification uses the data type EDGE, which is implemented by three readable representation variables, *source*, *dest*, and *data*. We assume that it contains a constructor EDGE(i, j, x), which sets *source* to i, *dest* to j, and *data* to x. It contains no other operations other than the three accessor operations, so it is an immutable structure. Although we place no restrictions on the values stored in its representation variables, the specification of

GRAPH.ALLFROM ensures that any EDGE in the CONSLIST returned by this operation will have natural numbers for *source* and *dest* and a non-nil value for *data*.

In the next two sections, we will consider two applications of the GRAPH ADT. Each of these applications will result in a graph algorithm. We will then examine two implementations of GRAPH and analyze the running times of their operations. We will also analyze the space usage of each implementation. Using these analyses, we will analyze the running times of the two algorithms with each of these implementations.

9.1   Universal Sink Detection

Our first example is somewhat contrived, but it serves as a useful introduction to graph algorithms. To begin, we define a *sink* in a directed graph $G = (V, E)$ to be a vertex v with no outgoing edges. A *universal sink* is a sink v such that for every vertex $u \neq v$, $(u, v) \in E$. In this section, we will examine the problem of finding a universal sink in a directed graph, if one exists.

We first observe that a directed graph can have at most one universal sink. Let us therefore consider the related problem of returning a universal sink in a nonempty graph if one exists, or returning an arbitrary vertex otherwise. We will then reduce the universal sink detection problem to this variant. Suppose we consider any two distinct vertices, u and v (if there is only one vertex, clearly it is a universal sink). If $(u, v) \in E$, then u cannot be a sink. Otherwise, v cannot be a universal sink. Let G' be the graph obtained by removing from G one vertex x that is not a universal sink, along with all edges incident on x. If G has a universal sink w, then w must also be a universal sink in G'. We have therefore transformed this problem to a smaller instance. Because this reduction is a transformation, we can implement it using a loop.

In order to implement this algorithm using the GRAPH ADT, we need to generalize the problem to a subgraph of G comprised of the vertices $i, \ldots, j$ and all edges between them. If $j > i$, we can then eliminate either i or j from the range of vertices, depending on whether (i, j) is an edge. Note that by generalizing the problem in this way, we do not need to modify the graph when we eliminate vertices — we simply keep track of i and j, the endpoints of the range of vertices we are considering. If there is an edge (i, j), we eliminate vertex i by incrementing i; otherwise, we eliminate vertex j by decrementing j. When all vertices but one have been eliminated (i.e., when $i = j$), the remaining vertex must be the universal sink if there is one.

Figure 9.4   An algorithm to find a universal sink in a directed graph

---

Precondition: G refers to a GRAPH.
Postcondition: Returns the universal sink in G, or -1 if G has no universal sink.

UNIVERSALSINK(G)
   if G.SIZE() $= 0$
      return -1
   else
      $i \leftarrow 0$; $j \leftarrow G$.SIZE() $- 1$
      // **Invariant:** If G has a universal sink k, then $i \le k \le j$.
      while $i < j$
         if G.GET(i, j) $=$ nil
            $j \leftarrow j - 1$
         else
            $i \leftarrow i + 1$
      // **Invariant:** For $0 \le k < j$, if $k \ne i$, then (k, i) is an edge,
      // but (i, k) is not.
      for $j \leftarrow 0$ **to** G.SIZE() $- 1$
         if $j \ne i$ **and** (G.GET(i, j) $\ne$ nil **or** G.GET(j, i) $=$ nil)
            return -1
      return i

We can therefore solve the original universal sink detection problem for a nonempty graph by first finding a candidate vertex i as described above. We know that if there is a universal sink, it must be i. We then check whether i is a universal sink by verifying that for every $j \ne i$, (j, i) is an edge but (i, j) is not. The resulting algorithm is shown in Figure 9.4.

9.2   Topological Sort

A *cycle* in a directed graph $G = (V, E)$ is a finite sequence of vertices $v_0, \ldots, v_k$ such that $(v_k, v_0) \in E$, and for $0 \le i < k$, $(v_i, v_{i+1}) \in E$. A directed graph with no cycles is said to be *acyclic*. These two terms apply analogously to undirected graphs as well, except that in this case all the edges in the sequence must be distinct. In either type of graph, a cycle in which all the vertices in the sequence are distinct is said to be *simple*.

Directed acyclic graphs are often used to model precedence relationships between objects or activities. Suppose, for example, that we have four jobs, A, B, C, and D. We must schedule these jobs sequentially such that A precedes C, B precedes A, and B precedes D. These precedence relationships

Figure 9.5 A directed acyclic graph modeling precedence relationships

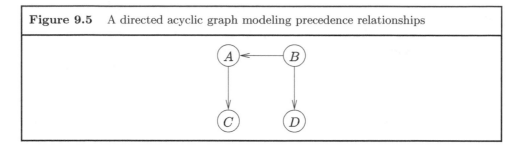

can be modeled by the directed acyclic graph shown in Figure 9.5. We need to find an ordering of the vertices such that for every edge (u, v), u precedes v in the ordering. Such an ordering is called a *topological sort* of the graph. Examples of topological sorts of the graph in Figure 9.5 are $\langle B, A, C, D \rangle$ and $\langle B, D, A, C \rangle$. In this section, we will present an algorithm for finding a topological sort of a given directed acyclic graph. First, we will show that every directed acyclic graph has a topological sort.

Lemma 9.1. *Every nonempty directed acyclic graph has at least one vertex with no incoming edges.*

Proof. By contradiction. Suppose every vertex in some nonempty directed acyclic graph G has incoming edges. Then starting from any vertex, we may always traverse an incoming edge backwards to its source. Because G has finitely many vertices, if we trace a path in this fashion, we must eventually repeat a vertex. We will have then found a cycle — a contradiction. $\square$

Theorem 9.2. *Every directed acyclic graph $G = (V, E)$ has a topological sort.*

Proof. By induction on the size of V.

Base: $V = \varnothing$. Then the empty ordering is a topological sort.

Induction Hypothesis: Suppose that for some $n > 0$, every directed acyclic graph with fewer than n vertices has a topological sort.

Induction Step: Let $G = (V, E)$ be a directed acyclic graph with n vertices. Because G is nonempty, it must have at least one vertex v_0 with no incoming edges. Let G' be the graph obtained from G by removing v_0 and all of its outgoing edges. By the induction hypothesis, G' has a topological sort $v_1, \ldots, v_{n-1}$. Because v_0 has no incoming edges in G, $v_0, \ldots, v_{n-1}$ must therefore be a topological sort for G. $\square$

The proof of Theorem 9.2 is constructive; i.e., it gives an algorithm for finding a topological sort. First, we find a vertex v_0 with no incoming edges. v_0 will come first in the topological sort. The remainder of the topological sort is obtained by removing v_0 and finding a topological sort of the resulting graph. We have therefore transformed the problem to a smaller instance.

The above sketch is missing a few details. For example, we need to know how to find a vertex with no incoming edges. Also, our GRAPH ADT provides no mechanism for removing vertices. In order to overcome these problems, we will maintain an array $incount[0..n-1]$ so that $incount[i]$ gives the number of edges to i from vertices not yet in the topological sort. When we add a vertex i to the topological sort, we do not need to remove it from the graph; instead, we can simply decrement $incount[j]$ for all j adjacent to i. To initialize $incount$, we can simply examine each edge (i,j) and increment $incount[j]$.

In order to speed up finding the next vertex in the topological sort, let us keep track of all vertices i for which $incount[i] = 0$. We can use a STACK for this purpose. After we initialize $incount$, we can traverse it once and push each i such that $incount[i] = 0$ onto the stack. Thereafter, when we decrement an entry $incount[i]$, we need to see if it reaches 0, and if so, push it onto the stack. The algorithm is shown in Figure 9.6.

9.3 Adjacency Matrix Implementation

Our first implementation of GRAPH will have a single representation variable:

* $edges[0..n-1, 0..n-1]$.

Our structural invariant will be that $edges[i, i] = \mathsf{nil}$ for $0 \leq i < n$. We interpret $edges[i, j]$ as giving the information associated with edge (i, j), provided this value is non-nil. We interpret a nil value for $edges[i, j]$ as indicating the absence of an edge (i, j). The full implementation is shown in Figure 9.7.

Each of the operations SIZE, PUT, and GET runs in $\Theta(1)$ time. The constructor is easily seen to run in $\Theta(n^2)$ time. The ALLFROM operation clearly runs in $\Theta(n)$ time, where n is the number of vertices in the graph. The space usage is clearly in $\Theta(n^2)$.

We can now analyze the running times of the algorithms given in the previous two sections. We will first consider UNIVERSALSINK from Figure 9.4. Let n be the number of vertices in G. The **while** loop begins with $j - i = n - 1$ and decreases $j - i$ each iteration. Because it terminates when

---

Figure 9.6   Topological sort algorithm

Precondition: G is a directed acyclic graph.
Postcondition: Returns an array listing the vertices of G in topological order.

$\textsc{TopSort}(G)$
    $n \leftarrow G.\textsc{Size}()$; $s \leftarrow$ **new** $\textsc{Array}[0..n-1]$
    $incount \leftarrow$ **new** $\textsc{Array}[0..n-1]$; $avail \leftarrow$ **new** $\textsc{Stack}()$
    for $i \leftarrow 0$ **to** $n-1$
       $incount[i] \leftarrow 0$
    // **Invariant:** For $0 \leq j < n$, $incount[j]$ gives the number of edges to j
    // from vertices $0, \ldots, i-1$.
    for $i \leftarrow 0$ **to** $n-1$
       $L \leftarrow G.\textsc{AllFrom}(i)$
       while not $L.\textsc{IsEmpty}()$
          $k \leftarrow L.\textsc{Head}().\textsc{Dest}()$; $incount[k] \leftarrow incount[k]+1$; $L \leftarrow L.\textsc{Tail}()$
    for $i \leftarrow 0$ **to** $n-1$
       if $incount[i] = 0$
          $avail.\textsc{Push}(i)$
    // **Invariant:** For $0 \leq j < n$, $incount[j]$ is the number of edges to j from
    // vertices not in $s[0..i-1]$, and if $incount[j] = 0$, then j is either in
    // $s[0..i-1]$ or $avail$, but not both.
    for $i \leftarrow 0$ **to** $n-1$
       $s[i] \leftarrow avail.\textsc{Pop}()$; $L \leftarrow G.\textsc{AllFrom}(s[i])$
       while not $L.\textsc{IsEmpty}()$
          $k \leftarrow L.\textsc{Head}().\textsc{Dest}()$; $incount[k] \leftarrow incount[k]-1$; $L \leftarrow L.\textsc{Tail}()$
          if $incount[k] = 0$
             $avail.\textsc{Push}(k)$
    return s

$j - i = 0$ it iterates $n - 1$ times. Because $\textsc{MatrixGraph}.\textsc{Get}$ runs in $\Theta(1)$ time, the entire loop runs in $\Theta(n)$ time. The **for** loop iterates at most n times, and each iteration runs in $\Theta(1)$ time. The entire algorithm therefore operates in $\Theta(n)$ time.

Let us now consider $\textsc{TopSort}$ from Figure 9.6. We will need to break the algorithm into the four **for** loops.

In the body of the second **for** loop, $\textsc{MatrixGraph}.\textsc{AllFrom}$ runs in $\Theta(n)$ time. The body of the **while** loop runs in $\Theta(1)$ time. Each iteration decreases the number of elements in L by 1 until L is empty. Because there can be at most $n - 1$ edges from any vertex, the **while** loop iterates at most $n - 1$ times. Its running time is therefore in $O(n)$. The body of the second

---

Figure 9.7 MATRIXGRAPH implementation of GRAPH

Structural Invariant: $edges[i, i] = \mathsf{nil}$ for $0 \le i < n$.

MATRIXGRAPH(n)
   $edges \leftarrow$ **new** ARRAY$[0..n - 1, 0..n - 1]$
   for $i \leftarrow 0$ **to** $n - 1$
      for $j \leftarrow 0$ **to** $n - 1$
         $edges[i, j] \leftarrow \mathsf{nil}$

MATRIXGRAPH.SIZE$()$
   return SIZEOF$(edges[0])$ // Number of columns

MATRIXGRAPH.PUT(i, j, x)
   if $i = j$
      error
   else
      $edges[i, j] \leftarrow x$

MATRIXGRAPH.GET(i, j)
   return $edges[i, j]$

MATRIXGRAPH.ALLFROM(i)
   $L \leftarrow$ **new** CONSLIST$()$
   for $j \leftarrow 0$ **to** $n - 1$
      if $edges[i, j] \ne \mathsf{nil}$
         $L \leftarrow$ **new** CONSLIST(**new** EDGE$(i, j, edges[i, j]), L)$
   return L

---

for loop therefore runs in $\Theta(n)$ time. Because it iterates n times, its running time is in $\Theta(n^2)$.

The first and third **for** loops clearly run in $\Theta(n)$ time. Furthermore, the analysis of the fourth **for** loop is similar to that of the second. Therefore, the entire algorithm runs in $\Theta(n^2)$ time.

Note that the second and fourth **for** loops in TOPSORT each contain a nested **while** loop. Each iteration of this **while** loop processes one of the edges. Furthermore, each edge is processed at most once by each **while** loop. The total number of iterations of each of the **while** loops is therefore the number of edges in the graph. While this number can be as large as $n(n - 1) \in \Theta(n^2)$, it can also be much smaller.

The number of edges does not affect the asymptotic running time, however, because MATRIXGRAPH.ALLFROM runs in $\Theta(n)$ time, regardless of how many edges it retrieves. If we can make this operation more efficient, we might be able to improve the running time for TOPSORT on graphs with few edges. In the next section, we will examine an alternative implementation that accomplishes this.

9.4   Adjacency List Implementation

In this section, we consider an implementation designed to improve the efficiency of the ALLFROM operation. The two-dimensional array used in the adjacency matrix implementation can be thought of as an array of arrays each containing the adjacency information for a single vertex. In the adjacency list implementation, we still use an array indexed by vertices to store the adjacency information for each vertex; however, we maintain this adjacency information in a CONSLIST instead of an array. In such a representation, the CONSLIST for vertex i is exactly the CONSLIST that needs to be returned by ALLFROM(i). Furthermore, because a CONSLIST is immutable, we can return it without violating security.

We again use a single representation variable:

- $elements[0..n-1]$: an array of CONSLISTs.

Our structural invariant will be that for $0 \le i < n$, $elements[i]$ refers to a CONSLIST containing EDGEs representing at most one (i, j) for each j such that $0 \le j < n$ and $j \ne i$, where each EDGE has a non-nil data item (see the specification for GRAPH.ALLFROM in Figure 9.3 for an explanation of this representation). We interpret the EDGEs in this structure as representing the edges in the graph, along with the information associated with each edge.

A partial implementation of LISTGRAPH is shown in Figure 9.8. In addition, the SIZE operation returns the size of $elements$, and ALLFROM(i) returns $elements[i]$.

It is easily seen that the SIZE and ALLFROM operations run in $\Theta(1)$ time, and that the constructor runs in $\Theta(n)$ time. Each iteration of the **while** loop in the GET operation reduces the size of L by 1. The length of L is initially the number of vertices adjacent to i. Because each iteration runs in $\Theta(1)$ time, the entire operation runs in $\Theta(m)$ time in the worst case, where m is the number of vertices adjacent to i. The worst case for GET occurs when vertex j is not adjacent to i. Similarly, it can be seen that the PUT operation

---

Figure 9.8   LISTGRAPH implementation (partial) of GRAPH

Structural Invariant: For $0 \leq i < n$, *elements*[i] refers to a CONSLIST containing EDGEs representing at most one (i, j) for each j such that $0 \leq j < n$ and $j \neq i$, where each EDGE has a non-nil data item.

LISTGRAPH(n)
    elements ← **new** ARRAY[$0..n-1$]
    for i ← 0 **to** $n - 1$
        elements[i] ← **new** CONSLIST()

LISTGRAPH.PUT(i, j, x)
    if $j \geq$ SIZEOF(*elements*) **or** $j < 0$ **or** $j = i$ **or** $x =$ nil
        error
    else
        elements[i] ← ADDEDGE(**new** EDGE(i, j, x), *elements*[i])

LISTGRAPH.GET(i, j)
    L ← *elements*[i]
    while not L.ISEMPTY()
        if L.HEAD().DEST() = j
            return L.HEAD().DATA()
        else
            L ← L.TAIL()
    return nil

— **Internal Functions Follow** —

Precondition: e refers to an EDGE and L refers to a CONSLIST of EDGEs each having the same source as e.
Postcondition: Returns a CONSLIST with the contents of L, plus the edge e. If the edge represented by e is already in L, it is replaced by e.

LISTGRAPH.ADDEDGE(e, L)
    if L.ISEMPTY()
        return new CONSLIST(e, L)
    else if L.HEAD().DEST() = e.DEST()
        return new CONSLIST(e, L.TAIL())
    else
        return new CONSLIST(L.HEAD(), ADDEDGE(e, L.TAIL()))

runs in $\Theta(m)$ time. Note that $\Theta(m) \subseteq O(n)$. The space usage of LISTGRAPH is easily seen to be in $\Theta(n + a)$, where a is the number of edges in the graph.

Let us now revisit the analysis of the running time of TOPSORT (Figure 9.6), this time assuming that G is a LISTGRAPH. Consider the second **for** loop. Note that running time of the nested **while** loop does not depend on the implementation of G; hence, we can still conclude that it runs in $O(n)$ time. We can therefore conclude that the running time of the second **for** loop is in $O(n^2)$. However, because we have reduced the running time of ALLFROM from $\Theta(n)$ to $\Theta(1)$, it is no longer clear that the running time of this loop is in $\Omega(n^2)$. Indeed, if there are no edges in the graph, then the nested **while** loop will not iterate. In this case, the running time is in $\Theta(n)$.

We therefore need to analyze the running time of the nested **while** loop more carefully. Note that over the course of the **for** loop, each edge is processed by the inner **while** loop exactly once. Therefore, the body of the inner loop is executed exactly a times over the course of the entire outer loop, where a is the number of edges in G. Because the remainder of the outer loop is executed exactly n times, the running time of the outer loop is in $\Theta(n + a)$.

We now observe that the fourth loop can be analyzed in exactly the same way as the second loop; hence, the fourth loop also runs in $\Theta(n + a)$ time. In fact, because the structure of these two loops is quite common for graph algorithms, this method of calculating the running time is often needed for analyzing algorithms that operate on LISTGRAPHs.

To complete the analysis of TOPSORT, we observe that the first and third loops do not depend on how G is implemented; hence, they both run in $\Theta(n)$ time. The total running time of TOPSORT is therefore in $\Theta(n + a)$. For graphs in which $a \in o(n^2)$, this is an improvement over the $\Theta(n^2)$ running time when G is implemented as a MATRIXGRAPH.

Let us now consider the impact of the LISTGRAPH implementation on the analysis of UNIVERSALSINK (Figure 9.4). Due to the increased running time of GET, the body of the **while** loop runs in $\Theta(m)$ time, where m is the number of vertices adjacent to i. This number cannot be more than $n - 1$, nor can it be more than a. Because this loop iterates $\Theta(n)$ times, we obtain an upper bound of $O(n \min(n, a))$. Likewise, it is easily seen that the **for** loop runs in $O(n \min(n, a))$ time.

To see that this bound is tight for the **while** loop, let us first consider the case in which $a \leq n(n - 1) - \lfloor n/2 \rfloor$. Suppose that from vertex 0 there is an edge to each of the vertices $1, \ldots, \min(a, \lfloor (n - 1)/2 \rfloor)$, but no edge to any other vertex. From vertices other than 0 we may have edges to any of the other vertices. Note that with these constraints, we can have up to $n(n-1) - \lfloor n/2 \rfloor$ edges. For such a graph, the first $\lfloor n/2 \rfloor$ iterations of the **while** loop will have $i = 0$, while j ranges from $n-1$ down to $\lfloor (n-1)/2 \rfloor + 1$. For each of these iterations, GET(i, j) runs in $\Theta(\min(a, n))$ time, because there are $\Theta(\min(a, n))$ vertices adjacent to 0, but j is not adjacent to 0. Because the number of these iterations is in $\Theta(n)$, the total time is in $\Theta(n \min(n, a))$.

Now let us consider the case in which $a > n(n-1) - \lfloor n/2 \rfloor$. In this case, we make sure that from each of the vertices $0, \ldots, \lfloor n/2 \rfloor - 1$, there is an edge to every other vertex. Furthermore, we make sure that in each of the CONSLISTS of edges from these first $\lfloor n/2 \rfloor$ vertices, the edge to vertex $n-1$ occurs last. From the remaining vertices we may have any edges listed in any order. For such a graph, the first $\lfloor n/2 \rfloor$ iterations of the **while** loop will have $j = n - 1$, while i ranges from 0 to $\lfloor n/2 \rfloor - 1$. For each of these iterations, GET(i, j) runs in $\Theta(n)$ time, because there are $\Theta(n)$ vertices adjacent to i, and $n - 1$ is the last of these. Because the total number of iterations is in $\Theta(n)$, the total time is in $\Theta(n^2)$. Because $a \geq n$, this is the same as $\Theta(n \min(a, n))$.

Based on the analyses of the two algorithms, we can see that neither implementation is necessarily better than the other. If an algorithm relies more heavily on GET than on ALLFROM, it is better to use MATRIXGRAPH. If an algorithm relies more heavily on ALLFROM, it is probably better to use LISTGRAPH, particularly if there is a reasonable expectation that the graph will be *sparse* — i.e., that it will have relatively few edges. Note also that for sparse graphs, a LISTGRAPH will use considerably less space.

9.5 Multigraphs

Let us briefly consider the building of a LISTGRAPH. We must first construct a graph with no edges, then add edges one by one using the PUT operation. The constructor runs in $\Theta(n)$ time. The PUT operation runs in $\Theta(m)$ time, where m is the number of vertices adjacent to the source of the edge. It is easily seen that the time required to build the graph is in $O(n + a \min(n, a))$, where a is the number of edges. It is not hard to match this upper bound using graphs in which the number of vertices with outgoing edges is minimized for the given number of edges. An example of a sparse graph (specifically, with $a \leq n$) that gives this behavior is a graph whose edge set is

$$\{(0, j) \mid 1 \leq j < a\}.$$

A dense graph giving this behavior is a complete graph — a graph in which every possible edge is present. Note that in terms of the number of vertices, the running time for building a complete graph is in $\Theta(n^3)$.

Building a LISTGRAPH is expensive because the PUT operation must check each edge to see if it is already in the graph. We could speed this activity considerably if we could avoid this check. However, the check is necessary not only to satisfy the operation's specification, but also to maintain the structural invariant. If we can modify the specification of PUT and weaken the structural invariant so that *parallel* edges (i.e., multiple edges from a vertex i to a vertex j) are not prohibited, then we can build the graph more quickly.

We therefore extend the definitions of undirected and directed graphs to allow parallel edges from one vertex to another. We call such a structure a *multigraph*. We can then define the MULTIGRAPH ADT by modifying the following postconditions in the specification of GRAPH:

- PUT(i, j, x): Adds the edge (i, j) and associates x with it.
- GET(i, j): Returns the data item associated with an edge (i, j), or nil if (i, j) is not in the graph.

We could also specify additional operations for retrieving all edges (i, j) or modifying the data associated with an edge, but this specification is sufficient for our purposes.

We will represent a MULTIGRAPH using adjacency lists in the same way as in the LISTGRAPH implementation. The structural invariant will be modified to allow parallel edges (i, j) for the same i and j. The implementation of the operations remains the same except for PUT, whose implementation is shown in Figure 9.9. It is easily seen that a LISTMULTIGRAPH can be built in $\Theta(n+a)$ time, where n is the number of vertices and a is the number of edges.

Because it is more efficient to build a LISTMULTIGRAPH than to build a LISTGRAPH, it may be advantageous to represent a graph using a

---

Figure 9.9 The PUT operation in the LISTMULTIGRAPH implementation of MULTIGRAPH

LISTMULTIGRAPH.PUT(i, j, x)
    if $j \geq$ SIZEOF(*elements*) **or** $j < 0$ **or** $x =$ nil
        error
    else
        elements$[i] \leftarrow$ **new** CONSLIST(**new** EDGE(i, j, x), *elements*$[i]$)

LISTMULTIGRAPH. If we are careful never to add parallel edges, we can maintain an invariant that the LISTMULTIGRAPH represents a graph. This transfers the burden of maintaining a valid graph structure from the PUT operation to the code that invokes the PUT operation.

Although we can use a LISTMULTIGRAPH to represent a graph, an interesting problem is how to construct a LISTGRAPH from a given LISTMULTIGRAPH. Specifically, suppose we wish to define a LISTGRAPH constructor that takes a LISTMULTIGRAPH as input and produces a LIST-GRAPH with the same vertices and edges, assuming the LISTMULTIGRAPH has no parallel edges. We may be able to do this more efficiently than simply calling LISTGRAPH.PUT repeatedly.

One approach would be to convert the LISTMULTIGRAPH to a MATRIX-GRAPH, then convert the MATRIXGRAPH to a LISTGRAPH. In fact, we do not really need to build a MATRIXGRAPH — we could simply use a two-dimensional array as a temporary representation of the graph. As we examine each edge of the LISTMULTIGRAPH, we can check to see if it has been added to the array, and if not, add it to the appropriate adjacency list. If we ever find parallel edges, we can immediately terminate with an error. Each edge can therefore be processed in $\Theta(1)$ time, for a total of $\Theta(a)$ time to process the edges. Unfortunately, $\Theta(n^2)$ time is required to initialize the array, and the space usage of $\Theta(n^2)$ is rather high, especially for sparse graphs. However, the resulting time of $\Theta(n^2)$ is still an improvement (in most cases) over the $\Theta(a \min(n, a))$ worst-case time for repeatedly calling LISTGRAPH.PUT.

In the above solution, the most natural way of processing the edges of the LISTMULTIGRAPH is to consider each vertex i in turn, and for each i, to process all edges proceeding from i. As we are processing the edges from vertex i, we only need row i of the array. We could therefore save a significant amount of space by replacing the 2D array with a singly-dimensioned array $A[0..n-1]$. Before we consider any vertex i, we initialize A. For each edge (i, j), we check to see if it has been recorded in $A[j]$. If so, we have found a parallel edge; otherwise, we record this edge in $A[j]$. Thus, we have reduced our space usage to $\Theta(n)$. However, because A must be initialized each time we consider a new vertex, the overall running time is still in $\Theta(n^2)$.

Note that if we ignore the time for initializing A, this last solution runs in $\Theta(n + a)$ time in the worst case. We can therefore use the virtual initialization technique of Section 7.1 to reduce the overall running time to $\Theta(n + a)$. However, the technique of virtual initialization was inspired by the need to avoid initializing large arrays, not to avoid initializing small arrays many times. If we are careful about the way we use the array, a single initialization should be sufficient. Thus, if we can find a way to avoid repeated initializations of A, we will be able to achieve $\Theta(n + a)$ running time without using virtual initialization.

Consider what happens if we simply omit every initialization of A except the first. If, when processing edge (i, j), we find edge (i', j), for some $i' < i$, recorded in $A[j]$, then we know that no other edge (i, j) has yet been processed. We can then simply record (i, j) in $A[j]$, as if no edge had been recorded there. If, on the other hand, we find that (i, j) has already been recorded in $A[j]$, we know that we have found a parallel edge.

As a final simplification to this algorithm, we note that there is really no reason to store EDGEs in the array. Specifically, the only information we need to record in $A[j]$ is the most recent (i.e., the largest) vertex i for which an edge (i, j) has been found. Thus, A can be an array of integers. We can initialize A to contain only negative values, such as -1, to indicate that no such edge has yet been found. The resulting LISTGRAPH constructor is shown in Figure 9.10. It is easily seen to run in $\Theta(n + a)$ time and use $\Theta(n)$

Figure 9.10   Constructor for building a LISTGRAPH from a LISTMULTIGRAPH

Precondition: G refers to a LISTMULTIGRAPH with no parallel edges.
Postcondition: Constructs a LISTGRAPH with the same vertices and edges as G.

LISTGRAPH(G)
    $size \leftarrow G$.SIZE(); $elements \leftarrow$ **new** ARRAY$[0..size - 1]$
    $A \leftarrow$ **new** ARRAY$[0..size - 1]$
    // **Invariant:** For $0 \le k < i$, $elements[k] = G$.ALLFROM(k) and
    // $A[k] = -1$.
    for $i \leftarrow 0$ **to** $size - 1$
        $elements[i] \leftarrow G$.ALLFROM(i); $A[i] \leftarrow -1$
    // **Invariant:** For $0 \le j < size$, $A[j] < i$. For $0 \le k < i$ and $0 \le j < size$,
    // $elements[k]$ has at most one edge to j.
    for $i \leftarrow 0$ **to** $size - 1$
        $L \leftarrow elements[i]$
        // **Invariant:** For $0 \le j < size$, $A[j] \le i$. If $A[j] = i$, then $elements[i]$
        // contains one more edge to j than does L; otherwise, they contain
        // the same number of edges to j.
        while not L.ISEMPTY()
            $j \leftarrow L$.HEAD().DEST()
            if $A[j] < i$
                $A[j] \leftarrow i$; $L \leftarrow L$.TAIL()
            else
                error

temporary space in the worst case, where n and a are the number of vertices and unique edges, respectively, in the given LISTMULTIGRAPH.

9.6 Summary

Graphs are useful for representing relationships between data items. Various algorithms can then be designed for manipulating graphs. As a result, we can often use the same algorithm in a variety of different applications.

Graphs may be either directed or undirected, but we can treat undirected graphs as directed graphs in which for every edge (u, v), there is a reverse edge (v, u). We then have two implementations of graphs. The adjacency matrix implementation has GET and PUT operations that run in $\Theta(1)$ time, but its ALLFROM operation runs in $\Theta(n)$ time, where n is the number of vertices in the graph. Its space usage is in $\Theta(n^2)$. On the other hand, the adjacency list implementation has an ALLFROM operation that runs in $\Theta(1)$ time, but its GET and PUT operations run in $\Theta(m)$ time in the worst case, where m is the number of vertices adjacent to the given source vertex. Its space usage is in $\Theta(n + a)$ where n is the number of vertices and a is the number of edges.

In order to improve the running time of the PUT operation — and hence of building a graph — when using an adjacency list, we can relax our definition to allow parallel edges. The resulting structure is known as a multigraph. We can always use a multigraph whenever a graph is required, though it might be useful to maintain an invariant that no parallel edges exist. Furthermore, we can construct a LISTGRAPH from a LISTMULTIGRAPH with no parallel edges in $\Theta(n + a)$ time and $\Theta(n)$ space, where n is the number of vertices and a is the number of edges. Figure 9.11 shows a summary of the running times of these operations for each of the implementations of GRAPH, as well as for LISTMULTIGRAPH.

9.7 Exercises

Exercise 9.1. Prove that UNIVERSALSINK, shown in Figure 9.4, meets its specification.

Exercise 9.2. Prove that TOPSORT, shown in Figure 9.6, meets its specification.

Exercise 9.3. Give an algorithm that takes as input a directed graph $G = (V, E)$ and returns a directed graph $G' = (V, E')$, where

$$E' = \{(u, v) \mid (v, u) \in E\}.$$

Figure 9.11   Comparison of running times for two implementations of GRAPH, along with LISTMULTIGRAPH

	constructor	GET	PUT	ALLFROM
MATRIXGRAPH	$\Theta(n^2)$	$\Theta(1)$	$\Theta(1)$	$\Theta(n)$
LISTGRAPH	$\Theta(n)$	$\Theta(m)$	$\Theta(m)$	$\Theta(1)$
LISTMULTIGRAPH	$\Theta(n)$	$\Theta(m)$	$\Theta(1)$	$\Theta(1)$

Notes:

- n is the number of vertices in the graph, and m is the number of vertices adjacent to the given source vertex.

- The constructor referenced above is the one that constructs a graph with no edges — the LISTGRAPH constructor that takes a LISTMULTIGRAPH as input runs in $\Theta(n+a)$ worst-case time, where n is the number of vertices and a is the number of edges in the graph, assuming there are no parallel edges.

- The SIZE operation runs in $\Theta(1)$ worst-case time for all implementations.

- All running times are worst-case.

Thus, G' contains the same edges as does G, except that they are reversed in G'. Express the running time of your algorithm as simply as possible using Θ-notation in terms of the number of vertices n and the number of edges a, assuming the graphs are implemented using

a. MATRIXGRAPH
b. LISTGRAPH
c. LISTMULTIGRAPH.

Exercise 9.4. Give an algorithm to compute the number of edges in a given graph. Express the running time of your algorithm as simply as possible using Θ-notation in terms of the number of vertices n and the number of edges a, assuming the graph is implemented using

a. MATRIXGRAPH
b. LISTGRAPH

Exercise 9.5. A directed graph is said to be *transitively closed* if whenever (u, v) and (v, w) are edges, then (u, w) is also an edge. Give an $O(n^3)$

algorithm to determine whether a given directed graph is transitively closed. You may assume the graph is implemented as a MATRIXGRAPH.

Exercise 9.6. An undirected graph is said to be *connected* if for every pair of vertices u and v, there is a path of edges leading from u to v. A *tree* is a connected undirected acyclic graph. Prove each of the following for an undirected graph G with n vertices:

a. If G is a tree, then G has exactly $n - 1$ edges.
b. If G is connected and has exactly $n - 1$ edges, then G is a tree.
c. If G is acyclic and has exactly $n - 1$ edges, then G is a tree.

Exercise 9.7. Prove that MATRIXGRAPH, shown in Figure 9.7, meets its specification.

Exercise 9.8. Prove that the LISTGRAPH constructor shown in Figure 9.10 meets its specification.

Exercise 9.9. Give an algorithm that takes as input a graph G and returns true iff G is undirected; i.e., if for every edge (u, v), (v, u) is also an edge. Give the best upper bound you can on the running time, expressed as simply as possible using big-O notation in terms of the number of vertices n and the number of edges a, assuming the graph is implemented using MATRIXGRAPH.

* Exercise 9.10. An *Euler path* in a connected undirected graph G is a path that contains every edge in G exactly once. Give an efficient algorithm to find an Euler path in a connected undirected graph, provided one exists. Your algorithm should return some representation of the Euler path, or nil if no Euler path exists. Your algorithm should run in $O(a)$ time, where a is the number of edges in G, assuming that G is implemented as a LISTGRAPH.

9.8 Notes

The study of graph theory began in 1736 with Leonhard Euler's famous study of the Königsberg Bridge Problem [38], which is simply the problem of finding an Euler path in a connected undirected graph (see Exercise 9.10). Good references on graph theory and graph algorithms include Even [39], Kocay and Kreher [85], and Tarjan [112]. In the early days of electronic computing, graphs were typically implemented using adjacency matrices. Hopcroft and Tarjan [65] first proposed using adjacency lists for sparse graphs. The topological sort algorithm of Section 9.2 is due to Knuth [82].

Part III

Algorithm Design Techniques

Chapter 10

Divide and Conquer

In Part I of this text, we introduced several techniques for applying the top-down approach to algorithm design. We will now take a closer look at some of these techniques. In this chapter, we will look at the *divide-and-conquer* technique.

As we stated in Chapter 3, the divide-and-conquer technique involves reducing a large instance of a problem to one or more instances having a fixed fraction of the size of the original instance. For example, recall that the algorithm MAXSUMDC, shown in Figure 3.3 on page 78, reduces large instances of the maximum subsequence sum problem to two smaller instances of roughly half the size.

Though we can sometimes convert divide-and-conquer algorithms to iterative algorithms, it is usually better to implement them using recursion. One reason is that typical divide-and-conquer algorithms implemented using recursion require very little stack space to support the recursion. If we divide an instance of size n into instances of size n/b whenever n is divisible by b, we can express the total stack usage due to recursion with the recurrence

$$f(n) \in f(n/b) + \Theta(1).$$

Applying Theorem 3.35 to this recurrence, we see that $f(n) \in \Theta(\lg n)$. The other reason for retaining the recursion is that when a large instance is reduced to more than one smaller instance, removing the recursion can be difficult and usually requires the use of a stack to simulate at least one recursive call.

Because divide-and-conquer algorithms are typically expressed using recursion, the analysis of their running times usually involves the asymptotic solution of a recurrence. Theorem 3.35 almost always applies to this recurrence. Not only does this give us a tool for analyzing running times,

331

it also can give us some insight into what must be done to make an algorithm more efficient. We will explain this concept further as we illustrate the technique by applying it to several problems.

10.1 Polynomial Multiplication

Suppose we are given two polynomials:

$$p(x) = \sum_{i=0}^{n-1} a_i x^i,$$

$$q(x) = \sum_{i=0}^{n-1} b_i x^i.$$

We wish to compute the product polynomial:

$$pq(x) = \sum_{i=0}^{2n-2} \left(\sum_{j=0}^{i} a_j b_{i-j} \right) x^i,$$

where we define $a_j = b_j = 0$ for $n \leq j < 2n$. We can clearly compute each of the $2n - 1$ coefficients in pq in $\Theta(n)$ time; hence, by Theorem 3.31, we can compute the entire product in $\Theta(n^2)$ time.

We wish to apply the divide-and-conquer technique to obtain a more efficient solution. Observe that if $n > 1$, then we can divide each polynomial into two smaller polynomials:

$$p(x) = p_0(x) + x^m p_1(x),$$
$$q(x) = q_0(x) + x^m q_1(x),$$

where

$$p_0(x) = \sum_{i=0}^{m-1} a_i x^i,$$

$$p_1(x) = \sum_{i=0}^{n-m-1} a_{m+i} x^i,$$

$$q_0(x) = \sum_{i=0}^{m-1} b_i x^i,$$

$$q_1(x) = \sum_{i=0}^{n-m-1} b_{m+i} x^i.$$

If we set $m = \lfloor n/2 \rfloor$, then each of the smaller polynomials has roughly $n/2$ terms.

The product polynomial is now

$$pq(x) = p_0(x)q_0(x) + x^m(p_0(x)q_1(x) + p_1(x)q_0(x)) + x^{2m}p_1(x)q_1(x). \quad (10.1)$$

To obtain the coefficients of pq, we can first compute the four products of the smaller polynomials. We can then obtain any given coefficient of pq by performing at most two additions. We can therefore obtain all $2n - 1$ coefficients in $\Theta(n)$ time after the four smaller products are computed. Setting $m = \lfloor n/2 \rfloor$, we can describe the running time of this divide-and-conquer algorithm with the following recurrence:

$$f(n) \in 4f(n/2) + \Theta(n), \quad (10.2)$$

when $n > 1$ is a power of 2. Unfortunately, applying Theorem 3.35 yields $f(n) \in \Theta(n^2)$, which is the same running time as the brute-force calculation.

This exercise illustrates an important point about the divide-and-conquer technique, namely, that the technique by itself does not guarantee improved running times. In order for the technique to be effective, it must save some work. Sometimes, as with MaxSumDC, the savings in work comes about naturally. In such cases, it may be rather hard to see how work was saved. In other cases, we must be more clever in order to save work.

As we suggested earlier, Theorem 3.35 can give insight into how a divide-and-conquer solution might be designed or improved. For example, consider recurrence (10.2). Because the third case of Theorem 3.35 applies, we cannot obtain a more efficient solution by reducing the $\Theta(n)$ overhead outside of the recursive calls. In order to improve the performance, we need either to reduce the number of recursive calls or decrease the size of the smaller instances. We will focus on reducing the number of recursive calls. In the exercises, we explore alternative solutions involving decreasing the size of the smaller instances.

The following observation gives us the insight we need in order to reduce the number of recursive calls:

$$(p_0(x) + p_1(x))(q_0(x) + q_1(x))$$
$$= p_0(x)q_0(x) + p_0(x)q_1(x) + p_1(x)q_0(x) + p_1(x)q_1(x).$$

Note that all four of the terms in the right-hand-side above appear in the product pq (see (10.1)). In order to make this fact useful, however, we need to be able to separate out the first and last terms. We can do this by computing the products $p_0(x)q_0(x)$ and $p_1(x)q_1(x)$, then subtracting. Thus, we can compute the product pq using the following three products:

$$P_1(x) = p_0(x)q_0(x),$$
$$P_2(x) = (p_0(x) + p_1(x))(q_0(x) + q_1(x)),$$
$$P_3(x) = p_1(x)q_1(x)$$

We can then compute any given coefficient of pq with at most two subtractions and one addition.

The algorithm is shown in Figure 10.1. This implementation uses the COPY function specified in Figure 1.18 on page 22. Note that when we divide the polynomials, the low-order parts will be of degree $m - 1$, and the high-order parts will be of degree $n - m - 1$. We cannot select m so that these two

---

Figure 10.1   Divide-and-conquer polynomial multiplication algorithm

Precondition: p and q are arrays of NUMBERs and n is a positive NAT.
Postcondition: Returns an array $P[0..2n - 2]$ such that $P[i]$ is the coefficient of x^i in the product pq, where $p[i]$ denotes the coefficient in p of x^i and $q[i]$ denotes the coefficient in q of x^i.

PolyMult($p[0..n - 1], q[0..n - 1]$)
  $P \leftarrow$ **new** Array$[0..2(n - 1)]$
  if $n = 1$
    $P[0] = p[0]q[0]$
  else
    $m \leftarrow \lceil n/2 \rceil$; $s \leftarrow$ **new** Array$[0..m - 1]$; $t \leftarrow$ **new** Array$[0..m - 1]$
    Copy($p[0..m - 1], s[0..m - 1]$); Copy($q[0..m - 1], t[0..m - 1]$)
    for $i \leftarrow m$ **to** $n - 1$
      $s[i - m] \leftarrow s[i - m] + p[i]$; $t[i - m] \leftarrow t[i - m] + q[i]$
    $P_1 \leftarrow$ PolyMult($p[0..m - 1], q[0..m - 1]$)
    $P_2 \leftarrow$ PolyMult($s[0..m - 1], t[0..m - 1]$)
    $P_3 \leftarrow$ PolyMult($p[m..n - 1], q[m..n - 1]$)
    Copy($P_1[0..2(m - 1)], P[0..2(m - 1)]$); $P[2m - 1] \leftarrow 0$
    Copy($P_3[0..2(n - m - 1)], P[2m..2(n - 1)]$)
    for $i \leftarrow 0$ **to** $2(m - 1)$
      $P[m + i] \leftarrow P[m + i] + P_2[i] - P_1[i]$
    for $i \leftarrow 0$ **to** $2(n - m - 1)$
      $P[m + i] \leftarrow P[m + i] - P_3[i]$
  return P

degrees are the same if n is odd. Therefore, we need to be careful to note the degrees of each polynomial we construct. By choosing $m = \lceil n/2 \rceil$, we ensure that $m \geq n - m$. Thus, we can add the two halves of a polynomial by first recording the low-order half, then adding in the high-order half, yielding a polynomial of degree $m - 1$. After the recursive multiplications, P_1 and P_2 will both have degree $2(m - 1)$, but P_3 will have degree $2(n - m - 1)$. To construct P, we can first copy P_1 and P_3 to the proper locations, and fill in 0 for the coefficient of x^{2m-1}. We can then add $P_2[i] - P_1[i] - P_3[i]$ to the coefficient of x^{m+i}; however, because P_3 has a different degree than P_1 and P_2, we use a separate loop to subtract this polynomial.

From Figure 10.1 and Exercise 3.26 (page 103), it is evident that a total of $\Theta(n)$ time is needed apart from the recursive calls. Thus, we can describe the running time with the following recurrence:

$$f(n) \in 3f(n/2) + \Theta(n),$$

whenever $n > 1$ is a power of 2. From Theorem 3.35, $f(n) \in \Theta(n^{\lg 3})$. Because $\lg 3 \approx 1.59$, this algorithm is an improvement over the brute-force calculation.

10.2   Merge Sort

In Section 5.6, we saw that we can sort using a worst-case running time in $\Theta(n \lg n)$ using heap sort (Figure 5.20). However, as was suggested by Exercise 5.25, heap sort is not *stable* when sorting KEYED items; i.e., items with equal keys can be reordered by heap sort. In this section, we will apply divide-and-conquer to obtain a stable sorting algorithm that also runs in $\Theta(n \lg n)$ time in the worst case.

We can apply divide-and-conquer to sorting by first dividing in half any array with more than one element and sorting the two halves. We then need to combine the two sorted halves into a single sorted array. We have therefore reduced the sorting problem to the problem of merging two sorted arrays into a single sorted array. Furthermore, in order to ensure stability, we require the following behavior for a merging algorithm:

- If two elements in the same input array have equal keys, they remain in the same order in the output array.
- If an element x from the first input array has a key equal to some element y in the second input array, then x must precede y in the output array.

Figure 10.2   The MERGESORT algorithm

Precondition: $A[1..n]$ is an array of KEYED items.
Postcondition: $A[1..n]$ is a permutation of its original values sorted in nondecreasing order. If initially, $x = A[i]$ and $y = A[j]$, where $x.\text{KEY}() = y.\text{KEY}()$ and $i < j$, then x precedes y in the result.

MERGESORT($A[1..n]$)
   if $n > 1$
      $m \leftarrow \lfloor n/2 \rfloor$; MERGESORT($A[1..m]$); MERGESORT($A[m + 1..n]$)
      $B[1..n] \leftarrow$ MERGE($A[1..m], A[m + 1..n]$)
      COPY($B[1..n], A[1..n]$)

Precondition: $A[1..m]$ and $B[1..n]$ are arrays of KEYED items sorted in nondecreasing order.
Postcondition: Returns an array $C[1..m + n]$ containing the elements of A and B in nondecreasing order, maintaining the same order as in the input arrays. If $A[i].\text{KEY}() = B[j].\text{KEY}()$, then $A[i]$ precedes $B[j]$ in C.

MERGE($A[1..m], B[1..n]$)
   $C \leftarrow$ **new** ARRAY$[1..m + n]$; $i \leftarrow 1$; $j \leftarrow 1$; $k \leftarrow 1$
   // **Invariant:** $C[1..k - 1]$ contains $A[1..i - 1]$ and $B[1..j - 1]$ in correct
   // order.
   while $i \leq m$ **and** $j \leq n$
      if $A[i].\text{KEY}() \leq B[j].\text{KEY}()$
         $C[k] \leftarrow A[i]$; $i \leftarrow i + 1$
      else
         $C[k] \leftarrow B[j]$; $j \leftarrow j + 1$
      $k \leftarrow k + 1$
   COPY($A[i..m], C[k..k + m - i]$); COPY($B[j..n], C[k..k + n - j]$)
   return C

Suppose we are given two sorted arrays. If either is empty, we can simply use the other. Otherwise, the element with minimum key in the two arrays needs to be first in the sorted result. The element with minimum key in each array is the first element in the array. We can therefore determine the overall minimum by comparing the keys of the first elements of the two arrays. If the keys are equal, in order to ensure stability, we must take the element from the first array. To obtain the remainder of the result, we merge the remainder of the two input arrays. We have therefore transformed a large instance of merging to a smaller instance.

Putting it all together, we have the MERGESORT algorithm shown in Figure 10.2. Note that in the MERGE function, when the loop terminates, either $i > m$ or $j > n$. Hence, either $A[i..m]$ or $B[j..n]$ is empty. As a result, only one of the two calls to COPY (see Figure 1.18 on page 22 for its specification) will have any effect.

It is easily seen that MERGE runs in $\Theta(m+n)$ time. Therefore, the time required for MERGESORT excluding the recursive calls is in $\Theta(n)$. For $n > 1$ a power of 2, the following recurrence gives the worst-case running time of MERGESORT:

$$f(n) \in 2f(n/2) + \Theta(n).$$

From Theorem 3.35, $f(n) \in \Theta(n \lg n)$.

10.3   Quick Sort

Though merge sort and heap sort both run in $\Theta(n \lg n)$ time in the worst case, another divide-and-conquer algorithm is more commonly used when stability is not required. As was suggested in Exercise 2.17, sorting can be reduced to the Dutch national flag problem, which was introduced in Section 2.4. We first select from the array to be sorted a *pivot* element p, which we use to determine the colors of the elements, as follows:

- If $x.\text{KEY}() < p.\text{KEY}()$, then x is red.
- If $x.\text{KEY}() = p.\text{KEY}()$, then x is white.
- If $x.\text{KEY}() > p.\text{KEY}()$, then x is blue.

By solving the resulting Dutch national flag problem, we will have partitioned the array into three sections:

- The first section consists of all elements with keys less than $p.\text{KEY}()$.
- The second section consists of all elements with keys equal to $p.\text{KEY}()$.
- The third section consists of all elements with keys greater than $p.\text{KEY}()$.

By sorting the first and third sections, we will have sorted the array. This general strategy is known as quick sort.

Following the divide-and-conquer paradigm, we would like to select the pivot so that after the array has been partitioned, the first and third sections have roughly the same number of elements. Thus, the median element would be a good choice for p. As we will show in the next section, it is possible to find the median in $\Theta(n)$ time in the worst case. We saw in Section 3.6 that the Dutch national flag problem can be solved in $\Theta(n)$ time. Because each

of the two subproblems is at most half the size of the original problem, we
can bound the running time of this sorting algorithm with the recurrence

$$f(n) \in 2f(n/2) + \Theta(n).$$

From Theorem 3.35, $f(n) \in \Theta(n \lg n)$.

However, it turns out that the overhead of choosing the median as the
pivot is too expensive in practice, so that heap sort, for example, outperforms
this algorithm. On the other hand, choosing an arbitrary element, such as the
first, degrades the worst case performance. For example, suppose that the
input array is already sorted and that all keys are distinct. If we always
choose the first element as the pivot, then we always choose the smallest
element. As a result, one of the two subproblems is empty, and the other
contains all but one of the original elements. Because the empty subproblem
can be sorted in $\Theta(1)$ time, we can describe the running time for such a case
with the following recurrence:

$$f(n) \in f(n-1) + \Theta(n).$$

From Theorem 3.34, $f(n) \in \Theta(n^2)$, so that the running time for this
algorithm is in $\Omega(n^2)$ in the worst case. Observing that each element is chosen
as a pivot at most once, we can easily see that $O(n^2)$ is an upper bound on
the running time, so that the algorithm runs in $\Theta(n^2)$ time in the worst
case. Because of this bad worst case, the most common implementations of
this algorithm combine it with a $\Theta(n \lg n)$ algorithm, usually heap sort, in
order to achieve $\Theta(n \lg n)$ performance in the worst case (see Exercise 10.10).
For the remainder of this section, we will focus on improving the quick sort
algorithm without combining it with another sorting algorithm.

Choosing the first element (or the last element) as the pivot is a bad
idea, because an already-sorted array yields the worst-case performance.
Furthermore, the performance is nearly as bad on a nearly-sorted array.
To make matters worse, it is not hard to see that when the running time
is in $\Theta(n^2)$, the stack usage is in $\Theta(n)$. Because we often need to sort a
nearly-sorted array, we don't want an algorithm that performs badly in such
cases.

The above analyses illustrate that it is better for the pivot element to be
chosen to be near the median than to be near the smallest (or equivalently,
the largest) element. More generally, it illustrates why divide-and-conquer is
often an effective algorithm design strategy: when a problem is reduced to
multiple subproblems, it is best if these subproblems are the same size. For

---

Figure 10.3   The randomized QuickSort algorithm

Precondition: $A[lo..hi]$ is an array of Keyed items, and lo and hi are Ints.

Postcondition: $A[lo..hi]$ is a permutation of its original values in nondecreasing order.

QuickSort($A[lo..hi]$)
    if $lo < hi$
        $p \leftarrow A[\text{RandomInteger}(lo, hi)].\text{Key}()$
        $r \leftarrow 0;\ w \leftarrow 0;\ b \leftarrow 0$
        // **Invariant:** $r, w, b \in \mathbb{N}$, $r + w + b \leq hi - lo + 1$, $A[i].\text{Key}() < p$
        // for $lo \leq i < lo + r$, $A[i].\text{Key}() = p$ for $hi - b - w < i \leq hi - b$, and
        // $A[i].\text{Key}() > p$ for $hi - b < i \leq hi$.
        while $r + w + b < hi - lo + 1$
            $j \leftarrow hi - b - w$
            if $A[j].\text{Key}() < p$
                $A[j] \leftrightarrow A[lo + r];\ r \leftarrow r + 1$
            else if $A[j].\text{Key}() = p$
                $w \leftarrow w + 1$
            else
                $A[j] \leftrightarrow A[hi - b];\ b = b + 1$
        QuickSort($A[lo..lo + r - 1]$)
        QuickSort($A[hi - b + 1..hi]$)

Precondition: i and j are integers, $i \leq j$.

Postcondition: Returns an integer k such that $i \leq k \leq j$. Each value in the range has an equal probability, independent of previous calls.

RandomInteger(i, j)

---

quick sort, we need a way to choose the pivot element quickly in such a way that it tends to be near the median.

One way to accomplish this is to choose the pivot element randomly. This algorithm is shown in Figure 10.3. In order to make the presentation easier to follow, we have specified the algorithm so that the array is indexed with arbitrary endpoints.

Let us now analyze the expected running time of QuickSort on an array of size n. We first observe that for any call in which $lo < hi$, the loop will execute at least once. Furthermore, by an easy induction on n, we can show that at most $n + 1$ calls have *lo* $\geq$ *hi*. Because each of these calls requires $\Theta(1)$ time, a total of at most $O(n)$ time is used in processing the base cases. Otherwise, the running time is proportional to the number of times the loop executes over the course of the algorithm.

Each iteration of the loop involves comparing one pair of elements. For a given call to QUICKSORT, the pivot is compared to all elements currently in the array, then is excluded from the subsequent recursive calls. Thus, once a pair of elements is compared, they are never compared again on subsequent loop iterations (though they may be compared twice in the same iteration — once in each **if** statement). The total running time is therefore proportional to the number of pairs of elements that are compared. We will only concern ourselves with pairs of distinct elements, as this will only exclude $O(n)$ pairs.

Let $F[1..n]$ be the final sorted array, and let *comp* be a discrete random variable giving the number of pairs (i, j) such that $1 \leq i < j \leq N$ and $F[i]$ is compared with $F[j]$. We wish to compute $E[comp]$. Let c_{ij} denote the event that $F[i]$ is compared with $F[j]$. Then

$$E[comp] = E\left[\sum_{i=1}^{n} \sum_{j=i+1}^{n} I(c_{ij})\right]$$

$$= \sum_{i=1}^{n} \sum_{j=i+1}^{n} E[I(c_{ij})]$$

$$= \sum_{i=1}^{n} \sum_{j=i+1}^{n} P(c_{ij}).$$

We observe that $F[i]$ is compared with $F[j]$ iff one of them is in the subarray being sorted when the other is chosen as the pivot. Furthermore, two elements $F[i]$ and $F[j]$ are in the same subarray as long as no element k such that

$$F[i].\text{KEY}() \leq F[k].\text{KEY}() \leq F[j].\text{KEY}()$$

is chosen as the pivot. Thus, the probability that $F[i]$ and $F[j]$ are compared is the probability that one of them is chosen as pivot before any other $F[k]$ satisfying the above inequality. Because there are at least $j - i + 1$ elements $F[k]$ satisfying the above inequality when $j > i$,

$$P(c_{ij}) \leq \frac{2}{j - i + 1}.$$

We therefore have

$$E[comp] = \sum_{i=1}^{n} \sum_{j=i+1}^{n} P(c_{ij})$$

$$\leq \sum_{i=1}^{n} \sum_{j=i+1}^{n} \frac{2}{j-i+1}$$

$$= 2 \sum_{i=1}^{n} \sum_{j=2}^{n-i+1} \frac{1}{j}. \qquad (10.3)$$

The inner sum above is closely related to the *harmonic series*:

$$H_n = \sum_{i=1}^{n} \frac{1}{i}.$$

Tight bounds for H_n are given by the following theorem, whose proof is left as an exercise.

Theorem 10.1. *For all $n \geq 1$:*

$$\ln(n+1) \leq H_n \leq 1 + \ln n.$$

Applying Theorem 10.1 to inequality (10.3), we have

$$E[comp] \leq 2 \sum_{i=1}^{n} \sum_{j=2}^{n-i+1} \frac{1}{j}$$

$$= 2 \sum_{i=1}^{n} (H_{n-i+1} - 1)$$

$$\leq 2 \sum_{i=1}^{n} \ln(n-i+1)$$

$$= 2 \sum_{i=1}^{n} \ln i$$

$$\in O(n \lg n),$$

from Theorem 3.31. For an array of distinct elements, a similar analysis shows that $E[comp] \in \Omega(n \lg n)$; hence, the expected running time of QUICKSORT on any array of n elements is in $\Theta(n \lg n)$.

The expected-case analysis of QUICKSORT suggests that it would work well in practice, and indeed, there are versions that outperform both heap sort and merge sort. The most widely-used versions, however, are not randomized. Instead of choosing the pivot element randomly, they use heuristics, such as choosing the median of the first, middle, and last elements. Such heuristics tend to choose pivot elements nearer to the median than those chosen randomly. Furthermore, they typically involve less overhead than generating a random (or *pseudorandom*) number.

Because of the $\Theta(n^2)$ worst-case running time and $\Theta(n)$ worst-case stack space usage of deterministic versions of quick sort, the most common implementations combine quick sort with two other sorting algorithms. In order to avoid the bad worst case, heap sort is typically used to handle subproblems in which the recursion gets too deep (see Exercise 10.10). In order to speed up sorting of small subproblems, insertion sort is typically used to sort small base cases. The most basic combination of these algorithms is called *introsort*.

10.4   Selection

In Section 1.1, we introduced the selection problem. Recall that this problem is to find the kth smallest element of an array of n elements. We showed that it can be reduced to sorting. Using either heap sort or merge sort, we therefore have an algorithm for this problem with a running time in $\Theta(n \lg n)$. In this section, we will improve upon this running time.

Section 2.4 shows that the selection problem can be reduced to the Dutch National Flag problem and a smaller instance of itself. This reduction is very similar to the reduction upon which quick sort is based. Specifically, we choose a pivot element p and solve the resulting Dutch national flag problem as we did for the quick sort reduction. Let r and w denote the numbers of red items and white items, respectively. We then have three cases:

- If $r \geq k$, we return the kth smallest red item.
- If $r < k$ and $r + w \geq k$, we return p.
- If $r + w < k$, we return the $(k - r - w)$th smallest blue element.

Due to the similarity of this algorithm to quick sort, some of the same problems arise in choosing the pivot element appropriately. For example, if we always use the first element as the pivot, then selecting the nth smallest element in a sorted array of n distinct elements always results in a recursive call with all but one of the original elements. As we saw in Section 10.3, this yields a running time in $\Theta(n^2)$. On the other hand, it is possible to show that selecting the pivot at random yields an expected running time in $\Theta(n)$ — the details are left as an exercise.

Our goal is to construct a deterministic algorithm with worst-case running time in $O(n)$. As we saw in Section 10.3, quick sort achieves a better asymptotic running time if the median is chosen as the pivot. It stands to reason that such a choice might be best for the selection algorithm. We mentioned in Section 10.3 that it is possible to find the median in $O(n)$ time. The way to do this is to use our linear-time selection algorithm to find the $\lceil n/2 \rceil$nd smallest element. However, this doesn't help us in designing the linear-time selection algorithm because the reduction is not to a smaller instance.

Instead, we need a way to approximate the median well enough so that the resulting algorithm runs in $O(n)$ time. Consider the following strategy for approximating the median. First, we arrange the n elements into an $M \times \lfloor n/M \rfloor$ array, where M is some fixed odd number. If n is not evenly divisible by M, we will have up to $M - 1$ elements that will not fit in the array — we will ignore these elements for now. Suppose we sort each column in nondecreasing order. Further suppose that we order the columns (keeping each column intact) so that the middle row is in nondecreasing order. We then select an element in the center of the array as the pivot p (see Figure 10.4).

By choosing p in this fashion, we ensure that all elements above and to the left of p are no greater than p, and that all elements below and to the right of p are no less than p. In other words, no more than about 3/4 of the elements can be greater than p, and no more than about 3/4 of the elements can be less than p. Thus, if we can find this p in $O(n)$ time, we have the following recurrence giving the running time of the algorithm:

$$f(n) \in f(\lfloor 3n/4 \rfloor) + \Theta(n).$$

Figure 10.4   Finding an approximate median

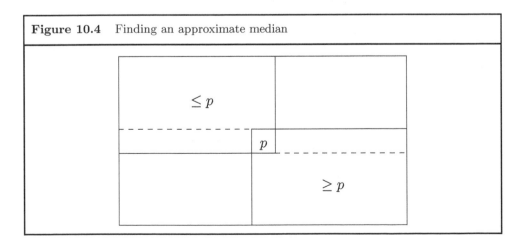

Unfortunately, Theorem 3.35 does not apply to this recurrence, as we would need $b = 4/3$, which is not a natural number. However, given Theorem 3.35, we might suspect that $f(n) \in \Theta(n)$, as this is the solution yielded by the theorem if we could use $b = 4/3$. We will soon show that this is, in fact, the case.

Let us now consider the time needed to find p. Sorting M elements using either heap sort or merge sort uses $\Theta(M \lg M)$ time. Because M is a fixed constant, however, $M \lg M$ is also a fixed constant, so that the time is in $\Theta(1)$. This must be done for each of the $\lfloor n/M \rfloor$ columns, so that the time to sort all of the columns is in $O(n)$. However, the time to sort the $\lfloor n/M \rfloor$ elements in the middle row is in $\Theta(n \lg n)$. On the other hand, we really don't need to sort the middle row in order to find p — we only need to find the median of this row. If $M > 1$, this row has strictly fewer than n elements, so that finding its median is a smaller instance of the selection problem.

If we use this technique for finding the median, we need two recursive calls — one to find the median of $\lfloor n/M \rfloor$ elements, and one to solve the smaller selection problem after the Dutch national flag algorithm has been applied. This latter recursive call has no more than about $3n/4$ elements. The recurrence describing the running time is therefore of the form

$$f(n) \in f(\lfloor 3n/4 \rfloor) + f(\lfloor n/M \rfloor) + \Theta(n), \tag{10.4}$$

for some odd number M.

We don't have a theorem that applies to the above recurrence. We can gain some intuition by comparing this recurrence with recurrences of the form

$$g(n) \in ag(\lfloor n/b \rfloor) + \Theta(n),$$

where b is an integer greater than 1. From Theorem 3.35, $g(n) \in \Theta(n)$ iff $a < b$, or equivalently, iff $a/b < 1$. If a is a positive integer, this condition is equivalent to

$$\sum_{i=1}^{a} \frac{1}{b} < 1.$$

The following theorem generalizes this condition to a sum of several different positive real numbers.

Theorem 10.2. *Let* $n_0 \geq 1$ *and* $m \geq 1$ *be integers, and let* $c_1, \ldots, c_m$ *be positive real numbers such that*

$$\sum_{i=1}^{m} c_i < 1.$$

Let $f : \mathbb{N} \to \mathbb{R}^{\geq 0}$ *be an eventually non-decreasing function satisfying*

$$f(n) \in \sum_{i=1}^{m} f(\lfloor c_i n \rfloor) + X(n)$$

whenever $n \geq n_0$, *where* X *is either* O, Ω, *or* Θ. *Then* $f(n) \in X(n)$.

Proof. If X is Ω, clearly we have $f(n) \in \Omega(n)$. In what follows, we will show that if X is O, then $f(n) \in O(n)$. It will then follow that if X is Θ, then $f(n) \in \Theta(n)$.

Suppose X is O. Then for some natural number n_1 and some positive real number a, we have

$$f(n) \leq \sum_{i=1}^{m} f(\lfloor c_i n \rfloor) + an$$

whenever $n \geq n_0$ and $n \geq n_1$. By Exercise 3.11, it is sufficient to show that for some positive real number b, $f(n) \leq bn$ whenever $n > 0$.

The technique we will use to prove this fact is called *constructive induction*. With this technique, we use the constant b as if it had already been fixed. As the proof progresses, we will need to assume certain constraints on b. Once the proof is finished, if the assumed constraints are consistent, we can then fix a value for b that satisfied all of the constraints.

Induction Hypothesis: Assume that for some n, if $0 < k < n$, then $f(k) \leq bk$.

Induction Step: First, we will assume that n is large enough to apply the recurrence, then to apply the induction hypothesis to each term in the resulting summation. If $n \geq \max(n_0, n_1)$,

$$f(n) \leq \sum_{i=1}^{m} f(\lfloor c_i n \rfloor) + an.$$

In order to be able to apply the induction hypothesis to each $f(\lfloor c_i n \rfloor)$, we need $\lfloor c_i n \rfloor > 0$. Therefore we assume that $n \geq n_2$, where

$$n_2 \geq \max\{n_0, n_1, 1/c_i \mid 1 \leq i \leq m\}.$$

Let

$$c = \sum_{i=1}^{m} c_i.$$

By the Induction Hypothesis,

$$f(n) \leq \sum_{i=1}^{m} b\lfloor c_i n \rfloor + an$$

$$\leq bn \sum_{i=1}^{m} c_i + an$$

$$= bcn + an$$

$$= (bc + a)n.$$

Thus, $f(n) \leq bn$ if

$$bc + a \leq b$$

$$a \leq b(1 - c)$$

$$\frac{a}{1-c} \leq b,$$

as $1 - c > 0$.

Base: We must still show the claim for $0 < n < n_2$. In other words, we need $b \geq f(n)/n$ for $0 < n < n_2$. We can satisfy this constraint and the one above if $b = \max\{a/(1 - c), f(n)/n \mid 0 < n < n_2\}$ (note that because this set is finite and nonempty, it must have a maximum element). $\qquad\square$

Returning to recurrence 10.4, we see that Theorem 10.2 applies if $M > 4$. Thus, if we set $M = 5$, we have $f(n) \in O(n)$. The entire algorithm is shown in Figure 10.5.

Now that we have described the algorithm precisely, let us analyze its running time more carefully to be sure that it is, in fact in $\Theta(n)$. It is easily seen that the running time is in $\Omega(n)$. We need for the recurrence

$$f(n) \in f(\lfloor n/5 \rfloor) + f(\lfloor 3n/4 \rfloor) + O(n) \tag{10.5}$$

Figure 10.5   A linear-time algorithm for the selection problem

---

LINEARSELECT($A[1..n], k$)
  if $n \leq 4$
    SORT($A[1..n]$)
    return $A[k]$
  else
    $m \leftarrow \lfloor n/5 \rfloor$; $T \leftarrow$ **new** ARRAY$[1..m]$
    for $i \leftarrow 1$ **to** m
      SORT($A[5i-4..5i]$); $T[i] \leftarrow A[5i-2]$
    $p \leftarrow$ LINEARSELECT($T[1..m], \lceil m/2 \rceil$); $r \leftarrow 0; w \leftarrow 0; b \leftarrow 0$
    // **Invariant:** $r, w, b \in \mathbb{N}$, $r + w + b \leq n$, and $A[i] < p$ for $1 \leq i \leq r$,
    // $A[i] = p$ for $n - b - w < i \leq n - b$, and $A[i] > p$ for $n - b < i \leq n$.
    while $r + w + b < n$
      $j \leftarrow n - b - w$
      if $A[j] < p$
        $r \leftarrow r + 1$; $A[j] \leftrightarrow A[r]$
      else if $A[j] = p$
        $w \leftarrow w + 1$
      else
        $A[j] \leftrightarrow A[n - b]$; $b = b + 1$
    if $r \geq k$
      return LINEARSELECT($A[1..r], k$)
    else if $r + w \geq k$
      return p
    else
      return LINEARSELECT($A[r + w + 1..n], k - r - w$)

---

to give an upper bound on the running time of the algorithm for sufficiently large n. Clearly, the number of elements in the first recursive call is $\lfloor n/5 \rfloor$. Furthermore, if we ignore the recursive calls, the time needed is in $O(n)$ (note that the time needed to sort 5 elements is bounded by a constant because the number of elements is constant). However, the number of elements in the second recursive call is not always bounded above by $\lfloor 3n/4 \rfloor$. Consider, for example, the array $A[1..13]$ with $A[i] = i$ for $1 \leq i \leq 13$. The values 3 and 8 will be placed in $T[1]$ and $T[2]$, respectively. The value assigned to p will therefore be 3. If $k > 3$, ten elements will be passed to the second recursive call, but $\lfloor 3 \cdot 13/4 \rfloor = 9$.

Returning to Figure 10.4, and taking the number of rows to be 5, we see that for each two columns (ten elements) that we add, at least three elements are excluded from the second recursive call. For example, when $5 \leq n \leq 14$, at least three elements are excluded, and when $15 \leq n \leq 24$, at least six elements are excluded. In general, at least $3i$ elements are excluded if $10i - 5 \leq n \leq 10i + 4$. We need to find the largest value of n such that $3i < n/4$, if such an n exists. If we can do so, then for all larger values of n, the number of elements in the second recursive call will be no more than $3n/4$. Because the number of elements must be an integer, it will then be bounded above by $\lfloor 3n/4 \rfloor$.

We therefore need to find the largest i such that

$$3i < (10i + 4)/4$$
$$12i < 10i + 4$$
$$i < 2.$$

The largest such n is therefore $10 + 4 = 14$. Then for all $n \geq 15$, recurrence (10.5) gives an upper bound on the running time of LinearSelect. From Theorem 10.2, the running time is in $O(n)$, and hence in $\Theta(n)$.

Various performance improvements can be made to LinearSelect. For example, if $n = 5$, there is no reason to apply the Dutch national flag algorithm after sorting the array — we can simply return $A[k]$. In other words, it would be better if the base case included $n = 5$, and perhaps some larger values as well. Furthermore, sorting is not the most efficient way to solve the selection problem for small n. We explore some alternatives in the exercises.

Even with these performance improvements, however, LinearSelect does not perform nearly as well as the randomized algorithm outlined at the beginning of this section. Better still is using a quick approximation of the median, such as finding the median of the first, middle, and last elements, as the value of p. This approach yields an algorithm whose worst-case running time is in $\Theta(n^2)$, but which typically performs better than even the randomized algorithm.

10.5   Integer Division

Exercise 4.14 on page 145 discussed an implementation of a BigNum ADT (specified in Figure 4.18, page 146) for arbitrary-precision natural numbers. This ADT is rather limited, in that its only arithmetic operations are addition and subtraction. Figure 10.6 specifies multiplication and division

Figure 10.6 Multiplication and division functions for use with the BigNum ADT defined in Figure 4.18 on page 146

Precondition: u and v are BigNums.
Postcondition: Returns a BigNum representing the product of the values of u and v.

Multiply(u, v)

Precondition: u is a BigNum and v is a positive BigNum.
Postcondition: Returns a BigNum representing the value $\lfloor u/v \rfloor$.

Divide(u, v)

---

functions for operating on BigNums. We leave it as an exercise to show that the polynomial multiplication algorithm of Section 10.1 can be adapted to form a BigNum multiplication algorithm that runs in $\Theta(n^{\lg 3})$ time, where n is the number of bits in the product. In this section and the next, we consider implementations of Divide.

Let us first consider the familiar long division algorithm from elementary school. Suppose the dividend u has m digits and the divisor v has n digits. We begin by finding the smallest prefix of the significant digits of u that gives us a number no smaller than v. If there is no such prefix, the quotient is 0. Otherwise,

> *Digits (or bits) are significant if they are not to the left of the leftmost nonzero digit (or bit, respectively). The most significant digit (or bit) is the leftmost of the significant digits (or bits, respectively).*

the next step is to obtain an approximation for the most significant digit of the result. Let k be the number of digits in the prefix formed above. We obtain the approximation by dividing the $k - n + 1$ most significant digits of u by the most significant digit of v. (Note that because k will always be either n or $n + 1$, $k - n + 1$ will be either 1 or 2.) This quotient is our approximation of the first significant digit of the result.

Because we only used one digit of v in approximating the first significant digit of the result, this approximation may be too large. We determine whether this is the case by multiplying this approximation by v, then comparing the product with the prefix of u. If the product is larger, we repeatedly subtract 1 from the approximation and recompute the product until the product is no larger than the prefix of u. The resulting digit is the first significant digit of the result.

Having obtained the first significant digit of the result, we need to obtain the rest of the result. We begin by subtracting the last product obtained above from the prefix of u. We then append the rest of u to this difference. Finally, we obtain the remaining digits of the quotient by dividing the resulting value by v. If we ensure that the result of this last division has exactly $m - k$ digits (by padding with zeros if necessary), then the digits we obtain complete the quotient. We have therefore reduced the division problem to a smaller instance of itself. The reduction is not quite a transformation, but it can easily be expressed as a loop.

This algorithm can easily be applied to the division of an m-bit binary number u by an n-bit binary number v. In fact, we really don't need to approximate the first significant bit — it can't be a 0, so it must be a 1. We do, however, need to determine the prefix of u as described above. We then subtract v from the prefix and append the remainder of u. We obtain the remaining bits by dividing this value by v and inserting zeros if necessary.

In the above algorithm, we perform a $\Theta(n)$-bit subtraction for each 1 bit of the quotient. Furthermore, each subtraction is preceded by at least one $\Theta(n)$-bit comparison. Because the number of 1 bits in the quotient may be as many as $m-n+1$, the worst-case number of comparisons and subtractions of $\Theta(n)$-bit numbers is $(m-n+1)$. The running time is therefore in $\Theta(n(m-n))$, which is worse than what we would like.

We can instead group the bits of u and v into digits of some radix r, where r is a power of 2. However, for any fixed radix r, this decreases the number of comparisons by at most a constant factor, so that the asymptotic running time does not improve. Applying the divide-and-conquer principle, we might try breaking v into two digits. For now, let's assume the number of bits n in v is even. Our radix is therefore $2^{n/2}$. To obtain an approximation of the first digit of the quotient, we recursively divide the first one or two digits of u by the first digit of v.

If n is odd and greater than 1, we can multiply both u and v by 2 without changing the quotient. These multiplications have the effect of appending a zero as the least significant bit, so that the resulting length is even. Because n is greater than 1, dividing the length of the resulting divisor by 2 yields a smaller subproblem. For $n = 1$, $v = 1$, so the quotient is simply u. We have therefore reduced the division problem to smaller instances of itself. The resulting algorithm is shown in Figure 10.7. We assume the existence of two constants **zero** and **one**, which refer to BigNums with values of 0 and 1, respectively.

We will now analyze the running time of DivideDC. We begin with the **while** loop. In order to analyze this loop, we need to know how large *prod*, *rem*, and *approx* might be. From the invariant of the main loop, $rem \leq v - 1$

Figure 10.7 Divide-and-conquer implementation of DIVIDE, specified in Figure 10.6

DIVIDEDC(u, v)
 $m \leftarrow u.$NUMBITS(); $n \leftarrow v.$NUMBITS()
 if $n = 1$
  return u
 else
  if n mod $2 = 1$
   $u \leftarrow u.$SHIFT(1); $m \leftarrow m + 1$
   $v \leftarrow v.$SHIFT(1); $n \leftarrow n + 1$
  $digLen \leftarrow n/2$; $numDig \leftarrow \lceil m/digLen \rceil$
  $qLen \leftarrow digLen \times (numDig - 1)$
  $qBits \leftarrow$ **new** ARRAY$[0..qLen - 1]$
  $vFirst \leftarrow$ **new** BIGNUM($v.$GETBITS($digLen, digLen$))
  $rem \leftarrow$ **new** BIGNUM($u.$GETBITS($qLen, digLen$))
  // **Invariant:** $rem < v$ and
  // $v \times$ **new** BIGNUM($qBits[i + digLen..qLen - 1]$) + $rem =$
  // **new** BIGNUM($u.$GETBITS($i + digLen, m - i - digLen$)).
  for $i \leftarrow qLen - digLen$ **to** 0 **by** $-digLen$
   $next \leftarrow$ **new** BIGNUM($u.$GETBITS($i, digLen$))
   $rem \leftarrow rem.$SHIFT($digLen$).ADD($next$)
   if $rem.$COMPARETO(v) < 0
    $qDig \leftarrow$ zero.GETBITS($0, digLen$)
   else
    $approx \leftarrow$ DIVIDEDC($rem.$SHIFT($-digLen$), $vFirst$)
    $prod \leftarrow$ MULTIPLY($v, approx$)
    // **Invariant:** $prod = v \times approx$, $approx \geq \lfloor rem/v \rfloor$, and the
    // invariant for the outer loop.
    while $prod.$COMPARETO(rem) > 0
     $approx \leftarrow approx.$SUBTRACT(one)
     $prod \leftarrow prod.$SUBTRACT(v)
    $qDig \leftarrow approx.$GETBITS($0, digLen$)
   COPY($qDig[0..digLen - 1]$, $qBits[i..i + digLen - 1]$)
  return new BIGNUM($qBits$)

at the top of the main loop. Before the **while** loop is executed, the value of rem is multiplied by $2^{n/2}$, and $next$ is added. Because $next$ contains at most $n/2$ significant bits, $next < 2^{n/2}$. Thus, when the **while** loop executes, $rem < v2^{n/2}$. Because v contains n significant bits, rem contains at most

$3n/2$ significant bits. Likewise, it is not hard to show that at the beginning of the **while** loop, *approx* contains at most $n/2+1$ significant bits, and that *prod* contains at most $3n/2+1$ significant bits. The body of the **while** loop therefore runs in $\Theta(n)$ time in the worst case.

In order to get a tight bound on the number of iterations of the **while** loop, we need a tighter bound on *approx*. In particular, we need to know how close *approx* is to $\lfloor rem/v \rfloor$. Let $r = \lfloor rem \times 2^{-n/2} \rfloor$. We first observe that

$$\left\lfloor \frac{r}{vFirst+1} \right\rfloor = \left\lfloor \frac{r \times 2^{n/2}}{(vFirst+1) \times 2^{n/2}} \right\rfloor$$

$$= \left\lfloor \frac{rem}{(vFirst+1) \times 2^{n/2}} \right\rfloor,$$

because the $n/2$ low-order bits of the numerator do not affect the value of the expression. Furthermore, the right-hand side above is no larger than $\lfloor rem/v \rfloor$. Thus,

$$approx - \lfloor rem/v \rfloor \leq \left\lfloor \frac{r}{vFirst} \right\rfloor - \left\lfloor \frac{r}{vFirst+1} \right\rfloor$$

$$\leq \frac{r}{vFirst} - \frac{r-vFirst}{vFirst+1}$$

$$= \frac{r(vFirst+1) - vFirst(r-vFirst)}{vFirst(vFirst+1)}$$

$$= \frac{r + vFirst^2}{vFirst(vFirst+1)}.$$

Now because $rem < v2^{n/2}$, it follows that $r < vFirst \times 2^{n/2}$. We therefore have

$$approx - \lfloor rem/v \rfloor \leq \frac{r + vFirst^2}{vFirst(vFirst+1)}$$

$$< \frac{vFirst \times 2^{n/2} + vFirst^2}{vFirst(vFirst+1)}$$

$$= \frac{2^{n/2} + vFirst}{vFirst+1}$$

$$= \frac{2^{n/2}}{vFirst+1} + \frac{vFirst}{vFirst+1}.$$

Because *vFirst* contains $n/2$ significant bits, its value must be at least $2^{n/2-1}$. The value of the first term on the right-hand side above is therefore strictly less than 2. Clearly, the value of the second term is strictly less than

1, so that the right-hand side is strictly less than 3. Because the left-hand side is an integer, its value must therefore be at most 2. It follows from the **while** loop invariant that the loop terminates when $approx = \lfloor rem/v \rfloor$. Because this loop decrements $approx$ by 1 each iteration, it must iterate at most twice. Its running time is therefore in $\Theta(n)$.

It is now easily seen that, excluding the recursive call, the running time of the body of the main loop is dominated by the running time of the multiplication. Because the result of the multiplication contains at most $3n/2 + 1$ significant bits, this multiplication can be done in $\Theta(n^{\lg 3})$ time using the multiplication algorithm suggested at the beginning of this section. If $m \geq n$, the number of iterations of the main loop is easily seen to be

$$numDig - 1 = \lceil m/digLen \rceil - 1$$
$$= \left\lceil \frac{m}{n/2} \right\rceil - 1$$
$$= \lceil 2m/n \rceil - 1.$$

Thus, the running time of the main loop, excluding the recursive call, is in

$$\Theta(n^{\lg 3} m/n) = \Theta(m n^{\lg 3 - 1}).$$

We now observe that for even n, there are in the worst case $\lceil 2m/n \rceil - 1$ recursive calls. For odd n, the worst-case number of recursive calls is $\lceil 2(m + 1)/(n + 1) \rceil - 1$. The resulting recurrence is therefore quite complicated. However, consider the parameters of the recursive call. We have already shown that $rem < v2^{n/2}$, and $vFirst = \lfloor v2^{-n/2} \rfloor$. This recursive call therefore divides a value strictly less than v by $\lfloor v2^{-n/2} \rfloor$. Thus, in any of these calls, the dividend is less than the divisor plus 1, multiplied by 2^n, where n is the number of bits in the divisor. In addition, it is easily seen that the dividend is never less than the divisor. Furthermore, if these relationships initially hold for odd n, they hold for the recursive call in this case as well. We therefore will first restrict our attention to this special case.

Let n, the number of significant bits in v, be even. If

$$v \leq u < (v + 1)2^n,$$

then m, the number of significant bits in u, is at most $2n$. The number of iterations of the outer loop is therefore at most

$$\lceil 2m/n \rceil - 1 \leq \lceil 4n/n \rceil - 1$$
$$= 3.$$

Because each iteration may contain a recursive call, this suggests that there are a total of at most 3 recursive calls. However, note that whenever a recursive call is made, the dividend is no less than the divisor, so that a nonzero digit results in the quotient. Suppose the first of the three digits of the quotient is nonzero. Because the first n bits of u are at most v, the only possible nonzero result for the first digit is 1. The remainder of the quotient is then formed by dividing a value strictly less than 2^n by v, which is at least 2^{n-1}. This result is also at most 1, so that the second digit must be 0. We conclude that no more than two recursive calls are ever made. In each of these recursive calls, the divisor has $n/2$ bits.

If n is odd and greater than 1, we increase the number of bits in v by 1. The above reasoning then applies to $n + 1$, where n denotes the original number of bits in v. We can therefore express the overall running time in terms of n via the recurrence

$$f(n) \in 2f(\lceil n/2 \rceil) + \Theta(n^{\lg 3})$$

for $n > 1$. Applying Theorem 3.35, we see that $f(n) \in \Theta(n^{\lg 3})$.

Let us now turn to the more general case. If $m < n$, it is easily seen that the running time is in $\Theta(n)$. If $m \geq n$, as we have already shown, the worst-case number of recursive calls is in $\Theta(m/n)$, and the overhead is in $\Theta(mn^{\lg 3 - 1})$. Because each of these recursive calls satisfies the special case analyzed above, each runs in $\Theta(n^{\lg 3})$ time. Thus, the overall running time is in $\Theta(mn^{\lg 3 - 1})$.

If we wish to express the running time in terms of the number of bits in the larger of the two operands, it is easily seen that the worst case occurs when m is larger, but n is a fixed fraction of m. If N denotes the number of bits in the larger operand, we then see that the running time is in $\Theta(N^{\lg 3})$, which is asymptotically the same as multiplication. Furthermore, it is not hard to see that if we can improve the running time of multiplication to $O(N^{1+\epsilon})$ for any fixed positive ϵ, the running time of division will also be in $O(N^{1+\epsilon})$ (or $O(mn^\epsilon)$).

In a later chapter, we will show that the running time of multiplication can be improved to $O(N \lg N \lg \lg N)$. When we use this running time, the recurrence for the case in which

$$v \leq u < (v + 1)2^n,$$

becomes

$$f(n) \in 2f(\lceil n/2 \rceil) + O(n \lg n \lg \lg n)$$

for $n > 1$. Applying Theorem 3.35 to this recurrence yields

$$f(n) \in O(n \lg^2 n \lg \lg n).$$

The running time of the division algorithm is then in $O(N \lg^2 N \lg \lg N)$, which is slightly worse than the running time of the multiplication algorithm used. In the next section, we will design a division algorithm whose asymptotic running time matches that of multiplication even for the asymptotically fastest known multiplication algorithm.

10.6 * Newton's Method

We can reduce division to multiplication in a straightforward way if we can compute a reciprocal. A reciprocal of an arbitrary positive integer is a fraction that may or may not have a finite binary representation. We therefore will have to settle for an approximation. In order to simplify the discussion of fixed-point fractions, it helps to scale the value of the divisor v to an appropriate range. Specifically, suppose v consists of n bits; i.e., $2^{n-1} \le v < 2^n$. Then

$$\left\lfloor \frac{u}{v} \right\rfloor = \left\lfloor u 2^{-n} \left(\frac{1}{v 2^{-n}} \right) \right\rfloor.$$

Note that $1/2 \le v 2^{-n} < 1$. Thus, if we can compute a close fixed-point approximation for the reciprocal of a value y such that $1/2 \le y < 1$, we can reduce the integer division problem to the integer multiplication problem. Note that due to the given range of y, the binary encoding of y has no bits to the left of the radix point, and the first bit to the right is a 1. Furthermore, because $1 < 1/y \le 2$, we can approximate $1/y$ with a value z such that $1 \le z < 2$; i.e., z has a single 1 bit to the left of the radix point. We can therefore use BIGNUMs to represent both y and $1/y$ with the interpretation that each contains a radix point at the appropriate position.

Because multiplying an approximation of the reciprocal of $v 2^{-n}$ by $u 2^{-n}$ gives only an approximation of $\lfloor u/v \rfloor$, we may need to correct our result. Suppose we can approximate the reciprocal to enough accuracy that the result of the multiplication is a value q such that

$$\left| q - \frac{u}{v} \right| \le 1.$$

Then it is not hard to see that

$$\left| \lfloor q \rfloor - \left\lfloor \frac{u}{v} \right\rfloor \right| \le 1.$$

Then if $v\lfloor q \rfloor \le u - v$, we know that the actual quotient is $\lfloor q \rfloor + 1$. If $v\lfloor q \rfloor > u$, we know that the quotient is $\lfloor q \rfloor - 1$. Otherwise, the quotient is $\lfloor q \rfloor$.

Suppose an error of ϵ is introduced in approximating the reciprocal. Then we need

$$\left| u2^{-n} \left(\frac{1}{v2^{-n}} + \epsilon \right) - \frac{u}{v} \right| \le 1$$

$$\left| \frac{u}{v} + \epsilon u 2^{-n} - \frac{u}{v} \right| \le 1$$

$$|\epsilon| \le 2^n / u.$$

Suppose u consists of m bits, so that $u < 2^m$. Then we can ensure that the approximation of u/v differs from the actual value of u/v by no more than 1 if our approximation of the reciprocal of $v2^{-n}$ differs from the actual reciprocal by at most 2^{n-m}.

The resulting algorithm is shown in Figure 10.8. We handle the case in which $u < v$ separately in order to ensure that the precondition for $u.\textsc{Subtract}(v)$ is met. As in the previous section, we use constants **zero** and **one**, which refer to BigNum representing 0 and 1, respectively. It is easily seen that the running time is simply the time for Reciprocal plus the time to do the two multiplications. The time to do the first multiplication depends on the size of the value returned by Reciprocal. Because the accuracy of the approximation is 2^{n-m}, we would expect the value to be not much more than $m - n$ significant bits.

In the remainder of this section, we will consider how to implement the Reciprocal function specified in Figure 10.8. The technique we apply is *Newton's method* for approximating a root of a function. Let I be some interval of the real numbers, and suppose $f : I \to \mathbb{R}$ has at least one root — a value $x \in I$ such that $f(x) = 0$. For example, if y is a fixed positive real number, the function $f(x) = 1/x - y$ over $\mathbb{R}^{>0}$ has exactly one root, namely, $x = 1/y$. Newton's method is an iterative approach to finding an approximation of a root of f.

Newton's method begins with an initial estimate x_0 of the root. If $f(x_0)$ is not sufficiently close to 0, a better approximation is found using the derivative of f, which we will denote by f'. Recall that $f'(x_0)$ gives the slope of the line tangent to f at x_0 (see Figure 10.9). We can easily find the intersection x_1 of this line with the x-axis, and for many functions, this intersection will be a better approximation to the root than the initial estimate. We then apply Newton's method using x_1 as the initial estimate. For many functions, this approach is guaranteed to approach a root very quickly. As we will see, the function $f(x) = 1/x - y$ is such a function.

Figure 10.8   Partial implementation of DIVIDE, specified in Figure 10.6, using an approximate reciprocal

---

DIVIDERECIP(u, v)
  if u.COMPARETO(v) < 0
    return zero
  else
    $m \leftarrow u$.NUMBITS(); $n \leftarrow v$.NUMBITS()
    $r \leftarrow$ RECIPROCAL($v, m - n$)
    $q \leftarrow$ MULTIPLY(u, r).SHIFT($1 - r$.NUMBITS() $- n$);
    $prod \leftarrow$ MULTIPLY(v, q)
    if $prod$.COMPARETO(u.SUBTRACT(v)) ≤ 0
      $q \leftarrow q$.ADD(one)
    else if $prod$.COMPARETO(u) > 0
      $q \leftarrow q$.SUBTRACT(one)
    return q

Precondition: y refers to a nonzero BIGNUM, and k refers to a natural number.
Postcondition: Returns a BIGNUM z such that

$$\left| z2^{1-z.\text{NUMBITS}()} - \frac{1}{y2^{-y.\text{NUMBITS}()}} \right| \leq 2^{-k}.$$

RECIPROCAL(y, k)

The line tangent to f at x_0 has slope $f'(x_0)$ and includes the point $(x_0, f(x_0))$. To find its x-intercept, we need to go to the left of x_0 a distance of $f(x_0)/f'(x_0)$ (or if this value is negative, we go to the right a distance of $-f(x_0)/f'(x_0)$). The new estimate x_1 is therefore given by

$$x_1 = x_0 - f(x_0)/f'(x_0).$$

If $f(x) = 1/x - y$, then $f'(x) = -x^{-2}$. The new estimate is therefore

$$x_1 = x_0 - \frac{1/x_0 - y}{-x_0^{-2}}$$
$$= x_0 + x_0 - yx_0^2$$
$$= 2x_0 - yx_0^2.$$

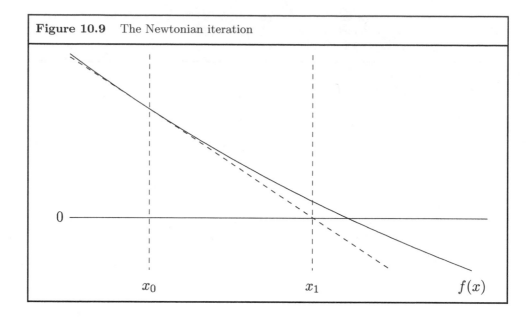

Figure 10.9   The Newtonian iteration

In order to see how quickly the Newtonian iteration converges to $1/y$, suppose we have an estimate $x_0 = (1 + \epsilon)/y$, where ϵ is some real number. Applying the iteration, we have

$$x_1 = 2x_0 - yx_0^2$$

$$= \frac{2(1+\epsilon)}{y} - y\left(\frac{1+\epsilon}{y}\right)^2$$

$$= \frac{2 + 2\epsilon - 1 - 2\epsilon - \epsilon^2}{y}$$

$$= \frac{1 - \epsilon^2}{y}. \qquad (10.1)$$

Thus, each iteration squares the error term ϵ. For $1/2 \leq y < 1$, it is not hard to show that an initial estimate of $3/2$ yields

$$-1/4 \leq \epsilon < 1/2;$$

hence, the number of bits of accuracy doubles with each iteration.

Although this technique does converge rapidly to $1/y$, the number of iterations depends on the degree of accuracy we require. Unfortunately, each iteration requires a multiplication by y, so that the time required cannot be proportional to the time for a single multiplication of values having roughly the same size as y. However, note that successive iterations give successively better approximations. For the earlier approximations, which will probably not be very accurate anyway, we need not use all of the bits of y in the computation.

This suggests the following approach. Suppose we need an approximation that differs from the actual reciprocal by no more than 2^{-k}. We will use k as the size of this problem instance. If k is not too small, we first solve a smaller instance in order to obtain a less-accurate approximation. The accuracy that we require of this approximation needs to be such that a single application of the Newtonian iteration will yield an accuracy of within 2^{-k}. In applying this iteration, we only use as many bits of y as we need in order to ensure the required accuracy. Finally, in order to keep the number of bits in the approximation from growing too rapidly, we return only as many bits as we need to ensure the required accuracy.

Let $\alpha \in \mathbb{R}$ denote the absolute error of some estimate; i.e., our estimate is $1/y + \alpha$. Let $\beta \in \mathbb{R}^{\geq 0}$ denote the absolute error introduced by truncating y, so that the value we use for y in the iteration is $y - \beta$. Finally, let $\gamma \in \mathbb{R}^{\geq 0}$ denote the absolute error introduced by truncating the result. The value computed by the iteration is therefore

$$2\left(\frac{1}{y} + \alpha\right) - (y - \beta)\left(\frac{1}{y} + \alpha\right)^2 - \gamma = \frac{1}{y} + \frac{\beta}{y^2} + \frac{2\alpha\beta}{y} + \alpha^2\beta - y\alpha^2 - \gamma.$$

We need for this value to differ from $1/y$ by at most 2^{-k}; i.e., we need

$$\left|\frac{\beta}{y^2} + \frac{2\alpha\beta}{y} + \alpha^2\beta - y\alpha^2 - \gamma\right| \leq 2^{-k}. \tag{10.2}$$

Note that because $y > 0$, $\beta \geq 0$, and $\gamma \geq 0$, all terms except the second are always non-negative. In order to ensure that the inequality holds when the value inside the absolute value bars is non-negative, we can therefore ignore the last two terms. We therefore need

$$\frac{\beta}{y^2} + \frac{2\alpha\beta}{y} + \alpha^2\beta \leq 2^{-k}.$$

If we replace α by $|\alpha|$ in the above inequality, the left-hand side does not decrease. For fixed α and β, the resulting left-hand side is maximized when y is minimized. Setting y to its minimum possible value of $1/2$, it therefore suffices to ensure that

$$4\beta + 4|\alpha|\beta + \alpha^2\beta \leq 2^{-k}.$$

In order to keep the first term sufficiently small, we need $\beta < 2^{-k-2}$. In order to leave room for the other two terms, let us take $\beta \leq 2^{-k-3}$. In other words, we will use the first $k+3$ bits of y in applying the iteration. Then as long as $|\alpha| \leq 1/2$, we have

$$4\beta + 4\alpha\beta + \alpha^2\beta \leq 2^{-k-1} + 2^{-k-2} + 2^{-k-5}$$
$$\leq 2^{-k}.$$

Let us now consider the case in which the value inside the absolute value bars in (10.2) is negative. We can now ignore the first and third terms. We therefore need

$$y\alpha^2 + \gamma - \frac{2\alpha\beta}{y} \leq 2^{-k}.$$

Here, we can safely replace α by $-|\alpha|$. For fixed α, β, and γ in the resulting inequality, the first term is maximized when y is maximized, but the third term is maximized when y is minimized. It therefore suffices to ensure that

$$\alpha^2 + \gamma + 4|\alpha|\beta \leq 2^{-k}.$$

Again taking $\beta \leq 2^{-k-3}$, we only need $|\alpha| \leq 2^{-(k+1)/2}$ and $\gamma \leq 2^{-k-2}$. We then have

$$\alpha^2 + \gamma + 4|\alpha|\beta \leq 2^{-k-1} + 2^{-k-2} + 2^{k-1-(k+1)/2}$$
$$\leq 2^{-k},$$

provided $k \geq 1$.

We can satisfy the constraints on α and γ by finding an approximation within $2^{-\lceil (k+1)/2\rceil}$, and returning $k+3$ bits of the result of applying the iteration (recall that the result has one bit to the left of the radix point). Note that if we take k as the size of the problem instance, we are reducing the problem to an instance roughly half the original size. We therefore have a divide-and-conquer algorithm.

In order to complete the algorithm, we need to handle the base cases. Because $\lceil (k+1)/2\rceil < k$ only when $k > 2$, these cases occur for $k \leq 2$. It turns out that these cases are important for ensuring that the approximation is at least 1 and strictly less than 2. From (10.1), the result of the iteration is never more than $1/y$ (here y denotes the portion we are actually using in computing the iteration). Thus, if $y > 1/2$, the estimate is less than 2. Furthermore, if $y = 1/2$, an initial estimate less than 2 will ensure that some error remains, so that the result is still strictly less than 2. Finally, provided $\epsilon < 1$, the result is always closer to $1/y$ than the initial estimate. Thus, if we make sure that our base case gives a value that is less than 2 and no worse an estimate than 1 would be, the approximation will always be in the proper range.

We leave it as an exercise to show that the estimate

$$\frac{11 - \lfloor 8y \rfloor}{4}$$

satisfies the specification and the requirements discussed above for $k \leq 2$. $\lfloor 8y \rfloor$ is simply the first 3 bits of y. Because $1/2 \leq y < 1$, $4 \leq \lfloor 8y \rfloor < 8$. The numerator is therefore always a 3-bit natural number. The final division by 4 simply puts the radix point in the proper place.

The algorithm is shown in Figure 10.10. We use the variable *len* to store the value $k + 3$, which, except in the base case, is both the number of bits we use from y and the number of bits we return. We assume the existence of a constant **eleven** referring to a BIGNUM with value 11. Before we do the subtraction, we must make sure the radix points in the operands line up. The approximation x_0 has one bit to the left of the implicit radix point. The multiplication of x_0 by 2 simply moves the radix point to the right one place. As a result, the implicit radix point in $2x_0$ is $x_0.\text{NUMBITS}() - 2$ from the right in x_0. The implicit radix point in the product yx_0^2 is $len + 2(x_0.\text{NUMBITS}() - 1)$ bits from the right. In order for the radix points to line up, we therefore need to pad the value stored in x_0 with $len + x_0.\text{NUMBITS}()$ zeros prior to subtracting.

Let us now analyze the running time of RECIPNEWTON. Suppose we use a multiplication algorithm that runs in $O(M(n))$ time, where n is the number

---

Figure 10.10 Implementation of RECIPROCAL, specified in Figure 10.8, using Newton's method with divide-and-conquer

---

RECIPNEWTON(y, k)
  $n \leftarrow y.\text{NUMBITS}()$; $len \leftarrow k + 3$
  if $k \leq 2$
      return eleven.$\text{SUBTRACT}(y.\text{SHIFT}(3 - n))$
  else
      $x_0 \leftarrow \text{RECIPNEWTON}(y, \lceil (k + 1)/2 \rceil)$
      $y \leftarrow y.\text{SHIFT}(len - n)$
      $t \leftarrow x_0.\text{SHIFT}(len + x_0.\text{NUMBITS}())$
      $x_1 \leftarrow t.\text{SUBTRACT}(\text{MULTIPLY}(y, \text{MULTIPLY}(x_0, x_0)))$
      return $x_1.\text{SHIFT}(len - x_1.\text{NUMBITS}())$

of bits in the product. For now, we will assume that $M(n)$ is a smooth function in $\Omega(n)$, but we will strengthen this assumption as the analysis proceeds. It is easily seen that for $k \geq 3$, the number of bits returned by RECIPNEWTON is $k + 3$. Therefore, for $k \geq 4$, the worst-case number of bits in the first product is $2k + 6$. Because we use $k + 3$ bits of y, the worst-case number of bits in the second product is $3k + 9$. Because M is smooth, from Exercise 3.21, the time required for the two multiplications is in $O(M(k))$.

Because the remainder of the operations, excluding the recursive call, run in linear time, the total time excluding the recursive call is in $O(M(k))$. The total running time is therefore given by the recurrence

$$f(k) \in f\left(\left\lceil\frac{k+1}{2}\right\rceil\right) + O(M(k)),$$

for $k \geq 4$. We can simplify this recurrence by defining $f_1(k) = f(k + 1)$. Thus, for $k \geq 4$,

$$
\begin{aligned}
f_1(k) &= f(k+1) \\
&\in f\left(\left\lceil\frac{k+2}{2}\right\rceil\right) + O(M(k+1)) \\
&= f\left(\left\lceil\frac{k}{2}\right\rceil + 1\right) + O(M(k+1)) \\
&= f_1(\lceil k/2 \rceil) + O(M(k+1)) \\
&= f_1(\lceil k/2 \rceil) + O(M(k)),
\end{aligned}
$$

because M is smooth.

In order to be able to apply Theorem 3.35 to f_1, we need additional assumptions on M. We therefore assume that $M(k) = k^q g(k)$, where $q \geq 1$ and $g_1(k) = g(2^{k+2})$ is smooth. (Note that the functions $k^{\lg 3}$ and $k \lg k \lg \lg k$ both satisfy these assumptions on M.) Then from Theorem 3.35, $f_1(k) \in O(M(k))$. Because M is smooth, $f(k) = f_1(k - 1) \in O(M(k))$.

We can now analyze the running time of DIVIDERECIP. If $m < n$, the running time is clearly in $\Theta(1)$. Suppose $m \geq n$. Then the value r returned by RECIPROCAL$(v, m - n)$ has $m - n + 3$ bits in the worst case. Hence, the result of the first multiplication has $2m - n + 3$ bits in the worst case. The worst-case running time of this multiplication is therefore in $O(M(m))$. q then has $m - n + 1$ bits in the worst case. The result of the second multiplication therefore has $m + 1$ bits in the worst case, and hence runs in $O(M(m))$ time. Because RECIPROCAL runs in $O(M(m - n))$ time, and the remaining operations run in $O(m)$ time, the overall running time is in $O(M(m))$. The running time for DIVIDERECIP is therefore the same as for multiplication, even if our multiplication algorithm runs in $O(n \lg n \lg \lg n)$ time.

10.7 Summary

The divide-and-conquer technique involves reducing large instances of a problem to one or more smaller instances, each of which is a fraction of the size of the original problem. The running time of the resulting algorithm can typically be analyzed by deriving a recurrence to which Theorem 3.35 applies. Theorem 3.35 can also suggest how to improve a divide-and-conquer algorithm.

Some variations of the divide-and-conquer technique don't completely fit the above description. For example, quick sort does not necessarily produce subproblems whose sizes are a fraction of the size of the original array. As a result, Theorem 3.35 does not apply. However, we still consider quick sort to be a divide-and-conquer algorithm because its goal is to partition an array into two arrays of approximately half the size of the input array, and to sort these arrays recursively. Likewise, in LINEARSELECT, the sizes of the two recursive calls are very different, but because they are both fractions of the original size, the analysis ends up being related to that of a more standard divide-and-conquer algorithm. Finally, DIVIDEDC does not divide the problem into a bounded number of subproblems; however, all of the recursive calls in turn yield at most two recursive calls, so we can analyze these calls using standard divide-and-conquer techniques.

10.8 Exercises

Exercise 10.1. Prove that POLYMULT, shown in Figure 10.1, meets its specification.

Exercise 10.2. POLYMULT is not particularly efficient when one polynomial has a degree much larger than that of the other. For example, if p has degree n and q has degree 1, a straightforward implementation of the definition of the product yields $\Theta(n)$ running time. Devise an algorithm that runs in $\Theta(mn^{\lg 3 - 1})$ time on polynomials of degree m and n with $m \geq n$. Your algorithm may use POLYMULT. Analyze the running time of your algorithm. [**_Hint:_** If $m > n$, divide the larger polynomial into polynomials of degree at most n.]

* Exercise 10.3. Construct a divide-and-conquer polynomial multiplication algorithm that performs 5 recursive calls on polynomials of 1/3 the size of the original polynomials. Show that your algorithm has a running time in $\Theta(n^{\log_3 5})$. (Note that $\log_3 5 < \lg 3$.)

** Exercise 10.4. Generalize Exercise 10.3 by showing that for sufficiently large n and any $k \geq 2$, the product of two degree-$(n-1)$ polynomials can be computed from the products of $2k - 1$ polynomials of degree approximately $(n/k) - 1$. Using this result, show that for any $\epsilon \in \mathbb{R}^{>0}$, there is an algorithm to multiply two degree-$(n - 1)$ polynomials in $O(n^{1+\epsilon})$ time.

Exercise 10.5. Adapt POLYMULT to implement MULTIPLY, as specified in Figure 10.6, in $\Theta(n^{\lg 3})$ time, where n is the number of bits in the product.

Exercise 10.6. Prove that MERGESORT, shown in Figure 10.2, meets its specification.

Exercise 10.7. Suppose we are given a tape containing a large number of KEYED items to be sorted. The number of items is too large to fit into main memory, but we have three additional tapes we can use, and we can rewrite the input tape. Give a bottom-up version of merge sort that produces the sorted output on one of the tapes. You may not assume that data items on the tapes can be accessed "randomly" — they must be accessed in sequence. Your algorithm must make at most $O(\lg n)$ passes through each tape.

Exercise 10.8. Prove that QUICKSORT, shown in Figure 10.3, meets its specification.

Exercise 10.9. Notice that one of the recursive calls in QUICKSORT is tail recursion. Taking advantage of this fact, convert one of the recursive calls to iteration. Notice that the calls can be made in either order, and so either may be converted to iteration. Make the proper choice so that the resulting algorithm uses $\Theta(\lg n)$ stack space in the worst case on an array of n elements.

Exercise 10.10. Suppose we modify QUICKSORT by introducing a second parameter d giving the depth of recursion and a third parameter giving the length N of the entire array (not just the portion currently being sorted). Then prior to selecting the pivot element, if $d \geq 2 \lg N$, instead of sorting using the given algorithm, sort $A[lo..hi]$ using a $\Theta(n \lg n)$ algorithm such as heap sort or merge sort. Show that this modification results in an algorithm that runs in $\Theta(n \lg n)$ in the worst case, even if $A[lo]$ is always used as the pivot element.

* **Exercise 10.11.** The goal of this exercise is to prove Theorem 10.1.

a. For $x \leq y$, let $[x, y]$ denote the set of all real numbers a such that $x \leq a \leq y$. For natural numbers $m < n$, let $f : [m, n] \to \mathbb{R}^{\geq 0}$ be a continuous function such that whenever $m \leq x < y \leq n$, $f(x) \geq f(y)$ (i.e., f is nonincreasing). Prove that

$$\sum_{i=m+1}^{n} f(i) \leq \int_{m}^{n} f(x)dx \leq \sum_{i=m}^{n-1} f(i).$$

b. Use the result of part (a). to prove Theorem 10.1.

Exercise 10.12. Prove that for an array of size n, QUICKSORT (shown in Figure 10.3) makes a total of at most $n + 1$ calls (including the initial call and all recursive calls, as appropriate) in which $lo \geq hi$.

Exercise 10.13. A randomized algorithm for the selection problem can be obtained by replacing the the first assignment statement of SELECTBY-MEDIAN (Figure 2.7 on page 42) with the statement:

$$p \leftarrow A[\text{RANDOMINTEGER}(1, n)]$$

Show that the expected running time of this algorithm is in $\Theta(n)$. [***Hint:*** Your analysis should be similar to the analysis of QUICKSORT in Section 10.3.]

Exercise 10.14. Let $n_0 \geq 1$ and $m \geq 1$ be integers, let q be a positive real number, and let $c_1, \ldots, c_m$ be positive real numbers such that

$$\sum_{i=1}^{m} c_i^q < 1.$$

Let $f : \mathbb{N} \to \mathbb{R}^{\geq 0}$ be an eventually non-decreasing function satisfying

$$f(n) \in \sum_{i=1}^{m} f(\lfloor c_i n \rfloor) + X(n^q)$$

whenever $n \geq n_0$, where X is either O, Ω, or Θ. Prove that $f(n) \in X(n^q)$.

* **Exercise 10.15.** Let $n_0 \geq 1$ and $m \geq 2$ be integers, let q be a positive real number, and let $c_1, \ldots, c_m$ be positive real numbers such that

$$\sum_{i=1}^{m} c_i^q = 1.$$

Let $f : \mathbb{N} \to \mathbb{R}^{\geq 0}$ be an eventually non-decreasing function satisfying

$$f(n) \in \sum_{i=1}^{m} f(\lfloor c_i n \rfloor) + O(n^q)$$

whenever $n \geq n_0$. Prove that $f(n) \in O(n^q \lg n)$.

Exercise 10.16. Prove that LINEARSELECT, shown in Figure 10.5, meets the specification given in Figure 1.2 (p. 7).

Exercise 10.17. Determine the number of comparisons used by each of the following algorithms when sorting 4 elements.

a. INSERTIONSORT, shown in Figure 1.7 on page 12.
b. MERGESORT, shown in Figure 10.2.

Exercise 10.18. Repeat Exercise 10.17 for 5 elements.

Exercise 10.19. Show that it is possible to find either the smallest or largest of n elements using at most $n - 1$ comparisons.

* Exercise 10.20. Show that it is possible to find either the second largest or second smallest of n elements using at most $n + \lceil \lg n \rceil - 2$ comparisons.

* Exercise 10.21. Show that it is possible to find the median of five elements using at most six comparisons.

* Exercise 10.22. Prove that DIVIDEDC, shown in Figure 10.7, meets is specification as given in Figure 10.6.

Exercise 10.23. Prove that DIVIDERECIP, shown in Figure 10.8, meets its specification as given in Figure 10.6.

* Exercise 10.24. Let $1/2 \leq y < 1$.

a. Show that if

$$x_0 = \frac{11 - \lfloor 8y \rfloor}{4},$$

then

$$\left| \frac{1}{y} - x_0 \right| \leq \frac{1}{4}.$$

b. Show that if x_0 is as defined in part 10.24, then

$$\left| \frac{1}{y} - x_0 \right| \leq \left| \frac{1}{y} - 1 \right|.$$

c. Prove that RECIPNEWTON meets is specification as given in Figure 10.8.

Figure 10.11   Additional functions for BigNums

Precondition: u is a BigNum and k is a Nat.
Postcondition: Returns a BigNum representing the value of u^k. We assume that $0^0 = 1$.

Power(u, k)

Precondition: u is a BigNum.
Postcondition: Returns a String (see Figure 4.17 and Exercise 4.13) containing the decimal representation u.

ToString(u)

Exercise 10.25. Design a divide-and-conquer algorithm that implements Power as specified in Figure 10.11. Your algorithm should run in $O(M(n))$ time, where n is the number of bits in the result and $M(n)$ is the time needed for Multiply when the product contains n bits. You may make reasonable assumptions about $M(n)$, provided $n^{\lg 3}$ and $n \lg n \lg \lg n$ satisfy these assumptions.

* Exercise 10.26. Design a divide-and-conquer algorithm that implements ToString as specified in Figure 10.11. Your algorithm should run in $O(n^q)$ time, where n is the number of bits in u, assuming Multiply needs $O(n^q)$ time to produce an n-bit product. You may assume q is a real number strictly larger than 1.

* Exercise 10.27. Given two natural numbers u and v which are not both 0, the *greatest common divisor* of u and v (or $\gcd(u, v)$) is the largest integer that evenly divides both u and v.

a. Prove that for any positive integers u and v, $\gcd(u, v) = \gcd(v, u \bmod v)$.
b. Design a divide-and-conquer algorithm that takes as input two positive integers u and v and returns $\gcd(u, v)$. Your algorithm should run in $O(\lg \max(u, v))$ time.

* Exercise 10.28. Given two positive integers u and m such that $u < m$, a *multiplicative inverse* of $u \bmod m$ is any positive integer v such that $1 \leq v < m$ and $(uv) \bmod m = 1$.

a. Prove that for any positive integers u and v, there exist integers a and b such that $au + bv = \gcd(u, v)$.

b. Prove that u has a multiplicative inverse mod m iff $\gcd(u, m) = 1$. [***Hint:*** See Lemma 7.4 on page 267.]

c. Prove that for $1 \leq u < m$, u has at most one multiplicative inverse mod m.

d. Give a efficient divide-and-conquer algorithm that takes as input positive integers u and m such that $u < m$ and returns the multiplicative inverse of u mod m, or nil if no inverse exists. Your algorithm should run in $O(\lg m)$ time. [***Hint:*** Modify the algorithm for Exercise 10.27 to find a and b as described in part (a).]

Exercise 10.29. The *Manhattan Skyline Problem* can be stated as follows. We are given a description of n rectangular buildings on the horizon. Each description is a triple, $\langle l_i, w_i, h_i \rangle$, where l_i is the x-coordinate of the building's left-hand edge, w_i is the width of the building, and h_i is the height above the horizon of the building's roof. (Note that the buildings may overlap.) We wish to construct the skyline produced by these buildings. The skyline is represented by a sequence of points $\langle (x_1, y_1), \ldots, (x_k, y_k) \rangle$, ordered by x-coordinate, representing the locations where a vertical segment of the skyline meets a horizontal segment leading to the right (see Figure 10.12). Note that the value of y_k must always be 0. Give a divide-and-conquer

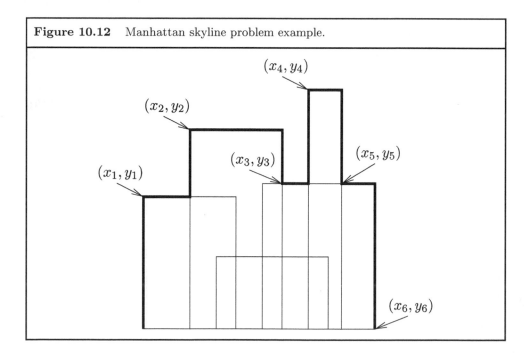

Figure 10.12   Manhattan skyline problem example.

algorithm to compute the Manhattan skyline, and show that your algorithm runs in $\Theta(n \lg n)$ time.

Exercise 10.30. A *majority element* of an array $A[1..n]$ is an element that occurs more than $n/2$ times in the array. Construct an efficient divide-and-conquer algorithm to find the majority element of A if one exists. Your algorithm may only compare elements for equality (hence, it may not sort the elements). Analyze the worst-case running time of your algorithm. ($\Theta(n)$ is possible.)

Exercise 10.31. Give a divide-and-conquer algorithm to construct a round-robin tournament involving n competitors. The tournament consists of a series of rounds. In each round, every competitor plays one other competitor if n is even; if n is odd, exactly one competitor is idle each round. Every competitor must play every other competitor exactly once in the tournament. Therefore, the number of rounds is $n-1$ if n is even, or n if n is odd. Let the competitors be identified by the natural numbers $0, \ldots, n-1$. Your algorithm should produce a 2D array A of natural numbers such that $A[i, j]$ indicates j's opponent in round i; if j is idle in round i, $A[i, j]$ should be n. Your algorithm should run in $\Theta(n^2)$ time. A possible output for $n = 5$ is shown below.

	0	1	2	3	4
0	1	0	5	4	3
1	2	4	0	5	1
2	3	2	1	0	5
3	4	5	3	2	0
4	5	3	4	1	2

* Exercise 10.32. Give a $\Theta(n \lg n)$ divide-and-conquer algorithm for determining the closest pair of points in a given collection. You may assume that the points are given via two arrays: $x[1..n]$ and $y[1..n]$, where $n \geq 2$. The n points are then $(x[1], y[1]), (x[2], y[2]), \ldots, (x[n], y[n])$. The distance between a pair of points (x, y) and (x', y') is given by

$$\sqrt{(x - x')^2 + (y - y')^2}.$$

Your algorithm should return the minimum distance separating any two distinct points.

* Exercise 10.33. Give a divide-and-conquer algorithm for computing $\lfloor\sqrt{n}\rfloor$, where n is a BIGNUM. Your algorithm's running time should be in $O(M(\lg n))$, where $M(n)$ is as defined in Section 10.6.

** Exercise 10.34. Give a $\Theta(n^{\lg 7})$ divide-and-conquer algorithm for multiplying two $n \times n$ matrices of real numbers. [**Hint:** Find a way to multiply two 2×2 matrices using only 7 scalar multiplications. Use this technique as the basis for a divide-and-conquer algorithm.]

* Exercise 10.35. A *Hamiltonian path* in a (directed or undirected) graph is a path that contains each vertex exactly once. A directed graph is said to be *complete* if for each pair of distinct vertices i and j, either (i, j) or (j, i) is an edge in the graph. It turns out that every complete directed graph has a Hamiltonian path. Give a divide-and-conquer algorithm that finds a Hamiltonian path in a given complete directed graph. Your algorithm should run in $O(n \lg n)$ time in the worst case, where n is the number of vertices in the graph, assuming the graph is implemented as a MATRIXGRAPH.

10.9   Notes

The POLYMULT algorithm is based on a $\Theta(n^{\lg 3})$ large-integer multiplication algorithm by Karatsuba and Ofman [76]. The DIVIDEDC algorithm is due to Burnikel and Ziegler [18]. The RECIPNEWTON algorithm is a top-down adaptation of an algorithm given by Knuth [83]; he credits the idea to Cook. Solutions to Exercises 10.3, 10.4, 10.25, and 10.26, can be found in Knuth [83].

Merge sort was one of the earliest algorithms developed for electronic computers, being developed by von Neumann in 1945 [80,114]. Exercise 10.7 is based on work by Eckert and Mauchly [34]. Quick sort was developed by Hoare [62]. Introsort was developed by Musser [95]. Pattern-defeating quicksort, or pdqsort, is an important variation of introsort developed by Peters [98].

Algorithm LINEARSELECT is due to Blum, *et al.* [14]. The solution to Exercise 10.20 is due to Aigner [4].

The solution to Exercise 10.32 is due to Bentley [11]. The solution to Exercise 10.34 is due to Strassen [109].

Chapter 11

Optimization I: Greedy Algorithms

In this chapter and the next, we consider algorithms for *optimization* problems. We have already seen an example of an optimization problem — the maximum subsequence sum problem from Chapter 1. We can characterize optimization problems as admitting a set of *candidate solutions*. In the maximum subsequence sum problem, the candidate solutions are the contiguous subsequences in the input array. An *objective function* then typically maps these candidate solutions to numeric values. The objective function for the maximum subsequence sum problem maps each contiguous subsequence to its sum. The goal is to find a candidate solution that either maximizes or minimizes, depending on the problem, the objective function. Thus, the goal of the maximum subsequence problem is to find a candidate solution that maximizes the objective function.

In this chapter, we will examine optimization problems which admit *greedy* solutions. A greedy algorithm builds a specific candidate solution incrementally. The aspect of a greedy algorithm that makes it "greedy" is how it chooses from among the different ways of incrementing the current partial solution. In general, the different choices are ordered according to some criterion, and the best choice according to this criterion is taken. Thus, the algorithm builds the solution by always taking the step that appears to be most promising at that moment. Though there are many problems for which greedy strategies do not produce optimal solutions, when they do, they tend to be quite efficient. In the next chapter, we will examine a more general technique for solving optimization problems when greedy strategies fail.

11.1   Job Scheduling

Consider the job scheduling problem discussed in Chapter 8. Recall that we are given n jobs, each requiring one unit of execution time and having its own deadline. Suppose that, in addition, each job has a positive integer *value*. We wish to schedule the jobs on a single server so as to maximize the total value of those jobs which meet their deadlines. Because jobs which do not meet their deadlines do not contribute any value, we will assume that no jobs are scheduled after their deadlines — if a job can't meet its deadline, we simply don't schedule it. At this point, we are not assuming any particular scheduling strategy, such as the one given in Chapter 8; instead, we are trying to find an optimal strategy.

In deriving a greedy algorithm in a top-down fashion, the first step is to generalize the problem so that a partial solution is given as input. We assume as a precondition that this partial solution can be extended to an optimal solution. Our task is then to extend it in some way so that the resulting partial solution can be extended to an optimal solution. If we characterize the size of such an instance as the difference between the size of a complete solution and the given partial solution, we will have reduced a large instance to a smaller instance.

The input to the generalized scheduling problem is a set $X = \{x_1, \ldots, x_m\}$ of jobs and a partial schedule *sched* of these jobs. To be more precise, let *sched*$[1..n]$ be an array of natural numbers such that if *sched*$[t] = 0$, then no job has been scheduled in the time slot ending at time t; otherwise, if *sched*$[t] = i$, then job x_i is scheduled in this time slot. If all the jobs in X either have been scheduled or cannot be scheduled, we are finished — the precondition that this schedule can be extended to an optimal schedule implies that it must be an optimal schedule. Otherwise, our task is to schedule some job x_i so that the resulting partial schedule can be extended to a schedule of maximum value. If we take the size of a partial schedule to be the number of unscheduled jobs in X, we will have reduced a large instance to a smaller instance.

We must now decide upon the criterion to use to extend a partial schedule. Of the remaining jobs that can meet their deadlines, it would make sense to schedule the one with the highest value. Furthermore, in order to impact the fewest deadlines of other jobs, it would make sense to schedule it as late as possible. In what follows, we will show that this selection criterion always results in an optimal schedule.

In order to simplify reasoning about this strategy, let us observe that because we will not be changing any scheduling decisions that have already been made, the values of the jobs scheduled so far have no effect on future decisions — their values are simply added to the total value of the schedule. As a result, all we really need to know about the schedule constructed so far is what time slots are still available. Furthermore, maximizing the values of jobs scheduled in the remaining slots will maximize the total value, because the values of all scheduled jobs are simply added together.

We can therefore focus our attention on the following version of the problem. The input consists of a set X of (unscheduled) jobs and an array avail$[1..n]$ of boolean values. A valid schedule either assigns a job x_i into a time slot t such that t is no more than the deadline of x_i and avail$[t] =$ true, or it does not schedule x_i. The goal is to maximize the total value of scheduled jobs. The following theorem shows that an optimal schedule can be constructed by selecting the job with maximum value and scheduling it at the latest possible time, assuming it can be scheduled.

Theorem 11.1. *Let* $X = \{x_1, \ldots, x_m\}$ *be a set of jobs, and let* avail$[1..n]$ *be an array of boolean values indicating the time slots at which jobs may be scheduled. Let* x_k *be a job having maximum value, and suppose there is some* t *no greater than the deadline of* x_k *such that* avail$[t] =$ true. *Let* t_0 *be the maximum such* t. *Then there is an optimal schedule in which* x_k *is scheduled at the time slot ending at time* t_0.

Proof. Let *sched*$[1..n]$ be an optimal schedule and suppose *sched*$[t_0] \neq k$. We consider two cases.

Case 1: *sched*$[t_1] = k$. Because t_0 is the latest available time slot for x_k, $t_1 < t_0$. Therefore, by swapping the values of *sched*$[t_1]$ and *sched*$[t_0]$, we violate no deadlines and do not change the value of the schedule. The resulting schedule must therefore be optimal.

Case 2: x_k is not scheduled in *sched*. Let $j =$ *sched*$[t_0]$. We first observe that $j \neq 0$, because in this case we could obtain a schedule with higher value by scheduling x_k in *sched*$[t_0]$. Because x_k is a job having maximum value, the value of x_k is at least the value of x_j. Therefore, by scheduling x_k at *sched*$[t_0]$ instead of x_j, we retain an optimal schedule. $\square$

Theorem 11.1 tells us that our greedy strategy results in an optimal schedule. To implement this strategy, we need to consider the jobs in non-increasing order of their values, and schedule each schedulable job at the latest time possible. Therefore, we should first sort the jobs in non-increasing order of their values. Using heap sort or merge sort, this can be done in $\Theta(m \lg m)$ time. SCHEDULE, shown in Figure 8.2, then implements the greedy strategy. Because SCHEDULE can be implemented to run in $O(n + m \lg n)$ time, if $m \in \Theta(n)$, the entire algorithm runs in $\Theta(n \lg n)$ time.

11.2 Minimum-Cost Spanning Trees

Suppose we wish to construct a communications network connecting a given set of nodes. Given the distances separating each pair of nodes, we wish to find the network topology that connects all of the nodes using as little cable as possible.

We can state the above problem as a graph problem. In Exercise 9.6, we defined a *tree* to be connected, acyclic, undirected graph. (Note that a tree is different from a rooted tree as defined on page 154, though we can form a rooted tree from a tree by selecting any vertex as the root.) Given a connected undirected graph $G = (V, E)$, a *spanning tree* is a tree (V, T) such that $T \subseteq E$; i.e., a spanning tree is a tree consisting of all of the vertices of G and a subset of the edges. Let $cost : E \to \mathbb{N}$ give a cost for each edge. We wish to find a *minimum-cost spanning tree (MST)* for G — i.e., a spanning tree whose edges have minimum total cost.

In order to develop a greedy algorithm, we first generalize the problem so that a portion of an MST is given as input. This partial MST will be a subset $E' \subseteq E$ such that (V, E') is acyclic, but not necessarily connected. In order to keep the cost as small as possible, we will use as our selection criterion the cost of the edge; i.e., we will always select a least-cost edge that does not introduce a cycle.

We need to show that the above strategy will result in an MST. In order to state the theorem that guarantees this fact, we need one definition. Let $G = (V, E)$ be an undirected graph. A *connected component* of G is any connected subset $C \subseteq V$ such that no vertex in C is adjacent to any vertex in $V \setminus C$. Thus, the connected component containing a vertex v is the set of all vertices reachable from v using zero or more edges. We can now state the following theorem, which validates our selection strategy.

Theorem 11.2. *Let $G = (V, E)$ be a connected undirected graph with cost function* cost $: E \to \mathbb{N}$, *and let $E' \subset E$ be such that for some MST (V, T) of G, $E' \subseteq T$. Suppose that (V, E') is not connected, and let C be a connected component of (V, E'). If $\{u, v\} \in E \setminus E'$ is a minimum-cost edge such that $u \in C$ and $v \notin C$, then there is an MST of G containing all the edges in $E' \cup \{\{u, v\}\}$.*

Before we prove Theorem 11.2, we note that it is stronger than we require. We state it in this way in order to justify a second greedy algorithm, which we will discuss a bit later. Note, however, that a minimum-cost edge that does not introduce a cycle certainly qualifies as the edge $\{u, v\}$ in the statement of the theorem.

Proof of Theorem 11.2. If $\{u, v\} \in T$, then there is nothing to show. Suppose $\{u, v\} \notin T$. We will show how to construct a set T' such that $E' \cup \{\{u, v\}\} \subseteq T'$ and (V, T') is an MST.

Because (V, T) is a tree, there is a path from u to v in T. However, this path cannot contain the edge $\{u, v\}$, because $\{u, v\} \notin T$. This path must therefore consist of:

- a (possibly empty) path in C from u to some vertex w;
- an edge $\{w, x\}$, where $x \notin C$; and
- a (possibly empty) path from x to v.

Note that even though either path above might be empty, they cannot both be empty, or we would have $\{w, x\} = \{u, v\}$. By the choice of $\{u, v\}$, cost$(\{w, x\}) \geq$ cost$(\{u, v\})$. Let $T' = (T \cup \{\{u, v\}\}) \setminus \{\{w, x\}\}$. Then the total cost of T' is no more than the total cost of T. From Exercise 9.6 a, T, and hence T', has exactly $|V| - 1$ edges. Furthermore, (V, T') is connected, as any path in T that contains $\{w, x\}$ can be modified to use the edge $\{u, v\}$ and the paths from u to w and x to v in T. From Exercise 9.6 b, (V, T') is a tree. Because its cost is no more than the cost of the MST (V, T), (V, T') is an MST containing all of the edges in $E' \cup \{\{u, v\}\}$. $\qquad\square$

In order to implement this algorithm, we need an efficient way to determine whether two vertices belong to the same connected component of (V, E'), where E' is the set of edges we have collected so far. The connected components form disjoint subsets of V. We can therefore maintain these connected components using a DISJOINTSETS structure. In order

---

Figure 11.1 Kruskal's algorithm for finding an MST

Precondition: G refers to a GRAPH which is undirected and connected, and whose edges contain their costs as data.

Postcondition: Returns a CONSLIST of EDGEs representing an MST of G. Each edge will occur once in the list.

KRUSKAL(G)
$\quad$ $n \leftarrow G$.SIZE(); $comp \leftarrow$ **new** DISJOINTSETS(n)
$\quad$ $q \leftarrow$ **new** INVERTEDPRIORITYQUEUE(); $T \leftarrow$ **new** CONSLIST()
$\quad$ **for** $i \leftarrow 0$ **to** $n - 1$
$\quad\quad$ $L \leftarrow G$.ALLFROM(i)
$\quad\quad$ **while not** L.ISEMPTY()
$\quad\quad\quad$ $e \leftarrow L$.HEAD(); q.PUT(e, e.DATA()); $L \leftarrow L$.TAIL()
$\quad$ // **Invariant:** T is a subset of the edges of an MST of G, the sets in
$\quad$ // $comp$ are the connected components of T, and q contains a subset of
$\quad$ // the edges of G ordered by cost, including at least all $\{u, v\}$ such that
$\quad$ // u and v are in different sets in $comp$.
$\quad$ **while not** q.ISEMPTY()
$\quad\quad$ $e \leftarrow q$.REMOVEMIN()
$\quad\quad$ $c_1 \leftarrow comp$.FIND(e.SOURCE()); $c_2 \leftarrow comp$.FIND(e.DEST())
$\quad\quad$ **if** $c_1 \neq c_2$
$\quad\quad\quad$ $T \leftarrow$ **new** CONSLIST(e, T); $comp$.MERGE(c_1, c_2)
$\quad$ **return** T

---

to determine whether u and v belong to the same component, we see if FIND(u) = FIND(v). If not, we include $\{u, v\}$ and merge the two components.

The algorithm, known as Kruskal's algorithm, is shown in Figure 11.1. Note that in using an INVERTEDPRIORITYQUEUE, we process the edges in nondecreasing order of cost. We could have achieved the same effect by sorting the edges by cost, but this presentation is somewhat simpler, and in fact amounts to sorting the edges with heap sort.

For the purpose of analyzing KRUSKAL, let n be the number of vertices in G, and let a be the number of edges. Let us first assume that G is implemented using LISTGRAPH. In the initialization code preceding the first loop, $\Theta(n)$ time is required to construct a new DISJOINTSETS structure, whereas the other operations each run in $\Theta(1)$ time. The **for** loop with the nested **while** simply traverses G in a manner similar to the loops found in TOPSORT (Figure 9.6). If we ignore for the moment the cost of the PUT operations on q, we see that this nested structure runs in $\Theta(n+a)$ time. Each edge is inserted into q; hence, because INVERTEDPRIORITYQUEUE.PUT runs in $\Theta(\lg i)$ time when there are i elements in the queue, the total time for all insertions is in $\Theta(a \lg a)$. Because G is connected, $n - 1 \le a \le n(n - 1)/2$. Furthermore, $\lg(n(n-1)/2) < 2 \lg n$, so that $\Theta(n+a) + \Theta(a \lg a) = \Theta(a \lg n)$. The last **while** loop is easily seen to run in $\Theta(a \lg n)$ time as well.

If G is implemented using MATRIXGRAPH, the ALLFROM operation requires $\Theta(n)$ time, so that the **for** loop requires $\Theta(n^2)$. The total running time is therefore in $\Theta(n^2 + a \lg n)$, which is worse than $\Theta(a \lg n)$ for sufficiently sparse graphs (i.e., when $a \in o(n^2/\lg n)$). Kruskal's algorithm therefore tends to be better-suited for the LISTGRAPH implementation, particularly when the graph is sparse.

As we suggested earlier, Kruskal's algorithm isn't the only greedy algorithm for finding MSTs. We arrive at a different algorithm if we generalize the original problem in a slightly different way. Rather than allowing our input to consist of any set of edges that can be extended to an MST, we instead require that this set of edges form a spanning tree on some subset of the vertices. Thus, when we add an edge, it must extend this spanning tree to another vertex; i.e., it must connect a vertex in the spanning tree to one that is not in the spanning tree. Our selection criterion will be to select such an edge having minimum cost. Theorem 11.2 tells us that such a strategy results in an MST.

The data structures needed to implement this algorithm, which is known as Prim's algorithm, are simpler than those needed to implement Kruskal's algorithm. We need to partition the vertices into two disjoint sets — the set of vertices in the spanning tree and those not in the spanning tree. A boolean array $inTree[0..n - 1]$ will suffice for this purpose. For each vertex k not in the spanning tree, we need an efficient way to find a least-cost edge $\{i, k\}$ such that i is in the spanning tree. For this purpose, we use two arrays:

- an array $bestCost[1..n - 1]$ such that if k is not in the spanning tree, then $bestCost[k]$ is the minimum cost of any edge to k from a vertex in the spanning tree, or ∞ if there is no such edge; and
- an array $best[1..n - 1]$ such that if k is not in the spanning tree and $bestCost[k] \ne \infty$, then $\{best[k], k\}$ is a least-cost edge from the spanning tree to k.

The spanning tree will initially contain only the vertex 0; hence, it is unnecessary to include the index 0 for the arrays $best$ and $bestCost$. We can then initialize each $best[k]$ to 0 and each $bestCost[k]$ to the cost of edge $\{0, k\}$, or to ∞ if there is no such edge. In order to find an edge to add to the spanning tree we can find the minimum $bestCost[k]$ such that k is not in the spanning tree. If we denote this index by $next$, then the edge

---

Figure 11.2 Prim's algorithm for finding an MST

Precondition: G refers to a GRAPH which is undirected and connected, and whose edges contain their costs as data.

Postcondition: Returns a CONSLIST of EDGEs representing an MST of G. Each edge will occur once in the list.

PRIM(G)
    $n \leftarrow G.\text{SIZE}()$; *inTree* $\leftarrow$ **new** ARRAY$[0..n-1]$; *inTree*$[0] \leftarrow$ true
    best $\leftarrow$ **new** ARRAY$[1..n-1]$; *bestCost* $\leftarrow$ **new** ARRAY$[1..n-1]$
    $T \leftarrow$ **new** CONSLIST()
    for $k \leftarrow 1$ **to** $n-1$
        inTree$[k] \leftarrow$ false; *best*$[k] \leftarrow 0$; *bestCost*$[k] \leftarrow G.\text{GET}(0, k)$
        if *bestCost*$[k] =$ *nil*
            bestCost$[k] \leftarrow \infty$
    // **Invariant:** T contains *count* edges forming a spanning tree for the
    // vertices k such that *inTree*$[k]$ is true, and there is an MST of G
    // containing all of the edges in T. For each k such that *inTree*$[k]$ is false,
    // *bestCost*$[k]$ is the minimum cost of any edge $\{i, k\}$ such that *inTree*$[i]$
    // is true, or ∞ if there is no such edge. For each k such that *inTree*$[k]$
    // is false and *bestCost*$[k] \neq \infty$, $\{$*best*$[k], k\}$ is a least-cost edge
    // leading to k from any vertex i such that *inTree*$[i]$ is true.
    for *count* $\leftarrow 0$ **to** $n-2$
        $m \leftarrow \infty$
        for $k \leftarrow 1$ **to** $n-1$
            if not *inTree*$[k]$ **and** *bestCost*$[k] < m$
                next $\leftarrow k$; $m \leftarrow$ *bestCost*$[k]$
        $e \leftarrow$ **new** EDGE(*best*$[next]$, *next*, m)
        $T \leftarrow$ **new** CONSLIST(e, T); *inTree*$[next] \leftarrow$ true
        for $k \leftarrow 1$ **to** $n-1$
            if not *inTree*$[k]$
                $d \leftarrow G.\text{GET}(next, k)$
                if $d \neq$ *nil* **and** $d <$ *bestCost*$[k]$
                    best$[k] \leftarrow$ *next*; *bestCost*$[k] \leftarrow d$
    return T

$\{$*best*$[next]$, *next*$\}$ is the next edge to be added, thus connecting *next* to the spanning tree. For each k that is still not in the spanning tree, we must then update *bestCost*$[k]$ by comparing it to the cost of $\{$*next*, $k\}$, and update *best*[k] accordingly. The algorithm is shown in Figure 11.2.

It is easily seen that if G is a MATRIXGRAPH, the running time is in $\Theta(n^2)$. This is an improvement over Kruskal's algorithm when a MATRIXGRAPH is used. If a LISTGRAPH is used, however, the running time is still in $\Omega(n^2)$, and can be as bad as $\Theta(n^3)$ for dense graphs. Thus, Kruskal's algorithm is preferred when a LISTGRAPH is used, but Prim's algorithm is preferred when a MATRIXGRAPH is used. If we have the freedom of choosing the GRAPH implementation, we should choose a LISTGRAPH and Kruskal's algorithm for sparse graphs, but a MATRIXGRAPH and Prim's algorithm for dense graphs.

11.3   Single-Source Shortest Paths

Consider a route finding program that we might find online or within GPS software. There are typically many possible routes leading from a given starting point to a given destination, but the software will typically try to optimize a particular objective function such as the total expected time. We can model such a problem as an instance of a shortest path problem. We model the various road segments as edges of a directed graph G whose vertices are the road intersections. We represent the starting point with a start vertex u and the destination with an end vertex v. A cost (representing, for example, the expected time) is associated with each edge. We wish to find a least-cost path from u to v in G.

We will use the term *length* to refer to the cost of an edge, regardless of what kind of cost is being represented. A least-cost path is then a shortest path. We will assume that edge lengths are positive integers. Note that if we have found a shortest path from u to v, and if vertex w occurs on this path, then the subpath from u to w is also a shortest path from u to w. As a result, when we find a shortest path from u to v, we typically find many other shortest paths from u as well. For this reason, it simplifies the discussion to generalize the problem to that of finding, for every vertex w, a shortest path from u to w.

We first observe that for each vertex $w \neq u$, if we consider only a single shortest path from u to w, then there is a unique predecessor x of w on this path. Furthermore, we can select the shortest paths in such a way that x precedes w on any shortest path on which w occurs. Thus, for each vertex in G, there is a unique sequence of these predecessors leading back to u. This predecessor relationship therefore gives the parent relationship of a tree rooted at u. This rooted tree can be used to represent the shortest paths.

Let us now generalize the problem so that a tree T rooted at u and containing a subset of the edges and vertices of the graph is provided as additional input. Suppose that this tree is a proper subtree of a shortest path tree; i.e., suppose that for each vertex w in the tree, the path from u to w in the tree is a shortest path from u to w in G. We need to add a vertex x

and an edge (w, x), where w is a vertex in T, so that the path from u to x in the resulting tree is a shortest path in G from u to x.

For each vertex w in T, let d_w give the length of the path from u to w in T. For each edge (x, y) in G, let $len(x, y)$ give the length of (x, y). Let (w, x) be an edge in G such that

- w is in T;
- x is not in T; and
- $d_w + len(w, x)$ is minimized.

Clearly, the path from u to w in T, followed by the edge (w, x) is a shortest path from u to x in G, as there can be no shorter paths from u to any vertex not in T.

Building a shortest path tree in this way is very similar to the way Prim's algorithm builds an MST. While Prim's algorithm is for undirected graphs, this algorithm — Dijkstra's algorithm — is for directed graphs. The computation for updating the *bestCost* array must use $d_w + len(w, x)$, rather than the cost of (w, x) (we assume that $len(w, x)$ will be stored in the *data* variable for edge (w, x)). Hence, the value d_w must be computed and stored as vertices are added to the tree. The resulting algorithm runs in $\Theta(n^2)$ time, the same as for Prim's algorithm; we leave the details as an exercise.

11.4   Huffman Codes

Compression algorithms are often used for data archival or for improving data transmission rates. In this section, we examine one of the key components of data compression. In order to simplify the discussion, we will assume we are dealing with character data, though the techniques apply more generally.

In a typical English-language text, some characters like "e" occur much more frequently than other characters like "X" or "π". It makes sense, then, to use a variable-width encoding when storing text in files, so that the more frequently occurring characters have shorter codes.

For example, consider the popular UTF-8 encoding scheme. In this scheme, each possible character is encoded using a number of bytes determined by expected character frequencies. For example, each of the English characters, the Arabic numerals, and common punctuation and special characters are encoded using one byte. Characters from other languages, such as Greek or Cyrillic characters, require two bytes, whereas most Chinese

Figure 11.3   A Huffman tree for the string, "Mississippi"

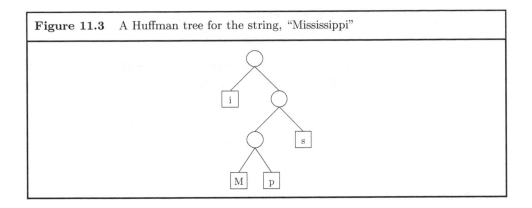

characters require three bytes. Various symbols and emoticons even require four bytes.

Two improvements to this approach can be made to reduce the length of a specific document. First, we can choose the encoding based on the actual character frequencies within that document. Second, we can use a variable number of bits, rather than a variable number of bytes. If we can make these improvements, the characters occurring most frequently in the document are likely to be encoded using fewer than eight bits.

The difficulty with variable-width encodings is choosing the encoding so that it is clear where one character ends and the next begins. For example, if we encode "n" with 11 and "o" with 111, then the encoding 11111 would be ambiguous — it could encode either "no" or "on". To overcome this difficulty, we arrange the characters as the leaves of a binary tree in which each non-leaf has two non-empty children (see Figure 11.3). The encoding of a character is determined by the path from the root to the leaf containing that character: each left child on the path denotes a 0 in the encoding, and each right child on the path denotes a 1 in the encoding. Thus, in Figure 11.3, "M" is encoded as 100. Because no path from the root to a leaf is a proper prefix of any other path from the root to a leaf, no ambiguity results.

Example 11.1. For example, we can use the tree in Figure 11.3 to encode "Mississippi" as 10001111011101011010. We parse this encoding by traversing the tree according to the paths specified by the encoding. Starting at the root, we go right-left-left, arriving at the leaf "M". Starting at the root again, we go left, arriving at the leaf "i". Continuing in this manner, we see that the bit-string decodes into "Mississippi". Note that because there are four distinct characters, a fixed-width encoding would require at least two bits per character, yielding a bit string of length 22. However, the bit string produced by the given encoding has length 21.

The specific problem we wish to address in this section is that of producing a tree that yields a minimum-length encoding for a given text. We will not concern ourselves with the counting of the characters in the text; rather, we will assume that a frequency table has been produced and is provided as our input. This frequency table gives the number of occurrences of each character in the text. To simplify matters, we will assume that none of the characters in the table has a frequency of 0. Furthermore, we will not concern ourselves with producing the encoding from the tree; i.e., our output consists solely of a binary tree storing the information we need in order to extract each character's code.

We first need to consider how we can determine the length of an encoded string for a particular encoding tree. Note that when we decode a bit string, we traverse exactly one edge in the tree for each bit of the encoding. One way to determine the length of the encoding is therefore to compute the number of times each edge would be traversed during decoding. A given edge (u, v) is traversed once for each occurrence of each character in the subtree rooted at v. For a subtree t, let us therefore define $weight(t)$ to be the total number of occurrences of all characters in t. For an encoding tree T, we can then define $cost(T)$ to be the sum of the weights of all proper subtrees of T. (Note that $weight(T)$ will always be the length of the given text.) $cost(T)$ then gives the length of the encoding based on T. For a given frequency table, we define a *Huffman tree* to be an encoding tree with minimum cost for that table.

Let us now generalize the problem so that the input is a collection of trees, $t_1, \ldots, t_n$, each of which encodes a portion of the frequency table. We assume that each character in the frequency table occurs in exactly one of the input trees, and that the frequency table has a Huffman tree that contains all of the input trees as subtrees. Note that if all of the trees are single nodes, this input is just the information from the frequency table. If the input consists of more than one tree, we need to merge two of the trees by making them the children of a new root. Furthermore, we need to be able to do this so that the frequency table has a Huffman tree containing all of the resulting trees as subtrees. We claim that merging two trees of minimum weight will produce such a tree.

Theorem 11.3. *Let T be a Huffman tree for a frequency table F, and let $t_1, \ldots, t_n$ be subtrees of T such that $n > 1$ and each leaf of T occurs in exactly* *one of* $t_1, \ldots, t_n$. *Suppose* $weight(t_1) \leq weight(t_2) \leq \cdots \leq weight(t_n)$. *Let* t_{n+1} *be the binary tree formed by making* t_1 *and* t_2 *the left and right children, respectively, of a new root. Then there is a Huffman tree* T' *for* F *containing* $t_3, t_4, \ldots, t_{n+1}$ *as subtrees.*

Proof. If t_{n+1} is a subtree of T, then we can let $T' = T$. Furthermore, if T has a subtree with t_1 as the right child and t_2 as the left child, we can simply swap t_1 with t_2 and let the resulting tree be T'. Otherwise, t_1 and t_2 are not siblings in T. Furthermore, neither can be a subtree of the other because they have no leaves in common. Let node x be the lowest common ancestor of t_1 and t_2 in T; i.e., x is an ancestor of both t_1 and t_2, but neither child of x is. We consider two cases.

Case 1: The path from x to t_1 is no longer than the path from x to t_2. Let t be the sibling of t_2 in T. Without loss of generality, assume t is the left child and t_2 is the right child (otherwise, we can swap them). Clearly, t can be neither t_1 nor t_2. Furthermore, it cannot be a proper subtree of any of $t_1, \ldots, t_n$, because then t_2 would also be a proper subtree of the same tree. Finally, t cannot contain t_1 as a proper subtree, because then the path from x to t_1 would be longer than the path from x to t_2. We conclude that t must contain one or more of $t_3, \ldots, t_n$. We can therefore swap t_1 with t, letting the result be T'.

Because t contains one or more of $t_3, \ldots, t_n$, $weight(t_1) \leq weight(t)$; hence, $weight(t) - weight(t_1) \geq 0$. The swap then causes the weights of all nodes except x on the path from x to the parent of t_1 in T to increase by $weight(t) - weight(t_1)$. Furthermore, it causes the weights of all nodes except x on the path from x to the parent of t_2 in T to decrease by $weight(t) - weight(t_1)$. No other nodes change weight. Because there are at least as many nodes on the path from x to t_2 in T as on the path from x to t_1 in T, the swap cannot increase the cost of the tree. Therefore T' is a Huffman tree.

Case 2: The path from x to t_1 is longer than the path from x to t_2. In this case we assume without loss of generality that t_1 is a left child, and we swap its sibling with t_2. Because Case 1 doesn't rely on the fact that $weight(t_1) \leq weight(t_2)$, the same reasoning holds for this case. □

We assume the frequency table is provided via two arrays:

- *chars*$[1..n]$, which contains the characters in the table; and
- *freq*$[1..n]$, which contains positive integers giving the frequencies of the corresponding characters.

Figure 11.4   Algorithm for constructing a Huffman tree

Precondition: $chars[1..n]$ is an array of CHARs, $n \geq 1$, and $freq[1..n]$ is an array of positive NATs.

Postcondition: Returns a BINARYTREENODE representing a Huffman tree for text including $freq[i]$ occurrences of $char[i]$, for $1 \leq i \leq n$.

HUFFMANTREE($chars[1..n]$, $freq[1..n]$)
    $q \leftarrow$ **new** INVERTEDPRIORITYQUEUE()
    for $i \leftarrow 1$ **to** n
        $t \leftarrow$ **new** BINARYTREENODE(); t.SETROOT($chars[i]$)
        q.PUT($t, freq[i]$)
    // **Invariant:** q contains BINARYTREENODEs which are subtrees of
    // some Huffman tree for the given frequency table, and whose priorities
    // are their weights as defined by the frequencies of the characters
    // contained in their leaves. Each character in $chars[1..n]$ occurs in
    // exactly one leaf of one tree.
    while q.SIZE() > 1
        $w_1 \leftarrow q$.MINPRIORITY(); $t_1 \leftarrow q$.REMOVEMIN()
        $w_2 \leftarrow q$.MINPRIORITY(); $t_2 \leftarrow q$.REMOVEMIN()
        $t \leftarrow$ **new** BINARYTREENODE(); t.SETLEFT(t_1); t.SETRIGHT(t_2)
        q.PUT($t, w_1 + w_2$)
    return q.REMOVEMIN()

The algorithm should then return a BINARYTREENODE representing a Huffman tree for the frequency table. The data in the leaves are characters, and all other data items in the tree are nil. The algorithm is shown in Figure 11.4. We maintain the trees in an INVERTEDPRIORITYQUEUE using the weights of the trees as priorities.

Because each iteration of the **for** loop adds an element to an initially empty priority queue, iteration i runs in $\Theta(\lg i)$ time. The **for** loop therefore runs in $\Theta(n \lg n)$ time. After the **for** loop completes, q contains n elements. Each iteration of the **while** loop removes two elements from q and adds one element. The loop therefore iterates $n - 1$ times. Each iteration runs in $O(\lg n)$ time. The running time of the **while** loop is therefore in $O(n \lg n)$, so that the algorithm runs in $\Theta(n \lg n)$ time.

11.5   Summary

Greedy algorithms provide an efficient mechanism for solving certain optimization problems. The major steps involved in the construction of a greedy algorithm are:

- Generalize the problem so that a partial solution is given as input.
- Decide upon a selection criterion for incrementally extending partial solutions.
- Prove that if a given partial solution can be extended to an optimal solution, then after extending this partial solution using the chosen selection criterion, the resulting partial solution can also be extended to an optimal solution.
- Implement the transformation suggested by the incremental extension using a loop.

Priority queues are often useful in facilitating quick access to the best extension, as determined by the selection criterion. In many cases, the extension involves joining pieces of a partial solution in a way that can be modeled effectively using a DISJOINTSETS structure.

Proving that the incremental extension can be extended to an optimal solution is essential, because it is not true for all selection criteria. In fact, there are optimization problems for which there is no greedy solution. In the next chapter, we will examine a more general, though typically more expensive, technique for solving optimization problems.

11.6   Exercises

Exercise 11.1. Prove that KRUSKAL, shown in Figure 11.1, meets its specification.

Exercise 11.2. Prove that PRIM, shown in Figure 11.2, meets its specification.

Exercise 11.3. Instead of using the arrays *best* and *bestCost*, Prim's algorithm could use a priority queue to store all of the edges from vertices in the spanning tree. As vertices are added to the spanning tree, all edges from these vertices would be added to the priority queue. As edges are removed from the priority queue, they would need to be checked to see if they connect a vertex in the spanning tree with one that is not in the spanning tree. Implement this algorithm and analyze its running time assuming the graph is implemented as a LISTGRAPH.

Exercise 11.4. Implement the single-source shortest path algorithm as outlined in Section 11.3. Your algorithm should take a GRAPH G and a natural number $u < G.\text{SIZE}()$ and return an array $pred[0..G.\text{SIZE}()-1]$ such that $pred[i]$ gives the parent of i in the shortest paths tree; $pred[u]$ should be -1.

Exercise 11.5. Modify your algorithm from Exercise 11.4 to use a priority queue as suggested in Exercise 11.3. Analyze its running time assuming the graph is implemented as a LISTGRAPH.

Exercise 11.6. Suppose we wish to solve the single-source shortest path problem for a graph with unweighted edges; i.e., each edge is understood to have a length of 1. Prove that the algorithm for Exercise 11.5 can be modified by replacing the priority queue with a queue (see Exercise 4.11, page 144) to yield an algorithm for the unweighted single-source shortest path problem. Analyze the running time of the resulting algorithm, assuming the graph is implemented as a LISTGRAPH. (This algorithm is known as *breadth-first search*.)

Exercise 11.7. Construct a Huffman tree for the string, "banana split", and give its resulting encoding in binary. Don't forget the blank character.

Exercise 11.8. Prove that HUFFMANTREE, shown in Figure 11.4, meets its specification.

Exercise 11.9. Suppose we have a set of jobs, each having a positive integer execution time. We must schedule all of the jobs on a single server so that at most one job occupies the server at any given time and each job occupies the server for a length of time equal to its execution time. Our goal is to minimize the sum of the finish times of all of the jobs. Design a greedy algorithm to accomplish this and prove that it is optimal. Your algorithm should run in $O(n \lg n)$ time, where n is the number of jobs.

Exercise 11.10. Extend the above exercise to k servers, so that each job is scheduled on one of the servers.

Exercise 11.11. Suppose we are given a set of events, each having a start time and a finish time. Each event requires a single room. We wish to assign events to rooms using as few rooms as possible so that no two events in the same room overlap (they may, however, be scheduled "back-to-back" with no break in between). Give a greedy algorithm to accomplish this and prove that it is optimal. Your algorithm should run in $O(n \lg n)$ time.

Exercise 11.12. Repeat the above exercise with the constraint that only one room is available. The goal is to schedule as many events as possible.

Exercise 11.13. We wish to plan a trip across country in a car that can go d miles on a full tank of gasoline. We have identified all of the gas stations along the proposed route. We wish to plan the trip so as to make as few stops for gasoline as possible. Design a greedy algorithm that gives an optimal set of stops when given d and an array $dist[1..n]$ such that $dist[i]$ gives the distance from the starting point to the ith gas station. Your algorithm should operate in $O(n)$ time.

* Exercise 11.14. The *fractional knapsack problem* is as follows. We are given a set of n items, each having a positive *weight* $w_i \in \mathbb{N}$ and a positive *value* $v_i \in \mathbb{N}$. We are also given a *weight bound* $W \in \mathbb{N}$. We wish to carry some of these items in a knapsack without exceeding the weight bound. Our goal is to maximize the total value of the items we carry. Furthermore, the items are such that we can take a fraction of the item if we wish. Thus, we wish to maximize

$$\sum_{i=1}^{n} a_i v_i,$$

for rational $a_1, \ldots, a_n$ such that for $1 \le i \le n$, $0 \le a_i \le 1$, and subject to the constraint that

$$\sum_{i=1}^{n} a_i w_i \le W.$$

a. Give a greedy algorithm to find an optimal packing, and prove that your algorithm is correct. Your algorithm should run in $O(n \lg n)$ time.

b. Show using a specific example that this greedy algorithm does not always give an optimal solution if we require that each a_i be either 0 or 1.

c. Using techniques from Chapter 10, improve the running time of your algorithm to $O(n)$.

11.7 Notes

Greedy algorithms were first identified in 1971 by Edmonds [36], though they actually existed long before then. The theory that underlies greedy algorithms — *matroid* theory — was developed by Whitney [120] in the 1930s. See, e.g., Lawler [89] or Papadimitriou and Steiglitz [96] for more information on greedy algorithms and matroid theory.

The first MST algorithm was given by Borůvka [15] in 1926. What is now known as Prim's algorithm was first discovered by Jarník [70], and over 25 years later rediscovered independently by Prim [99] and Dijkstra [27]; the latter paper also includes the single-source shortest paths algorithm outlined in Section 11.3. Kruskal's algorithm was given by Kruskal [88].

Other MST algorithms have been given by Yao [124], Cheriton and Tarjan [21], Tarjan [112], Karger [77], and Chazelle [20]. Other improvements for single-source shortest paths have been given by Johnson [74, 75], Tarjan [112], and Fredman and Tarjan [46].

Huffman coding was developed by Huffman [68]. See Lelewer and Hirschberg [90] and Sayood [103] for surveys of compression algorithms. On the website for this textbook is a tool for constructing and displaying a Huffman tree for a given text.

Chapter 12

Optimization II: Dynamic Programming

In the last chapter, we saw that greedy algorithms are efficient solutions to certain optimization problems. However, there are optimization problems for which no greedy algorithm exists. In this chapter, we will examine a more general technique, known as *dynamic programming*, for solving optimization problems.

Dynamic programming is a technique of implementing a top-down solution using bottom-up computation. We have already seen several examples of how top-down solutions can be implemented bottom-up. Dynamic programming extends this idea by saving the results of many subproblems in order to solve the desired problem. As a result, dynamic programming algorithms tend to be more costly, in terms of both time and space, than greedy algorithms. On the other hand, they are often much more efficient than straightforward recursive implementations of the top-down solution. Thus, when greedy algorithms are not possible, dynamic programming algorithms are often the most appropriate.

12.1 Making Change

Suppose we wish to produce a specific value $n \in \mathbb{N}$ from a given set of coin denominations $d_1 < d_2 < \cdots < d_k$, each of which is a positive integer. Our goal is to achieve a value of exactly n using a minimum number of coins. To ensure that it is always possible to achieve a value of exactly n, we assume that $d_1 = 1$ and that we have as many coins in each denomination as we need.

An obvious greedy strategy is to choose at each step the largest coin that does not cause the total to exceed n. For some sets of coin denominations, this strategy will result in the minimum number of coins for any n. However, suppose $n = 30, d_1 = 1, d_2 = 10$, and $d_3 = 25$. The greedy strategy

389

first takes 25. At this point, the only denomination that does not cause the total to exceed n is 1. The greedy strategy therefore gives a total of six coins: one 25 and five 1s. This solution is not optimal, however, as we can produce 30 with three 10s.

Let us consider a more direct top-down solution. If $k = 1$, then $d_k = 1$, so the only solution contains n coins. Otherwise, if $d_k > n$, we can reduce the size of the problem by removing d_k from the set of denominations, and the solution to the resulting problem is the solution to the original problem. Finally, suppose $d_k \leq n$. There are now two possibilities: the optimal solution either contains d_k or it does not. In what follows, we consider these two cases separately.

Let us first consider the case in which the optimal solution does not contain d_k. In this case, we do not change the optimal solution if we remove d_k from the set of denominations. We therefore have reduced the original problem to a smaller problem instance.

> These two possibilities are not exclusive — there could be one optimal solution that contains d_k and another that does not.

Now suppose the optimal solution contains d_k. Suppose we remove one d_k coin from this optimal solution. What remains is an optimal solution to the instance with the same set of denominations and a target value of $n - d_k$. Now working in the other direction, if we have the optimal solution to the smaller instance, we can obtain an optimal solution to the original instance by adding a d_k coin. Again, we have reduced the original problem to a smaller problem instance.

To summarize, when $d_k \leq n$, the optimal solution can be obtained from the optimal solution to one of two smaller problem instances. We have no way of knowing in advance which of these smaller instances is the right one; however, if we obtain both of them, we can compare the two resulting candidate solutions. The one with fewer coins is the optimal solution. In fact, if we could quickly determine which of these smaller instances would yield fewer coins, we could use this test as the selection criterion for a greedy algorithm. Therefore, let us focus for now on the more difficult aspect of this problem — that of determining the minimum number of coins in an optimal solution.

Based on the above discussion, the following recurrence gives the minimum number of coins needed to obtain a value of n from the denominations $d_1, \ldots, d_k$:

$$C(n, k) = \begin{cases} n & \text{if } k = 1 \\ C(n, k-1) & \text{if } k > 1, d_k > n \\ \min(C(n, k-1), C(n-d_k, k) + 1) & \text{if } k > 1, n \geq d_k. \end{cases} \quad (12.1)$$

This recurrence gives us a recursive algorithm for computing $C(n,k)$. However, the direct recursive implementation of this recurrence is inefficient. In order to see this, let us consider the special case in which $d_i = i$ for $1 \leq i \leq k$ and $n \geq k^2$. Then for $k > 1$, the computation of $C(n,k)$ requires the computation of $C(n, k-1)$ and $C(n-k, k)$. The computation of $C(n-k, k)$ then requires the computation of $C(n-k, k-1)$. Furthermore,

$$
\begin{aligned}
n - k &\geq k^2 - k \\
&= k(k-1) \\
&\geq (k-1)^2,
\end{aligned}
$$

for $k \geq 1$. Thus, when $n \geq k^2$, the computation of $C(n,k)$ requires the computation of two values, $C(n_1, k-1)$ and $C(n_2, k-1)$, where $n_1 \geq (k-1)^2$ and $n_2 \geq (k-1)^2$. It is then easily shown by induction on k that $C(n,k)$ requires the computation of 2^{k-1} values $C(n_i, 1)$, where $n_i \geq 1$ for $1 \leq i \leq 2^{k-1}$. In such cases, the running time is exponential in k.

A closer look at the above argument reveals that a large amount of redundant computation is taking place. For example, the subproblem $C(n - 2k + 2, k - 2)$ must be computed twice:

1. $C(n,k)$ requires the computation of $C(n, k-1)$, which requires $C(n - k + 1, k - 1)$, which requires $C(n - 2k + 2, k - 1)$, which requires $C(n - 2k + 2, k - 2)$; and
2. $C(n,k)$ also requires $C(n - k, k)$, which requires $C(n - k, k - 1)$, which requires $C(n - k, k - 2)$, which requires $C(n - 2k + 2, k - 2)$.

Applying this reasoning again to both computations of $C(n - 2k + 2, k - 2)$, we can see that $C(n - 4k + 8, k - 4)$ must be computed four times. More generally, for even $i < k$, $C(n - ik + i^2/2, k - i)$ must be computed $2^{i/2}$ times for $n \geq k^2$.

In order to avoid the redundant computation that leads to exponential running time, we can compute all values $C(i, j)$ for $0 \leq i \leq n$, $1 \leq j \leq k$, saving them in an array. If we compute recurrence (12.1) bottom-up, rather than top-down, we will have all of the values we need in order to compute each $C(i, j)$ in constant time. All $(n+1)k$ of these values can therefore be computed in $\Theta(nk)$ time. Once all of these values have been computed, then the optimal collection of coins can be constructed in a greedy fashion, as suggested above. The algorithm is shown in Figure 12.1. This algorithm is easily seen to use $\Theta(nk)$ time and space.

Figure 12.1 Algorithm for computing the minimum number of coins needed to achieve a given value

---

Precondition: $d[1..k]$ is an array of INTs such that $1 = d[1] < d[2] < \cdots < d[k]$, and n is a NAT.

Postcondition: Returns an array $A[1..k]$ such that $A[i]$ gives the number of coins of denomination $d[i]$ in a minimum-sized collection of coins with value n.

CHANGE($d[1..k], n$)

    $C \leftarrow$ **new** ARRAY$[0..n, 1..k]$; $A \leftarrow$ **new** ARRAY$[1..k]$

    for $i \leftarrow 0$ **to** n

        $C[i, 1] \leftarrow i$

    for $i \leftarrow 0$ **to** n

        for $j \leftarrow 2$ **to** k

            if $i < d[j]$

                $C[i, j] \leftarrow C[i, j - 1]$

            else

                $C[i, j] \leftarrow$ MIN($C[i, j - 1], C[i - d[j], j] + 1$)

    for $j \leftarrow 1$ **to** k

        $A[j] \leftarrow 0$

    $i \leftarrow n$; $j \leftarrow k$

    // **Invariant:** $\sum_{l=1}^{k} A[l]d[l] = n - i$, and there is an optimal solution

    // that includes all of the coins in $A[1..k]$, but no additional coins from

    // $d[j + 1..k]$.

    while $j > 1$

        if $i < d[j]$ **or** $C[i, j - 1] < C[i - d[j], j] + 1$

            $j \leftarrow j - 1$

        else

            $A[j] \leftarrow A[j] + 1$; $i \leftarrow i - d[j]$

    $A[1] \leftarrow i$

    return $A[1..k]$

A characteristic of this problem that is essential in order for the dynamic programming approach to work is that it is possible to decompose a large problem instance into smaller problem instances in a way that optimal solutions to the smaller instances can be used to produce an optimal solution to the larger instance. This is, of course, one of the main principles of the top-down approach. However, this characteristic may be stated succinctly for optimization problems: For any optimal solution, any portion of that solution is itself an optimal solution to a smaller instance. This principle is known as the *principle of optimality*. It applies to the change-making problem because any sub-collection of an optimal collection of coins is itself an optimal collection for the value it yields; otherwise, we could replace the sub-collection with a smaller sub-collection yielding the same value, and obtain a better solution to the original instance.

The principle of optimality usually applies to optimization problems, but not always in a convenient way. For example, consider the problem of

> A simple path in a graph is a path in which each vertex appears at most once.

finding a longest simple path in a graph from a given vertex u to a given vertex v. If we take a portion of the longest path, say from x to y, this subpath is not necessarily the longest simple path from x to y in the original graph. However, it is guaranteed to be the longest simple path from x to y in the subgraph consisting of only those vertices on that subpath and all edges between them in the original graph. Thus, a subproblem consists of a start vertex, a final vertex, and a subset of the vertices. Because a graph with n vertices has 2^n subsets of vertices, there are an exponential number of subproblems to solve. Thus, in order for dynamic programming to be an effective design technique, the principle of optimality must apply in a way that yields relatively few subproblems.

One characteristic that often leads to relatively few subproblems, while at the same time causing direct recursive implementations to be quite expensive, is that the top-down solution results in *overlapping subproblems.* As we have already discussed, the top-down solution for the change-making problem can result in two subproblems which have a subproblem in common. This overlap results in redundant computation in the direct recursive implementation. On the other hand, it reduces the total number of subproblems, so that the dynamic programming approach is more efficient.

12.2 Chained Matrix Multiplication

Recall that the product AB, where A is a $k \times m$ matrix and B is an $m \times n$ matrix, is the $k \times n$ matrix C such that

$$C_{ij} = \sum_{l=1}^{m} A_{il} B_{lj} \quad \text{for } 1 \leq i \leq k, 1 \leq j \leq n.$$

If we were to compute the matrix product by directly computing each of the kn sums, we would perform a total of kmn scalar multiplications.

Now suppose we wish to compute the product,

$$M_1 M_2 \cdots M_n,$$

where M_i is a $d_{i-1} \times d_i$ matrix for $1 \leq i \leq n$. Because matrix multiplication is associative, we have some choice over the order in which the multiplications are performed. For example, to compute $M_1 M_2 M_3$, we may either

- first compute $M_1 M_2$, then multiply on the right by M_3; or
- first compute $M_2 M_3$, then multiply on the left by M_1.

In other words, we may compute either $(M_1 M_2) M_3$ or $M_1 (M_2 M_3)$.

Now suppose $d_0 = 2$, $d_1 = 3$, $d_2 = 4$, and $d_3 = 1$. Then the three matrices are dimensioned as follows:

- M_1: 2×3;
- M_2: 3×4; and
- M_3: 4×1.

If we compute $(M_1 M_2) M_3$, we first multiply a 2×3 matrix by a 3×4 matrix, then we multiply the resulting 2×4 matrix by a 4×1 matrix. The total number of scalar multiplications is

$$2 \cdot 3 \cdot 4 + 2 \cdot 4 \cdot 1 = 32.$$

On the other hand, if we compute $M_1 (M_2 M_3)$, we first multiply a 3×4 matrix by a 4×1 matrix, then we multiply the resulting 3×1 matrix by a 2×3 matrix. The total number of scalar multiplications is

$$3 \cdot 4 \cdot 1 + 2 \cdot 3 \cdot 1 = 18.$$

Thus, the way in which the matrices are parenthesized can affect the number of scalar multiplications performed in computing the matrix product. This fact motivates an optimization problem: Given a sequence of positive integer dimensions $d_0, \ldots, d_n$, determine the minimum number of scalar multiplications needed to compute the product $M_1 \ldots M_n$, assuming M_i is a $d_{i-1} \times d_i$ matrix for $1 \leq i \leq n$, and that the number of scalar multiplications required to multiply two matrices is as described above.

Various greedy strategies might be applied to this problem, but none can guarantee an optimal solution. Let us therefore look for a direct top-down solution to the problem of finding the minimum number of scalar multiplications for a product $M_i \ldots M_j$. Let us focus on finding the last matrix multiplication. This multiplication will involve the products $M_i \ldots M_k$ and $M_{k+1} \ldots M_j$ for some k, $1 \leq k < n$. The sizes of these two matrices are $d_{i-1} \times d_k$ and $d_k \times d_j$. Therefore, once these two matrices are computed, an additional $d_{i-1} d_k d_j$ scalar multiplications must be performed. The principle of optimality clearly holds for this problem, as a better way

---

Figure 12.2 Chained matrix multiplication algorithm

Precondition: $d[0..n]$ is an array of positive NATs, and n is a positive NAT.
Postcondition: Returns the minimum number of scalar multiplications needed to compute the product $M_1 \cdots M_n$, where M_i is a $d[i-1] \times d[i]$ matrix for $1 \leq i \leq n$.

CHAINEDMATRIXMULT($d[0..n]$)
   $m \leftarrow$ **new** ARRAY$[1..n, 1..n]$
   for $i \leftarrow n$ **to** 1 **by** -1
     $m[i, i] \leftarrow 0$
     for $j \leftarrow i + 1$ **to** n
       $m[i, j] \leftarrow \infty$
       for $k \leftarrow i$ **to** $j - 1$
         $m[i, j] \leftarrow$ MIN($m[i, j], m[i, k] + m[k + 1, j] + d[i-1]d[k]d[j]$)
   return $m[1, n]$

---

of computing either sub-product results in fewer total scalar multiplications. Therefore, the following recurrence gives the minimum number of scalar multiplications needed to compute $M_i \cdots M_j$:

$$
m(i, j) = \begin{cases} 0 & \text{if } i = j \\ \min_{i \leq k < j} \left(m(i, k) + m(k + 1, j) + d_{i-1}d_k d_j \right) & \text{if } i < j. \end{cases} \quad (12.2)
$$

In order to compute $m(i, j)$, $2(j - i)$ subproblems need to be solved. It is easily seen that there is a great deal of overlap between these subproblems. Therefore, dynamic programming is appropriate for computing $m(i, j)$. We need a matrix $m[1..n, 1..n]$. In order to compute $m[i, j]$, we need to use values in row i to the left of column j and values in column j below row i. It therefore makes sense to compute m by rows from bottom to top, and left to right within each row. The algorithm is given in Figure 12.2. It is easily seen to run in $\Theta(n^3)$ time and to use $\Theta(n^2)$ space.

12.3 All-Pairs Shortest Paths

In Section 11.3, we discussed the single-source shortest paths problem for directed graphs. In this section, we generalize the problem to all pairs of vertices; i.e., we wish to find, for each pair of vertices u and v, a shortest path from u to v. An obvious solution is to apply Dijkstra's algorithm n times, each time using a different vertex as the source. This would result in an algorithm with running time in $\Theta(n^3)$. Although the algorithm we present in this section is no faster asymptotically, it serves as a good example of how certain space optimizations can sometimes be made for dynamic programming algorithms. It also serves as an illustration of how dynamic programming can be applied to problems that are not optimization problems in the strictest sense of the word.

Let $G = (V, E)$ be a directed graph, and let $len : V^2 \to \mathbb{N} \cup \{\infty\}$ be a function giving the length of each edge, so that

- $len(u, u) = 0$ for $u \in V$; and
- $len(u, v) = \infty$ iff $u \neq v$ and $(u, v) \notin E$, for $(u, v) \in V^2$.

We wish to find, for each ordered pair $(u, v) \in V^2$, the length of the shortest path from u to v; if there is no such path, we define the length to be ∞. Note that we have simplified the problem so that instead of finding the actual paths, we will only be finding their lengths.

This optimization problem is somewhat nonstandard in that the objective function is not a numeric-valued function. Instead, its range can be thought of as a matrix of values. However, the optimum is well-defined, as it occurs when all values are simultaneously minimized, and this is always possible.

Let p be a shortest path from i to j, and consider any vertex k other than i or j. Then either k is in p or it isn't. If k is not in p, then p remains the shortest path from i to j if we remove k from the graph. Otherwise, we can break p into a path from i to k and a path from k to j. Clearly, each of these paths are shortest paths between their endpoints. Thus, if we can find the shortest path from i to k and the shortest path from k to j, we can determine the shortest path from i to j.

A shortcoming to this approach is that we haven't actually reduced the size of the problem, as the shortest paths from i to k and k to j are with respect to the original graph. One way to avoid this shortcoming is to generalize the problem so that a set of possible intermediate vertices is given as additional input. The problem is then to find, for each ordered pair (i, j) of vertices, the length of the shortest path from i to j such that all vertices other than i and j on this path belong to the given set. If the given set is V, then the result is the solution to the all-pairs shortest paths problem. In order to keep the number of subproblems from being too large, we can restrict the sets we allow as input. Specifically, our additional input can be a natural number k, which denotes the set of all natural numbers strictly less than k.

Let $L_k(i,j)$ denote the length of the shortest path from i to j with intermediate vertices strictly less than k, where $0 \le i < n$, $0 \le j < n$, and $0 \le k \le n$. Using the above reasoning, we have the following recurrence for $L_k(i,j)$:

$$L_k(i,j) = \begin{cases} len(i,j) & \text{if } k = 0 \\ \min(L_{k-1}(i,j), L_{k-1}(i,k-1) + L_{k-1}(k-1,j)) & \text{if } k > 0. \end{cases}$$
(12.3)

We can then implement a dynamic programming algorithm to compute all $L_k(i,j)$ using a 3D array. However, we can save a great deal of space by making some observations. Note that in order to compute an entry $L_k(i,j)$, for $k > 0$, we only use entries $L_{k-1}(i,j)$, $L_{k-1}(i,k-1)$, and $L_{k-1}(k-1,j)$. We claim that $L_{k-1}(i,k-1) = L_k(i,k-1)$ and that $L_{k-1}(k-1,j) = L_k(k-1,j)$. To see this, note that

$$\begin{aligned} L_k(i,k-1) &= \min(L_{k-1}(i,k-1), L_{k-1}(i,k-1) + L_{k-1}(k-1,k-1)) \\ &= L_{k-1}(i,k-1), \end{aligned}$$

and

$$\begin{aligned} L_k(k-1,j) &= \min(L_{k-1}(k-1,j), L_{k-1}(k-1,k-1) + L_{k-1}(k-1,j)) \\ &= L_{k-1}(k-1,j). \end{aligned}$$

As a result, we can use a 2D array $L[0..n-1, 0..n-1]$ to represent L_{k-1}. We can then transform this array into L_k by updating each value in turn. The algorithm, known as Floyd's algorithm, is shown in Figure 12.3. We assume that the length of each edge is given by its key. It is easily seen that, regardless of whether G is implemented as a MATRIXGRAPH or a LISTGRAPH, the algorithm runs in $\Theta(n^3)$ time and uses only a constant amount of space other than what is required for input and output.

12.4 The Knapsack Problem

In Exercise 11.14 (page 387), we introduced the fractional knapsack problem. One part of this exercise was to show that the greedy algorithm for the fractional knapsack problem does not extend to the so-called 0-1 knapsack problem — the variation in which the items cannot be broken. Specifically, in this variation we are given a set of n items, each having a positive weight $w_i \in \mathbb{N}$ and a positive value $v_i \in \mathbb{N}$, and a weight bound $W \in \mathbb{N}$. We wish to

---

Figure 12.3   Floyd's algorithm for all-pairs shortest paths

Precondition: G refers to a GRAPH in which the data associated with each edge is a NAT giving its length.
Postcondition: Returns an array $L[0..n-1, 0..n-1]$ such that $L[i,j]$ is the length of the shortest path from i to j in G.

FLOYD(G)
    $n \leftarrow G$.SIZE(); $L \leftarrow$ **new** ARRAY$[0..n-1, 0..n-1]$
    for $i \leftarrow 0$ **to** $n-1$
        for $j \leftarrow 0$ **to** $n-1$
            if $i = j$
                $L[i,j] \leftarrow 0$
            else
                $d \leftarrow G$.GET(i,j)
                if $d = $ nil
                    $L[i,j] \leftarrow \infty$
                else
                    $L[i,j] \leftarrow d$
    for $k \leftarrow 1$ **to** n
        for $i \leftarrow 0$ **to** $n-1$
            for $j \leftarrow 0$ **to** $n-1$
                $L[i,j] \leftarrow$ MIN$(L[i,j], L[i,k-1] + L[k-1,j])$
    return $L[0..n-1, 0..n-1]$

---

find a subset $S \subseteq \{1, \ldots, n\}$ that maximizes

$$\sum_{i \in S} v_i,$$

subject to the constraint that

$$\sum_{i \in S} w_i \leq W.$$

To solve this problem, first note that either item n is in an optimal solution, or it isn't. If it is, then we can obtain an optimal solution by solving the problem in which item n has been removed and the weight bound has been decreased by w_n. Otherwise, we can obtain an optimal solution by solving the problem in which item n has been removed. We therefore have the following recurrence giving the optimal value $V_i(j)$ that can be obtained from the first i items with a weight bound of j, where $0 \leq i \leq n$ and

$0 \leq j \leq W$:

$$
V_i(j) = \begin{cases} 0 & \text{if } i = 0 \\ V_{i-1}(j) & \text{if } i > 0, \, j < w_i \\ \max(V_{i-1}(j), V_{i-1}(j - w_i) + v_i) & \text{otherwise.} \end{cases} \qquad (12.4)
$$

The optimal value is then given by $V_n(W)$.

It is not hard to see that the optimal value can be computed in $\Theta(nW)$ time and space using dynamic programming — the details are left as an exercise. However, suppose W is much larger than the values of the items. In this case, another approach might be more appropriate. Let

$$
V = \sum_{i=1}^{n} v_i.
$$

Let us then compute the minimum weight required to achieve each possible value $v \leq V$. The largest value v yielding a minimum weight no larger than W is then our optimal value.

Taking this approach, we observe that item n is either in the set of items for which value v can be achieved with minimum weight, or it isn't. If it is, then the minimum weight can be computed by removing item n and finding the minimum weight needed to achieve a value of $v - v_n$. Otherwise, the minimum weight can be computed by removing item n. The following recurrence therefore gives the minimum weight $W_i(j)$ needed to achieve a value of exactly j from the first i items, for $0 \leq i \leq n$, $0 \leq j \leq V$:

$$
W_i(j) = \begin{cases} 0 & \text{if } j = 0 \\ \infty & \text{if } i = 0, \, j > 0 \\ W_{i-1}(j) & \text{if } i > 0, \, 0 < j < v_i \\ \min(W_{i-1}(j), W_{i-1}(j - v_i) + w_i) & \text{otherwise.} \end{cases} \qquad (12.5)
$$

The optimal value is then the maximum $j \leq V$ such that $W_n(j) \leq W$.

It is not hard to see that a dynamic programming algorithm based on this recurrence can find the optimal value in $\Theta(nV)$ time and space. Again, we leave the details as an exercise. Note that we could potentially improve the algorithm further if we could first find a better upper bound than V for the optimal value. This would allow us to reduce the number of columns we need to compute in our array. We will explore this idea further in Chapter 17.

12.5   Summary

Dynamic programming algorithms provide more power for solving optimization problems than do greedy algorithms. Efficient dynamic programming algorithms can be found when the following conditions apply:

- The principle of optimality can be applied to decompose the problem into subinstances of the same problem.
- There is significant overlap between the subinstances.
- The total number of subinstances, including those obtained by recursively decomposing subinstances, is relatively small.

Although dynamic programming algorithms proceed bottom-up, the first step in formulating a dynamic programming algorithm is to formulate a top-down solution. This top-down solution usually takes the form of a recurrence for computing the optimal value of the objective function. The top-down solution is then implemented bottom-up, storing all of the solutions to the subproblems. In some cases, we optimize the space usage by discarding some of these solutions.

Because dynamic programming algorithms typically solve subinstances that are not used in the optimal solution, they tend to be less efficient than greedy algorithms. Hence, greedy algorithms are preferred when they exist. However, for many problems, there are no greedy algorithms that guarantee optimal solutions. In such cases, dynamic programming algorithms may be the most efficient.

Although the examples in this chapter have all been optimization problems, it is not hard to see that dynamic programming can be applied to other problems as well. Any computation that can be expressed as a recurrence can be computed bottom-up, yielding a dynamic programming solution. We explore some examples in the exercises.

12.6   Exercises

Exercise 12.1. Prove by induction on $n + k$ that $C(n, k)$, as defined in recurrence (12.1), gives the minimum number of coins needed to give a value of exactly n if the denominations are $d_1 < d_2 < \cdots < d_k$ and $d_1 = 1$.

Exercise 12.2. Prove that CHANGE, shown in Figure 12.1, meets its specification. You do not need to focus on the first half of the algorithm; i.e., you can assume that $C(i, j)$, as defined in recurrence (12.1), is assigned to $C[i, j]$. Furthermore, you may use the result of Exercise 12.1 in your proof.

* Exercise 12.3. As we have seen, the greedy algorithm suggested in Section 12.1 works for some sets of coin denominations but not for others.

a. Prove that for denominations $d_1 < d_2 < \cdots < d_k$, where $k > 1$, if the greedy algorithm fails for some value, then it must fail for some value $n < d_k + d_{k-1}$.

b. Devise an efficient dynamic programming algorithm which takes as input a set of denominations and returns **true** if the greedy algorithm always works for this set, or returns **false** otherwise. You may assume that the denominations are given in increasing order. Your algorithm should use $O(Mk)$ time and space, where M is the largest denomination and k is the number of denominations.

Exercise 12.4. Prove by induction on $j - i$ that $m(i, j)$, as defined in recurrence 12.2, is the minimum number of scalar multiplications needed to compute a product $M_i \cdots M_j$, where M_k is a $d_{k-1} \times d_k$ matrix for $i \le k \le j$.

Exercise 12.5. Prove by induction on k that $L_k(i, j)$, as defined in recurrence 12.3, gives the length of the shortest path from i to j in which all intermediate vertices are strictly less than k.

Exercise 12.6.

a. Modify Floyd's algorithm (Figure 12.3) so that it returns an array $S[0..n-1, 0..n-1]$ such that for $i \ne j$, $S[i, j]$ gives the vertex k such that (i, k) is the first edge in a shortest path from i to j. If there is no path from i to j, or if $i = j$, then $S[i, j]$ should be -1.

b. Give an algorithm that takes the array $S[0..n-1, 0..n-1]$ defined above, along with i and j such that $0 \le i < n$ and $0 \le j < n$, and prints the vertices along a shortest path from i to j. The first vertex printed should be i, followed by the vertices in order along the path, until the last vertex j is printed. If $i = j$, only i should be printed. If there is no path from i to j, a message to that effect should be printed. Your algorithm should run in $O(n)$ time.

Exercise 12.7. Give an algorithm for the 0-1 knapsack problem that runs in $O(nW)$ time and space, where n is the number of items and W is the weight bound. Your algorithm should use dynamic programming to compute recurrence (12.4) for $0 \le i \le n$ and $0 \le j \le W$, then use these values to guide a greedy algorithm for selecting the items to put into the knapsack. Your algorithm should return an array $selected[1..n]$ of booleans such that $selected[i]$ is **true** iff item i is in the optimal packing.

Exercise 12.8. Repeat Exercise 12.7 using recurrence (12.5) instead of (12.4). Your algorithm should use $\Theta(nV)$ time and space, where n is the number of items and V is the total value of all the items.

Exercise 12.9. Let $A[1..n]$ be an array of integers. An *increasing subsequence* of A is a sequence of indices $\langle i_1, \ldots, i_k \rangle$ such that $i_j < i_{j+1}$ and $A[i_j] < A[i_{j+1}]$ for $1 \leq j < k$. (Note that the indices in the subsequence are not necessarily contiguous.) A *longest increasing subsequence* of A is an increasing subsequence of A with maximum length.

a. Give a recurrence for $L(i)$, the length of the longest increasing subsequence of $A[1..i]$ that ends with i, where $1 \leq i \leq n$.
b. Give a dynamic programming algorithm that prints the indices of a longest increasing subsequence of $A[1..n]$. Your algorithm should operate in $O(n^2)$ time.

Exercise 12.10. Let $A[1..m]$ and $B[1..n]$ be two arrays. An array $C[1..k]$ is a *common subsequence* of A and B if there are two sequences of indices $\langle i_1, \ldots, i_k \rangle$ and $\langle j_1, \ldots, j_k \rangle$ such that

- $i_1 < i_2 < \cdots < i_k$;
- $j_1 < j_2 < \cdots < j_k$; and
- $C[l] = A[i_l] = B[j_l]$ for $1 \leq l \leq k$.

A *longest common subsequence* of A and B is a common subsequence of A and B with maximum size.

a. Give a recurrence for $L(i, j)$, the length of the longest common subsequence of $A[1..i]$ and $B[1..j]$.
b. Give a dynamic programming algorithm that returns the longest common subsequence of $A[1..m]$ and $B[1..n]$. Your algorithm should operate in $O(mn)$ time.

Exercise 12.11. A *palindrome* is a string that reads the same from right to left as it does from left to right ("abcba", for example). Give a dynamic programming algorithm that takes a STRING (see Figure 4.17 on page 145) s as input, and returns a longest palindrome contained as a substring within s. Your algorithm should operate in $O(n^2)$ time, where n is the length of s. You may use the results of Exercise 4.13 (page 144) in analyzing your algorithm. [**Hint:** For each pair of indices $i \leq j$, determine whether the substring from i to j is a palindrome.]

* **Exercise 12.12.** Suppose we have two k-dimensional boxes A and B whose k dimensions are $a_1, \ldots, a_k$ and $b_1, \ldots, b_k$, respectively. We say that A fits inside of B if there is a permutation $a_{i_1}, \ldots, a_{i_k}$ of the dimensions of A such that $a_{i_j} < b_j$ for $1 \leq j \leq k$. Design a dynamic programming algorithm that takes as input a positive integer k and the dimensions of n k-dimensional boxes, and returns the maximum size of any subset of the boxes that can be ordered such that each box (except the last) in the ordering fits inside of the next. Your algorithm should run in $O(\max(n^2 k, nk \lg k))$ time in the worst case. Note that your algorithm doesn't need to return a subset or an ordering — only the size of the subset.

Exercise 12.13. Let $G = (V, E)$ be a directed graph. The *transitive closure* of G is a directed graph $G' = (V, E')$, where E' is the set of all $(u, v) \in V^2$ such that $u \neq v$ and there is a path from u to v in G. Give an $O(n^3)$ dynamic programming algorithm to produce a MATRIXGRAPH that is the transitive closure of a given MATRIXGRAPH.

Exercise 12.14. A *convex polygon* is a polygon whose interior angles are all less than 180 degrees. For example, in Figure 12.4, polygon a is convex, but polygon b is not. A *triangulation* of a convex polygon is a set of non-intersecting diagonals that partition the polygon into triangles, as shown in Figure 12.4 (c). Give a dynamic programming algorithm that takes as input a convex polygon and produces a triangulation that minimizes the sum of the lengths of the diagonals, where the length of an edge $(x_1, y_1), (x_2, y_2)$ is given by

$$\sqrt{(x_1 - x_2)^2 + (y_1 - y_2)^2}.$$

You may assume that the polygon is represented as a sequence of points in the Cartesian plane $\langle p_1, p_2, \ldots, p_n \rangle$ such that the edges of the polygon are $(p_1, p_2), (p_2, p_3), \ldots, (p_{n-1}, p_n)$, and (p_n, p_1). You may further assume that $n \geq 3$. Your algorithm should run in $O(n^3)$ time.

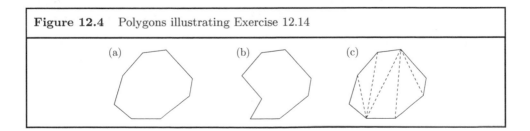

Figure 12.4 Polygons illustrating Exercise 12.14

(a)   (b)   (c)

Figure 12.5   An example illustrating Exercise 12.15

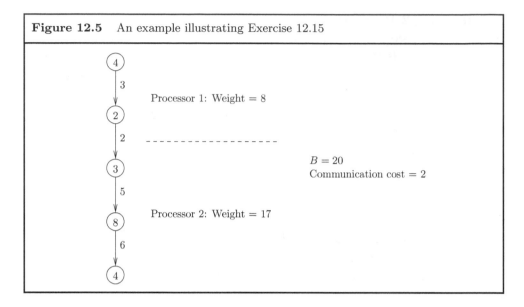

* Exercise 12.15. A *chain* is a rooted tree with exactly one leaf. We are given a chain representing a sequence of n pipelined processes. Each node i in the chain represents a process and has a positive *execution time* $e_i \in \mathbb{N}$. Each edge (i, j) has a positive *communication cost* $c_{ij} \in \mathbb{N}$. For edge (i, j), if processes i and j are executed on separate processors, the time needed to send data from process i to process j is c_{ij}; if the processes are executed on the same processor, this time is 0. We wish to assign processes to processors such that each processor has total weight no more than a given value $B \in \mathbb{N}$. The weight of a processor is given by the sum of the execution times of the processes assigned to that processor, plus the sum of the communication costs of edges between tasks on that processor and tasks on *other* processors (see Figure 12.5). The *communication cost* of an assignment is the sum of the communication costs of edges that connect nodes assigned to different processors.

Give a dynamic programming algorithm that finds the minimum communication cost of any assignment of processes to processors such that each processor has weight no more than B. Note that we place no restriction on the number of processors used. Your algorithm should run in $O(n^2)$ time. Prove that your algorithm is correct.

Exercise 12.16. Given two strings x and y, we define the *edit distance* from x to y as the minimum number of operations required to transform x into y, where the operations are chosen from the following:

- insert a character;
- delete a character; or
- change a character.

**a. Prove that there is an optimal sequence of operations transforming x to y in which the edits proceed from left to right.

b. Using the above result, give a dynamic programming algorithm that takes as input x and y and returns the edit distance from x to y. Your algorithm should run in $O(mn)$ time, where m is the length of x and n is the length of y. Prove that your algorithm is correct.

Exercise 12.17. Suppose we wish to store n keys, $k_1 < k_2 < \cdots < k_n$, in a binary search tree (see Chapter 6). We define the *cost* of a look-up of key k_i as $d_i + 1$, where d_i is the depth of k_i in the tree. Thus, the cost of a look-up is simply the number of nodes examined. Suppose further that we are given, for $1 \le i \le n$, the probability $p_i \in \mathbb{R}^{>0}$ that any given look-up is for key k_i. We assume that

> The depth of a node in a tree is the number of edges in the path from the root to that node.

$$\sum_{i=1}^{n} p_i = 1.$$

We say that a binary search tree containing these keys is *optimal* if the expected cost of a look-up in this tree is minimum over the set of all binary search trees containing these keys.

a. Let us extend the definition of the cost of a look-up to pertain to a specific subtree, so that the cost with respect to subtree T is the number of nodes in T examined during that look-up. For $i \le j$, let S_{ij} be the set of all binary search trees with keys $k_1, \ldots, k_n$ such that there is a subtree containing exactly the keys $k_i, \ldots, k_j$. Let C_{ij} denote the minimum over S_{ij} of the expected cost of a look-up with respect to the subtree containing keys $k_i, \ldots, k_j$. Prove that

$$
C_{ij} = \begin{cases}
p_i & \text{if } i = j \\
\displaystyle\min_{i \le k \le j}(C_{i,k-1} + C_{k+1,j}) + \sum_{k=i}^{j} p_k & \text{if } i < j
\end{cases}
$$

*b. Give a dynamic programming algorithm that takes as input $p_1, \ldots, p_n$ and returns the expected cost of a look-up for an optimal binary search tree whose keys $k_1 < k_2 < \cdots < k_n$ have the given probabilities. (Note that we don't need the values of the keys in order to compute this value.) Your algorithm should run in $O(n^3)$ time and $O(n^2)$ space.

**c. Suppose r_{ij} is the root of an optimal binary search containing the keys $k_i, \ldots, k_j$, where $i \leq j$. Prove that $r_{i,j-1} \leq r_{ij} \leq r_{i+1,j}$ for $1 \leq i < j \leq n$.

*d. Using the above result, improve your algorithm to run in $O(n^2)$ time.

Exercise 12.18. Give a dynamic programming algorithm that takes as input two natural numbers $k \leq n$ and returns the probability that flipping a fair coin n times yields at least k heads. Your algorithm should run in $O(n)$ time. Prove that your algorithm is correct.

* Exercise 12.19. Give a dynamic programming algorithm that takes as input a natural number n and returns the number of different orderings of n elements using $<$ and/or $=$. For example, for $n = 3$, there are 13 orderings:

$$x < y < z \quad x < z < y \quad y < x < z \quad y < z < x$$

$$z < x < y \quad z < y < x \quad x = y < z \quad z < x = y$$

$$x = z < y \quad y < x = z \quad y = z < x \quad x < y = z$$

$$x = y = z.$$

Your algorithm should run in $O(n^2)$ time and use $O(n)$ space. Prove that your algorithm is correct.

* Exercise 12.20. Suppose we have a mathematical structure containing three elements, a, b, and c, and a multiplication operation given by the following table:

	a	b	c
a	a	c	a
b	c	b	b
c	a	c	b

Note that this multiplication operation is neither commutative nor associative. Give a dynamic programming algorithm that takes as input a string over a, b, and c, and returns a boolean indicating whether it is possible to parenthesize the string so that the result is a. (For example, if we parenthesize $abca$ as $(a(bc))a$, we get a result of a.) Your algorithm should run in $O(n^3)$ time, where n is the length of the input string. Prove that your algorithm is correct.

* Exercise 12.21. Suppose we are given an array $L[1..n]$ of positive integers representing the lengths of successive words in a paragraph. We wish to format the paragraph so that each line contains no more than m characters, including a single blank character between adjacent words on the same line. Furthermore, we wish to minimize a "sloppiness" criterion. Specifically, we wish to minimize the following objective function:

$$\sum_{i=1}^{k-1} f(m - c_i),$$

where k is the total number of lines used, $f : \mathbb{N} \rightarrow \mathbb{N}$ is some nondecreasing function, and c_i is the number of characters (including blanks between adjacent words) on line i. Give an efficient dynamic programming algorithm for computing the optimal arrangement. Your algorithm should run in $O(n^2)$ time and use $O(n)$ space. [***Hint:*** Reduce this problem to the problem for which the measure of sloppiness includes the last line — i.e., the optimization function is as above, but with $k - 1$ replaced by k.]

* Exercise 12.22. We are given a set of n points (x_i, y_i), where each x_i and y_i is a real number and all the x_is are distinct. A *bitonic tour* of these points is a cycle that begins at the rightmost point, proceeds strictly to the left to the leftmost point, then proceeds strictly to the right to return to the rightmost point; furthermore, this cycle contains every point exactly once (see Figure 12.6). We wish to find the bitonic tour having minimum Euclidean length; i.e., the distance between two points (x_1, y_1) and (x_2, y_2) is given by

$$\sqrt{(x_1 - x_2)^2 + (y_1 - y_2)^2}.$$

Give an efficient dynamic programming algorithm for finding a minimum-length bitonic tour. Your algorithm should use $O(n^2)$ time and space. [***Hint:*** Reduce this problem to that of finding a minimum-length bitonic path that includes all the points exactly once, but does not return to the starting point.]

* Exercise 12.23. Suppose we were to modify the scheduling problem of Section 11.1 so that each job also has a natural number *execution time*, which must be fulfilled without interruption. Thus, a schedule including job i must have job i scheduled for e_i contiguous time units lying between time 0 and time d_i, where e_i is the execution time and d_i is the deadline of job i. Give an efficient dynamic programming algorithm to generate a schedule with maximum value. Your algorithm should use $O(n(m + \lg n))$ time and $O(mn)$ space, where n is the number of jobs and m is the maximum deadline.

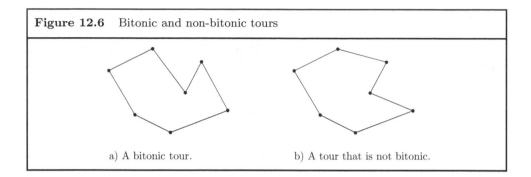

Figure 12.6   Bitonic and non-bitonic tours

a) A bitonic tour.   b) A tour that is not bitonic.

12.7   Notes

The mathematical foundation for dynamic programming was given by Bellman [10]. The CHANGE algorithm in Figure 12.1 is due to Wright [123]. The CHAINEDMATRIXMULT algorithm in Figure 12.2 is due to Godbole [56]. Floyd's algorithm (Figure 12.3) is due to Floyd [40], but is based on a theorem due to Warshall [118] for computing the transitive closure of a boolean matrix. Because a boolean matrix can be viewed as an adjacency matrix for a directed graph, this is the same as finding the transitive closure of a directed graph (Exercise 12.13).

The algorithm suggested by Exercise 12.3 is due to Kozen and Zaks [86]. Exercise 12.10 is solved by Chvatal *et al.* [22]. Wagner and Fischer [117] solved Exercise 12.16 and provided an alternative solution to Exercise 12.10. Exercise 12.17 is solved by Gilbert and Moore [55] and Knuth [81], but a more elegant solution is given by Yao [125]. Exercises 12.19 and 12.20 are from Brassard and Bratley [17].

Part IV

Common Reduction Targets

Chapter 13

Depth-First Search

As we have seen in earlier chapters, many problems can be characterized as graph problems. Graph problems often require the searching of the graph for certain structural characteristics. For example, one problem which we will examine in this chapter is searching a connected undirected graph for vertices whose removal would disconnect the graph. Such vertices are called *articulation points*.

In order to find articulation points, an algorithm must extract a great deal of information involving the paths connecting the various vertices in the graph. One way of organizing this information is by constructing a certain kind of rooted spanning tree, called a *depth-first* spanning tree. One advantage to processing a rooted spanning tree as opposed to a graph is that a rooted tree fits more naturally with the top-down approach. Furthermore, as we will see later in this chapter, a depth-first spanning tree has properties that are helpful for extracting connectivity information. We therefore find that many problems can be reduced to finding one or more depth-first spanning trees. These spanning trees are found using a technique called *depth-first search*.

Because algorithms using depth-first search operate on rooted trees, we begin by studying the problem of determining ancestry in rooted trees. The technique we use to solve this problem will motivate the depth-first search technique. We will then show how depth-first search can be used to find articulation points in a connected undirected graph. Finally, we will show how the technique can be extended to problems for directed graphs.

13.1   Ancestry in Rooted Trees

Suppose we are given two nodes, x and y, in a rooted tree T. We wish to determine whether x is an ancestor of y. By traversing the subtree rooted at x (see Section 6.1), we can determine whether y is in that subtree. In the worst case, y is not in the subtree, so we have to traverse the entire subtree. If the subtree contains most of the nodes in T, the traversal will take $\Theta(n)$ time, where n is the number of nodes in the tree.

It seems unlikely that we would be able to solve this problem in $o(n)$ time. However, note that we can traverse the entire tree in $\Theta(n)$ time. This fact might help us to solve efficiently the problem of determining ancestry for several pairs of nodes. Perhaps we can do a single traversal in $\Theta(n)$ time, and save enough information that only constant additional time is needed to decide ancestry for any pair of nodes in the tree.

We can get some insight into how to accumulate the necessary information by reviewing preorder and postorder traversals, as outlined in Section 6.1. A preorder traversal visits a node x before visiting any of its proper descendants, whereas a postorder traversal visits x after visiting all of its proper descendants. Therefore, if x is a proper ancestor of y, a preorder traversal will visit x before visiting y, and a postorder traversal will visit x after visiting y. If we could combine a preorder traversal with a postorder traversal and keep track of the order in which the visits were made, we could then efficiently check a necessary condition for x being a proper ancestor of y.

We will show that the above condition is also sufficient for x being a proper ancestor of y. First, however, let us present an algorithm for calculating this information in order to be able to reason about it more precisely. In order to describe the algorithm, we need a simple data structure called a VISITCOUNTER, whose definition is shown in Figure 13.1. It has two representation variables, an integer *count* and an array *num*$[0..n-1]$. Its structural invariant is that for $0 \leq i < n$, *num*$[i]$ is a natural number, and that

$$count = \max_{0 \leq i < n} num[i].$$

We interpret the size of the structure to be the size of *num*, and we interpret the value of *num*$[i]$ as the value associated with i. Clearly, the constructor runs in $\Theta(n)$ time, and the operations all run in $\Theta(1)$ time.

The algorithm shown in Figure 13.2 combines the preorder and postorder traversals of the tree T. We use a (directed) GRAPH to represent T. *pre* is a VISITCOUNTER that records the order in which nodes are visited in the

---

Figure 13.1 The data structure VISITCOUNTER

Structural Invariant: For $0 \leq i < n$, $num[i]$ is a NAT, and

$$count = \max_{0 \leq i < n} num[i].$$

Precondition: n is a NAT.
Postcondition: Constructs a VISITCOUNTER of size n, all of whose values are 0.

VISITCOUNTER(n)
   $count \leftarrow 0$; $num \leftarrow$ **new** ARRAY$[0..n - 1]$
   for $i \leftarrow 0$ **to** $n - 1$
     $num[i] \leftarrow 0$

Precondition: i is a NAT strictly less than SIZE().
Postcondition: Associates with i a value of $m + 1$, where m is the largest value initially associated with any j, $0 \leq j <$ SIZE().

VISITCOUNTER.VISIT(i)
   $count \leftarrow count + 1$; $num[i] \leftarrow count$

Precondition: i is a NAT strictly less than SIZE().
Postcondition: Returns the value associated with i.

VISITCOUNTER.NUM(i)
   return $num[i]$

Precondition: true.
Postcondition: Returns the size of this VISITCOUNTER.

VISITCOUNTER.SIZE()
   return SIZEOF(num)

---

preorder traversal, and *post* is a VISITCOUNTER that records the order in which nodes are visited in the postorder traversal.

Note that PREPOSTTRAVERSE is different from most recursive algorithms in that there is no explicit base case. However, a base case does exist — the case in which i has no outgoing edges. In this case, the loop will not iterate, and no recursive call will be made. The lack of an explicit base case is reflected in the following correctness proof, which likewise does not contain a separate base case.

Figure 13.2 Preprocessing algorithm for ancestry test

Precondition: T is a GRAPH representing a rooted tree with edges directed from parents to children. *pre* and *post* are VISITCOUNTERs whose size n is the number of nodes in T, and i is a NAT strictly less than n.

Postcondition: Let S be the set of descendants of i. For every $j \in S$ and every node $k \notin S$, *pre*.NUM$(j) >$ *pre*.NUM(k) and *post*.NUM$(j) >$ *post*.NUM(k). For any $j, k \in S$, j is a proper ancestor of k iff *pre*.NUM$(j) <$ *pre*.NUM(k) and *post*.NUM$(j) >$ *post*.NUM(k). If node $k \notin S$, then *pre*.NUM(k) and *post*.NUM(k) are unchanged.

PREPOSTTRAVERSE$(T, i, pre, post)$
    pre.VISIT(i); $L \leftarrow T$.ALLFROM(i)
    // **Invariant:** The postcondition holds with S denoting the set of
    // proper descendants of i that are not descendants of any node in L,
    // except that *pre*.NUM(i) has been changed to be larger than
    // *pre*.NUM(k) for every $k \notin S \cup \{i\}$.
    while not L.ISEMPTY$()$
        next $\leftarrow L$.HEAD$()$.DEST$()$; $L \leftarrow L$.TAIL$()$
        PREPOSTTRAVERSE$(T, next, pre, post)$
    post.VISIT(i)

Theorem 13.1. PREPOSTTRAVERSE *satisfies its specification.*

Proof.   By induction on n, the size of T.

Induction Hypothesis: Assume that PREPOSTTRAVERSE satisfies its specification for every tree with strictly fewer than n nodes.

Induction Step: Assume the precondition is satisfied. We must show the correctness of the invariant.

Initialization: The call to *pre*.VISIT(i) makes *pre*.NUM(i) larger than any other values in *pre*. Otherwise, no other values in *pre* or *post* have been changed from their initial values. At the beginning of the loop, L contains the children of i and $S = \varnothing$. The invariant is therefore satisfied.

Maintenance: Suppose the invariant holds at the beginning of an iteration. Clearly, the precondition holds for the recursive call. Because the subtree rooted at *next* has strictly fewer nodes than does T, from the Induction Hypothesis, the recursive call satisfies the postcondition with S denoting the set of descendants of *next*. Let R be the set of descendants of *next*. Let S' denote the value of S at the end of the iteration; i.e., $S' = S \cup R$. We must show that the invariant holds for S' at the end of the iteration.

Let us first determine the values in *pre* and *post* that have changed from their initial values by the time the iteration completes. From the invariant, only *pre*.NUM(i), *pre*.NUM(j), and *post*.NUM(j) such that $j \in S$ have changed prior to the beginning of the iteration. From the Induction Hypothesis, the recursive call only changes the values of *pre*.NUM(j) and *post*.NUM(j) for $j \in R$. Thus, the only values to have changed from their initial values are *pre*.NUM(i), *pre*.NUM(j), and *post*.NUM(j) such that $j \in S'$. Furthermore because only values for $j \in R$ are changed by the iteration, it is still the case that *pre*.NUM(i) > *pre*.NUM(k) for all $k \notin S' \cup \{i\}$.

Let $j \in S'$ and $k \notin S'$. If $j \notin R$, then *pre*.NUM(j), *post*.NUM(j), *pre*.NUM(k) and *post*.NUM(k) are unchanged by the iteration. Therefore, because $j \in S$, from the invariant, it is still the case that *pre*.NUM(j) > *pre*.NUM(k) and *post*.NUM(j) > *post*.NUM(k). On the other hand, suppose $j \in R$. Because $k \notin R$, by the Induction Hypothesis, *pre*.NUM(j) > *pre*.NUM(k) and *post*.NUM(j) > *post*.NUM(k) at the end of the iteration.

Now let $j, k \in S'$. We must show that j is a proper ancestor of k iff *pre*.NUM(j) < *pre*.NUM(k) and *post*.NUM(j) > *post*.NUM(k).

$\Rightarrow$: Suppose j is a proper ancestor of k. Then either j and k are both in R or neither is in R. If neither j nor k is in R, then the iteration changes none of their *pre* or *post* values. Hence, from the invariant, *pre*.NUM(j) < *pre*.NUM(k) and *post*.NUM(j) > *post*.NUM(k). On the other hand, if $j, k \in R$ then from the Induction Hypothesis, *pre*.NUM(j) < *pre*.NUM(k) and *post*.NUM(j) > *post*.NUM(k).

$\Leftarrow$: Suppose *pre*.NUM(j) < *pre*.NUM(k) and *post*.NUM(j) > *post*.NUM(k). If $j \in R$, then from the Induction Hypothesis, $k \in R$, for if not, *pre*.NUM(j) > *pre*.NUM(k). Thus, from the Induction Hypothesis, j is a proper ancestor of k. If $j \notin R$, then from the Induction Hypothesis, $k \notin R$, for otherwise, *post*.NUM(k) > *post*.NUM(j). Then none of their *pre* or *post* values is changed by the iteration. From the invariant, j is a proper ancestor of k.

Termination: Because L contains finitely many elements and each iteration removes one element from L, the loop must eventually terminate.

Correctness: Assume the invariant holds and that L is empty when the loop terminates. We need to show that the postcondition holds when the algorithm finishes. Let S denote the set of descendants of i.

Let us first consider which values in *pre* and *post* have been changed by the algorithm. From the invariant, only *pre*.NUM(i), *pre*.NUM(j), and *post*.NUM(j), where $j \in S \setminus \{i\}$, have changed by the time the loop terminates. The final call to *post*.VISIT(i) changes *post*.NUM(i). Therefore, the only values to have been changed by the algorithm are *pre*.NUM(j) and *post*.NUM(j) such that $j \in S$.

Let $j \in S$ and $k \notin S$. If $j \neq i$, then from the invariant, *pre*.NUM(j) > *pre*.NUM(k) and *post*.NUM(j) > *post*.NUM(k). If $j = i$, then from the invariant *pre*.NUM(j) > *pre*.NUM(k). Furthermore, the call to *post*.VISIT(i) makes *post*.NUM(j) > *post*.NUM(k).

Now let $j, k \in S$. We must show that j is a proper ancestor of k iff *pre*.NUM(j) < *pre*.NUM(k), and *post*.NUM(j) > *post*.NUM(k).

$\Rightarrow$: Suppose j is a proper ancestor of k. Then $k \neq i$, because i is an ancestor of every node in S. If $j \neq i$, then it follows from the invariant that *pre*.NUM(j) < *pre*.NUM(k) and *post*.NUM(j) > *post*.NUM(k). If $j = i$ then from the invariant *pre*.NUM(j) < *pre*.NUM(k), and the final call to *post*.VISIT(i) makes *post*.NUM(j) > *post*.NUM(k).

$\Leftarrow$: Suppose *pre*.NUM(j) < *pre*.NUM(k) and *post*.NUM(j) > *post*.NUM(k). If neither $j = i$ nor $k = i$, then from the invariant, j is a proper ancestor of k. If $j = i$, then clearly j is a proper ancestor of k. Finally, $k \neq i$ because the final call to *post*.VISIT(i) would then make *post*.NUM(k) > *post*.NUM(j).

$\square$

In order to analyze the running time of PREPOSTTRAVERSE, let us assume that T is represented as a LISTGRAPH. Then the call to ALLFROM runs in $\Theta(1)$ time. Furthermore, the **while** loop iterates exactly m times, where m is the number of children of i. Because each iteration of the **while** loop results in one recursive call, it is easily seen that the running time is proportional to the total number of calls to PREPOSTTRAVERSE. It is easily shown by induction on n, the number of nodes in the subtree rooted at i, that a call in which the second parameter is i results in exactly n total calls. The running time is therefore in $\Theta(n)$.

Figure 13.3   Algorithm for testing ancestry for multiple pairs of nodes in a rooted tree

---

Precondition: T refers to a GRAPH representing a tree rooted at i with edges directed from parents to children, and $x[1..m]$ and $y[1..m]$ are arrays of NATs less than T.SIZE().
Postcondition: Returns an array $ancestor[1..m]$ of BOOLs such that $ancestor[i]$ is **true** iff $x[i]$ is a proper ancestor of $y[i]$.

ANCESTORS$(T, i, x[1..m], y[1..m])$
    $n \leftarrow T.$SIZE(); $ancestor \leftarrow$ **new** ARRAY$[1..m]$
    $pre \leftarrow$ **new** VISITCOUNTER(n); $post \leftarrow$ **new** VISITCOUNTER(n)
    PREPOSTTRAVERSE$(T, i, pre, post)$
    for $j \leftarrow 1$ **to** m
        $condPre \leftarrow pre.$NUM$(x[j]) < pre.$NUM$(y[j])$
        $condPost \leftarrow post.NUM(x[j]) > post.NUM(y[j])$
        $ancestor[j] \leftarrow condPre$ **and** $condPost$
    return $ancestor$

The algorithm for testing ancestry for multiple pairs of nodes is given in Figure 13.3. The initialization prior to the call to PREPOSTTRAVERSE clearly runs in $\Theta(n)$ time, as does the call to PREPOSTTRAVERSE. The body of the loop runs in $\Theta(1)$ time. Because the loop iterates m times, the entire algorithm runs in $\Theta(n + m)$ time.

13.2   Reachability in a Graph

We will now show how the technique used in the last section can be applied to graph problems. Consider the problem of determining whether there is a path from a given vertex i to a given vertex j in an undirected graph. Viewing the problem top-down, we first note that there is a path if $i = j$. Otherwise, we can retrieve all of the vertices adjacent to i and remove i from the graph. For each vertex k that was adjacent to i, we can then determine whether there is a path from k to j in the resulting graph. We must be careful, however, because each of these tests is destructive — it removes all of the vertices it reaches. As a result, we must be sure a node k is still in the graph before we solve that subproblem. Note that if it has been removed, then it must have been reachable from one of the other vertices adjacent to i; hence all nodes reachable from k have been removed. Thus, if j were reachable from k, we would have already found that it was reachable from i.

In order to avoid deleting vertices from the graph, we need a mechanism for selecting a subgraph based on a given subset of the vertices. More precisely, let $G = (V, E)$ be a (directed or undirected) graph, and let $V' \subseteq V$. We define the subgraph of G *induced* by V' to be $G' = (V', E')$, where E' is the set of edges connecting vertices from V'. We therefore need a mechanism for selecting a subset of the vertices in the graph.

For this purpose, we define the data structure SELECTOR. A SELECTOR represents a set of n elements numbered $0, \ldots, n-1$, each of which is either selected or unselected. The constructor and operations for SELECTOR are specified in Figure 13.4. It is a straightforward matter to implement SELECTOR using an array of booleans so that the constructor, SELECTALL, and UNSELECTALL run in $\Theta(n)$ time, where n is the number of elements represented, and so that the remaining operations run in $\Theta(1)$ time.

Figure 13.4   Specification of the SELECTOR data structure

Precondition: n is a NAT.
Postcondition: Constructs a SELECTOR of size n, all of whose elements are selected.

SELECTOR(n)

Precondition: true.
Postcondition: Selects all elements.

SELECTOR.SELECTALL()

Precondition: true.
Postcondition: Unselects all elements.

SELECTOR.UNSELECTALL()

Precondition: i is a NAT less than the number of elements.
Postcondition: Selects element i.

SELECTOR.SELECT(i)

Precondition: i is a NAT less than the number of elements.
Postcondition: Unselects element i.

SELECTOR.UNSELECT(i)

Precondition: i is a NAT less than the number of elements.
Postcondition: Returns true if element i is selected, or false otherwise.

SELECTOR.ISSELECTED(i)

Figure 13.5   Reachability algorithm for undirected graphs

Precondition: G refers to an undirected GRAPH, and i and j are NATs strictly less than G.SIZE().
Postcondition: Returns true iff there is a path in G from i to j.

REACHABLE(G, i, j)
   $n \leftarrow G$.SIZE(); *sel* $\leftarrow$ **new** SELECTOR(n)
   pre $\leftarrow$ **new** VISITCOUNTER(n); *post* $\leftarrow$ **new** VISITCOUNTER(n)
   REACHDFS($G, i, sel, pre, post$)
   return not *sel*.ISSELECTED(j)

Precondition: G refers to an undirected graph, i is a NAT such that $i < G$.SIZE(), *sel* refers to a SELECTOR of size G.SIZE(), *pre* and *post* refer to VISITCOUNTERs of size G.SIZE(), and *sel*.ISSELECTED(i) = true.
Postcondition: Unselects each j such that j is reachable from i in G', where G' denotes the subgraph of G induced by the set of selected vertices.

REACHDFS($G, i, sel, pre, post$)
   sel.UNSELECT(i); *pre*.VISIT(i); $L \leftarrow G$.ALLFROM(i)
   while not L.ISEMPTY()
      next $\leftarrow L$.HEAD().DEST(); $L \leftarrow L$.TAIL()
      if *sel*.ISSELECTED(*next*)
         REACHDFS($G, next, sel, pre, post$)
   post.VISIT(i)

We can now traverse the graph using almost the same algorithm as PREPOSTTRAVERSE — the only differences are that *pre* and *post* are not needed, and we must check that a vertex has not already been visited before we traverse it. We call this traversal a *depth-first search* (DFS). The entire algorithm is shown in Figure 13.5. We retain *pre* and *post* in order to maintain a close relationship between REACHDFS and PREPOSTTRAVERSE.

Let G be an undirected GRAPH, and let $i \in \mathbb{N}$ such that $i < G$.SIZE(). Further let *sel* be a SELECTOR of size G.SIZE() in which all elements are selected, and let *pre* and *post* be VISITCOUNTERs of size G.SIZE() in which all values are 0. Suppose we invoke REACHDFS($G, i, sel, pre, post$). We define a directed graph G' as follows, based on the behavior of this invocation:

- G' has the same vertices as G;
- G' has the edge (j, k) iff a call REACHDFS($G, j, sel, pre, post$) is made, which in turn calls REACHDFS($G, k, sel, pre, post$).

Let us consider the structure of G'. We first observe that for each vertex $k \neq i$, there is some edge (j, k) in G' iff k is reachable from i in G. Furthermore, a call to REACHDFS$(G, k, sel, pre, post)$ can be made only if $sel.$IsSELECTED$(k) =$ true. Because this call immediately unselects k, and because the algorithm never selects a vertex, it follows that REACHDFS$(G, k, sel, pre, post)$ can be called at most once. Hence, each vertex in G' has at most one incoming edge. Finally, i can have no incoming edges. Therefore, G' forms a tree rooted at i. The vertices of G' are exactly the vertices reachable from i in the subgraph of G induced by the selected vertices. G' is therefore a rooted spanning tree of the connected component containing i in the subgraph of G induced by the selected vertices.

It should now be clear that the calls to REACHDFS$(G, i, sel, pre, post)$ and PREPOSTTRAVERSE$(G', i, pre, post)$ produce exactly the same values in pre and $post$. In essence, REACHDFS performs both a preorder traversal and a postorder traversal on a rooted tree. This rooted tree is a spanning tree of a particular connected component of a given graph. The given graph is the subgraph of the input graph G induced by the selected vertices, and the connected component is specified by the input vertex i. The spanning tree is not specified, but is implied by the behavior of REACHDFS. We call this spanning tree the *depth-first spanning tree* generated by the call to REACHDFS$(G, i, sel, pre, post)$.

We can use the correspondence between REACHDFS and PREPOSTTRA-VERSE in order to analyze the running time of REACHDFS. Suppose G is implemented as a LISTGRAPH. Let G' be the subgraph of G induced by the selected vertices, and let G'' be the connected component of G' containing i; thus, the vertices in G'' are the vertices visited by REACHDFS. Let n be the number of vertices in G''. Certainly, REACHDFS runs in $\Omega(n)$ time. The only difference in the two algorithms is that in REACHDFS, the loop may iterate more times. Thus, if we ignore the iterations in which no recursive call is made, the running time is the same as that of PREPOSTTRAVERSE: $\Theta(n)$.

In the call REACHDFS$(G, j, sel, pre, post)$, the loop iterates m times, where m is the number of vertices adjacent to j in G. The total number of iterations in all recursive calls is therefore $2a_1 + a_2$, where a_1 is the number of edges in G'' and a_2 is the number of edges in G from vertices in G'' to vertices not in G''. The time for a single iteration that does not make a recursive call is in $\Theta(1)$. Because G'' is connected, $a_1 \geq n - 1$; hence, the total running time of REACHDFS$(G, i, sel, pre, post)$ is in $\Theta(a)$, where a is the number of edges in G incident on vertices in G''.

13.3 A Generic Depth-First Search

Due to its hierarchical nature, a rooted tree is more amenable to the top-down approach to algorithm design than is a graph. Furthermore, as we will see shortly, a depth-first spanning tree has several additional properties that can prove useful for designing graph algorithms. For this reason, it makes sense to generalize REACHDFS to a general-purpose depth-first search algorithm. With such an algorithm, we can then design our algorithms as traversals of depth-first spanning trees.

In order to generalize this algorithm, we need an ADT for defining various ways of processing a depth-first spanning tree. Upon examining REACHDFS, we see that there are five places where processing might occur:

- Preorder processing of vertices can occur prior to the loop.
- Preorder processing of tree edges might occur prior to the recursive call.
- Postorder processing of tree edges might occur following the recursive call.
- Though the **if** statement in REACHDFS has no **else**-block, we might include an **else**-block for processing other edges.
- Postorder processing of vertices can occur following the loop.

We therefore have the ADT specified in Figure 13.6. The generic depth-first search is shown in Figure 13.7.

Let us now consider the useful properties of depth-first spanning trees. These properties concern the non-tree edges. First, we show the following theorem regarding undirected graphs.

Theorem 13.2. *Let G be a connected undirected graph with n vertices, and let sel be a* SELECTOR *of size n in which all elements are selected. Suppose we call* DFS(G, i, sel, s), *where s is a* SEARCHER *of size n. Then for every edge $\{j, k\}$ processed as a non-tree edge, either j is an ancestor of k or k is an ancestor of j.*

Proof. Without loss of generality, assume j is unselected before k is. Consider the call to DFS on vertex j. Initially, j is preorder processed while k is still selected. We consider two cases.

Case 1: $\{j, k\}$ is processed as a non-tree edge in the call to DFS on j. Then when this happens, k must be unselected. There must therefore have been a call to DFS on k which unselected k. This call resulted in k being both preorder processed and postorder processed after j was preorder processed, but before j was postorder processed. j is therefore a proper ancestor of k.

Figure 13.6   The SEARCHER ADT for facilitating depth-first search

---

Precondition: n is a NAT.
Postcondition: Constructs a new SEARCHER of size n.

SEARCHER(n)

Precondition: i is a NAT less than the size of this SEARCHER.
Postcondition: true.

SEARCHER.PREPROC(i)

Precondition: i is a NAT less than the size of this SEARCHER.
Postcondition: true.

SEARCHER.POSTPROC(i)

Precondition: e is an EDGE whose vertices are less than the size of this SEARCHER.
Postcondition: true.

SEARCHER.TREEPREPROC(e)

Precondition: e is an EDGE whose vertices are less than the size of this SEARCHER.
Postcondition: true.

SEARCHER.TREEPOSTPROC(e)

Precondition: e is an EDGE whose vertices are less than the size of this SEARCHER.
Postcondition: true.

SEARCHER.OTHEREDGEPROC(e)

Case 2: $\{j, k\}$ is processed as a tree edge in the call to DFS on j, but is processed as a non-tree edge in the call to DFS on k. In this case, k is by definition a child of j.   □

The above theorem gives the property of depth-first spanning trees that makes depth-first search so useful for connected undirected graphs. Given a connected undirected graph G and a depth-first spanning tree T of G, let us refer to edges of G that correspond to edges in T as *tree edges*. We will call all other edges *back edges*. By definition, tree edges connect parents with children. Theorem 13.2 tells us that back edges connect ancestors with descendants.

Figure 13.7   A generic depth-first search algorithm

Precondition: G refers to a GRAPH, i is a NAT less than G.SIZE(), *sel* refers to a SELECTOR with size G.SIZE() such that i is selected, and s refers to a SEARCHER with size G.SIZE().

Postcondition: Traverses a depth-first spanning tree rooted at i on the connected component containing i in the subgraph of G induced by the selected vertices. Each vertex j in this tree is processed by calling s.PREPROC(j) before any of j's proper descendants are processed and by calling s.POSTPROC(j) after all of j's descendants are processed. Each edge (j, k) in the tree is processed by calling s.TREEPREPROC((j, k)) before k is processed and by calling s.TREEPOSTPROC((j, k)) after k is processed. All other edges e from j to any node in G are processed by calling s.OTHEREDGEPROC(e).

DFS(G, i, sel, s)
   sel.UNSELECT(i); s.PREPROC(i); $L \leftarrow G$.ALLFROM(i)
   while not L.ISEMPTY()
      edge $\leftarrow L$.HEAD(); *next* $\leftarrow$ *edge*.DEST(); $L \leftarrow L$.TAIL()
      if *sel*.ISSELECTED(*next*)
         s.TREEPREPROC(*edge*)
         DFS(G, *next*, *sel*, s)
         s.TREEPOSTPROC(*edge*)
      else
         s.OTHEREDGEPROC(*edge*)
   s.POSTPROC(i)

However, Theorem 13.2 does not apply to depth-first search on a directed graph. To see why, consider the graph shown in Figure 13.8. The solid edges in part (b) show a depth-first search tree for the graph in part (a); the remaining edges of the graph are shown with dashed lines in part (b). Because 0 is the root and all other vertices are reachable from 0, all other vertices are descendants of 0. Suppose $(0, 1)$ is the first edge from 0 to be processed. Because 2 is the only vertex reachable from 1, it is the only proper descendant of 1. Of the remaining edges from 0, only $(0, 3)$ leads to a vertex that has not yet been reached, so 3 is the only other child of 0. Finally, because 4 is reachable from 3, 3 is the parent of 4. In the resulting depth-first spanning tree, 3 is neither an ancestor nor a descendant of 1, but there is an edge $(3, 1)$ in the graph.

The point at which the proof of Theorem 13.2 fails for directed graphs is the initial assumption that j is unselected before k is. For an undirected graph, one of the endpoints of the edge will be unselected first, and it doesn't matter which endpoint we call j. However, with a directed edge, either the source or the destination may be unselected first, and we must consider both cases. Given the assumption that the source is unselected first, the remainder of the proof follows. We therefore have the following theorem.

Theorem 13.3. *Let G be a directed graph with n vertices such that all vertices are reachable from i, and let sel be a SELECTOR of size n in which all elements are selected. Suppose we call $\text{DFS}(G, i, sel, s)$, where s is a SEARCHER of size n. Then for every edge (j, k) processed as a non-tree edge, if j is unselected before k is, then j is an ancestor of k.*

Thus, if we draw a depth-first spanning tree with subtrees listed from left to right in the order we unselect them (as in Figure 13.8), there will be no edges leading from left to right. As we can see from Figure 13.8, all three remaining possibilities can occur, namely:

- edges from ancestors to descendants (we call these *forward edges* if they are not in the tree);
- edges from descendants to ancestors (we call these *back edges*); and
- edges from right to left (we call these *cross edges*).

Theorem 13.3 gives us the property we need to make use of depth-first search with directed graphs.

As a final observation, we note that back edges in directed graphs always form cycles, because there is always a path along the tree edges from a vertex to any of its descendants. Hence, a directed acyclic graph cannot have back edges.

Figure 13.8   Example of depth-first search on a directed graph

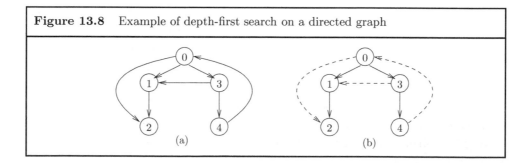

(a)   (b)

In the next three sections, we will show how to use depth-first search to design algorithms for connected undirected graphs, directed acyclic graphs, and directed graphs.

13.4   Articulation Points

As we mentioned at the beginning of this chapter, an *articulation point* in a connected undirected graph is any vertex whose removal yields a disconnected graph. If, for example, a given graph represents a communications network, then an articulation point is a node whose failure would partition the network. It would therefore be desirable to know if a given network contains any articulation points.

Let G be a connected undirected graph, and let T be a depth-first spanning tree for G. We first note that it is easy to tell if the root of T is an articulation point. If T has only one child, then the removal of its root from G cannot disconnect G — the tree edges continue to connect the graph. On the other hand, from Theorem 13.2, G can have no edges between different subtrees of T. Thus, if T has more than one child, its root must be an articulation point of G. We therefore conclude that the root of T is an articulation point of G iff it has more than one child.

The above property suggests the following algorithm. Let n be the number of vertices and a be the number of edges in G. We do n separate depth-first searches, using a different vertex as the root for each search. As we process the tree edges (either in preorder or in postorder), we count the number of children of the root. After the search completes, we then determine whether the root is an articulation point by examining the number of children it has. It is not hard to see that we could construct such an algorithm with running time in $\Theta(na)$, provided G is implemented as a LISTGRAPH.

In order to obtain a more efficient algorithm, let us consider some vertex i other than the root of T. If there are no back edges in G, then the removal of i disconnects G if i has at least one child. In this case, G is partitioned into one connected component for each child of i, plus a connected component containing all vertices that are not descendants of i. If, however, there are back edges, these back edges may connect all of these partitions together. Note, however, that from Theorem 13.2, no back edge can connect partitions containing two different children of i. In particular, if a back edge does connect a partition containing a child of i with another partition, it leads from a proper descendant of i to a proper ancestor of i. We therefore conclude that i is an articulation point iff i has at least one child j in T such that no descendant of j is adjacent to a proper ancestor of i.

If we can efficiently test the above property, then we should be able to find all articulation points with a single depth-first search. Note that it is sufficient to know, for each vertex j other than the root, the highest ancestor k of j that is adjacent to some descendant of j. The parent i of j is an articulation point if $k = i$. On the other hand, if for each child j of i, the highest ancestor k adjacent to some descendant of j is a proper ancestor of i, then i is not an articulation point. Because a vertex is preorder processed before all of its descendants, we can determine which of a given set of ancestors of a vertex is the closest to the root by determining which was preorder processed first. Thus, let us use a VISITCOUNTER *pre* to keep track of the order the vertices are preorder processed. We then need to compute the following value for each vertex i other than the root:

$$highest[i] = \min\{pre.\text{NUM}(k) \mid k \text{ is adjacent to a descendant of } i\}. \quad (13.1)$$

Let us consider a top-down approach to computing $highest[i]$. We first observe that if j is a child of i, then $highest[i] \leq highest[j]$. Furthermore, the vertex k determining $highest[i]$ is adjacent to either i or some proper descendant of i. If k is adjacent to a proper descendant of i, then $highest[i] = highest[j]$ for some child j of i. Finally, because i is adjacent to its parent, which has a smaller value in *pre* than does any child of i, we can ignore the *pre* values of the children of i in computing $highest[i]$. We therefore conclude that

$$highest[i] = \min(\{pre.\text{NUM}(k) \mid \{i, k\} \text{ is a back edge}\}$$

$$\cup \{highest[j] \mid j \text{ is a child of } i\}). \quad (13.2)$$

We can now build a SEARCHER s so that $\text{DFS}(G, 0, sel, s)$ will find the articulation points of G, where *sel* is an appropriate SELECTOR. (Note that it doesn't matter which node is used as the root of the depth-first search, so we will arbitrarily use 0.) Let n be the number of vertices in G. We need as representation variables a VISITCOUNTER *pre* of size n, an array $highest[0..n-1]$, a readable array $artPoints[0..n-1]$ of booleans to store the results, and a natural number *rootChildren* to record the number of children of the root. Note that making *artPoints* readable makes this data structure insecure, because code that can read the reference to the array can change values in the array. We will discuss this issue in more detail shortly.

To implement the SEARCHER operations, we only need to determine when the various calculations need to be done. Initialization should go in the constructor; however, because the elements of the arrays are not needed until the corresponding vertices are processed, we can initialize these elements in PREPROC. We want the processing of a vertex i to compute $highest[i]$. In order to use recurrence (13.2), we need $pre.\text{NUM}(k)$ for each back edge $\{i, k\}$ and $highest[j]$ for each child j of i. We therefore include the code to compute $highest[i]$ in OTHEREDGEPROC and TREEPOSTPROC. The determination of whether a vertex i other than the root is an articulation point needs to occur once we have computed $highest[j]$ for each child j of i; hence, we include this code in TREEPOSTPROC. To be able to determine whether the root is an articulation point, we count its children in TREEPOSTPROC. We can then make the determination once all of the processing is complete, i.e., in the call to POSTPROC for the root.

The implementation of ARTSEARCHER is shown in Figure 13.9. We have not given an implementation of the TREEPREPROC operation — it does

---

Figure 13.9   ARTSEARCHER implementation of SEARCHER

```
ARTSEARCHER(n)
    artPoints ← new ARRAY[0..n − 1]; highest ← new ARRAY[0..n − 1]
    pre ← new VISITCOUNTER(n); rootChildren ← 0


ARTSEARCHER.PREPROC(i)
    pre.VISIT(i); artPoints[i] ← false; highest[i] ← ∞


ARTSEARCHER.TREEPOSTPROC(e)
    i ← e.SOURCE(); j ← e.DEST(); highest[i] ← MIN(highest[i], highest[j])
    if i = 0
        rootChildren ← rootChildren + 1
    else if highest[j] = pre.NUM(i)
        artPoints[i] ← true


ARTSEARCHER.OTHEREDGEPROC(e)
    i ← e.SOURCE(); k ← e.DEST()
    highest[i] ← MIN(highest[i], pre.NUM(k))


ARTSEARCHER.POSTPROC(i)
    if i = 0 and rootChildren > 1
        artPoints[i] ← true
```

Figure 13.10   Algorithm for finding articulation points in a connected undirected graph

---

Precondition: G refers to a connected undirected GRAPH.
Postcondition: Returns an array $A[0..G.\text{SIZE}() - 1]$ of booleans such that $A[i]$ is **true** iff i is an articulation point in G.

ARTPTS(G)
    $n \leftarrow G.\text{SIZE}()$; $s \leftarrow$ **new** ARTSEARCHER(n); $sel \leftarrow$ **new** SELECTOR(n)
    DFS($G, 0, sel, s$)
    return $s.\text{ARTPOINTS}()$

---

nothing. We have also not specified any preconditions or postconditions for the constructor or any of the operations. The reason for this is that we are only interested in what happens when we use this structure with a depth-first search. It therefore doesn't make sense to prove its correctness in every context. As a result, we don't need to make this structure secure. Furthermore, the code in each of the operations is so simple that specifying preconditions and postconditions is more trouble than it is worth. As we will see, it will be a straightforward matter to prove that the algorithm that uses this structure is correct.

We can now construct an algorithm that uses depth-first search to find the articulation points in a connected undirected GRAPH G. The algorithm is shown in Figure 13.10. Let n be the number of vertices and a be the number of edges in G, and suppose G is implemented as a LISTGRAPH. Because each of the operations in ARTSEARCHER runs in $\Theta(1)$ time, it is easily seen that the call to DFS runs in $\Theta(a)$ time, the same as REACHDFS. The remaining statements run in $\Theta(n)$ time. Because G is connected, $n \in O(a)$, so the entire algorithm runs in $\Theta(a)$ time.

To prove that ARTPTS is correct, we need to show that the call to DFS results in $s.artPoints$ containing the correct boolean values. In order to prove this, it is helpful to prove first that $s.highest$ contains the correct values. This proof uses the fact that DFS performs a traversal of a depth-first spanning tree of G.

Lemma 13.4. *Let G be a connected undirected GRAPH with n vertices. Let sel be a SELECTOR of size n in which all elements are selected, and let s be a newly-constructed ARTSEARCHER of size n. Then DFS($G, 0, sel, s$) results in $s.highest[i]$ having the value specified in Equation (13.1) for $1 \leq i < n$.*

Proof. Let $1 \leq i < n$. We first observe that $s.highest[i]$ is only changed by PREPROC(i), TREEPOSTPROC(e), and OTHEREDGEPROC(e), where e is an edge from i; i.e., $s.highest[i]$ is only changed during the processing of vertex i. We will show by induction on m, the number of descendants of i in the depth-first spanning tree, that the processing of vertex i gives $s.highest[i]$ the correct value.

Induction Hypothesis: Assume that for any j with fewer than m descendants, the processing of vertex j gives $s.highest[j]$ the correct value.

Induction Step: Suppose i has m descendants. It is easily seen that the processing of vertex i assigns to $s.highest[i]$ the value,

$$\min(\{s.pre.\text{NUM}(k) \mid \{i, k\} \text{ is a back edge}\} \cup$$

$$\{s.highest[j] \mid j \text{ is a child of } i\}).$$

We must show that $s.pre.\text{NUM}(k)$ and $s.highest[j]$ have the correct values when they are used. $s.pre.\text{NUM}(k)$ is used in OTHEREDGEPROC(e), where $e = (i, k)$. This operation is only called

> We are denoting edges as directed edges because a GRAPH uses only directed edges (see p. 321).

when k is unselected, and hence after PREPROC(k) has been called. $s.pre.\text{NUM}(k)$ has therefore been set to its correct value. $s.highest[j]$ is used in TREEPOSTPROC(e), where $e = (i, j)$. Hence, j is a child of i that has been processed. Because j is a child of i, it has strictly fewer than m descendants. Thus, by the Induction Hypothesis, its processing sets it to its correct value. Thus, the processing of vertex i sets $s.highest[i]$ to the value given in Equation (13.2), which we have shown to be equivalent to Equation (13.1). $\qquad \square$

The proof of Lemma 13.4 relies heavily on known properties of depth-first search and depth-first spanning trees. As a result, it is quite straightforward. Often proofs of correctness for algorithms using depth-first search don't even require induction. Such is the case for the proof of the following theorem.

Theorem 13.5. ARTPTS *satisfies its specification.*

Proof. Let $0 \leq i < n$. We must show that the call to DFS results in $s.artPoints[i]$ being **true** if i is an articulation point, or **false** otherwise. We first note that $artPoints[i]$ is changed only during the processing of i. Furthermore, it is initialized to **false** in PREPROC(i). We must therefore show that it is set to **true** iff i is an articulation point. We consider two cases.

Case 1: $i = 0$. Then $artPoints[i]$ is set to **true** iff $rootChildren > 1$ in the call to PostProc(0). $rootChildren$ is only changed during the processing of vertex 0. It is initialized in $PreProc(0)$ to 0 and incremented by 1 in TreePostProc(e) for each tree edge $(0, j)$. When PostProc(0) is called, $rootChildren$ therefore contains the number of children of vertex 0, which is the root of the depth-first spanning tree. As we have observed earlier, the root is an articulation point iff it has more than one child.

Case 2: $i > 0$. Then $artPoints[i]$ is set to **true** iff $s.highest[j]$ has a value equal to $s.pre.\textsc{Num}(i)$ in the call to TreePostProc(e), where $e = (i, j)$ for some vertex j. Because (i, j) is passed to TreePostProc, j must be a child of i. From Lemma 13.4, the call to Dfs sets $s.highest[j]$ to the correct value, as defined in Equation (13.1). Furthermore, an examination of the proof of Lemma 13.4 reveals that this value is set by the processing of vertex j. This processing is done prior to the call to TreePostProc(e), so that $s.highest[j]$ has the correct value by the time it is used. Furthermore, $s.pre.\textsc{Num}(i)$ is set to its proper value by PreProc(i), which is also called before TreePostProc(e). As we have already shown, i is an articulation point iff $s.highest[j] = s.pre.\textsc{Num}(i)$ for some child j of i. $\square$

13.5 Topological Sort Revisited

In Section 9.2, we gave an algorithm for finding a topological sort of a directed acyclic graph. This algorithm ran in $\Theta(n+a)$ time for a ListGraph with n vertices and a edges. In this section, we give an alternative algorithm that illustrates the use of depth-first search on directed acyclic graphs.

We first note that a shortcoming of the Dfs algorithm is that it only processes vertices that are reachable from the root. In an arbitrary graph, there may be no vertex from which every vertex is reachable; hence it may be impossible to find a depth-first spanning tree (or any spanning tree) for the graph.

To remedy this shortcoming, we provide the algorithm DfsAll, shown in Figure 13.11. In order to understand its postcondition, it helps compare its behavior with that of Dfs. In particular, suppose G has n vertices, and let G' be the graph obtained by adding a new vertex n to G and edges from n to every other vertex in the graph. Notice that the behavior of the **for** loop in DfsAll(G, s) is exactly the same as the behavior of Dfs(G', n, sel, s), except that DfsAll only processes the vertices and edges in G. In particular, each time Dfs is called by DfsAll, it traverses a subtree of G' rooted

---

Figure 13.11   Algorithm for processing an entire graph with depth-first search

---

Precondition: G is a GRAPH and s is a SEARCHER with size G.SIZE().
Postcondition: Traverses a depth-first spanning forest on G. Each vertex j in this forest is processed by calling s.PREPROC(j) before any of j's proper descendants are processed and by calling s.POSTPROC(j) after all of j's descendants are processed. Each edge (j, k) in the forest is processed by calling s.TREEPREPROC((j, k)) before k is processed and by calling s.TREEPOSTPROC((j, k)) after k is processed. All other edges e from j to any node in G are processed by calling s.OTHEREDGEPROC(e).

DFSALL(G, s)
   $n \leftarrow G$.SIZE(); $sel \leftarrow$ **new** SELECTOR(n)
   for $i \leftarrow 0$ **to** $n - 1$
     if sel.ISSELECTED(i)
      DFS(G, i, sel, s)

---

at a child of the root n. For this reason, we call the collection of trees traversed by DFSALL a *depth-first spanning forest*. In particular, note that either Theorem 13.2 or Theorem 13.3, depending on whether G is undirected or directed, can be extended to apply to this forest.

Let G be a LISTGRAPH with n vertices and a edges. A graph G' constructed by adding a new vertex and $n - 1$ new edges to G then has $n + a - 1$ edges. Therefore, the running time of DFSALL(G, s) is easily seen to be in $\Theta(n+a)$, provided each of the vertex and edge processing operations in s runs in $\Theta(1)$ time.

Now consider the depth-first spanning forest for a directed acyclic graph. Because there are no cycles, the spanning forest can have no back edges. This leaves only tree edges, forward edges and cross edges. Furthermore, for each of these types of edge (i, j), j is postorder processed before i. This property suggests a straightforward algorithm for topological sort, namely, to order the vertices in the reverse of the order in which they are postorder processed by a depth-first search.

The SEARCHER for this algorithm needs as representation variables a readable array $order[0..n-1]$ for storing the listing of vertices in topological order and a natural number loc for storing the location in $order$ of the last vertex to be inserted. Only the constructor and the POSTPROC operation are nonempty; these are shown in Figure 13.12. The topological sort algorithm is shown in Figure 13.13. If G is implemented as a LISTGRAPH, the algorithm's

---

Figure 13.12   TopSortSearcher implementation of Searcher

TopSortSearcher(n)
   order ← **new** Array$[0..n-1]$; *loc* ← n

TopSortSearcher.PostProc(i)
   loc ← *loc* − 1; *order*[*loc*] ← i

Figure 13.13   Topological sort algorithm using depth-first search

---

Precondition: G is a directed acyclic graph.
Postcondition: Returns an array listing the vertices of G in topological order.

DfsTopSort(G)
   n ← G.Size(); s ← **new** TopSortSearcher(n)
   DfsAll(G, s)
   return s.Order()

---

running time is clearly in $\Theta(n + a)$, where n is the number of vertices and a is the number of edges in G. We leave the proof of correctness as an exercise.

13.6   Strongly Connected Components

Let $G = (V, E)$ be a directed graph. We say that G is *strongly connected* if for each pair of vertices u and v, there is a path from u to v. For an arbitrary directed graph G, let $S \subseteq V$. We say that S is a *strongly connected component* of G if

- the subgraph of G induced by S is strongly connected; and
- for any subset $S' \subseteq V$, if $S \subseteq S'$ and the subgraph of G induced by S' is strongly connected, then $S' = S$.

Thus, the strongly connected component containing a given vertex i is the set of vertices j such that there are paths from i to j and from j to i.

It is easily seen that the strongly connected components of a directed graph $G = (V, E)$ partition the V into disjoint subsets. We wish to design an algorithm to find this partition.

Let us consider a depth-first spanning forest of a directed graph G. We will begin by trying to find one strongly connected component. We first note that from any vertex i, we can reach all descendants of i. Depending on which back edges exist, we may be able to reach some ancestors of i. Depending on which cross edges exist, we may be able to reach some other vertices as well; however, we cannot reach any vertices in a tree to the right of the tree containing i (i.e., vertices in a tree that is processed later).

This suggests that we might focus on either the first or the last tree processed. Consider the last tree processed. Let i be the root, and let j be any vertex such that there is a path from j to i. Then j must be in the same tree as i, and hence must be a descendant of i. There is therefore a path from i to j. As a result, the strongly connected component containing i is the set of vertices j such that there is a path from j to i. We generalize this fact with the following theorem.

Theorem 13.6. *Let G be a directed graph, and let F be a depth-first spanning forest of G. Let S be a strongly connected component of G, and let i be the vertex in S that is postorder processed last. Let G' be the subgraph of G induced by set of vertices postorder processed no later than i. Then S is the set of vertices j such that there is a path from j to i in G'.*

Proof. Clearly, for every vertex $j \in S$, there is a path from j to i that stays entirely within S. Because i is postorder processed last of the vertices in S, this path stays within G'. Therefore, let j be a vertex such that there is a path from j to i in G'. We will show that $j \in S$. Specifically, we will show that j is a descendant of i, so that there is a path from i to j. The proof is by induction on n, the length of the shortest path from j to i in G'.

Base: $n = 0$. Then $j = i$, so that j is a descendant of i.

Induction Hypothesis: Let $n > 0$, and assume that for every $m < n$, if there is a path of length m from k to i in G', then k is a descendant of i.

Induction Step: Suppose there is a path of length n from j to i in G'. Let (j, k) be the first edge in this path. Then there is a path of length $n - 1$ from k to i in G'. From the Induction Hypothesis, k is a descendant of i. We now have three cases.

Case 1: (j, k) is a back edge. Then j is clearly a descendant of i.

Case 2: (j, k) is either a forward edge or a tree edge. Then i and j are both ancestors of k. Because j is in G', it can be postorder processed no later than i. Therefore, j cannot be a proper ancestor of i. j must therefore be a descendant of i.

Case 3: (j, k) is a cross edge. Then k is postorder processed before j is. Because j is postorder processed between k and i, and because k is a descendant of i, j must also be a descendant of i. $\qquad\square$

The above theorem suggests the following approach to finding the connected components of G. We first do a depth-first search on the entire graph using a postorder VISITCOUNTER *post*. We then select all of the vertices. To see how we might find an arbitrary strongly-connected component, suppose some of the components have been found and unselected. We find the selected vertex i that has maximum *post*.NUM(i). We then find all vertices j from among the selected vertices such that there is a path from j to i containing only selected vertices.

We have to be careful at this point because the set of selected vertices may not be exactly the set of vertices that are postorder processed no later than i. Specifically, there may be a vertex j that belongs to one of the components that have already been found, but which is postorder processed before i. However, Theorem 13.6 tells us that because j belongs to a different component than i, there is no path from j to i. Therefore, eliminating such nodes will not interfere with the correct identification of a strongly connected component. We conclude that the vertices that we find comprise the strongly connected component containing i.

In order to be able to implement this algorithm, we need to be able to find all vertices j from which i is reachable via selected vertices. This is almost the same as the reachability problem covered in Section 13.2, except that the edges are now directed, and we must follow the edges in the wrong direction. It is not hard to see that we can use depth-first search to find all vertices reachable from a given vertex i in a directed graph. In order to be able to use this algorithm to find all vertices j from which i is reachable, we must reverse the direction of the edges.

Because DFSALL processes all of the edges in the graph, we can use it to build a new graph in which all of the edges have been reversed. In fact, we can use the same depth-first search to record the order of the postorder processing of the vertices. We use three representation variables:

- a readable LISTMULTIGRAPH *reverse* (recall from Section 9.5 that if we know we will not attempt to add parallel edges, it is more efficient to add edges to a LISTMULTIGRAPH and construct a LISTGRAPH from it);
- a readable array *order*[$0..n-1$]; and
- a natural number *loc*.

As we process each edge, we add its reverse to *reverse*. As we postorder process each vertex, we add it to *order* as we did for topological sort (Figure 13.12). The resulting REVSEARCHER is shown in Figure 13.14.

Once DFSALL is called with a REVSEARCHER, we need to perform a second depth-first search on the entire reversed graph. The SEARCHER we need for this search uses a readable array *components*[$0..n-1$] in which it will store values indicating the component to which a given vertex belongs, along with a natural number *count* to keep track of the number of strongly connected components completely found. It also includes an operation NEXTCOMP, used to indicate that a strongly connected component has been found completely. Its implementation is shown in Figure 13.15.

Because the second depth-first search must start each tree at a particular vertex, we need to modify DFSALL slightly. The resulting algorithm is shown in Figure 13.16. We leave it as an exercise to show that this algorithm runs

---

Figure 13.14   REVSEARCHER implementation of SEARCHER

REVSEARCHER(n)
    reverse ← **new** LISTMULTIGRAPH(n)
    order ← **new** ARRAY[$0..n-1$]; *loc* ← n

REVSEARCHER.TREEPREPROC(e)
    reverse.PUT(e.DEST(), e.SOURCE(), e.DATA())

REVSEARCHER.OTHEREDGEPROC(e)
    reverse.PUT(e.DEST(), e.SOURCE(), e.DATA())

REVSEARCHER.POSTPROC(i)
    loc ← *loc* − 1; *order*[*loc*] ← i

Figure 13.15   SccSearcher implementation of Searcher

SccSearcher(n)
   components ← **new** Array$[0..n-1]$; *count* ← 0

SccSearcher.PreProc(i)
   components$[i]$ ← *count*

SccSearcher.NextComp()
   count ← *count* + 1

Figure 13.16   An algorithm for finding strongly connected components in a directed graph

---

Precondition: G refers to a directed Graph.
Postcondition: Returns an array $C[0..n-1]$, where n is the number of vertices in G, such that $C[i] = C[j]$ iff i and j belong to the same strongly connected component.

StronglyConnComp(G)
   n ← G.Size(); *rs* ← **new** RevSearcher(n)
   DfsAll(G, rs)
   order ← *rs*.Order(); G' ← **new** ListGraph(*rs*.Reverse())
   ss ← **new** SccSearcher(n); *sel* ← **new** Selector(n)
   for i ← 0 **to** $n-1$
     if *sel*.IsSelected(*order*$[i]$)
       Dfs(G', *order*$[i]$, *sel*, *ss*); *ss*.NextComp()
   return *ss*.Components()

---

in $\Theta(n + a)$ time, where n is the number of vertices and a is the number of edges.

13.7   Summary

Many graph problems can be reduced to depth-first search. In performing the reduction, we focus on a depth-first spanning tree or a depth-first spanning forest. Because a rooted tree is more amenable to the top-down approach than is a graph, algorithmic design is made easier. Furthermore, depth-first spanning trees have structural properties that are often useful in designing graph algorithms.

The implementation of a reduction to depth-first search consists mainly of defining an implementation of the SEARCHER ADT. This data structure defines what processing will occur at the various stages of the traversal of the depth-first spanning tree. Proofs of correctness can then focus on the traversal, utilizing induction as necessary.

13.8 Exercises

Exercise 13.1. Analyze the worst-case running time of the algorithm PRE-POSTTRAVERSE, shown in Figure 13.2, assuming the tree T is implemented as a MATRIXGRAPH.

Exercise 13.2. Prove that DFSTOPSORT, shown in Figures 13.12 and 13.13, meets its specification.

Exercise 13.3. Show that STRONGLYCONNCOMP, shown in Figures 13.14–13.16, runs in $\Theta(n + a)$ time, where n is the number of vertices and a is the number of edges in the given graph, assuming the graph is implemented as a LISTGRAPH.

Exercise 13.4. Prove that STRONGLYCONNCOMP, shown in Figures 13.14–13.16, meets its specification.

Exercise 13.5. Give an algorithm that decides whether a given directed graph G contains a cycle. Your algorithm should return a boolean value that is **true** iff G has a cycle. Assuming G is implemented as a LISTGRAPH, your algorithm should run in $O(n+a)$ time, where n is the number of vertices and a is the number of edges in G.

Exercise 13.6. A *bridge* in a connected undirected graph is an edge whose removal disconnects the graph. Give an algorithm that returns a CONSLIST containing all bridges of a given connected undirected graph. Your algorithm should run in $O(a)$ time in the worst case, where a is the number of edges in the graph, assuming the graph is implemented as a LISTGRAPH.

Exercise 13.7. A connected undirected graph is said to be *biconnected* if it is impossible to disconnect the graph by removing a single vertex; i.e., it is biconnected iff it has no articulation points. A *biconnected component* of a connected undirected graph G is a maximal biconnected subgraph G' of G (by "maximal", we mean that there is no biconnected subgraph of G that contains all of G' plus other vertices and/or edges).

    a. Prove that each edge in a connected undirected graph G belongs to exactly one biconnected component of G.

* b. Give an algorithm to identify the biconnected components of a given connected undirected graph G. Specifically, your algorithm should set the *data* field of each EDGE in G to a natural number so that $e.data = f.data$ iff e and f belong to the same biconnected component. Your algorithm should run in $O(a)$ time in the worst case, where a is the number of edges in the graph, assuming the graph is implemented as a LISTGRAPH.

* **Exercise 13.8.** A directed graph is *semiconnected* if for each pair of vertices i and j, there is either a path from i to j or a path from j to i. Give an algorithm to decide whether a given directed graph G is semiconnected. Your algorithm should return a boolean that is **true** iff G is semiconnected. Your algorithm should run in $O(n+a)$ time, where n is the number of vertices and a is the number of edges in G.

* **Exercise 13.9.** An *arborescence* of a directed graph $G = (V, E)$ is a subset $E' \subseteq E$ such that (V, E') is a rooted tree with edges directed from parents to children. Give an algorithm to determine whether a given directed graph G contains an arborescence, and if so, returns one. If G contains an arborescence, your algorithm should return an array $parent[0..n-1]$ such that $parent[i]$ gives the parent of vertex i for all vertices other than the root, and such that $parent[i] = -1$ if i is the root of the arborescence. If G does not contain an arborescence, your algorithm should return nil. You algorithm should operate in $O(n + a)$ time, where n is the number of vertices and a is the number of edges in G.

* **Exercise 13.10.** Give an algorithm that takes a connected undirected graph $G = (V, E)$ as input and produces as output a strongly connected directed graph $G' = (V, E')$ such that

- if $\{i, j\} \in E$, then exactly one of (i, j) and (j, i) is in E'; and
- if $\{i, j\} \notin E$, then neither (i, j) nor (j, i) is in E'.

Thus, G' is obtained from G by assigning a direction to each edge of G. If no such G' exists, your algorithm should return nil. Your algorithm should run in $O(a)$ time, where a is the number of edges in the graph, assuming G is implemented as a LISTGRAPH.

* **Exercise 13.11.** A directed graph is *singly connected* if for each pair of vertices i and j, there is at most one simple path from i to j. Give an efficient algorithm to determine whether a given directed graph G is singly connected. Your algorithm should return a boolean that is **true** iff G is singly connected. Analyze the worst-case running time of your algorithm assuming that G is implemented as a LISTGRAPH.

* Exercise 13.12. A *coloring* of an undirected graph is an assignment of labels to the vertices such that no two adjacent vertices have the same label. A *k-coloring* is a coloring that uses no more than k distinct labels. Give an efficient algorithm to find a 3-coloring for a given connected undirected graph G such that no vertex in G is adjacent to more than 3 vertices, and at least one vertex is adjacent to strictly fewer than 3 vertices (a 3-coloring always exists for such a graph). Your algorithm should run in $O(n)$ time, where n is the number of vertices in G, assuming G is implemented as a LISTGRAPH.

Exercise 13.13. An undirected graph is said to be *bipartite* if its vertices can be partitioned into two disjoint sets such that no two vertices belonging to the same partition are adjacent. (Note that such a partitioning is a 2-coloring, as defined in Exercise 13.12.) Give an efficient algorithm to find such a partitioning if one exists. Your algorithm should run in $O(n+a)$ time, where n is the number of vertices and a is the number of edges in the graph.

13.9 Notes

The depth-first search technique was developed in the nineteenth century by Trémaux, as reported by Lucas [92]. Its properties were studied by Tarjan [110], who presented an algorithm he credits to Hopcroft for finding articulation points and biconnected components (Exercise 13.7); see also Hopcroft and Tarjan [65]. The algorithm given in Section 13.6 for finding strongly connected components is due to Sharir [105].

Chapter 14

Network Flow and Matching

In this chapter, we examine the *network flow* problem, a graph problem to which many problems can be reduced. In fact, some problems that don't even appear to be graph problems can be reduced to network flow, yielding efficient algorithms. We begin by defining the problem.

Let $\mathbb{Z}$ denote the set of integers, and let $\mathbb{Z}^{>0}$ denote the set of positive integers. A *flow network* is a 4-tuple (G, u, v, C), where

- $G = (V, E)$ is a directed graph;
- $u \in V$ is the *source vertex*;
- $v \in V$ is the *sink vertex*; and
- $C : E \rightarrow \mathbb{Z}^{>0}$ gives a positive integer *capacity* for each edge.

For example, Figure 14.1 shows a flow network whose source is 0, whose sink is 5, and whose edges all have capacity 1. Intuitively, the capacities represent the maximum flow that the associated edges can support. We are interested in finding the maximum total flow from u to v that the network can support.

The above definition is more general than what is typical. The standard definition prohibits incoming edges to the source and outgoing edges from the sink. However, this more general definition is useful for the development of our algorithms.

In order to define formally a network flow, we need some additional notation. For a vertex x in a directed graph, let

- $x^{\leftarrow} = \{(w, x) \in E\}$, the set of incoming edges to x; and
- $x^{\rightarrow} = \{(x, y) \in E\}$, the set of outgoing edges from x.

A *flow* for a flow network $((V, E), u, v, C)$ is function $F : E \rightarrow \mathbb{N}$ such that

- for each $e \in E$, $F(e) \leq C(e)$; and

Figure 14.1   A flow network

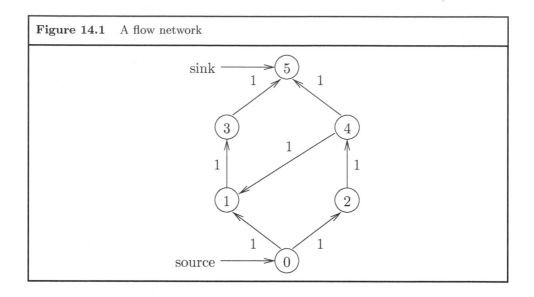

- for each vertex $x \in V \setminus \{u, v\}$,

$$\sum_{e \in x^{\leftarrow}} F(e) = \sum_{e \in x^{\rightarrow}} F(e).$$

Thus, the flow on each edge is no more than that edge's capacity, and the total flow into a vertex other than the source or the sink is the same as the total flow out of that vertex. An example of a flow on the network shown in Figure 14.1 would have a flow of 1 on every edge except $(4, 1)$; this edge would have a flow of 0.

We leave it as an exercise to show that for any flow F of a flow network (G, u, v, C),

$$\sum_{e \in u^{\rightarrow}} F(e) - \sum_{e \in u^{\leftarrow}} F(e) = \sum_{e \in v^{\leftarrow}} F(e) - \sum_{e \in v^{\rightarrow}} F(e). \qquad (14.1)$$

We therefore define the *value* of a flow to be the above difference — the net flow out of the source, or equivalently, the net flow into the sink. Thus, the flow described above for the network in Figure 14.1 has a value of 2. Given a flow network, the *network flow problem* is to find a network flow with maximum value. Clearly, 2 is the maximum value of any flow for the network in Figure 14.1.

In the next two sections, we will examine algorithms for the network flow problem. In the remainder of the chapter, we will consider the *bipartite matching* problem, and show how to reduce it to network flow.

14.1   The Ford–Fulkerson Algorithm

A flow for a given network can be found by finding a simple path (i.e., one in which no vertices are repeated) from the source to the sink. We will refer to such a path as an *augmenting path*. If no augmenting path exists, then the maximum flow must be 0. Otherwise, suppose m is the minimum capacity of any edge in some particular augmenting path. We can clearly place a flow of m on each edge in that path. We can then solve the smaller network flow problem obtained by reducing the capacity of each edge on the augmenting path by m, and removing any edge whose capacity would become 0. If we measure the size of a problem instance as the value of a maximum flow, then the resulting problem instance is clearly smaller. We can then combine the flow obtained from the solution to the smaller problem with the first flow we obtained.

The above approach clearly finds a flow for a given network. Unfortunately, that flow is not guaranteed to be a maximum flow. To see why, consider the flow network in Figure 14.1. Suppose the first augmenting path found is $\langle 0, 2, 4, 1, 3, 5 \rangle$. We can put a flow of 1 on each of these edges. In the smaller instance, each of these edges would be removed, so that there is no augmenting path in the resulting network. The flow found on the smaller instance is therefore empty, so that the final flow has value 1. As we have already seen, a maximum flow for this network has value 2.

The most obvious approach to repairing this algorithm is to be more careful in how we choose the augmenting path. However, it turns out that a more straightforward approach is to be more careful in how we construct the smaller problem instance. The problem with the reduction described above is that once we decide to place a flow on an edge, we cannot reverse that decision. If we are more careful, we can construct a smaller instance that allows us to reverse these decisions.

Specifically, when we decrease the capacity of an edge by m, we also increase by m the capacity of the edge going the opposite direction. If there is no such edge, we add it to the graph. When we combine the two flows, we allow flows in opposite directions to cancel each other; i.e., if edge (x, y) has flow k and edge (y, x) has flow $k' \leq k$, we set the flow on (x, y) to $k - k'$ and the flow on (y, x) to 0. Note that because any edge added to the graph by the reduction will have a capacity of m, and the initial flow will be m in the opposite direction, the combination of the two flows will result in no flow on any edge that was added to the graph. We can therefore remove these edges from the resulting flow.

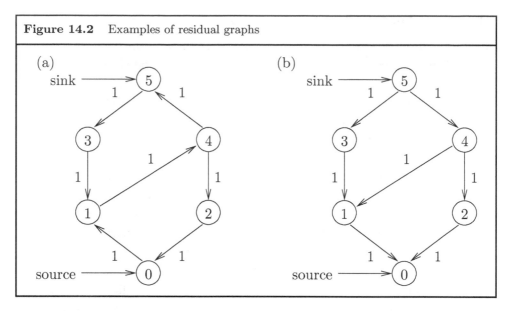

Figure 14.2 Examples of residual graphs

Let us now formalize the construction outlined above. Let (G, u, v, C) be a flow network, and let P be the set of edges in some augmenting path. Let m be the minimum capacity of any edge in P. We define the *residual network* of (G, u, v, C) with respect to P to be the flow network (G', u, v, C'), where G' and C' are defined as follows:

- G' is constructed from G by removing any edges in P with capacity m and by adding edges (y, x) such that $(x, y) \in P$ and (y, x) is not an edge in G.
- $C'((x, y))$ is defined as follows for each edge $(x, y) \in G'$:
  - If $(x, y) \in P$, $C'((x, y)) = C((x, y)) - m$.
  - If $(y, x) \in P$ and (x, y) is an edge in G, $C'((x, y)) = C((x, y)) + m$.
  - If $(y, x) \in P$ and (x, y) is not an edge in G, $C'((x, y)) = m$.
  - Otherwise, $C'((x, y)) = C((x, y))$.

Thus, Figure 14.2(a) shows the residual network for the flow network in Figure 14.1 with respect to the augmenting path $\langle 0, 2, 4, 1, 3, 5 \rangle$. This graph has an augmenting path: $\langle 0, 1, 4, 5 \rangle$. The residual network with respect to this augmenting path is shown in Figure 14.2(b). There is no augmenting path in this graph. If we combine the flows obtained by assigning a flow of 1 to each edge in the respective paths, the flows on the edges $(4, 1)$ in the original graph and $(1, 4)$ in the graph in Figure 14.2(a) cancel each other out. The resulting flow therefore has a flow of 1 on each edge except $(4, 1)$ in the original network. This flow has a value of 2, which is maximum.

We now need to prove the correctness of this reduction. We begin by showing the following lemma.

Lemma 14.1. *Let (G, u, v, C) be a flow network, and let P be the set of edges on some augmenting path. Let F_1 be the flow obtained by adding a flow of m to each edge in P, where m is the minimum capacity of any edge in P. Let F_2 be a maximum flow on the residual graph of (G, u, v, C) with respect to P, and suppose F_2 has value k. Then the combination of F_1 and F_2 is a flow with value $k + m$ on (G, u, v, C).*

Proof. We must first show that the combination of the two flows does not give a flow where there is no edge in G. This can only happen if there is a flow in F_2 on an edge (x, y) that is not in G. Then (y, x) must be an edge in P. The capacity of (x, y) in the residual graph is therefore m. Because the flow on (y, x) in F_1 is m, the combination of F_1 and F_2 cannot give a positive flow on (x, y).

We will now show that in the combination of F_1 with F_2, the flow on each edge (x, y) is no more than $C((x, y))$. The only way this can happen is if there is positive flow on (x, y) in F_2. We consider three cases.

Case 1: $(x, y) \in P$. Then $C'((x, y)) = C((x, y)) - m$. The sum of the two flows on (x, y) is therefore at most $C((x, y))$.

Case 2: $(y, x) \in P$. Then $C'((x, y)) = C((x, y)) + m$. In the combination of F_1 with F_2, the flow on (x, y) is its flow in F_2, minus m. This total flow can be no more than $C((x, y))$.

Case 3: $(x, y) \notin P$ and $(y, x) \notin P$. Then $C'((x, y)) = C((x, y))$. In the combination of F_1 with F_2, the flow on (x, y) is simply its flow in F_2, which can be no more than $C((x, y))$.

Finally, it is clear that for each vertex w in G other than u and v, the total flow into w must equal the total flow out of w, and that the total flow out of u is $k + m$. □

Using the above Lemma, we can prove the theorem below. Combined with Lemma 14.1, this theorem ensures that the reduction yields a maximum flow for the given network.

Theorem 14.2. *Let (G, u, v, C) be a flow network with maximum flow k, and let P be the set of edges in some augmenting path. Let m be the minimum* *capacity of any edge in P, and let (G', u, v, C') be the residual network of (G, u, v, C) with respect to P. Then the maximum flow for (G', u, v, C') has value $k - m$.*

Proof. Let F_1 be a maximum flow for (G, u, v, C). Then F_1 has value k. To simplify our discussion, let us interpret F_1 as a function $F_1 : V \times V \to \mathbb{Z}$, where V is the set of vertices in G, such that $F_1(x, y)$ gives the flow over (x, y) minus the flow over (y, x); if either of these edges does not exist, we use 0 for this edge's flow.

Let us assign flows to the edges of G' as follows:

1. If $(x, y) \in P$ and $F_1(x, y) \geq m$, assign a flow of $F_1(x, y) - m$ to (x, y). Because $C'((x, y)) = C((x, y)) - m$, the flow on this edge does not exceed the capacity.
2. If $(x, y) \in P$ and $F_1(x, y) < m$, assign a flow of $m - F_1(x, y)$ to (y, x). Because $C'((y, x)) = C((y, x)) + m$ if $(y, x) \in G$, or $C'((y, x)) = m$ if $(y, x) \notin G$, the flow on this edge does not exceed the capacity.
3. If $(x, y) \notin P$, $(y, x) \notin P$, and $F_1(x, y) > 0$, assign a flow of $F_1(x, y)$ to (x, y). Because $C'((x, y)) = C((x, y))$, the flow on this edge does not exceed its capacity.
4. Assign a flow of 0 to all other edges.

Because the above construction essentially reduces the flow F_1 by m along P, the sum of incoming flows equals the sum of outgoing flows for all vertices in G' except u and v. This assignment is therefore a network flow, which we will denote F_2. Furthermore, P contains exactly one edge incident on u — the first edge, which we will call (u, w). The effect of Steps 1 and 2 therefore decreases the net flow from u by m. The value of F_2 is therefore $k - m$. From Lemma 14.1, the combination of F_2 with a flow of m along P gives a flow of k for (G, u, v, C). Because this is true for any flow on (G', u, v, C'), and because k is the maximum flow for (G, u, v, C), we conclude that F_2 must be a maximum flow for (G', u, v, C'). $\square$

Though this reduction is not a transformation, we can implement it using a loop by maintaining a graph in which the flows on augmenting paths are combined as they are found. The resulting algorithm, known as the Ford–Fulkerson algorithm, is shown in Figure 14.3. Because the GRAPH ADT (see Figure 9.3 on page 311) provides no operation for removing an edge, we will allow the residual graph to have edges with capacity 0. The proof of correctness is easily shown using Theorem 14.2; the details are left as an exercise.

Figure 14.3   The Ford–Fulkerson algorithm for network flow

Precondition: G is directed GRAPH in which each edge contains a NAT giving its capacity, and *source* and *sink* are distinct NATs less than the number of vertices in G.

Postcondition: Returns a directed graph F in which the contents of the edges give a maximum flow for G from *source* to *sink*.

NETWORKFLOW(G, *source*, *sink*)
    $F \leftarrow$ COPYGRAPH(G, true); $R \leftarrow$ COPYGRAPH(G, false)
    $P \leftarrow$ FINDPATH(R, *source*, *sink*)
    // **Invariant:** F combined with a maximum flow for R gives a maximum
    // flow for G. P is a CONSLIST containing the EDGEs of a path from
    // *source* to *sink* in R if there is such a path; otherwise, $P = $ nil.
    while $P \neq$ nil
        $m \leftarrow$ MINVAL(P); ADDFLOW(F, P, R, m)
        $P \leftarrow$ FINDPATH(R, *source*, *sink*)
    return F

Precondition: G is a GRAPH, and *zeroEdges* is a boolean.

Postcondition: Returns a copy of G. If *zeroEdges* is true, the contents of all edges are set to 0; otherwise, they are unchanged.

COPYGRAPH(G, *zeroEdges*)

Precondition: G is a GRAPH whose edges contain natural numbers, and i and j are distinct natural numbers strictly less than the number of vertices in G.

Postcondition: Returns a CONSLIST P containing the EDGEs in a simple path of non-zero EDGEs from i to j in G. If no such path exists, returns nil.

FINDPATH(G, i, j)

Precondition: L is a CONSLIST of EDGEs containing positive integers.

Postcondition: Returns the minimum integer stored on any EDGE in L.

MINVAL(L)

Precondition: F and R are directed GRAPHS having the same number of vertices and whose edges contain natural numbers, P is a CONSLIST of EDGEs forming a simple path in R, and m is a positive integer.

Postcondition: Adds a flow of m to each edge in F that appears in P and sets R to the resulting residual graph. Edges are added to each GRAPH if necessary.

ADDFLOW(F, P, R, m)

Four auxiliary functions are specified in Figure 14.3. We leave it as exercises to show that if G is represented as a LISTGRAPH, then

- COPYGRAPH can be implemented to return a LISTGRAPH and to run in $O(n + a)$ time, where n is the number of vertices and a is the number of edges in G; and
- ADDFLOW can be implemented to run in $O(n + a)$ time, where n is the number of vertices in F (or equivalently R) and a is the number of edges in F and R together, assuming F and R are implemented as LISTGRAPHs.

Furthermore, MINVAL can clearly be implemented to run in $O(n)$ time, where n is the number of EDGEs in L, and FINDPATH can be implemented to run in $O(n+a)$ time using either depth-first search or breadth-first search (see Exercise 11.6), where n is the number of vertices and a is the number of edges in its first argument G.

Note that FINDPATH does not specify which augmenting path will be chosen. As a result, the Ford–Fulkerson algorithm can perform very poorly. Consider, for example, the flow network shown in Figure 14.4(a), where k is some large integer. It is easily seen by inspection that the maximum flow is $2k$. Suppose the algorithm first selects the augmenting path $\langle 0, 1, 2, 3 \rangle$. The minimum capacity on this path is 1, and the resulting residual graph is shown in Figure 14.4(b). Suppose the algorithm then chooses the augmenting path $\langle 0, 2, 1, 3 \rangle$. The minimum capacity is again 1, and the resulting residual graph is shown in Figure 14.4(c). It is easily seen that this process can continue increasing the flow by 1 until the maximum flow of $2k$ is achieved. On the other hand the algorithm could have achieved the same flow with two augmenting paths: $\langle 0, 1, 3 \rangle$ and $\langle 0, 2, 3 \rangle$.

Figure 14.4   A flow network on which NETWORKFLOW can perform poorly

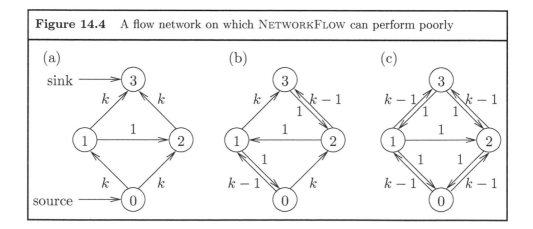

In Section 14.2, we will consider how to make good augmenting path choices. For now, we note that in the worst case, the loop in NETWORKFLOW can iterate M times, where M is the value of the maximum flow. Assuming the initialization and the body of the loop are implemented to run in $\Theta(n+a)$ time, where n is the number of vertices and a is the number of edges in G, the algorithm runs in $\Theta(M(n + a))$ time in the worst case. If we assume that all vertices are reachable from the source, then $a \geq n - 1$, and we can simplify the running time to $\Theta(Ma)$.

Before we move on to a discussion on finding augmenting paths, we note one additional property of the Ford–Fulkerson algorithm. As long as each augmenting path found is simple — and there is no reason a path-finding algorithm would find a path containing a cycle — the path will not contain any edges to the source or any edges from the sink. The obvious consequence is that if the graph contains edges into the source or out of the sink, they will not be used. A less obvious consequence is that after such edges are introduced into the residual graph, they will not be used. Thus, once a flow is added to an edge from the source or to the sink, the flow on that edge will never be decreased.

14.2   The Edmonds–Karp Algorithm

We have seen that the way augmenting paths are chosen by the Ford–Fulkerson algorithm can significantly impact its performance. In this section, we consider how to select augmenting paths in order to avoid very bad performance. One might suppose that we should try to select edges with high capacity; however, the approach we take does not even consider the edge capacities. Rather, we instead select a shortest augmenting path, in terms of the number of edges. The resulting network flow algorithm is known as the Edmonds–Karp algorithm.

Exercise 11.6 on page 386 outlined the breadth-first search technique for finding a shortest path in $\Theta(n+a)$ time, where n is the number of vertices and a is the number of edges. We will therefore focus on analyzing the running time of the Edmonds–Karp algorithm. We first show the following lemma.

Lemma 14.3. *No iteration of the Edmonds–Karp algorithm can bring any vertex nearer to the source.*

Proof.   By contradiction. Let R be the residual graph at the beginning of an iteration, and let R' be the residual graph at the end of the iteration. Suppose some vertex x is closer to the source u in R' than in R. Specifically, let x be a vertex that is closest to u in R' of all such vertices. There must be some edge on the shortest path from u to x in R' that is not in R, for otherwise this path would also be a path from u to x in R. Specifically, the last edge (w, x) on this path must have been added, for otherwise w, which is closer than x to u in R', would also be closer to u in R' than in R. This means that (x, w) is on a shortest augmenting path in R, so that x is closer than w to u in R. Therefore, w is closer to u in R' than in R — a contradiction. $\qquad\square$

Knowing that no vertex ever gets any closer to the source over the course of the Edmonds–Karp algorithm, we will now prove a lemma that shows when a vertex must get farther away from the source. If a vertex is farther than $n - 1$ edges from the source, where n is the number of vertices, then it must be unreachable. By Lemma 14.3, once a vertex becomes unreachable, it will never become reachable. This next lemma will therefore enable us to bound the number of iterations of the Edmonds–Karp algorithm.

Lemma 14.4. *Suppose that when some vertex x is at a distance d from the source u, the Edmonds–Karp algorithm removes an edge (x, y). Suppose that later this edge is added again. Then after this edge is added, the distance from u to x is at least $d + 2$.*

Proof. If (x, y) is removed, then this edge must be on a shortest augmenting path. Then before this edge is removed, the distance from u to y is $d + 1$. When (x, y) is added again, (y, x) must be on a shortest augmenting path. From Lemma 14.3, the distance from u to y is still at least $d + 1$ when this path is found. The distance to x is therefore at least $d + 2$. From Lemma 14.3, the distance from u to x must still be at least $d + 2$ after the edge (x, y) is added. $\qquad\square$

Theorem 14.5. *In the worst case, the Edmonds–Karp algorithm iterates no more than na times, where n is the number of vertices and a is the number of edges in G.*

Proof. Because a flow equal to the minimum edge capacity on a shortest augmenting path is added by each iteration, each iteration removes at least one edge. By Lemmas 14.3 and 14.4, no edge can be removed more than $n/2$ times. When edges are added, they are always added in the opposite direction of an existing edge; hence, at most $2a$ distinct edges ever appear in the residual graph. The loop can therefore iterate at most na times. $\qquad\square$

If the initialization and the body of the loop are implemented to run in $\Theta(n + a)$ time, we can conclude that the algorithm runs in $O(na(n + a))$ time in the worst case. Furthermore, the analysis of the last section still applies, so that the running time is in $O(\min(M, na)(n + a))$, where M is the value of the maximum flow. If we assume that every vertex is reachable from the source, we can simplify this to $O(\min(Ma, na^2))$.

14.3 Bipartite Matching

A *matching* in an undirected graph is a subset of the edges such that no two edges are incident on the same vertex. In this section, we consider the problem of finding a matching of maximum size in a given bipartite graph, as defined in Exercise 13.13 on page 439. Specifically, we will show that this problem can be reduced to the network flow problem.

As an example, consider the bipartite graph shown in Figure 14.5. We claim that the heavier edges, namely, $\{0, 4\}, \{2, 5\}$, and $\{3, 7\}$, form a matching of maximum size. Clearly, these edges form a matching because no two of them share a common vertex. To see that it is of maximum size, we first note that any larger matching must contain all of the vertices in $\{0, 1, 2, 3\}$ as endpoints. However, the only edges incident on 1 and 3 are $\{1, 7\}$ and $\{3, 7\}$, respectively, and they share a common vertex. Hence, any matching must exclude either 1 or 3. Therefore, there is no matching of size larger than 3.

We will now show how to reduce bipartite matching to network flow. Given a bipartite graph G, we construct an instance of network flow as follows. For simplicity, we will assume that the vertices of the bipartite graph have already been partitioned into the sets V_1 and V_2 (see Exercise 13.13). We first direct all of the edges from V_1 to V_2. We then add a new source vertex u and edges from u to each vertex in V_1. Next, we add a new sink vertex v and edges from each vertex in V_2 to v. Finally, we assign a capacity of 1 to each edge. See Figure 14.6 for the result of applying this reduction to the graph in Figure 14.5.

Figure 14.5   A maximum-sized matching in a bipartite graph

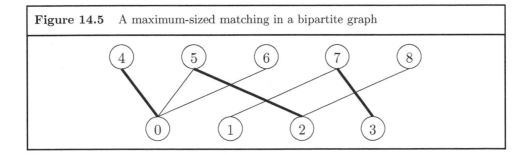

Figure 14.6   The flow network constructed from the bipartite graph shown in Figure 14.5

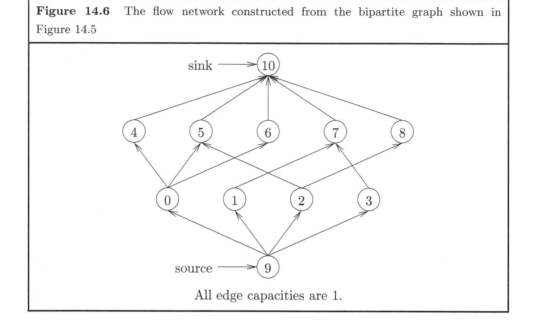

All edge capacities are 1.

Consider any matching in the given bipartite graph. We can construct a flow in the constructed network by adding a flow of 1 to each edge in the matching, as well as to each edge leading to a matched vertex in V_1 and to each edge leading from a matched vertex in V_2. Clearly, any unmatched vertex from the bipartite graph will have a flow of 0 on all of its incoming and outgoing edges. Furthermore, each matched vertex in V_1 will have a flow of 1 on its incoming edge and a flow of 1 on the single outgoing edge in the matching. Likewise, each matched vertex in V_2 will have a flow of 1 on the single incoming edge in the matching and a flow of 1 on its outgoing edge. Thus, we have constructed a flow whose value is the number of edges in the matching.

Conversely, consider any flow on the constructed network. Because any vertex in V_1 can have an incoming flow of at most 1, at most one of its outgoing edges will contain a positive flow. Likewise, because any vertex in V_2 can have an outgoing flow of at most 1, at most one of its incoming edges will contain a positive flow. The edges from V_1 to V_2 containing positive flow therefore correspond to a matching in the bipartite graph. Furthermore, the value of the flow is the number of edges in the matching.

We conclude that the edges from V_1 to V_2 in a maximum flow for the constructed network are the edges in a maximum-sized matching for the given bipartite graph. The resulting flow network has $n+2$ vertices and $n+a$

edges, where n and a are the number of vertices and edges, respectively, in the bipartite graph. The Edmonds–Karp algorithm will therefore solve the constructed network flow instance in $O(M(n + a))$ time, where M is the number of edges in the maximum-sized matching. Because M can be no more than $n/2$, if we assume that each vertex is incident on at least one edge, the running time is in $O(na)$. Furthermore, it is not hard to construct the flow network in $O(n + a)$ time, so the bipartite matching problem can be solved in $O(na)$ time.

Rather than presenting the code for the reduction, let us first examine the reduction more carefully to see if we can optimize the bipartite matching algorithm. For example, the addition of new vertices and edges is only needed to form a flow network. We could instead adapt one of the network flow algorithms to operate without the source and/or the sink explicitly represented.

We also note that as flow is added, the edges containing the flow — which are the edges of a matching — have their direction reversed. Rather than explicitly reversing the direction of the edges, we could keep track of which edges have been included in the matching in some other way. For example, we could use an array $matching[0..n - 1]$ such that $matching[i]$ gives the vertex to which i is matched, or is -1 if i is unmatched. Because a matching has at most one edge incident on any vertex, this may end up being a more efficient way of keeping track of the vertices adjacent (in the flow network) to vertices in V_2. The maximum-sized matching could also be returned via this array.

As we observed at the end of Section 14.1, once flow is added to any edge from the source or to any edge to the sink, that flow is never removed. To put this in terms of the matching algorithm, once a vertex is matched, it remains matched, although the vertex to which it is matched may change. Furthermore, we claim that if we ever attempt to add a vertex $w \in V_1$ to the current matching M and are unable to do so (i.e., there is no path from w to an unmatched vertex in V_2), then we will never be able to add w to the matching.

To see why this is true, notice that if there were a maximum-sized matching containing all currently matched vertices and w, then there is a matching M' containing no other vertices from V_1. If we delete all vertices from V_1 that are unmatched in M', then M' is clearly a maximum-sized matching for the resulting graph. The Ford–Fulkerson algorithm must therefore be able to find a path that yields M' from M.

Figure 14.7   The MATCHINGGRAPH for the bipartite graph shown in Figure 14.5 with matching $\{\{0,5\},\{3,7\}\}$

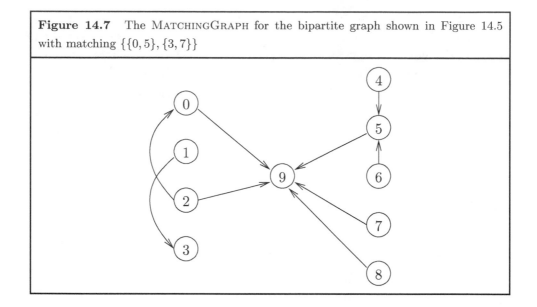

As a result, we only need to do a single search from each vertex in V_1. The following theorem summarizes this property.

Theorem 14.6. *Let G be a bipartite graph, and let S be the set of vertices in some matching on G. Suppose some maximum-sized matching includes all of the vertices in S. Let i be some vertex not in S. Then there is a maximum-sized matching including $S \cup \{i\}$ if there is a matching including $S \cup \{i\}$.*

In order to implement the above optimizations, it is helpful to define a data structure called MATCHINGGRAPH, which implements the GRAPH ADT. Its purpose is to represent a particular directed graph G' derived from a given bipartite graph G and a matching on G. Suppose G has vertices $0, 1, \ldots, n-1$. G' then contains the vertices $0, 1, \ldots, n$. If $\{i, j\}$ is an edge in G and j is unmatched, then G' will contain the edge (i, n). Every other edge in G' will represent two edges in G — an edge not in the matching followed by an edge in the matching. Thus, for $0 \leq i < n$, $0 \leq j < n$, and $i \neq j$, G' contains the edge (i, j) iff there is a vertex k in G such that $\{k, j\}$ is in the matching and $\{i, k\}$ is an edge in G. For example, Figure 14.7 shows the MATCHINGGRAPH for the bipartite graph of Figure 14.5 with matching $\{\{0,5\},\{3,7\}\}$.

Suppose the two partitions of G are V_1 and V_2. Then augmenting paths in the flow network constructed by the reduction correspond to paths from unmatched vertices in V_1 to n in G'. In order to find an augmenting path in the flow network, we need to find a path to n in G' from an unmatched vertex in G. For example, consider the MATCHINGGRAPH shown in Figure 14.7. We can add vertex 2 to the matching by finding a path from 2 to 9 in G'. Taking the path $\langle 2, 0, 9 \rangle$ could yield the augmenting path $\langle 2, 5, 0, 4 \rangle$, which produces the matching shown in Figure 14.5. This path could also yield the augmenting path $\langle 2, 5, 0, 6 \rangle$ because 0 is adjacent to two unmatched vertices, 4 and 6. Alternatively, taking the path $\langle 2, 9 \rangle$ would yield the augmenting path $\langle 2, 8 \rangle$.

Note that G' actually represents two flow networks. If (i, j) is an edge in G' and $j \neq n$, then i and j must both be in the same partition. Therefore, the subgraph induced by $V_1 \cup \{n\}$ represents the flow network in which edges in the matching lead from V_2 to V_1. Symmetrically, the subgraph induced by $V_2 \cup \{n\}$ represents the flow network in which edges in the matching lead from V_1 to V_2 — i.e., the flow network that would be constructed by swapping V_1 with V_2. Thus, 4 could be added to the matching by finding a path from 4 to 9 in G'. The only such path, $\langle 4, 5, 9 \rangle$, would also yield the matching shown in Figure 14.5.

To implement a MATCHINGGRAPH, we need two representation variables:

- a GRAPH *bipartite* representing the bipartite graph; and
- a readable array *matching*$[0..n-1]$ representing the matching, so that *matching*$[i]$ gives the vertex to which i is matched, or -1 if i is unmatched.

Its structural invariant will be that for $0 \leq i < n$, if *matching*$[i] \neq -1$, then *matching*$[matching[i]] = i$.

A partial implementation is shown in Figure 14.8 — we only include implementations of those operations we will actually be using. These operations include an additional operation for adding an edge to the matching, while removing any edges that might be incident on either endpoint. We also include a constructor that constructs a MATCHINGGRAPH from a given bipartite graph with an empty matching. We use the *data* variable of an EDGE to store the intermediate vertex between the two edges of the bipartite graph represented by that EDGE.

Note that this implementation is not secure, because its constructor allows an outside reference to *bipartite*, and because *matching* is readable. We could easily modify the implementation so that the constructor stores a copy of its input graph and the MATCHING operation returns a copy of *matching*; however, if we write our matching algorithm so that it doesn't

---

Figure 14.8 MATCHINGGRAPH implementation of GRAPH (partial)

Structural Invariant: For $0 \leq i < n$, if $matching[i] \neq -1$, then $matching[matching[i]] = i$.

Precondition: G refers to a bipartite GRAPH.
Postcondition: Constructs a MATCHINGGRAPH representing G with an empty matching.

MATCHINGGRAPH(G)
   $n \leftarrow G$.SIZE(); $bipartite \leftarrow G$; $matching \leftarrow$ **new** ARRAY$[0..n-1]$
   for $i \leftarrow 0$ **to** $n - 1$
      $matching[i] \leftarrow -1$

MATCHINGGRAPH.SIZE()
   return $bipartite$.SIZE() $+ 1$

MATCHINGGRAPH.ALLFROM(i)
   $n \leftarrow bipartite$.SIZE(); $L \leftarrow$ **new** CONSLIST()
   if $i < n$
      $foundUnmatched \leftarrow$ false; $adj \leftarrow bipartite$.ALLFROM(i)
      while not adj.ISEMPTY()
         $e \leftarrow adj$.HEAD(); $adj \leftarrow adj$.TAIL()
         $k \leftarrow e$.DEST(); $j \leftarrow matching[k]$
         if $j = -1$ **and not** $foundUnmatched$
            $L \leftarrow$ **new** CONSLIST(**new** EDGE(i, n, k), L)
            $foundUnmatched \leftarrow$ true
         else if $j \neq -1$
            $L \leftarrow$ **new** CONSLIST(**new** EDGE(i, j, k), L)
   return L

Precondition: i and j are distinct NATs representing vertices in the bipartite graph.
Postcondition: Adds $\{i, j\}$ to the matching, removing from the matching any edge incident on i or j.

MATCHINGGRAPH.MATCH(i, j)
   if $matching[i] \neq -1$
      $matching[matching[i]] \leftarrow -1$
   if $matching[j] \neq -1$
      $matching[matching[j]] \leftarrow -1$
   $matching[i] \leftarrow j$; $matching[j] \leftarrow i$

Figure 14.9   PATHSEARCHER implementation of SEARCHER

PATHSEARCHER(n)
  incoming ← **new** ARRAY$[0..n-1]$

PATHSEARCHER.TREEPREPROC(e)
  incoming$[e.$DEST$()]$ ← e

---

change these items except via operations in MATCHINGGRAPH, we can avoid this extra copying.

In order to complete the matching algorithm, we need to be able to find a path from i to j in a directed graph. Because the maximum flow on the constructed flow network is no more than $n/2$, where n is the number of vertices in the bipartite graph, the Ford–Fulkerson algorithm will not perform badly. Therefore, we will use depth-first search to find paths. (We leave it as an exercise to implement the algorithm using breadth-first search.) We therefore need a SEARCHER with the following representation variable:

- *incoming*$[0..n-1]$: a readable array of EDGEs giving the incoming edge in the depth-first spanning tree for each vertex reached.

The implementation of PATHSEARCHER is shown in Figure 14.9.

By Theorem 14.6, a depth-first search of a MATCHINGGRAPH can be used to determine whether a given vertex can be safely matched. Note that this theorem doesn't specify which partition the vertex comes from. In particular, we really don't need to know the partition to which any vertex belongs — we can simply test them in any order, and add the ones that can be safely added. We therefore no longer need to require that the first k vertices form the first partition. The algorithm is shown in Figure 14.10. Note that *in* and *M* maintain references to the *incoming* variable in *s* and the *matching* variable of *matchGraph*, respectively (this would not be possible if PATHSEARCHER and MATCHINGGRAPH were secure). Note also that as long as an augmenting path is not found, we do not need to select any unselected nodes because no unselected node leads to n.

Let n be the number of vertices and a be the number of edges in G. To simplify the analysis of the running time, suppose each vertex has at least one incident edge, so that $n \in O(a)$. Let us first focus on a single iteration of the **for** loop. Clearly, the running time of the call to DFS is in $O(a)$.

Figure 14.10   Bipartite matching algorithm

Precondition: G is a bipartite graph.
Postcondition: Returns an array $M[0..n-1]$ describing a maximum-sized matching of G, so that $M[i] = j$ if j and i are matched, and $M[i] = -1$ if i is unmatched.

MATCHING(G)
    $n \leftarrow G$.SIZE(); $sel \leftarrow$ **new** SELECTOR(n)
    $s \leftarrow$ **new** PATHSEARCHER($n+1$)
    $matchGraph \leftarrow$ **new** MATCHINGGRAPH(G)
    $in \leftarrow s$.INCOMING(); $M \leftarrow matchGraph$.MATCHING()
    // **Invariant:** M represents a matching, and there is no matching
    // containing the matched vertices in M and any unmatched vertex $j < i$.
    for $i \leftarrow 0$ **to** $n-1$
        if $M[i] = -1$
            DFS($matchGraph, i, sel, s$)
            if not sel.ISSELECTED(n)
                $j \leftarrow n$
                while $j \neq i$
                    $e \leftarrow in[j]$; $k \leftarrow e$.SOURCE()
                    $matchGraph$.MATCH(k, e.DATA()); $j \leftarrow k$
                sel.SELECTALL()
    return M

The number of iterations of the inner loop is at most the current size of the matching, so its running time is in $O(n) \subseteq O(a)$. The call to SELECTALL also runs in $O(n) \subseteq O(a)$ time. We therefore conclude that a single iteration of the **for** loop runs in $O(a)$ time, so that the entire algorithm runs in $O(na)$ time.

To show that the running time of the algorithm is in $\Omega(na)$, we will first construct a graph with $4k$ vertices and $4k - 1$ edges for $k \in \mathbb{N}$. We will show that the algorithm runs in $\Omega(k^2)$ time for these graphs. We will then generalize the construction to an arbitrary number n of vertices and a edges such that $n - 1 \leq a < n(n + 20)/32$. We will show that the algorithm runs in $\Omega(na)$ time for these graphs.

We begin by setting $V = \{i \mid 0 \leq i < 4k\}$ (refer to Figure 14.11 for the case in which $k = 4$). We then add the following edges:

- for $0 \leq i < k$, the edges $\{2i, 2k + i\}$ and $\{2i + 1, 2k + i\}$;
- for $0 < i < k$, the edge $\{2i, 2k + i - 1\}$; and
- for $0 \leq i < k$, the edge $\{2k - 1, 3k + i\}$.

Figure 14.11 An illustration of the lower bound for MATCHING

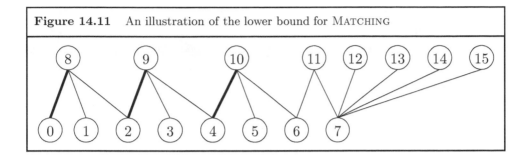

We arrange the edges so that when we try to add vertex $2i$ for $0 \leq i < k$, we first encounter the edge $\{2i, 2k + i\}$. Because $2k + i$ is not in the matching, it is added. It will then be impossible to add vertex $2i + 1$, but each node $2k + j$, for $0 \leq j < i$, will be reached in the search for an augmenting path. (For example, consider the search when trying to add 5 to the matching $\{\{0, 8\}, \{2, 9\}, \{4, 10\}\}$ in Figure 14.11.) Constructing this matching therefore uses $\Omega(k^2)$ time.

We can now generalize the above construction to arbitrary n by adding or removing a few vertices adjacent to $2k - 1$. Furthermore, we can add edges $\{2i, 2k + j\}$ for $0 \leq i < k$ and $0 \leq j < i - 1$ without increasing the size of the maximum-sized matching. However, these additional edges must all be traversed when we try to add vertex $2i+1$ to the matching. This construction therefore forces the algorithm to use $\Omega(na)$ time. Furthermore, the number of edges added can be as many as

$$\sum_{i=0}^{k-1}(i - 1) = \frac{k(k - 1)}{2} - k$$

$$= \frac{k^2 - 3k}{2}$$

$$= \frac{n^2 - 12n}{32}.$$

Including the $n - 1$ original edges, the total number of edges a is in the range

$$n - 1 \leq a < \frac{n(n + 20)}{32}.$$

The above construction is more general than we really need, but its generality shows that some simple modifications to the algorithm won't improve its asymptotic running time. For example, the graph is connected, so processing connected components separately won't help. Also, the two partitions are the same size, so processing the smaller (or larger) partition first won't help either. Furthermore, using breadth-first search won't help because it will process just as many edges when no augmenting path exists. On the other hand, this algorithm is not the most efficient one known for this problem. In the exercises, we explore how it might be improved.

Although the optimizations we made over a direct reduction to network flow did not improve the asymptotic running time of the algorithm, the resulting algorithm may have other advantages. For example, suppose we are trying to match jobs with job applicants. Each applicant may be qualified for several jobs. We wish to fill as many jobs as possible, but still assign jobs so that priority is given to those who applied earlier. If we process the applicants in the order in which they applied, we will obey this priority.

14.4   Summary

The network flow problem is a general combinatorial optimization problem to which many other problems can be reduced. Although the Ford–Fulkerson algorithm can behave poorly when the maximum flow is large in comparison to the size of the graph, its flexibility makes it useful for those cases in which the maximum flow is known to be small. For cases in which the maximum flow may be large, the Edmonds–Karp algorithm, which is simply the Ford–Fulkerson algorithm using breadth-first search to find augmenting paths, performs adequately.

The bipartite matching problem is an example of a problem which occurs quite often in practice and which can be reduced to network flow to yield a reasonably efficient algorithm. Furthermore, a careful study of the reduction yields insight into the problem that leads to a more general algorithm.

14.5   Exercises

Exercise 14.1. Prove Equation (14.1) on page 442. [**Hint:** Show by induction that the net flow out of any set of vertices including the source but not the sink is equal to the left-hand side.]

Exercise 14.2. Prove that NETWORKFLOW, shown in Figure 14.3, meets its specification.

Exercise 14.3. Implement COPYGRAPH, specified in Figure 14.3, to return a LISTGRAPH and run in $O(n + a)$ time, where n is the number of vertices and a is the number of edges in the given graph.

Exercise 14.4. Implement ADDFLOW, specified in Figure 14.3, to run in $O(n + a)$ time, where n is the number of vertices in F and a is the number of edges in F and R together. For the purposes of your analysis, you may assume that F and R are implemented as LISTGRAPHS, and that the EDGES in P form a simple path in R.

* Exercise 14.5. Suppose we generalize the network flow problem to allow positive rational edge capacities. Prove that the Ford–Fulkerson algorithm always finds a maximum flow for such a network.

** Exercise 14.6. Suppose we generalize the network flow problem to allow positive real edge capacities. Give such a flow network for which the Ford–Fulkerson algorithm does not terminate and does not converge to a maximum flow.

Exercise 14.7. Implement the matching algorithm using breadth-first search (see Exercise 11.6) to find augmenting paths.

** Exercise 14.8. Let G be a bipartite graph whose partitions are $\{i \mid 0 \le i < k\}$ and $\{i \mid k \le i < n\}$, and let M be a matching on G smaller than the maximum size. Suppose the minimum length of any augmenting path in G is l. Let $S = \{P_1, \ldots, P_m\}$ be a maximal set of vertex-disjoint augmenting paths of length l; i.e., any augmenting path of length l shares at least one vertex with some path in S. We define the *symmetric difference* of two sets A and B as

$$A \oplus B = (A \cup B) \backslash (A \cap B);$$

thus, the symmetric difference is the set of elements in exactly one of the two sets.

a. Prove that $M' = M \oplus (P_1 \cup \cdots \cup P_m)$ is a matching with m more edges than M.
b. Prove that any augmenting path in M', where M' is as defined above, has more than l edges. [**Hint:** For the case in which P shares a vertex with some P_i, define $T = (M \oplus M') \oplus P$. Prove that $T = (P_1 \cup \cdots \cup P_m) \oplus P$ and that T has at least $(m + 1)l$ edges.]
c. Prove that the size of every matching exceeds the size of M by no more than n/l.
d. Give an algorithm to find a maximal set of minimum-length augmenting paths. Your algorithm should run in $O(a)$ time, where a is the number of edges in G, assuming G is represented as a LISTGRAPH and $n \in O(a)$. [**Hint:** Use both breadth-first search and a modified depth-first search.]

e. Give an $O(a\sqrt{n})$ algorithm to find a maximum-sized matching in G.

Exercise 14.9. Suppose we modify the network flow problem so that the input includes an array $cap[0..n-1]$ of integers such that for each vertex i, $cap[i]$ gives an upper bound on the flow we allow to go to and from vertex i. Show how to reduce this problem to the ordinary network flow problem. Your reduction must run in $O(n+a)$ time, where n is the number of vertices and a is the number of edges in the graph.

Exercise 14.10. We define an $n \times n$ *grid* to be an undirected graph (V, E) where $V = \{(i, j) \mid 1 \le i \le n, 1 \le j \le n\}$, and two vertices (i, j) and (i', j') are adjacent iff either $i = i'$ and $j = j' \pm 1$ or $j = j'$ and $i = i' \pm 1$. Thus, each vertex in a grid has at most 4 neighbors. We call the vertices with fewer than 4 neighbors *boundary vertices* (i.e., these are vertices $(1, j)$, (n, j), $(i, 1)$, or (i, n)). Give an $O(mn^2)$ algorithm which takes a value $n \in \mathbb{N}$ and $m \le n^2$ starting vertices $(i, j) \in [1..n] \times [1..n]$ and determines whether there exists a set of m vertex-disjoint paths in the $n \times n$ grid, each connecting a starting node with a boundary node. You may assume you have an algorithm for the problem stated in Exercise 14.9.

* Exercise 14.11. A *path cover* of a directed graph is a set of paths such that every vertex is included in exactly one path. The *size* of a path cover is the number of paths in the set. Show how to reduce the problem of finding a minimum-sized path cover in a directed acyclic graph to the problem of finding a maximum-sized matching in a bipartite graph. The total running time of the algorithm should be in $O(na)$.

* Exercise 14.12. We are given two arrays of integers, $R[1..m]$ and $C[1..n]$ such that

$$\sum_{i=1}^{m} R[i] = \sum_{i=1}^{n} C[i] = k.$$

Give an $O(kmn)$ algorithm that returns an $m \times n$ matrix of 0s and 1s such that row i contains exactly $R[i]$ 1s and column j contains exactly $C[j]$ 1s, for all $1 \le i \le m$ and $1 \le j \le n$. If there is no such matrix, your algorithm should return nil.

** Exercise 14.13. Given a connected undirected graph G, the *edge connectivity* of G is the minimum number of edges whose removal would disconnect the graph. Give an $O(n^2 a)$ algorithm to find the edge connectivity of a given connected undirected GRAPH with n vertices and a edges. For

your running time analysis, you may assume the graph is represented as a
LISTGRAPH. Prove the correctness of your algorithm.

14.6 Notes

The NETWORKFLOW algorithm is due to Ford and Fulkerson [42]. The
running-time analysis of the use of breadth-first search in the Ford–Fulkerson
algorithm is due to Edmonds and Karp [37] and Dinic [30]. Asymptotically
faster algorithms exist — to date, the fastest known is due to Goldberg and
Rao [57]. Their algorithm has a running time in

$$O(\min(n^{2/3}, a^{1/2})a \lg(n^2/a + 2) \lg C),$$

where C is the maximum capacity of any edge.

The technique of finding a maximum-sized matching using augmenting
paths is due to Berge [13]. He showed that in an arbitrary undirected graph,
a matching is of maximum size iff no augmenting path exists. Finding
augmenting paths in arbitrary undirected graphs is more challenging,
however, because we must avoid returning to the same vertex from which we
started. The first efficient algorithm for finding an augmenting path in an
arbitrary undirected graph is due to Edmonds [35]. The algorithm suggested
by Exercise 14.8 is due to Hopcroft and Karp [64], and is the asymptotically
fastest known algorithm for finding a maximum-sized matching in a bipartite
graph. The structure of this exercise is based on a problem in Cormen, *et al.*
[25]. An $O(a\sqrt{n})$ algorithm for arbitrary undirected graphs was later given
by Micali and Vazirani [93].

A solution to Exercise 14.6 is given by Ford and Fulkerson [43].

Chapter 15

* The Fast Fourier Transform

In this chapter, we examine an algorithm whose discovery has had a profound impact on several areas of science and engineering. Although we will not delve into these application areas, we will show how it has been used to design an arbitrary-precision natural number multiplication algorithm which runs in $O(n \lg n \lg \lg n)$ time, where n is the number of bits in the product. Along the way, we will examine some properties of the complex numbers as well as the natural numbers. We begin by examining the computation of a *convolution*, the fundamental problem that is solved by the fast Fourier transform.

15.1   Convolutions

Let $a = \langle a_0, \ldots, a_{m-1} \rangle$ and $b = \langle b_0, \ldots, b_{n-1} \rangle$ be two vectors. We define the *convolution* of a and b as the vector $c = \langle c_0, \ldots, c_{m+n-2} \rangle$, where

$$c_j = \sum_{i=\max(0,j-n+1)}^{\min(j,m-1)} a_i b_{j-i}.$$

Many applications require the computation of a convolution. For example, if a and b represent the coefficients of two polynomials, where a_i and b_i are the respective coefficients for x^i, then the convolution of a and b gives the coefficients of their product.

We desire an efficient algorithm for computing a convolution. We can gain some insight into how this might be done by examining the polynomial multiplication problem. Clearly, the $\Theta(n^{\lg 3})$ algorithm of Section 10.1 can be used to compute a convolution. Furthermore, the solution to Exercise 10.4 shows that this can be done in $O(n^{1+\epsilon})$ time for any $\epsilon \in \mathbb{R}^{>0}$ (though in fact the hidden constant becomes quite large as ϵ approaches 0). We wish to improve on these algorithms.

It is a well-known fact that a polynomial of degree $n - 1$ is uniquely determined by its values at any n distinct points. Therefore, one way to multiply two polynomials $p(x)$ and $q(x)$ whose product has degree $n - 1$ is as follows:

1. Evaluate $p(x_i)$ and $q(x_i)$ for n distinct values x_i, $0 \le i < n$.
2. Compute $r(x_i) = p(x_i)q(x_i)$ for $0 \le i < n$.
3. Construct the unique polynomial $r(x)$ of degree $n - 1$ determined by the values $r(x_i)$ for $0 \le i < n$.

Note that step 2 can be done in $\Theta(n)$ time, assuming each multiplication can be done in $\Theta(1)$ time. We need to show how steps 1 and 3 can be done efficiently.

The evaluation of a polynomial of degree less than n at n distinct points can be viewed as a linear transformation — i.e., a multiplication of a $1 \times n$ vector by an $n \times n$ matrix. Specifically, let p be the $1 \times n$ vector representing the coefficients of a polynomial $p(x)$ as described above (if the degree is less than $n - 1$, we can use coefficients of 0 for the high-order terms). Let A be the $n \times n$ matrix such that $A_{ij} = x_j^i$ for $0 \le i < n$, $0 \le j < n$, where $x_0, \ldots, x_{n-1}$ are distinct values. Then the product pA yields the $1 \times n$ vector $v = \langle v_0, \ldots, v_{n-1} \rangle$ such that

$$v_j = \sum_{i=0}^{n-1} p_i A_{ij}$$

$$= \sum_{i=0}^{n-1} p_i x_j^i$$

$$= p(x_j).$$

Furthermore, if A has an inverse A^{-1}, then this transformation is invertible:

$$vA^{-1} = pAA^{-1}$$

$$= p.$$

Thus, given the values of a polynomial at the n points $x_0, \ldots, x_{n-1}$, we can compute the polynomial by multiplying the vector of values by A^{-1}. The product of two polynomials $p(x)$ and $q(x)$ is therefore represented by the vector

$$(pA \cdot qA)A^{-1},$$

where "·" denotes the component-wise product of two vectors of the same size.

The main problem with this approach is that the multiplications of a $1 \times n$ vector with an $n \times n$ array would appear to require $\Omega(n^2)$ time. However, this running time can be improved if we choose the points $x_0, \ldots, x_{n-1}$ cleverly. In order to do this, we need to allow them to be chosen from the set of complex numbers, $\mathbb{C}$. We also need to define, for any $n \geq 1$, a *principal nth root of unity* as any value $\omega \in \mathbb{C}$ such that

- $\omega^n = 1$; and
- for $1 \leq j < n$,

$$\sum_{i=0}^{n-1} \omega^{ij} = 0.$$

We will show how to find such values in $\mathbb{C}$. First, however, let us consider why having a principal nth root of unity might be helpful. Given a principal nth root of unity ω, let A be the $n \times n$ matrix such that $A_{ij} = \omega^{ij}$. Given a $1 \times n$ vector p, the product pA is said to be the *discrete Fourier transform* of p with respect to ω. Note that if p is the coefficient vector for a polynomial $p(x)$, then pA gives the values of $p(\omega^j)$ for $0 \leq j < n$.

In what follows, we will develop a divide-and-conquer algorithm for computing a DFT. To simplify matters, let's assume that n is a power of 2. The following theorem shows an important property of principal nth roots of unity when n is a power of 2. We will use this property in designing our divide-and-conquer algorithm.

Theorem 15.1. *Let ω be a principal nth root of unity, where $n \geq 2$ is a power of 2. Then ω^2 is a principal $(n/2)$nd root of unity.*

Proof. Because $\omega^n = 1$, $(\omega^2)^{n/2} = 1$. Let $1 \leq j < n/2$. Then $1 \leq 2j < n$. Because ω is a principal nth root of unity, we have

$$\sum_{i=0}^{n-1} \omega^{i(2j)} = 0.$$

Note that for $i \geq n/2$,

$$\omega^{i(2j)} = \omega^{nj}\omega^{(2i-n)j}$$

$$= \omega^{(2i-n)j},$$

because $\omega^n = 1$. Therefore, we can write

$$\sum_{i=0}^{n-1} \omega^{i(2j)} = \sum_{i=0}^{\frac{n}{2}-1} \omega^{2ij} + \sum_{i=n/2}^{n-1} \omega^{2ij}$$

$$= \sum_{i=0}^{\frac{n}{2}-1} \omega^{2ij} + \sum_{i=n/2}^{n-1} \omega^{(2i-n)j}$$

$$= \sum_{i=0}^{\frac{n}{2}-1} \omega^{2ij} + \sum_{i=0}^{\frac{n}{2}-1} \omega^{(2(i+n/2)-n)j}$$

$$= 2\sum_{i=0}^{\frac{n}{2}-1} \omega^{2ij}.$$

Because the above value is 0, it follows that

$$\sum_{i=0}^{\frac{n}{2}-1} (\omega^2)^{ij} = 0.$$

Hence, ω^2 is a principal $(n/2)$nd root of unity.   □

Knowing that ω^2 is a principal $n/2$nd root of unity, we can now reduce the problem of computing a DFT for a $1 \times n$ vector to two smaller instances. We form these two smaller instances by dividing a given $1 \times n$ vector p into its odd components $p' = \langle p_1, p_3, \ldots, p_{n-1} \rangle$ and its even components $p'' = \langle p_0, p_2, \ldots, p_{n-2} \rangle$. Thus,

$$\sum_{i=0}^{n-1} p_i \omega^{ij} = \sum_{i=0}^{\frac{n}{2}-1} (p_{2i}\omega^{2ij} + p_{2i+1}\omega^{(2i+1)j})$$

$$= \sum_{i=0}^{\frac{n}{2}-1} p_{2i}\omega^{2ij} + \omega^j \sum_{i=0}^{\frac{n}{2}-1} p_{2i+1}\omega^{2ij}.$$

Note that each sum on the right-hand side is the jth component of the DFT with respect to ω^2 of a $1 \times n/2$ vector. Specifically, let d' and d'' be the DFTs of p' and p'', respectively, with respect to ω^2, and let d be the DFT of p with respect to ω. Then for $0 \leq j < n/2$, we have

$$d_j = d''_j + \omega^j d'_j. \tag{15.1}$$

Furthermore,

$$d_{j+n/2} = \sum_{i=0}^{\frac{n}{2}-1} p''_i \omega^{2i(j+n/2)} + \omega^{j+n/2} \sum_{i=0}^{\frac{n}{2}-1} p'_i \omega^{2i(j+n/2)}$$

$$= \sum_{i=0}^{\frac{n}{2}-1} p''_i \omega^{2ij} + \omega^{j+n/2} \sum_{i=0}^{\frac{n}{2}-1} p'_i \omega^{2ij}$$

$$= d''_j + \omega^{j+n/2} d'_j. \tag{15.2}$$

The above equation can be simplified somewhat by applying the following theorem.

Theorem 15.2. *Let $n > 1$ be a power of 2. Then ω is a principal nth root of unity iff $\omega^{n/2} = -1$.*

Proof. $\Rightarrow$ Suppose ω is a principal nth root of unity. It follows from Theorem 15.1 by induction on n that $\omega^{n/2}$ is a principal 2nd root of unity. It is therefore sufficient to show that if ω is a principal 2nd root of unity, then $\omega = -1$.

Suppose ω is a principal 2nd root of unity. Then from the definition, we have

$$0 = \sum_{i=0}^{1} \omega^i$$

$$= 1 + \omega.$$

Rearranging terms, we have $\omega = -1$.

$\Leftarrow$: Let $n = 2^k$. We will show by induction on $k \geq 1$ that if $\omega^{n/2} = -1$, then ω is a principal nth root of unity.

Base: $k = 1$. Then $n = 2$, and $n/2 = 1$. Because -1 is a principal 2nd root of unity, the result follows.

Induction Hypothesis: Assume for some $k > 1$ that whenever $1 \leq k' < k$ and $n = 2^{k'}$, if $\omega^{n/2} = -1$, then ω is a principal nth root of unity.

Induction Step: Suppose $n = 2^k$ and $\omega^{n/2} = -1$. Clearly, $\omega^n = 1$. Let $1 \leq j < n$. We consider two cases.

Case 1: j is odd. We therefore have

$$\sum_{i=0}^{n-1} \omega^{ij} = \sum_{i=0}^{\frac{n}{2}-1} \omega^{ij} + \sum_{i=n/2}^{n-1} \omega^{ij}$$

$$= \sum_{i=0}^{\frac{n}{2}-1} \omega^{ij} + \sum_{i=0}^{\frac{n}{2}-1} \omega^{(i+n/2)j}$$

$$= \sum_{i=0}^{\frac{n}{2}-1} \omega^{ij} + \sum_{i=0}^{\frac{n}{2}-1} \omega^{ij}(\omega^{n/2})^j$$

$$= \sum_{i=0}^{\frac{n}{2}-1} \omega^{ij} + \sum_{i=0}^{\frac{n}{2}-1} \omega^{ij}(-1)^j$$

$$= 0.$$

Case 2: j is even. Then because $1 \leq j < n$, n must be at least 4. We first observe that

$$(\omega^2)^{n/4} = \omega^{n/2}$$

$$= -1.$$

By the Induction Hypothesis, ω^2 is a principal $(n/2)$nd root of unity. We then have

$$\sum_{i=0}^{n-1} \omega^{ij} = \sum_{i=0}^{n-1} (\omega^2)^{ij/2}$$

$$= \sum_{i=0}^{\frac{n}{2}-1} (\omega^2)^{ij/2} + \sum_{i=n/2}^{n-1} (\omega^2)^{ij/2}$$

$$= \sum_{i=n/2}^{n-1} (\omega^2)^{ij/2},$$

because ω^2 is a principal $(n/2)$nd root of unity. Re-indexing the above equality, we have

$$\sum_{i=0}^{n-1} \omega^{ij} = \sum_{i=n/2}^{n-1} (\omega^2)^{ij/2}$$

$$= \sum_{i=0}^{\frac{n}{2}-1} (\omega^2)^{(i+n/2)j/2}$$

$$= \sum_{i=0}^{\frac{n}{2}-1} (\omega^2)^{(n/2)j/2} (\omega^2)^{ij/2}$$

$$= \sum_{i=0}^{\frac{n}{2}-1} (\omega^2)^{ij/2}$$

$$= 0.$$

We conclude that ω is a principal nth root of unity. $\qquad\square$

Using the fact that $\omega^{n/2} = -1$, we can now rewrite (15.2) for $0 \le j < n/2$ as

$$d_{j+n/2} = d_j'' - \omega^j d_j'. \tag{15.3}$$

We therefore have the divide-and-conquer algorithm, known as the *Fast Fourier Transform*, shown in Figure 15.1. Note that we use the type COMPLEX to represent a complex number.

Because FFT should only be called with a vector whose size n is a power of 2, n is not a good measure of the size of the problem instance for the purpose of analyzing the algorithm. Instead, we will use $k = \lg n$. Assuming each arithmetic operation on complex numbers can be performed in $\Theta(1)$ time, it is easily seen that the running time excluding the recursive calls is in $\Theta(2^k)$. The worst-case running time is therefore given by the recurrence

$$f(k) \in 2f(k-1) + \Theta(2^k).$$

From Theorem 3.34, $f(k) \in \Theta(k2^k)$.

In order to use FFT to compute a convolution, we need to be able to compute the inverse transform. Let A be the $n \times n$ matrix defining a DFT. In order to compute the inverse transform, we need to know that A^{-1} exists, and we need an efficient way to multiply a given $1 \times n$ vector on the right by A^{-1}. The following theorem gives A^{-1}.

Figure 15.1 The Fast Fourier Transform algorithm

Precondition: $p[0..n-1]$ is an array of COMPLEXes, n is a NAT containing a power of 2, and ω is a COMPLEX containing a principal nth root of unity.
Postcondition: Returns the DFT of p with respect to ω.

FFT($p[0..n-1], \omega$)
    $d \leftarrow$ **new** ARRAY$[0..n-1]$; $mid \leftarrow n/2$
    if $n = 1$
        $d[0] \leftarrow p[0]$
    else
        $p' \leftarrow$ **new** ARRAY$[0..mid-1]$; $p'' \leftarrow$ **new** ARRAY$[0..mid-1]$
        for $i \leftarrow 0$ **to** $mid - 1$
            $p''[i] \leftarrow p[2i]$; $p'[i] \leftarrow p[2i+1]$
        $d' \leftarrow$ FFT(p', ω^2)
        $d'' \leftarrow$ FFT(p'', ω^2)
        $v \leftarrow 1$
        // **Invariant:** $d[0..i-1]$ and $d[mid..mid+i-1]$ contain the correct
        // values for the DFT of p, and $v = \omega^i$.
        for $i \leftarrow 0$ **to** $mid - 1$
            $d[i] \leftarrow d''[i] + v(d'[i])$
            $d[i + mid] \leftarrow d''[i] - v(d'[i])$
            $v \leftarrow v\omega$
    return d

Theorem 15.3. *Let A be the $n \times n$ matrix such that for $0 \le i < n$ and $0 \le j < n$, $A_{ij} = \omega^{ij}$, where ω is a principal nth root of unity. Then A^{-1} is the matrix B, where $B_{ij} = \omega^{-ij}/n$.*

Proof. We must show that $AB = I$, where

$$I_{ij} = \begin{cases} 1 & \text{if } i = j \\ 0 & \text{otherwise,} \end{cases}$$

for $0 \le i < n$ and $0 \le j < n$. Let $C = AB$. Then

$$C_{ij} = \sum_{k=0}^{n-1} A_{ik} B_{kj}$$

$$= \sum_{k=0}^{n-1} \omega^{ik} \omega^{-kj}/n$$

$$= \frac{1}{n} \sum_{k=0}^{n-1} \omega^{k(i-j)}.$$

We now consider three cases.

Case 1: $i = j$. Then

$$C_{ij} = \frac{1}{n} \sum_{k=0}^{n-1} \omega^{k(i-j)}$$

$$= \frac{1}{n} \sum_{k=0}^{n-1} \omega^0$$

$$= 1.$$

Case 2: $i > j$. Then $1 \le i - j < n$. Because ω is a principal nth root of unity, we have

$$C_{ij} = \frac{1}{n} \sum_{k=0}^{n-1} \omega^{k(i-j)}$$

$$= 0.$$

Case 3: $i < j$. Then $1 \le i - j + n < n$. Because $\omega^n = 1$, $\omega^{k(i-j)} = \omega^{k(i-j+n)}$. Hence, as in Case 2, $C_{ij} = 0$.

We conclude that $C = I$, so that $B = A^{-1}$. $\qquad\square$

Note that the matrix A^{-1} can be written A'/n, where $A'_{ij} = \omega^{-ij}$. The following theorem shows that ω^{-1} is also a principal nth root of unity, so that multiplication by A' is also a DFT. As a result, we can use FFT to compute the inverse transform.

Theorem 15.4. *Let ω be a principal nth root of unity, where $n \ge 2$ is a power of 2. Then ω^{-1} is a principal nth root of unity.*

Proof. From Theorem 15.2, we need only to show that $\omega^{-n/2} = -1$. Because $\omega^n = 1$, we have

$$\omega^{-n/2} = \omega^{n-n/2}$$

$$= \omega^{n/2}$$

$$= -1$$

from Theorem 15.2. ω^{-1} is therefore a principal nth root of unity. $\qquad\square$

In order to complete the convolution algorithm, we need a principal nth root of unity for each n that is a power of 2. The following theorem provides these values. The theorem actually holds for all positive n, but the proof is simpler when n is a power of 2.

Theorem 15.5. *Let n be a power of 2. Then*

$$\cos\frac{2\pi}{n} + i\sin\frac{2\pi}{n}$$

is a principal nth root of unity.

Proof.   We first observe that if $n = 1$, then

$$\cos\frac{2\pi}{n} + i\sin\frac{2\pi}{n} = 1 + 0i$$

$$= 1.$$

Thus, from Theorem 15.2, it suffices to show that

$$\left(\cos\frac{2\pi}{n} + i\sin\frac{2\pi}{n}\right)^{n/2} = -1$$

whenever $n > 1$ is a power of 2. We proceed by induction on n.

Base: $n = 2$. Then

$$\left(\cos\frac{2\pi}{n} + i\sin\frac{2\pi}{n}\right)^{n/2} = \cos\pi + i\sin\pi$$

$$= -1 + 0i$$

$$= -1.$$

Induction Hypothesis: Assume for some $n > 2$, where n is a power of 2, that for any k such that $1 < k < n$, if k is a power of 2, then

$$\left(\cos\frac{2\pi}{k} + i\sin\frac{2\pi}{k}\right)^{k/2} = -1.$$

Induction Step:

$$\left(\cos\frac{2\pi}{n} + i\sin\frac{2\pi}{n}\right)^{n/2} = \left(\left(\cos\frac{2\pi}{n} + i\sin\frac{2\pi}{n}\right)^2\right)^{n/4}$$

$$= \left(\cos^2\frac{2\pi}{n} - \sin^2\frac{2\pi}{n} + 2i\left(\cos\frac{2\pi}{n}\sin\frac{2\pi}{n}\right)\right)^{n/4}.$$

We now apply the following trigonometric identities:

$$\cos^2 x - \sin^2 x = \cos 2x$$

and

$$2(\cos x \sin x) = \sin 2x.$$

We therefore have

$$\left(\cos\frac{2\pi}{n} + i\sin\frac{2\pi}{n}\right)^{n/2} = \left(\cos\frac{4\pi}{n} + i\sin\frac{4\pi}{n}\right)^{n/4}$$

$$= \left(\cos\frac{2\pi}{n/2} + i\sin\frac{2\pi}{n/2}\right)^{\frac{n/2}{2}}$$

$$= -1$$

by the Induction Hypothesis. $\square$

Before we give the algorithm for computing a convolution, let us consider a slight generalization of the problem. We have defined a convolution to be a vector whose size is the sum of the sizes of two given vectors. In order to apply FFT, we must pad the two input vectors with enough zeros so that each has a size n, where n is a power of 2 and is at least as large as the size of the convolution. It would be somewhat easier to do this if we required the input vectors to be padded with enough zeros so that they were both the size of the convolution.

Let us therefore consider the value of the vector $(pA \cdot qA)A^{-1}$ when p and q are arbitrary $1 \times n$ vectors over $\mathbb{C}$ and A is the DFT matrix with respect to ω. The jth component of the vector pA is given by

$$\sum_{i=0}^{n-1} p_i A_{ij} = \sum_{i=0}^{n-1} p_i \omega^{ij}.$$

The jth component of the component-wise product $(pA \cdot qA)$ is therefore

$$\sum_{i=0}^{n-1} p_i \omega^{ij} \sum_{k=0}^{n-1} q_k \omega^{kj} = \sum_{i=0}^{n-1}\sum_{k=0}^{n-1} p_i q_k \omega^{(i+k)j}.$$

Finally, multiplying the above summation on the right by A^{-1}, we obtain a vector whose jth component is

$$\sum_{l=0}^{n-1}\sum_{i=0}^{n-1}\sum_{k=0}^{n-1} p_i q_k \omega^{(i+k)l} \omega^{-lj} / n = \frac{1}{n}\sum_{l=0}^{n-1}\sum_{i=0}^{n-1}\sum_{k=0}^{n-1} p_i q_k \omega^{(i+k-j)l}$$

$$= \frac{1}{n}\sum_{i=0}^{n-1}\sum_{k=0}^{n-1} p_i q_k \sum_{l=0}^{n-1} \omega^{(i+k-j)l}.$$

We now observe that in the exponent for ω above, $1 - n \leq i + k - j \leq 2n - 2$. Because $\omega^n = 1$, we can multiply any of the terms by either ω^n or ω^{-n} without changing its value. Hence, because ω is a principal nth root of unity,

$$\sum_{l=0}^{n-1} \omega^{(i+k-j)l} = \begin{cases} n & \text{if } i+k-j = 0 \text{ or } i+k-j = n \\ 0 & \text{otherwise.} \end{cases}$$

Therefore, the jth component of $(pA \cdot qA)A^{-1}$ is

$$\sum_{i=0}^{j} p_i q_{j-i} + \sum_{i=j+1}^{n-1} p_i q_{j-i+n}.$$

We will refer to this vector as the *positive wrapped convolution* of p and q. We will denote this operation by $p \otimes q$. Note that if either p_i or q_j is 0 whenever $i + j \geq n$, the second summation in the above definition is 0, so that we can reduce the problem of computing an ordinary convolution to the problem of computing a positive wrapped convolution.

Figure 15.2 gives an algorithm for computing a positive wrapped convolution using the Fast Fourier Transform. Note that m is the smallest power of 2 no larger than n, so that $n \leq m < 2n$. Assuming each arithmetic operation can be performed in $\Theta(1)$ time, the running time excluding the calls to FFT is in $\Theta(n)$. If $k = \lg m$, the running time for each call to FFT is in $\Theta(k2^k) = \Theta(n \lg n)$. The overall running time is therefore in $\Theta(n \lg n)$. It is easily seen that this algorithm can be used to multiply two polynomials over $\mathbb{C}$ in $\Theta(n \lg n)$ time, where n is the degree of the product.

Throughout this discussion, we have been assuming that we can store arbitrary complex numbers and perform arithmetic operations on them in $\Theta(1)$ time. These assumptions are rather dubious. However, for most scientific and engineering applications, it is sufficient to use floating-point

Figure 15.2 Algorithm for computing a positive wrapped convolution over $\mathbb{C}$ using the Fast Fourier Transform

---

Precondition: $p[0..n-1]$ and $q[0..n-1]$ are arrays of COMPLEXes, and n is a positive NAT.
Postcondition: Returns the positive wrapped convolution of p and q.

CONVOLUTION($p[0..n-1], q[0..n-1]$)
    $m \leftarrow 2^{\lceil \lg n \rceil}$; $p' \leftarrow$ **new** ARRAY$[0..m-1]$; $q' \leftarrow$ **new** ARRAY$[0..m-1]$
    COPY($p[0..n-1], p'[0..n-1]$); COPY($q[0..n-1], q'[0..n-1]$)
    for $i \leftarrow n$ **to** $m-1$
        $p'[i] \leftarrow 0$; $q'[i] \leftarrow 0$
    $\omega \leftarrow \cos(2\pi/m) + \mathrm{i}\sin(2\pi/m)$
    $ptrans \leftarrow$ FFT(p', ω); $qtrans \leftarrow$ FFT(q', ω)
    $rtrans \leftarrow$ **new** ARRAY$[0..m-1]$
    for $i \leftarrow 0$ **to** $m-1$
        $rtrans[i] \leftarrow ptrans[i]\,qtrans[i]$
    $r' \leftarrow$ FFT($rtrans, 1/\omega$); $r \leftarrow$ **new** ARRAY$[0..n-1]$
    for $i \leftarrow 0$ **to** $n-1$
        $r[i] \leftarrow r'[i]/m$
    return r

---

approximations. The CONVOLUTION algorithm is therefore very useful in practice.

15.2 Commutative Rings

In Exercise 10.5 (page 364), we suggested that the polynomial multiplication algorithm of Section 10.1 could be adapted to multiply two arbitrary-precision natural numbers in $\Theta(n^{\lg 3})$ time, where n is the number of bits in the product. Because we now have a $\Theta(n \lg n)$ algorithm for multiplying polynomials, we might conclude that it could be used to multiply arbitrary-precision natural numbers in $\Theta(n \lg n)$ time. However, there are two problems with this conclusion. First, CONVOLUTION uses complex numbers having infinite binary representations. It turns out that if we are careful, we can use finite approximations and still obtain correct results for arbitrary-precision multiplication. The second problem is more serious, though. Note that both CONVOLUTION and FFT perform multiplications involving values derived from the vectors they are processing. These values can become much larger than the original elements of the vectors, so that recursive calls would need to be made to do these multiplications. This has the effect of increasing the running time.

In view of the above complications, we will take a somewhat different approach. In this section, we will show that the results of the previous section can be extended to various other mathematical structures, including some involving only natural numbers. In the next section, we will develop a multiplication algorithm that uses the Fast Fourier Transform over certain of these structures. This algorithm will have a running time in $O(n \lg^2 n)$. In the following section, we will show how to improve it to achieve a running time in $O(n \lg n \lg \lg n)$. This algorithm is asymptotically the fastest known algorithm for arbitrary-precision multiplication.

In order to show how the results of the previous section extend to other mathematical structures, we need a few definitions. Let S be a set, and let $+$ be any binary operation on S; i.e., for every $x, y \in S, x + y \in S$. The pair $\langle S, + \rangle$ is said to be a *group* if the following properties hold:

- **Associativity:** For every $x, y, z \in S, (x + y) + z = x + (y + z)$.
- **Identity:** There is an element $0 \in S$ such that for every $x \in S, 0 + x = x + 0 = x$.
- **Inverse:** For every element $x \in S$, there is an element $-x \in S$ such that $x + (-x) = -x + x = 0$.

If, in addition *commutativity* holds — for every $x, y \in S, x + y = y + x$ — then we say $\langle S, + \rangle$ is an *abelian group*.

Example 15.1. $\langle \mathbb{Z}, + \rangle$, the set of integers with addition, is an abelian group.

Example 15.2. $\langle \mathbb{N}, + \rangle$, the set of natural numbers with addition, is not a group because only 0 has an inverse.

Example 15.3. For a positive integer m, let $\mathbb{Z}_m$ denote the set of natural numbers strictly less than m, and let $+$ denote addition mod m. It is not hard to see that $\langle \mathbb{Z}_m, + \rangle$ is an abelian group, with 0 being the identity and $m - i$ being the inverse of i.

Example 15.4. Let S_3 be the set of permutations of three distinct elements, and let $\circ$ denote composition. We denote a permutation by the result of applying it to $\langle 1, 2, 3 \rangle$; for example, the permutation that swaps the first and second elements is denoted by $\langle 2, 1, 3 \rangle$. Then $\langle 2, 1, 3 \rangle \circ \langle 1, 3, 2 \rangle = \langle 2, 3, 1 \rangle$, but $\langle 1, 3, 2 \rangle \circ \langle 2, 1, 3 \rangle = \langle 3, 1, 2 \rangle$. Hence, $\langle S_3, \circ \rangle$ is not commutative. However, it is not hard to see that it is a group, with $\langle 1, 2, 3 \rangle$ being the identity element, $\langle 2, 3, 1 \rangle$ being the inverse of $\langle 3, 1, 2 \rangle$ and vice versa, and every other element being its own inverse.

Let $\langle S, + \rangle$ be an abelian group, and let $\cdot$ be a binary operation on S. Then $\langle S, +, \cdot \rangle$ is said to be a *ring* if the following properties hold for every x, y, and z in S:

- **Associativity:** $(x \cdot y) \cdot z = x \cdot (y \cdot z)$.
- **Distributivity:** $x \cdot (y + z) = x \cdot y + x \cdot z$ and $(x + y) \cdot z = x \cdot z + y \cdot z$.

If, in addition, commutativity holds for $\cdot$, $\langle S, +, \cdot \rangle$ is said to be a *commutative ring*. If a ring $\langle S, +, \cdot \rangle$ has an element $1 \in S$ such that for every $x \in S$, $x \cdot 1 = 1 \cdot x = x$, then 1 is said to be a *unit element*.

Example 15.5. It is not hard to see that $\langle \mathbb{C}, +, \cdot \rangle$, where $+$ and $\cdot$ denote ordinary addition and multiplication, respectively, is a commutative ring with unit element 1.

Example 15.6. For a positive integer m, consider $\langle \mathbb{Z}_m, +, \cdot \rangle$, where $+$ is addition mod m and $\cdot$ is multiplication mod m. As we observed in Example 15.3, $\langle \mathbb{Z}_m, + \rangle$ is an abelian group. It is not hard to see that $\langle \mathbb{Z}_m, +, \cdot \rangle$ is a commutative ring, and that 1 is a unit element. We will be using commutative rings of this form for the multiplication algorithms of the next two sections.

Example 15.7. Let $S = \{0, 2, 4, 6\}$, and let $+$ and $\cdot$ denote addition and multiplication, respectively, mod 8. Then it is not hard to see that $\langle S, +, \cdot \rangle$ is a commutative ring. However, it does not have a unit element, because $0 \cdot 2 = 0$, $2 \cdot 4 = 0$, and $6 \cdot 2 = 4$.

Example 15.8. Let S be the set of 2×2 matrices over $\mathbb{R}$, and let $+$ and $\cdot$ denote matrix addition and multiplication, respectively. Then It is not hard to show that $\langle S, +, \cdot \rangle$ is a ring, and that the identity matrix is a unit element. However, the ring is not commutative; for example,

$$\begin{pmatrix} 1 & 1 \\ 0 & 1 \end{pmatrix} \begin{pmatrix} 1 & 0 \\ 1 & 1 \end{pmatrix} = \begin{pmatrix} 2 & 1 \\ 1 & 1 \end{pmatrix},$$

but

$$\begin{pmatrix} 1 & 0 \\ 1 & 1 \end{pmatrix} \begin{pmatrix} 1 & 1 \\ 0 & 1 \end{pmatrix} = \begin{pmatrix} 1 & 1 \\ 1 & 2 \end{pmatrix}.$$

In what follows, we will show that the results of the previous section extend to an arbitrary commutative ring $R = \langle S, +, \cdot \rangle$ with unit element 1. For convenience, we will typically abbreviate $x \cdot y$ as xy. We will also abbreviate $x + (-y)$ as $x - y$.

We first observe that for $x \in S$ and $n \in \mathbb{N}$, we can define x^n as follows:

$$x^n = \begin{cases} 1 & \text{if } n = 0 \\ xx^{n-1} & \text{otherwise.} \end{cases}$$

Hence, the definition of a principal nth root of unity makes sense for R. Furthermore, the definition of a discrete Fourier transform also makes sense over this ring. The following theorem states that some familiar properties of exponentiation must hold for any ring with unit element; its proof is left as an exercise.

Theorem 15.6. *Let R be any ring with unit element. Then the following properties hold for any x in R and any $m, n \in \mathbb{N}$:*

a. $x^m x^n = x^{m+n}$.
b. $(x^m)^n = x^{(mn)}$.

Theorem 15.1 can be shown using only the properties given in the definition of a ring, together with Theorem 15.6. It therefore applies to R. The derivations of Equations (15.1) and (15.2) use the properties of a ring, together with commutativity, so that they also hold for R. The proof of Theorem 15.2 applies for arbitrary rings with unit elements, so equation (15.3) holds for R. The algorithm FFT therefore can be used to compute a DFT over R, provided ω is a principal nth root of unity for that ring, and that addition and multiplication on elements of the ring are the $+$ and $\cdot$ operations from R.

In order to extend Theorem 15.3 to R, we must consider what it would mean to divide by n in that ring. First of all the ring might not contain n as an element. However, we can always embed the integers into a ring with unit element as follows. First, if the ring has a unit element 1, it also contains -1 (the additive inverse of 1) and 0 (the additive identity). For $n > 1$, if $n - 1$ is in the ring, we can give the element $(n - 1) + 1$ the name n, and we can give the element $-(n - 1) - 1$ the name $-n$. Thus, each integer refers to some element of the ring. Note that a particular element of the ring might not correspond to any integer, or it might correspond to more than one. If it does correspond to more than one integer, it is not hard to show that it corresponds to infinitely many integers.

Now that we have identified n with some element in the ring, we can define division by n as multiplication by n^{-1}, provided n has a multiplicative inverse. We note that if ω is a principal nth root of unity, then $\omega\omega^{n-1} = 1$, so that $\omega^{-1} = \omega^{n-1}$. Then the proof of Theorem 15.3 can easily be seen to apply to an arbitrary ring with unit element, provided n has a multiplicative inverse in that ring. Because the proof of Theorem 15.4 also applies to an arbitrary ring with unit element, FFT can be used to compute an inverse DFT over R.

In order to compute a convolution over R, we need to be able to find a principal nth root of unity when n is a power of 2. Unfortunately, not every commutative ring with unit element has a principal nth root of unity whenever n is a power of 2. In the next section, we will focus on particular commutative rings and determine when they have principal nth roots of unity. We will then show how to multiply arbitrary-precision natural numbers by using the fast Fourier transform over these rings.

15.3 Integer Multiplication

Suppose we wish to multiply two BigNums, u and v, as specified in Exercise 4.14 on page 145. If uv contains n bits, and $m \geq 2^n$, then the product uv in the ring $\langle \mathbb{Z}_m, +, \cdot \rangle$ is the same as the ordinary product over $\mathbb{N}$. We have therefore reduced arbitrary-precision multiplication to multiplication in a ring of the form $\langle \mathbb{Z}_m, +, \cdot \rangle$. In this section and the next, we show how to use the Fast Fourier Transform to compute a product over such a ring for specific values of m.

We first need to choose m in such a way that we can find principal nth roots of unity in the ring, when n is a power of 2. Because Theorem 15.2 holds for any ring with unit element, we need to find m and ω such that $\omega^{n/2} \bmod m = m - 1$, the inverse of 1 in $\langle \mathbb{Z}_m, + \rangle$. One way of satisfying this constraint is to select $m = 2^k + 1$ for some positive integer k. Then $2^{2k/n}$ is a principal nth root of unity, provided $2k$ is divisible by n. Because n is a power of 2, we should require k to be a power of 2 such that $2k \geq n$.

We also need to be able to find the multiplicative inverse of n in this ring. Because $2^{2k/n}$ is a principal nth root of unity, $2^{2k} = 1$ in this ring. Therefore, $n^{-1} = 2^{2k}/n$. We therefore have the following theorem.

Theorem 15.7. *Let k and n be powers of 2 such that $1 \leq n \leq 2k$, and let $m = 2^k + 1$. In the ring $\langle \mathbb{Z}_m, +, \cdot \rangle$:*

a. $2^{2k/n}$ *is a principal nth root of unity; and*
b. $n^{-1} = 2^{2k}/n$.

Note that if k and n are both powers of 2 such that $1 \leq n \leq 2k$, both $2^{2k/n}$ and $2^{2k}/n$ are also powers of 2. This fact is advantageous because

---

Figure 15.3   Implementation of MULTIPLY (specified in Figure 10.6, p. 349) using modular multiplication

---

MULTFFT(u, v)
    $n \leftarrow$ MAX($1, u$.NUMBITS() $+ v$.NUMBITS()); $k \leftarrow 2^{\lceil \lg n \rceil}$
    return MODMULT(u, v, k)

Precondition: u and v are BIGNUMs each having at most k bits, and k is a NAT containing a power of 2.
Postcondition: Returns a BIGNUM representing

$$uv \bmod (2^k + 1).$$

MODMULT(u, v, k)

---

multiplying a BIGNUM by a power of 2 can be done very efficiently via the SHIFT operation.

In order to complete the reduction of arbitrary-precision multiplication to multiplication in a ring $\langle \mathbb{Z}_m, +, \cdot \rangle$, we must select a specific m. Suppose the natural numbers u and v together have a total of n bits. Then uv will have at most n bits. We can therefore set k to the smallest power of 2 no smaller than n, and let $m = 2^k + 1$. The resulting algorithm is shown in Figure 15.3 (see Figure 10.6 on page 349 for its specification).

Let us consider how to multiply two k-bit numbers, u and v, mod $2^k + 1$, where k is a power of 2. Suppose we break u and v into b blocks of l bits each. Let these blocks be $u_0, \ldots, u_{b-1}$ and $v_0, \ldots, v_{b-1}$, so that

$$u = \sum_{i=0}^{b-1} u_i 2^{il}$$

and

$$v = \sum_{i=0}^{b-1} v_i 2^{il}.$$

The product $uv \bmod (2^k + 1)$ is then given by

$$uv \bmod (2^k + 1) = \left(\sum_{j=0}^{2b-1} \sum_{i=\max(0, j-b+1)}^{\min(j, b-1)} u_i v_{j-i} 2^{jl} \right) \bmod (2^k + 1).$$

Note that the last term in the above sum (i.e., for $j = 2b-1$) is 0. We include it in order to simplify the derivation that follows.

Because $k = bl$, $2^{bl} = -1$ in the ring $\langle Z_m, +, \cdot \rangle$, where $m = 2^k + 1$. We can therefore write the product uv in this ring as

$$
uv = \left(\sum_{j=0}^{b-1} \sum_{i=0}^{j} u_i v_{j-i} 2^{jl} \right) - \left(\sum_{j=b}^{2b-1} \sum_{i=j-b+1}^{b-1} u_i v_{j-i} 2^{(j-b)l} \right)
$$

$$
= \left(\sum_{j=0}^{b-1} \sum_{i=0}^{j} u_i v_{j-i} 2^{jl} \right) - \left(\sum_{j=0}^{b-1} \sum_{i=j+1}^{b-1} u_i v_{j-i+b} 2^{jl} \right)
$$

$$
= \sum_{j=0}^{b-1} 2^{jl} \left(\sum_{i=0}^{j} u_i v_{j-i} - \sum_{i=j+1}^{b-1} u_i v_{j-i+b} \right).
$$

Let $p = \langle p_0, \ldots, p_{b-1} \rangle$, where

$$
p_j = \sum_{i=0}^{j} u_i v_{j-i} - \sum_{i=j+1}^{b-1} u_i v_{j-i+b}.
$$

Thus, in $\langle Z_m, +, \cdot \rangle$,

$$
uv = \sum_{j=0}^{b-1} p_j 2^{jl}.
$$

Furthermore, the vector p closely resembles the positive wrapped convolution $\langle u_0, \ldots, u_{b-1} \rangle \otimes \langle v_0, \ldots, v_{b-1} \rangle$. The only difference is that the two sums are subtracted, rather than added. For this reason, we define p to be the *negative wrapped convolution* of the two vectors. The following theorem shows how computing a negative wrapped convolution can be reduced to computing a positive wrapped convolution.

Theorem 15.8. *Let R be a commutative ring with unit element, and suppose ψ is a principal $(2n)$th root of unity in R. Let p and q be $1 \times n$ vectors over R, and let Ψ and Ψ' be $1 \times n$ vectors such that $\Psi_j = \psi^j$ and $\Psi'_j = \psi^{2n-j}$ for $0 \le j < n$. Then the negative wrapped convolution of p and q is given by*

$$
\Psi' \cdot ((\Psi \cdot p) \otimes (\Psi \cdot q)), \tag{15.1}
$$

where $\cdot$ denotes the component-wise product of two vectors over R.

Proof.   Let $0 \leq j < n$. Then the jth component (15.1) is

$$\psi^{2n-j} \left(\sum_{i=0}^{j} \psi^{i} p_{i} \psi^{j-i} q_{j-i} + \sum_{i=j+1}^{n-1} \psi^{i} p_{i} \psi^{j-i+n} q_{j-i+n} \right)$$

$$= \psi^{2n} \sum_{i=0}^{j} p_{i} q_{j-i} + \psi^{3n} \sum_{i=j+1}^{n-1} p_{i} q_{j-i+n}$$

$$= \sum_{i=0}^{j} p_{i} q_{j-1} + \psi^{n} \sum_{i=j+1}^{n-1} p_{i} q_{j-i+n}$$

$$= \sum_{i=0}^{j} p_{i} q_{j-1} - \sum_{i=j+1}^{n-1} p_{i} q_{j-i+n}.$$

$\square$

Let us therefore reduce multiplication in the ring $\langle \mathbb{Z}_m, +, \cdot \rangle$ to computing a negative wrapped convolution. In order to do this, the negative wrapped convolution must be computed over a commutative ring with a principal $(2b)$th root of unity. If we are to use a ring $\langle \mathbb{Z}_{m'}, +, \cdot \rangle$, where $m' = 2^{k'} + 1$ and k' is a power of 2, then from Theorem 15.7, we must have $k' \geq b$.

Furthermore, m' must be large enough so that

$$\left(\sum_{i=0}^{j} u_{i} v_{j-i} - \sum_{i=j+1}^{b-1} u_{i} v_{j-i+b} \right) \bmod m'$$

uniquely determines

$$\sum_{i=0}^{j} u_{i} v_{j-i} - \sum_{i=j+1}^{b-1} u_{i} v_{j-i+b}.$$

Because each component of u and v is strictly less than 2^{l}, the above expression is strictly less than $b2^{2l}$ and strictly greater than $-b2^{2l}$. We therefore need

$$2^{k'} + 1 \geq 2b2^{2l}$$

$$k' \geq \lg(b2^{2l+1} - 1).$$

The above inequality is satisfied if $k' \geq \lg b + 2l + 1$. Because our convolution algorithm works on vectors whose size is a power of 2, it makes sense to choose b as a power of 2. Because k is a power of 2, this implies that

$l = k/b$ is also a power of 2. Because k' must also be a power of 2, we can satisfy this inequality by taking $k' \geq 4l$, provided $\lg b + 1 \leq 2l$.

In order to make k' as small as possible and still at least $\max(b, 4l)$, we should choose b and $4l$ to be roughly equal. If k is an even power of 2, we can set $l = \sqrt{k}/2$ and $b = 2\sqrt{k}$. In this case, both will be powers of 2, and we can set $k' = b = 4l$. Otherwise, we can set $l = \sqrt{k/2}$ and $b = \sqrt{2k}$. Again, both are powers of 2, and in this case we can set $k' = 4l$. Furthermore, it is easily seen that for these choices, $\lg b + 1 \leq 2l$ whenever $k \geq 16$.

Finally, the computation of the negative wrapped convolution will involve arithmetic, including multiplication, over the ring we choose. Thus, this computation will be reduced to modular multiplication. In order to avoid a circular reduction, we must make sure we choose $k' < k$. It is easily seen that when $k \geq 16$, this constraint is satisfied.

The reduction of modular multiplication to a negative wrapped convolution is shown in Figure 15.4. For the base case, it uses some other multiplication algorithm satisfying the spec given in Figure 10.6. It uses a function TORING to apply the mod $2^k + 1$ operation. It also uses a function EVAL, which coverts the negative wrapped convolution into the product mod $2^k + 1$. We will consider the design of these two functions shortly.

The NEGCONV function can now be implemented by directly applying Theorem 15.8. Its implementation is shown in Figure 15.5. In order to multiply a BIGNUM x by ψ^j, which is a power of 2, we shift x to the right by $j \lg \psi$ bits. We use the variable *lgPsi* to store the value $\lg \psi$.

NEGCONV uses the function POSCONV, whose implementation is shown in Figure 15.6. This algorithm is simply a modification of CONVOLUTION for the modular ring; however, because the precondition requires that n is a power of 2, we don't need to copy the elements to arrays of such a size. In order to facilitate multiplication by n^{-1}, we use the variable *lgInv* to store $\lg(n^{-1})$. Also, recall that the precondition for MODMULT (Figure 15.3) requires that each argument is at most k bits. However, the discrete Fourier transforms may contains elements equal to 2^k, which has $k+1$ bits. We must therefore handle this case separately.

The principal nth root of unity used for computing the DFT will be $2^{2k/n}$. For computing the inverse DFT, we therefore must use the multiplicative inverse of $2^{2k/n}$. Because $2^{2k} \bmod (2^k + 1) = 1$, $(2^{2k/n})^{-1} = 2^{2k - 2k/n}$. For reasons of efficiency and ease of analysis, we use a boolean to indicate which of these roots the function MODFFT is to use.

The implementation of MODFFT is shown in Figure 15.7. It is a fairly straightforward adaptation of FFT (Figure 15.1) to the ring $\langle \mathbb{Z}_m, +, \cdot \rangle$. We

---

Figure 15.4 Implementation of MODMULT, specified in Figure15.3

MODMULTFFT(u, v, k)
   if $k < 16$
     return TORING(MULTIPLYADHOC$(u, v), k)$
   else
     if $(\lg k) \bmod 2 = 0$
       $b \leftarrow 2\sqrt{k}; l \leftarrow \sqrt{k}/2$
     else
       $b \leftarrow \sqrt{2k}; l \leftarrow \sqrt{k/2}$
     $uarray \leftarrow$ **new** ARRAY$[0..b-1]$; $varray \leftarrow$ **new** ARRAY$[0..b-1]$
     for $j \leftarrow 0$ **to** $b - 1$
       $uarray[j] \leftarrow$ **new** BIGNUM$(u.\text{GETBITS}(jl, l))$
       $varray[j] \leftarrow$ **new** BIGNUM$(v.\text{GETBITS}(jl, l))$
     $conv \leftarrow$ NEGCONV$(uarray, varray, 4l)$
     return EVAL$(conv, k, l)$

Precondition: x is a BIGNUM and k is a positive NAT.
Postcondition: Returns a BIGNUM representing $x \bmod (2^k + 1)$.

TORING(x, k)

Precondition: $p[0..n-1]$ and $q[0..n-1]$ are arrays of BIGNUMs each having at most k bits, k is a NAT containing a power of 2, and n is a NAT containing a power of 2 such that $n \le k$.
Postcondition: Returns a BIGNUM representing the negative wrapped convolution of p and q over the ring $\langle \mathbb{Z}_m, +, \cdot \rangle$, where $m = 2^k + 1$.

NEGCONV$(p[0..n-1], q[0..n-1], k)$

Precondition: $v[0..n-1]$ is an array of BIGNUMs no larger than 2^{4l}, n, k, and l are NATs containing powers of 2.
Postcondition: Returns a BIGNUM representing

$$\left(\sum_{j=0}^{n-1} u_j 2^{jl} \right) \bmod (2^k + 1),$$

where $u_j = v[j]$ if $v[j] \le 2^{4l-1}$, or $u_j = v[j] - (2^{4l} + 1)$ otherwise.

EVAL$(v[0..n-1], k, l)$

---

must be careful, however, when subtracting $\omega^i d'[i]$ from $d''[i]$ in order to obtain $d[i + mid]$, because $\omega^i d'[i]$ may be greater than $d''[i]$. In order to satisfy the precondition of BIGNUM.SUBTRACT (Figure 4.18 on page 146), we first subtract $\omega^i d'[i]$ from m, then add the result, mod m, to $d''[i]$. In

---

Figure 15.5   Implementation of NegConv, as specified in Figure 15.4

NegConv($p[0..n-1], q[0..n-1], k$)
    $lgPsi \leftarrow k/n$; $p' \leftarrow$ **new** Array$[0..n-1]$; $q' \leftarrow$ **new** Array$[0..n-1]$
    for $j \leftarrow 0$ **to** $n-1$
        $p'[j] \leftarrow$ ToRing($p[j]$.Shift($j \cdot lgPsi$), k)
        $q'[j] \leftarrow$ ToRing($q[j]$.Shift($j \cdot lgPsi$), k)
    $r' \leftarrow$ PosConv(p', q', k)
    $r \leftarrow$ **new** Array$[0..n-1]$
    for $j \leftarrow 0$ **to** $n-1$
        $r[j] \leftarrow$ ToRing($r'[j]$.Shift($(2n-j)lgPsi$), k)
    return r

Precondition: $p[0..n-1]$ and $q[0..n-1]$ are arrays of BigNums each no larger than 2^k, k is a Nat containing a power of 2, and n is a Nat containing a power of 2 such that $n \leq k$.
Postcondition: Returns a BigNum representing the positive wrapped convolution of p and q over the ring $\langle \mathbb{Z}_m, +, \cdot \rangle$, where $m = 2^k + 1$.

PosConv($p[0..n-1], q[0..n-1], k$)

---

order to compute m, we assume the existence of a constant **one**, which refers to a BigNum representing 1.

Let us now turn to the implementation of ToRing, specified in Figure 15.4. A straightforward way of computing $x \bmod m$ is to divide x by m using long division, and return the remainder. Fortunately, the form of m makes this long division easy. Suppose we break m and x into k-bit digits. Then the representation of m in this radix is 11.

In order to see how each step of the long division can proceed, suppose $x = a2^k + b$, where $b < 2^k$ and $a < m$. We first approximate the quotient as a. If $a \leq b$, the quotient is, in fact a, and the remainder is $b - a$. If $a > b$, we try $a - 1$ as the quotient. Then because $a < m$, $a \leq 2^k$, so that

$$(a-1)(2^k+1) = a2^k + a - 2^k - 1$$

$$\leq a2^k - 1$$

$$\leq a2^k + b.$$

Then $a - 1$ is the quotient, and the remainder is

$$a2^k + b - (a-1)(2^k+1) = b + 2^k - a + 1$$

$$= b + m - a.$$

Figure 15.6   Implementation of PosConv, specified in Figure 15.5

$\text{PosConv}(p[0..n-1], q[0..n-1], k)$
    $lgInv \leftarrow 2k - \lg n$
    $ptrans \leftarrow \text{ModFft}(p, k, \mathsf{false})$
    $qtrans \leftarrow \text{ModFft}(q, k, \mathsf{false})$
    $rtrans \leftarrow \mathbf{new}\ \text{Array}[0..m-1]$
    for $i \leftarrow 0$ **to** $n - 1$
        if $ptrans[i].\text{NumBits}() > k$
            $rtrans[i] \leftarrow \text{ToRing}(qtrans[i].\text{Shift}(k), k)$
        else if $qtrans[i].\text{NumBits}() > k$
            $rtrans[i] \leftarrow \text{ToRing}[i](ptrans[i].\text{Shift}(k), k)$
        else
            $rtrans[i] \leftarrow \text{ModMult}(ptrans[i], qtrans[i], k)$
    $r \leftarrow \text{ModFft}(rtrans, k, \mathsf{true})$
    for $i \leftarrow 0$ **to** $n - 1$
        $r[i] \leftarrow \text{ToRing}(r[i].\text{Shift}(lgInv), k)$
    return r

Precondition: $p[0..n-1]$ is an array of BigNums, each no larger than 2^k, n and k are Nats containing powers of 2 such that $n \leq 2k$, and *inv* is a Bool.
Postcondition: Returns the DFT of p over $\langle \mathbb{Z}_m, +, \cdot \rangle$ with respect to $2^{-2k/n}$ if *inv* = true, or with respect to $2^{2k/n}$ otherwise.

$\text{ModFft}(p[0..n-1], k, inv)$

We can therefore compute $x \bmod m$ using only addition and subtraction of BigNums, as shown in Figure 15.8. We assume the existence of a constant one referring to a BigNum representing 1.

Finally, we need to implement Eval, specified in Figure 15.4. A straightforward implementation by adding and shifting would be too inefficient, because numbers with up to k bits would need to be copied each iteration. Instead, we should try to generate the result one l-bit block at a time. We can store the resulting bits in an array, then convert the result to a BigNum. A difficulty with this approach is that some elements of the input array may represent negative values. It therefore makes sense to accumulate the positive terms in one array and the negative terms in another. We can then combine the two arrays into a single BigNum. The algorithm is shown in Figure 15.9.

To analyze the running time of our multiplication algorithm, we begin by analyzing ToRing. From the loop invariant, the value of *rem* never exceeds 2^k; hence, the value of *next* never exceeds 2^{k+1}. Thus, the body of the loop

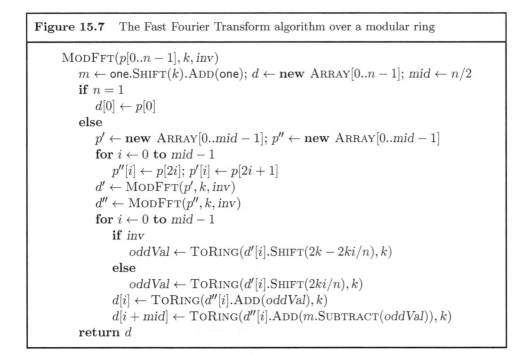

Figure 15.7   The Fast Fourier Transform algorithm over a modular ring

```
MODFFT(p[0..n − 1], k, inv)
    m ← one.SHIFT(k).ADD(one); d ← new ARRAY[0..n − 1]; mid ← n/2
    if n = 1
        d[0] ← p[0]
    else
        p′ ← new ARRAY[0..mid − 1]; p″ ← new ARRAY[0..mid − 1]
        for i ← 0 to mid − 1
            p″[i] ← p[2i]; p′[i] ← p[2i + 1]
        d′ ← MODFFT(p′, k, inv)
        d″ ← MODFFT(p″, k, inv)
        for i ← 0 to mid − 1
            if inv
                oddVal ← TORING(d′[i].SHIFT(2k − 2ki/n), k)
            else
                oddVal ← TORING(d′[i].SHIFT(2ki/n), k)
            d[i] ← TORING(d″[i].ADD(oddVal), k)
            d[i + mid] ← TORING(d″[i].ADD(m.SUBTRACT(oddVal)), k)
    return d
```

Figure 15.8   Algorithm for computing $x \bmod (2^k + 1)$

```
TORING(x, k)
    numDig ← ⌈x.NUMBITS()/k⌉; m ← one.SHIFT(k).ADD(one)
    rem ← x.GETBITS(k(numDig − 1), k)
    // Invariant:
    // rem = x.GETBITS((i + 1)k, x.NUMBITS() − (i + 1)k) mod m
    for i ← numDig − 2 to 0 by −1
        next ← x.GETBITS(ik, k)
        if rem.COMPARETO(next) > 0
            next ← next.ADD(m)
        rem ← next.SUBTRACT(rem)
    return rem
```

clearly runs in $\Theta(k)$ time. The number of iterations is $\lceil n/k \rceil - 1$, where n is the number of bits in x. The loop therefore runs in $\Theta(n)$ time, provided $n > k$. Because the initialization runs in $\Theta(k)$ time, the entire algorithm runs in $\Theta(\max(n, k))$ time.

In order to analyze MODFFT, let us first ignore the computations whose running times depend on k, namely, the calculation of m and the calls to

---

Figure 15.9   Implementation of EVAL, specified in Figure 15.4

EVAL($v[0..n-1], k, l$)
  $m \leftarrow$ one.SHIFT(k).ADD(one); $m' \leftarrow$ one.SHIFT($4l$).ADD(one)
  $half \leftarrow m'$.SHIFT(-1)
  $pos \leftarrow$ **new** ARRAY$[0..nl-1]$; $neg \leftarrow$ **new** ARRAY$[0..nl-1]$
  $posCarry \leftarrow$ zero; $negCarry \leftarrow$ zero
  for $j \leftarrow 0$ **to** $n-1$
    if $v[j]$.COMPARETO($half$) > 0
      $negCarry \leftarrow negCarry$.ADD($m'$.SUBTRACT($v[j]$))
    else
      $posCarry \leftarrow posCarry$.ADD($v[j]$)
    $negBits \leftarrow negCarry$.GETBITS($0, l$); $negCarry \leftarrow negCarry$.SHIFT($l$)
    $posBits \leftarrow posCarry$.GETBITS($0, l$); $posCarry \leftarrow posCarry$.SHIFT($l$)
    COPY($negBits[0..l-1], neg[jl..j(l+1)-1]$)
    COPY($posBits[0..l-1], pos[jl..j(l+1)-1]$);
  $posNum \leftarrow posCarry$.SHIFT($nl$).ADD(**new** BIGNUM($pos$))
  $negNum \leftarrow negCarry$.SHIFT($nl$).ADD(**new** BIGNUM($neg$))
  return TORING($posNum$.ADD(m.SUBTRACT(TORING($negNum, k$))), k)

TORING, ADD, and SUBTRACT. Thus, if we let $n = 2^N$, the running time of the remaining code is in $\Theta(N2^N)$. Specifically, we can conclude that the total number of iterations of each of the **for** loops is in $\Theta(N2^N)$.

Now let $k = 2^K$, and let us analyze the running time of a single iteration of the second **for** loop, including the calls to TORING, ADD, and SUBTRACT. We first observe that for all i, $d'[i] \leq 2^k$ and $d''[i] \leq 2^k$. Because the number of bits added by the SHIFT is at most $2k$, the SHIFT therefore runs in $O(2^K)$ time. Because the result of the SHIFT has $O(2^K)$ bits, the call to TORING runs in $\Theta(2^K)$ time. Likewise, it is easily seen that the remaining operations run in $O(2^K)$ time as well. A single iteration of the second **for** loop therefore runs in $\Theta(2^K)$ time. We conclude that MODFFT runs in $\Theta(N2^{N+K})$ time.

It is easily seen that the running time of POSCONV, excluding the calls to MODFFT and MODMULT, is in $\Theta(2^{N+K})$. Because the first two arguments to MODMULT must have at most 2^K bits, we can describe the running time of MODMULT in terms of K. In particular, let $f(K)$ denote the worst-case running time of MODMULT, assuming it is implemented using MODMULTFFT. Because MODMULT is called no more than 2^K times, the running time of POSCONV is bounded above by a function in $O(N2^{N+K}) + 2^N f(K)$. Likewise, it is easily seen that NEGCONV has the same asymptotic running time.

In order to analyze EVAL, let $l = 2^L$. It is easily seen that excluding the **return** statement, this function runs in $\Theta(\max(2^K, 2^{N+L}))$ time. Furthermore, it is not hard to see that when the **return** statement is executed, *posNum* and *negNum* each contain at most $n(3 + l)$ bits; hence, TORING($negNum, k$) runs in $\Theta(\max(2^K, 2^{N+L}))$ time. Likewise, it is not hard to see that the entire **return** statement runs in $\Theta(\max(2^K, 2^{N+L}))$ time.

We can now obtain an asymptotic recurrence for $f(K)$, the worst-case running time of MODMULT. In what follows, we assume $K \geq 4$. We first observe that if K is even, then $b = 2^{(K/2)+1}$ and $l = 2^{(K/2)-1}$. Likewise, if K is odd, $b = 2^{(K+1)/2}$, and $l = 2^{(K-1)/2}$. We can combine these two cases by saying that $b = 2^{\lceil (K+1)/2 \rceil}$ and $l = 2^{\lfloor (K-1)/2 \rfloor}$. The running time of the **for** loop is therefore in

$$\Theta(bl) = \Theta(2^{\lceil (K+1)/2 \rceil + \lfloor (K-1)/2 \rfloor})$$
$$= \Theta(2^K).$$

In the call to NEGCONV, the number of elements in the arrays is $b = 2^{\lceil (K+1)/2 \rceil}$, and the third parameter is $4l = 2^{\lfloor (K-1)/2 \rfloor + 2}$. Applying the our analysis of NEGCONV, we see that the running time of this call is in $O(K2^K) + 2^{\lceil (K+1)/2 \rceil} f(\lfloor (K-1)/2 \rfloor + 2)$. Likewise, the call to EVAL runs in $\Theta(2^K)$ time. We therefore have

$$f(K) \in O(K2^K) + 2^{\lceil (K+1)/2 \rceil} f(\lfloor (K-1)/2 \rfloor + 2). \tag{15.2}$$

In order to simplify the above recurrence, let $g(K) = f(K + 3)/2^K$ for $K \geq 1$. Then

$$g(K) \in \frac{O((K+3)2^{K+3}) + 2^{\lceil (K+4)/2 \rceil} f(\lfloor (K+2)/2 \rfloor + 2)}{2^K}$$
$$= O(K) + \frac{4f(\lfloor K/2 \rfloor + 3)}{2^{\lfloor K/2 \rfloor}}$$
$$= O(K) + 4g(\lfloor K/2 \rfloor). \tag{15.3}$$

Applying Theorem 3.35, we have $g(K) \in O(K^2)$. Thus, for $K \geq 4$,

$$f(K) = 2^{K-4} g(K - 3)$$
$$\in 2^{K-4} O(K^2)$$
$$\subseteq O(2^K K^2).$$

The running time of MODMULT is therefore in $O(2^K K^2)$. We can therefore conclude that the running time of MULTFFT is in

$$O(2^{\lceil \lg n \rceil} \lceil \lg n \rceil^2) = O(n \lg^2 n),$$

where n is the number of bits in the product.

The above analysis is almost sufficient to show that the running time of MULTFFT is in $\Theta(n \lg^2 n)$. Specifically, we only need to show that there are inputs for each sufficiently large n such that the call to MODMULT is made on each iteration of the first loop in POSCONV. Unfortunately, such a proof would be quite difficult. On the other hand, it seems unlikely that our upper bound on this algorithm's worst-case running time can be improved.

15.4 The Schönhage–Strassen Algorithm

In this section, we will show how to improve the multiplication algorithm of the preceding section to achieve a running time in $O(n \lg n \lg \lg n)$. In order to see what we need to improve, consider recurrence (15.2). Specifically, consider the $2^{\lceil (K+1)/2 \rceil} f(\lfloor (K - 1)/2 \rfloor + 2)$ term. The coefficient is b, the number of calls made to MODMULT in POSCONV, and the argument to f is $\lg(4l)$, the size of each recursive call. If we add $\lg b$ to the size of the recursive calls, we get $K + 2$, where the 2 is the lg of the multiplier for l that we use to define the ring in which the FFT will be computed.

Let us suppose, more generally, that $b = 2^{\lceil (K+c)/2 \rceil}$ and that the size of the recursive call is $\lfloor (K - c)/2 \rfloor + d$, where c and d are natural numbers. Then the recurrence becomes

$$f(K) \in O(K2^K) + 2^{\lceil (K+c)/2 \rceil} f(\lfloor (K - c)/2 \rfloor + d). \qquad (15.1)$$

Now letting $g(K) = f(K - c + 2d)/2^K$, we have

$$g(K) = \frac{f(K - c + 2d)}{2^K}$$

$$\in \frac{O((K - c + 2d)2^{K-c+2d}) + 2^{\lceil (K+2d)/2 \rceil} f(\lfloor (K - 2c + 2d)/2 \rfloor + d)}{2^K}$$

$$= O(K) + \frac{2^d f(\lfloor K/2 \rfloor - c + 2d)}{2^{\lfloor K/2 \rfloor}}$$

$$= O(K) + 2^d g(\lfloor K/2 \rfloor).$$

By Theorem 3.35, if $d > 1$, $g(K) \in O(K^d)$, as for recurrence (15.3); however, if $d = 1$, then $g(K) \in O(K \lg K)$. It then follows that $f(K) \in$

$O(2^K K \lg K)$, and the running time of the resulting multiplication algorithm would be in $O(n \lg n \lg \lg n)$. Thus, in order to improve the running time of MODMULT, it suffices to reduce the size of the ring we use from $2^{4l} + 1 = 2^{2^{2l}} + 1$ to $2^{2l} + 1$.

The difficulty with such an approach is that we have already shown that $\lceil \lg(b2^{2l+1} - 1) \rceil$ bits are required so that the elements of the negative wrapped convolution over the given ring uniquely determine the negative wrapped convolution over the integers. We need an additional result result that will allow us to extract the elements of the negative wrapped convolution over the integers from their values over a modular ring. This result is the *Chinese Remainder Theorem*.

Theorem 15.9 (Chinese Remainder Theorem). *Let a_1, a_2, m_1, and m_2 be natural numbers such that $a_1 < m_1$, $a_2 < m_2$, where m_1 and m_2 are relatively prime. Then there is a unique natural number $i < m_1 m_2$ such that $i \bmod m_1 = a_1$ and $i \bmod m_2 = a_2$.*

Before we prove this theorem, let's see why it might useful. We need to compute the negative wrapped convolution of two vectors u and v, each of size b and consisting of natural numbers less than 2^l. Let w_j denote the jth component of the negative wrapped convolution. As we have already shown, $-b2^{2l} < w_j < b2^{2l}$. Suppose we were to compute the negative wrapped convolution over two separate rings $\langle \mathbb{Z}_{m_i}, +, \cdot \rangle$, where $m_1 = 2^{2l} + 1$ and $m_2 = 2b$, as shown in Figure 15.10. (As we will see, it is possible to compute the second convolution with relatively little overhead.) Then the results of these convolutions give us

$$conv[j] = w_j \bmod (2^{2l} + 1), \tag{15.2}$$

and

$$conv'[j] = w_j \bmod (2b), \tag{15.3}$$

for $0 \le j < b$.

Because $2b$ is a power of 2 and $2^{2l} + 1$ is odd, they are relatively prime. Theorem 15.9 therefore guarantees that if $w_j \ge 0$, then it is the only natural number less than $2b(2^{2l} + 1)$ that satisfies (15.2) and (15.3). Furthermore, it is not hard to see that $w_j + 2b(2^{2l} + 1)$ also satisfies these constraints. Thus, Theorem 15.9 guarantees that if $w_j < 0$, then $w_j + 2b(2^{2l} + 1)$ is the only natural number less than $2b(2^{2l} + 1)$ that satisfies these constraints. The proof of Theorem 15.9 will be constructive, so that we will be able to compute the value that it guarantees. Finally, because $w_j < b(2^{2l} + 1) < w_j + 2b(2^{2l} + 1)$,

Figure 15.10 Implementation of MODMULT, specified in Figure 15.3, using two negative wrapped convolutions

```
MODMULTSS(u, v, k)
    if k < 8
        return TORING(MULTIPLYADHOC(u, v), k)
    else
        if (lg k) mod 2 = 0
            b ← √k; l ← √k
        else
            b ← √2k; l ← √(k/2)
        uarray ← new ARRAY[0..b − 1]; varray ← new ARRAY[0..b − 1]
        uarray' ← new ARRAY[0..b − 1]; varray' ← new ARRAY[0..b − 1]
        for j ← 0 to b − 1
            uarray[j] ← new BIGNUM(u.GETBITS(jl, l))
            varray[j] ← new BIGNUM(v.GETBITS(jl, l))
            uarray'[j] ← new BIGNUM(u.GETBITS(jl, lg b + 1))
            varray'[j] ← new BIGNUM(v.GETBITS(jl, lg b + 1))
        conv ← NEGCONV(uarray, varray, 2l)
        conv' ← NEGCONVSS(uarray', varray', lg b + 1)
        return EVALSS(conv, conv', k, l)
```

Precondition: $p[0..n−1]$ and $q[0..n−1]$ are arrays of BIGNUMs each having at most k bits, and k and n are NATs such that n is a power of 2.

Postcondition: Returns a BIGNUM representing the negative wrapped convolution of p and q over the ring $\langle \mathbb{Z}_m, +, \cdot \rangle$, where $m = 2^k$.

NEGCONVSS$(p[0..n − 1], q[0..n − 1], k)$

Precondition: $u[0..n − 1]$ is an array of BIGNUMs no larger than 2^{2l}, $v[0..n − 1]$ is an array of BIGNUMs less than $2n$, and n, k, and l are NATs containing powers of 2.

Postcondition: Returns a BIGNUM representing

$$\left(\sum_{j=0}^{n-1} w_j 2^{jl} \right) \bmod (2^k + 1),$$

where $w_j \bmod (2^{2l} + 1) = u[j]$, $w_j \bmod 2n = v[j]$, and $-n(2^{2l} + 1) \le w_j < n(2^{2l} + 1)$.

EVALSS$(u[0..n − 1], v[0..n − 1], k, l)$

we can determine whether the value guaranteed by Theorem 15.9 is w_j or $w_j + 2b(2^{2l} + 1)$.

In order to prove Theorem 15.9, we need the following lemma.

Lemma 15.10. *Let a be an integer, and let b and m be positive integers. Then $(a \bmod bm) \bmod m = a \bmod m$.*

Proof. Let $r_1 = a \bmod bm$, so that for some integer p, $bmp + r_1 = a$. Let $r_2 = a \bmod m$, so that for some integer q,

$$mq + r_2 = a$$

$$= r_1 + bmp,$$

$$m(q - bp) = r_1 - r_2.$$

Because r_1 and r_2 differ by a multiple of m, and because $0 \le r_2 < m$, $r_1 \bmod m = r_2$. Thus, $(a \bmod bm) \bmod m = a \bmod m$. $\qquad\square$

Proof of Theorem 15.9 Let $f : \mathbb{Z}_{m_1 m_2} \to \mathbb{Z}_{m_1} \times \mathbb{Z}_{m_2}$ be defined so that $f(i) = (i \bmod m_1, i \bmod m_2)$. We will show that f is a one-to-one and onto function.

In order to show that f is onto, let $a_1 \in \mathbb{Z}_{m_1}$ and $a_2 \in \mathbb{Z}_{m_2}$. From Theorem 7.4,

$$m_1 x \bmod m_2 = 1$$

has a natural number solution $x = c$. Let

$$i = (m_1 c((a_2 - a_1) \bmod m_2) + a_1) \bmod m_1 m_2. \tag{15.4}$$

Clearly, $0 \le i < m_1 m_2$. Because $m_1 c((a_2 - a_1) \bmod m_2)$ is a multiple of m_1, from Lemma 15.10, $i \bmod m_1 = a_1$. Also, from Lemma 15.10, we have

$$i \bmod m_2 = (m_1 c((a_2 - a_1) \bmod m_2) + a_1) \bmod m_2$$

$$= ((m_1 c \bmod m_2)((a_2 - a_1) \bmod m_2) + a_1) \bmod m_2$$

$$= a_2 \bmod m_2$$

$$= a_2.$$

Therefore, $f(i) = (a_1, a_2)$. Because the choice of a_1 and a_2 was arbitrary, we conclude that f is onto.

Because $\mathbb{Z}_{m_1 m_2}$ and $\mathbb{Z}_{m_1} \times \mathbb{Z}_{m_2}$ are finite sets with the same number of elements, and f is a mapping from $\mathbb{Z}_{m_1 m_2}$ onto $\mathbb{Z}_{m_1} \times \mathbb{Z}_{m_2}$, it follows that f is one-to-one. $\qquad\square$

Let us now consider how to implement EVALSS. Let $m_1 = 2^{2l} + 1$ and $m_2 = 2b$. In order to apply (15.4), we need to have a value c such that $m_1 c \bmod m_2 = 1$. Because $b \le 2l$ is a power of 2, $(2^{2l} + 1) \bmod 2b = 1$. We can therefore use $c = 1$. Furthermore, because $0 \le a_1 < m_1$, $0 \le$

Figure 15.11   Implementation of EVALSS, specified in Figure 15.10

EVALSS($u[0..n-1], v[0..n-1], k, l$)
  $m \leftarrow$ one.SHIFT($2l$).ADD(one)
  $m' \leftarrow$ one.SHIFT($\lg n + 1$)
  half $\leftarrow m$.SHIFT($\lg n$); *full* $\leftarrow$ *half*.SHIFT(1)
  pos $\leftarrow$ **new** ARRAY[$0..nl-1$]; *neg* $\leftarrow$ **new** ARRAY[$0..nl-1$]
  posCarry $\leftarrow$ zero; *negCarry* $\leftarrow$ zero
  for $j \leftarrow 0$ **to** $n-1$
    if $v[j] \geq u[j]$
      diff $\leftarrow v[j]$.SUBTRACT($u[j]$)
    else
      $t \leftarrow u[j]$.SUBTRACT($v[j]$).GETBITS($0, \lg n + 1$)
      diff $\leftarrow m'$.SUBTRACT(**new** BIGNUM(t))
    $w \leftarrow$ *diff*.SHIFT($2l$).ADD(*diff*).ADD($u[j]$)
    if w.COMPARETO(*half*) > 0
      negCarry $\leftarrow$ *negCarry*.ADD(*full*.SUBTRACT(w))
    else
      posCarry $\leftarrow$ *posCarry*.ADD(w)
    negBits $\leftarrow$ *negCarry*.GETBITS($0, l$); *negCarry* $\leftarrow$ *negCarry*.SHIFT(l)
    posBits $\leftarrow$ *posCarry*.GETBITS($0, l$); *posCarry* $\leftarrow$ *posCarry*.SHIFT(l)
    COPY(*negBits*[$0..l-1$], *neg*[$jl..j(l+1)-1$])
    COPY(*posBits*[$0..l-1$], *pos*[$jl..j(l+1)-1$])
  posNum $\leftarrow$ *posCarry*.SHIFT(nl).ADD(**new** BIGNUM(*pos*))
  negNum $\leftarrow$ *negCarry*.SHIFT(nl).ADD(**new** BIGNUM(*neg*))
  $M \leftarrow$ one.SHIFT(k).ADD(1)
  return TORING(*posNum*.ADD(M.SUBTRACT(TORING(*negNum*, k))), k)

$m_1((a_2 - a_1) \bmod m_2) + a_1 < m_1 m_2$. The value guaranteed by Theorem 15.9 is therefore

$$(2^{2l} + 1)((v[j] - u[j]) \bmod 2b) + u[j].$$

We can multiply by $2^{2l} + 1$ using a bit shift and an addition. We can then determine w_j by comparing the above value with $b(2^{2l+1})$ and subtracting $2b(2^{2l} + 1)$ if necessary. The algorithm is shown in Figure 15.11.

In order to implement NEGCONVSS, we must be able to compute a negative wrapped convolution over a ring $\langle \mathbb{Z}_m, +, \cdot \rangle$, where m is a power of 2. However, because the values of the vectors are much smaller than those used in the other convolution, we don't need to be quite as careful regarding the efficiency of this algorithm. Specifically, we don't need to use the FFT. Instead, we can first compute a non-wrapped convolution mod 2^k. Let us

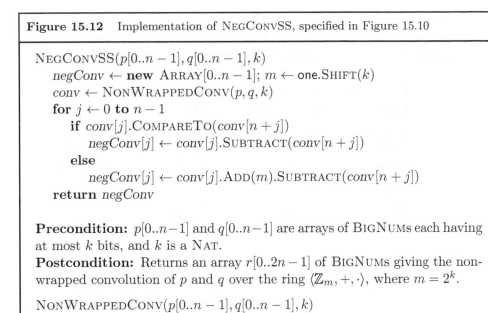

Figure 15.12   Implementation of NEGCONVSS, specified in Figure 15.10

NEGCONVSS($p[0..n-1], q[0..n-1], k$)
   $negConv \leftarrow$ **new** ARRAY$[0..n-1]$; $m \leftarrow$ one.SHIFT(k)
   $conv \leftarrow$ NONWRAPPEDCONV(p, q, k)
   for $j \leftarrow 0$ **to** $n-1$
      if $conv[j]$.COMPARETO($conv[n+j]$)
         $negConv[j] \leftarrow conv[j]$.SUBTRACT($conv[n+j]$)
      else
         $negConv[j] \leftarrow conv[j]$.ADD($m$).SUBTRACT($conv[n+j]$)
   return $negConv$

Precondition: $p[0..n-1]$ and $q[0..n-1]$ are arrays of BIGNUMs each having at most k bits, and k is a NAT.
Postcondition: Returns an array $r[0..2n-1]$ of BIGNUMs giving the non-wrapped convolution of p and q over the ring $\langle \mathbb{Z}_m, +, \cdot \rangle$, where $m = 2^k$.

NONWRAPPEDCONV($p[0..n-1], q[0..n-1], k$)

refer to this convolution as $conv[0..2b-1]$. Element j of the negative wrapped convolution is then $(conv[j] - conv[n+j]) \bmod 2^k$. The algorithm is shown in Figure 15.12.

Recall that POLYMULT (Figure 10.1 on page 334) computes a non-wrapped convolution of two vectors over $\langle Z, +, \cdot \rangle$. We can therefore modify this algorithm to operate on BIGNUMs such that all operations are mod 2^k. In order for the resulting algorithm to satisfy the specification of NONWRAPPEDCONV, we would also need to modify it to return an array whose size is larger by one element, whose value will be 0. We leave the details as an exercise.

In order to analyze the Schönhage–Strassen algorithm, which is simply the MULTIPLY algorithm of Figure 15.3 with MODMULT implemented using MODMULTSS, we first observe that the analysis of EVALSS is similar to the analysis of EVAL in the previous section. Hence, its running time is in $\Theta(\max(2^K, 2^{N+L}))$, where $k = 2^K$, $n = 2^N$, and $l = 2^L$. Because POLYMULT runs in $\Theta(n^{\lg 3})$ time, where n is the degree of the product, NONWRAPPEDCONV can be implemented to run in $O(n^{\lg 3}M(k))$ time, where $M(k)$ is the time needed to multiply two k-bit BIGNUMs mod 2^k. Because $M(k)$ must be in $\Omega(k)$, NEGCONVSS then runs in $O(n^{\lg 3}M(k))$ time.

To analyze MODMULTSS, we first recall that the running time of NEGCONV is in $O(N2^{N+K}) + 2^N f(K)$, where $f(K)$ denotes the worst-case running time of MODMULT; here, we will assume that MODMULT is implemented with MODMULTSS. If we now let 2^K be the value of k in the call to MODMULTSS, then the call to NEGCONV runs in $O(K2^K) + 2^{\lceil K/2 \rceil} f(\lfloor K/2 \rfloor + 1)$, and NEGCONVSS runs in $O(2^{\lceil K/2 \rceil} \lg 3 M(K))$ time. Hence, even if $M(K)$ is in $\Theta(K^2)$, the running time for these two calls together is in $O(K2^K) + 2^{\lceil K/2 \rceil} f(\lfloor K/2 \rfloor + 1)$. Because the call to EVALSS runs in $\Theta(2^K)$ time, the total running time of MODMULTSS is easily seen to be given by the recurrence

$$f(K) \in O(K2^K) + 2^{\lceil K/2 \rceil} f(\lfloor K/2 \rfloor + 1),$$

when $K \geq 3$.

The above recurrence fits the form of (15.7) with $d = 1$; hence, as we showed at the beginning of this section, the running time of the Schönhage–Strassen algorithm is in $O(n \lg n \lg \lg n)$, where n is the number of bits in the product.

15.5   Summary

The Fast Fourier Transform is an efficient algorithm for computing a convolution, a problem which arises in a variety of applications. For numerical applications, applying the FFT over $\langle \mathbb{C}, +, \cdot \rangle$ is appropriate; however, for number-theoretic applications like arbitrary-precision integer multiplication, other algebraic structures are more appropriate. The algorithm extends to any commutative ring containing a principal nth root of unity, and over which n has a multiplicative inverse, where n is a power of 2 giving the number of elements in the vectors.

Some rings that are particularly useful for number-theoretic applications are rings of the form $\langle \mathbb{Z}_m, +, \cdot \rangle$, where m is of the form $2^k + 1$. The properties of these rings contribute in several ways to the efficiency of the Schönhage–Strassen integer multiplication algorithm. First, we can compute n mod $(2^k + 1)$ efficiently. Second, the principal nth roots of unity in these rings are powers of 2, so that we can use bit shifting to multiply by these roots. Third, when n is a power of 2, it has a multiplicative inverse that is also a power of 2. Fourth, we can compute a product in this ring with a negative wrapped convolution of vectors with half as many elements as would be needed to compute a non-wrapped convolution. Finally, because any power of 2 is relatively prime to $2^k + 1$, we can reduce by half the number of bits we use in computing the negative wrapped convolution if we instead perform some computation on a few bits of each value and apply the Chinese Remainder Theorem.

15.6   Exercises

Exercise 15.1. Prove Theorem 15.6. [*Hint:* Use induction on either m or n.]

Exercise 15.2. Suppose that in multiplying two BigNums mod $2^k - 1$, where k is a power of 2, instead of making b and $4l$ as nearly equal as possible (as in Section 15.3), we were to make b as small as possible. Analyze the running time of the algorithm that results if we set b to 8 and l to $k/8$.

Exercise 15.3.

a. Prove Theorem 15.9 by showing that for any $a_1 \in \mathbb{Z}_{m_1}$ and any $a_2 \in \mathbb{Z}_{m_2}$, if $i = (m_2 c_2 a_1 + m_1 c_1 a_2) \bmod m_1 m_2$, where $(m_1 c_1) \bmod m_2 = 1$ and $(m_2 c_2) \bmod m_1 = 1$, then $i \bmod m_1 = a_1$ and $i \bmod m_2 = a_2$.

* b. Extend the above idea to prove the following. Let $m_1, \ldots, m_n$ be positive integers that are all relatively prime to each other, and let

$$M = \prod_{j=1}^{n} m_j.$$

Then for natural numbers $a_1, \ldots, a_n$ such that each $a_j < m_j$, there is a unique natural number $i < M$ such that for $1 \le j \le n$, $i \bmod m_j = a_j$.

Exercise 15.4. Modify POLYMULT (Figure 10.1 on page 334) to implement NONWRAPPEDCONV, specified in Figure 15.12. Show that the algorithm runs in $O(n^{\lg 3} M(k))$ time, where $M(k)$ is the time required to multiply to k-bit BigNums.

* Exercise 15.5. For $c \in \mathbb{C}$ and $p = \langle p_0, \ldots, p_{n-1} \rangle \in \mathbb{C}^n$, the *chirp transform* of p with respect to c is the vector $q \in \mathbb{C}^n$ such that for $0 \le i < n$,

$$q_j = \sum_{i=0}^{n-1} p_i c^{ij}.$$

Thus, if c is a principal nth root of unity, then the chirp transform with respect to c is a DFT. Show how to reduce the problem of computing a chirp transform for arbitrary $c \in \mathbb{C}$ to the problem of computing a convolution. Using this reduction, give an $O(n \lg n)$ algorithm for evaluating a chirp transform.

Exercise 15.6. A *Toeplitz matrix* is an $n \times n$ array A such that for $1 \leq i < n$ and $1 \leq j < n$, $A_{ij} = A_{i-1,j-1}$. Thus, we can describe a Toeplitz matrix by giving only its first row and its first column. Give an algorithm for multiplying an $n \times n$ Toeplitz matrix over $\mathbb{C}$ by an n-element vector over $\mathbb{C}$. You may choose an appropriate representation for the Toeplitz matrix. Your algorithm should run in $O(n \lg n)$ time, assuming each operation on complex numbers can be performed in $O(1)$ time.

* Exercise 15.7. Let

$$p(x) = \sum_{i=0}^{n-1} a_i x^i$$

be a polynomial of degree strictly less than n, where each $a_i \in \mathbb{R}$, and let $x_0 \in \mathbb{R}$. Give an algorithm for computing all of the derivatives of $p(x)$ at x_0 (i.e., your algorithm should find, for $0 \leq j < n$, the jth derivative of $p(x)$ at x_0). Your algorithm should run in $O(n \lg n)$ time, assuming that all operations on complex numbers run in $O(1)$ time. [*Hint:* Define $q(x) = p(x_0 + x)$, and find all of the derivatives of $q(x)$ at 0. You will probably find the Binomial Theorem ((6.15) on page 242) helpful.]

15.7 Notes

Heideman, Johnson, and Burrus [61] credit Gauss with the discovery of the fast Fourier transform in 1805. Its importance to computation was shown by Cooley and Tukey [24]. The multiplication algorithm of Section 15.4 is due to Schönhage and Strassen [104].

Though we have referred to Theorem 15.9 as the Chinese Remainder Theorem, it is usually stated in the more general form suggested by Exercise 15.3. The process of solving so-called simultaneous congruences in this way dates back to the third or fourth century AD, when the Chinese mathematician Sun Zi (or Sun Tsŭ) showed how to solve a specific instance of simultaneous congruences. The technique was published as a general theorem by Qin Jiushao (or Chhin Chiu-Shao) in 1247.

Part V

Intractable Problems

Chapter 16

$\mathcal{NP}$-Completeness

Up to now, we have focused on developing efficient algorithms for solving problems. The word "efficient" is somewhat subjective, and the degree of efficiency has varied depending on the problem. Still, in each case, we have shown a running time that was no worse than a low-order polynomial in some natural description of the problem size.

It is possible to prove, however, that some problems cannot be solved by any algorithm with polynomial running time. In fact, it is possible to prove that some problems cannot be solved by any algorithm at all. We will not be examining any of these problems, but in this chapter and the next, we will take a look at a very interesting class of problems for which no efficient algorithms are known. Part of the reason that this class of problems is interesting is that if a polynomial-time algorithm were to be found for any one of these problems, then we could derive polynomial-time algorithms for *all* of the problems in this class. Furthermore, no one to date has given a convincing proof that there are no such algorithms. At the heart of these issues is the most famous open question in computational complexity theory.

16.1 Boolean Satisfiability

Suppose we are given an expression $\mathcal{F}$ containing boolean variables and the following operators:

- $\neg$: logical negation;
- $\vee$: logical **or**; and
- $\wedge$: logical **and**.

There are two questions we might ask regarding $\mathcal{F}$:

- Is $\mathcal{F}$ *valid*? That is, does $\mathcal{F}$ evaluate to true for every possible assignment of true or false to the variables in $\mathcal{F}$?
- Is $\mathcal{F}$ *satisfiable*? That is, does there exist some assignment of true or false to the variables in $\mathcal{F}$ so that $\mathcal{F}$ evaluates to true?

For example, let $\mathcal{F} = \neg x \vee (y \wedge x)$. This expression is not valid, because setting x to true and y to false yields

$$\neg\mathsf{true} \vee (\mathsf{false} \wedge \mathsf{true}) = \mathsf{false} \vee \mathsf{false}$$
$$= \mathsf{false}.$$

However, $\mathcal{F}$ is satisfiable — in fact, any other assignment of values to x and y makes $\mathcal{F}$ true.

Note that it follows immediately from the definitions of validity and satisfiability that for any expression $\mathcal{F}$, $\mathcal{F}$ is valid iff $\neg\mathcal{F}$ is unsatisfiable. Because of this duality, we will focus on only one of these problems, the satisfiability problem. We would like to find a satisfiability algorithm whose worst-case running time is bounded by some polynomial in the size of the given expression, where the size is defined to be the total number of occurrences of variables and operators. However, as of this writing, no such algorithm has been found. Indeed, as we will see shortly, there is good reason to believe that no such algorithm is possible. On the other hand, there currently exists no proof that such an algorithm is impossible.

Before we look at the satisfiability problem in more detail, let us first consider a simpler problem, that of evaluating a boolean expression $\mathcal{F}$, given boolean values for its variables. We first observe that $\mathcal{F}$ must be of one of the following forms:

- a single variable;
- the negation of an expression, i.e., $\neg\mathcal{F}_1$;
- the **or** of two expressions, i.e., $\mathcal{F}_1 \vee \mathcal{F}_2$; or
- the **and** of two expressions, i.e., $\mathcal{F}_1 \wedge \mathcal{F}_2$.

It is therefore convenient to represent the formula using a binary tree in which the leaves represent variables and the internal nodes represent operators. For the $\neg$ operator, the right-hand child will always be empty. To make this representation more concrete, we can use special constants not, and, and or to represent the three operators, and we can represent the variables using positive integers. In order to avoid unnecessary complications, we will assume that if j represents a variable in the expression, then for

---

Figure 16.1   Binary trees representing the formula $\neg x \vee (y \wedge x)$

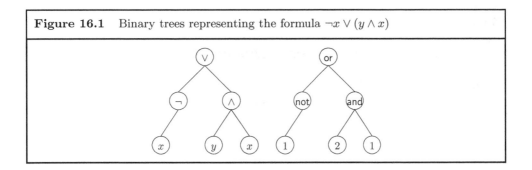

$1 \leq i \leq j$, i represents some variable in the expression (note, however, that we cannot apply this assumption to arbitrary subtrees). For example, Figure 16.1 shows the tree representing the formula $\neg x \vee (y \wedge x)$, first in a more abstract form, then in a more concrete form using 1 to represent x and 2 to represent y. Finally, we can represent an assignment of truth values to the variables using an array $A[1..n]$ of boolean values, where $A[i]$ gives the value assigned to the variable represented by i.

Given an expression tree for $\mathcal{F}$ and an array representing an assignment of truth values, we can then evaluate $\mathcal{F}$ using BOOLEVAL, shown in Figure 16.2. It is not hard to see that this algorithm runs in $\Theta(m)$ time, where m is the number of operators in $\mathcal{F}$ (note that the number of leaves in the expression tree can be no more than $m + 1$).

Returning to the satisfiability problem, we now point out some characteristics that this problem has in common with the other problems we will study in this chapter. First, it is a *decision problem* — the output is either "yes" or "no". Second, when the answer is "yes", there is a relatively short proof of this fact — an assignment of truth values that satisfies the expression. Third, given a proposed proof of satisfiability (i.e., some assignment of truth values to the variables), we can efficiently verify whether it does, in fact, prove the satisfiability of the expression. However, finding such a proof, or proving that none exists, appears to be an expensive task in the worst case (note that there are 2^n possible assignments of truth values to n variables).

16.2   The Set $\mathcal{P}$

We have suggested that the boolean satisfiability problem may not be efficiently solvable. However, we have not yet formalized what this means. In this section we will define a set of decision problems that we will consider to be those that are efficiently decidable.

Figure 16.2   Algorithm for evaluating a boolean expression.

Precondition: $\mathcal{F}$ is a BINARYTREENODE referring to the root of a nonempty boolean expression tree, and $A[1..n]$ is an array of BOOLs.
Postcondition: Returns the value of $\mathcal{F}$ assuming that the variable represented by i has value $A[i]$ if $i \leq n$, or false if $i > n$.

BOOLEVAL($\mathcal{F}, A[1..n]$)
   if $\mathcal{F}$.LEFTCHILD() = nil
      if $\mathcal{F}$.ROOT() $\leq n$
         return $A[\mathcal{F}.$ROOT$()]$
      else
         return false
   else if $\mathcal{F}$.DATA() = not
      return not BOOLEVAL($\mathcal{F}$.LEFTCHILD(), A)
   else
      $l \leftarrow$ BOOLEVAL($\mathcal{F}$.LEFTCHILD(), A)
      $r \leftarrow$ BOOLEVAL($\mathcal{F}$.RIGHTCHILD(), A)
      if $\mathcal{F}$.ROOT() = and
         return l and r
      else
         return l or r

We will begin by adopting a couple of conventions. First, we will assume that each problem instance is a bit string. Certainly, we can encode other types of input data as bit strings, provided the set of all instances is countable. We do need to ensure,

> An artificially long input would result in an artificially low running time when expressed in terms of the length of the input.

however, that this encoding is done in such a way that the length of the encoding is not unnecessarily long. With this convention, we can now express the running time of an algorithm in terms of the length of its input string. This gives us a uniform way of expressing the running times of all algorithms for all problems. Second, we will view a decision problem as a subset of its instances. Specifically, let I denote the set of all bit strings that encode boolean expressions. We can then let SAT denote the set of all expressions in I that are satisfiable. It will also be convenient to use SAT to denote the problem itself. In general, given a set of instances I, we will refer to any subset $X \subseteq I$ as a decision problem over I.

We must now address the question of how efficient is "efficient". We will somewhat arbitrarily delineate the "efficient" algorithms as those that operate within a running time bounded by some polynomial in the length of the input. This delineation, however, is not entirely satisfactory. On the one hand, one could make a persuasive argument that an algorithm with a running time in $\Theta(n^{1000})$ is not "efficient". On the other hand, suppose some algorithm has a running time in $\Theta(n^{\lceil \alpha(n)/4 \rceil})$, where α is as defined in Section 8.4. Because $n^{\lceil \alpha(n)/4 \rceil} \leq n$ for every positive n that can be coded in binary within our universe, such an algorithm might reasonably be considered to be "efficient". However, $n^{\lceil \alpha(n)/4 \rceil}$ is not bounded above by any polynomial.

The main reason we equate polynomial running time with efficiency is that polynomials have several useful closure properties. Specifically, if $p_1(n)$ and $p_2(n)$ are polynomials, then so are $p_1(n) + p_2(n)$, $p_1(n)p_2(n)$, and $p_1(p_2(n))$. As we will see, these closure properties make the theory much cleaner. Furthermore, if we can say that a particular decision problem cannot be solved by any polynomial-time algorithm, then we can be fairly safe in concluding that there is no algorithm that will terminate in a reasonable amount of time on large inputs in the worst case.

Before we formalize this idea, we need to be careful about one aspect of our running-time measures. Specifically, we have assumed in this text that arithmetic operations can be performed in a single step. This assumption is valid if we can reasonably expect the numbers to fit in a single machine word. For larger values, we should use the BigNum type in order to get an appropriate measure of the running time. Also note that all of the algorithms in this text except those using real or complex numbers can be expressed using only booleans and natural numbers as primitive types (i.e., those not defined in terms of other types). Furthermore, only the algorithms of Section 15.1 require real or complex numbers — all other algorithms can be restricted to rational numbers, which can be expressed as a pair of natural numbers and a sign bit. Thus, it will make sense to stipulate that an "efficient" algorithm contains only boolean or natural number variables, along with other types built from these, and that each natural number variable will contain only a polynomial number of bits.

We can now formalize our notion of "efficient". We say that an algorithm A is a *polynomial-time algorithm* if there is a polynomial $p(n)$ such that

- A always completes within $p(n)$ steps, where n is the number of bits in the input string; and
- all primitive variables used by A are either booleans or natural numbers whose values remain strictly less than $2^{p(n)}$.

We then define $\mathcal{P}$ to be the set of all decision problems X such that there exists a deterministic (i.e., not randomized) polynomial-time algorithm A

deciding X. It is this set $\mathcal{P}$ that we will consider to be the set of efficiently solvable decision problems.

The decision to define $\mathcal{P}$ using only deterministic algorithms is rather arbitrary. Indeed, there is a branch of computational complexity theory that focuses on efficient randomized algorithms. However, the study of deterministic algorithms is more fundamental, and therefore is a more reasonable starting point for us.

As one final note on the set $\mathcal{P}$, we should emphasize that we are focusing on worst-case running time. This focus sometimes is too pessimistic in practice. For example, we have already seen from Theorem 7.1 that in the worst case, a hash table provides lookups in $\Theta(n)$ time, but that in practice the lookups tend to run in $\Theta(1)$ time. Likewise, there are problems for which no known algorithm runs in polynomial time in the worst case, but because the worst case occurs so rarely, practical algorithms exist. We discuss this issue further in Section 16.11.

16.3 The Set $\mathcal{NP}$

SAT is clearly a decision problem, but as we have suggested, it is currently not known whether or not it belongs to $\mathcal{P}$. In this section, we will define a related set called $\mathcal{NP}$ that includes all of $\mathcal{P}$, but also includes SAT, as well as many other problems not known to be in $\mathcal{P}$. Furthermore, $\mathcal{NP}$ will have the property that if SAT is, in fact, in $\mathcal{P}$, then $\mathcal{P} = \mathcal{NP}$.

In order to extend the definition of $\mathcal{P}$ to include problems like SAT, we need to formalize the idea that each element of a decision problem X has a short proof which can be efficiently checked. For the sake of concreteness, let us assume that all proofs will be encoded as bit strings. We then denote the set of all bit strings by $\mathcal{B}$.

We now define $\mathcal{NP}$ to be the set of all decision problems X for which there exist:

- a polynomial $p(n)$; and
- a decision problem $Y \subseteq I \times \mathcal{B}$, where I is the set of instances for X;

such that

- $Y \in \mathcal{P}$;
- for each $x \in I$, $x \in X$ iff there is a proof $\phi \in \mathcal{B}$ such that $(x, \phi) \in Y$; and
- for each $x \in X$, there is a proof $\phi \in \mathcal{B}$ such that $(x, \phi) \in Y$ and $|\phi| \leq p(|x|)$.

From our earlier discussion, it follows that $\text{SAT} \in$
$\mathcal{NP}$. We can clearly consider any array $A[1..n]$ of

> We use $|x|$ to denote the length of the encoding of x.

boolean values to be a bit string, and vice versa. We
then let the decision problem Y be the problem solved by BOOLEVAL. Hence,
$Y \in \mathcal{P}$. We can then let $p(n) = n$. Then a given expression $\mathcal{F}$ is satisfiable
iff there is a proof ϕ such that $(x, \phi) \in Y$. Because we have assumed that
whenever an integer j represents a variable in $\mathcal{F}$, all positive integers less
than j also represent variables in $\mathcal{F}$, it follows that if a proof ϕ exists, there
will always be one with length no more than $|\mathcal{F}|$.

We therefore have an example of a problem in $\mathcal{NP}$ that may or may not
be in $\mathcal{P}$. The following theorem gives the relationship between $\mathcal{P}$ and $\mathcal{NP}$.

Theorem 16.1. $\mathcal{P} \subseteq \mathcal{NP}$.

Proof. Let $X \in \mathcal{P}$, and let I be the set of instances of X. We then define
$Y = X \times \mathcal{B}$. Thus, Y is comprised of all pairs (x, ϕ) such that $x \in X$ and
$\phi \in \mathcal{B}$. We can therefore decide whether $(x, \phi) \in I \times \mathcal{B}$ belongs to Y by
simply deciding whether $x \in X$. Because $X \in \mathcal{P}$, it follows that $Y \in \mathcal{P}$. Let
$p(n) = 1$. Then $x \in X$ iff $(x, 0) \in Y$, and the length of 0 is 1. Therefore
$X \in \mathcal{NP}$. $\qquad \square$

It is currently unknown whether the above containment is proper, or
whether $\mathcal{P} = \mathcal{NP}$. In fact the "$\mathcal{P} = \mathcal{NP}$" question is the most famous open
question in computational complexity theory. Most complexity theorists
believe that these sets are not equal. Though many of the reasons for this
belief are beyond the scope of this book, we will soon see one compelling
reason. For now, let us simply state that we take as a working hypothesis
that $\mathcal{P} \neq \mathcal{NP}$. Thus, if we can show that some particular statement implies
that $\mathcal{P} = \mathcal{NP}$, we take this as strong evidence that the statement is false.

In order to focus on the relationship between $\mathcal{P}$ and $\mathcal{NP}$, it is useful
to identify problems that seem more likely to be in $\mathcal{NP} \setminus \mathcal{P}$. In some sense,
we want to identify the hardest problems in $\mathcal{NP}$. We can do this using
a refinement of the notion of problem reduction. Specifically, let X and
Y be two decision problems whose instances comprise the sets I and J,
respectively. We say that X is *polynomially many-one reducible* to Y, written
$X \leq^p_m Y$, if there is a function $f : I \to J$ such that

- for all $x \in I$, $x \in X$ iff $f(x) \in Y$; and
- there is a deterministic polynomial-time algorithm for computing f.

Note that polynomial many-one reductions are transformations — given
an instance x of problem X, we can decide whether $x \in X$ simply by

computing $f(x)$ and deciding whether $f(x) \in Y$. The notation may seem confusing at first, because when we use the word "reduce", we usually think of decreasing the size. As a result, denoting a reduction from X to Y by $X \leq_m^p Y$ seems backwards. The proper way to understand the notation is to realize that when there is a polynomial many-one reduction from X to Y, then in some sense, X is no harder than Y. This idea is formalized by the following theorem.

Theorem 16.2. *If $X \leq_m^p Y$ and $Y \in \mathcal{P}$, then $X \in \mathcal{P}$.*

Proof. Let I and J be the sets of instances of X and Y, respectively, and let $f : I \to J$ be the function computing the polynomial many-one reduction from X to Y. Let $p_1(n)$ be a polynomial bounding the running time and the values of variables for some algorithm to compute f, and let $p_2(n)$ be a polynomial bounding the running time and the values of variables for some algorithm to decide Y. We can then decide whether a given $x \in I$ belongs to X by first computing $f(x)$, then deciding whether $f(x) \in Y$. Let A denote this algorithm.

The time required to compute $f(x)$ is no more than $p_1(|x|)$. The time required to decide whether $f(x) \in Y$ is no more than $p_2(|f(x)|)$. Because $f(x)$ is computed using at most $p_1(|x|)$ steps, $|f(x)| \leq cp_1(|x|)$, where c is some positive integer constant bounding the number of bits that can be written in a single step. The total time required by A is therefore no more than

$$p(|x|) = p_1(|x|) + p_2(cp_1(|x|)),$$

which is a polynomial in $|x|$. Furthermore, the values of the variables in A do not exceed $\max(p_1(|x|), p_2(|x|))$. Because $p(n)$, $p_1(n)$, and $p_2(n)$ must be nonnegative for all $n \in \mathbb{N}$, all are bounded above by the polynomial $p(n) + p_1(n) + p_2(n)$. Therefore, $X \in \mathcal{P}$. $\qquad\square$

Note that Theorem 16.2 does not say that if Y can be decided in $O(f(n))$ time, then X can be decided in $O(f(n))$ time. Indeed, in the proof of the theorem, the bound on the time to decide X can be much larger than the time to decide Y. Thus, if we interpret $X \leq_m^p Y$ as indicating that X is no harder than Y, we must understand "no harder than" in a very loose sense — simply that if $Y \in \mathcal{P}$, then $X \in \mathcal{P}$.

We will often utilize Theorem 16.2 in the following equivalent form.

Corollary 16.3. *If $X \leq_m^p Y$ and $X \notin \mathcal{P}$, then $Y \notin \mathcal{P}$.*

Suppose we have some problem $Y \in \mathcal{NP}$ such that for every $X \in \mathcal{NP}$, $X \leq_m^p Y$. If $\mathcal{P} \neq \mathcal{NP}$, then there is some $X \in \mathcal{NP} \setminus \mathcal{P}$. Because $X \leq_m^p Y$ and $X \notin \mathcal{P}$, Corollary 16.3 tells us that $Y \notin \mathcal{P}$. This fact motivates the following definitions.

Definition 16.3.1. If Y is a decision problem such that for every $X \in \mathcal{NP}$, $X \leq_m^p Y$, then we say that Y is $\mathcal{NP}$-*hard*.

Definition 16.3.2. If $Y \in \mathcal{NP}$ is $\mathcal{NP}$-hard, then we say that Y is $\mathcal{NP}$-*complete*.

Suppose we have some $\mathcal{NP}$-hard problem Y, and also suppose that $\mathcal{P} \neq \mathcal{NP}$. Then there is some $X \in \mathcal{NP} \setminus \mathcal{P}$. Because $X \in \mathcal{NP}$ and Y is $\mathcal{NP}$-hard, $X \leq_m^p Y$. Hence, from Corollary 16.3, $Y \notin \mathcal{P}$. We therefore have the following theorem and its corollary.

Theorem 16.4. *If Y is $\mathcal{NP}$-hard and $\mathcal{P} \neq \mathcal{NP}$, then $Y \notin \mathcal{P}$.*

Corollary 16.5. *If Y is $\mathcal{NP}$-complete and $\mathcal{P} \neq \mathcal{NP}$, then $Y \in \mathcal{NP} \setminus \mathcal{P}$.*

It turns out that thousands of $\mathcal{NP}$-complete problems in a wide variety of problem domains have been identified. If we could find a polynomial-time algorithm for any one of these problems, Corollary 16.5 would then imply that $\mathcal{P} = \mathcal{NP}$. The fact that this has not been accomplished is one reason to suspect that $\mathcal{P} \neq \mathcal{NP}$. Let us now identify an $\mathcal{NP}$-complete problem.

Theorem 16.6 (Cook's Theorem). SAT *is $\mathcal{NP}$-complete.*

The idea of the proof of Cook's Theorem is to give a method for constructing, from an arbitrary $X \in \mathcal{NP}$, a polynomial-time algorithm that takes as input an instance x of X and produces as output a boolean expression $\mathcal{F}$ such that $\mathcal{F}$ is satisfiable iff $x \in X$. In constructing this algorithm, we can use the polynomial $p(n)$ bounding the size of a proof ϕ and the algorithm for deciding whether ϕ proves that $x \in X$. In order to complete the construction, we must carefully define the computational model so that the boolean formula can encode the algorithm. Due to the large amount of work involved, we will delay the proof of Cook's Theorem until Section 16.8.

Fortunately, once we have one $\mathcal{NP}$-complete problem, the task of showing other problems to be $\mathcal{NP}$-complete becomes much easier. The reason for this is that polynomial many-one reducibility is transitive, as we show in the following theorem. Its proof is similar to the proof of Theorem 16.2, and is therefore left as an exercise. Its corollary then gives us a proof technique for showing $\mathcal{NP}$-hardness, provided we already have at least one $\mathcal{NP}$-hard problem.

Theorem 16.7. *If $X \leq_m^p Y$ and $Y \leq_m^p Z$, then $X \leq_m^p Z$.*

Corollary 16.8. *If X is $\mathcal{NP}$-hard and $X \leq_m^p Y$, then Y is $\mathcal{NP}$-hard.*

Thus, to show a decision problem Y to be $\mathcal{NP}$-hard, we need only to show that $X \leq_m^p Y$ for some $\mathcal{NP}$-hard problem X. This is the technique that we will use for all subsequent $\mathcal{NP}$-hardness proofs. Note also that the more problems we have shown to be $\mathcal{NP}$-complete, the more tools we have for showing additional problems to be $\mathcal{NP}$-complete. For this reason, we will devote the next few sections to identifying a variety of $\mathcal{NP}$-complete problems.

16.4 Restricted Satisfiability Problems

In order to illustrate the technique of proving $\mathcal{NP}$-hardness using a polynomial many-one reduction from a known $\mathcal{NP}$-hard problem, we consider in this section two special cases of boolean satisfiability. In the first special case, the expression is in *conjunctive normal form (CNF)*; i.e., the expression is of the form

$$\bigwedge_{i=1}^{n} \bigvee_{j=1}^{k_i} \alpha_{ij},$$

where each α_{ij} is a *literal* — either a variable or the negation of a variable. Let us refer to this problem as CSAT. We will now show that CSAT is $\mathcal{NP}$-complete. The proof of $\mathcal{NP}$-hardness will consist of showing that SAT $\leq_m^p$ CSAT.

It makes sense to represent the input for CSAT using a data structure that follows the form of a CNF formula more closely than does an expression tree. Specifically, we represent a CNF formula as a CONSLIST of *clauses*, each of which is a disjunction of literals. We then represent a clause as a CONSLIST of literals. Finally, we represent each literal as an integer as follows. For a non-negated variable, we simply use a positive integer, as in an expression tree. For a negated variable $\neg x$, we use $-i$, where i is the integer representing the variable x. We will again assume that for an input formula $\mathcal{F}$, if j represents a variable in $\mathcal{F}$, then for $1 \leq i \leq j$, i represents a variable in $\mathcal{F}$. Again, this assumption will not apply to arbitrary sub-formulas.

One obvious way of reducing SAT to CSAT is to convert a given boolean expression to an equivalent expression in CNF. However, there are boolean expressions for which the shortest equivalent CNF expression has size exponential in the size of the original expression. As a result, any such conversion algorithm must require at least exponential time in the worst case.

Fortunately, our reduction doesn't need to construct an equivalent expression, but only one that is satisfiable iff the given expression is satisfiable. In fact, the constructed expression isn't even required to contain the same variables. We will use this flexibility in designing our reduction.

For the first step of our reduction, we will construct an equivalent formula in which negations are applied only to variables. Because of this restriction, we can simplify our representation for this kind of expression by allowing leaves to contain either positive or negative integers, as in our representation of CNF formulas. Using this representation, we no longer need nodes representing the $\neg$ operation. We will refer to this representation as a *normalized expression tree*.

Fortunately, there is a polynomial-time algorithm for normalizing a boolean expression tree. The algorithm uses DeMorgan's laws:

- $\neg(x \lor y) = \neg x \land \neg y$; and
- $\neg(x \land y) = \neg x \lor \neg y$.

The algorithm is shown in Figure 16.3. This algorithm solves a slightly more general problem for which the input includes a boolean *neg*, which indicates whether the normalized expression should be equivalent to $\mathcal{F}$ or $\neg \mathcal{F}$. It is easily seen that its running time is proportional to the number of nodes in the tree, which is in $O(m)$, where m is the number of operators in $\mathcal{F}$.

As the second step in our reduction, we need to find the largest integer used to represent a variable in a normalized expression tree. We need this value in order to be able to introduce new variables. Such an algorithm is shown in Figure 16.4. Clearly, its running time is in $O(|\mathcal{F}|)$.

As the third step in our reduction, we will construct from a normalized expression tree $\mathcal{F}$ and a value larger than any integer representing a variable in $\mathcal{F}$, a CNF expression $\mathcal{F}'$ having the following properties:

P_1: $\mathcal{F}'$ contains all of the variables in $\mathcal{F}$;

P_2: for any satisfying assignment A for $\mathcal{F}$, there is a satisfying assignment A' for $\mathcal{F}'$ in which all the variables in $\mathcal{F}$ have the same values as in A; and

P_3: for any satisfying assignment A' for $\mathcal{F}'$, the assignment A for $\mathcal{F}$ in which each variable in $\mathcal{F}$ is assigned its value from A' satisfies $\mathcal{F}$.

Figure 16.3 Algorithm to normalize a boolean expression tree

Precondition: $\mathcal{F}$ is a BINARYTREENODE referring to the root of a boolean expression tree, and *neg* is a BOOL.
Postcondition: Returns a normalized expression tree $\mathcal{F}'$ such that if *neg* is false, $\mathcal{F}' \equiv \mathcal{F}$, and if *neg* is true, $\mathcal{F}' \equiv \neg\mathcal{F}$.

NORMALIZE($\mathcal{F}$, *neg*)
  $\mathcal{F}' \leftarrow$ **new** BINARYTREENODE(); $op \leftarrow \mathcal{F}$.ROOT()
  if $\mathcal{F}$.LEFTCHILD() = nil
    if *neg*
      $\mathcal{F}'$.SETROOT($-op$)
    else
      $\mathcal{F}'$.SETROOT(op)
  else if op = not
    $\mathcal{F}' \leftarrow$ NORMALIZE($\mathcal{F}$.LEFTCHILD(), **not** *neg*)
  else
    $\mathcal{F}'$.SETLEFTCHILD(NORMALIZE($\mathcal{F}$.LEFTCHILD(), *neg*))
    $\mathcal{F}'$.SETRIGHTCHILD(NORMALIZE($\mathcal{F}$.RIGHTCHILD(), *neg*))
    if (op = and **and** *neg*) **or** (op = or **and** **not** *neg*)
      $\mathcal{F}'$.SETROOT(or)
    else
      $\mathcal{F}'$.SETROOT(and)
  return $\mathcal{F}'$

Thus, $\mathcal{F}'$ will be satisfiable iff $\mathcal{F}$ is satisfiable. We consider three cases.

Case 1: $\mathcal{F}$ is a literal. Then because $\mathcal{F}$ is in CNF, we let $\mathcal{F}' = \mathcal{F}$.

Case 2: $\mathcal{F} = \mathcal{F}_1 \wedge \mathcal{F}_2$. We then construct CNF formulas $\mathcal{F}'_1$ and $\mathcal{F}'_2$ from $\mathcal{F}_1$ and $\mathcal{F}_2$, respectively, such that properties P_1-P_3 are satisfied. Then $\mathcal{F}' = \mathcal{F}'_1 \wedge \mathcal{F}'_2$ is in CNF and clearly satisfies properties P_1-P_3 with respect to $\mathcal{F}$.

Case 3: $\mathcal{F} = \mathcal{F}_1 \vee \mathcal{F}_2$. We then construct CNF formulas $\mathcal{F}'_1$ and $\mathcal{F}'_2$ from $\mathcal{F}_1$ and $\mathcal{F}_2$, respectively, such that properties P_1-P_3 are satisfied. Let u be a variable that is contained in neither $\mathcal{F}'_1$ nor $\mathcal{F}'_2$. We construct $\mathcal{F}''_1$ by including u in each clause of $\mathcal{F}'$, and we construct $\mathcal{F}''_2$ by including $\neg u$ in each clause of $\mathcal{F}'_2$. We then let $\mathcal{F}' = \mathcal{F}''_1 \wedge \mathcal{F}''_2$. Clearly, $\mathcal{F}'$ is in CNF. Furthermore, it is not hard to show that $\mathcal{F}'$ satisfies properties P_1-P_3 with respect to $\mathcal{F}$.

Figure 16.4   Algorithm to find the largest integer representing a variable in a normalized expression tree

---

Precondition: $\mathcal{F}$ is a BINARYTREENODE representing a normalized expression tree.
Postcondition: Returns the largest absolute value of any integer in $\mathcal{F}$.

MAXVAR($\mathcal{F}$)
     if $\mathcal{F}$.ROOT() = **and or** $\mathcal{F}$.ROOT() = **or**
         $l \leftarrow$ MAXVAR($\mathcal{F}$.LEFTCHILD())
         $r \leftarrow$ MAXVAR($\mathcal{F}$.RIGHTCHILD())
         return MAX(l, r)
     else
         return $|\mathcal{F}$.ROOT()$|$

The algorithm for constructing $\mathcal{F}'$ is shown in Figure 16.5. It uses a data type MUTABLENAT, which contains a single readable and writable representation variable *data*, which is a NAT. It also uses the function APPEND specified in Figure 4.15.

It is not hard to see that ADDTOCLAUSES operates in $O(n)$ time, where n is the number of clauses in $\mathcal{F}$. Furthermore, NORMALIZEDTOCNF only constructs a new clause when processing a literal; hence, the number of clauses in the CNF formula is no more than $|\mathcal{F}|$. As suggested in Exercise 4.3, APPEND can be implemented to run in $O(n)$ time, where n is the number of elements in its first argument. It follows that the time for a single call to NORMALIZEDTOCNF, excluding recursive calls, runs in $O(|\mathcal{F}|)$ time. Because NORMALIZEDTOCNF is called once for every node in the expression tree $\mathcal{F}$, its overall running time is in $O(|\mathcal{F}|^2)$.

The reduction is implemented in Figure 16.6. It clearly runs in $O(|\mathcal{F}|^2)$ time, so that SAT $\leq_m^p$ CSAT. We can therefore show the following theorem.

Theorem 16.9. CSAT *is $\mathcal{NP}$-complete.*

Proof. By the above discussion, CSAT is $\mathcal{NP}$-hard. In order to show CSAT to be in $\mathcal{NP}$, we use essentially the same reasoning as we did in showing SAT to be in $\mathcal{NP}$. The only difference is that we need an algorithm to evaluate a CNF expression, rather than an expression tree. It is a straightforward matter to adapt BOOLEVAL (Figure 16.2) to evaluate a CNF expression $\mathcal{F}$ in $O(|\mathcal{F}|)$ time — the details are left as an exercise. It follows that CSAT $\in \mathcal{NP}$. CSAT is therefore $\mathcal{NP}$-complete. $\qquad\square$

Figure 16.5 Algorithm for constructing a CNF formula from a normalized expression tree

---

Precondition: $\mathcal{F}$ is a BINARYTREENODE referring to a normalized boolean expression tree, and m refers to a MUTABLENAT larger than the absolute value of any variable in $\mathcal{F}$.

Postcondition: Returns a CONSLIST representing a CNF formula $\mathcal{F}'$ that satisfies properties P_1-P_3 with respect to $\mathcal{F}$. m has a value larger than the absolute value of any variable in the returned formula.

NORMALIZEDTOCNF($\mathcal{F}, m$)
  $root \leftarrow \mathcal{F}$.ROOT()
  if $root =$ **and** or $root =$ **or**
    $l \leftarrow$ NORMALIZEDTOCNF($\mathcal{F}$.LEFTCHILD(), m)
    $r \leftarrow$ NORMALIZEDTOCNF($\mathcal{F}$.RIGHTCHILD(), m)
    if $root =$ **or**
      $x \leftarrow m$.DATA(); $l \leftarrow$ ADDTOCLAUSES(l, x)
      $r \leftarrow$ ADDTOCLAUSES($r, -x$); m.SETDATA($x + 1$)
    return APPEND(l, r)
  else
    $c \leftarrow$ **new** CONSLIST($root$, **new** CONSLIST())
    return new CONSLIST(c, **new** CONSLIST())

Precondition: $\mathcal{F}$ is a (possibly empty) CONSLIST representing a CNF formula, and α is a nonzero INT.

Postcondition: Returns a CONSLIST obtained by adding the literal α to each clause in $\mathcal{F}$.

ADDTOCLAUSES($\mathcal{F}, \alpha$)
  if $\mathcal{F}$.ISEMPTY()
    return $\mathcal{F}$
  else
    $h \leftarrow$ **new** CONSLIST($\alpha, \mathcal{F}$.HEAD())
    $t \leftarrow$ ADDTOCLAUSES($\mathcal{F}$.TAIL(), α)
    return new CONSLIST(h, t)

As a second example, let us further restrict our inputs by limiting the number of literals in each clause. We say that a CNF formula is in *k-conjunctive normal form* (or *k-CNF*) if no clause contains more than k literals. We then define *k*-SAT to be the problem of determining satisfiability for a given *k*-CNF formula. Though we won't show it here, it turns out that 2-SAT $\in \mathcal{P}$. In what follows, we will show that 3-SAT is $\mathcal{NP}$-complete.

Figure 16.6 The reduction from SAT to CSAT

Precondition: $\mathcal{F}$ is BINARYTREENODE referring to a boolean expression tree.

Postcondition: Returns a CONSLIST representing a CNF formula that is satisfiable iff $\mathcal{F}$ is satisfiable.

SATTOCSAT($\mathcal{F}$)
    $\mathcal{F}' \leftarrow$ NORMALIZE($\mathcal{F}$, false)
    $m \leftarrow$ **new** MUTABLEINT(); m.SETDATA(MAXVAR($\mathcal{F}'$) + 1)
    return NORMALIZEDTOCNF($\mathcal{F}'$, m)

The fact that 3-SAT $\in \mathcal{NP}$ follows immediately from the fact that CSAT $\in \mathcal{NP}$, as 3-SAT is the same problem as CSAT, only with more restrictions placed on the input. Thus, the proof that CSAT $\in \mathcal{NP}$ also proves that 3-SAT $\in \mathcal{NP}$.

In order to show that 3-SAT is $\mathcal{NP}$-hard, we have two choices: we can reduce either SAT or CSAT to 3-SAT. Reducing CSAT to 3-SAT would appear to be less work, as instances of CSAT are already in CNF. All that remains is to ensure that the number of literals in each clause is no more than 3. We will therefore show that CSAT $\leq_m^p$ 3-SAT.

As in the previous reduction, we will not produce an equivalent formula. Instead, we will again introduce new variables. In addition, we will break up clauses that are too long into clauses containing only 3 literals.

Suppose our formula contains a clause $C = \alpha_1 \vee \cdots \vee \alpha_m$, where $m > 3$. We first introduce $m - 3$ new variables, $u_1, \ldots, u_{m-3}$. We then construct the following clauses to replace C:

- $\alpha_1 \vee \alpha_2 \vee u_1$;
- $\neg u_i \vee \alpha_{i+2} \vee u_{i+1}$ for $1 \leq i \leq m - 4$; and
- $\neg u_{m-3} \vee \alpha_{m-1} \vee \alpha_m$.

We first claim that any assignment of boolean values that satisfies C can be extended to an assignment that satisfies each of the new clauses. To see why, first observe that if C is satisfied, then α_i must be true for some i. We can then set $u_1, \ldots, u_{i-2}$ to true and $u_{i-1}, \ldots, u_{m-3}$ to false. Then each of the first $i - 2$ clauses is satisfied because $u_1, \ldots, u_{i-2}$ are true. The $(i-1)$st clause, $\neg u_{i-2} \vee \alpha_i \vee u_{i-1}$ is satisfied because α_i is true. Finally, the remaining clauses are satisfied because $\neg u_{i-1}, \ldots, \neg u_{m-3}$ are true.

We now claim that any assignment that satisfies the new clauses will also satisfy C. Suppose to the contrary that all the new clauses are satisfied, but that C is not satisfied — i.e., that $\alpha_1, \ldots, \alpha_m$ are all **false**. Then in order for the first clause to be satisfied, u_1 must be **true**. Likewise, it is easily shown by induction on i that each u_i must be **true**. Then the last clause is not satisfied — a contradiction.

If we apply the above transformation to each clause having more than 3 literals in a CNF formula $\mathcal{F}$ and retain those clauses with no more than 3 literals, then the resulting 3-CNF formula is satisfiable iff $\mathcal{F}$ is satisfiable. Furthermore, it is not hard to implement this reduction in $O(|\mathcal{F}|)$ time — the details are left as an exercise. Hence, CSAT $\leq_m^p$ 3-SAT. We therefore conclude that 3-SAT is $\mathcal{NP}$-complete.

16.5 Vertex Cover and Independent Set

So far, all of the problems that we have shown to be $\mathcal{NP}$-complete are satisfiability problems for various kinds of boolean formulas. As we have seen in earlier chapters, it is sometimes possible to reduce a problem A to another problem B that at first looks nothing like problem A. By applying this technique to polynomial many-one reducibility, we can identify $\mathcal{NP}$-complete problems in other domains.

For example, let us consider the *vertex cover* problem, which we will denote VC. Let $G = (V, E)$ be an undirected graph. A vertex cover for G is a subset $C \subseteq V$ such that for each edge $\{u, v\} \in E$, $C \cap \{u, v\} \neq \varnothing$; i.e., at least one endpoint of each edge is contained in the vertex cover. The vertex cover problem is to decide whether a given undirected graph has a vertex cover of size k, where k is a given positive integer.

To show that VC $\in \mathcal{NP}$, we will treat bit strings as arrays $A[0..m-1]$ of boolean values. We can interpret an array $A[0..m-1]$ as describing a subset S of the vertices $\{0, 1, \ldots, n-1\}$ such that for $0 \leq i < n$, $i \in S$ iff $i < m$ and $A[i]$ is **true**. It is then an easy matter to check, in time linear in the size of a graph G, whether $A[0..m-1]$ denotes a vertex cover of G with size k — the details are left as an exercise. Therefore, VC $\in \mathcal{NP}$.

In order to show that VC is $\mathcal{NP}$-hard, we need to reduce one of the three satisfiability problems to it. We will use 3-SAT because 3-CNF formulas have a simpler structure than either CNF or arbitrary boolean formulas. Still, it is not immediately clear how we can construct, from a given 3-CNF formula $\mathcal{F}$, an undirected graph G and a positive integer k such that G has a vertex cover of size k iff $\mathcal{F}$ is satisfiable.

One rather simplistic approach is first to decide whether $\mathcal{F}$ is satisfiable, then to construct one of two fixed graphs — one that has a vertex cover of size 1, or one that does not. However, because 3-SAT is $\mathcal{NP}$-hard, we cannot decide in polynomial time whether $\mathcal{F}$ is satisfiable unless $\mathcal{P} = \mathcal{NP}$. As a result, such an approach will probably never work.

Instead, we need to construct an instance of VC whose solution will give us a solution to our original instance of 3-SAT. In order to do this, we should try to see what the two problems have in common. A particularly useful technique is to compare the proofs of membership in $\mathcal{NP}$. Often we can find a reduction that has the side-effect of transforming each proof $\phi \in \mathcal{B}$ for one problem to a proof ϕ' for the other.

Let $\mathcal{F}$ be a given 3-CNF formula with n clauses, $C_1, \ldots, C_n$. For $1 \le i \le n$, let α_{i1}, α_{i2}, and α_{i3} be the three literals in clause C_i (if there are fewer than three literals in C_i, we set α_{i3} and, if necessary, α_{i2} to equal α_{i1}). A proof for this instance of 3-SAT represents an assignment of boolean values to the variables. A proof for an instance of VC represents a set of vertices. Perhaps we can associate the selection of a boolean value to the selection of one of two possible vertices. In particular, let us construct, for each variable x_i in $\mathcal{F}$, two vertices x_i and $\neg x_i$, together with an edge $\{x_i, \neg x_i\}$. Then any vertex cover must include either x_i or $\neg x_i$. Furthermore, by choosing an appropriate size for the vertex cover, we might be able to prohibit the simultaneous inclusion of both x_i and $\neg x_i$.

In order to complete the reduction, we need to ensure that any vertex cover of size k describes a satisfying assignment for $\mathcal{F}$, and that for any satisfying assignment for $\mathcal{F}$, there is a vertex cover of size k that describes it. To this end, we will add more structure to the graph we are constructing. We know that for a satisfying assignment, each clause contains at least one **true** literal. In order to model this constraint with a graph, let us construct, for each clause C_i, the vertices c_{i1}, c_{i2}, and c_{i3}, along with the edges $\{c_{i1}, c_{i2}\}$, $\{c_{i2}, c_{i3}\}$, and $\{c_{i3}, c_{i1}\}$. Then any vertex cover must contain at least two of these three vertices.

Finally, for $1 \le i \le n$ and $1 \le j \le 3$, we construct an additional edge $\{c_{ij}, \alpha_{ij}\}$. For example, Figure 16.7 shows the graph constructed from the 3-CNF formula $(x_1 \vee \neg x_2 \vee x_3) \wedge (\neg x_1 \vee x_3)$. By setting $k = m + 2n$, where m is the number of variables and n is the number of clauses in $\mathcal{F}$, we force any vertex cover of size k to contain exactly one of the two vertices constructed for each variable and exactly two of the three vertices constructed for each clause. In order to cover all of the edges $\{c_{ij}, \alpha_{ij}\}$, the vertex cover must be such that in each clause C_i, there is at least one literal α_{ij} that belongs to

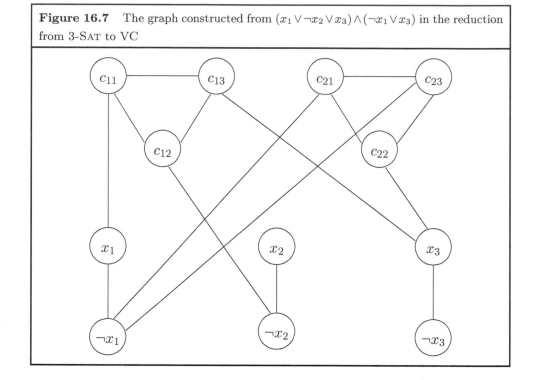

Figure 16.7   The graph constructed from $(x_1 \lor \neg x_2 \lor x_3) \land (\neg x_1 \lor x_3)$ in the reduction from 3-SAT to VC

the vertex cover. Thus, we can represent an assignment of **true** to a literal by including it in the vertex cover. We can now show the following lemma.

Lemma 16.10. *Let $\mathcal{F}$ be a 3-CNF formula with m variables and n clauses, and let G and k be the graph and positive integer resulting from the above construction. Then G has a vertex cover of size k iff $\mathcal{F}$ is satisfiable.*

Proof.   We must show the implication in both directions.

$\Rightarrow$: Suppose G has a vertex cover S of size $k = m + 2n$. Then S must contain at least one of the two vertices x_i and $\neg x_i$ for $1 \leq i \leq m$, plus at least two of the three vertices c_{i1}, c_{i2}, and c_{i3} for $1 \leq i \leq n$. Because this gives a total of at least k vertices, we conclude that S must contain exactly one of x_i and $\neg x_i$ and exactly two of c_{i1}, c_{i2}, and c_{i3}. Let us set x_i to **true** iff $x_i \in S$. Consider any clause C_i. Let j be such that $c_{ij} \notin S$. Because the edge $\{c_{ij}, \alpha_{ij}\}$ must be covered, α_{ij} must be in S. Therefore, at least one literal in C_i is **true**. We conclude that $\mathcal{F}$ is satisfiable.

$\Leftarrow$: Suppose $\mathcal{F}$ is satisfiable. Let A be a satisfying assignment. We can then construct a vertex cover S as follows. First, for $1 \leq i \leq m$, if x_i is true in A, we include x_i in S; otherwise, we include $\neg x_i$. Thus, each of the edges $\{x_i, \neg x_i\}$ is covered. Then for $1 \leq i \leq n$, we include in S two of c_{i1}, c_{i2}, and c_{i3}, so that the vertex that is not included is adjacent to an $\alpha_{ij} \in S$ (note that because A is a satisfying assignment, such a vertex exists for each clause). Thus, S is of size $m + 2n = k$ and covers all edges in G. $\square$

It is easily seen that the above construction can be implemented to run in $O(m+n)$ time, or linear in the size of the formula — the details are left as an exercise. From Lemma 16.10, 3-SAT $\leq_m^p$ VC. Because 3-SAT is $\mathcal{NP}$-hard, it follows that VC is $\mathcal{NP}$-hard. Because we have shown that VC $\in \mathcal{NP}$, we have the following theorem.

Theorem 16.11. VC *is $\mathcal{NP}$-complete.*

A problem closely related to VC is the *independent set* problem, which we denote IS. An independent set in an undirected graph G is a subset S of the vertices such that no pair of vertices in S is adjacent in G. The independent set problem is to decide, for a given undirected graph G and natural number k, whether G has an independent set of size k. The relationship between IS and VC is shown by the following theorem.

Theorem 16.12. *Let $G = (V, E)$ be an undirected graph and $S \subset V$. Then S is an independent set iff $V \setminus S$ is a vertex cover.*

Proof.   We must show the implication in both directions.

$\Leftarrow$: Suppose S is an independent set. Let $\{u, v\} \in E$. Because u and v cannot both be in S, at least one of them is in $V \setminus S$. It follows that $V \setminus S$ is a vertex cover.

$\Rightarrow$: Suppose $V \setminus S$ is a vertex cover. Let u and v be two vertices in S. Because $V \setminus S$ is a vertex cover containing neither u nor v, u cannot be adjacent to v. It follows that S is an independent set. $\square$

Given this close relationship between the two problems, it is an easy matter to modify the proof that VC $\in \mathcal{NP}$ to show that IS $\in \mathcal{NP}$. Furthermore,

> If $k > n$, we can use $n+1$ instead.

it follows from Theorem 16.12 that for an undirected graph G with n vertices and a positive integer k, G has an independent set of size $n - k$ iff G has a vertex cover of size k. Clearly, we can construct $n - k$ in polynomial time; hence, VC $\leq_m^p$ IS. We therefore have the following theorem.

Theorem 16.13. IS *is $\mathcal{NP}$-complete.*

16.6 Three-Dimensional Matching

In this section, we will study a problem closely related to the bipartite matching problem of Section 14.3. The input will consist of three non-empty disjoint sets, X, Y, and Z, each having the same number of elements, and a set of triples $W \subseteq X \times Y \times Z$. We wish to decide if there is a subset $M \subseteq W$ such that each element of $X \cup Y \cup Z$ occurs in exactly one triple in M. We call this problem the *3D matching* (3DM) problem.

Note that if we were to use two disjoint sets instead of three, we could think of the two sets as the two vertex sets of a bipartite graph. The set of pairs (instead of triples) would then be directed edges. Our problem would then be that of deciding whether there is a matching including all the vertices of this directed graph. 3DM is then the natural extension of this problem to 3D *hypergraphs*. Using the algorithm MATCHING (Figure 14.10 on page 458), we can decide the two-dimensional version (2DM) in $O(na)$ time, where n is the number of vertices and a is the number of edges in the graph; thus, 2DM $\in \mathcal{P}$. However, we will now show that 3DM is $\mathcal{NP}$-complete.

In order to show that 3DM $\in \mathcal{NP}$, let us first denote an instance by

$$X = \{x_1, \ldots, x_m\}$$
$$Y = \{y_1, \ldots, y_m\}$$
$$Z = \{z_1, \ldots, z_m\}$$
$$W = \{w_1, \ldots, w_n\}.$$

We interpret a bit string ϕ as encoding an array $A[1..k]$ such that each block of b bits encodes an element of A, where b is the number of bits needed to encode n. Any bit string that does not have length exactly bm will be considered to be invalid. To verify that the array A encoded by ϕ is a proof, we can check that

- ϕ is valid;
- $1 \leq A[i] \leq n$ for $1 \leq i \leq m$; and
- each element of $X \cup Y \cup Z$ belongs to some triple $w_{A[i]}$, where $1 \leq i \leq m$.

This can easily be done in $O(bm^2)$ time — the details are left as an exercise. Hence, 3DM $\in \mathcal{NP}$.

In order to show that 3DM is $\mathcal{NP}$-hard, we need to reduce some $\mathcal{NP}$-complete problem to it. So far, we have identified five $\mathcal{NP}$-complete problems: three satisfiability problems and two graph problems. However, none of these bears much resemblance to 3DM. We therefore make use of a principle that has proven to be quite effective over the years: when in doubt, try 3-SAT.

As we did in showing 3-SAT $\leq_m^p$ VC, we will begin by focusing on the proofs of membership in $\mathcal{NP}$ for the two problems. Specifically, we want to relate the choice of a subset of W to the choice of truth values for boolean variables. Let's start by considering two triples, $\langle x, a_x, b_x \rangle$ and $\langle \neg x, a_x, b_x \rangle$, where x is some boolean variable. If these are the only two triples containing a_x or b_x, any matching must include exactly one of these triples. This choice could be used to set the value of x.

If we were to construct two such triples for each variable, we would then need to construct triples to represent the clauses. Using a similar idea, we could introduce, for a given clause $\alpha_{i1} \vee \alpha_{i2} \vee \alpha_{i3}$, the triples $\langle \alpha_{i1}, c_i, d_i \rangle$, $\langle \alpha_{i2}, c_i, d_i \rangle$, and $\langle \alpha_{i3}, c_i, d_i \rangle$ — one triple for each literal in the clause. Again, any matching must contain exactly one of these triples. If we let x be false when $\langle x, a_x, b_x \rangle$ is chosen, then the triple chosen for the clause must contain a true literal.

This construction has a couple of shortcomings, however. First, because each literal must occur exactly once in a matching, we can use a given variable to satisfy only one clause. Furthermore, if more than one literal is true in a given clause, there may remain literals that are unmatched. These shortcomings should not be too surprising, as we could do essentially the same construction producing pairs instead of triples — the third components are redundant. Thus, if this construction had worked, we could have used the same technique to reduce 3-SAT to 2DM, which belongs to $\mathcal{P}$. We would have therefore proved that $\mathcal{P} = \mathcal{NP}$.

In order to overcome the first shortcoming, we need to enrich our construction so that we have several copies of each literal. To keep it simple, we will make one copy for each clause, regardless of whether the literal appears in the clause. We must be careful, however, so that when we choose the triples to set the boolean value, we must either take all triples containing x or all triples containing $\neg x$. Because we are constructing triples rather than pairs, we can indeed accomplish these goals.

Figure 16.8   Triples for setting boolean values in the reduction from 3-SAT to 3DM, with $n = 4$

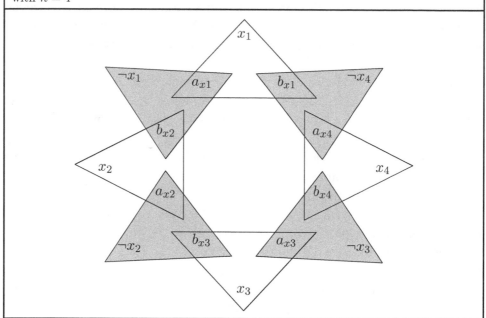

Let $x_1, \ldots, x_n$ denote all the copies of the literal x, and let $\neg x_1, \ldots, \neg x_n$ denote all the copies of the literal $\neg x$. We then introduce the following triples (see Figure 16.8):

- $\langle x_i, a_{xi}, b_{xi} \rangle$ for $1 \leq i \leq n$;
- $\langle \neg x_i, a_{xi}, b_{x,i+1} \rangle$ for $1 \leq i \leq n - 1$; and
- $\langle \neg x_n, a_{xn}, b_{x1} \rangle$.

It is not too hard to see that in order to match all of the a_{xi}s and b_{xi}s, a matching must include either those triples containing the x_is or those triples containing the $\neg x_i$s.

We can now use the construction described earlier for building triples from clauses, except that for clause i, we include the ith copy of each literal in its triple. Thus, in any matching, there must be for each clause at least one triple containing a copy of a literal. However, there still may be unmatched copies of literals. We need to introduce more triples in order to match the remaining copies.

Suppose our 3-CNF formula $\mathcal{F}$ has n clauses and m variables. Then our construction so far contains:

- $2mn$ copies of literals;
- mn as and n cs; and
- mn bs and n ds.

In order to make the above three sets of equal size, we add e_i to the second set and f_i to the third set, for $1 \le i \le (m-1)n$. We then include all possible triples $\langle x_i, e_j, f_j \rangle$ and $\langle \neg x_i, e_j, f_j \rangle$ for $1 \le i \le n$ and $1 \le j \le (m-1)n$. Using this construction, we can now show the following theorem.

Theorem 16.14. 3DM *is* $\mathcal{NP}$-*complete.*

Proof.   We have shown that 3DM $\in \mathcal{NP}$. We will show that it is $\mathcal{NP}$-hard by showing that 3-SAT $\le_m^p$ 3DM. Specifically, we will show that the above construction is a polynomial-time many-one reduction.

We will first show that the construction can be computed in polynomial time. It is easily seen that the time required for the construction is proportional to the number of triples produced. Suppose the CNF formula $\mathcal{F}$ contains m variables and n clauses. The triples produced include

- $2mn$ triples for setting truth values;
- one triple for each literal in each clause, or at most $3n$ triples; and
- triples $\langle x_i, e_j, f_j \rangle$ and $\langle \neg x_i, e_j, f_j \rangle$ for each variable x, each i such that $1 \le i \le n$, and each j such that $1 \le j \le (m-1)n$, or $2(m-1)mn^2$ triples.

Thus, the total number of triples produced is at most

$$2mn + 3n + 2(m-1)mn^2.$$

Because this value is polynomial in the size of $\mathcal{F}$, the construction can be done in polynomial time.

Let W be the set of triples constructed. In order to complete the proof, we must show that W contains a matching iff $\mathcal{F}$ is satisfiable.

$\Rightarrow$: Suppose W contains a matching M. As we have argued above, for each variable x, M must contain either those triples $\langle x_i, a_{xi}, b_{xi} \rangle$ or those triples $\langle \neg x_i, a_{xi}, b_{xi} \rangle$, for $1 \le i \le n$. Let us set x to false iff the triples $\langle x_i, a_{xi}, b_{xi} \rangle$ belong to M. M must also contain some triple $\langle \alpha_{ij}, c_i, d_i \rangle$ for $1 \le i \le n$. Because α_{ij} cannot also be in another triple in M, α_{ij} must be true. Thus, each clause contains at least one true literal, so that $\mathcal{F}$ is satisfiable.

$\Leftarrow$: Suppose $\mathcal{F}$ is satisfiable, and let A denote a satisfying assignment of boolean values to the variables in $\mathcal{F}$. We construct a matching M as follows. First, if x is false in A, we include $\langle x_i, a_{xi}, b_{xi} \rangle$ for $1 \le i \le n$; otherwise, we include $\langle \neg x_i, a_{xi}, b_{xi} \rangle$ for $1 \leq i \leq n$. Thus, each a_{xi} and b_{xi} is included exactly once. Then for clause i, because A is a satisfying assignment there is at least one literal α_{ij} that is **true** in A. Because α_{ij} has not yet been included in M, we can include the triple $\langle \alpha_{ij}, c_i, d_i \rangle$ in M. Thus, M includes each c_i and d_i exactly once.

At this point M includes no item more than once, but does not include any of the e_is or f_is. Furthermore, because exactly $mn+n$ of the x_is and $\neg x_i$s have been included, $(m-1)n$ have not yet been included. Let $\beta_1, \ldots, \beta_{(m-1)n}$ denote the x_is and $\neg x_i$s that have not yet been included. We complete M by including $\langle \beta_i, e_i, f_i \rangle$ for $1 \leq i \leq (m-1)n$. It is now easily seen that M is a matching. $\qquad \square$

16.7 Partitioning and Strong $\mathcal{NP}$-Completeness

In this section, we will look at partitioning problems related to the 0-1 knapsack problem of Section 12.4. These are the first $\mathcal{NP}$-complete problems we will have seen in which numbers play a significant role. As we will see, the $\mathcal{NP}$-completeness of a number problem does not always imply intractability. For this reason, we will introduce a stronger notion of $\mathcal{NP}$-completeness.

The most basic partitioning problem consists of a set of items, each having a positive integer *weight*. The problem is to decide whether the items can be partitioned into two disjoint subsets having identical total weight. More formally, let $w_1, \ldots, w_n$ denote the weights of the items. We wish to decide whether there is a subset $S \subseteq \{1, \ldots, n\}$ such that

$$\sum_{i \in S} w_i = \sum_{i \notin S} w_i.$$

The problem is known as the *partition problem*, or PART. We leave it as an exercise to show that PART $\in \mathcal{NP}$. We will show that PART is $\mathcal{NP}$-hard, and therefore $\mathcal{NP}$-complete.

Before showing the $\mathcal{NP}$-hardness of PART, however, we first observe that this problem is a special case of the 0-1 knapsack problem in which the values are equal to the weights and the weight bound W is half the total weight. In Section 12.4, we sketched an algorithm to solve this problem in $O(nW)$ time. Clearly, this same algorithm can be applied to PART. This would seem to imply that PART $\in \mathcal{P}$, so that showing PART to be $\mathcal{NP}$-hard would amount to showing $\mathcal{P} = \mathcal{NP}$.

However, the $O(nW)$ algorithm does not prove that PART $\in \mathcal{P}$. The reason is that we have defined $\mathcal{P}$ to be the set of decision problems that can be decided in a time polynomial in the length of their inputs. We claim that nW is not necessarily polynomial in the length of the input to PART. To see why, note that the number of bits required to encode an integer is logarithmic in the value of the integer; hence, the value is exponential in the length of the encoding. Because W is one of the integers given as input, nW is not bounded by a polynomial in the length of the input.

The relationship between the value of an integer and the length of its binary encoding is essential to the $\mathcal{NP}$-hardness of PART, as its proof will illustrate. We will now present that proof, which is a reduction from 3DM.

Let W, X, Y, and Z represent an instance of 3DM, where

- $X = \{x_0, \ldots, x_{m-1}\}$;
- $Y = \{y_0, \ldots, y_{m-1}\}$;
- $Z = \{z_0, \ldots, z_{m-1}\}$; and
- $W = \{w_0, \ldots, w_{n-1}\}$ such that each $w_i \in X \times Y \times Z$.

We will construct a weight for each triple, plus two additional weights.

Suppose $\langle x_i, y_j, z_k \rangle \in W$. The weight we construct for this triple will be

$$(n + 1)^{2m+i} + (n + 1)^{m+j} + (n + 1)^k.$$

If we were to express this weight in radix $n + 1$, it would consist entirely of 1s and 0s and have exactly three 1s. The positions of the three 1s in this encoding determine the three components of the triple as follows:

$$\overbrace{1\,00\cdots0}^{i \text{ digits}}\underbrace{00\cdots01}_{m \text{ digits}}\overbrace{00\cdots0}^{j \text{ digits}}\underbrace{00\cdots01}_{m \text{ digits}}\overbrace{00\cdots0}^{k \text{ digits}}.$$

Consider any subset $S \subseteq W$. Clearly, no element of $X \cup Y \cup Z$ can occur in more than n triples in S. Thus, when viewed in radix $n + 1$, the sum of the weights corresponding to the elements of S describes the number of occurrences of each element of $X \cup Y \cup Z$ in S. Specifically, if we number the digits beginning with 0 for the least significant digit, then

- digit $2m + i$ gives the number of occurrences of x_i in S, for $0 \leq i < m$;
- digit $m + j$ gives the number of occurrences of y_j in S, for $0 \leq j < m$; and
- digit k gives the number of occurrences of z_k is S, for $0 \leq k < m$.

It follows that S is a matching iff the sum of its corresponding weights is

$$M = \sum_{i=0}^{3m-1} (n+1)^i,$$

which in radix $n+1$ is simply $3m$ 1s.

In order to complete the construction, we need two more weights. Let C denote the sum of the n weights constructed so far. We construct the following two weights:

$$A = 2C - M$$

and

$$B = C + M.$$

Thus, the sum of all $n+2$ weights is $4C$. Because $A + B = 3C > 2C$, A and B cannot belong to the same subset in a partition. Furthermore, the subset containing A must also contain items corresponding to elements of W having total weight M. Because these elements must form a matching, the weights we have constructed contain a partition iff W contains a matching.

To see that the time needed to construct the instance of PART is polynomial in the size of the instance of 3DM, we first observe that

$$2C \leq 2 \sum_{i=0}^{3m-1} n(n+1)^i$$
$$< 2(n+1)^{3m}.$$

Therefore, each weight constructed has a binary encoding with no more than $1 + \lceil 3m \lg(n+1) \rceil$ bits. Because addition, subtraction, multiplication, and exponentiation can all be performed in a time polynomial in the number of bits in their operands (see Exercise 4.14, Section 10.1, Exercise 10.25, and Sections 15.3–15.4), the construction can clearly be performed in time polynomial in the size of the instance of 3DM. We therefore have the following theorem.

Theorem 16.15. PART *is $\mathcal{NP}$-hard.*

Note that in the above construction, the weights can become extremely large, though their lengths are all polynomial in the size of the instance of 3DM. It is not too hard to imagine that we might want to solve the partition problem for a large number of weights — thousands or perhaps even millions. However, when numbers represent physical quantities — including time —

we don't expect them to be very long. For example, about 300 bits are sufficient to encode in binary the estimated number of elementary particles in the universe. Thus, because there is an algorithm for PART whose running time is a low-order polynomial in the length of the input and the values encoded in the input, it seems unreasonable to consider this problem to be intractable.

In order to accommodate numbers in the input, we say that an algorithm is *pseudopolynomial* if its running time is bounded by some polynomial in the length of the input and the largest integer encoded in the input. Thus, the $O(nW)$ algorithm for 0-1 knapsack (and hence partition) is pseudopolynomial. Whenever the numbers in a decision problem's input refer to physical quantities, we consider the problem to be tractable if it has a pseudopolynomial algorithm. However, if the numbers are purely mathematical entities (as, for example, in cryptographic applications), we consider the problem to be tractable only if it belongs to $\mathcal{P}$.

We would also like to extend the notion of $\mathcal{NP}$-hardness to account for numbers in the input. To this end, we first define a way to restrict a decision problem so that no integer in an instance is too large. Specifically, for a decision problem X and a function $f : \mathbb{N} \to \mathbb{R}^{\geq 0}$, we define X_f to be the restriction of X to instances x in which no integer has a value larger than $f(|x|)$. We then say that X is $\mathcal{NP}$-hard *in the strong sense* if there is a polynomial p such that X_p is $\mathcal{NP}$-hard. If, in addition, $X \in \mathcal{NP}$, we say that X is $\mathcal{NP}$-complete in the strong sense.

Suppose we were to find a pseudopolynomial algorithm for a strongly $\mathcal{NP}$-hard problem. When we restrict the problem so that its instances have integers bounded by some polynomial, the pseudopolynomial algorithm becomes truly polynomial, so that the restricted problem would be in $\mathcal{P}$. Furthermore, this restricted problem is still $\mathcal{NP}$-hard in the ordinary sense. Thus, by Theorem 16.4, we would have shown that $\mathcal{P} = \mathcal{NP}$. It therefore seems highly unlikely that there is a pseudopolynomial algorithm for any strongly $\mathcal{NP}$-hard problem.

In order to show a problem to be $\mathcal{NP}$-hard in the strong sense, we must ensure that the reduction produces numbers whose values are bounded above by some polynomial in the length of the instance we construct. The proof of Cook's Theorem in Section 16.8 does not construct large integers; hence, SAT is $\mathcal{NP}$-complete in the strong sense. Furthermore of all of the $\mathcal{NP}$-hardness proofs we have presented so far, only the proof that PART is $\mathcal{NP}$-hard constructs integers whose values are not bounded by some polynomial in the length of the input. As a result, CSAT, 3SAT, VC, IS, and 3DM are all $\mathcal{NP}$-complete in the strong sense. However, these results are rather uninteresting because none of their instances contain numbers that can become large in comparison to the length of the input without rendering the problem trivial.

In what follows, we will show a problem with potentially large numbers to be $\mathcal{NP}$-complete in the strong sense. We will use a restricted form of polynomial many-one reduction motivated by the following theorem.

Theorem 16.16. *Let f be a polynomial many-one reduction from problem X to problem Y, where X is $\mathcal{NP}$-hard in the strong sense. Suppose that f satisfies the following properties:*

(1) there is a polynomial p_1 such that $p_1(|f(x)|) \geq |x|$ for every instance x of X; and

(2) there is a two-variable polynomial p_2 such that each integer constructed has a value no greater than $p_2(|x|, \mu(x))$, where $\mu(x)$ denotes the maximum value of any integer in x.

Then Y is $\mathcal{NP}$-hard in the strong sense.

Proof. Because X is $\mathcal{NP}$-hard in the strong sense, there is some polynomial p such that X_p is $\mathcal{NP}$-hard. If the reduction is then applied to X_p, all numbers constructed will have values bounded by $p_2(|x|, p(|x|))$, by Property 2. Furthermore, by Property 1, these values are no more than $p_2(p_1(|f(x)|), p(p_1(|f(x)|)))$, which is a polynomial in the length of the instance constructed. The reduction from X_p to Y therefore shows that Y is $\mathcal{NP}$-hard in the strong sense. $\square$

We say that a polynomial many-one reduction is a *pseudopolynomial* reduction, denoted by $\leq_m^{pp}$, if it satisfies the properties given in Theorem 16.16.

Let us now consider other partitioning problems. For a fixed natural number $k > 1$, the k-partition problem (k-PART) is defined as follows. The input consists of kn items, each having a positive integer weight, such that the sum of the weights is Bn for some positive integer B. Furthermore, each weight w must satisfy

$$\frac{B}{k+1} < w < \frac{B}{k-1}.$$

The question we ask is whether the kn items can be partitioned into n disjoint subsets, each having total weight exactly B. Note that the constraints on the weights imply that each subset will contain exactly k items.

In what follows, we will show that 4-PART is $\mathcal{NP}$-hard in the strong sense. We leave it as exercises to show that

- k-PART $\in \mathcal{NP}$ for all $k > 1$;
- 3-PART is $\mathcal{NP}$-complete in the strong sense; and
- 2-PART $\in \mathcal{P}$.

We will show that 3DM $\leq_m^{pp}$ 4-PART. The reduction will be somewhat similar to the reduction from 3DM to PART, but we must be careful that the weights we construct are not too large. Let us describe an instance of 3DM using the same notation as we did for the earlier reduction. We will assume that each element occurs in at least one triple. Otherwise, there is no matching, and we can create an instance with seven items having weight 6 and one item having weight 8, so that the total weight is 50, and $B = 25$. Clearly, $25/5 < 6 < 8 < 25/3$; hence, this is a valid instance, but there is clearly no way to form a subset with weight 25.

We will construct, for each triple $\langle x_i, y_j, z_k \rangle \in W$, four weights: one weight for each of x_i, y_j, and z_k, plus one weight for the triple itself. Because each element of $X \cup Y \cup Z$ can occur in several triples, we may construct several items for each element. Exactly one of these will be a *matching item*. All non-matching items constructed from the same element will have the same weight, which will be different from that of the matching item constructed from that element. We will construct the weights so that in any 4-partition, the item constructed from a triple must be grouped with either the matching items constructed from the elements of the triple, or three non-matching items — one corresponding to each element of the triple. In this way, a 4-partition will exist iff W contains a matching.

As in the previous reduction, it will be convenient to view the weights in a particular radix r, which we will specify later. In this case, however, the weights will contain only a few radix-r digits. We will choose r to be large enough that when we add any four of the weights we construct, each column of digits will have a sum strictly less than r; hence, we will be able to deal with each digit position independently in order to satisfy the various constraints. Note that if we construct the weights so that for every triple, the sum of the four weights constructed is the same, then this sum will be B.

We will use the three low-order digits to enforce the constraint that the four items within any partition must be derived from some triple and its three components. To this end, we make the following assignments:

- For any weight constructed from $x_i \in X$, we assign $i + 1$ to the first digit and 0 to the second and third digits.
- For any weight constructed from $y_j \in Y$, we assign $j + 1$ to the second digit and 0 to the first and third digits.
- For any weight constructed from $z_k \in Z$, we assign $k + 1$ to the third digit and 0 to the first two digits.
- For a triple $\langle x_i, y_j, z_k \rangle$, we assign the first three digits the values $2m - i$, $2m - j$, and $2m - k$, respectively.

B will therefore have $2m + 1$ as each of its three low-order digits.

Note that because each weight constructed from a triple has a value of at least $m + 1$ in each of its three low-order digits, no two of these weights can be grouped together. Furthermore, because all three low-order digits of any weight constructed from an element of $X \cup Y \cup Z$ have values no more than m, and at least two of these values are 0, in order to reach a sum of B with only four weights, at least one must correspond to a triple. Thus, in any 4-partition, each group must contain exactly one weight corresponding to a triple, and the other three weights must correspond to the elements of that triple.

We will use the fourth digit to enforce the constraint that for any four items grouped together, the items corresponding to elements from $X \cup Y \cup Z$ are either all matching items or all non-matching items. We therefore assign the fourth digits as follows:

- for each matching item: 1;
- for each non-matching item from $X \cup Y$: 0;
- for each non-matching item from Z: 3; and
- for each item from W: 0.

The fourth digit of B will therefore be 3. Furthermore, because any group must have one item from each of W, X, Y, and Z, it must contain either three matching items or three non-matching items. Setting the digits in this way therefore ensures that the set of weights has a 4-partition iff W contains a matching.

Finally, in order to ensure that each weight is greater than $B/5$ and less than $B/3$, we set the fifth digit of all weights to 1. As a result, the fifth digit of B is 4. We will see that by choosing r to be sufficiently large, all weights will be within the proper range.

To summarize, for a triple $\langle x_i, y_j, z_k \rangle$, we have the weight

$$r^4 + (2m - k)r^2 + (2m - j)r + 2m - i.$$

For the elements $x_i \in X$, $y_j \in Y$, and $z_k \in Z$, we have for the matching items the weights

$$
\begin{aligned}
&r^4 + r^3 && + i + 1 \\
&r^4 + r^3 && + (j+1)r \\
&r^4 + r^3 + (k+1)r^2
\end{aligned}
$$

and for any non-matching item the weights

$$
\begin{aligned}
&r^4 + && + i + 1 \\
&r^4 + && + (j+1)r \\
&r^4 + 3r^3 + (k+1)r^2
\end{aligned}
$$

Furthermore,

$$
B = 4r^4 + 3r^3 + (2m+1)r^2 + (2m+1)r + 2m + 1.
$$

To complete the reduction, we must assign a value to r. As we have observed, r must be larger than the sum of any four digits occurring in the same column. Thus, r must be strictly larger than both $8m$ and 12. Because $m \geq 1$, we can satisfy these constraints by setting $r = 13m$. We then have

$$
\begin{aligned}
B/5 &< (4r^4 + 4r^3)/5 \\
&< (4r^4 + r^4)/5 \\
&= r^4,
\end{aligned}
$$

so that every weight is larger than $B/5$. Furthermore, each weight is less than

$$
\begin{aligned}
r^4 + 4r^3 &< r^4 + r^4/3 \\
&= 4r^4/3 \\
&< B/3.
\end{aligned}
$$

We must now show that the above reduction is pseudopolynomial. We first observe that no weight is larger than $2r^4 = 2(13m)^4$, which is polynomial in the size of the instance of 3DM. Furthermore, it is easily seen that all the weights can be constructed in a time linear in the size of the instance of 3DM. We therefore have the following theorem.

Theorem 16.17. *4-*PART *is* $\mathcal{NP}$*-hard in the strong sense.*

16.8   Proof of Cook's Theorem

In this section, we will present a proof of Cook's Theorem, namely, that SAT is $\mathcal{NP}$-complete. As we have already observed in Section 16.1, SAT $\in \mathcal{NP}$. It therefore remains to be shown that SAT is $\mathcal{NP}$-hard. Furthermore, because we have used Cook's Theorem either directly or indirectly to show all of our $\mathcal{NP}$-hardness results, we cannot use any of these results to prove Cook's Theorem. Because we cannot show the $\mathcal{NP}$-hardness of SAT by reducing any known $\mathcal{NP}$-hard problem to it, we must directly use the definition of $\mathcal{NP}$-hardness — that is, we must directly show that for *every* problem $X \in \mathcal{NP}$, $X \leq_m^p$ SAT.

Our proof will therefore involve a *generic* reduction. This kind of reduction is more abstract in that we begin with an arbitrary $X \in \mathcal{NP}$. Specifically, the same reduction should work for any problem X that we might choose from $\mathcal{NP}$. Thus, the only assumption we can make about X is that it satisfies the definition of $\mathcal{NP}$: there exist a polynomial $p(n)$ and a decision problem $Y \subseteq I \times \mathcal{B}$, where I is the set of instances of X, such that

- $Y \in \mathcal{P}$ — that is, there exist a polynomial $p'(n)$ and an algorithm A that takes an element $x \in I$ and an element $\phi \in \mathcal{B}$ as its inputs and decides within $p'(|x| + |\phi|)$ steps whether $(x, \phi) \in Y$;
- for each $x \in I$, $x \in X$ iff there is a proof $\phi \in \mathcal{B}$ such that $(x, \phi) \in Y$; and
- for each $x \in X$, there is a proof $\phi \in \mathcal{B}$ such that $(x, \phi) \in Y$ and $|\phi| \leq p(|x|)$.

For our reduction, we need to construct, for a given instance $x \in I$, a boolean formula $\mathcal{F}$ that is satisfiable iff $x \in X$. Equivalently, $\mathcal{F}$ must be satisfiable iff there is a $\phi \in \mathcal{B}$ such that $|\phi| \leq p(|x|)$ and $(x, \phi) \in Y$. Our reduction therefore will construct from x a formula $\mathcal{F}$ that in some sense simulates the algorithm A on x and some unknown ϕ, where $|\phi| \leq p(|x|)$.

The input for our reduction is the instance x. However, because our reduction is generic, it must work for any algorithm A and any polynomials $p(n)$ and $p'(n)$ satisfying the above constraints. Therefore, A, p, and p' are in a sense additional inputs to our reduction. What makes constructing such a reduction rather difficult is the fact that one of these additional inputs is an algorithm. In order to be able to handle an algorithm as input to an algorithm, we need to define more precisely what we mean by an algorithm.

Rather than formalizing all of the constructs we have been using in our algorithms, we will instead simplify matters by defining a lower-level model of computation, which we will call a *random access machine*, or *RAM*. Thus, in constructing a boolean formula to simulate a RAM, we will in essence be defining an interpreter for a simple machine language. Such a task is much simpler than defining an interpreter for a high-level language, such as the notation we have been using to present our algorithms.

In order to maintain some consistency between this computational model and the algorithms we have designed, we will assume that a RAM consists of the following:

- a fixed program consisting of a sequence of $P > 0$ instructions numbered 0 through $P - 1$;
- a program counter, which is initially 0 and can store any natural number less than P;
- countably infinitely many memory locations, each of which is initially 0 and can store any natural number;
- two input streams from which values may be read one bit at a time; and
- a single output bit, which is produced when the program terminates.

Because we will be using this model only for representing an algorithm for deciding whether $(x, \phi) \in Y$, we need exactly two input streams, one for x and one for ϕ. Furthermore, we can represent a "yes" output by setting the output bit to 1.

We will assume that each memory location is addressed by a unique natural number. Each machine will then have the following instruction set:

- INPUT(i, l): Stores the next bit from input stream i, where i is either 0 or 1, in memory location l. If all of the input has already been read, the value 2 is stored.
- LOAD(n, l): Stores the natural number n at memory location l.
- COPY(l_1, l_2): Copies the value stored at location l_1 into location l_2.
- GOTO(p): Changes the value of the program counter to p.
- IFLEQ(l_1, l_2, p): If the value at location l_1 is less than or equal to the value at location l_2, changes the value of the program counter to p.
- ADD(l_1, l_2): Adds the value in location l_1 to the value in location l_2, saving the result in location l_2.
- SUBTRACT(l_1, l_2): Subtracts the value in location l_1 from the value in location l_2, saving the result in location l_2.
- SHIFT(l): Replaces the value n stored in location l with $\lfloor n/2 \rfloor$.
- HALT(b): Terminates the program with output b, which must be either 0 or 1.

In addition, wherever a memory location is used, an *indirection operator* "$*$" may be added. The expression "$*l$" indicates that the location referenced by the value stored in location l should be used. Thus, for example, if 21 is stored at 0, 2 is stored at 1, and 52 is stored at 2, the instruction

$$\text{ADD}(0, *1)$$

will add 21 (stored at 0) to 52 (stored at 2, the value referenced by 1), and store the sum 73 in location 2. Indirection operators cannot be nested.

Each instruction that does not explicitly change the program counter will increment it by 1. We will assume that any time an instruction cannot be executed (e.g., because a larger number is subtracted from a smaller number or the program counter would index beyond the program), the program will immediately terminate with output 0.

We will now argue somewhat informally that for any decision problem X, there is a deterministic polynomial-time algorithm deciding X iff there is a polynomial-time RAM deciding X. First, if we have a deterministic polynomial-time algorithm A, we can build a RAM to execute A using standard compiling techniques. Some statements in an algorithm may require much more time when compiled to a RAM. For example, to implement a multiplication, we can use the following top-down formulation:

$$ab = \begin{cases} 0 & \text{if } b = 0 \\ (a+a)\frac{b}{2} & \text{if } b \text{ is positive and even} \\ (a+a)\frac{b-1}{2} + a & \text{if } b \text{ is odd.} \end{cases}$$

To determine whether $b = 0$, we can simply check whether $b \leq 0$. To determine whether b is even, we can copy b to c, shift c yielding $d = \lfloor b/2 \rfloor$, and subtract $d + d$ from b. If the result is less than or equal to 0, then b is even; otherwise, b is odd. This technique can be implemented with a loop that runs in time linear in the number of bits in b.

In order to implement data structures, we need a memory manager for a RAM. Because we have infinitely many memory locations, only finitely many of which may be in use at any given time, we can use one memory location l_1 to store a value *avail* such that for every $l \geq avail$, l is unused. If we need to allocate n locations, we can copy l_1 to some memory location l_2 and add n to l_1. To access the ith of these n locations, we add i to l_2 and use the indirection operator on the result. Thus, it is a straightforward matter to implement the data structures in this text. Specifically, because we can implement a STACK, we can implement function and operation calls, including recursion.

It is important to realize that even though some operations are less efficient on a RAM, there is some polynomial $p(n)$ that bounds the running time of any simulation of an algorithmic step. Thus, if we have an algorithm that runs in $p'(n)$ steps, the RAM simulation will run in no more than $p'(p(n))$ steps, which is still polynomial in n. Furthermore, if the values of the natural numbers in the algorithm are bounded by $p'(n)$, then so are the values in the memory locations of the RAM.

Conversely, it is not hard to write an algorithm to simulate a polynomial-time RAM. We can use variables to store the value of the program counter and the indices of the next available bits of the two

> We must also make sure that $2^{p(n)}$ bounds each constant appearing in the RAM program.

input streams. In addition, we can use a VARRAY (see Section 9.5) to store the memory locations used by the RAM. Note that because the values of all memory locations must always be less than $2^{p(n)}$, where $p(n)$ is some polynomial in the number of bits in the two input streams, all memory locations that can be accessed have addresses strictly less than $2^{p(n)}$. We can therefore use a VARRAY of size $2^{p(n)}$ to keep track of the RAM's memory. It is then a straightforward matter to simulate the RAM using constant time for each instruction, plus some constant time for initialization.

Using RAMs, we now have a slightly different characterization of NP. Specifically, NP is the set of all decision problems X such that there exist

- polynomials $p(n)$ and $p'(n)$; and
- a RAM M deciding a problem $Y \subseteq I \times B$, where I is the set of instances for X;

such that

- M terminates within $p'(|x| + |\phi|)$ steps on input (x, ϕ);
- all memory locations of M maintain values strictly less than $2^{p'(|x|+|\phi|)}$ given input (x, ϕ);
- for each $x \in I$, $x \in X$ iff there is a proof $\phi \in B$ such that $(x, \phi) \in Y$; and
- for each $x \in X$, there is a $\phi \in B$ such that $(x, \phi) \in Y$ and $|\phi| \leq p(|x|)$.

Thus, to reduce an arbitrary problem $X \in NP$ to SAT, we need to construct from a given $x \in I$, where I is the set of instances of X, a boolean formula $\mathcal{F}$ such that $\mathcal{F}$ is satisfiable iff there is a $\phi \in B$ with $|\phi| \leq p(|x|)$ such that M outputs 1 on input (x, ϕ). Furthermore, the running time of the construction of $\mathcal{F}$ must be bounded by some polynomial in $|x|$. In designing the construction, we may utilize $p(n)$, $p'(n)$, and M, which depend only on the problem X; however, the instance x is the input for the construction, so that we cannot know it in advance.

Because we can use any polynomial-time M that decides Y, we can simplify matters further by making a couple of assumptions about M. First, we can assume that M contains at least one HALT(1) instruction — if there is no input yielding a "yes" answer, we can always include such an instruction at an unreachable location. Second, because statements that cannot be executed due to error conditions have the same effect as HALT(0), and because the instruction set is powerful enough to check any run-time error conditions, we can assume that all statements can be executed without error.

In addition, we make some simplifying assumptions regarding the polynomials p and p'. First, we note that by removing any negative terms from p', we obtain a polynomial that is nondecreasing and never less than the original polynomial. Thus, we can assume that p' is nondecreasing, so that $p'(|x|+p(|x|))$ will give an upper bound on the number of steps executed by M on an input (x, ϕ) with $|\phi| \leq p(|x|)$. Furthermore, because $p'(n+p(n))$ is a polynomial, we can assume that $p'(n)$ is an upper bound on the number of steps taken by M on any input (x, ϕ) such that $|x| = n$ and $|\phi| \leq p(n)$. Note that with these assumptions, $p'(n) \geq p(n)$ for all n. We can therefore choose $p(n) = p'(n)$, so that we can use a single polynomial p to bound both $|\phi|$ and the number of steps executed by M. Finally, we can choose p so that $p(n) \geq n$ for all $n \in \mathbb{N}$.

As the first step in our construction, we need boolean variables to represent the various components of the state of M at various times in its execution. First, we need variables describing the input sequences x and ϕ. For x, we will use the variables $\overline{x}[k]$ for $1 \leq k \leq n$, where n is the length of x. Because ϕ is unknown, even during the execution of the construction, we cannot know its exact length; however, we do know that its length is no more than $p(n)$. We therefore will use the variables $\overline{\phi}[k]$ for $1 \leq k \leq p(n)$ to represent ϕ.

We also need variables to keep track of which bits are unread at each step of the execution of M. For this purpose, we will use the variables $\widehat{x}_i[k]$ for $0 \leq i \leq p(n)$ and $0 \leq k \leq n$, plus the variables $\widehat{\phi}_i[k]$ for $0 \leq i \leq p(n)$ and $0 \leq k \leq p(n)$. We want $\widehat{x}_i[k]$ to be **true** iff the kth bit of x has not been read after i execution steps. Likewise, we want $\widehat{\phi}_i[k]$ to be **true** iff the kth bit of ϕ exists and has not been read after i execution steps.

We then need to record the value of the program counter at each execution step. We will use the variables p_{ij} for $0 \leq i \leq p(n)$ and $0 \leq j < P$ for this purpose, where P denotes the number of instructions in the program of M. We want p_{ij} to be true iff the program counter has a value of j after i execution steps.

Recording the values of the memory locations at each execution step presents more of a challenge. Because a memory location can contain any value less than $2^{p(n)}$, M can access any memory location with an address less than $2^{p(n)}$. If we were to construct variables for each of these locations, we would end up with exponentially many variables. We cannot hope to construct a formula containing this many variables in a polynomial amount of time. However, the number of memory locations accessed by any instruction is at most four — the number accessed by $\text{COPY}(*l_1, *l_2)$ in the worst case. As a result, M can access a total of no more than $4p(n)$ different memory locations. We can therefore use a technique similar to the implementation of a VARRAY (see Section 9.5) in order to keep track of the memory locations actually used.

Specifically, we will let the variables $a_j[k]$, for $1 \leq j \leq 4p(n)$ and $1 \leq k \leq p(n)$, denote the value of the kth bit of the address of some location l_j, where the first bit is the least significant bit. Here, we will let true represent 1 and false represent 0. Then the variables $v_{ij}[k]$, for $0 \leq i \leq p(n)$, $1 \leq j \leq 4p(n)$, and $1 \leq k \leq p(n)$, will record the value of the kth bit of the value stored at location l_j after i execution steps. We will make no requirement that location l_j actually be used by M, nor do we require that l_j be a different location from $l_{j'}$ when $j \neq j'$.

Finally, we will use the additional variables $c_i[0..p(n)]$ and $d_i[1..p(n)]$ for $1 \leq i \leq p(n)$. We will explain their purposes later.

Before we describe the formula $\mathcal{F}$ that we will construct, let us first define some abbreviations, or "macros", that will make the description of $\mathcal{F}$ simpler. First, we will define the following:

$$\text{IF}(y, z) = \neg y \vee z.$$

This abbreviation specifies that if y is true, then z must also be true. However, if y is false, then no constraint is placed upon z. Note that such an expression can be constructed in $O(1)$ time.

We can extend the above abbreviation to specify an if-then-else construct:

$$\text{IFELSE}(y, z_1, z_2) = \text{IF}(y, z_1) \wedge \text{IF}(\neg y, z_2).$$

This specifies that if y is true, then z_1 is true, but if not, then z_2 is true. Clearly it can be constructed in $O(1)$ time.

We will now define an abbreviation for the specification that two variables y and z are equal:

$$\text{EQ}(y, z) = \text{IFELSE}(y, z, \neg z).$$

Again, such an expression can be constructed in $O(1)$ time.

We can extend this abbreviation in a couple of ways. First, we can use one of the constants true or false in place of one of the variables. This will be useful, for example, if we want to specify that some variable has the same value as some specific bit of the input x, say $x[k]$. Because $x[k]$ is not a variable in the formula, it cannot appear in the formula; however, when we're designing the construction, we don't know this value. It would therefore be convenient to be able to write $\text{EQ}(y, x[k])$, and to let the construction fill in the appropriate value for $x[k]$. We then define

$$\text{EQ}(y, \text{true}) = y$$

and

$$\text{EQ}(y, \text{false}) = \neg y.$$

We can also extend the abbreviation to arrays of variables as follows:

$$\text{EQ}(y[1..n], z[1..n]) = \bigwedge_{k=1}^{n} \text{EQ}(y[k], z[k]).$$

Such an expression can be constructed in $O(n)$ time. For different sizes of arrays, the running time will be proportional to the number of elements. To aid in readability, we will typically drop the range of subscripts when the entire array is used.

When we specify the behavior of a program step, we need a way of checking to see if a_j records some particular memory location l. Let $l[1..p(n)]$ be the bits comprising l. We can check whether a given $a_j[1..p(n)] = l[1..p(n)]$ using the EQ abbreviation. However, we may in many cases need to check whether a_j records the memory location indirectly addressed by l. For this test, we use the following abbreviation:

$$\text{IND}(i, j, l) = \bigvee_{j'=1}^{4p(n)} (\text{EQ}(a_{j'}, l) \wedge \text{EQ}(a_j, v_{ij'})).$$

Because a_j, a_j', l, and $v_{ij'}$ are arrays of $p(n)$ elements, this expression can be constructed in $O(p^2(n))$ time.

Finally, we will need some abbreviations for specifying the behavior of arithmetic and comparison instructions. We can express all of these behaviors using the specification of a sum. Thus, we need to express that the sum of $y[1..p(n)]$ and $z[1..p(n)]$ is $s[1..p(n)]$. In order to express this constraint, we will need to represent the "carry" bits used to compute the sum. For this purpose, we will use the variables $c_i[0..p(n)]$ for some i. Specifically, for $1 \le k \le p(n)$, $c_i[k]$ will be the carry from the sum of $y[k]$, $z[k]$, and $c_i[k-1]$, and the value of $c_i[0]$ will be false, denoting 0.

We first observe that the low-order bit of the sum of $y[k]$, $z[k]$, and $c_i[k-1]$ is the exclusive-or of the three bits. We therefore first define an abbreviation for specifying exclusive-or:

$$\textsc{Xor}(y, z) = (y \vee z) \wedge \neg(y \wedge z).$$

We then observe that the carry bit of this sum is 1 iff at least two of the three bits are 1. Stated another way, the carry bit is 1 iff either

- both $y[k]$ and $z[k]$ are 1; or
- $c_i[k-1]$ is 1 and either $y[k]$ or $z[k]$ is 1.

We therefore define the following abbreviation:

$$\textsc{Sum}(y, z, s, i) = \neg c_i[0] \wedge \neg c_i[p(n)] \wedge$$

$$\bigwedge_{k=1}^{p(n)} (\textsc{Eq}(s[k], \textsc{Xor}(\textsc{Xor}(y[k], z[k]), c_i[k-1])) \wedge$$

$$\textsc{Eq}(c_i[k], (y[k] \wedge z[k]) \vee (c_i[k-1] \wedge (y[k] \vee z[k])))).$$

This expression states that $y[1..p(n)] + z[1..p(n)] = s[1..p(n)]$ and that $c_i[0..p(n)]$ give the carry bits of this sum. This expression can be constructed in $O(p(n))$ time.

Let us now begin to construct our formula $\mathcal{F}$. This formula will be the conjunction of a number of sub-formulas, each of which will specify some constraint on the values of the boolean variables. These constraints together will encode the requirement that M gives a "yes" answer on input (x, ϕ), where x is the given input for problem X. Because we will not specify the value of ϕ, the formula will be satisfiable iff there is some ϕ with length at most $p(n)$ such that M yields an output of 1 on (x, ϕ). Furthermore, we will show that we can construct this formula within a polynomial amount of time.

For the first constraint, we will specify that for $0 \le i \le p(n)$, there is at most one j such that p_{ij} is true. Thus, there will be no ambiguity as to the value of the program counter at each execution step. We specify this constraint with the sub-formula,

$$\mathcal{F}_1 = \bigwedge_{i=0}^{p(n)} \bigwedge_{j=0}^{P-2} \bigwedge_{j'=j+1}^{P-1} \text{IF}(p_{ij}, \neg p_{ij'}).$$

Because P is a constant depending only on the problem X, this sub-formula can be constructed in $O(p(n))$ time.

We now need to specify some initialization constraints. The first is simply that the program counter has an initial value of 0. We specify this constraint with the sub-formula,

$$\mathcal{F}_2 = p_{0,0}.$$

Clearly, this sub-formula can be constructed in $O(1)$ time.

We also need to specify that the variables $\overline{x}[1..n]$ encode the input string x. Let the kth bit of x be denoted by $x[k]$ for $1 \leq k \leq n$. We then construct

$$\mathcal{F}_3 = \text{EQ}(\overline{x}, x).$$

Because x and $\overline{x}$ are arrays of n elements, this sub-formula can be constructed in $O(n)$ time.

In addition, we need to specify that all bits in both input streams are initially unread. Notice that for each i, we have defined a variable $\widehat{x}_i[0]$, but there is no $\overline{x}[0]$. The purpose of these variables is so that whenever $x[k]$ is the next bit to be read, $\widehat{x}_i[k-1]$ is false and $\widehat{x}_i[k]$ is true. In order to enforce this constraint initially, we construct

$$\mathcal{F}_4 = \neg\widehat{x}_0[0] \wedge \bigwedge_{k=1}^{n} \widehat{x}_0[k].$$

Clearly, this sub-formula can be constructed in $O(n)$ time.

We need a similar specification for ϕ; however, we don't know the exact length of ϕ. We want $\widehat{\phi}_0[k]$ to be true iff $1 \leq k \leq |\phi|$. Thus, we need $\widehat{\phi}_0[0]$ to be false. Then as k increases, $\widehat{\phi}_0[k]$ may be true for a while, but as soon as we encounter a false $\widehat{\phi}_0[k]$, these variables must be false for all greater values of k. We can enforce this constraint with the following sub-formula:

$$\mathcal{F}_5 = \neg\widehat{\phi}_0[0] \wedge \bigwedge_{k=1}^{p(n)-1} \text{IF}(\neg\widehat{\phi}_0[k], \neg\widehat{\phi}_0[k+1]).$$

We can clearly construct this sub-formula in $O(p(n))$ time.

As the final initialization specification, we need to specify that all memory locations are initially 0. We therefore construct

$$\mathcal{F}_6 = \bigwedge_{j=1}^{4p(n)\,p(n)} \bigwedge_{k=1}^{p(n)} \neg v_{0,j}[k].$$

Clearly, we can construct this sub-formula in $O(p^2(n))$ time.

We now need a constraint specifying that at some point, a HALT(1) instruction is executed. Let A be the set of program locations at which a HALT(1) instruction appears. We then construct

$$\mathcal{F}_7 = \bigvee_{i=0}^{p(n)-1} \bigvee_{j\in A} p_{ij}.$$

Because the size of A depends only on the problem X, this sub-formula can be constructed in $O(p(n))$ time.

To complete the formula, we need constraints specifying the correct behavior of M. To this end, we will construct one sub-formula for each instruction in the program of M. These sub-formulas will depend on the particular instruction. Let $0 \le q < P$, where P is the number of instructions in the program. In what follows, we will describe how the sub-formula $\mathcal{F}'_q$ is constructed depending on the instruction at program location q.

Regardless of the specific instruction, the sub-formula will have the same general form. In each case, $\mathcal{F}'_q$ must specify that some particular behavior occurs whenever the program counter has a value of q. $\mathcal{F}'_q$ will therefore have the following form:

$$\mathcal{F}'_p = \bigwedge_{i=1}^{p(n)} \text{IF}(p_{i-1,q}, \psi_q(i)), \tag{16.1}$$

where $\psi_q(i)$ is a predicate specifying the result of executing the ith instruction.

Each $\psi_q(i)$ will be a conjunction of predicates, each specifying some aspect of the result of executing the ith instruction. In particular, $\psi_q(i)$ will be the conjunction of the following predicates:

- $\mathcal{U}_q(i)$, which specifies how the memory locations are updated;
- $\mathcal{E}_q(i)$, which specifies what memory locations must be represented in $\mathcal{F}$ in order for this instruction to be simulated (this specification is needed to prevent $\mathcal{U}_q(i)$ from being vacuously satisfied);
- $\mathcal{I}_q(i)$, which specifies which input bits remain unread; and

- $\mathcal{P}_q(i)$, which specifies the new value of the program counter.

$\psi_q(i)$ is then defined as follows:

$$\psi_q(i) = \mathcal{U}_q(i) \wedge \mathcal{E}_q(i) \wedge \mathcal{I}_q(i) \wedge \mathcal{P}_q(i). \tag{16.2}$$

There are some instances of the above predicates that occur for more than one type of instruction.

- If the instruction at location q is not an INPUT instruction, then

$$\mathcal{I}_q(i) = \text{EQ}(\widehat{x}_i, \widehat{x}_{i-1}) \wedge \text{EQ}(\widehat{\phi}_i, \widehat{\phi}_{i-1}). \tag{16.3}$$

- If this instruction is neither a GOTO, an IFLEQ, nor a HALT, then

$$\mathcal{P}_q(i) = p_{i,q+1}. \tag{16.4}$$

- If this instruction is either a GOTO or a HALT, then

$$\mathcal{U}_q(i) = \bigwedge_{j=1}^{4p(n)} \text{EQ}(v_{ij}, v_{i-1,j}), \tag{16.5}$$

and

$$\mathcal{E}_q(i) = \mathsf{true}. \tag{16.6}$$

In what follows, we will define the remaining predicates for several of the possible instructions. We leave the remaining cases as exercises.

Let us first consider an instruction LOAD(n, l). Because l is the only memory location that is accessed, we can define

$$\mathcal{E}_q(i) = \bigvee_{j=1}^{4p(n)} \text{EQ}(a_j, l).$$

Because its value changes to n, we can define

$$\mathcal{U}_q(i) = \bigwedge_{j=1}^{4p(n)} \text{IFELSE}(\text{EQ}(a_j, l), \text{EQ}(v_{ij}, n), \text{EQ}(v_{ij}, v_{i-1,j})).$$

Note that the above expression specifies that every v_{ij} such that $a_j = l$ has its value changed to n.

Let us now compute the time needed to construct the resulting sub-formula $\mathcal{F}'_q$. Because the arrays a_j and l each contain $p(n)$ elements, $\mathcal{E}_q(i, j)$ can be constructed in $O(p^2(n))$ time. It is not hard to verify that $\mathcal{U}_q(i)$ can be constructed in $O(p^2(n))$ time as well. Clearly, $\mathcal{P}_q(i)$ as defined in (16.4) can be constructed in $O(1)$ time. Finally, $\mathcal{I}_q(i)$ as defined in (16.3) can be constructed in $O(p(n))$ time. Thus, $\psi_q(i)$ can be constructed in $O(p^2(n))$ time. The sub-formula $\mathcal{F}'_q$ can therefore be constructed in $O(p^3(n))$ time.

We can handle an instruction $\text{LOAD}(n, *l)$ in a similar way, but using the IND abbreviation. Thus, we define

$$\mathcal{E}_q(i) = \bigvee_{j=1}^{4p(n)} \text{IND}(i-1, j, l),$$

and

$$\mathcal{U}_q(i) = \bigwedge_{j=1}^{4p(n)} \text{IF}(\text{IND}(i-1, j, l), \text{EQ}(v_{ij}, n), \text{EQ}(v_{ij}, v_{i-1,j})).$$

In this case, $\mathcal{E}_q(i)$ and $\mathcal{U}_q(i)$ can be constructed in $O(p^3(n))$ time, so that $\mathcal{F}'_q$ can be constructed in $O(p^4(n))$ time.

Let us now consider an instruction $\text{IFLEQ}(l_1, l_2, q')$. Because the memory locations l_1 and l_2 are referenced, we define

$$\mathcal{E}_q = \bigvee_{j=1}^{4p(n)} \text{EQ}(a_j, l_1) \wedge \bigvee_{j=1}^{4p(n)} \text{EQ}(a_j, l_2).$$

This statement will cause the program counter to be set to q' if the value stored at l_1 is less than or equal to the value stored at l_2; otherwise, the program counter will be set to $q + 1$. We first observe that for natural numbers v_1 and v_2, $v_1 \leq v_2$ iff $v_2 - v_1 \geq 0$. We can therefore use the variable d_i to record $|v_2 - v_1|$ using the SUM abbreviation as follows:

$$\mathcal{U}_q(i) = \bigwedge_{j=1}^{4p(n)} \text{EQ}(v_{ij}, v_{i-1,j})$$

$$\wedge \bigwedge_{j=1}^{4p(n)} \bigwedge_{j'=1}^{4p(n)} \text{IF}(\text{EQ}(a_j, l_1) \wedge \text{EQ}(a_{j'}, l_2),$$

$$\text{SUM}(v_{ij}, d_i, v_{ij'}) \vee \text{SUM}(v_{ij'}, d_i, v_{ij})).$$

We can now define $\mathcal{P}_q(i)$ as follows:

$$\mathcal{P}_q(i) = \text{IFELSE} \left(\bigvee_{j=1}^{4p(n)} \bigvee_{j'=1}^{4p(n)} \text{EQ}(a_j, l_1) \wedge \text{EQ}(a_{j'}, l_2) \wedge \text{SUM}(v_{ij}, d_i, v_{ij'}), \right.$$

$$\left. p_{iq'}, p_{i,q+1} \right).$$

$\mathcal{E}_q(i)$ can be constructed in $O(p^2(n))$ time, and both $\mathcal{U}_q(i)$ and $\mathcal{P}_q(i)$ can be constructed in $O(p^3(n))$ time. Furthermore, $\mathcal{I}_q(i)$ as given in (16.3) can be constructed in $O(p(n))$ time. The total time needed to construct $\mathcal{F}'_q$ is therefore in $O(p^4(n))$.

Finally, let us consider a HALT instruction. For a HALT instruction, we have already defined $\mathcal{I}_q(i)$ (16.3), $\mathcal{U}_q(i)$ (16.5), and $\mathcal{E}_q(i)$ (16.6). To define $\mathcal{P}_q(i)$, we need to specify that for all $i' > i$, each $p_{i'j}$ is false:

$$\mathcal{P}_q(i) = \bigwedge_{i'=i+1}^{p(n)} \bigwedge_{j=0}^{P-1} \neg p_{i'j}.$$

Because P is a constant depending only on X, $\mathcal{P}_q(i)$ can be constructed in $O(p(n))$ time. Furthermore, $\mathcal{I}_q(i)$ can be constructed in $O(p(n))$ time, $\mathcal{U}_q(i)$ can be constructed in $O(p^2(n))$ time, and $\mathcal{E}_q(i)$ can be constructed in $O(1)$ time. The sub-formula $\mathcal{F}'_q$ can therefore be constructed in $O(p^3(n))$ time.

We leave it as exercises to show that the sub-formula $\mathcal{F}'_q$ can be constructed for each of the other cases in a time in $O(p^5(n))$. We now define the formula $\mathcal{F}$ as the conjunction of all of the sub-formulas:

$$\mathcal{F} = \bigwedge_{q=1}^{7} \mathcal{F}_q \wedge \bigwedge_{q=0}^{P-1} \mathcal{F}'_q.$$

Because P is a constant depending only on X, $\mathcal{F}$ can be constructed in $O(p^5(n))$ time.

We must now show that $\mathcal{F}$ is satisfiable iff there is some $\phi \in \mathcal{B}$ such that M executes a HALT(1) instruction on input (x, ϕ). Suppose $\mathcal{F}$ is satisfiable. Let us fix some satisfying assignment to the variables of $\mathcal{F}$. Because $\mathcal{F}_5$ must be true by this assignment, there must be some k, $1 \leq k \leq p(n)$, such that $\widehat{\phi}[k']$ is true for $1 \leq k' \leq k$ and $\widehat{\phi}[k']$ is false for $k < k' \leq p(n)$. Let $\phi = \overline{\phi}[1..k]$. By the above construction, for $1 \leq i \leq p(n)$ and $0 \leq j < P$, p_{ij} is true iff the ith instruction executed by M on input (x, ϕ) is the instruction at program location j. Finally, because $\mathcal{F}_7$ must be satisfied, one of these instructions must be a HALT(1) instruction.

Now suppose that for some $\phi \in \mathcal{B}$, M executes a HALT(1) instruction on input (x, ϕ). By our choice of the polynomial $p(n)$, we can assume that $|\phi| \leq p(|x|)$. Let us now set $\overline{x} = x$ and $\overline{\phi}[1..|\phi|] = \phi$. We will also set $\widehat{\phi}[k] = \mathsf{true}$ for $1 \leq k \leq |\phi|$ and $\widehat{\phi}[k] = \mathsf{false}$ for $|\phi| < k \leq p(n)$. We can clearly assign truth values to the variables in the sub-formulas $\mathcal{F}_q$ for $2 \leq q \leq 6$ so that all of these sub-formulas are satisfied. By the above construction, we can then assign truth values to the variables in each of the sub-formulas $\mathcal{F}'_q$ for $1 \leq q \leq p(n)$ so that these formulas, along with $\mathcal{F}_1$, are satisfied. Such an assignment will yield $p_{ij} = \mathsf{true}$ iff p_j is the ith instruction executed by M on input (x, ϕ). Because M executes a HALT(1) instruction on this input, $\mathcal{F}_7$ must also be satisfied. Therefore, $\mathcal{F}$ is satisfied by this assignment.

We have therefore shown that $X \leq_m^p \text{SAT}$. Because X can be any problem in $\mathcal{N P}$, it follows that SAT is $\mathcal{N P}$-hard. Because SAT $\in \mathcal{N P}$, it follows that SAT is $\mathcal{N P}$-complete.

16.9 Summary

The $\mathcal{N P}$-complete problems comprise a large class of decision problems for which no polynomial-time algorithms are known. Furthermore, if a polynomial time algorithm were found for any one of these problems, we would be able to construct polynomial-time algorithms for all of them. For this reason, along with many others that are beyond the scope of this book, we tend to believe that none of these problems can be solved in polynomial time. Note, however, that this conjecture has not been proven. Indeed, this question — whether $\mathcal{P} = \mathcal{N P}$ — is the most famous open question in theoretical computer science.

Proofs of $\mathcal{N P}$-completeness consist of two parts: membership in $\mathcal{N P}$ and $\mathcal{N P}$-hardness. Without knowledge of any $\mathcal{N P}$-complete problems, it is quite tedious to prove a problem to be $\mathcal{N P}$-hard. However, given one or more $\mathcal{N P}$-complete problems, the task of proving additional problems to be $\mathcal{N P}$-hard is greatly eased using polynomial-time many-one reductions.

Some general guidelines for finding a reduction from a known $\mathcal{N P}$-complete problem to a problem known to be in $\mathcal{N P}$ are as follows:

- Look for a known $\mathcal{N P}$-complete problem that has similarities with the problem in question.
- If all else fails, try reducing from 3-SAT.

- Look at the proofs of membership in $\mathcal{NP}$ and try to transform proofs $\phi \in \mathcal{B}$ for the known $\mathcal{NP}$-complete problem to proofs $\phi' \in \mathcal{B}$ for the problem in question.

Large numbers play an interesting role in the theory of $\mathcal{NP}$-completeness. In particular, some problems become $\mathcal{NP}$-hard simply because very large numbers can be given as input using comparatively few bits. The definitions of strong $\mathcal{NP}$-completeness and strong $\mathcal{NP}$-hardness exclude such problems. A refinement of polynomial many-one reducibility, namely, pseudopolynomial reducibility, is used to prove strong $\mathcal{NP}$-hardness.

16.10 Exercises

Exercise 16.1. Prove that if X, Y, and Z are decision problems such that $X \leq_m^p Y$ and $Y \leq_m^p Z$, then $X \leq_m^p Z$.

Exercise 16.2. Adapt BoolEval (Figure 16.2) to evaluate a CNF expression $\mathcal{F}$ in $O(|\mathcal{F}|)$ time.

Exercise 16.3. Implement the reduction from CSAT to 3-SAT, as outlined in Section 16.4, to run in $O(n)$ time, where n is the size of the given CNF formula.

Exercise 16.4. Give an algorithm that takes as input an undirected graph G, a natural number k, and an array $A[0..m-1]$ of booleans, and determines whether A denotes a vertex cover of G with size k. Your algorithm must run in $O(n + a)$ time, where n and a are the number of vertices and edges, respectively, of G. For the purpose of analyzing the running time, you may assume that G is implemented as a ListGraph.

Exercise 16.5. Implement the reduction from 3-SAT to VC, as outlined in Section 16.5, to run in $O(m + n)$ time, where m is the number of variables and n is the number of clauses in the given 3-CNF formula.

* Exercise 16.6. Let NotAllEqual-3-SAT be the problem of deciding, for a given 3-CNF formula f, whether there is an assignment of boolean variables such that each clause in f contains at least one true literal and at least one false literal. Prove that this problem is $\mathcal{NP}$-complete.

Exercise 16.7. A *clique* is a complete undirected graph — i.e., a graph such that for every pair of distinct vertices u and v, $\{u, v\}$ is an edge. The *clique problem* (Clique) is the problem of deciding, for a given undirected graph G and natural number k, if G has a subgraph that is a clique with k vertices. Show that CLIQUE is $\mathcal{NP}$-complete.

Exercise 16.8. Two graphs G and G' are said to be *isomorphic* if the vertices of G can be renamed so that the resulting graph is G'. Given two graphs G and G' and a natural number k, we wish to decide whether G and G' contain isomorphic subgraphs with k vertices. Show that this problem is $\mathcal{NP}$-complete. You may use the result of Exercise 16.7.

** Exercise 16.9. A *Hamiltonian cycle* in a graph G is a cycle that contains each vertex in G exactly once. Prove that the problem of deciding whether a given undirected graph contains a Hamiltonian cycle is $\mathcal{NP}$-complete. [**Hint:** Reduce VC to this problem.]

Exercise 16.10. Repeat Exercise 16.9 for directed graphs. You may use the result of Exercise 16.9.

Exercise 16.11. As was defined in Exercise 10.35, a *Hamiltonian path* in a graph G is a simple path that contains each vertex in G exactly once. Prove that the problem of deciding whether a given undirected graph has a Hamiltonian path is $\mathcal{NP}$-complete. You may use the results of Exercises 16.9 and 16.10.

Exercise 16.12. Repeat Exercise 16.11 for directed graphs. You may use the results of Exercises 16.9–16.11.

Exercise 16.13. Given a directed graph $G = (V, E)$ and a positive integer k, we wish to determine whether there is a subset $V' \subseteq V$ of size k such that every cycle in G contains at least one vertex in V'. Show that this problem is $\mathcal{NP}$-complete.

* Exercise 16.14. Given an undirected graph $G = (V, E)$ and a positive integer k, we wish to decide whether V can be partitioned into two disjoint sets, V_1 and V_2, such that V_1 contains exactly k vertices and for every vertex $u \in V_2$, there is a vertex $v \in V_1$ such that $\{u, v\} \in E$. Show that this problem is $\mathcal{NP}$-complete.

Exercise 16.15. Give an algorithm that takes an instance (X, Y, Z, W) of 3DM and a bit string ϕ and determines whether ϕ is a proof that (X, Y, Z, W) has a matching, as defined in Section 16.6. You may assume that (X, Y, Z, W) is represented by a natural number m and an array $W[1..n]$ of triples of the form (i, j, k) such that $m \leq n$ and each i, j, and k is a positive integer no greater than m. Your algorithm should run in $O(m^2 \lg n)$ time.

Exercise 16.16. Given a finite sequence of finite sets and a natural number k, we wish to decide whether the sequence contains at least k mutually disjoint sets. Show that this problem is $\mathcal{NP}$-complete.

Exercise 16.17. Prove that PART, as defined in Section 16.7, is in $\mathcal{NP}$.

Exercise 16.18. Suppose we modify the 0-1 knapsack problem (see Section 12.4) by including a target value V as an additional input. The problem then is to decide whether there is a subset of the items whose total weight does not exceed the weight bound W and whose total value is at least V. Prove that this problem is $\mathcal{NP}$-complete.

Exercise 16.19. Suppose we are given a set of items $a_1, \ldots, a_n$, each having a positive integer weight w_i, and positive integers k and W. We wish to decide whether the items can be partitioned into k mutually disjoint subsets $A_1, \ldots, A_k$, such that

$$\sum_{j=1}^{k} \left(\sum_{a_i \in A_j} w_i \right)^2 \leq W.$$

Show that this problem is $\mathcal{NP}$-complete.

** Exercise 16.20. Suppose we are given a sequence $S_1, \ldots, S_n$ of finite sets. We wish to partition

$$\bigcup_{i=1}^{n} S_i$$

into two disjoint sets S and S' such that for $1 \leq i \leq n$, $S_i \not\subseteq S$ and $S_i \not\subseteq S'$. Show that this problem is $\mathcal{NP}$-complete. [***Hint:*** Reduce 3-SAT to this problem.]

** Exercise 16.21. Suppose we are given an undirected graph $G = (V, E)$ with exactly $3k$ vertices. We wish to partition V into k disjoint subsets such that each subset forms a path of length 2 in G. Show that this problem is $\mathcal{NP}$-complete. [***Hint:*** Reduce 3DM to this problem.]

** Exercise 16.22. Given a directed graph $G = (V, E)$, we wish to decide whether each vertex $v_i \in V$ can be assigned a label $L_i \in \mathbb{N}$ such that L_i is the least natural number that is not in the set

$$\{L_j \mid (v_i, v_j) \in E\}.$$

Show that this problem is $\mathcal{NP}$-complete. [***Hint:*** Reduce 3-SAT to this problem.]

** **Exercise 16.23.** Show that the problem of deciding whether a given undirected graph has a 3-coloring is NP-complete. (See Exercise 13.12 for the definition of a 3-coloring.) [**Hint:** Reduce 3-SAT to this problem.]

Exercise 16.24. Show that the problem of deciding whether a given undirected graph has a k-coloring is NP-complete for each fixed $k \geq 4$. You may use the result of Exercise 16.23.

** **Exercise 16.25.** Certain aspects of the board game Axis and Allies^{TM} can be modeled as follows. The game is played on an undirected graph. The playing pieces include fighters and aircraft carriers, each of which has a natural number range. These pieces are each assigned to a vertex of the graph. Each vertex may be assigned any number of pieces. A combat scenario is valid if it is possible to move each piece to a new vertex (possibly the same one) so that

- for each move, the distance (i.e., number of edges) from the starting vertex to the ending vertex is no more than the range of piece moved; and
- after the pieces are moved, each vertex has no more than twice as many fighters as aircraft carriers.

Prove that the problem of determining whether a combat scenario is valid is NP-complete.

Exercise 16.26. Let k-PART be as defined in Section 16.7.

   a. Prove that k-PART $\in NP$ for all $k \geq 1$.
b. Prove that 3-PART is NP-complete in the strong sense. [Hint:** Show that 4-PART $\leq_m^{pp}$ 3-PART.]
   c. Prove that 2-PART $\in P$.

Exercise 16.27. The *bin packing* (BP) problem is to decide whether a given set of items, each having a weight w_i, can be partitioned into k disjoint sets each having a total weight of at most W, where k and W are given positive integers. Show that BP is NP-complete in the strong sense.

Exercise 16.28. Suppose we are given a complete undirected graph G with positive integer edge weights and a positive integer k. The *traveling salesperson problem* (TSP) is to determine whether there is a Hamiltonian cycle in G with total weight no more than k. Show that this problem is NP-complete in the strong sense. You may use the result of Exercise 16.9.

* **Exercise 16.29.** We are given a set of n tasks, each having an execution time $e_i \in \mathbb{N}$, a ready time $r_i \in \mathbb{N}$, and a deadline $d_i \in \mathbb{N}$. We wish to decide

whether there is a non-preemptive schedule that meets the constraints of all of the tasks. In other words, we wish to know if there is a function $f : [1..n] \to \mathbb{N}$ such that for $1 \leq i \leq n$,

- $r_i \leq f(i)$;
- $f(i) + e_i \leq d_i$; and
- for $1 \leq j \leq i$ and $j \neq i$, either $f(j) + e_j \leq f(i)$ or $f(j) \geq f(i) + e_i$.

Show that this problem is $\mathcal{NP}$-complete in the strong sense.

* Exercise 16.30. We are given an undirected graph $G = (V, E)$, a sequence $\langle w_1, \ldots, w_{|E|} \rangle$ of natural numbers, and a positive integer k. We wish to decide whether there is a 1-1 function $f : E \to \{1, \ldots, |E|\}$ such that if each edge $e \in E$ is assigned a length of $w_{f(e)}$, then for every pair of vertices u and v, there is a path from u to v with length at most k. Prove that this problem is $\mathcal{NP}$-complete in the strong sense.

Exercise 16.31. Define the predicate $\mathcal{P}_q(i)$ for the case in which the instruction at location q is $\mathrm{GOTO}(q')$. Show that the resulting sub-formula $\mathcal{F}'_q$ can be constructed in $O(p(n))$ time.

Exercise 16.32. Define the predicates $\mathcal{E}_q(i)$ and $\mathcal{U}_q(i)$ for the case in which the instruction at location q is $\mathrm{COPY}(l_1, l_2)$. Show that the resulting sub-formula $\mathcal{F}'_q$ can be constructed in $O(p^4(n))$ time.

Exercise 16.33. Define the predicates $\mathcal{E}_q(i)$ and $\mathcal{U}_q(i)$ for the case in which the instruction at location q is $\mathrm{COPY}(*l_1, *l_2)$. Show that the resulting sub-formula $\mathcal{F}'_q$ can be constructed in $O(p^5(n))$ time.

Exercise 16.34. Define the predicates $\mathcal{E}_q(i)$, $\mathcal{U}_q(i)$, and $\mathcal{P}_q(i)$ for the case in which the instruction at location q is $\mathrm{IFLEQ}(*l_1, *l_2, q')$. Show that the resulting sub-formula $\mathcal{F}'_q$ can be constructed in $O(p^5(n))$ time.

Exercise 16.35. Define the predicates $\mathcal{E}_q(i)$ and $\mathcal{U}_q(i)$ for the case in which the instruction at location q is $\mathrm{ADD}(*l_1, *l_2)$. Show that the resulting sub-formula $\mathcal{F}'_q$ can be constructed in $O(p^5(n))$ time.

Exercise 16.36. Define the predicates $\mathcal{E}_q(i)$ and $\mathcal{U}_q(i)$ for the case in which the instruction at location q is $\mathrm{SUBTRACT}(*l_1, *l_2)$. Show that the resulting sub-formula $\mathcal{F}'_q$ can be constructed in $O(p^5(n))$ time.

Exercise 16.37. Define the predicates $\mathcal{E}_q(i)$ and $\mathcal{U}_q(i)$ for the case in which the instruction at location q is $\mathrm{SHIFT}(*l)$. Show that the resulting sub-formula $\mathcal{F}'_q$ can be constructed in $O(p^4(n))$ time.

* Exercise 16.38. Define the predicates $\mathcal{I}_q(i)$, $\mathcal{E}_q(i)$, and $\mathcal{U}_q(i)$ for the case in which the instruction at location q is INPUT$(1, *l)$. Show that the resulting sub-formula $\mathcal{F}'_q$ can be constructed in $O(p^5(n))$ time.

16.11 Notes

$\mathcal{NP}$-completeness was introduced by Cook [23], who proved that SAT and CSAT are $\mathcal{NP}$-complete. Karp [78] then demonstrated the importance of this topic by proving $\mathcal{NP}$-completeness of 21 problems, including VC, 3DM, PART, and the problems described in Exercises 16.7, 16.9, 16.10, 16.13, 16.16, 16.18, and 16.23. The original definition of $\mathcal{NP}$ was somewhat different from the one given here — it was based on non-deterministic Turing machines, rather than on algorithms or RAMs. The definition given in Section 16.1 is based on a definition given by Brassard and Bratley [17]. All of these definitions are equivalent.

SAT is an example of an $\mathcal{NP}$-complete problem for which practical algorithms exist. Even though each of these algorithms requires exponential time in the worst case, they have been used to solve large instances arising in fields such as software verification and scheduling. For a survey of SAT-solvers, see Gong and Zhou [58].

The notion of strong $\mathcal{NP}$-completeness was introduced by Garey and Johnson [53]. They provided the definitions of strong $\mathcal{NP}$-completeness, pseudopolynomial algorithms, and pseudopolynomial reductions. They had earlier given $\mathcal{NP}$-completeness proofs for k-PART for $k \geq 3$ [51] and for the problem described in Exercise 16.29 [52]. As it turned out, their reductions were pseudopolynomial. Their book on $\mathcal{NP}$-completeness [54] is an excellent resource.

Exercise 16.20 is solved by Lovasz [91]. Exercise 16.21 is solved by Kirkpatrick and Hell [79]. Exercise 16.22 is solved by van Leeuwen [115]. The solution to Exercise 16.30 is attributed to Perl and Zaks by Garey and Johnson [54].

Axis and Allies[TM] (mentioned in Exercise 16.25) is a registered trademark of Hasbro, Inc.

Chapter 17

Approximation Algorithms

In Chapter 16, we examined decision problems that appear to be intractable. As we might expect, there are other types of problems that are also intractable. For example, consider the following version of the vertex cover problem (cf. Section 16.5). Instead of being given a target size as input, we are given simply an undirected graph from which we must find a vertex cover of minimum size. Let us call this optimization problem VCOPT. We can easily reduce VC to VCOPT, though because an optimization problem is not a decision problem, the reduction is not a many-one reduction. However, it is clear that if VCOPT has a polynomial-time solution, then so does VC. We can therefore conclude that unless $\mathcal{P} = \mathcal{NP}$, VCOPT cannot be solved in polynomial time.

With hard optimization problems, however, it may not be necessary to obtain an exact solution. In this chapter, we will explore techniques for obtaining approximate solutions to hard optimization problems. We will see that for some problems, we can obtain reasonable approximation algorithms. On the other hand, we will use the theory of $\mathcal{NP}$-completeness to show limitations to these techniques. Before looking at specific problems, however, we must first extend some of the definitions from Chapter 16 to include problems other than decision problems.

17.1 Polynomial Turing Reducibility

In this section, we will extend the definition of $\mathcal{NP}$-hardness to include problems that are not decision problems. As we have already observed, we can reduce VC to VCOPT in a way that proves that VCOPT cannot be solved in polynomial time unless $\mathcal{P} = \mathcal{NP}$; however, this reduction is not a many-one reduction. We will therefore define a new kind of reducibility that will include this kind of reduction.

Suppose we can reduce a problem X to another problem Y in such a way that for some polynomial $p(n)$ and any instance x of X:

- the time required to obtain a solution for x, excluding any time needed to solve instances of Y, is bounded above by $p(|x|)$; and
- the values of all variables are bounded above by $p(|x|)$.

We then say that X is *polynomially Turing reducible* to Y, or $X \leq_T^p Y$. Note that if $X \leq_m^p Y$, then clearly $X \leq_T^p Y$.

It is easily seen that VC $\leq_T^p$ VCOPT. More generally, consider any minimization problem Y with objective function f. We can construct a decision problem X from Y by adding an additional natural number input, k. X is simply the set of all pairs (y, k) such that y is an instance of Y with a candidate solution s for which $f(s) \leq k$. It is easily seen that $X \leq_T^p Y$, for if we can find the minimum value of f for a given instance y, then we can quickly decide whether there is a candidate solution s for which $f(s) \leq k$.

We can now extend the notion of $\mathcal{NP}$-hardness by saying that Y is $\mathcal{NP}$-hard with respect to Turing reducibility if for every $X \in \mathcal{NP}$, $X \leq_T^p Y$. Note that we have not modified the definition of $\mathcal{NP}$ — it contains only decision problems. As a result, it makes no sense to extend the definition of $\mathcal{NP}$-completeness beyond decision problems. Because $\mathcal{NP}$-hardness with respect to Turing reducibility is the natural version of $\mathcal{NP}$-hardness to use when discussing optimization problems, we will simply refer to this version as "$\mathcal{NP}$-hardness" in this chapter. The following theorem can now be shown in a manner similar to the proof of Theorem 16.2.

Theorem 17.1. *If $X \leq_T^p Y$ and there is a deterministic polynomial-time algorithm for solving Y, then there is a deterministic polynomial-time algorithm for solving X.*

The above theorem shows that if there is a deterministic polynomial-time algorithm for solving an $\mathcal{NP}$-hard problem Y, then there is a deterministic polynomial-time algorithm for deciding every problem in $\mathcal{NP}$. We therefore have the following corollary, which highlights the importance of the notion of $\mathcal{NP}$ hardness with respect to Turing reducibility.

Corollary 17.2. *If Y is $\mathcal{NP}$-hard and there is a deterministic polynomial-time algorithm for solving Y, then $\mathcal{P} = \mathcal{NP}$.*

17.2 Knapsack

The first problem we will examine is the 0-1 knapsack problem, as defined in Section 12.4. As is suggested by Exercise 16.18, the associated decision problem is $\mathcal{NP}$-complete; hence, the optimization problem is $\mathcal{NP}$-hard.

Consider the following greedy strategy for filling the knapsack. Suppose we take an item whose ratio of value to weight is maximum. If this item won't fit, we discard it and solve the remaining problem. Otherwise, we include it in the knapsack and solve the problem that results from removing this item and decreasing the capacity by its weight. We have thus reduced the problem to a smaller instance of itself. Clearly, this strategy results in a set of items whose total weight does not exceed the weight bound. Furthermore, it is not hard to implement this strategy in $O(n \lg n)$ time, where n is the number of items.

Because the problem is $\mathcal{NP}$-hard, we would not expect this greedy strategy to yield an optimal solution in all cases. What we need is a way to measure how good an approximation to an optimal solution it provides. In order to motivate an analysis, let us consider a simple example. Consider the following instance consisting of two items:

- The first item has weight 1 and value 2.
- The second item has weight 10 and value 10.
- The weight bound is 10.

The value-to-weight ratios of the two items are 2 and 1, respectively. The greedy algorithm therefore takes the first item first. Because the second item will no longer fit, the solution provided by the greedy algorithm consists of the first item by itself. The value of this solution is 2. However, it is easily seen that the optimal solution is the second item by itself. This solution has a value of 10.

A common way of measuring the quality of an approximation is to form a ratio with the actual value. Specifically, for a maximization problem, we define the *approximation ratio* of a given approximation to be the ratio of the optimal value to the approximation. Thus, the approximation ratio for the above example is 5. For a minimization problem, we use the reciprocal of this ratio, so that the approximation ratio is always at least 1. As the approximation ratio approaches 1, the approximation approaches the optimal value.

Note that for a minimization problem, the approximation ratio cannot take a finite value if the optimal value is 0. For this reason, we will restrict our attention to optimization problems whose optimal solutions always make their objective functions positive. In addition, we will restrict our attention to problems whose objective functions have integer values for all candidate solutions.

We would like to show some fixed upper bound on the approximation ratio of our greedy algorithm. However, we can modify the above example by replacing 10 with an arbitrarily large x in order to achieve an arbitrarily large approximation ratio of $x/2$. Thus, this approximation algorithm can perform arbitrarily poorly.

With a bit more work, however, we can modify this algorithm so that it has a bounded approximation ratio. Specifically, we find n different packings and take the one with the highest value. For the ith packing, we take the ith item first, then apply the greedy strategy to finish the packing. Thus, we expend additional work in making sure that we get started correctly. The algorithm is shown in Figure 17.1. For simplicity, we assume that the

---

Figure 17.1   An approximation algorithm for the 0-1 knapsack problem

---

Precondition: W is a positive NAT, $n \geq 1$, and $w[1..n]$ and $v[1..n]$ are arrays of positive NATs such that for $1 \leq i \leq j \leq n$, $v[i]/w[i] \geq v[j]/w[j]$ and $w[i] \leq W$.

Postcondition: Returns an array $A[1..n]$ of BOOLs such that if

$$S = \{i \mid 1 \leq i \leq n, A[i] = \text{true}\},$$

then

$$\sum_{i \in S} w[i] \leq W.$$

KNAPSACKAPPROX($W, w[1..n], v[1..n]$)
    $maxValue \leftarrow 0$
    for $i \leftarrow 1$ **to** n
        $A \leftarrow$ **new** ARRAY$[1..n]$
        for $j \leftarrow 1$ **to** n
            $A[j] \leftarrow$ false
        $A[i] \leftarrow$ true; $value \leftarrow v[i]$; $weight \leftarrow w[i]$
        for $j \leftarrow 1$ **to** n
            if $j \neq i$ **and** $weight + w[j] \leq W$
                $weight \leftarrow weight + w[j]$; $value \leftarrow value + v[j]$; $A[j] \leftarrow$ true
        if $value > maxValue$
            $M \leftarrow A$
    return M

items are given in nondecreasing order of value-to-weight ratios, and that no item's weight exceeds the weight bound. It is easily seen that this algorithm produces a solution in $\Theta(n^2)$ time. The following theorem shows how well it approximates an optimal solution in the worst case.

Theorem 17.3. KNAPSACKAPPROX *yields an approximation ratio of at most 2 on all inputs that satisfy the precondition. Furthermore, for every $\epsilon \in \mathbb{R}^{>0}$, there is some input for which the approximation ratio is at least $2 - \epsilon$.*

Proof. We begin by showing the lower bound. Let $\epsilon \in \mathbb{R}^{>0}$, and without loss of generality, assume $\epsilon < 1$. We first define the weight bound as

$$W = 2 \left\lceil \frac{4}{\epsilon} \right\rceil.$$

We then construct the following set of three items:

- The first item has weight 1 and value 2.
- The second and third items each have a weight and value of $W/2$.

The optimal solution clearly consists of the second and third items. This solution has value W. Each iteration of the outer loop of KNAPSACKAPPROX yields a solution containing the first item and one of the other two. The solution returned by this algorithm therefore has a value of $W/2 + 2$. The approximation ratio is therefore

$$\frac{W}{\frac{W}{2} + 2} = \frac{2W}{W + 4}$$

$$= 2 - \frac{8}{W + 4}$$

$$= 2 - \frac{8}{2\lceil 4/\epsilon \rceil + 4}$$

$$\geq 2 - \frac{8}{8/\epsilon}$$

$$= 2 - \epsilon.$$

Now consider an arbitrary input to KNAPSACKAPPROX. For a given solution X, let $V(X)$ denote the value of X. Suppose KNAPSACKAPPROX returns a solution A, and let S be an optimal solution. Let i be the index of some element with maximum value in S, and consider iteration i of the outer loop. Let A_i be the solution chosen by this iteration. We will show A_i has an approximation ratio of at most 2. Because $V(A) \geq V(A_i)$, the theorem will follow.

In computing an upper bound on $V(S) - V(A_i)$, we can ignore all items that belong to $S \cap A_i$. Suppose these common items have a total weight of C. Suppose further that $V(A_i) < V(S)$. Then the greedy loop must reject at least one element belonging to S. Let item k be the first element from S to be rejected by the greedy loop in the construction of A_i. Then the total weight of all items in $A_i \setminus S$ chosen prior to item k is greater than $W - C - w[k]$. Because their value-to-weight ratios are all at least $v[k]/w[k]$, their total value is greater than

$$\frac{v[k](W - C - w[k])}{w[k]}.$$

The items in $S \setminus A_i$ must have total weight at most $W - C$. Furthermore, all of their value-to-weight ratios are at most $v[k]/w[k]$; hence their total value is at most

$$\frac{v[k](W - C)}{w[k]}.$$

We therefore have

$$V(S) - V(A_i) < \frac{v[k](W - C)}{w[k]} - \frac{v[k](W - C - w[k])}{w[k]}$$

$$= v[k].$$

Because items i and k both belong to S and $v[i] \geq v[k]$, $v[k] \leq V(S)/2$. We therefore have

$$V(S) - V(A_i) < V(S)/2$$
$$V(S) < 2V(A_i)$$
$$V(S)/V(A_i) < 2$$
$$V(S)/V(A) < 2.$$

$\square$

Though we have a bounded approximation ratio, an approximation ratio of 2 may seem unsatisfactory, as in the worst case we may only achieve half the actual maximum value. It turns out that we can improve the approximation ratio by examining all pairs of items, then using the greedy algorithm to complete each of these packings. More generally, we can achieve an upper bound of $1 + \frac{1}{k}$ by examining all sets of k items and completing each packing using the greedy algorithm. (If there are fewer than k items, we simply do an exhaustive search and return the optimal solution.) The proof is a straightforward generalization of the proof of Theorem 17.3 — the details are left as an exercise.

It is not hard to see that the algorithm outlined above can be implemented to return a solution in $\Theta(n^{k+1})$ time. If k is a fixed constant, the running time is polynomial. We therefore have an infinite sequence of algorithms, each of which is polynomial, such that if an approximation ratio of $1 + \epsilon$ is needed (for some positive ϵ), then one of these algorithms will provide such an approximation. Such a sequence of algorithms is called a *polynomial approximation scheme*.

Although each of the algorithms in the above sequence is polynomial in the length of the input, it is somewhat unsatisfying that to achieve an approximation ratio of $1 + \frac{1}{k}$, a running time in $\Theta(n^{k+1})$ is required. We would be more satisfied with a running time that is polynomial in both n and k. More generally, suppose we have an approximation algorithm that takes as an extra input a natural number k such that for any fixed k, the algorithm yields an approximation ratio of no more than $1 + \frac{1}{k}$. Suppose further that this algorithm runs in a time polynomial in k and the length of its input. We call such an algorithm a *fully polynomial approximation scheme*.

We can obtain a fully polynomial approximation scheme for the 0-1 knapsack problem using one of the dynamic programming algorithms suggested in Section 12.4. The algorithm based on recurrence (12.5) on page 399 runs in $\Theta(nV)$ time, where n is the number of items and V is the sum of their values. We can make V as small as we wish by replacing each value v by $\lfloor v/d \rfloor$ for some positive integer d. If some of the values become 0, we remove these items. Observe that because we don't change any weights or the weight bound, any packing for the new instance is a packing for the original. However, because we take the floor of each v/d, the optimal packing for the new instance might not be optimal for the original. The smaller we make d, the better our approximation, but the less efficient our dynamic programming algorithm.

In order to determine an appropriate value for d, we need to analyze the approximation ratio of this approximation algorithm. Let S be some optimal set of items. The optimal value is then

$$V^* = \sum_{i \in S} v_i.$$

With the modified values, this packing has a value of

$$\sum_{i \in S} \left\lfloor \frac{v_i}{d} \right\rfloor \geq \sum_{i \in S} \frac{v_i - d}{d}$$

$$= \sum_{i \in S} \frac{v_i}{d} - \sum_{i \in S} 1$$

$$\geq \frac{V^*}{d} - n.$$

If we remove from S the items whose new values are 0, we obtain a packing for the revised instance with same value as above. Because the dynamic programming algorithm selects an optimal packing for the revised instance, it will yield a packing with a value at least this large. If we substitute the original values into the packing chosen by the dynamic programming algorithm, we obtain a value of at least $V^* - nd$. The approximation ratio is therefore at most

$$\frac{V^*}{V^* - nd}.$$

We need to ensure that the approximation ratio is at most $1 + \frac{1}{k}$ for some positive integer k. We therefore need

$$\frac{V^*}{V^* - nd} \leq 1 + \frac{1}{k}$$

$$V^* \leq V^* - nd + \frac{V^* - nd}{k}$$

$$0 \leq \frac{V^* - (k+1)nd}{k}$$

$$0 \leq V^* - (k+1)nd$$

$$d \leq \frac{V^*}{(k+1)n}.$$

Let v be the largest value of any item in the original instance. Assuming that no item's weight exceeds the weight bound, we can conclude that $V^* \geq v$. Thus, if $v \geq (k+1)n$, we can satisfy the above inequality by setting d to $\lfloor v/((k+1)n) \rfloor$. However, if $v < (k+1)n$, this value becomes 0. In this case, we can certainly set d to 1, as the dynamic programming algorithm would then give the optimal solution. We therefore set

$$d = \max \left(\left\lfloor \frac{v}{(k+1)n} \right\rfloor, 1 \right).$$

We can clearly compute the scaled values in $O(n)$ time. If $v \geq 2(k+1)n$, the sum of the scaled values is no more than

$$\frac{nv}{d} = \frac{nv}{\left\lfloor \frac{v}{(k+1)n} \right\rfloor}$$

$$\leq \frac{nv}{\frac{v-(k+1)n}{(k+1)n}}$$

$$= \frac{(k+1)n^2 v}{v - (k+1)n}$$

$$\leq \frac{(k+1)n^2 v}{v/2}$$

$$= 2(k+1)n^2.$$

In this case, the dynamic programming algorithm runs in $O(kn^3)$ time.

If $v < 2(k+1)n$, then $d = 1$, so that we use the original values. In this case, the sum of the values is no more than

$$nv < 2(k+1)n^2,$$

so that again, the dynamic programming algorithm runs in $O(kn^3)$ time. Thus, the total running time of the approximation algorithm is in $O(kn^3)$. Because this running time is polynomial in k and n, and because the approximation ratio is no more than $1+\frac{1}{k}$, this algorithm is a fully polynomial approximation scheme.

17.3 Bin Packing

Exercise 16.27 introduced the bin packing problem as a decision problem. Its input consists of a set of items, each having a positive integer weight w_i, a positive integer weight bound W, and a positive integer k. The question we ask is whether the items can be partitioned into k disjoint subsets, each having a total weight of no more than W. The corresponding optimization problem does not include the input k, but instead asks for the minimum number of subsets into which the items can be partitioned such that the weight bound is satisfied. As is suggested by Exercise 16.27, the decision problem BP is strongly $\mathcal{NP}$-complete. As a result, it is easily seen that the optimization problem is $\mathcal{NP}$-hard in the strong sense.

Ideally, we would like to have a fully polynomial approximation scheme for bin packing. However, the following theorem tells us that unless $\mathcal{P} = \mathcal{NP}$, a fully polynomial approximation scheme does not exist.

Theorem 17.4. *Let $p(x, y)$ be an integer-valued polynomial, and let X be an optimization problem whose optimal value on any input x is a natural number bounded above by $p(|x|, \mu(x))$. If there is a fully polynomial approximation scheme for X, then there is a pseudopolynomial algorithm for obtaining an optimal solution for X.*

> Recall that $|x|$ denotes the number of bits in the encoding of x and $\mu(x)$ denotes the maximum value of any integer encoded within x.

Proof. The pseudopolynomial algorithm operates as follows. Given an input x, it first computes $k = p(|x|, \mu(x))$. It then uses the fully polynomial approximation scheme to approximate a solution with an approximation ratio bounded by $1 + \frac{1}{k}$. Let V be the value of the approximation, and let V^* be the value of an optimal solution. If the problem is a minimization problem, we have

$$\frac{V}{V^*} \leq 1 + \frac{1}{k},$$

$$V \leq V^* + \frac{V^*}{k},$$

$$V - V^* \leq \frac{V^*}{k}$$

$$< 1.$$

Because both V and V^* are natural numbers and $V \geq V^*$, we conclude that $V = V^*$. Furthermore, because the fully polynomial approximation scheme runs in time polynomial in $|x|$ and $p(|x|, \mu(x))$, it is a pseudopolynomial algorithm.

An analogous argument applies to maximization problems. □

Because the minimum number of bins needed is clearly no more than the length of the input to the bin packing problem, Theorem 17.4 applies to this problem. Indeed, the condition that the optimal solution is bounded by a polynomial in the length of the input and the largest integer in the input holds for most optimization problems. In these cases, if the given problem is strongly $\mathcal{NP}$-hard (as is bin packing), there can be no fully polynomial approximation scheme unless $\mathcal{P} = \mathcal{NP}$.

If we cannot obtain a fully polynomial approximation scheme for bin packing, we might still hope to find a polynomial approximation scheme. However, the theory of $\mathcal{NP}$-hardness tells us that this is also unlikely. In particular, for a fixed positive integer k, let k-BP denote the problem of deciding whether, for a given instance of bin packing, there is a solution using at most k bins. It is easily seen that PART $\leq_m^p$ 2-BP, so that 2-BP is

$\mathcal{NP}$-hard. Now for a fixed positive real number ϵ, let ϵ-APPROXBP be the problem of approximating a solution to a given instance of bin packing with an approximation ratio of no more than $1 + \epsilon$. We will now show that for any $\epsilon < 1/2$, 2-BP $\leq_T^p \epsilon$-APPROXBP, so that ϵ-APPROXBP is $\mathcal{NP}$-hard. As a result, there can be no polynomial approximation scheme for bin packing unless $\mathcal{P} = \mathcal{NP}$.

Theorem 17.5. *For $0 < \epsilon < 1/2$, ϵ-APPROXBP is $\mathcal{NP}$-hard.*

Proof. As we noted above, we will show that 2-BP $\leq_T^p \epsilon$-APPROXBP. Given an instance of 2-BP, we first find an approximate solution with approximation ratio at most $1 + \epsilon$. If the approximate solution uses no more than 2 bins, then we can answer "yes". If the approximate solution uses 3 or more bins, then the optimal solution uses at least

$$\frac{3}{1+\epsilon} > \frac{3}{3/2}$$
$$= 2$$

bins. We can therefore answer "no".

Ignoring the time needed to compute the approximation, this algorithm runs in $\Theta(1)$ time. Therefore, 2-BP $\leq_T^p \epsilon$-APPROXBP, and ϵ-APPROXBP is $\mathcal{NP}$-hard. $\square$

From Theorem 17.5, we can conclude that there is no approximation algorithm for bin packing with approximation ratio less than $3/2$ unless $\mathcal{P} = \mathcal{NP}$. As a result, there can be no polynomial approximation scheme for bin packing unless $\mathcal{P} = \mathcal{NP}$.

On the other hand, there do exist approximation algorithms which yield approximation ratios that come close to the lower bound of $3/2$ for bin packing. The algorithm we will present here is a simple greedy strategy known as *first fit*. For each item, we try each bin in turn to see if the item will fit. If we find a bin in which the item fits, we place it in that bin; otherwise, we place it in a new bin. The algorithm is shown in Figure 17.2. This algorithm is easily seen to run in $\Theta(n^2)$ time in the worst case. We will now show that it yields an approximation ratio of at most 2.

Theorem 17.6. BINPACKINGFF *yields an approximation ratio of no more than 2 on all inputs that satisfy the precondition.*

Proof. We will first show as an invariant of the **for** loop that at most one bin is no more than half full. This clearly holds initially. Suppose it holds at the beginning of some iteration. If $w[i] > W/2$, then no matter where $w[i]$

Figure 17.2   First-fit approximation algorithm for bin packing

---

Precondition: W is a positive NAT, and $w[1..n]$ is an array of positive NATs such that for $1 \leq i \leq n$, $w[i] \leq W$.

Postcondition: Returns an array $B[1..k]$ of CONSLISTs of NATs i such that $1 \leq i \leq n$. For $1 \leq i \leq n$, i occurs in exactly one CONSLIST in $B[1..k]$. For $1 \leq i \leq k$, if S is the set of integers in $B[i]$, then

$$\sum_{j \in S} w_j \leq W.$$

BINPACKINGFF(W, $w[1..n]$)
  $B \leftarrow$ **new** ARRAY$[1..n]$; *slack* $\leftarrow$ **new** ARRAY$[1..n]$; *numBins* $\leftarrow 0$
  for $i \leftarrow 1$ **to** n
    $j \leftarrow 1$
    while $j \leq$ *numBins* **and** $w[i] >$ *slack*$[j]$
      $j \leftarrow j + 1$
    if $j >$ *numBins*
      numBins $\leftarrow$ *numBins* $+ 1$; $B[j] \leftarrow$ **new** CONSLIST(); *slack*$[j] \leftarrow W$
    $B[j] \leftarrow$ **new** CONSLIST($i, B[j]$); *slack*$[j] \leftarrow$ *slack*$[j] - w[i]$
  return $B[1..numBins]$

---

is placed, it cannot increase the number of bins that are no more than half full. Suppose $w[i] \leq W/2$. Then if there is a bin that is no more than half full, $w[i]$ will fit into this bin. Thus, the only case in which the number of bins that are no more than half full increases is if there are no bins that are no more than half full. In this case, the number cannot be increased to more than one.

We conclude that the packing returned by this algorithm has at most one bin that is no more than half full. Suppose this packing consists of k bins. The total weight must therefore be strictly larger than $(k-1)W/2$. The optimal packing must therefore contain more than $(k-1)/2$ bins. Thus, the number of bins in the optimal packing is at least

$$\left\lfloor \frac{k-1}{2} \right\rfloor + 1 = \left\lfloor \frac{k+1}{2} \right\rfloor$$
$$\geq k/2.$$

The approximation ratio is therefore at most 2.   □

It can be shown via a much more complicated argument that if the optimal packing uses B^* bins, then BINPACKINGFF gives a packing using no more than $\lceil \frac{17}{10} B^* \rceil$ bins. Thus, as B^* increases, the upper bound on the approximation ratio approaches $17/10$. If we first sort the items by nonincreasing weight, it can be shown that this strategy (known as *first-fit decreasing*) gives a packing using no more than $\frac{11}{9} B^* + \frac{2}{3}$ bins. Note that although this upper bound is less than $3/2$ as B^* increases, this does not give a polynomial-time algorithm for ϵ-APPROXBP for any $\epsilon < 3/2$, as the proof of Theorem 17.5 essentially shows the hardness of deciding whether $B^* = 2$. Furthermore, Theorem 17.5 does not preclude the existence of a pseudopolynomial algorithm with an approximation ratio bounded by some value less than $3/2$. We leave it as an exercise to show that dynamic programming can be combined with the first-fit decreasing strategy to yield, for any positive ϵ, an approximation algorithm with an approximation ratio bounded by $\frac{11}{9} + \epsilon$.

17.4 The Traveling Salesperson Problem

Exercise 16.28 introduced the traveling salesperson problem as a decision problem, TSP. Its input consists of a complete undirected graph G with positive integer edge weights and a positive integer k. The question we ask is whether there is a Hamiltonian cycle in G with total weight no more than k. As is suggested by Exercise 16.28, TSP is strongly $\mathcal{NP}$-complete. The corresponding optimization problem does not include the input k, but instead asks for the Hamiltonian cycle in G with minimum weight. It is easily seen that this problem is $\mathcal{NP}$-hard in the strong sense. Clearly, a minimum weight Hamiltonian cycle has weight no more than nW, where n is the number of vertices in G and W is the maximum weight of any edge in G; hence, by Theorem 17.4, there can be no fully polynomial approximation scheme for the optimization problem unless $\mathcal{P} = \mathcal{NP}$.

For $\epsilon > 0$, let ϵ-APPROXTSP be the problem of finding, for a given undirected graph G with positive integer edge weights, a Hamiltonian cycle with approximation ratio no more than $1 + \epsilon$. In what follows, we will show that ϵ-APPROXTSP is $\mathcal{NP}$-hard in the strong sense for every positive ϵ. As a result, there can be no polynomial or pseudopolynomial algorithm for finding an approximation with any bounded approximation ratio unless $\mathcal{P} = \mathcal{NP}$.

Theorem 17.7. *For every positive ϵ, ϵ-APPROXTSP is $\mathcal{NP}$-hard in the strong sense.*

Proof. Let $\epsilon > 0$, and let HC be the problem of deciding whether a given undirected graph G contains a Hamiltonian cycle. By Exercise 16.9, *HC* is $\mathcal{NP}$-complete. Since there are no integers in the problem instance, it is strongly $\mathcal{NP}$-complete. We will show that HC $\leq_T^{pp}$ ϵ-ApproxTSP, where $\leq_T^{pp}$ denotes a pseudopolynomial Turing reduction. It will then follow that ϵ-ApproxTSP is $\mathcal{NP}$-hard in the strong sense.

Let $G = (V, E)$ be an undirected graph. We first construct a complete undirected graph $G' = (V, E')$. Let $k = \lfloor \epsilon \rfloor + 2$. We define the weight of an edge $e \in E'$ as follows:

- If $e \in E$, then the weight of e is 1.
- If $e \notin E$, then the weight of e is nk, where n is the size of V.

Note that because k is a fixed constant, the weights are bounded by a polynomial in the size of G.

We now show how we can use an approximation of a minimum-weight Hamiltonian cycle in G' to decide whether G has a Hamilton cycle. Suppose we can obtain an approximation with an approximation ratio of no more than $1 + \epsilon$. If the weight of this approximation is n, then the corresponding Hamiltonian cycle must contain only edges with weight 1; hence, it is a Hamiltonian cycle in G, so we can answer "yes". Otherwise, the approximation contains at least one edge with weight nk, and $n > 0$. The weight of the approximation is therefore at least $nk + n - 1$. Because the approximation ratio is no more than $1 + \epsilon$, the minimum-weight Hamiltonian path has a weight of at least

$$\frac{nk + n - 1}{1 + \epsilon} = \frac{n(\lfloor \epsilon \rfloor + 2) + n - 1}{1 + \epsilon}$$
$$> \frac{n(1 + \epsilon)}{1 + \epsilon}$$
$$= n.$$

Hence, there is no Hamiltonian cycle whose edge weights are all 1. Because this implies that G contains no Hamiltonian cycle, we can answer "no".

The running time for this algorithm, excluding any time needed to compute the approximation, is linear in the size of G. Furthermore, all integers constructed have values polynomial in the size of G. We therefore conclude that ϵ-ApproxTSP is $\mathcal{NP}$-hard in the strong sense. $\square$

As a result of Theorem 17.7, we have little hope of finding a polynomial-time approximation algorithm yielding a bounded approximation ratio for the traveling salesperson problem. However, if we make a certain restriction to the problem, we can find such an algorithm. The *metric traveling salesperson problem* is the restriction of the traveling salesperson problem to inputs in which the edges of the graph satisfy the triangle inequality; i.e., if u, v, and w are vertices, then

$$weight(\{u, w\}) \leq weight(\{u, v\}) + weight(\{v, w\}).$$

The triangle inequality is satisfied, for example, if the vertices represent points in the plane, and the edge weights represent distances. In what follows, we will present a polynomial-time approximation algorithm yielding an approximation ratio bounded by 2 for this problem.

We first observe that if we remove any edge from a Hamiltonian cycle, we obtain a spanning tree of the graph. Furthermore, the weight of this spanning tree must be less than the weight of the Hamiltonian cycle. Hence, an MST will have a weight strictly less than the weight of a minimum-weight Hamiltonian cycle. Now consider a tour of an MST that follows a depth-first search — that is, we go from vertex u to vertex v when the call on u makes a call on v, and we go from v to u when the call on v returns. In this way, we traverse each edge exactly twice and reach each vertex at least once, returning to the vertex from which we started. Clearly, the weight of the edges in this tour (counting each edge exactly twice) is less than twice the weight of a minimum-weight Hamiltonian cycle.

We now wish to convert this tour to a Hamiltonian cycle by taking shortcuts. Specifically, when the tour would return to a vertex that it has already reached, we skip ahead to the next vertex in the tour that has not yet been reached (see Figure 17.3). When we have reached all vertices, we return to the starting point.

It is easily seen by induction that if the triangle inequality is satisfied, then the weight of edge $\{u, v\}$ is no more than the sum of the weights of the edges on any simple path from u to v. It is easily seen that when a path from u to v is replaced by edge $\{u, v\}$ in the above conversion, that path is a simple path, because all edges in the tour that reach vertices that have already been reached must go from children to parents; hence, the path in the tour from u to v takes edges from children to parents, followed by a single edge from a parent to v, which is reached for the first time in the tour. Clearly, no vertex can be repeated in such a path. As a result, the weight of this Hamiltonian cycle is less than twice the weight of an optimal Hamiltonian cycle.

Notice that because this Hamiltonian cycle reaches the vertices in the same order that they are first reached in the depth-first search, the

Figure 17.3   Conversion of an MST to a Hamiltonian cycle

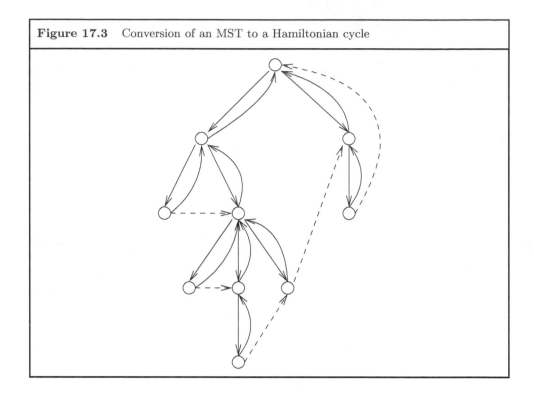

Figure 17.4   An implementation of SEARCHER for use in the metric traveling salesperson approximation algorithm

METRICTSPSEARCHER(n)
    pre ← **new** VISITCOUNTER(n); *order* ← **new** ARRAY$[0..n - 1]$

METRICTSPSEARCHER.PREPROC(i)
    pre.VISIT(i); *order*[*pre*.NUM(i)] ← i

vertices are ordered by their preorder traversal numbers. Therefore, it is easy to construct this Hamiltonian cycle while doing the depth-first search on the MST. A SEARCHER for the depth-first search needs only a VISITCOUNTER *pre* for recording the preorder traversal numbers and a readable array *order*$[0..n - 1]$ such that the Hamiltonian cycle will be $\langle order[0], order[1], \ldots, order[n - 1], order[0]\rangle$. Such a SEARCHER is defined in Figure 17.4.

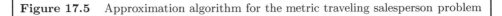

Figure 17.5   Approximation algorithm for the metric traveling salesperson problem

---

Precondition: G is a GRAPH representing a complete undirected graph with at least one vertex, whose edges contain positive NAT weights satisfying the triangle inequality.

Postcondition: Returns an array $order[0..n-1]$ in which each NAT less than n occurs exactly once. The sum of the weights of the edges $\{order[0], order[1]\}, \{order[1], order[2]\}, \ldots, \{order[n-1], order[0]\}$ is less than twice the weight of an optimal Hamiltonian cycle.

METRICTSP(G)
    $n \leftarrow G.$SIZE; $L \leftarrow$ PRIM(G)
    $G' \leftarrow$ **new** LISTMULTIGRAPH(n)
    while not $L.$ISEMPTY()
        $e \leftarrow L.$HEAD(); $L \leftarrow L.$TAIL()
        $i \leftarrow e.$SOURCE(); $j \leftarrow e.$DEST(); $x \leftarrow e.$DATA()
        $G'.$PUT(i,j,x); $G'.$PUT(j,i,x)
    $G'' \leftarrow$ **new** LISTGRAPH(G'); $sel \leftarrow$ **new** SELECTOR(n)
    $s \leftarrow$ **new** METRICTSPSEARCHER(n); DFS($G'', 0, sel, s$)
    return $s.$ORDER()

For constructing an MST, we can use either Kruskal's algorithm (Figure 11.1, page 376) or Prim's algorithm (Figure 11.2, page 378). Our graph is complete, so that the number of edges is in $\Theta(n^2)$, where n is the number of vertices. If we are using a LISTGRAPH representation, Kruskal's algorithm is more efficient, running in $\Theta(n^2 \lg n)$ time. However, if we are using a MATRIXGRAPH representation, Prim's algorithm is more efficient, running in $\Theta(n^2)$ time. Because we can construct a MATRIXGRAPH from a LISTGRAPH in $\Theta(n^2)$ time, we will use Prim's algorithm. The entire algorithm is shown in Figure 17.5.

Assuming G is a MATRIXGRAPH, the call to PRIM runs in $\Theta(n^2)$ time. The LISTMULTIGRAPH constructor then runs in $\Theta(n)$ time. Because the CONSLIST returned by PRIM contains exactly $n-1$ edges, and the LISTMULTIGRAPH.PUT operation runs in $\Theta(1)$ time, the loop runs in $\Theta(n)$ time. As was shown in Section 9.5, the LISTGRAPH constructor runs in $\Theta(n)$ time. The SELECTOR constructor runs in $\Theta(n)$ time, and the METRICTSPSEARCHER constructor clearly runs in $\Theta(1)$ time. Because the METRICTSPSEARCHER.PREPROC operation runs in $\Theta(1)$ time and G'' is a LISTGRAPH, with $n-1$ edges, the call to DFS runs in $\Theta(n)$ time. The total running time is therefore in $\Theta(n^2)$.

17.5 The Maximum Cut and Minimum Cluster Problems

We conclude this chapter by examining two optimization problems that are essentially the same, but which yield entirely different results with respect to approximation algorithms. Let $G = (V, E)$ be a complete undirected graph with positive integer edge weights. For a natural number $k \geq 2$, a *k-cut* for G is a partition of V into k disjoint sets, $S_1, S_2, \ldots, S_k$. The *weight* of this cut is the sum of the weights of all edges $\{u, v\} \in E$ such that u and v are in different partitions. The *maximum cut problem* is to find, for a given natural number $k \geq 2$ and complete undirected graph $G = (V, E)$ with edge weights and more than k vertices, a k-cut with maximum weight. The *minimum cluster* problem is to find a k-cut that minimizes the sum of the weights of all edges $\{u, v\} \in E$ such that u and v are in the same partition. Clearly, a k-cut has maximum weight iff it minimizes this latter sum.

Let CUT be the problem of deciding, for given natural numbers $k \geq 2$ and B, and complete undirected graph $G = (V, E)$ with positive integer edge weights and more than k vertices, whether there is a k-cut with weight at least B. For each $k \geq 2$, we also define the k-CUT problem to be the CUT problem restricted to cuts of exactly k sets (i.e, k is not given as input, but is fixed). We further define the CLUSTER and k-CLUSTER problems analogously. We leave as exercises to show that k-CLUSTER is strongly $\mathcal{NP}$-complete for every $k \geq 2$, and that CLUSTER is strongly $\mathcal{NP}$-complete. It then follows that CUT and k-CUT for $k \geq 2$ are all strongly $\mathcal{NP}$-complete.

Given the above results, the problems of finding either a maximum cut or a minimum cluster are $\mathcal{NP}$-hard in the strong sense. Thus, from Theorem 17.4, there is no fully polynomial approximation scheme for either of these problems unless $\mathcal{P} = \mathcal{NP}$. However, there is a simple greedy strategy that yields good approximation ratios for maximum cut. We begin with k empty sets, and add vertices one by one to the set that gives us the largest cut. The algorithm is shown in Figure 17.6. Note that this algorithm actually uses the amount by which the total weight of the clusters would increase when choosing the set in which to place a given vertex — these values are easier to compute than the weights of the resulting cuts. It is easily seen that this algorithm runs in $\Theta(n^2)$ time, if G is represented by a MATRIXGRAPH. The following theorem gives bounds for its approximation ratio.

Theorem 17.8. *For each $k \geq 2$, MAXCUT yields an approximation ratio of no more than*

$$1 + \frac{1}{k-1};$$

thus, the approximation ratio is never more than 2.

Figure 17.6   Approximation algorithm for maximum cut

Precondition: G is a GRAPH representing a complete undirected graph with positive NAT edge weights, and k is a NAT such that $2 \leq k < n$, where n is the number of vertices in G.

Postcondition: Returns an array $cut[0..n-1]$ such that for $0 \leq i < n$, $1 \leq cut[i] \leq k$. If W is the sum of the weights of the edges in G, then the weight of the cut described by $cut[0..n-1]$ is at least $W(k-1)/k$.

MAXCUT(G, k)
    $n \leftarrow G.\text{SIZE}()$; $cut \leftarrow$ **new** ARRAY$[0..n-1]$
    $clusterInc \leftarrow$ **new** ARRAY$[1..k]$
    for $i \leftarrow 0$ **to** $n - 1$
        for $j \leftarrow 1$ **to** k
            $clusterInc[j] \leftarrow 0$
        for $j \leftarrow 0$ **to** $i - 1$
            $clusterInc[cut[j]] \leftarrow clusterInc[cut[j]] + G.\text{GET}(i, j)$
        $m \leftarrow 1$
        for $j \leftarrow 2$ **to** k
            if $clusterInc[j] < clusterInc[m]$
                $m \leftarrow j$
        $cut[i] \leftarrow m$
    return $cut[0..n-1]$

Proof.   For a given vertex i, let W_i denote the sum of the weights of all edges $\{i, j\}$ such that $0 \leq j < i$. At the end of iteration i, the value of the cut increases by $W_i - clusterInc[m]$, where $clusterInc[m]$ is the sum of the weights of the edges from i to other vertices in partition m. m is chosen so that $clusterInc[m]$ is minimized; hence, for each partition other than m, the sum of the weights of the edges from i to vertices in that partition is at least $clusterInc[m]$. We therefore have

$$clusterInc[m] \leq W_i/k.$$

The value of the cut therefore increases by at least $W_i(k-1)/k$ on iteration i. Because the value of the cut is initially 0, the final value of the cut is at least

$$\sum_{i=0}^{n-1} \frac{W_i(k-1)}{k} = \frac{k-1}{k} \sum_{i=0}^{n-1} W_i$$

$$= \frac{k-1}{k} W,$$

where W is the sum of all edge weights in G. Clearly, the maximum cut can be no more than W. The approximation ratio is therefore bounded above by

$$\frac{W}{(k-1)W/k} = \frac{k}{k-1}$$

$$= 1 + \frac{1}{k-1}.$$

□

Though the algorithm MAXCUT yields a fixed bound on the approximation ratio for approximating a maximum cut, it is perhaps surprising that the same algorithm yields unbounded approximation ratios for approximating a minimum cluster, even though the two optimization problems are essentially the same. We can see why this is the case by examining instances that cause the approximation ratio for MAXCUT to approach the upper bound shown in Theorem 17.8.

For $k \geq 2$, consider a complete undirected graph $G = (V, E)$, where $V = \{i \in \mathbb{N} \mid i < k^2\}$. We partition V into k groups such that for $0 \leq j < k$, group j is the set $\{i \in \mathbb{N} \mid jk \leq i < (j+1)k\}$; thus, each group contains k vertices. We now assign weights to the edges in G such that if vertices u and v are in the same group, then $\{u, v\}$ has weight 1; otherwise, $\{u, v\}$ has weight x, where x is some sufficiently large natural number. (See Figure 17.7 for the case in which $k = 2$.)

Figure 17.7 A bad case for MAXCUT

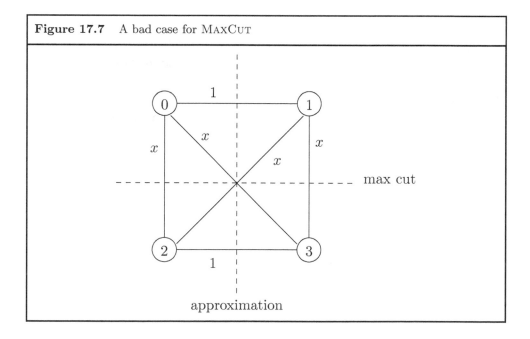

We claim that if $x \geq k^3$, the maximum cut for G partitions the vertices so that each group forms a cluster. To see this, first note that when we partition G in this way, the resulting cut includes exactly those edges with weight x. Because the sum of all other edges is less than x, the maximum cut must contain all of the edges with weight x. Note that connecting any two of the vertices $0, k, \ldots, k^2 - k$ is an edge with weight x; hence, a maximum cut must place all of these k vertices into different clusters. Then for $0 \leq i < k$ and $1 \leq j < k$, there is an edge of weight x between vertex $ik + j$ and $i'k$ for each $i' \neq i$. As a result, vertex $ik + j$ must be placed in the same cluster as vertex ik. Hence, the maximum cut partitions the vertices so that each group forms a cluster.

Now consider the behavior of MAXCUT on G. It will first place vertices $0, 1, \ldots, k - 1$ into different clusters. Then vertex k is adjacent to exactly one vertex in each of the clusters via an edge with weight x. Because placing k in any of the clusters would increase the weight of that cluster by x, k is placed in the first cluster with vertex 0. Placing $k + 1$ in this cluster would increase its weight by $x + 1$; however, placing $k + 1$ in any other cluster would increase that cluster's weight by only x. As a result, $k + 1$ is placed in the second cluster with vertex 1. It is easily seen that the algorithm continues by placing vertices into clusters in round-robin fashion, so that each cluster ultimately contains exactly one vertex from each group.

We can use symmetry to help us to evaluate the approximation ratio of MAXCUT on G. In the maximum cut, each vertex is adjacent to $(k - 1)k$ vertices in other clusters via edges whose weights are all x. In the cut produced by MAXCUT, each vertex is also adjacent to $(k - 1)k$ vertices in other clusters; however, only $(k - 1)^2$ of these edges have weight x, while the remaining edges each have weight 1. The approximation ratio is therefore

$$\frac{(k-1)kx}{(k-1)^2 x + k - 1} = \frac{kx}{(k-1)x + 1},$$

which approaches

$$\frac{k}{k-1} = 1 + \frac{1}{k-1}$$

as x approaches ∞. The bound of Theorem 17.8 is therefore tight.

Let us now analyze the approximation ratio for MAXCUT as an approximation algorithm for the minimum cluster problem. Again we can use symmetry to simplify the analysis. In the optimal solution, each vertex is adjacent to $k - 1$ vertices in the same cluster via edges whose weights are all 1. In the solution given by MAXCUT, each vertex is adjacent to $k - 1$

vertices in the same cluster via edges whose weights are all x. Thus, the approximation ratio is x, which can be chosen to be arbitrarily large. We can therefore see that even though the maximum cut and minimum cluster optimization problems are essentially the same, the MAXCUT algorithm yields vastly different approximation ratios relative to the two problems.

To carry this idea a step further, we will now show that the minimum cluster problem has no approximation algorithm with a bounded approximation ratio unless $\mathcal{P} = \mathcal{NP}$. For a given $\epsilon \in \mathbb{R}^{>0}$ and integer $k \geq 2$, let the ϵ-APPROX-k-CLUSTER problem be the problem of finding, for a given complete undirected graph G with positive integer edge weights, a k-cut whose sum of cluster weights is at most $W^*(1 + \epsilon)$, where W^* is the minimum sum of cluster weights. Likewise, let ϵ-APPROX-CLUSTER be the corresponding problem with k provided as an input. We will show that for every positive ϵ and every integer $k \geq 3$, the ϵ-APPROX-k-CLUSTER problem is $\mathcal{NP}$-hard in the strong sense. Because ϵ-APPROX-3-CLUSTER $\leq_T^{pp} \epsilon$-APPROX-CLUSTER, it will then follow that this latter problem is also $\mathcal{NP}$-hard in the strong sense. Whether the result extends to ϵ-APPROX-2-CLUSTER is unknown at the time of this writing.

Theorem 17.9. *For every $\epsilon \in \mathbb{R}^{>0}$ and every $k \geq 3$, ϵ-APPROX-k-CLUSTER is $\mathcal{NP}$-hard in the strong sense.*

Proof. As is suggested by Exercises 16.23 and 16.24, the problem of deciding whether a given undirected graph is k-colorable is $\mathcal{NP}$-complete for each $k \geq 3$. Let us refer to this problem as k-COL. Because k-COL contains no large integers, it is $\mathcal{NP}$-complete in the strong sense. We will now show that k-COL $\leq_T^{pp} \epsilon$-APPROX-k-CLUSTER, so that ϵ-APPROX-k-CLUSTER is $\mathcal{NP}$-hard in the strong sense for $k \geq 3$.

Let $G = (V, E)$ be a given undirected graph. Let n be the number of vertices in G. We can assume without loss of generality that $n > k$, for otherwise G is clearly k-colorable. We construct $G' = (V, E')$ to be the complete graph on V. We assign an edge weight of $n^2\lceil 1 + \epsilon \rceil$ to edge $\{u, v\} \in E'$ if $\{u, v\} \in E$; otherwise, we assign it a weight of 1. Clearly, this construction can be completed in time polynomial in n. Furthermore, because ϵ is a fixed constant, all integers have values polynomial in n.

Suppose we have a k-cut of G' such that the ratio of its cluster weight to the minimum cluster weight is at most $1 + \epsilon$. If the given cluster weight is less than $n^2\lceil 1 + \epsilon \rceil$, then all edges connecting vertices in the same cluster must have weight less than $n^2\lceil 1 + \epsilon \rceil$; hence none of them belong to E.

This k-cut is therefore a k-coloring of G. In this case, we can answer "yes". Suppose the cluster weight is at least $n^2 \lceil 1 + \epsilon \rceil$. Because the approximation ratio is no more than $1 + \epsilon$, the minimum sum of cluster weights is at least n^2. It is therefore impossible to k-color G, for a k-coloring of G would be a k-cut of G' in which each cluster contains only edges with weight 1, and which would therefore have total weight less than n^2. In this case, we can answer "no". We conclude that k-COL $\leq_T^{pp}$ ϵ-APPROX-k-CLUSTER, so that ϵ-APPROX-k-CLUSTER is $\mathcal{NP}$-hard in the strong sense. $\qquad\square$

17.6 Summary

Using Turing reducibility, we can extend the definition of $\mathcal{NP}$-hardness from Chapter 16 to apply to problems other than decision problems in a natural way. We can then identify certain optimization problems as being $\mathcal{NP}$-hard, either in the strong sense or the ordinary sense. One way of coping with $\mathcal{NP}$-hard optimization problems is by using approximation algorithms.

For some $\mathcal{NP}$-hard optimization problems we can find polynomial approximation schemes, which take as input an instance x of the problem and a positive real number ϵ and return, in time polynomial in $|x|$, an approximate solution with approximation ratio no more than $1 + \epsilon$. If this algorithm runs in time polynomial in $|x|$ and $1/\epsilon$, it is called a fully polynomial approximation scheme.

However, Theorem 17.4 tells us that for most optimization problems, if the problem admits a fully polynomial approximation scheme, then there is a pseudopolynomial algorithm to solve the problem exactly. As a result, we can use strong $\mathcal{NP}$-hardness to show for a number of problems that unless $\mathcal{P} = \mathcal{NP}$, that problem cannot have a fully polynomial approximation scheme. Furthermore, by showing $\mathcal{NP}$-hardness of certain approximation problems, we can show that unless $\mathcal{P} = \mathcal{NP}$, the corresponding optimization problem has no approximation algorithm with approximation ratio bounded by some — or in some cases any — given value.

Finally, there are some pairs of optimization problems, such as the maximum cut problem and the minimum cluster problem, that are essentially the same problem, but which yield vastly different results concerning approximation algorithm. For example, the maximum k-cut, can be approximated in $\Theta(n^2)$ time with an approximation ratio of no more than $1 + \frac{1}{k-1}$; however, unless $\mathcal{P} = \mathcal{NP}$, there is no polynomial-time algorithm with any bounded approximation ratio for finding the minimum weight of clusters formed by a k-cut if $k \geq 3$.

17.7 Exercises

Exercise 17.1. Give an approximation algorithm that takes an instance of the knapsack problem and a positive integer k and returns a packing with an approximation ratio of no more than $1 + \frac{1}{k}$. Your algorithm must run in $O(n^{k+1})$ time. Prove that both of these bounds (approximation ratio and running time) are met by your algorithm.

Exercise 17.2. Suppose we were to modify the knapsack problem to allow as many copies as we wish of any of the items. Show that the greedy algorithm yields an approximation ratio of no more than 2 for this variation.

Exercise 17.3. The *best-fit* algorithm for bin packing considers the items in the given order, always choosing the largest-weight bin in which the item will fit. Show that the approximation ratio for this algorithm is no more than 2.

** Exercise 17.4. Let ϵ be any fixed positive real number. Demonstrate how dynamic programming can be combined with the first-fit-decreasing algorithm to obtain a pseudopolynomial-time approximation algorithm for bin packing with approximation ratio no more than $\frac{11}{9} + \epsilon$. You may use the fact that the first-fit-decreasing algorithm always produces a packing using at most $\frac{11}{9}B^* + \frac{2}{3}$ bins, where B^* is the minimum number of bins possible.

* Exercise 17.5.

a. Prove that NotAllEqual-3-Sat $\leq_m^{pp}$ k-Cluster for each fixed $k \geq 2$, so that, from the result of Exercise 16.6, k-Cluster is $\mathcal{NP}$-hard in the strong sense for $k \geq 2$.

b. Prove that Cluster is strongly $\mathcal{NP}$-complete.

* Exercise 17.6. Give an approximation algorithm with approximation ratio bounded by 2 for the problem of finding a minimum-sized vertex cover. Your algorithm should run in $O(n + a)$ time, assuming the graph is implemented as a ListGraph. Prove both the approximation ratio and the running time.

* Exercise 17.7.

a. Given an undirected graph $G = (V, E)$, we define $G^2 = (V^2, E')$ such that for $u = \langle u_1, u_2 \rangle$ and $v = \langle v_1, v_2 \rangle$ in V^2, $\{u, v\} \in E'$ iff for every i, $1 \leq i \leq 2$, either $u_i = v_i$ or $\{u_i, v_i\} \in E$. Prove that the size of the largest clique in G^2 is k^2, where k is the size of the largest clique in G.

b. Use part (a) to prove that if there is a polynomial-time algorithm with a bounded approximation ratio for approximating the size of a largest clique in a given graph, then there is a polynomial approximation scheme for this problem.

17.8 Notes

The concept of a polynomial-time approximation algorithm was first formalized by Garey *et al.* [50] and Johnson [73]. In fact, much of the foundational work in this area is due to Garey and Johnson — see their text [54] for a summary of the early work. For example, they proved Theorem 17.4 [53]. A detailed analysis of bin packing, including an $\frac{11}{9}B^* + 4$ upper bound on the approximation ratio for first-fit decreasing, is given by Johnson [72]. This bound was later improved to $\frac{11}{9}B^* + \frac{2}{3}$ by Dósa [31], who showed this bound to be tight. The $\lceil \frac{17}{10}B^* \rceil$ upper bound for the first-fit algorithm is due to Garey *et al.* [49], and a close relationship between best-fit and first-fit was established by Johnson *et al.* [71]. Dósa and Sgall [32] later showed that the upper bound for best-fit is also $\lceil \frac{17}{10}B^* \rceil$.

The polynomial approximation scheme suggested by Exercise 17.1 for the knapsack problem is due to Sahni [102]. The fully polynomial approximation scheme of Section 17.2 is due to Ibarra and Kim [69]. Theorem 17.7 was shown by Sahni and Gonzalez [101].

Bibliography

[1] G. M. Adel'son-Vel'skiĭ and E. M. Landis. An algorithm for the organization of information. *Soviet Mathematics Doklady*, 3:1259–1263, 1962.

[2] A. V. Aho, John E. Hopcroft, and Jeffrey D. Ullman. *The Design and Analysis of Computer Algorithms*. Addison Wesley, 1974.

[3] A. V. Aho, Monica S. Lam, Ravi Sethi, and Jeffrey D. Ullman. *Compilers: Principles, Techniques, and Tools*, 2nd edition. Pearson Education Limited, 2014.

[4] M. Aigner. *Combinatorial Search*. Wiley-Teubner, 1988.

[5] A. Andersson. Balanced search trees made simple. In *Proceedings of the Third Workshop on Algorithms and Data Structures*, number 709 in Lecture Notes in Computer Science, pp. 60–71. Springer-Verlag, 1993.

[6] K. R. Apt and E.-R. Olderog. *Verification of Sequential and Concurrent Programs*, 3rd edition. Springer-Verlag, 2009.

[7] P. G. H. Bachmann. *Analytische Zahlentheorie, Bd 2: Die Analysische Zahlentheorie*. Teubner, Leipzig, Germany, 1894.

[8] R. Bayer. Symmetric binary B-trees: Data structure and maintenance algorithms. *Acta Informatica*, 1:290–306, 1972.

[9] R. Bayer and E. M. McCreight. Organization and maintenance of large ordered indexes. *Acta Informatica*, 1:173–189, 1972.

[10] R. E. Bellman. *Dynamic Programming*. Princeton University Press, 1957.

[11] J. L. Bentley. Multidimensional divide-and-conquer. *Communications of the ACM*, 23:214–229, 1980.

[12] J. L. Bentley. *Programming Pearls*, 2nd edition. Addison-Wesley, Reading, MA, 2000.

[13] C. Berge. Two theorems in graph theory. *Proceedings of the National Academy of Sciences*, 43:842–844, 1957.

[14] M. Blum, R. W. Floyd, V. R. Pratt, R. L. Rivest, and R. E. Tarjan. Time bounds for selection. *Journal of Computer and System Sciences*, 7:448–461, 1972.

[15] O. Borůvka. O jistém problému minimálnim. *Práce Moravské Přírodověd Spolecnosti*, 3:37–58, 1926.

[16] G. Brassard. Crusade for a better notation. *ACM SIGACT News*, 17:60–64, 1985.

[17] G. Brassard and P. Bratley. *Fundamentals of Algorithmics*. Prentice Hall, 1996.

[18] C. Burnikel and J. Ziegler. Fast recursive division. Research Report MPI-I-98-1-022, Max-Planck-Institut für Informatik, 1998.

[19] J. L. Carter and M. N. Wegman. Universal classes of hash functions. *Journal of Computer and System Sciences*, 18:143–154, 1979.

[20] B. Chazelle. A minimum spanning tree algorithm with inverse-ackermann type complexity. *Journal of the ACM*, 47:1028–1047, 2000.

[21] D. Cheriton and R. E. Tarjan. Finding minimum spanning trees. *SIAM Journal on Computing*, 5:724–742, 1976.

[22] V. Chvatal, D. A. Klarner, and D. E. Knuth. Selected combinatorial research problems. Technical Report STAN-CS-72-292, Stanford University, 1972.

[23] S. A. Cook. The complexity of theorem-proving procedures. In *Proceedings of the 3rd Annual ACM Symposium on Theory of Computing*, pp. 151–158, 1971.

[24] J. W. Cooley and J. W. Tukey. An algorithm for the machine calculation of complex Fourier series. *Mathematics of Computation*, 19:297–301, 1965.

[25] T. H. Cormen, C. E. Leiserson, R. L. Rivest, and C. Stein. *Introduction to Algorithms*, 2nd edition, McGraw-Hill, 2001.

[26] C. A. Crane. Linear lists and priority queues as balanced binary trees. Technical Report STAN-CS-72-259, Computer Science Department, Stanford University, Stanford, CA, 1972.

[27] E. W. Dijkstra. A note on two problems in connexion with graphs. *Numerische Mathematik*, 1:269–271, 1959.

[28] E. W. Dijkstra. The structure of "THE"-multiprogramming system. *Communications of the ACM*, 11:341–346, 1968.

[29] E. W. Dijkstra. *A Discipline of Programming*. Prentice-Hall, Englewood Cliffs, NJ, 1976.

[30] E. A. Dinic. Algorithm for solution of a problem of maximum flow in a network with power estimation. *Soviet Mathematics Doklady*, 11:1277–1280, 1970.

[31] G. Dósa. The tight bound of first fit decreasing bin-packing algorithm is $FFD(I) \leq 11/9OPT(I) + 6/9$. In B. Chen, M. Paterson, and G. Zhang (eds), *Combinatorics, Algorithms, Probabilistic and Experimental Methodologies*, pp. 1–11, Springer Berlin Heidelberg, 2007.

[32] G. Dósa and J. Sgall. Optimal analysis of best fit bin packing. In J. Esparza, P. Fraigniaud, T. Husfeldt, and E. Koutsoupias (eds), *Automata, Languages, and Programming*, pp. 429–441, Springer Berlin Heidelberg, 2014.

[33] A. I. Dumey. Indexing for rapid random access memory systems. *Computers and Automation*, 5:6–9, 1956.

[34] J. P. Eckert and J. W. Mauchly. Progress report on the edvac, September 1945.

[35] J. Edmonds. Paths, trees, and flowers. *Canadian Journal of Mathematics*, 17:449–467, 1965.

[36] J. Edmonds. Matroids and the greedy algorithm. *Mathematical Programming*, 1:127–136, 1971.

[37] J. Edmonds and R. M. Karp. Theoretical improvements in algorithmic efficiency for network flow problems. *Journal of the ACM*, 19:248–264, 1972.

[38] L. Euler. Solutio problematis ad geometriam situs pertinentis. *Commetarii Academiae Scientiarum Imperialis Petropolitanae*, 8:128–140, 1736.

[39] S. Even. *Graph Algorithms*, 2nd edition. Cambridge University Press, 2012.

[40] R. W. Floyd. Algorithm 97: Shortest path. *Communications of hte ACM*, 5:345, 1962.

[41] R. W. Floyd. Algorithm 245: Treesort. *Communications of the ACM*, 7:701, 1964.

[42] L. R. Ford and D. R. Fulkerson. Maximal flow through a network. *Canadian Journal of Mathematics*, 8:399–404, 1956.

[43] L. R. Ford and D. R. Fulkerson. *Flows in Networks*. Princeton University Press, 1962.

[44] N. Francez. *Program Verification*. Addison-Wesley, 1992.

[45] M. L. Fredman, J. Komlós, and E. Szermerédi. Storing a sparse table with $O(1)$ worst case access time. *Journal of the ACM*, 31:538–544, 1984.

[46] M. L. Fredman and R. E. Tarjan. Fibonacci heaps and their use in improved network optimization algorithms. *Journal of the ACM*, 34:596–615, 1987.

[47] B. A. Galler and M. J. Fischer. An improved equivalence algorithm. *Communications of the ACM*, 7:301–303, 1964.

[48] A. Gambin and A. Malinowski. Randomized meldable priority queues. In *Conference on Current Trends in Theory and Practice of Informatics*, pp. 344–349, 1998.

[49] M. R. Garey, R. L. Graham, D. S. Johnson, and A. C.-C. Yao. Resource constrained scheduling as generalized bin packing. *Journal of Combinatorial Theory, Series A*, 21:257–298, 1976.

[50] M. R. Garey, R. L. Graham, and J. D. Ullman. Worst-case analysis of memory allocation algorithms. In *Proceedings of the Fourth ACM Symposium on Theory of Computing*, pp. 143–150, 1972.

[51] M. R. Garey and D. S. Johnson. Complexity results for multiprocessor scheduling under resource constraints. *SIAM Journal on Computing*, 4:397–411, 1975.

[52] M. R. Garey and D. S. Johnson. Two-processor scheduling with start-times and deadlines. *SIAM Journal on Computing*, 6:416–426, 1977.

[53] M. R. Garey and D. S. Johnson. "Strong" NP-Completeness results: Motivation, examples, and implications. *Journal of the ACM*, 25:499–508, 1978.

[54] M. R. Garey and D. S. Johnson. *Computers and Intractability: A Guide to the Theory of NP-Completeness*. W. H. Freeman and Company, New York, 1979.

[55] E. N. Gilbert and E. F. Moore. Variable length encodings. *Bell System Technical Journal*, 38:933–968, 1959.

[56] S. S. Godbole. On efficient computation of matrix chain products. *IEEE Transactions on Computers*, C-22:864–866, 1973.

[57] A. V. Goldberg and S. Rao. Beyond the flow decomposition barrier. *Journal of the ACM*, 45:783–797, 1998.

[58] W. Gong and X. Zhou. A survey of SAT solver. In *AIP Conference Proceedings*, volume 1836, 020059, 2017.

[59] R. L. Graham, D. E. Knuth, and O. Patashnik. *Concrete Mathematics*, 2nd edition. Addison-Wesley, Reading, Massachusetts, 1994.

[60] L. J. Gubias and R. Sedgewick. A dichromatic framework for balanced trees. In *Proceedings of the 19th Annual Symposium on Foundations of Computer Science*, pp. 8–21. IEEE Computer Society, 1978.

[61] M. T. Heideman, D. H. Johnson, and C. Sidney Burrus. Gauss and the history of the fast fourier transform. *IEEE ASSP Magazine*, pp. 14–21, 1984.

[62] C. A. R. Hoare. Quicksort. *Computer Journal*, 5:10–15, 1962.

[63] C. A. R. Hoare. An axiomatic basis for computer programming. *Communications of the ACM*, 12:576–580, 1969.

[64] J. E. Hopcroft and R. M. Karp. An $n^{5/2}$ algorithm for maximum matchings in bipartite graphs. *SIAM Journal on Computing*, 2:225–231, 1973.

[65] J. E. Hopcroft and R. E. Tarjan. Efficient algorithms for graph manipulation. *Communications of the ACM*, 16:372–378, 1973.

[66] J. E. Hopcroft and J. D. Ullman. Set merging algorithms. *SIAM Journal on Computing*, 2:294–303, 1973.

[67] R. R. Howell. On asymptotic notation with multiple variables. Technical Report 2007-4, Kansas State University, 2007. https://people.cs.ksu.edu/~rhowell/asymptotic.pdf.

[68] D. A. Huffman. A method for the construction of minimum-redundancy codes. *Proceedings of the IRE*, 40:1098–1101, 1952.

[69] O. H. Ibarra and C. E. Kim. Fast approximation algorithms for the knapsack and sum of subset problems. *Journal of the Association for Computing Machinery*, 22:463–468, 1975.

[70] V. Jarník. O jistém problému minimálnim. *Práce Moravské Přírodověd Spolecnosti*, 6:57–63, 1930.

[71] D. S. Johnson, A. Demers, J. D. Ullman, M. R. Garey, and R. L. Graham. Worst-case performance bounds for simple one-dimensional packing algorithms. *SIAM Journal on Computing*, 3:299–325, 1974.

[72] D. S. Johnson. *Near-Optimal Bin Packing Algorithms*. Doctoral thesis, dept. of mathematics, Massachusetts Institute of Technology, Cambridge, MA, 1973.

[73] D. S. Johnson. Approximation algorithms for combinatorial problems. *Journal of Computer and System Sciences*, 9:256–278, 1974.

[74] D. B. Johnson. Priority queues with update and finding minimum spanning trees. *Information Processing Letters*, 4:53–57, 1975.

[75] D. B. Johnson. Efficient algorithms for shortest paths in sparse networks. *Journal of the ACM*, 24:1–13, 1977.

[76] A. A. Karatsuba and Y. Ofman. Multiplication of multidigit numbers on automata. *Doklady Akademii Nauk SSSR*, 145:293–294, 1962.

[77] D. R. Karger, P. N. Klein, and R. E. Tarjan. A randomized linear-time algorithm to find minimum spanning trees. *Journal of the Association for Computing Machinery*, 42:321–328, 1995.

[78] R. M. Karp. Reducibility among combinatorial problems. In R. E. Miller and J. W. Thatcher (eds), *Complexity of Computer Computations*, pp. 85–103. Plenum Press, 1972.

[79] D. G. Kirkpatrick and P. Hell. On the complexity of a generalized matching problem. In *Proceedings of the 10th Annual ACM Symposium on Theory of Computing*, pp. 240–245. Association for Computing Machinery, 1978.

[80] D. E. Knuth. Von Neumann's first computer program. *ACM Computing Surveys*, 2:247–260, 1970.

[81] D. E. Knuth. Optimal binary search trees. *Acta Informatica*, 1:14–25, 1971.

[82] D. E. Knuth. *Fundamental Algorithms*, volume 1 of *The Art of Computer Programming*, 3rd edition. Addison-Wesley, 1997. [The 1st edition was published in 1968. The second edition was published in 1973.]

[83] D. E. Knuth. *Seminumerical Algorithms*, volume 2 of *The Art of Computer Programming*, 3rd edition. Addison-Wesley, 1998. [The 1st edition was published in 1969. The second edition was published in 1981.]

[84] D. E. Knuth. *Sorting and Searching*, volume 3 of *The Art of Computer Programming*, 2nd edition. Addison-Wesley, 1998. [The 1st edition was published in 1973.]

[85] W. L. Kocay and D. L. Kreher. *Graphs, Algorithms, and Optimization*, 2nd edition. CRC Press, 2017.

[86] D. Kozen and S. Zaks. Optimal bounds for the change-making problem. *Theoretical Computer Science*, 123:377–388, 1994.

[87] D. C. Kozen. *The Design and Analysis of Algorithms*. Springer-Verlag, 1992.

[88] J. B. Kruskal, Jr. On the shortest spanning subtree of a graph and the traveling salesman problem. *Proceedings of the American Mathematical Society*, 7:48–50, 1956.

[89] E. L. Lawler. *Combinatorial Optimization: Networks and Matroids*. Holt, Rinehart, and Winston, 1976.

[90] D. A. Lelewer and D. S. Hirschberg. Data compression. *ACM Computing Surveys*, 19:261–296, 1987.

[91] L. Lovasz. Coverings and colorings of hypergraphs. In *Proceedings of the 4th Southeastern Conference on Combinatorics, Graph Theory, and Computing*, pp. 3–12. Utilitas Mathematica Publishing, 1973.

[92] E. Lucas. *Récréations Mathématiques*, volume 1. Gauthier-Villars, 1883.

[93] S. Micali and V. V. Vazirani. An $O(\sqrt{|V|} \cdot |E|)$ algorithm for finding maximal matchings in general graphs. In *Proceedings of the 21st Annual IEEE Symposium on Foundations of Computer Science*, pp. 17–27, 1980.

[94] S. S. Muchnick. *Advanced Compiler Design & Implementation*. Morgan Kaufmann, 1997.

[95] D. R. Musser. Introspective sorting and selection algorithms. *Software: Practice and Experience*, 27:983–993, 1997.

[96] C. H. Papadimitriou and Kenneth Steiglitz. *Combinatorial Optimization: Algorithms and Complexity*. Prentice-Hall, 1982.

[97] L. C. Paulson. *ML for the Working Programmer*, 2nd edition. Cambridge University Press, 1996.

[98] O. R. L. Peters. Pattern-defeating quicksort. *CoRR*, 2021. https://arxiv.org/abs/2106.05123.

[99] R. C. Prim. Shortest connection networks and some generalizations. *Bell System Technical Journal*, 36:1389–1401, 1957.

[100] W. Pugh. Skip lists: A probabilistic alternative to balanced trees. *Communications of the ACM*, 33:668–676, 1990.

[101] S. Sahni and T. Gonzalez. P-complete approximation problems. *Journal of the Association for Computing Machinery*, 23:555–565, 1976.

[102] S. Sahni. Approximate algorithms for the 0/1 knapsack problem. *Journal of the Association for Computing Machinery*, 22:115–124, 1975.

[103] K. Sayood. *Introduction to Data Compression*, 5th edition. Morgan Kaufmann Publishers, 2018.

[104] A. Schönhage and V. Strassen. Schnelle multiplikation grosser zahlen. *Computing*, 7:281–292, 1971.

[105] M. Sharir. A strong-connectivity algorithm and its applications in data flow analysis. *Computers and Mathematics with Applications*, 7:67–72, 1981.

[106] E. Silberstang. *The Winner's Guide to Casino Gambling*, 4th edition. Henry Holt and Company, LLC, 2005.

[107] D. D. Sleator and R. E. Tarjan. A data structure for dynamic trees. *Journal of Computer and System Sciences*, 26:362–391, 1983.

[108] D. D. Sleator and R. E. Tarjan. Self-adjusting heaps. *SIAM Journal on Computing*, 15:52–69, 1986.

[109] V. Strassen. Gaussian elimination is not optimal. *Numerische Mathematik*, 13:354–356, 1969.

[110] R. E. Tarjan. Depth-first search and linear graph algorithms. *SIAM Journal on Computing*, 1:146–160, 1972.

[111] R. E. Tarjan. On the efficiency of a good but not linear set merging algorithm. *Journal of the ACM*, 22:215–225, 1975.

[112] R. E. Tarjan. *Data Structures and Network Algorithms*. Society for Industrial and Applied Mathematics, 1983.

[113] R. E. Tarjan. Amortized computational complexity. *SIAM Journal on Algebraic and Discrete Methods*, 6:306–318, 1985.

[114] A. H. Taub (ed). *John Von Neumann: Collected Works*, volume 5, Pergamon Press, 1961.

[115] J. van Leeuwen. Having a Grundy-numbering is NP-complete. Report 207, Pennsylvania State University, University Park, PA, 1976.

[116] J. Vuillemin. A data structure for manipulating priority queues. *Communications of the ACM*, 21:309–315, 1978.

[117] R. A. Wagner and M. J. Fischer. The string-to-string correction problem. *Journal of the ACM*, 21:168–173, 1974.

[118] S. Warshall. A theorem on Boolean matrices. *Journal of the ACM*, 9:11–12, 1962.

[119] E. W. Weisstein. Collatz problem. From *MathWorld* — A Wolfram Web Resource. http://mathworld.wolfram.com/CollatzProblem.html.

[120] H. Whitney. On the abstract properties of linear dependence. *American Journal of Mathematics*, 57:509–533, 1935.

[121] J. W. J. Williams. Algorithm 232: Heapsort. *Communications of the ACM*, 7:347–348, 1964.

[122] N. Wirth. Program development by stepwise refinement. *Communications of the ACM*, 14:221–227, 1971.

[123] J. W. Wright. The change-making problem. *Journal of the ACM*, 22:125–128, 1975.

[124] A. C.-C. Yao. An $O(|E| \log \log |V|)$ algorithm for finding minimum spanning trees. *Information Processing Letters*, 4:21–23, 1975.

[125] F. F. Yao. Efficient dynamic programming using quadrangle inequalities. In *Proceedings of the 12th Annual ACM Symposium on Theory of Computing*, pp. 429–435, 1980.

Index

A

abstract data type (ADT), 110
abstraction, 6
accessor operations, 118
Ackermann's function, 304
Adel'son-Vel'skiĭ, G. M., 208, 244
Aho, A. V., 147, 288
Aigner, M., 370
aliasing, 147
Amdahl, G. M., 288
amortized analysis, 124–125, 131–141
Andersson, A., 244
approximation ratio, 557
Apt, K. R., 54
arbitrary-precision arithmetic, 145–147,
    348–363
    division, 348–356, 366
    exponentiation, 367
    multiplication, 364, 477–478, 481–498
    radix conversion, 367
    reciprocal, 355–362, 366
arithmetic series, 48
asymptotic notation
    Θ, 61
    o, 89
    Ω, 61
    ω, 89
    O, 57
    limits and, 92–95
    multiple variables, 82–89
    operations using, 67–68
    properties, 59, 62–63, 65, 93, 98–104

recurrences and, 68, 74–81
summations and, 69

B

Bachman, P. G. H., 104
Bayer, R., 244
Bellman, R. E., 408
Bentley, J. L., 24, 370
Berge, C., 463
big-Oh, 57
big-Omega, 61
big-Theta, 61
bin packing problem, 551, 563–567, 578
binary search, 150–153
binomial coefficients, 242
binomial theorem, 242
bitonic tour, 407
Blum, M., 370
Boehme, E. M., 288
BOOL, 126
boolean expressions
    conjunctive normal form, 512
    DeMorgan's laws, 513
    k-conjunctive normal form, 516
    literal, 512
    satisfiability, 503–518, 534–547
        not all equal, 548
    validity, 504
boolean satisfiability
    conjunctive normal form
        clauses, 512
Borůvka, O, 387

587

Brassard, G., 104–105, 307, 408, 553
Bratley, P., 307, 408, 553
Burnikel, C., 370
Burrus, C. S., 500

C

Carter, J. L., 288
change-making problem, 389–393
Chazelle, B., 388
Cheriton, D., 388
Chinese Remainder Theorem, 493
chirp transform, 499
Chiu-Shao, C., 500
Chvatal, V., 408
clique, 548, 578, 579
clique problem, 548
cloning, 125
    shallow, 125
Collatz problem, 33, 54
Collatz, L., 54
collision (*see* hashing, collision), 249
compression map (*see* hashing, compression map), 259
conditional probability, 177
ConsList, 126
constructive induction, 345
convolution, 465–477
    negative wrapped, 483
    positive wrapped, 476
Cook, S. A., 370, 553
Cooley, J. W., 500
Cormen, T. H., 54, 104, 288, 307, 463
correctness
    algorithms, 53
    data structures, 113
countable set, 170
Crane, C. A., 195
craps, 194
cut, 572

D

3-dimensional matching, 522–526
design patterns, 20, 109
Dijkstra, E. W., 24, 54, 387
Dinic, E. A., 463
discrete Fourier transform, 467
discrete probability space, 170
disjoint set, 289

disjoint set structures, 289–307
divide-and-conquer, 75, 151, 331–370
Dumey, A. I., 288
Dutch national flag, 37–43, 50–51, 53, 54, 337
dynamic programming, 389–408
Dósa, G., 579

E

Eckert, J. P., 370
Edmonds, J., 387, 463
Euler, L., 327
Even, S., 327
event, 172
    independence of, 176
        pairwise, 232
events
    independence of
        mutual, 232
eventually non-decreasing, 69, 88
eventually positive, 69, 88
EXPAND function, 151
expandable array, 122
expected value, 171
expected-case analysis, 170

F

factorial, 49
Fast Fourier Transform, 465–500
Fibonacci sequence, 49
Fischer, M. J., 307, 408
Floyd, R. W., 195, 408
for loops, 32
Ford, L. R., 463
Francez, N., 54
Fredman, M. L., 195, 288, 388
Fulkerson, D. R., 463
fully polynomial approximation scheme, 561

G

Galler, B. A., 307
Gambin, A., 195
Garey, M. R., 553, 579
Gauss, C. F., 500
generalization, 39–43
geometric series, 48
Gilbert, E. N., 408
Godbole, S. S., 408

Goldberg, A. V., 463
golden ratio, 49
Gong, W., 553
Gonzalez, T., 579
Graham, R. L., 105
graphs, 309–327
    acyclic, 313
    adjacency list, 318–321, 325
    adjacency matrix, 315–318, 325
    articulation points, 425–430
    biconnected, 437
    bipartite, 439
    breadth-first search, 386
    bridges, 437
    coloring, 439, 551
    connected components of, 374
    connected undirected, 327
    cycle in, 313
    edge connectivity, 462
    Euler paths in, 327
    Hamiltonian cycle, 549
    Hamiltonian path, 370
    independent set, 521–522
    induced subgraph, 418
    isomorphic, 549
    matching, 451–460, 522
    path cover, 462
    reachability, 417–425
    semiconnected, 438
    shortest paths, 379–380, 385–386, 395–398
    simple cycle in, 313
    simple path in, 443
    singly connected, 438
    sink in, 312
    sparse, 321
    strongly connected components, 432–436
    topological sort, 313–315, 430–432
    transitive closure, 403
    transitively closed, 326
    universal sink detection, 312–313
    universal sink in, 312
    vertex cover, 518–522, 578
greatest common divisor, 367
group, 478
    abelian, 478
Gubias, L. J., 244

H
harmonic series, 341
hashing, 248–288
    c-universal, 272
    collision, 249
    compression map, 259
    division method, 255–259, 284
    load factor, 254
    perfect, 275–283
    polynomial, 259–261, 284
    rehashing, 254
    universal, 261–275, 284
heaps, 153–187
    binary, 179–187
    leftist, 159–165
Heideman, M. T., 500
Hell, P., 553
Hirschberg, D. S., 388
Hoare, C. A. R., 53, 370
Hopcroft, J. E., 307, 327, 439, 463
Huffman, D. A., 388

I
Ibarra, O. H., 579
immutable structure, 126
indicator random variable, 236
induction, 27–29
    constructive, 345
insecure data structure, 120
insertion sort (*see* sorting, insertion sort), 6
INT, 38
interface, 110
internal function, 118
invariant
    loop, 12
    structural, 112
inversion, 103
INVERTEDPRIORITYQUEUE, 149
iteration operator, 300

J
Jarník, V., 387
Jiushao, Q., 500
Johnson, D. B., 388
Johnson, D. H., 500
Johnson, D. S., 553, 579

K

k-cut, 572
Karatsuba, A., 370
Karger, D. R, 388
Karp, R. M., 463, 553
KEYED type, 149
Kim, C. E., 579
Kirkpatrick, D. G., 553
knapsack problem, 387, 397–399, 401–402,
    557–563, 578
Knuth, D. E., 104, 105, 195, 288, 307, 327,
    370, 408
Kocay, W. L, 327
Komlós, J., 288
Kozen, D. C., 307, 408
Kreher, D. L., 327
Kruskal, J. B., Jr., 387

L

L'Hôpital's rule, 93
Landis, E. M., 208, 244
Lawler, E. L., 387
Lelewer, D. A., 388
lg, 70
limit, 92
linearity of expectation, 178
linked list, 131
little-oh, 89
little-omega, 89
load factor, *see* hashing, load factor, 254
logarithm
    base e, 94
    base 2, 70
    natural, 94
Lovasz, L., 553
Lucas, E., 439
Luhn, H. P., 288

M

Malinowski, A., 195
Markov's Inequality, 194
matching
    bipartite, 451–460
matrix multiplication
    chained, 393–395
Mauchly, J. W., 370
maximum cut problem, 572–577

maximum subsequence sum, 13–19, 24,
    29–32, 49–50, 58–60, 63–66, 68, 70–79,
    95, 331, 371
McCreight, E. M., 244
McIlroy, M. D., 307
Micali, S., 463
minimum cluster problem, 572–577,
    578
mod, 33
modular multiplicative inverse, 367
Moore, E. F., 408
Morris, 307
most significant bit, 349
most significant digit, 349
Muchnick, S. S., 147
multigraphs, 321–325, 325
multiset, 149
Musser, D. R., 370

N

natural number (NAT), 4–5
network flow, 441–451, 460
    augmenting path, 443
    residual network, 444
Newton's method, 356–363
nondestructive updates, 126
$\mathcal{NP}$-complete problem, 511
    strong sense, 529
$\mathcal{NP}$-hard problem, 511
    non-decision problem, 556
    strong sense, 529
null path length, 159
NUMBER, 5

O

object-oriented design, 24
object-oriented programming, 24
Ofman, Y., 370
Olderog, E.-R., 54
optimization problem, 371

P

palindrome, 22, 402
Papadimitriou, C. H., 387
partition problem, 526–533
Patashnik, O., 105
Paulson, L. C., 147
Perl, Y., 553
Peters, O. R. L., 370

polynomial approximation scheme, 561
    fully, 561
polynomial multiplication, 332–335,
    465–477
polynomial-time algorithm, 507
postcondition, 4
precondition, 4
Prim, R. C., 387
prime number, 258
principal roots of unity, 467
principle of optimality, 392
priority queue, 149–195
PRIORITYQUEUE, 149
probability, 170
probability space, 170
pseudopolynomial, 529
Pugh, W., 244

Q

queue, 144
quick sort (*see* sorting, quick sort),
    53

R

random access machine (RAM), 534
random variable, discrete, 171
Rao, S., 463
recurrence, 68
    asymptotic solution to (*see*
        asymptotic notation, recurrences
        and), 74
reduction, 6
    polynomial
        many-one, 509
        Turing, 555–556
    pseudopolynomial, 530
rehashing (*see* hashing, rehashing), 254
ring, 479
    commutative, 479
    unit element, 479
Rochester, N., 288

S

Sahni, S., 579
Samuel, A. L., 288
Sayood, K., 388
Schönhage, A., 500
scheduling, 289–292, 372–374
Sedgewick, R., 244

selection problem, 3–6, 25–27, 37–39,
    45–46, 73, 342–348
selection sort (*see* sorting, selection sort),
    22
self-adjusting, 216
sentinel element, 181
Sgall, J., 579
Sharir, M., 439
significant bit, 349
significant digit, 349
skip lists, 226–239
Sleator, D., 147, 195, 244
smooth function, 69, 88, 105
sorting
    heap sort, 179–187, 335, 338, 342
    insertion sort, 6–12, 27–29, 32–37,
        72–73, 342
    introsort, 342, 370
    merge sort, 335, 337, 370
    pdqsort, 370
    quick sort, 53, 337–342, 370
    selection sort, 22–23
    stable, 193, 335
specification, 3
    of an algorithm, 4
state of a data structure, 113
Steiglitz, K., 387
Strassen, V., 370, 500
STRING, 144–145
summations
    arithmetic series, 48
    asymptotic solution to (*see*
        asymptotic notation, summations
        and), 69
    geometric series, 48

T

tail recursion, 10
Tarjan, R. E., 147, 195, 244, 307, 327,
    388, 439
TOARRAY, 256
Toeplitz matrix, 500
top-down, 3, 6, 24
topological sort, 316–318, 320
Trémaux, 439
transformation, 10
traveling salesperson problem, 551,
    567–571
    metric, 568–571

trees, 327, 374
    AVL, 207–216, 294
    binary, 155
    binary search, 200–226
    leftist, 160–165
    red-black, 241
    rooted, 154
      height of, 155
      leaf, 155
      size of, 155
      traversals, 203, 412–416
    spanning, 374
      depth-first, 420
      minimum-cost, 374–379
    splay, 216–226
Tritter, A. L., 307
Tsǔ, S., 500
Tukey, J. W., 500

U

Ullman, J. D., 307
universal family, 261, 284
universal sink detection, 315–316

V

van Leeuwen, J., 553
Vazirani, V. V., 463

virtual initialization, 245–247
VISITOR interface, 197
visitor pattern, 197
von Neumann, J., 370
Vuillemin, J., 195

W

Wagner, R. A., 408
Warshall, S., 408
Wegman, M. N., 288
Weisstein, E., 54
Whitney, H., 387
Williams, J., 195
Wirth, N., 24
worst case, 56
Wright, J. W., 408

Y

Yao, A. C.-C., 388
Yao, F. F., 408

Z

Zaks, S., 408, 553
Zhou, X., 553
Zi, S., 500
Ziegler, J., 370

CPSIA information can be obtained
at www.ICGtesting.com
Printed in the USA
LVHW060922270123
737651LV00004B/14

9 789811 263835